# Conrad's Shadow

STUDIES IN VIOLENCE, MIMESIS, AND CULTURE

SERIES EDITOR
William A. Johnsen

The Studies in Violence, Mimesis, and Culture Series examines issues related to the nexus of violence and religion in the genesis and maintenance of culture. It furthers the agenda of the Colloquium on Violence and Religion, an international association that draws inspiration from René Girard's mimetic hypothesis on the relationship between violence and religion, elaborated in a stunning series of books he has written over the last forty years. Readers interested in this area of research can also look to the association's journal, *Contagion: Journal of Violence, Mimesis, and Culture.*

# Conrad's Shadow

**Catastrophe, Mimesis, Theory**

**Nidesh Lawtoo**

Michigan State University Press · *East Lansing*

♾ The paper used in this publication meets the minimum requirements of ANSI/NISO Z39.48-1992
(R 1997) (Permanence of Paper).

Michigan State University Press
East Lansing, Michigan 48823-5245

Printed and bound in the United States of America.

22  21  20  19  18  17  16      1  2  3  4  5  6  7  8  9  10

LIBRARY OF CONGRESS CATALOGING-IN-PUBLICATION DATA
Names: Lawtoo, Nidesh, author.
Title: Conrad's shadow : catastrophe, mimesis, theory / Nidesh Lawtoo.
Description: East Lansing : Michigan State University Press, [2016] | Series: Studies in violence, mimesis,
and culture | Includes bibliographical references and index.
Identifiers: LCCN 2015041932| ISBN 9781611862188 (pbk. : alk. paper) | ISBN 9781609175030 (pdf) | ISBN
9781628952766 (epub) | ISBN 9781628962765 (kindle)
Subjects: LCSH: Conrad, Joseph, 1857–1924—Criticism and interpretation.
Classification: LCC PR6005.O4 Z76465 2016 | DDC 823/.912—dc23 LC record available at http://lccn.loc.
gov/2015041932

Book design by Charlie Sharp, Sharp Des!gns, Lansing, Michigan
Cover design by David Drummond, Salamander Design, www.salamanderhill.com.
Cover artwork is a still frame taken from *L'Homme sans ombre* (The Man with No Shadow—2004),
directed by Georges Schwizgebel and is used with permission from Georges Schwizgebel.

Michigan State University Press is a member of the Green Press Initiative and is committed to developing
and encouraging ecologically responsible publishing practices. For more information about the Green
Press Initiative and the use of recycled paper in book publishing, please visit *www.greenpressinitiative.org.*

Visit Michigan State University Press at *www.msupress.org*

*To Kim and Nia,*
*for harbors to come*
. . .

# Contents

# Acknowledgments

Shadows do not appear without material, intellectual, artistic, and affective support—and even then, one needs to be on the move to catch up with them. I am very grateful to the graduate students in my seminar "The Secret Shadow" in 2012 at the University of Lausanne for helping me sketch the main outlines of this book; to the Swiss National Science Foundation for granting me a generous fellowship that single-handedly funded my entire research at Johns Hopkins University from 2013 to 2016, during which time this book was written; and to The Humanities Center for continuing to provide—fifty years after the birth of theory—heterogeneous theoretical foundations that allowed me to keep up with the conceptual protagonist of this book, as it moves from literary to psychological, anthropological to philosophical territories.

I am particularly grateful to Hent de Vries, Paola Marrati, Ruth Leys, and Michael Fried for their warm support and stimulating theoretical exchanges; to Dick Macksey for sharing stories about Girard, Derrida, and other suspects; to Gaby Spiegel for inviting me to contribute to the Andrew W. Mellon Seminar, and to all of its participants—Rachel Galvin, Leo Lisi, Yi-Ping Ong, Anne Moss, Jeanne-Marie Jackson, Sharon Achinstein, among others—for putting up with the avatars of mimesis. Doug Mao I thank for inviting me to present my brand of "bad modernism" in the English Department; Jane Bennett and Bill Connolly for animating a magical summer-night reading group that generated vital matter to ruminate (in the Nietzschean sense), for inviting me to contribute to their seminars, and for the vitalism of their friendship; and Paul Delnero for our ritual after-work theoretical conversations, occasional Freudian skirmishes, and regular drinks.

And over the years, I have gotten unflagging support from Conradians of all stripes and persuasions on both sides of the Atlantic. The four Joseph Conrad Societies (of America, UK and Ireland, Poland, and France) provided the most welcoming and stimulating contexts to test out ideas still in embryonic stages. In particular, Anne Luyat, Richard Ruppel, Jack Peters, Richard Richardson, Paul Armstrong, and Lissa Rebozo-Schneider have actively contributed to giving substance to theoretical shadows by repeatedly inviting me to present papers at the MLA on subjects as diverse as Conrad and Darwin, Conrad and Narrative, Conrad and the Brain, and Conrad and Ecology. Jonathan Dollimore, Martine Hennard, Keith Carabine, Hugh Epstein, and J. Hillis Miller, I thank for reading portions of this manuscript and for providing valuable feedback; Gary Handwerk, Henry Staten, Mikkel Borch-Jacobsen at the University of Washington, I thank for steering me early on toward turbulent theoretical currents and for their persistent professional help; and Rachel Falconer and Martine Hennard for joining the club of phantom supporters and for participating in a stimulating reading group at the University of Lausanne. On the side of mimetic theory, I am grateful to the participants of the COV&R for their openness to the different forms mimesis can take and for encouraging me to end—rather than start—battles. Last but not least, thanks to Anastasia Wraight at Michigan State University Press for her careful editorial work, and my editor, Bill Johnsen, for providing a timely editorial echo no Conradian could possibly resist: just after the *Phantom of the Ego* had appeared, Johnsen gave voice to Garnett's mythical question, "Why not write another?"

Another? Yes, I could do that. I would do that. But it takes an artist to capture, in perfect brushstrokes, the moving silhouette of Conrad's shadow. That the Swiss animation film director Georges Schwizgebel had the audacity to cut a photogram from the original 35 mm of *The Man Without Shadow* (2004), which he sent across the ocean to the critic to reproduce on the cover of this book, is a telling tribute to the power of shadows to move—chameleon-like—across genres, media, and material supports. The lovers of shadows to whom this study is addressed will find a magical representation of the moving soul of this book in Schwizgebel's wonderful animation. The man may be without his shadow, but the traces of the journey remain to be seen. And, of course, my family: my mother for giving me independence early on and for putting up with a nomadic son later on; and my children, Kim and Nia, for, well, many things, but also for illustrating the first version of this book with mesmerizing drawings that made me see how shadows are not at all debased copies of original forms; rather, they are the secret source of original artistic transformations. My *donna duplex*, Michi Lawtoo, I cannot thank enough for remaining on board during multiple transatlantic crossings, while being the most supportive, patient, and insightful traveling companion. It's all too apt that she chose the luminous screen onto which a split, yet moving shadow is now projected.

Portions of this book have appeared as articles in the following journals:

- "Conrad's Neuroplasticity." *Modernism/modernity* 23.4 (2016).
- "Dueling to the End/Ending 'The Duel.'" Girard *avec* Conrad." *Contagion* 22 (2015): 153–84.
- "Fear of the Dark: Surrealist Shadows in *The Nigger of the 'Narcissus.'"* *Modern Fiction Studies* 60.2 (2014): 227–50.
- "A Picture of Africa: Frenzy, Counter-Narrative, *Mimesis.*" *Modern Fiction Studies* 59.1 (2013): 26–52.
- "A Picture of Europe: Possession Trance in *Heart of Darkness.*" *Novel: A Forum on Fiction* 45.3 (2012): 409–32.

# The Secret Shadow

Homo duplex has, in my case, more than one meaning.

—Joseph Conrad, *Collected Letters*

t is not a secret that shadows, doubles, and phantoms haunt Joseph Conrad's fictions. The romantic topos of the homo duplex looms so large on his modernist tales that we can hardly claim to reveal an original topic of investigation. And yet Conrad also blurred the line dividing mimetic figures from original configurations as he famously said: "Homo duplex has, in my case, more than one meaning" (*CL*, III, 89). This statement makes us wonder: is the meaning of the homo duplex more than one in the sense that it is already double, and thus indicative of a divided identity—as the trope clearly suggests? Or, rather, is this meaning more than one in the sense that it is already plural, and thus open to protean transformations—as Conrad seems to imply? And if both senses simultaneously in-*form* Conrad's representations of the homo duplex, which approach, then, would be best suited to unmask secret transformations that blur the shadow-line between double and protean figures? You will have guessed it. This book proposes a mimetic approach to the old romantic subject of the doppelgänger and, by doing so, attempts to illuminate the protean meanings of Conrad's shadow in a kaleidoscope of constantly changing light.

A mimetic perspective to a writer as impressionistically opaque as Joseph Conrad might initially surprise. Rarely, if ever, have his fictions been explicitly approached from the angle of mimesis—unsurprisingly so, since Conrad's early-modernist poetics is clearly antimimetic in its refusal to depict transparently realistic representations of reality. But mimesis, not unlike the homo duplex, also has more than one meaning. This is, once again, not an original view. What Socrates says of the actor at the origins of literary theory continues to capture the eminently mimetic qualities of mimesis itself: like the mime (*mimos*) from which it derives its name, mimesis is a figure "just like Proteus," for it "twist[s] and turn[s], this way and that, assuming every shape."[1] From antiquity to modernity mimesis has, indeed, continued to function as a protean conceptual protagonist on the literary and theoretical scene that changes shape, name, and identity at will, adapting—chameleon-like—to a variety of different backgrounds. Born from an ancient marriage between visual representations and bodily impersonations, reframed in terms of *imitatio* of exemplary models, central to the imitation of the ancients, mimesis continues to animate the imitation of the moderns as well, albeit under different masks and personae: from psychic identification to affective contagion, hypnotic suggestion to entranced possessions, restricted mimesis to general mimesis, mimetic desire to mimetic pathos, mirror neurons to the mimetic unconscious, recent developments in the heterogeneous field of "mimetic theory" confirm from different perspectives that mimesis is, indeed, a protean concept in search of an identity.[2] Let us thus resist the automatic reflex of identifying mimesis at the outset, especially since the author under consideration is one who escapes singular identifications. Instead, in this book I propose to follow what Socrates calls the twists and turns of a conceptual identity that is not one, in the sense that it leads to double manifestations and, above all, protean transformations.

*Conrad's Shadow*, then, does not propose a return to a homogeneous account of mimetic "realism"—though the real implications of imitative behavior will be considered in some detail. Nor is it restricted to a "journey within" a psychoanalytical unconscious haunted by archetypal shadows or uncanny doppelgängers—though mimetic doubles will provide the most direct door to reopen the labyrinth of the unconscious in Conrad's work. Instead, this book follows-up on a recent mimetic turn in Conrad and new modernist studies[3] in order to diagnose the different forms of mimetic pathos, pathologies, and patho-logies manifested in Conrad's corpus as a whole. In the process, I consider the psychological, ethical, anthropological, and metaphysical implications of contagious affects that, for better and worse, have the power to trouble the boundaries of individuation, generating secret continuities at the heart of discontinuities. For Conrad, in fact, a journey within the unconscious is always simultaneously a journey without individual consciousness; human doubles that haunt fictional egos are always framed against larger ethical, political, and environmental shadows cast on the real world. From the escalation of violence to the threat of catastrophic storms, contagious epidemics to communal solidarity, rituals of (dis)possession in (post)colonial Africa to the horrorism of terrorism in the post-9/11 West, among other subjects, there is an entire zone of Conrad's oeuvre that has so far remained in the background of critical discussions, yet immediately springs to the foreground if we adopt interdisciplinary lenses to see the different shadows constitutive of Conrad's poetics. My mimetic hypothesis will thus be Janus-faced. It suggests that looking back to an ancient concept that has been neglected in the twentieth century will help us fully move Conrad studies into the twenty-first century.

In an attempt to reach a certain blending of formal and semantic preoccupations, my approach will also be double in the sense that it has both a critical and a theoretical side. On the one hand, I use the theoretical filter of mimesis to offer new critical readings of Conrad's fictions. I do so via close formal analyses that trace the protean manifestations of mimetic shadows as they appear within a single text, reappear across a number of Conradian texts, and, sometimes, resurface unexpectedly in postcolonial and cinematic intertexts. On the other hand, I use Conrad's tales as a privileged artistic medium to theorize mimesis in new ways. Time and again, we shall see that Conrad's fictions are good to think with. As such, they do not require any theory to be applied to them. Instead, they hold up a theoretical mirror to us. While not fully realistic in its reflections, this mirror remains, in formally complex ways, true to reality and urges us to reflect on the shadows that haunt the contemporary world. If the critical side of this book has been written for readers interested in knowing why Conrad's untimely tales continue to cast such a spell on our contemporary imagination, the theoretical side is also looking toward a more general readership interested in knowing why mimesis continues to be one of the most urgent concepts to rethink today. These two sides are not meant to be mutually exclusive but to supplement one another. My wager is that as both the critical and the theoretical sides are joined, a new picture of Conrad and of mimetic theory will progressively take form.

Before embarking on this journey, then, let me outline, in broad brush-strokes, why Conrad's dark pictures of reality offer such illuminating case studies for a Janus-faced diagnostic that looks back to the old concept of mimesis in order to reflect on the protean shadows that now loom large ahead of us.

## The Artist as Double

Prior to representing the homo duplex in his fictions, Conrad embodied mimetic principles in his own protean life. As his name indicates, and his career confirms, Joseph Conrad, born Józef Teodor Konrad Korzeniowski (1857–1924), had an identity that was not one but dual and multiple instead. What Conrad says of his favorite alter ego, Charlie Marlow, equally applies to the artist himself: Conrad was, indeed, "not typical," and this accounts for the untypical nature of his tales. The only child of revolutionary Polish patriots, Conrad was sent in exile to Siberia with his parents at the age of four, lost his mother a few years later, and his father by the time he was twelve. He was thus left an orphan in a country that had also lost its national identity. A child without parents, a subject without a country: early on Conrad was deprived of stable familial and national origins. But if this loss of models failed to provide him with a stabilizing and unifying upbringing, it also rendered him paradoxically open to the possibility of impressive linguistic, cultural, and professional transformations.

Bookish and introverted, melancholic and multilingual, haunted by the shadow of his enthusiastic, revolutionary, and poetic father, while taken in custody by a pragmatic, conservative, and rational uncle, Conrad suffered from tragic personal losses, psychic tensions, and cultural deprivations, which, in turn, led to adventurous nautical, geographical, and, above all, literary explorations. Moving from Poland to France in his midteens in order to embark on an improbable career as a seaman, which, for nearly two decades, took him across the world—around Cape Horn to India and Malaysia and back, with decisive stops in Mauritius and the Congo—switching to English

midroute while at the same time working his way up from steward to second
mate, first mate to captain, only to switch, once again, in his midthirties to
start an even more improbable literary career in a new country, in his third
language, and turn, not without struggles, from master mariner to master
of English prose—as he navigated through these perilous and breathtaking
maneuvers—Conrad must have realized that identity, for him, was not given
at the outset, as a fixed origin to rely on but had to be given form progressively, in medias res, while he sailed toward unknown destinations. As he
later said in his memoir, *A Personal Record* (1912), at his core there was no
hard kernel hidden inside but a "still plastic character" (5) receptive to adoptions coming from the outside.

Given these chameleon-like metamorphoses in an author who admittedly
thinks of writing in terms of "laying one's soul more or less bare to the world"
(*PR* 14), it is no wonder that underlying continuities exist between Conrad's
untypical character in real life and the literary characters he represents in his
untypical fictions. As Virginia Woolf famously put it, this doubling of the
self is at the heart of what she called Conrad's "double vision"—that is, his
ability to "be at once inside and out" of his characters.[4] And thinking of his
duality as a "sea captain" and as a "subtle, refined and fastidious analyst" that
often goes by the name of Marlow, Woolf perceptively added: "Conrad alone
was able to live that double life, for Conrad was compound of two men."[5]
Echoing Woolf, a number of critics have commented on Conrad as a "divided
man" (Guerard), a "double-personality" (Najder), a "double man" (Watts)
capable of navigating the "dynamic, fluid process of life" (Said), a stylist who
could trace "the movement of an alienated character outwards from the self"
(Watt), and, more recently, a "novelist of identification" who "locates himself,
his own authentic essence, outside himself, in another being" (Harpham).[6] All
these insights lend support to Conrad's confessional claim about the homo
duplex: "I—who have a double life, one of them peopled only by shadows
growing more precious as the years pass—know what that is" (*CL*, III, 491).

Double lives and divided souls, fluidity and janiformity, alienation of
the self and protean identifications with others: these are, indeed, eminently
mimetic qualities. While not yet identified under the ancient rubric of mimesis, some of the best readers of Conrad agree that the general problematic of
behavioral imitation—often restricted to the psychoanalytical concept of
"identification"—constitutes what Albert Guerard influentially called "the

central chapter of Conrad's psychology."[7] Conrad, for one, was fully aware that this chapter was at the heart of his artistic practice, if only because he consciously used the medium of writing to trigger mimetic effects. As he puts it in an essay on Henry James, novels provide an echo for the reader's "cry" to the novelist: "Take me out of myself!" (*NLL* 16). This ecstatic inclination that pushes inspired artists, enthusiastic protagonists, and sympathetic readers outside of themselves, to become someone other, I have argued elsewhere, is essentially mimetic in orientation and already takes protean forms in Conrad's most influential novella, *Heart of Darkness* (1899).[8] What we will explore in this book is how mimesis continues to unfold its protean identities as we uncover the multiple meanings of the homo duplex that traverse, like an undercurrent, Conrad's corpus as a whole. These meanings include a well-known Conradian fascination with doppelgängers and psychic identifications, but also less-known diagnostics of what I group under the rubric of "mimetic *pathos*," understood in the classical sense as a secret force that penetrates the ego, dispossesses it of its presence to self, generating what Nietzsche calls "an ever increasing widening of distance within the soul itself."[9] Symptomatic expressions of mimetic pathos include enthusiastic outbreaks, affective contagion, ritual sacrifices, shared sympathy, communal frenzy, and reciprocal violence—not to speak of previously unstudied mimetic affects and effects such as panic, possession trance, depersonalization, hypnotic suggestion (or rapport), psychic dissolution (or psychasthenia), mirroring reflexes (or mirror neurons), and brain plasticity (or neuroplasticity), to name just the major protean manifestations of mimesis that, for better and worse, cast such a long shadow on Conrad's fictions. Taken together, these symptoms are not only a reflection that Conrad lived a double life as seaman and writer. They also indicate that throughout his career, he continued to rely on his mimetic faculties to reflect on both the logical and pathological consequences of being oneself—while being (dis)possessed by someone other. This is, in a nutshell, the Janus-faced critical diagnostic that orients this book.

## The Critic as Janus

This double-faced orientation has been invoked by critics before, most notably by Cedric Watts, who, already in the 1970s, perceptively recognized that "Janus is a crafty usher to Proteus" and set out to articulate "janiform interpretations" of Conrad's work.[10] Informed by all such interpretations can offer us, I take some steps back—to leap farther ahead. As my preliminary reference to Socrates suggested, I shall repeatedly look back to the origins of mimetic theory in classical antiquity in order to look ahead to the future Conrad invites us to consider. If Janus is such a crafty usher to Proteus, it is, in fact, because both mythic figures have been informed by the same artistic principle, a mimetic principle that both *divides* and *multiplies* the ego—thereby leading the homo duplex (Janus) to have more than one meaning (Proteus). I argue that what is true of ancient mythic figures is equally true of Conrad's modernist literary figures: mimesis *is* the secret shadow that turns homo duplex into homo multiplex. Consequently, as we follow the twists and turns of its chameleon-like transformations, we shall progressively realize that mimesis can no longer be restricted to fictions that explicitly deal with the romantic topos of the doppelgänger but, rather, in-*forms* (gives form to) Conrad's poetics as a whole—both in its homogeneous and heterogeneous manifestations.

Unlike, say, the psychoanalytical notion of "identification," which as critics observed, "dominated his work for only a brief period, from 1897 to 1900,"[11] I argue that mimesis continues to serve as a *fil rouge* that strings together Conrad's labyrinthine literary explorations of the mimetic unconscious across his entire career. Mimetic theory shall help us follow this thread unraveled throughout the labyrinth of Conrad's mythic fictions. René Girard, for instance, one of the most original contemporary representatives of this theoretical tradition, usefully points out that "a writer's career, like that of a scientific researcher . . . often revolves, or seems to revolve entirely around a small number of themes and problems take up again and again by the author."[12] This general insight, as we shall see, equally applies to the case of Conrad, a writer Girard does not discuss but who provides numerous occasions to confirm, refine, and supplement contemporary research on imitation. Indeed, if one starts paying attention to the ways mimesis operates in Conrad's corpus, it is surprising to see how insistently, persistently, we could even say obsessively, he returns to the same problems, scenes, and images, changing perspective to illuminate a different facet of what I consider to be the same protean shadow.

In order to illustrate these underlying mimetic continuities, some of Conrad's texts shall be treated at greater length than others. One of the hermeneutical ambitions of my account of fictions like "The Duel," "The Secret Sharer," *The Shadow-Line, The Nigger of the "Narcissus," Heart of Darkness*, as well as its postcolonial double, Chinua Achebe's *Things Fall Apart*, is to trace the twists and turns of mimesis—beginning, middle, and end—in order to reframe, sometimes quite radically, our understanding of these complex texts, while simultaneously bringing into the foreground shadows that have so far been left in the background. In the case of other texts, such as *Almayer's Folly, The Secret Agent, Under Western Eyes, A Personal Record*, as well as Francis Ford Coppola's *Apocalypse Now*, my approach will be more strategically selective, as I zoom in on culminating moments of mimetic pathos in order to bring to the fore the theoretical implications of founding scenes Conrad obsessively returns to in his oeuvre. I can only regret that two major novels remained in the background of this study: both *Nostromo* and *Lord Jim* are used primarily as co-texts to illuminate other texts. This is not because these novels are not relevant for my mimetic inquiry, but simply because doing critical and theoretical justice to these immensely protean works would have required another study altogether.

Despite the shifts of perspectives necessary to keep up with the twists and turns of Conrad's shadow, my mimetic hypothesis remains firmly anchored on Janus-faced critical principles that orient my investigations everywhere. These principles will become progressively clear as we proceed, but I list three at the outset. First, this approach is double in a *diagnostic* sense that shows how mimesis, for Conrad, has two clinically opposed yet connected sides. One side is dark and pathological: it is generative of split identities, schizophrenic reactions, unconscious states, hypnotic swoons, as well as maddening, violent, and contagious symptoms. These symptoms infect individual characters in isolation, are secretly shared with privileged others (friends, models, lovers), turn antithetical characters (and sometimes authors) into rivals, and threaten to spread to the entire social microcosm Conrad depicts (the community, the ship, or the "small planet" the ship represents). The other side is luminous and therapeutic: it offers diagnostic insights into the pathological infections that penetrate the boundaries of the ego, dissolves its contours, turning it into someone—or something—other. It does so by convoking different types of critical discourses (or *logoi*)—be they psychological, anthropological, or ontological—to dissect the power of mimetic affect (or *pathos*) to tie the ego, in quite intimate ways, to others. This side is, thus, strictly speaking, not pathological but, rather, "patho-*logical.*"[13] As it is also the case for other writers that belong to an immanent modernist tradition—from Friedrich Nietzsche to Oscar Wilde, D. H. Lawrence to Georges Bataille, among others—there is no contradiction between these two seemingly opposed sides. It is because Conrad suffered from mimetic pathologies that threatened the stability of his ego from within that he could accurately re-present and diagnose such symptoms in his fictional characters from without. Either way, for us reading Conrad today, his fictions offer illuminating case studies for Janus-faced diagnostics of the mimetic patho(-)logies—now understood as both sickness and clinical discourse—that inform his protean writings.

Second, this approach is Janus-faced in the *epistemological* sense in that it is as much critically oriented as it is theoretically oriented. On the critical side, mimesis provides a sharp and far-reaching lens to illuminate shadows that have so far remained unseen (such as the shadow of catastrophe), answer hermeneutical riddles that have remained unsolved (such as the role of shadows in Conrad's poetics), and reframe much-discussed disciplinary quarrels (such as the postcolonial quarrel with Nigerian novelist Chinua Achebe). Given the amount of controversy generated by such issues within the field of Conrad studies, modernist studies, and postcolonial studies, this critical side should amply justify a mimetic approach to Conrad. But there is also a more general, theoretical side. Conrad's tales are, in fact, full of illuminating diagnostic insights into the workings of mimetic symptoms, and these insights stretch beyond the boundaries of the literary field, opening up Conrad studies to the outside. They include, for instance, the escalation of violence, contagious affects, unconscious communication, postcolonial imitation, but also the agentic power of environmental catastrophes, epidemic contagion, the "horrorism" of international terrorism, the (de)formative power of media simulations, as well as the plasticity of the human brain. Such topics have often been neglected, or have simply never been addressed before. They certainly go beyond the narrow territorial boundaries imposed by an increasingly specialized academic field and call for deterritorializing, interdisciplinary, or, better, transdisciplinary moves. Yet they are internal to Conrad's fictions nonetheless and become visible via a hermeneutical effort attentive to the protean manifestations of mimesis within the texts themselves.

And third, this approach is Janus-faced in the *theoretical* sense in that it looks back to mimetic principles that originate in classical antiquity, most notably in Plato's thought, in order to cast new light on Conrad's modernist fictions. It is true that at the dawn of the modern period, antiquity and modernity tended to be considered as rivalrous, antithetical parties: *les Anciens*, we were told, are on the side of imitation of the classics, *les Modernes*, on the side of the innovations of modernity. And yet, already in the context of this legendary *querelle* that dominated the European scene during the seventeenth and eighteenth centuries (and implicitly continues to inform contemporary takes on theory), the opposition between the ancients and the moderns was never simply clear-cut. As Marc Fumaroli puts it in *Les abeilles et les araignées*, surveying the key advocates on both sides of the mimetic/antimimetic fence, "one can be Modern with the Ancients, thanks to the Ancients, just as one can be against them."[14] Along similar lines, but reloading such old artistic quarrels from a new philosophical perspective, the French philosopher Philippe Lacoue-Labarthe has demonstrated in *L'imitation des modernes* that it is not at all oxymoronic to join modernity and imitation. On the contrary, he says that "we are obliged to think and rethink mimesis" in the modernist and postmodern period.[15] Following this injunction, and building on the work of key figures in mimetic theory—including Friedrich Nietzsche, Gabriel Tarde, Georges Bataille, René Girard, Jean Baudrillard, and Mikkel Borch-Jacobsen—I have argued in *The Phantom of the Ego* that a modernist approach to the old yet always new concept of mimesis should go beyond ancient or modern quarrels in order to articulate the reemergence of old rivalries, theoretical echoes, and aesthetic re-presentations that turn the ego into what Nietzsche—writing with and contra Plato—calls "a phantom of the ego." Conrad, writing with and against the same philosophical tradition, but from a distinctive literary, and thus artistic, perspective, calls these phantoms "shadows." To be sure, as a modernist artist framing mimetic shadows with a mimetic medium, Conrad is fundamentally modern with the ancients, thanks to the ancients, especially in his diagnostic awareness that mimesis is a concept that has both poisonous and therapeutic effects. If the moderns would say that mimesis generates both pathologies and pathologies, the ancients would say that it works as both a poison and a cure—that is, as a *pharmakon*.[16]

Once joined, these threefold diagnostic, epistemic, and theoretical oscillations point in the same theoretical direction and open up new fields of investigation. After a prolonged tendency in modernist studies either to confine mimesis to narrow aesthetic concerns with realism or to circumvent its discussion altogether in an echo of modernist anxieties of influence, mimesis is coming back to haunt the literary and theoretical scene. In addition to theorists such as Girard and Lacoue-Labarthe, who explicitly advocate a return to mimesis to better understand the contemporary world, different "turns" in critical theory are, in fact, implicitly reloading old mimetic problems in new conceptual terms—be it under the rubric of "mimicry" (postcolonial studies and gender studies), "affect" (affect theory), "vibrant matter" (new materialism), "contagion" (environmental studies), "mirror neurons" and "neuroplasticity" (neurosciences). These innovative turns open up exciting new lines of inquiry, promote a distinctly interdisciplinary approach that resonates with the study at hand, and we will be engaging with some of their most prominent representatives as I articulate the protean manifestations of Conrad's shadow.

And yet while we look ahead to new and timely theoretical twists, we shall not lose sight of old and untimely philosophical turns. My ambition is in fact never to simply apply new theoretical turns to the texts, but rather to trace the "twists and turns" of a concept that—as Socrates reminds us—has been turning for quite some time. Mimesis, we should not forget, is born at the same time as literary theory; or better, it is the very concept that gave birth to literary theory. Over the centuries, it has shown considerable resilience, a striking capacity of adaptation to new artistic media, and a deterritorializing power of contagion that flowed between the humanities, the human sciences and, in recent years, the neurosciences as well. For these and other reasons, mimesis continues to hold an enormous theoretical potential to account for perhaps the most characteristically distinctive human faculty, what Walter Benjamin aptly called "the mimetic faculty."[17] Many things have changed over the centuries, but humans have indeed remained thoroughly mimetic animals—and this faculty accounts for humans' chameleon-like penchant for conformism and docile adaptation but also change and creative transformation. It is perhaps no accident, then, that mimesis now *re*-turns on the theoretical front to secretly inform contemporary "discoveries" in the humanities, social sciences, and hard sciences, silently contributing to the revival of interest in human, all too human forms of imitation. And here is where the Janus-faced critic turns—chameleon-like—into a protean theorist.

## The Theorist as Proteus

Theory and Conrad, Conrad and theory: the mirroring connection is familiar enough. If influential literary theorists—such as Edward Said, Fredric
Jameson, and J. Hillis Miller, to name a few—found in Conrad's fictions
an original source of theoretical inspiration, Conrad's fictions have also
turned into exemplary case studies to test out various theoretical perspectives—such as postcolonial studies, Marxism, and deconstruction, to name
the corresponding few. Either way, the Conrad-theory connection rests on
solid foundations. Irrespective of the theory/antitheory oscillations that
continue to rock literary studies, there is no doubt that Conrad studies has
profited from theoretical readings, just as much as theorists have profited
from Conrad's fictions. The Polish expatriate has, in fact, attracted some of
the most influential advocates of critical theory, helped inaugurate new fields
of inquiry, and generated passionate debates, far-reaching insights, as well
as animated controversies that continue to make him a privileged figure to
introduce new theoretical turns. There are thus good reasons to return to
Conrad if we want to contribute to the "theory renaissance"[18] that is currently under way from the interdisciplinary angle of the mimetic turn.

   The reception of Conrad often generated contradictory evaluations, and
these contradictions contributed, paradoxically, to his critical and theoretical fortune. Conrad, in fact, has been critiqued for his "misty" style (Forster)
and heavy-handed "adjectival insistence" (Leavis), yet he has also been celebrated for promoting an "impressionistic" aesthetics (Watt) and is generally
considered a "master" (Harpham) of English prose. Conrad is an exemplary
author who was readily included in the "great tradition" of British literature
(Leavis again), but at the same time he is also recognized as an *"émigré"*
writer in "exile" (Eagleton). He was famously condemned as a "thoroughgoing racist" for his denigrating representations of African people (Achebe),
but prominent anthropologists affirmed their mimetic desire "to be the Conrad" of anthropology (Malinowski), admitted that they "would have liked to
write his books" (Lévi-Strauss), and continue to claim that "anthropology
is still waiting for its Conrad" (Clifford). On yet another front, Conrad's
psychological insights have been interpreted as explorations of a universal,
"archetypal" unconscious (Guerard), but he is also at the origin of a deeply
historical conception of a "political unconscious" (Jameson). His account of

darkness has been read as a "metaphysical" insight into the Dionysian horror of death (Miller) but also as the product of "self-conscious" Apollonian
"visions" of the horror of "imperialism" (Said). And if an influential artist
qua rival once suggested that Conrad's most controversial novella, *Heart of
Darkness*, should be banned from the ideal canon (yes, Achebe), eminent
continental philosophers have recently reclaimed the same text as a "classic
of horrorism" (Cavarero), as well as "one of the greatest texts of Western
literature" (Lacoue-Labarthe).[19] The list is far from exhaustive, but it should
suffice to make my point: given such heterogeneous evaluations, I think it
is no exaggeration to say that Conrad has generated some of the most contradictory, at times polemical, but always thought-provoking discussions in
critical theory in the twentieth century. It is thus no wonder that at the dawn
of the twenty-first century, Conrad continues to be celebrated as a writer
who "holds great and plural interest in the contemporary moment" and is at
the source of innovative philosophical debates in "contemporary thought."[20]

Mimetic theory draws from this long and heterogeneous tradition,
engages with its major advocates, and, in the process, gives new twists to old
theoretical turns as it articulates some of the underlying continuities that
inform these discontinuous accounts. Born from an "ancient quarrel" (Plato's
term) between philosophy and art, mimesis is, indeed, a concept that both
connects and disconnects competing perspectives thereby allowing us to
cast new light on some of the major contradictions at the heart of Conrad's
fictions. It is useful to recall, for instance, that already as an aesthetic figure
in classical antiquity, mimesis has both a visual and an affective side: it is
both on the side of (Apollonian) representations and of (Dionysian) impersonations. Consequently, opposed categories such as light and darkness, seeing and feeling, origins and shadows, form and formlessness, harmony and
violence, sameness and difference, truth and lies, are quite constitutive of
this Janus-faced concept. And as mimesis takes protean forms in the modern
period, and animates new sciences of man under the conceptual masks of
identification (psychoanalysis), contagion (sociology), hypnosis (psychology), or trance (anthropology), stretching to include concerns with mimicry
(postcolonial studies), simulation (media studies), affect (affect theory), or
the brain (neurology), we shall see that the protean *logoi* that inform mimesis
will illuminate different manifestations of the same chameleon-figure that
traverses Conrad's corpus, revealing surprising theoretical continuities where

we previously saw contradictory critical discontinuities. This book shall thus take literally Gebauer and Wulf's affirmation that "the productive side of mimesis, lies in the new connections it forges among art, philosophy, and science."[21]

The characteristic interdisciplinary scope of mimetic theory, in conjunction with the protean nature of the author under consideration, will lead us to cross over various fields of knowledge in order to establish bridges and conversations across disciplinary boundaries that have so far split discussions in different and competing areas of investigation. For instance, if the psychological dimension of mimesis understood as affective contagion will reopen the problematic of the mimetic unconscious that animated the modernist period, it shall also engage with the contagious violence that threatens to escalate to the point of catastrophe in the contemporary period (part 1). Alternatively, mimesis understood in its frenzied, ritualistic side will lead us to reframe the race quarrel that dominated postcolonial studies in the last decades of the twentieth century from an anthropological perspective that reconciles Achebe with Conrad while opening up a new conception of postcolonial mimesis that accounts for hybrid cross-fertilizations in the twenty-first century (part 2). And if the metaphysical implications of Conrad's take on darkness have been marginalized by recent commentators, mimesis understood in both its Apollonian and Dionysian manifestations offers an alternative account of the birth of Conrad's tragic metaphysics that brings it up-to-date with the horrorism of terrorism (part 3). In the process, contradictions that have dominated discussions in the past shall not be resolved in a grand, unifying, and homogeneous synthesis. Instead, adopting a Janus-faced perspective to Conrad's fictions will allow us to look back to a past conception of mimesis that is more interdisciplinary and future-oriented than previously realized, for it has psychological, ethical, anthropological, metaphysical, and neurological implications that directly inform the heterogeneous preoccupations of modernity. As we shift perspectives to keep up with the twists and turns of Conrad's shadow, the different shades of the same heterogeneous phenomenon will be played out in a kaleidoscopic spectrum of constantly changing light.

At the level of method, what was true of this book's janiform critical side is equally true of its protean theoretical side: I consider literature as a source of theoretical insights that emerge from the texts themselves. I am, of course, not alone in adopting such a double literary/theoretical perspective. Some of the most perceptive theorists of mimesis have paved the way. For instance, in his first book, *Deceit, Desire, and the Novel*, René Girard makes an exemplary point as he argues that "novelistic genius begins with the collapse of the 'autonomous' self" and sets out to derive his theory of "mimetic desire" from novelists from Cervantes to Dostoevsky.[22] Reframing the terms of the debate around mimesis, Girard specifies: "The enormous emphasis on mimesis through the entire history of Western literature cannot be a mere mistake," and he adds that "the great masterpieces are 'more mimetic' than other works" in the sense that they expand the definition of mimesis to account for the "entire range of imitative behavior,"[23] a range, we should specify, that is constitutive of the origins of mimetic theory. Given Conrad's striking affinities with the writers Girard discusses (most notably Dostoevsky), his persistent exploration of themes at the center of Girard's system (from doubles to rivalries, sacrifices to contagion), and, last but not least, his anticipation of some of Girard's most recent theoretical intuitions (such as the escalation of violence), Girard could certainly have enlisted Conrad's novelistic genius to expand his pantheon of "great novelists." Since Girard did not write about Conrad, *Conrad's Shadow* sets out to do it for him, in his company, but in my own way—that is, not by "applying" Girard but by inferring mimetic theory from Conrad.[24] As we shall see, this connection will prove rewarding for both parties. On one side, Girard will help us bring into focus pathological principles concerning the laws of violence at the heart of Conrad's dark fictions (bad mimesis); on the other side, Conrad will help us nuance, balance, sometimes counter, and, more often, supplement mimetic theory from a patho-*logical* perspective that promotes the laws of sympathy that keep the same heart beating (good mimesis).

But Girard is not alone in deriving mimetic theory directly from literature. Writing from a different philosophical perspective, but with Girard very much in his radar, the French philosopher Philippe Lacoue-Labarthe pursues the challenge to an "autonomous" conception of the subject from the angle of what he calls "unchained mimesis" (*mimèsis déchaînée*). Lacoue-Labarthe's answer to Jean-Luc Nancy's influential theoretical question, "who comes after the subject?," is worth mentioning in a book about a sailor turned protean writer, if only because this answer is actually an echo of Ulysses—another sailor far from home whose mythic journey, in a sense, is re-presented in Conrad's fictions. Ulysses's famous reply to Polyphemus's interrogation of identity, for Lacoue-Labarthe, sums up who comes after the so-called death of the subject: namely, "No one [*personne*]."[25] This ancient answer to poststructuralist concerns with a subject that has already always been decentered, deconstructed, deterritorialized, and is thus no longer, strictly speaking, one subject (unitary, monadic, self-contained), suggests that in order to know who comes after it is actually important to recall who comes before. It also indicates that, for Lacoue-Labarthe, literature provides a philosophical starting point to think about the mimetic foundations of the subject. Mimesis, in his view, turns the subject into a person who is "no one" (*personne*) in particular and, for this reason, is paradoxically open to the mimetic experience of becoming—not one, but everyone. Lacoue-Labarthe, as a careful reader of *Heart of Darkness* who recognized that Kurtz is precisely such a *personne*, perfectly knows that this could have been Conrad's answer as well. It is thus no accident that in *La Réponse d'Ulysse*, a posthumous collection of essays that convokes a literary tradition that goes from the *Odyssey* to *Heart of Darkness*, Lacoue-Labarthe gives the following piece of advice to his philosophical homo duplex, Nancy, as he says: "Maybe we should leave it up to literature (I would willingly say, to writings [*écritures*], without further identification) the care of asking this question [*lancer cet appel*]: 'who?'"[26] *Conrad's Shadow* takes this advice literally. I shall thus set out to infer mimetic theory from Conrad's exemplary writings in order to find out who, indeed, is this subject that is no(t) one.

I am aware that interrogating the texts directly for theoretical answers is no longer the dominant way of "doing" theory today. Bringing this realization to bear on Conrad studies, J. Hillis Miller writes, not without regrets, that "the almost unanimous assumption is that extrinsic criticism is the way to go these days."[27] This dominant "cultural" perspective is an extension of concerns with identity politics that reached their peak in the 1990s, is primarily concerned with the race-gender-class triad, and emphasizes political contexts over the so-called intrinsic, formal, or rhetorical qualities of the texts. The reader will see for herself that I do my share of unmasking operations concerning identity politics in what follows and that I am far from inimical to cultural studies. Still, I generally agree with Miller that a balancing swing of the pendulum from context back to the text, from theory back to literature, can help us bring Conrad studies fully into the twenty-first century. Reading closely, as I see it, is not inimical to theory. On the contrary, it is the very soul of theory. It is also the practical foundation for breaking new theoretical ground. Mimesis obliges that my focus will thus be intrinsic in its initial orientation. It considers that even politically oriented problems—such as colonialism, total wars, environmental catastrophes, and international terrorism—do not need to be considered from the *outside-in*, but already in-*form* Conrad's texts and intertexts from the *inside-out*. Consequently, this book zeroes in on the primary texts first, subjecting them to considerable hermeneutical and formal scrutiny along lines that concern both the theoretical message and the aesthetic medium of Conrad's Janus-faced tales.

And yet the reader who worries that reading might be an aesthetic end in itself intended to seal off "the text" from context, literature from life, by enveloping Conrad's modernist fictions in a halo of autonomous aesthetic self-sufficiency has no reason to worry. The ultimate aim of this intrinsic approach is to derive mimetic laws, principles, and insights that will allow us to reflect critically on the exterior world. This shift from text to context, artistic form to the referential world, might initially surprise for it seemingly contradicts my previous claim about the importance of intrinsic reading. It's ill advised, I know, to take formal principles outside the text, let alone the class, and I'm the first to remind students that characters are not people, plots not stories. A few years later though, as the same students are getting ready to enter the "real world," I welcome their mirroring interrogations, as they ask: why theorize if there is no practical relation to the world outside? To which I remind them that from Plato and Aristotle onward, theory is, indeed, not opposed to practice, but has always been practice's underlying presupposition. Close attention to literary analysis shall thus not be synony-mous with a disinterested formal exercise, no matter how important these exercises remain. My assumption is that entering deep into the aesthetic form of texts allows us to better see the outlines of matters that lie outside the texts. Learning how to read literature critically, and thus theoretically, is not simply an informative but also a *formative* and, sometimes, transformative activity that educates us to decipher the increasingly complex, indeterminate, and unstable world that surrounds us and—for the moment—still sustains us.

Ultimately, then, this book sets out to transgress the intrinsic/ extrinsic, textual/contextual, physical/metaphysical binary opposition.

Unsurprisingly so, since my goal is to focus on a Janus-faced concept (mimesis) that is as much oriented toward interior formal configurations as it is toward protean exterior ethical, anthropological, and ontological manifestations. Not unlike the shadow-line dividing the seaman and the writer, for Conrad, the line between intrinsic and extrinsic perspectives, texts and contexts, fiction and history, is shady at best. This is true at the level of the content (*logos*) of Conrad's mythic fictions, but is also true at the level of their narrative form (*lexis*). In my attempt to follow Conrad's shadow, I have thus attempted to do justice to both sides. At times, this involved departing from a standard academic discourse predicated on an impersonal diegetic distance in order to experiment with mimetic narrative, rhetorical, and dramatic forms that implicate the critic as well the reader in what is being discussed. If you worry that my formal attempt to shadow Conrad's shadow is based on a secret desire to become an artist, you have no cause for concern. It is rather based on the Janus-faced critical/theoretical impulse to dramatize some of the manifestations of mimesis in aesthetic forms that are congruent with the protean subject matter at hand. Hence a critical account of "The Duel" turns into a theoretical duel; an evaluation of the case of Leggatt takes the form of a juridical trial; a mirroring reflection between colonial and a postcolonial narrative is framed in mirroring terms, and so on. This strategy of redoubling introduces continuities between fiction and criticism in views reflecting theoretically on Conrad's shadow as its blurs the line between fiction and reality. Not the critic as artist then, but the theorist as mime, a *homo mimeticus* who re-enacts some of the protean manifestations of mimesis via performative narrative techniques that remain strictly subordinated to the moving contours of Conrad's original shadow. In the process, my hope is that mimetic theory—with its double concern with the reality of fictions and the fiction of reality—can become a Janus-faced locus of productive articulation of two perspectives that have been opposed in the past but can be joined in the future.

But there is another twist to the mimetic turn. Following the twists and turns of Conrad's shadow as it moves through his fictions allows us to balance a theoretical bias that has been shared by both extrinsic and extrinsic approaches alike in the twentieth century, but is becoming increasingly difficult to sustain in the twenty-first century. For all their emphases on different forms of decentering operations, theoretical approaches that have dominated the so-called rise of theory from the 1970s to the 1990s tend to share the same anthropocentric bias. Namely, they center their attention on the human actions, ideological phantoms, and politicized shadows (be they linked to race or gender, language or sexuality) in the foreground of Conrad's fictions, without paying much attention to the nonhuman forces (be they linked to the environment, epidemics, or nature) in the background.[28] Taking some distance from this all-too-human perspective, part 1 starts by showing that the nonhuman background, for Conrad, is never simply background. Rather, it in-*forms* in the most subtle, suggestive, and formally complex ways human figures in the foreground. As we follow the movement of this chameleon-like concept across different texts—blending against lush forests, muddy grounds, overcast skies, turbulent seas, or terrific storms—foreground and background, the human and the nonhuman, shall be articulated more carefully than, I believe, has been done so far. It is in fact this interplay between figure and ground that gives form to mimesis in the first place. In the process, shadows that appear, at first sight, to be the product of human figures, psychic phantoms, or ideological projections will progressively reveal less visible, but not less fundamental, nonhuman matters that both sustain and threaten to dissolve human forms in the first place. And here is where Conrad welcomes us in the age of the Anthropocene.

## Conrad in the Anthropocene

Conrad's fictions have repeatedly been accused of logocentrism, phallocentrism, and, especially, ethnocentrism in the twentieth century. Yet it is arguably Conrad who can best help us navigate past the fallacy of anthropocentrism that must be avoided in the twenty-first century. This anthropocentric bias is becoming particularly visible as we are entering a geological age defined by the "central role of mankind in geology and ecology," namely, the age of the "Anthropocene."[29] If *Anthropos* is at the center of an age in which humans are operating as a geological force on the environment, it is becoming increasingly clear that we are in the process of being decentered by nonhuman forces in a more fundamental way than ever before: climate change and its symptoms (polar caps melting, rising waters, hurricanes, and so forth) are not simply the effects of human actions; they also work as powerful causes that retroact on such actions. To be sure, Conrad is not writing in a period haunted by the shadow of climate change yet, is generally not describing anthropogenic "natural" catastrophes, and I will be careful not to project contemporary anxieties onto his texts, for the intrinsic reasons stated above. Still, one extrinsic point is worth bearing in mind. As a writer who spent a good part of his life on board ships, as part of a community of men who, if they wanted to survive, had to be extremely attentive to environmental forces—sea currents, winds, storms, typhoons—the recent, and quite vital, theoretical realizations that nature is endowed with "agentic" power, that we should pay more attention to "nonhuman" forces, and that the shadow-line dividing nature and culture is shady at best, must not have sounded radically new to Conrad. As Michel Serres also recognized, "Those who used to live out in the weather's rain and wind, whose habitual acts brought forth long-lasting cultures out of local experiences—peasants and sailors—have had no say for a long time now, if they ever had it."[30] If Conrad, as a sailor turned writer, is a unique voice in the age of the Anthropocene, it is because he had a say, always had it—and we are now in a position to listen.

Probably more than any other modernist writer, in his fictions Conrad consistently represents the environment's power to act on human actions—with a vengeance. Recent developments in ecocriticism and new materialism have warned us against "anthropocentric" fallacies resting on a monadic and egocentric conception of the subject that limits agency to humans alone in order to become "perceptively open" to what Jane Bennett calls the "vitality of matter," or "vibrant matter."[31] Conrad's fictions not only resonate with such vibrations; they also offer a narrative-based mimetic supplement to theorists of catastrophe. In particular, he makes us see how in the context of what Jean Luc Nancy calls the "equivalence of catastrophe," contagious—and in this sense mimetic—continuities break down structural oppositions that divide self and others, nature and culture, human and nonhuman forces, generating a turbulent spiral of actions and reactions his fictions encourage us to diagnose first, before attempting any ethical reevaluation. Mimesis, and the loss of differentiation it entails, is, indeed, in the maelstrom of Conrad's representations of catastrophe. As we follow Conrad's account of the dynamic interplay between human and nonhuman forces—be it during a storm, a total war, or an epidemic—we are thus encouraged to sail past the Scylla and Charybdis of binary distinctions that simply oppose good and evil, nature and culture, cause and effect, in order to adopt systemic lenses to follow the whirlpool of feedback loops that inform the complex ecology of mimetic actions and reactions in potentially catastrophic contexts.

And yet if Conrad's fictions invite us to think about the possibility of catastrophe that looms on the horizon of many of his tales of the sea—from *Typhoon* to "The Secret Sharer" to *The Shadow-Line*—it is not to fall prey to apocalyptic despair. Instead, Conrad promotes what the philosopher and mimetic theorist Jean-Pierre Dupuy calls "enlightened doomsaying." That is, a skill that consists in making us "see catastrophe as our *fate*—only a fate that we may yet choose to avoid."[32] Dupuy does not talk about Conrad but confirms an epistemic point I made above as he says that "there is no better preparation for acquiring this skill than a classical literary education," and urges "every engineer, every technocrat, and every business executive . . . to read at least one novel and see at least one film a week."[33] This is a welcome reminder coming from a philosopher working at the juncture where catastrophe and mimesis meet. It could also prompt critics in the humanities to reciprocate the gesture and take a step toward a nonacademic readership so as to meet halfway. Let us in fact remember that Marlow has no problems talking to businessmen and administrators within Conrad's fictions. Perhaps, then, critics, at one additional remove, should have no problems addressing the same audience as they comment on these fictions in the real world. For both parties interested in such a step, Conrad offers a good place to start. His fictions help us bridge the divide between two unnecessarily antagonistic cultures, and for two reasons: he not only had firsthand knowledge of catastrophic scenarios as a seaman; he also knew how to frame images of catastrophe to promote the possibility of survival as a novelist.

Reading Conrad's novels provides thus a good training to see catastrophe as our avoidable fate. But one needs to learn how to read (them) first and this book aims to contribute to this learning process. I might as well admit that I was tempted to subtitle part 1 "An Inquiry into Some Points of Seamanship in Catastrophic Contexts" in honor of the nautical manual Marlow finds on the shore of the Congo River—but this is a mimetic temptation I resisted in the end. Confessions apart, in what follows we shall familiarize ourselves with Conrad's sophisticated literary diagnostics of environmental and affective contagion, promotion of effective leadership, sustained ethical interrogations, and communal forms of cooperation he mobilizes in his stormy fictions in order to help us think about ways to avoid the shadow of catastrophe. Training our reading skills might well be training our survival skills.

Interestingly, from this new perspective, seemingly past-oriented values central to Conrad's poetics—such as solidarity, communal sharing, and universal kinship—turn out to be more future oriented than previously realized. In the wake of transnational issues such as climate change, international terrorism, or global pandemics, Conrad's appeal to what he calls "that mysterious fellowship which unities in a community of hopes and fears all the dwellers of this earth" (*PR* 23–24) has a new and timely ring. To be sure, his fictions do not offer ready-made solutions that can easily be applied to present-day catastrophic scenarios. Yet his emphasis on the microcosm of the ship understood as a "small planet" offers immanent, real to life, situational case studies to account for the formation of cooperative communities in which shared feelings of solidarity emerge in order to affirm the possibility of common survival during shared catastrophes. Once again, the two sides of mimesis are in the eye of Conrad's maelstrom: if one side generates violent, contagious pathologies that accentuate what Girard calls "escalation to extremes"[34] leading to catastrophic ends, the other side generates shared feelings of solidarity that open up a relational, communal, and systemic understanding that points toward new beginnings. In the process, Conrad's diagnostic of contagious pathologies also urges us to interrogate the value of ethical values in catastrophic scenarios. Above all, it reminds us that the practical possibility of survival rests on shared affective, intersubjective, and communal foundations.

Finally, reframing mimesis along these immanent lines makes us wonder about the ontological foundations of Conrad's shadow we are setting out to track. Traditionally, artists have in fact been relegated to makers of illusory "shadows" far removed from what philosophers call "truth" and scientists call "facts." But does this Platonic ontology that sets up a hierarchy between ideal Forms, material phenomena, and aesthetic forms still hold today? Can shadows still be dismissed as debased copies of a more original, physical, or metaphysical reality? Or should we rather say that these are "prejudices of philosophers," to borrow a phrase from a philosopher-poet

Conrad had many secret affinities with and who will loom large in this study?[35] Perhaps in an age of constant transformation in which fluxes of becoming are driving us toward an uncertain future at an increasing speed, moving artistic shadows might actually be able to adapt, conform, and give new form to changing ideas about what the "truth" is, or might possibly become. Pondering on such elusive questions, toward the end of this study I came to a better understanding of what Conrad had been saying from the beginning. As he puts it in his famous Preface to *The Nigger of the "Narcissus,"* such ontological concerns are shared by artists, philosophers, and scientists alike: "The artist then, like the thinker or the scientist, seeks the truth and makes his appeal" (*NN* xi), says Conrad. But a fundamental difference in perspective defines these exemplary seekers of truth. If "the thinker plunges into ideas, the scientist into facts," Conrad specifies that "it is otherwise with the artist" (xi). This untimely figure, in fact, "descends within himself" in order to "appeal" to what he calls "*our* less obvious capacities" (xii; my emphasis), implying that these capacities are human, very human capacities. Less obvious, less visible, and less tangible, our capacities are introverted and qualitative in nature. Hence they do not fare well in a culture that is extraverted and quantitative in spirit. And yet Conrad insists that they are no less profound, essential, or vital, especially in a world increasingly overwhelmed by new scientific "facts" that render philosophical "ideas" about what the "truth" is, or should be, in need of constant reframing, adaptation, and reconfiguration.

Whether we call these capacities "imagination," "creativity," or—and this is the term I prefer—"intuition," they affirm a will to truth that, for Conrad, is above all a will to see, and perhaps also a will to feel. As he concludes the Preface with a well-known phrase that still requires meditation, the goal of the artist is "to make you feel it is, before all, to make you *see*" (*NN* xiv). Not unlike the claim about the homo duplex, this phrase has been repeated so often that it may hardly sound original. But originality is, once again, not the point. Artists have in fact always known that both feeling and seeing are, indeed, mimetic capacities par excellence: if artists make us see via visual images (mimesis as representation), they also make us feel via affective dramatizations (mimesis as impersonation). Given the centrality of both sides of mimesis in Conrad's fictions, it is perhaps not surprising that this Janus-faced concept turns out to be at the palpitating heart of Conrad's poetics—animating both its double (critical) twists and protean (theoretical) turns.

## Twists and Turns

This book traces the protean articulations of mimesis in their psycho-ethical (part 1), anthropological (part 2), and metaphysical (part 3) manifestations. Schematically put, a perspectival, transdisciplinary, and comparative take on mimesis allows us to supplement three main theoretical approaches that have dominated Conrad studies in the second part of the twentieth century: psychoanalysis, postcolonial studies, and cultural studies. Let us proceed in order.

Since Albert Guerard's influential *Conrad the Novelist* (1958), psychoanalytical approaches have been immensely productive in uncovering the personal, familial, archetypal, and, more recently, imaginary, symbolic, and traumatic shadows that are internal to Conrad's fictions. *Conrad's Shadow* pursues this journey within in order to travel farther in the labyrinth of Conrad's fictional unconscious. This move follows naturally from the modernist brand of mimetic theory I have been advocating. Let us not forget that mimetic theory not only emerges out of a sustained critical engagement with psychoanalysis; it also uncovers its repressed genealogical foundations in pre-Freudian theories of hypnosis and imitative contagion that dominated nineteenth-century Europe. In fact, the idea that the essence of the subject is located in the other, that the subject, even in its most intimate affects, is born out of a mimetic identification, hypnotic rapport, or suggestive communication with privileged others (*socii*), or, more radically, that the "subject *is* the other," the ego is a "phantom *of* the ego," is first and foremost what Mikkel Borch-Jacobsen and the present author—building on the work of René Girard and Philippe Lacoue-Labarthe—have called a "mimetic hypothesis."[36]

And yet mimetic theory also takes a step back from psychoanalysis to leap farther ahead as it reminds us that every imposing approach casts a long shadow. In particular, psychoanalysis's territorial, familial, and Oedipal tendencies have tended to obscure the immanent, affective, interpersonal, and communal forces that trigger unconscious reactions in specific social, ethical, and political contexts. Conrad will help us bring this anti-Oedipal side of the unconscious, which I qualify as the "mimetic unconscious," out of the shadow. In particular, Conrad's diagnostic monocle zeroes in to dissect the elusive sphere of intersubjective, psychosomatic, and contagious forms of communication that are not under the control of consciousness and lead the ego to reproduce, share, and assimilate the qualities of privileged others so as to be caught in the affective experience of becoming—other, plural, multiple.[37] For Conrad, in fact, as for other modernists before and after him, the unconscious is mimetic in the sense that it leads subjects to be imitative, that is, to unconsciously or semiconsciously reproduce, shadow-like—but with real pathos nonetheless—the behavior, expressions, feelings, gestures, and thoughts of others, especially privileged others or *socii*, though not only. This is a psychic side of Conrad that has so far been neglected since psychoanalysis claimed to offer the only door to the unconscious. Yet other doors are now available. If pre-Freudian thinkers found in automatic, hypnotic reflexes the main road to the unconscious, neuroscientists have now located the neurological sources of these mimetic reflexes in so-called mirror neurons that fire in the brain at the sight of gestures and expressions performed by others. Conrad, as an experienced seaman, was particularly attentive to these nonverbal, psychosomatic reactions, and in his fictions he diagnoses such mimetic phenomena in real-life social situations. There is a strong theoretical potential in this narrative gesture. In fact, Conrad's fictions of the double encourage us to take mirror neurons outside the confines of the lab in order to reflect on the broader ethical and political implications of mimesis. The mimetic unconscious is thus, in this sense, already a political unconscious; it affects doubles and rivals, the dominant and the subaltern, the crew and the captains, the crowd and the individual alike, introducing secret continuities at the heart of discontinuities, especially in collective, affective, and potentially catastrophic contexts.

Part 1, "Ethics of Catastrophe," puts the old romantic trope of the doppelgänger to new theoretical use to face the catastrophic shadows that haunt Conrad's tales of the double. Chapter 1 focuses on a "Military Tale," titled "The Duel" (1908), that looks back to the Napoleonic Wars but also anticipates—via Carl Clausewitz's definition of war as "extended duel"—the "escalation of violence" René Girard sees as the destiny of global wars. While Conrad agrees with Girard that mimetic actions and reactions can lead to duels to the end, he also looks for therapeutic ways to put an end to duels.

Chapter 2 reframes the problematic of mimetic escalation in the context of what Conrad calls "end of the world" storms that inform *Typhoon* (1902) and, especially, "The Secret Sharer" (1912). Re-reading Conrad's stormy fictions in light of an emerging ethics of catastrophe in the age of the Anthropocene allows us to diagnose the contagious affects and effects at the heart of catastrophic scenarios that have remained largely unstudied so far and to revisit what Hillis Miller calls "the most secret secret" of Conrad's tale: namely, the basis of ethical decisions. Chapter 3 reframes what is arguably the best of Conrad's late novels, *The Shadow-Line* (1916), in light of a contagious epidemic that generates shared feelings of cooperative community. This chapter supplements what Jean-Luc Nancy calls "inoperative community" in light of mimetic forms of cooperation that affirm the possibility of survival. Across the shifts of perspective, in this part we shall see that, for Conrad, war and peace, splitting and doubling, infection and affection continue to operate according the Janus-faced laws of imitation.

If part 1 takes us on a journey inside to face environmental shadows outside, part 2 takes the opposite route. It starts from images of racial darkness all too visible from the outside in order to revisit the invisible mimetic forces that inaugurated postcolonial approaches to Conrad from the inside. Postcolonial studies have visibly contributed to Conrad studies over the past forty years. Initiated by Nigerian novelist Chinua Achebe in a controversial and still influential essay titled "An Image of Africa: Racism in Conrad's *Heart of Darkness*" (1977), postcolonial approaches have rendered us attentive to the violent implications of ethnocentric representations of racial otherness. They have also called attention to the subversive force of "mimicry" in destabilizing the relation between the dominant and the subaltern, thereby establishing mimesis at the center of theoretical debates on self-other relations. And yet within Conrad studies, with some notable exceptions—the most prominent being Edward Said—critical debates have tended to remain polarized around two competing fronts that simply pit Achebe contra Conrad. This is especially true when it comes to the notorious images of "frenzy" whereby African subjects dance to the sound of drums. This polarization eventually led to an image of Achebe's first and most influential novel, *Things Fall Apart* (1958), as the "antithesis" of Conrad's *Heart of Darkness*. Mimesis prompts us to reopen the race dossier and offer a more nuanced perspective to this much-discussed quarrel. In fact, an ancient theoretical tradition that goes from Plato to Nietzsche, Girard to Lacoue-Labarthe, has taught us that behind rivalrous quarrels often lies the shadow of imitation. I argue that what was true of ancient quarrels between philosophers and poets is equally true of race quarrels between colonial and postcolonial authors. Namely, that striking continuities exist between seemingly antagonistic images. The question I ask is thus not, can the subaltern speak? For Achebe did not only speak—he wrote. But, rather, can the subaltern mime? And if she or he mimes, then, which form of postcolonial imitation accounts for powerful counternarratives that reframe images of Africa via the same images they set out to counter?

In order to answer such troubling questions, part 2, "Anthropology of Frenzy," turns the postcolonial controversy triggered by Achebe's critique of Conrad into a less-polarized diagnostic of the mimetic patho-logy inform-ing the creation of postcolonial pictures of Africa. There will be two sides to this picture of Africa: one sketched by Conrad in *Heart of Darkness*, the other by Achebe in *Things Fall Apart*. And only when these two pictures are joined will they turn out to paint different faces on the same Janus-faced coin. Chapter 4 argues that before automatically denouncing Conrad's image of Africa depicting African subjects dancing in a state of "frenzy" as an exemplary case of racism, it is actually important to see more clearly into the anthropological phenomenon he is trying to represent. This ritual, collective, musical phenomenon has remained buried under critical layers of ideological accusations on both sides of the fence and has so far remained hidden in the background; yet if we take a step aside to a neighboring field, we realize that anthropologists specialized in sub-Saharan Africa have long defined such frenzied states in terms of "possession trance." If images of frenzy turn out to have ritual referents, and these rituals are enacted by European shadows qua leaders, then the picture not only changes but begins to operate as a disquiet-ing mirror of the self, not the other. In a second moment, the consequences of this anthropological reframing allow us to reflect more critically on the postcolonial side of the picture as well, which occupies us in chapter 5. What is striking about this much-discussed controversy is that no one seems to have noticed that even the most disputed Conradian images of African "frenzy" Achebe denounces in "An Image of Africa" inform the very images of frenzy he, Achebe, had previously depicted in *Things Fall Apart*. Far from being a case of colonial "mimicry," I argue that this is a form of postcolonial mimesis that generates pictures that are almost the opposite—but not quite.

After the psychic, ethical, and anthropological sides of mimesis, part 3 of this study revisits the underlying metaphysics that informs Conrad's modernist account of tragedy. Cultural approaches to identity politics that have dominated critical discussions in the last decades of the twentieth century have tended to disregard what J. Hillis Miller calls the "'metaphysical' dimension of Conrad's work."[38] More recently, however, figures as diverse as J. Hillis Miller, Philippe Lacoue-Labarthe, Jonathan Dollimore, and Adriana Cavarero have provided new and timely perspectives to revisit the metaphysical foundation of "the horror of the West" (Lacoue-Labarthe's term), which go beyond the borders of "the West," for the twenty-first century. These readings mark a philosophical turn, or a return of the philosophical, in Conrad studies. Reframed in this light, the atrocities of colonialism and imperialism, as well as the horror of the Holocaust and of contemporary terrorism, turn out to depict a type of horror that is as physical as it is ontological, as political as it is philosophical, as fictional as it is real. I suggest that despite, or rather because of, its ongoing modern manifestations, the horror, for Conrad, rests on tragic metaphysical foundations.

Building on this philosophical turn from a distinctively Nietzschean perspective, part 3, "Metaphysics of Tragedy," traces Conrad's account of the rebirth of tragedy—out of Dionysian and Apollonian mimesis. Chapter 6 reframes the ontological foundations of Conrad's impressionistic poetics in light of the surrealist principles that latently inform it. I argue that the images of darkness that cast an ethico-political shadow on *The Nigger of the "Narcissus"* (1897) are symptomatic of what the French anthropologist and surrealist writer Roger Caillois calls "mimetism or legendary psychasthenia."[39] This chapter reveals an image of Conrad as a protosurrealist writer *avant la lettre*. Chapter 7 shows how Conrad's surrealist metaphysics gives birth to a view of tragedy (out of Dionysian sacrifice) that finds in Nietzsche and his philosophical avatars—from Georges Bataille to Jean Baudrillard, René Girard to Philippe Lacoue-Labarthe—its most acute interlocutors. In particular, looking back to Conrad's aesthetic origins in his first novel, *Almayer's Folly* (1895), allows us to uncover a view of tragedy that is ancient in its sacrificial origins, stretches as far back as Euripides's *The Bacchae* (405 BC), yet continues to inform the most obscure side of *Heart of Darkness* and finds its ritual culmination in Francis Ford Coppola's *Apocalypse Now* (1979). Chapter 8 considers how this formless, Dionysian metaphysics is given new aesthetic form in explosive images of disfiguration in *The Secret Agent* (1907) that are constitutive of what Adriana Cavarero calls the "horrorism" of contemporary terrorism. But Conrad goes further. His take on terrorism shows that horrorism is mediated by mass media that no longer operate on ontological principles grounded in reality (Cavarero) or hyperreality (Baudrillard). Rather, the ontology of terrorism, for Conrad, emerges from the realization that virtual simulations have real, embodied, mimetic, or, as I shall call them, hypermimetic effects.

The book ends with a Coda that shows how Conrad's diagnostic of mimesis contributes to the emerging dialogue between literature and science. Recent developments in the neurosciences have proved that the human brain remains "plastic" throughout our lives; and French philosopher Catherine Malabou has been quick to remind us that "we do not know it." I argue that Conrad, as he spoke of "his still plastic character," knew it—and wanted others to know it too. A diagnostic of *Under Western Eyes* (1911) read in the company of *A Personal Record* (1912) shows that looking back to what Plato called the "plasticity" of the soul allows Conrad to look ahead to the "plasticity" of what he also calls the "brain." Conversely, Conrad's neuro-turn to the brain is actually also a return to a mimetic diagnostic of the soul, understood in its material, immanent, and malleable nature. In the process, he joins personal and fictional principles to give aesthetic form to what is perhaps the latest and most fundamental rediscovery of the plasticity characteristic of mimesis. The reader who is looking for a secret key to Conrad's adaptable, impressionable, and plastic poetics might well start at the end, before turning to the beginning.

·         ·         ·

Rather than restricting mimesis to one of its singular or double manifestations, I have attempted to trace its protean transformations as this chameleon concept crosses over into different fictional and theoretical territories. My concern throughout is to outline the general movement of mimesis in its multiple, protean, and plastic transformations. While writing each singular, chapter I thus had to resist the temptation to stop this movement, freeze the shadow, trace its contours, and pin it to the wall to dissect it further.

Each manifestation of Conrad's shadow could, indeed, have been expanded in order to take on a singular life in a book of its own: Conrad and violence, Conrad and the Anthropocene, Conrad and epidemics, Conrad and community, Conrad and trance, Conrad and postcolonial mimesis, Conrad and psychasthenia, Conrad and surrealism, Conrad and tragedy, Conrad and horrorism, Conrad and simulation, Conrad and plasticity, and so on—the doors mimesis opens are, indeed, plural. Ultimately, however, I resisted this temptation, not only because the chameleon in Conrad's fictions kept me on the move but also because I hoped others would follow up on such lines of inquiry. Indeed, *Conrad's Shadow* confirms the contemporary realization that the critical potential of Conrad for the twenty-first century "looks limitless."[40] A secret ambition of this book is to provide a protean, adaptable, and resilient theory to delineate new fields of critical investigation for the future.

As we will soon realize, Conrad's diagnostic of both human and nonhuman forms of imitation makes him, more than ever, "one of us." In his attempt to "make us see" the shadow of mimesis that takes shape ahead of us, lies, perhaps, his greatest originality.

# Abbreviations

Unless specified otherwise, I refer to the Cambridge edition of the *Collected Works of Joseph Conrad*. When the latter edition was not yet available, I referred to the Doubleday, Page & Co. (1925) uniform edition, which I signal below with the symbol (*). Conrad's works are abbreviated as follows:

| | |
|---|---|
| *AF* | *Almayer's Folly* |
| *LJ* | *Lord Jim* |
| *MS* | *The Mirror of the Sea* |
| *N\** | *Nostromo* |
| *NLL* | *Notes on Life and Letters* |
| *NN\** | *The Nigger of the "Narcissus"* |
| *PR* | *A Personal Record* |
| *SA* | *The Secret Agent* |
| *SL* | *The Shadow-Line* |
| *SoS* | *A Set of Six* |
| *TH\** | *Tales of Hearsay* |
| *TLS* | *'Twixt Land and Sea* |
| *TOS\** | *Typhoon and Other Stories* |

*TU**     *Tales of Unrest*
*UWE*    *Under Western Eyes*
*V**      *Victory*
*YOS*    *Youth and Other Stories*

The abbreviation *CL* has been used to refer to the *Collected Letters of Joseph Conrad* (Cambridge University Press, 1983–2005).
   Works by other authors are abbreviated as follows:

*B*      Euripides, *The Bacchae*
*BE*    René Girard, *Battling to the End*
*BGE*   Friedrich Nietzsche, *Beyond Good and Evil*
*BT*    Friedrich Nietzsche, *The Birth of Tragedy*
*CI*     Edward Said, *Culture and Imperialism*
*DM*   Charles Darwin, *The Descent of Man*
*EC*    Jean-Luc Nancy, *L'Équivalence des catastrophes (Après Fukushima)*
*H*      Adriana Cavarero, *Horrorism*
*HM*   Georges Bataille, "Hegel, la mort, le sacrifice"
*HW*   Philippe Lacoue-Labarthe, "The Horror of the West"
*IA*     Chinua Achebe, "An Image of Africa: Racism in Conrad's *Heart of Darkness*"
*IC*     Jean-Luc Nancy, *The Inoperative Community*
*LC*    Homi Bhabha, *The Location of Culture*
*LI*     Gabriel Tarde, *Les Lois de l'imitation* (*The Laws of Imitation*)
*MH*   Roger Caillois, *Le Mythe et l'homme*
*OW*   Carl von Clausewitz, *On War*
*P*      Aristotle, *Poetics*
*PP*    Jacques Derrida, "Plato's Pharmacy"
*R*      Plato, *Republic*
*RU*    Philippe Lacoue-Labarthe, *La Réponse d'Ulysse*
*SS*     Jean Baudrillard, *Simulacres et simulation*
*TFA*   Chinua Achebe, *Things Fall Apart*
*VS*     René Girard, *Violence and the Sacred*
*WSW*   Catherine Malabou, *What Should We Do with Our Brain?*
*WWI*   Arthur Schopenhauer, *The World as Will and Idea*

# PART 1

# Ethics of Catastrophe

# CHAPTER 1

# Dueling to the End/Ending "The Duel": Clausewitz *avec* Girard

War is nothing but a duel on a larger scale.

—Carl von Clausewitz, *On War*

[A] story of duelling, which became a legend in the army, runs through the epic of imperial wars.

—Joseph Conrad, "The Duel"

"The Duel" (1908) is generally considered a minor tale that is not often read, let alone studied. It has been primarily interpreted as a historical fiction concerned with the Napoleonic Wars. And quite rightly so, since the historicity of "The Duel" is at least double: this "Military Tale" deals with a historically documented relation between two officers in the Napoleonic army who fought a series of legendary duels for nearly two decades; and these personal duels follow, shadowlike, the Napoleonic Wars that plagued Europe as a whole. In a sense, then, this is a past-oriented story whose relative neglect might stem from the reassuring feeling that it deals with historical ideals, revolutions, and conflicts we have long left behind. And yet, as anticipated, Conrad's fictions tend to be Janus-faced and often look in two opposed directions: both behind, to what is past, and ahead, to what is yet to come.

This is equally true of "The Duel," a text that entails not only a timely historical reflection on the "universal carnage" produced by past total wars but also, and perhaps more important, an untimely theoretical reflection on the escalating violence characteristic of our contemporary global wars.

The innovative theoretical potential of "The Duel" emerges once it is put in perspective with both past and contemporary theorists who have taken the duel as their paradigmatic starting point to think about the violence of war. On the one hand, Conrad's representation of the Napoleonic Wars as a duel clearly echoes what is arguably still the most influential theoretical text on military strategy in the West: Karl Clausewitz's *Vom Kriege* (1832–1934).[1] In particular, Conrad considers the seemingly antiquated practice of the duel as a diagnostic mirror to reflect (on) the larger reciprocal and contagious dynamic responsible for what Clausewitz calls the "escalation" of violence. In a deft move, Conrad also goes beyond Clausewitz as he puts the old romantic trope of the homo duplex to new theoretical use to unmask the characteristically mimetic logic that secretly animates the homo bellicus. On the other hand, Conrad's emphasis on the mimetic nature of the duelists is framed against the background of what he calls in "Autocracy and War," "the Napoleonic episode as a school of violence" (*NLL* 73). This school already looks ahead to a more recent account of war concerned with the contemporary escalation of violence: René Girard's *Achever Clausewitz* (2007).[2] As Girard reminds us, after "two world wars, the invention of the atomic bomb, several genocides and an imminent ecological disaster" (*BE* x), Clausewitz's realization that violence is reciprocal, contagious, and thus bound to escalate to extremes still deserves a good listen. This used to be an unfashionable perspective, but Girard is now no longer alone in his view that mimesis and violence are intimately related. The growing concern with nuclear wars, climate change, global epidemics, and related anthropogenic catastrophes that threaten to escalate rightly preoccupies some of the leading intellectuals of our time.[3] Furthering this emerging line of inquiry from the angle of mimetic theory, we shall see that Conrad's neglected tale casts new light on the affective logic of contagious violence that continues to haunt our contemporary post-9/11 times. It does so by turning back to the romantic trope of the doppelgänger in order to look ahead to the double binds violence increasingly generates in our precarious times. As we shall see, there are numerous echoes between Conrad's Napoleonic tale and Girard's most recent take on violence, unsurprisingly so since both Conrad and Girard have Clausewitz's trope of war qua duel as their theoretical starting points. And yet if Girard focuses on apocalyptic battles to the end, Conrad is primarily interested in the end of the battle. I argue that in this life-affirmative inversion of perspectives lies Conrad's originality.

Conrad, Clausewitz, Girard. As might be expected, bringing these three theorists of war together will not only lead to friendly handshakes and pats on the back; it might also generate a field of tension in which dissenting views and theoretical skirmishes can be played out, in a nonviolent mood. Conrad may not have been much of a duelist himself. But when it comes to fictional duels, he can defend himself quite deftly. Perhaps he even manages to use his pen as a "cold steel" (*PR* 85) to score a few points against such experienced swashbucklers. D'Hubert contra Feraud, Clausewitz contra Napoleon, Conrad contra Girard: indeed, this duel may turn out to be as fictional and historical as it is critical and theoretical. And in this doubling and redoubling of duels on the violent nature of imitation we shall not only hear the echoes of old historical battles but also the possibility for new theoretical beginnings.

Let the duel begin.

## Mimetic Antipodes

From the opening of the narrative, Conrad makes clear that his focus on the duel is at least double, in the sense that it is as personal and psychological as it is collective and historical. The first lines tightly join these competing sides of the story, suggesting that they are mirror images of each other. "The Duel" opens as follows:

> Napoleon I, whose career had the quality of a duel against the whole of Europe, disliked duelling between the officers of his army. The great military emperor was not a swashbuckler, and had little respect for tradition.
>
> Nevertheless, a story of duelling, which became a legend in the army, runs through the epic of imperial wars. (165)

That this is a "historical fiction" (x) is clear from the outset.[4] But this fiction is not simply historical because it is based on a real and somewhat absurd duel between two French officers in Napoleon's Grand Army. It is also historical in the more general sense that it reflects (on) what Conrad calls, in the "Author's Note," "the Spirit of the Epoch" (xi). The personal duel in the foreground is thus immediately situated against the larger historical context of the Napoleonic Wars in the background; this move suggests a direct continuity between the intersubjective dynamic of the duel, on the one hand, and the collective dynamic of war, on the other. It is thus no accident that the protagonists' multiple duels—which move from France to Germany to Russia and back, from 1801 to 1816—parallel the rise and fall of the Napoleonic Wars. Clearly, the image of two "insane" (165) individuals dueling *usque ad finem* functions as a mirror that reflects Conrad's larger concerns with the violent dynamic responsible for what he calls the "years of universal carnage" (165).


## Homo Bellicus

And yet the opening lines also make clear that this historical fiction about the Napoleonic Wars is equally a theoretical fiction on the nature of war tout court. In fact, Conrad immediately situates his narrative in a relation of theoretical continuity with a foundational text that also emerges out of a careful scrutiny of the Napoleonic Wars. Written by a Prussian officer who partook in the wars against Napoleon, Carl von Clausewitz's *On War* provides an influential, and so far largely unexplored theoretical frame to reread Conrad's Napoleonic tale. Conrad's opening lines clearly echo Clausewitz's beginning. As the latter famously puts it in chapter 1 of Book I, "On the Nature of War:" "I shall not begin by expounding a pedantic, literary definition of war, but go straight to the heart of the matter, to the duel. War is nothing but a duel on a larger scale [*erweiterter Zweikampf*]" (*OW* 13). The connection between Conrad's "The Duel" and Clausewitz's *On War* could not be more direct: both authors focus on the Napoleonic Wars; both authors take the duel as a model to think about war; and, above all, both authors are interested in forms of escalating violence that go on *usque ad finem*.

To be sure, Conrad's Napoleonic fiction is equally in line with a long tradition of narratives of the duel—from Pushkin's "The Shot" to Chekov's "The Duel," passing by Tolstoy's *War and Peace* and Dostoevsky's *The Possessed*[5]—whose concern is also to illuminate the obscure logic of violence, a logic that will continue to haunt Conrad's imagination in his last and arguably less successful fictions such as *Suspense* and *The Rover*. Yet in "The Duel" Conrad's modernist lenses add a theoretical supplement to this romantic tradition. In fact, Conrad's focus on two antagonistic characters that are clear antipodes dramatizes Clausewitz's definition of war in terms of an "interaction with opposites" (*OW* 84). And, by doing so, he makes us see the dynamic responsible for the ongoing and escalating dimension of the Napoleonic Wars in particular and of total wars in general.

That Armand D'Hubert and Gabriel Feraud—the two cavalry officers in question—are polar opposites is clear from the outset. The narrator describes them as follows: "two officers, one tall, with an interesting face and a moustache the colour of ripe corn [D'Hubert], the other, short and sturdy, with a hooked nose and a thick crop of black curly hair [Feraud]" (173). And their opposed physical appearance reflects their opposed psychological disposition: D'Hubert, we are told, is a "Northman" who was "born sober," Feraud a "Southerner" who was "born intoxicated" (176); the former is endowed with an "equable temper," the latter is characterized by "exuberance" (193); D'Hubert is defined by his "natural kindness" (167), Feraud possesses the "inferior faculties of a tiger" (180). North versus south, reason versus passion, mind versus body, culture versus instinct: the opposition could not be more clearly drawn. And not surprisingly so. This structural polarity, in fact, is not only personal but also mirrors the wider collective interplay between rational and emotional forces that, for Clausewitz, animate the logic of war itself: "Savage peoples are ruled by passion, civilized peoples by the mind" (*OW* 14), he writes in Book I. And in Book II he specifies: "Psychological forces exert a decisive influence on the elements involved in war" (73). "The Duel" is a careful diagnostic of the role of such antithetical psychological forces in the articulation of the intersubjective and reciprocal dynamic of war qua duel. Conrad, in fact, dramatizes a personal polarity between reason and passion, mind and body, not only in order to mirror the opposing forces that animate historical wars but also, and for us more importantly, to offer a theoretical account of the cold-blooded and hot-blooded principles of the art of war itself.

And yet, for Conrad, the opposition between the duelists is not clear-cut; an underlying mimetic continuity runs through these seemingly antithetical figures. D'Hubert and Feraud, in fact, fight on the same front are both "officers of cavalry" (Hussars), and their similarities progressively increase as the story unfolds. The narrative begins by calling attention to their "connection with the high-spirited but fanciful animal" (165) they ride, perhaps in order to indicate that the same "high-spirited" passion runs through these two seemingly different cavalry officers. They are certainly "both intensely warlike" (166) and obsessed with "the care of their honor" (194); they wear the same uniform, and, above all, their military careers lead them, step by step, through the same ranks: from lieutenant to captain, colonel to general. To be sure, these characters might be polar opposites. But like all opposites, they attract each other in such a way that difference progressively gives way to sameness, opposed images turn out to be mirror images—antipodes become doppelgängers.[6]

### Homo Duplex

Conrad's fascination with the homo duplex is well known and traverses most of the fictions we will later encounter, but the connection between the homo duplex and the homo bellicus has so far gone unnoticed, surprisingly so since it informs other Conradian fictions as well. For instance, in "An Outpost of Progress" (1896), an early short story collected in *Tales of Unrest* (1898) that also depicts an "ex-non-commissioned officer of cavalry in an army" (88) as one of its protagonists, Conrad had already articulated the mimetic logic that generates violence among seemingly antithetical figures. As their names already suggest, Kayerts and Carlier, two opposed colonial characters, or better, caricatures (the former is "short and fat," the latter "tall" with "thin legs" [86]), progressively turn out to be mirror images of each other. And in a final fight to the death over a decent cup of tea, their differences are blurred (we are told that Kayerts "saved himself just in time from becoming Carlier" [115]), and they end up destroying one another. Conrad's theoretical insight into the mimetic dynamic of violence is already contained in this scene, in a nutshell. But there is also an important aesthetic principle to be learned from such clear mimetic re-presentations. In a narrative echo that is constitutive of his writing technique and, as we shall repeatedly confirm, in-*forms* his poetic praxis as a whole, Conrad picks up a motif initiated in an earlier fiction and develops it further, generating an underlying mimetic continuity that strings together seemingly different texts—from *Almayer's Folly* (1895) to *Heart of*

*Darkness* (1899), *Typhoon* (1902) to "The Secret Sharer" (1910), *The Nigger of the "Narcissus"* (1897) to *The Secret Agent* (1907), *Under Western Eyes*
(1911) to *A Personal Record* (1912) to *The Shadow-Line* (1917).

This structural feature out of which Conrad's fictions emerge from
mimetic principles nested in an earlier tale is perfectly visible in "The Duel."
Taking a motif embryonic in "An Outpost of Progress" as a starting point,
Conrad further develops the logical principle responsible for turning antithetical figures into mirroring characters caught up in a spiral of reciprocal
and escalating violence. In fact, the more duels D'Hubert and Feraud fight,
the more their differences disappear and give way to sameness. After the
first duel, for instance, the military Doctor gives the following diagnostic
advice to the otherwise cool-tempered and rational D'Hubert: "There!—
there! Don't be so quick in flourishing the sword. It doesn't pay in the long
run" (188). During the Russian Campaign, we are told that D'Hubert and
Feraud are "invested both with the appearance of a heroic pair in the eyes of
their comrades" (212). And later, as D'Hubert is wounded, it is Feraud who
steps into his shoes: "Colonel Feraud, promoted this moment to general,
had been sent to replace him [D'Hubert] at the head of his brigade" (219).
Finally, just prior to fighting the last duel, D'Hubert, in an echo of Kayerts,
saves himself just in time from becoming his antipode. After a labyrinthine,
surreal passage through a winding staircase that metaphorically reflects the
interior topography of his mind—and of his brain, too—D'Hubert has a
moment of self-recognition via a psychotic episode whereby his consciousness splits in two and he sees himself from the outside. And what he sees
is that the violent other has taken possession of his rational self, revealing
a "horrible and humiliating scene in which an infuriated madman with
blood-shot eyes and a foaming mouth played inconceivable havoc with
everything inanimate that may be found in a well-appointed dining-room"
(247). Indeed, the violent "madman" is no longer Feraud here, but turns
out to be the kindhearted D'Hubert. This mirroring scene of psychic (mis)
recognition at a culminating turning point in the narrative is indicative of
a mimetic continuity tying these two antipodes so intimately together that
the violence of the other is revealed to be at the heart of the self. It also indicates that the logic of the duel, and more generally of war, generates what
Conrad calls, in his major historical novel *Nostromo* (1904), the "intimacy
of antagonism" (253)—an oxymoronic phrase that turns the disjunction

of antagonism into the conjunction of intimacy, difference into sameness, antipodes into mimetic doubles.[7]

In the chapters that follow, we will encounter more explicit representations of Conrad's modernist recuperation of the romantic figure of the doppelgänger. But "The Duel" already makes us see that Conrad puts the old trope of the homo duplex to new fictional and theoretical use in order to cast light on the madness of the homo bellicus. Conrad, in fact, transgresses narrative conventions as he transposes the supernatural figure of the doppelgänger into a historical fiction in order to show that the psychic distinctions between self and other, rational and irrational characters, sane and insane men, no longer hold as the antipodes are infected by the contagious "*pathos*" of war. The mimetic emphasis on a "shadow" (255), or "shadowy ghost" (246), at times reflected in a "looking-glass" (253), confirms that D'Hubert and Feraud are, indeed, mirror images. Thus, as they face one another, they generate symmetrical inversions characteristic of mirroring reflections. More generally, if we take seriously Conrad's Clausewitzian intuition that the "private warfare" (192) of the duelists functions as a magnifying glass, or mirror, that reflects the "universal carnage" generated by the public dynamic of warfare, then at stake in this narrative are not only past-oriented, historical concerns but also future-oriented theoretical insights. But in order to look ahead, we first need to cast a retrospective glance back to the origins of this duel.

## Mimetic Origins

Critics have often wondered about the initial spark that triggered the duelists' explosion of personal violence that echoed collectively throughout the entire Napoleonic Wars; and quite rightly so, since this curiosity is generated by the text itself. From the "Author's Note" onward, in fact, Conrad puts readers and critics on the search for such mysterious origins. We are told that there is a "universal curiosity as to the origin of their quarrel" (190), a "mystery surrounding this deadly quarrel" (202), and the narrative asks, in a direct speech that addresses the reader: "But what could it be?" (189). Such a mystery is indeed bound to prick critics' ears, offering them a hermeneutical problem to resolve; all the more so since in the "Author's Note" Conrad adds an additional mystery by saying that "the pretext [of the historical duel] was never disclosed" and he "had therefore to invent it" (vii), thereby suggesting that an answer is buried within the text itself. But if this search for origins is already stimulated at the critical level, it is all the more relevant at the theoretical level. In fact, if Conrad joins arms with Clausewitz in order to cast light on the mysterious dynamic of war via the paradigmatic model of the duel, then, in these origins lies perhaps the solution to the riddle of mimetic violence.

## "The Hidden Reason of Things"

"The Duel" opens up a number of possible origins of this "deadly quarrel" in order to explain the prolonged outbreak of violence that ensues. Fictional hypotheses are not lacking: from "a quarrel of long standing envenomed by time," to the "transmigration of souls," to the possibility that "there might have been some woman in the case" (190), the reader is faced with a number of hermeneutical possibilities. What, then, could it be? In this context, a rivalrous, romantic affair seems a likely explanation, for reasons that are as literary as they are theoretical: literary because, as critics have pointed out, in fictions "most duels are provoked by the volatile stimulation of love";[8] theoretical because, as René Girard has shown in *Deceit, Desire, and the Novel* (1966), mimesis, desire, and violence are structurally linked. Let us recall that, for Girard, human desires are not original but imitative, and that "mimetic desire" is at the origin of a triangulation that can be summarized as follows: the subject desires what the model (or "mediator") desires, and since two different desires reach for the same object a violent conflict is bound to ensue, turning the model into an opponent (or "rival"). Ultimately, this mimetic rivalry leads both antagonists to lose sight of the desired object herself, as they are progressively caught up in the spiral of mimetic violence which renders them more and more alike (or "monstrous doubles").

For these literary and theoretical reasons, then, "mimetic desire," as Girard understands it, appears as a likely explanation of the origins of the violent quarrel between these two antagonistic figures qua doubles. A number of textual clues in "The Duel" seem to support this hypothesis. It is in fact during an armistice in Strasbourg, in the salon of Madame de Lionne, "a woman," we are told, "with a reputation for sensibility and elegance" (170), that the quarrel between D'Hubert and Feraud breaks out. And indeed, the text alludes to a possible triangulation of desire when, upon realizing that Feraud is at the salon, D'Hubert exclaims: "By thunder! . . . The general goes there sometimes. If he happens to find the fellow making eyes at the lady, there will be the devil to pay!" (170). Conversely, in a mirroring move, Feraud, stepping in for the general, addresses the potential rival in a tone that betrays his own personal jealousy, as he says: "If you are thinking of displaying your airs and graces to-night in Madame de Lionne's *salon* you are very much mistaken" (176). Indeed, Conrad forecasts the Girardian hypothesis that at the origin of violence is a mimetic desire that converges toward the same object, triggering a form of mimetic rivalry that opens up the infernal gates of "the royal road [*voie royale*] to violence."[9]

But if Conrad tampers with these gates, he does not follow through them. Numerous elements in the text suggest that for the two doubles qua rivals, the origins of the duel do not lie in mimetic desire. Madame de Lionne, for instance, is the first to admit that "her personality could by no stretch of reckless gossip be connected with this affair" (190). Since this madame speaks as a disappointed coquette who would have loved to be at the origin of such a legendary duel, the hurt pride of having her "personality" disconnected from this "affair" has the ring of authenticity. And in order to convince readers that not even an unconscious, mimetic desire is latently at work here, the narrator specifies that upon knowing that Feraud is at the salon, D'Hubert's "opinion of Madame de Lionne *went down* several degrees" (170; my emphasis), a clear indication that mimetic desire has failed to operate—if only because, for Girard, mimesis causes desire to go up, not down. Moreover, if this is true at the level of the private warfare (the origin of the duel), the mirroring structure of the text encourages us to think that it is equally true at the level of collective warfare (the origin of war). It is thus no accident that Madame de Lionne's salon is located in Strasbourg, a contested and thus divided city that is historically the object of competing Napoleonic and anti-Napoleonic political desires. But as Madame de Lionne is not the object of rivalry between the two competing officers, so, by metonymic extension, we are given to think that the possession of Strasbourg is not itself the origin of the quarrel between the two competing political forces. In sum, if the duelists are mimetic doubles whose "private warfare" (192) mirrors the warlike "Spirit of the Epoch" (xi), Conrad does not posit mimetic desire at the origin of mimetic violence.

And yet this does not mean that mimesis itself, and the contagious, unconscious pathos it generates, is not central to understanding the mysterious origins of the duel and, by extension, of the pathological violence of war. We should in fact not forget that Feraud and D'Hubert's first duel is itself a mimetic reproduction of yet another duel between Feraud and a civilian that had taken place early that day. There is thus a duel before the duel, an original arche-duel that generates "this private contest through the years of universal carnage" (165). Little is known about this mysterious origin, and the little we know is shrouded in a mist of highly subjective, unreliable memories. The narrative voice tells us that "though he [Feraud] had no clear recollection how the quarrel had originated (it was begun in an establishment where beer and wine are drunk late at night), he had not the slightest doubt of being himself the outraged party" (172). A bar, alcoholic drinks, and a violent quarrel: clearly this originary scene fails to offer a reliable starting point to develop an objective, historically informed genealogy of the origins of this mimetic "quarrel."

But the fact that this origin lacks objective, historical value does not mean that it is not revealing of the origins of subjective, infective principles constitutive of the logic of violent pathos, as Conrad understands it. These diagnostic principles can be schematically summarized as follows. First, this passage indicates that at the origin of D'Hubert and Feraud's first duel there is no mimetic desire, but mimesis itself. This first duel is already a mimetic reproduction of yet another duel, in a movement of regress that fails to point to a final, single, illuminating origin. As the clinical figure of the Doctor later suggests, countering the hypothesis that it all started in Strasbourg, "the origin of the quarrel . . . went much farther back" (194). The theoretical lesson of this statement is clear: such a claim makes the search for a final, mythical, and ultimately indemonstrable origin vain. Yet the indication of an origin before the origin is revealing of a mimetic principle nonetheless. Namely, that a pathological reproduction of violent pathos ensues once the motor of reciprocal violence is set in motion, generating a sequel of duels that go on *usque ad finem*. Second, the emphasis on "beer" and "wine," and the "establishments" that go along, indicates that there is nothing rational about this dispute, no true, objective cause that would logically justify the quarrel, but something that is of the order of irrational, contagious, and unconscious emotions, or better—since these emotions are not confined within a unitary subject—affects, or as I also call them, using a more ancient term, *pathoi* that take possession of subjects, projecting them outside of themselves, against each other.[10] This scene, then, might not give us the true, objective logic of the duel's origin. But, for Conrad, the lack of logos caused by an excess of pathos that takes possession of egos is precisely at the origin of this violent pathology. Third, while Feraud is ready to risk his life in the duel, the reasons for the quarrel quickly fade from his memory. This suggests that the pathos of violence spreads contagiously, generating an unconscious, infective dynamic that is cut loose from the conscious "reasons" that might have initially motivated it. And finally, the unshakable feeling "of being himself the outraged party," of being in the right while the other is in the wrong, is revealing of a generalized tendency to see the straw in the other's eyes, but not the beam in one's own eyes. In sum, for Conrad—as for a long tradition in mimetic theory that goes from Plato to Nietzsche, Tarde to Girard to Lacoue-Labarthe—at the "origin" of violent conflicts there is not so much reason but unreason, no conscious actions but unconscious, mimetic reactions.

## The Laws of Mimesis

If we return to dissect D'Hubert and Feraud's first duel with these mimetic laws in mind, we notice that Feraud reproduces the same irrational, contagious pathos as in the original quarrel. Yet, this time, Conrad pitches this Southern (fiery) temperament against a Northern (cold) temperament in order to explore how the interactive, affective, and infective dynamic of the duel generates an unconscious mimesis that is difficult, even for rational D'Hubert, to fend off. Upon their return from Madame De Lionne's salon, Feraud, offended by D'Hubert's interference, challenges the latter to a duel—the second in a day. And here is how "sober" D'Hubert is pulled into the spiral of irrational violence that will last for nearly two decades. We are told that "at first he [D'Hubert] had been only vexed, and somewhat amused; but now his face got clouded. He was asking himself seriously how he could manage to get away" (176). And then the narrator, entering the contest via free indirect speech, incisively adds: "It was impossible to run from a man with a sword" (176). Moving deftly from D'Hubert's exterior physiology to his interior psychology via a narrative *lexis* that is both diegetic in form and mimetic in its affective content, Conrad's steel traces the shift from the latter's ironic distance ("amused" face) to his worried realization of the force of *pathos* ("clouded" face). In the process, he casts light on the interactive, contagious logic of the duel that reveals the difficulty not to respond to an attack of the other—no matter how irrational this attack actually is. Conrad is here dramatizing an intersubjective double bind that illustrates a general principle of war: the duel is based on a reciprocal, mimetic bond whereby the action of the other inevitably generates a reaction in the self, binding the antagonists in a spiral of violence. Thinking back to the duel, D'Hubert will later say: "I had no option; I had no choice whatever, consistent with my dignity as a man and an officer" (200). And the narrator corroborates this point: "And Lieut. D'Hubert did follow. He could do nothing else" (178).

In the series of duels that follow, D'Hubert will inevitably reproduce this absurd, pathological pattern; but we now know that the pattern of this pathos is not without logical explanation. On the contrary, it dramatizes a reciprocal, affective patho(-)logy that perfectly captures Clausewitz's theoretical understanding of the art of war. In Book I of *On War*, Clausewitz articulates the following principle that will inform his entire treatise:

> If one side uses force without compunction, undeterred by the bloodshed it involves, while the other side refrains, the first will gain the upper hand. That side will force the other to follow suit; each will drive its opponent toward extremes [*so steigern sich beide bis zum äußersten*], and the only limiting factors are the counterpoises inherent in war. (14)[11]

Here we have, in a nutshell, what for Clausewitz, Conrad, and later, as we shall see, Girard is the theoretical crux of the matter. Namely, that in the duel, as in war, violence cannot be thought of in unilateral, linear terms. On the contrary, it generates what Clausewitz calls a "reciprocal action" [*Wechselwirkung*] (15) that must be thought in relational, spiraling, or, as Clausewitz puts it, "escalating" terms.[12] What is important to realize here is that this dynamic is not based on a subject-object, billiard-ball causal relation. Rather, as Clausewitz puts it, the subject's "will is directed at an animal object that *reacts*" (100), generating thus a "collision of two living forces" (16). This "reciprocity," in turn, locks, nolens volens, the two opposed parties together in a deadlock that leads the self to act like the other, generating a widening gyre of violence that leads "towards extremes." Hence a violent, irrational attack triggers an equally violent defense—no matter how rational the defender is—which, in turn, will continue to fuel the initial attack. And once this interplay of attack and defense, action and reaction, is set in motion between two parties endowed with an equal force, a feedback loop generates a spiral of reciprocal violence fueled by an affective, contagious, and thus highly infective mimetic pathology. The duelists are thus not in control of violence; it is the reciprocal logic of violence that controls them.

Critics have often wondered at the absurdity of a duel that lasts through-out the entire Napoleonic Wars, but for Conrad, as for Clausewitz before him, this absurdity is intrinsic to the escalating logic of war itself. As the narrator puts it: "A duel, whether regarded as a ceremony in the cult of honor, or even when reduced to its moral essence to a form of manly sport, demands a *perfect singleness of intention, a homicidal austerity of mood*" (180; my emphasis). Along similar lines, Clausewitz had already made clear that the laws of war conceived as duel require a "*violent resolution of the crisis*, the wish to annihilate the enemy's forces" (*OW* 43). Summing up this theoretical principle in a nutshell, he states: "war is an act of force, and there is no logical limit to the application of that force. Each side, therefore, compels its opponent to follow suit; a reciprocal action is started which must lead, in theory, to extremes" (15). The mysterious dynamic of war qua duel is thus based on a principle of reciprocity that leads the defender to strike back, generating an escalation of violence that "in theory"—that is, in the case of a perfect symmetrical balance between the two parties who immediately strike back—leads to a duel *usque ad finem*. With its sequences of escalating duels between two mimetic doubles caught in the inescapable double bind of reciprocal actions and reactions, Conrad's "The Duel" is an admirable fictional representation of Clausewitz's theoretical insight into the reciprocal, escalating, and thus contagious logic of violence. Clausewitz calls this "theoretical war" or "abstract war"; Raymond Aron dubs it "philosophical war."[13]

Now, this is the moment to recall the god Janus who is presiding over this duel, and stress that Conrad—fictional duelist that he is—is not only looking back to Clausewitz's account of abstract war derived from the Napoleonic total wars; he is also looking ahead, to recent theoretical developments in mimetic theory concerned with the catastrophes caused by our contemporary global wars. In fact, by introducing two characters that mirror each other in order to reflect on the imitative logic of a type of violence that escalates to extremes, Conrad is anticipating, by more than a century, Girard's reconceptualization of mimetic violence as it is formulated in *Battling to the End*. Insofar as Girard develops his new theory of violence on the basis of a reading of *On War* in general, and of Clausewitz's definition of war as a duel in particular, a theoretical confrontation becomes essential to articulate Girard's contribution to Conrad studies, as well as Conrad's contribution to mimetic theory. Let us thus add to these fictional and historical duels a third, theoretical duel.

### Incipit: The Theoretical Duel

In *Battling to the End*, Girard returns to Clausewitz's definition of war as an "extended duel" in order to reframe the logic of mimetic violence that already preoccupied him in *Violence and the Sacred*. He does so by confronting the "escalating" dynamic of reciprocal violence, which, for Clausewitz, is constitutive of abstract wars. Girard's interest in Clausewitz is thus less historical than it is theoretical. For the French theorist, in fact, *On War* is an untimely treatise that should be re-read today in order to think through the escalating logic of contemporary wars that cast a shadow on our own apocalyptic times. But Girard does not simply offer a critical commentary of *On War*. As the French title *Achever Clausewitz* suggests, for Girard, Clausewitz needs to be "*finished* [*achevé*]" (*BE* xiv) by foregrounding mimetic principles the latter had intuited, but had not fully taken hold of. This thought-provoking gesture is not deprived of theoretical violence: "*achever*" means to finish but also to finish off.

In order to finish (off) Clausewitz, Girard stresses two related principles that, in his view, are latent, and thus not fully manifest, in *On War*. First, Girard foregrounds the mimetic principle at work in Clausewitz's account of the reciprocal dimension of violence. As Girard points out, "Reciprocal action and the mimetic principle concern the same reality, even though Clausewitz, strangely, never spoke of imitation" (*BE* 10). And second, Girard takes literally Clausewitz's definition of "theoretical war," as well as the idea that through reciprocal action violence is bound to escalate to extremes. As Girard puts it, for Clausewitz, "The 'trend to extremes' is indeed imaginable only 'theoretically,' in other words, when the adversaries are rigorously similar" (8), but this mimetic hypothesis, he subsequently argues, should be taken as a real possibility. For Girard, then, mimesis, while not explicitly discussed by Clausewitz, is at the center of two of his most fundamental intuitions: the dynamic of the duel makes visible the mimetic principle responsible for the reciprocity of violence, and it is because of this reciprocal mimesis that violence is bound to escalate to extremes.

Girard does not mention Conrad's "The Duel," but this neglected tale marvelously supports his theory. In fact, by grounding his "Military Tale" on Clausewitz's definition of war as a duel via the literary trope of the double, the British modernist had manifestly dramatized the key mimetic principles the French theorist outlines. For Conrad, in fact, the homo duplex reveals the fundamentally mimetic, reciprocal, and escalating dimension of violence, generating the "universal carnage" characteristic of total wars. Conversely, Conrad shows that this theoretical trend to extremes works only fictionally, in other words, when the adversaries are perfectly similar—that is, when they are doppelgängers. Well before Girard's innovative intervention in mimetic theory, Conrad, in a somewhat neglected tale, envisions the possibility to further Clausewitz's account of war by introducing a mimetic principle at the heart of his account of war qua duel. This does not mean that Conrad finishes, or finishes off, Clausewitz. The idea of a definitive and violent closure to the open and indeterminate dynamic of history is foreign to both writers. Instead, Conrad supplements Clausewitz by exploring the principle of reciprocity in terms of a detailed, narrative-based account of behavioral mimesis that uncannily foreshadows Girard's key insights in *Battling to the End*.

But Conrad adds another twist to this theoretical turn. In fact, by zeroing in on the unconscious dimension of mimetic reciprocity of the duel in terms that are based on real, life-and-blood psycho-physiological principles, he goes beyond Girard's theoretical and still abstract definition of reciprocity. Let us see how Conrad, on the shoulders of Clausewitz, supplements Girard's theoretical account.

## The Mimetic Unconscious

There is, of course, nothing conscious, or rational, in D'Hubert and Feraud's mirroring reflexes that generate sameness where there once was difference, leading the defender to strike back in a gesture that mindlessly reproduces the violence of the attacker. Clausewitz, for one, had already specified that "even the most educated of peoples [*gebildetsten Völker*] . . . can be fired with passionate hatred of each other" (*OW* 14; trans. modified), adding that "if war is an act of force, the emotions cannot fail to be involved" (15).[14] Girard corroborates this view as he says that "passions do indeed rule the world, and the revolutionary and Napoleonic Wars released them" (*BE* 9). Granted. This is, after all, an old story; it goes back to the origins of mimetic theory in Plato's *Republic*.[15]

There is, however, a more specific lesson reflected in "The Duel." Conrad, in fact, offers an incisive diagnostic of the psycho-physiological principles informing the emergence of violence, an affective, unconscious emergence that reveals, at the level of microanalysis of the duel, the larger macrodynamic of mimetic contagion of war. Let us zoom in and take a closer look at their first duel. Upon hearing D'Hubert's initial refusal to fight, Feraud quips:

> "Ah, you won't?" hissed the Gascon. "I suppose you prefer to be made infamous. Do you hear what I say? . . . Infamous! Infamous! Infamous!" he shrieked, rising and falling on his toes and getting very red in the face. Lieut. D'Hubert, on the contrary, became very pale at the sound of the unsavoury word for a moment, *then flushed pink to the roots of his fair hair.* (177; my emphasis)

These are comic narrative exchanges critics rightly treat with ironic distance, but there is also a tragic pathos at work here that has yet to be diagnosed. Once caught up in the excessive logic of the duel, which, as we have seen, for Conrad has less to do with mimetic desire than with mimetic pathos, an irrational character "red in the face" manages to affect the other rational and originally "pale" character in such a way that he also "flushed pink," introducing a mimetic sameness at the heart of difference. This seemingly anecdotal passage supports Clausewitz's point that "the most powerful springs for actions in men lie in his emotions" (*OW* 60). Yet it also qualifies this claim by revealing the immanent, psycho-physiological, affective principle of mimetic contagion responsible for turning these antipodes into remarkably similar characters. Conrad, in fact, shows that the similarities between the two duelists qua doubles are an unconscious symptom, not a cause, of the contagious dimension of violent emotions. The duelists do not fight because they are doubles; they become doubles because they fight.

Consistently throughout his works we shall see that Conrad shows a remarkable awareness that affects are contagious and transgress the barrier that divides self and others, generating an affective communication that is not under the control of consciousness, happens against the best intentions of the ego, and is, in this sense, *un*-conscious. Preceding the so-called Freudian discovery, this model of the unconscious is not based on a repressive hypothesis that has dreams as its *via regia*; nor does it entail an Oedipal triangulation of desire. Rather, it is based on the untimely diagnostic insight that human beings respond involuntarily to the affects of others, reproducing gestures, expressions, and the corresponding pathos proper to the other within the ego itself. But what is untimely, as Nietzsche taught us, is only so because it is ahead of its time. The mimetic realization that humans, from the first hours of life onward, automatically reproduce expressions of others is now supported by empirical investigations in developmental psychology.[16] And the discovery of "mirror neurons" in the 1990s by a group of Italian neurologists offers an empirical account of the importance of mimesis in intersubjective, affective relations. Mirror neurons, we are told, "fire" not only when we perform a gesture but also when we see others performing it, triggering an unconscious reflex to mimetically reproduce gestures and expressions of the other. This is how feelings can be shared from the outside-in, via a nonverbal communication that leads the self to reproduce inside the gestures and expressions we see outside. As the neurologist Marco Iacoboni succinctly puts it in *Mirroring People*, mirror neurons "map the actions of the other onto the self. They make the other 'another self.'"[17] And he specifies: "Mirror neurons are the brain cells that fill the gap between self and other by enabling some sort of simulation or inner imitation of the actions of others."[18]

These are now well-known, revolutionary discoveries that are contributing to the stimulating dialogue between "mimesis and science."[19] They do not only force us to rethink the foundations of subjectivity in relational terms.

Nor do they solely confirm the mimetic nature of desire and violence. They also give us new insights into mimetic phenomena such as sympathy, compassion, identification, and, more generally, all forms of affective contagion and nonverbal communication that are so central to even begin to understand self-other relations. Less known, however, is that these are actually revolutionary confirmations of mimetic principles modernist writers like Conrad have known all along. As I have argued elsewhere, modernists from Nietzsche to Conrad, Lawrence to Bataille, contribute to making our understanding of the psyche new on the basis of a pre-Freudian model of the unconscious that has precisely such mimetic reflexes as its main door and which I have called, for lack of a better term, the "mimetic unconscious." This door gives us access to an embodied, relational, and immanent approach to the ego that opens up its boundaries to external influences, shared affects, and unconscious reactions that were at the center of interdisciplinary investigations in fin de siècle Europe; it also provides a wider historical, sociological, and philosophical understanding of the implications of appearing to be oneself while being someone other. Conrad helps us further this line of inquiry by representing the role of unconscious mimesis outside the confines of the lab in a complex, real-life, sociopolitical scenario such as war, in which one's survival depends precisely on the way mirror neurons unconsciously fire—or misfire. The mimetic unconscious is thus already a political unconscious, for it is a relational, intersubjective, and thus systemic unconscious.

Well before the revolutionary discovery of mirror neurons, Conrad shows a fundamental awareness that the mimetic similarities between the two duelists are a psycho-physiological effect of the human tendency to unconsciously reproduce the gestures of the other, especially if this gesture is imbued with pathos. Girard had already implicitly suggested this point as he says that "violent imitation . . . *makes adversaries more and more alike*" (*BE* 10), but Conrad specifies this claim by explicitly revealing the unconscious, mirroring principle that makes adversaries alike. What Conrad shows, in fact, is that these characters do not fight because they are similar, or have similar desires that converge on the same object. Rather, they fight because their nervous systems unconsciously respond to the contagious pathos of violence. Such a mimetic principle follows, shadowlike, Conrad's diagnostic of the homo duplex as it appears throughout his corpus. It can be schematically summarized as follow: an external, psycho-physiological manifestation of an affect (or pathos) in the other generates an automatic, mirroring reflex in the self, triggered by the all-too-human tendency to involuntarily mirror people (or mimetic unconscious). This unconscious reflex, in turn, generates an affective flow of nonverbal communication that blurs the boundaries that divide self and others (or individuation). The violent affect present in the self is thus triggered in the other as well, catching the antipode in a double bind that turns him into a mimetic double (or homo duplex)—no matter how rational, temperate, and self-controlled this other is, or may want to be. Thus the "pale" Northerner's mirror neurons are involuntarily triggered by the violent gestures and expressions of his Southern counterpart, and unconsciously fire, infecting him with the same pathology he had previously diagnosed in terms of "madness." The mirroring dynamic of the duel turns difference into sameness, antipodes into doubles.

Conrad does not reveal a singular origin of violence that can be framed in an abstract, transcendental form. Yet he shows how the mimetic unconscious triggers a violent, immanent pathos that turns homo duplex into homo bellicus. In an untimely theoretical gesture, Conrad puts the old fictional trope of the doppelgänger to new theoretical use in order to reveal the mimetic principles that continue to lead individuals and nations to fire, at the sight of others firing. If neuroscientists have so far tended to emphasize the role of mirror neurons in "understanding the meaning of the actions of others," this being their *"primary* role,"[20] Conrad reminds us that there are always two sides to imitation: one is logical, sympathetic and central to the idea of homo sapiens; the other is pathological, violent, and central to the practices of homo bellicus. As we entered the twenty-first century, the horrors of the twentieth century behind us, it seems that individuals and nations alike are far from having overcome this mimetic principle. Hence the urgency of diagnosing this mirroring, pathological dynamic more closely. Hence the timeliness of an author who sets up a mirror to reflect critically on the logic of unconscious violence.

From the very beginning of the tale, Conrad represents Clausewitz's account of war as a duel via the principle of an unconscious, reciprocal mimesis that turns polar opposites into mirror images of each other. The perfectly balanced, mirroring structure of the duel and the reciprocity that ensues allow Conrad to dramatize the escalation to extremes, which, for Clausewitz, we should not forget, is possible only in theory. Conrad, then, gives a fictional, empirical life to an abstract theoretical principle in order to better dissect its affective logic on the basis of what I call mimetic pathology. The escalation to extremes, for him, ensues when the two adversaries are perfectly equal and have the possibility to immediately strike back due to the mirroring reflex of the mimetic unconscious that generates symmetrical actions and reactions. That this is a perfectly symmetrical battle bound to escalate is already suggested by the outcome of the first duel. Thus, upon noticing D'Hubert scratched face, the Doctor clinically observes: "Both sides, too—and symmetrical" (185). The symmetry of the scratches reflects the symmetry of the psychic lives of the duelists themselves. And indeed, during the entire narrative, whether the officers fight with swords or sabers, on foot or on horseback, their actions are perfectly balanced and reciprocal. This is because the duelists are doubles, of course, but also because these modes of combat require immediate, unreflective, automatic reactions that are only bound to escalate. For instance, in the third duel, fought in Silesia with a cavalry saber, we are told:

> If not fought to a finish, it was, at any rate, fought to a standstill. . . . Both had many cuts which bled profusely. Both refused to have the combat stopped, time after time, with what appeared the most deadly animosity. This appearance was caused on the part of Captain D'Hubert by a rational desire to be done once for all with this worry; on the part of Captain Feraud by a tremendous exaltation of his pugnacious instincts and the incitement of wounded vanity. At last, disheveled, their shirts in rags, covered with gore and hardly able to stand, they were led away forcibly by their marveling and horrified seconds. (204)

This is a revealing passage not only for what it says but also for how it says it. The symmetrical opposition of the duelists is accentuated by Conrad's symmetrical sentence structure, a chiastic, linguistic structure that reflects the mimetic principle responsible for turning antipodes into mirroring figures. Captain D'Hubert's "rational desire" has, in fact, its mirroring counterpart in Captain Feraud's "pugnacious instincts." That desire tends to be instinctual and pugnaciousness can be rationally planned indicates an underlying continuity that hides behind the first layer of straightforward opposition between rational and irrational principles. Mimesis, in other words, cuts through the boundary that divides reason from unreason. And, as the narrative suggests, this mirroring effect brings their "homicidal austerity" to the extreme: "Asked whether the quarrel was settled this time, they gave it out as their conviction that it was a difference which could only be settled by one of the parties remaining lifeless on the ground" (205). For Conrad, then, as for Clausewitz and Girard, the mirroring escalation of violence leads to a battle *usque ad finem*. And what he makes us see is that violence continues to escalate to extremes for two related reasons: first, because the two adversaries are mirror images of each other; second, because the duels they fight call for unconscious mirroring reactions. The fictional trope of the homo duplex, then, dramatizes what Clausewitz and, later, Girard articulate in pure theoretical and somewhat abstract terms: namely, that the mimetic and unconscious reciprocity between the two adversaries is responsible for the spiraling escalation of violence characteristic of abstract war.

Rereading Conrad's "The Duel" in the company of both Clausewitz and Girard reveals that this much-neglected historical fiction articulates a timely theoretical account of the origins of contagious forms of violence, both at the interpersonal and collective levels. It does so by dramatizing mimetic principles that are not only in line with but also further classical and contemporary theoretical accounts of war. In a way, what Conrad writes in "The Warrior's Soul," another tale dealing with the Napoleonic Wars, also applies to "The Duel" and the other texts we shall consider later: "Poets do get close to truth somehow—there is no denying that" (*TH* 9). What we must add now is that if Girard attempts to "finish (off)" Clausewitz by bringing to the fore the mimetic principle already envisioned by Conrad, Conrad continues to supplement, nuance, and, eventually, subvert Girard's apocalyptic insights into the escalating logic of mimetic violence and the catastrophic ending that derives from it. "The Duel," in fact, accelerates the reciprocal action of abstract war only to suspend it at the end, in a move that is faithful to Clausewitz's account of real war. Consequently, "The Duel" does not end with a battle to the end, but with the end of the battle—which does not mean that the two antipodes will be easily reconciled.

## Theoretical Skirmishes

We have seen that Girard's reading of Clausewitz's account of reciprocity ties in well with Conrad's image of a duel that, in the context of the Napoleonic Wars, escalates to extremes. In a deft fictional move, Conrad offers a theoretical dramatization of this unconscious escalation of violence, revealing the underlying psycho-physiological principles responsible not only for the violence of two individuals but also for the collective violence that animates what he calls "the years of universal carnage" (165). If the personal duels are fought against the background of Napoleon's historical wars, it is because the mimetic patho(-)logy in the (fictional) foreground is meant to illuminate, mirror, and help us reflect on the mimetic principle at work in the (historical) background. Thus all the duels up to the Russian Campaign of 1912 operate according to the principle of escalation to extremes that also animates the Napoleonic Wars. This mimetic hypothesis is also internal to both Clausewitz's and Girard's accounts of war and should not be too lightly dismissed, especially in an age of globalized violence on the rise such as ours. Writing in the aftermath of two world wars, the threat of nuclear escalation, international terrorism, climate change, infectious pandemics, and other impending global catastrophes, Girard warns us, in a dark mood: "we have to have the lucidity to say that humanity itself tends towards annihilation. This is the implacable law of the duel" (*BE* 19). This is also the mimetic law Conrad lucidly outlines in so many of his darkly textured fictions in general, and in "The Duel" in particular. Writing from the perspective of fin de siècle Europe, Conrad already warns us about the possibility of global destructions that haunt the contemporary world.

### What Is Theory For?

And yet it is precisely at such precarious and vulnerable times that we should be careful not to fall prey to apocalyptic despair, taking the nihilistic possibility concerning the (likely) destruction of the whole planet as the only inevitable destiny toward which we are driven. Girard, it should be noticed, does hermeneutic violence to *On War* by positing the primacy of "theoretical war" over "real war," the "escalation to extremes" over the striving for "peace" (*BE* 19). Girard's account of the "possibility of an end of Europe, the Western world and the world as a whole" (ix) is certainly in line with the apocalyptic bent that drives his own admittedly Christian thought.[21] But in following a "religious interpretation" (xii) of a secular text such as *On War*, Girard distorts Clausewitz's more realistic, immanent, and a-theological approach. Girard complains that "no one seems to read" (xiii) Clausewitz. But it is sufficient to read attentively chapter 1 of Book I, titled "What Is War?"—the only chapter Clausewitz himself "regard[ed] as finished" (*OW* 9)—to find out that the Prussian officer considers the possibility of the escalation to extremes as an "abstraction" (17) that does not match the reality of real war. As Clausewitz clearly puts it, this possibility is "nothing but a play of the imagination [*Spiel der Vorstellungen*] issuing from an almost invisible sequence of logical subtleties" (16). And he adds: "the human mind is unlikely to consent to being ruled by such a logical fantasy [*Träumerei*]" (17). Writing in a pragmatic, immanent, and realistic mood characteristic of a man who experienced war firsthand for most of his life, he specifies: "the very nature of war impedes the *simultaneous concentration of all forces*" (19). For Clausewitz, then, there is no straight, ascending path that leads to an apocalyptic escalation to extremes. Once an abstract, ideal plan is put in practice, a number of down-to-earth "frictions" (65) emerge that shift war from the perfect formal symmetry of conceptual designs to the uneven roughness of the battlefield, from "abstract war" to "real war." Consequently, for Clausewitz at least, "the world of reality takes over from the world of abstract thought; material calculations take the place of hypothetical extremes" (18). And as he hammers the point home throughout the book, "*actual war is often far removed from the pure concept postulated by the theory*" (33). Thus he concludes with a diagnostic that, while offering a serious challenge to Girard's hypothesis, confirms our understanding of what theory is for:

> A theory, then, that dealt exclusively with absolute war would either have to ignore any case in which the nature of war had been deformed by outside influences, or else it would have to dismiss them all as misconstrued. That cannot be what theory is for. Its purpose is to demonstrate what war is in practice, not what its ideal nature ought to be. (240)

Indeed, for anyone who has read *On War*, it should be clear that, for Clausewitz, the real practice is far removed from the ideal model.[22]

Clausewitz and Girard share certain fundamental assumptions about the reciprocal dynamic of war in abstract theory. But when it comes to the fundamental ontology which in-*forms* their takes of reality, their perspectives could not be more antithetical: one is an empirical, a-theological officer qua strategist who is ultimately concerned with the material basis of "real war"; the other is an idealist, theological theorist qua prophet who is fascinated by the apocalyptic potential of "theoretical war." No wonder that despite their mimetic affinities, Girard does violence to Clausewitz and tries to finish him off in order to promote his own prophetic insight into the "imminence of the Second Coming" (*BE* xi) culminating with the final revelation that "the apocalypse has begun" (210).

Now what about Conrad? "The Duel" is a fictional confirmation of Girard's mimetic hypothesis that invites us to take the danger of escalations of violence seriously, and other apocalyptic texts we subsequently consider reinforce this view. But differences of orientation need to be signaled too. When it comes to the driving telos of Conrad's historical and theoretical narrative, it is clear that he is much closer to Clausewitz's pragmatism than to Girard's idealism, to the former's desire for peace than to the latter's vision of the Apocalypse. If I have said that Conrad was probably not much of a duelist in real life, he is certainly a duelist in the Nietzschean sense that "he challenges problems to a duel."[23] In addition to the personal, psychological duel that mirrors the collective, historical duel, a third, theoretical duel— somewhat twice removed from its fictional and historical origins—is now added to this scene of mimetic contestation.

## From Fiction to Theory

There is in fact a sense in which Girard, not unlike Feraud, is intensely warlike, is on the side of Napoleon, and privileges, at least in theory, the escalation to extremes over and against more peaceful, diplomatic solutions. Conrad, on the other hand, is clearly on the side of D'Hubert, a much more complex, dynamic character endowed with a psychological sensibility, strategic capacity, and desire for peace that is present in Clausewitz but is missing in the Napoleonic Feraud. If he envisions the possibility of escaping the logic of mimetic violence, and putting an end to the duel, it is thus on the basis of a strategy aligned with D'Hubert, a figure who is nicknamed "The Strategist," for "he could think in the presence of the enemy" (*SoS* 251). Thus, if it is true that he reveals the mimetic dimension of the escalation of violence character- istic of abstract war, it is equally true that he, Conrad, strategically sides with Clausewitz so as to consider a theoretical solution to the problem of violence in the context of real war. Contrary to Girard's claim that violence "always wins" (*BE* xvii), Conrad's narrative telos is driven by Clausewitz's realization that "not every war needs to be fought until one side collapses" (*OW* 33) and that "with the conclusion of peace the purpose of the war has been achieved and its business is at an end" (32). Hence, if The Strategist wants to live up to his reputation, he must find a way out from the mimetic escalation of vio- lence. It is in fact worth recalling that in Conrad's oeuvre, even ferociously dim-witted characters—like General Sotillio in *Nostromo*—who have not much intellectual power to restrain violent reflexes have a certain "reluctance at the notion of proceeding to extremes" (*N* 446). Rather than following "the royal road of violence," we shall thus follow Clausewitz's strategic attempt to open up what he calls "a short cut on the road to peace" (*OW* 35). This is how Conrad finishes—without finishing off—Girard.

What, then, is Conrad's strategic solution to put an end to the duel? Clearly, in light of a representation of a romantic duel animated by an unconscious pathos that lasts through "the years of universal carnage," Conrad does not opt for a reassuring return to the logos of enlightened and diplomatic reason as the diagnostic solution to the poison of irrational violence. The whole narrative functions as an illustration that rationality repeatedly fails to contain the unconscious pathology of mimetic escala- tion. Conrad's solution will thus not be an idealist or a rationalist one. Nor does Conrad propose a Christian conversion based on an *imitatio Christi* as the ultimate form of salvific revelation. As he helps us "continue the work" (*BE* 2) Girard initiated, his solution shall thus not be Christian or theologi- cal either.[24] Rather, in an immanent, a-theological move that is constitutive of the modernist, Nietzschean writers that interest me, Conrad will seek a solution to the riddle of mimetic violence in the problem itself—that is, in the human, all too human tendency to imitate. Aware that there is no outside of mimesis, that there is no easy idealist, rationalist, theological, or eschatological way out from the pathological spiral of violence, Conrad seeks in the pathology of mimesis a possible patho-*logical* solution to the problem of mimetic escalation.

Rather than seeking the end of the battle beyond the mimetic principle, Conrad recognizes that mimesis itself might be both the problem of and the solution to violence. This diagnostic point, which serves as the structuring feature of modernist mimetic theory in general and this book in particular, is still in line with the Girardian realization that mimesis is at least two-faced, depending on whether it operates in absolute war or real war. Benoît Chantres usefully suggests to Girard in *Battling to the End*: "Perhaps . . . we have to think of reciprocal action *both as what provokes the trend to extremes and as that which suspends it* [la diffère]" (*BE* 10). And Girard momentarily agrees as he echoes: "reciprocal action *simultaneously provokes and suspends* [diffère] the escalation to extremes. This is indeed one of the consequences of imitation, namely to have these two opposite effects" (11). And a bit later Girard specifies:

> It is therefore true that reciprocal action both *provokes and suspends* the trend to extremes. It provokes it when both adversaries behave in the same way, and *respond immediately* by each modeling his tactics, strategy and policy on those of the other. By contrast, if each is speculating on the intentions of the other, advancing, withdrawing, hesitating, taking into account time, space, fog, fatigue and all the constant interactions that define real war, reciprocal action then suspends [*diffère*] the trend to extremes. (13)

Girard is here differing with himself. This is, in fact, a life-affirming move that nuances his apocalyptic account of abstract war, and opens up a possible mimetic way out from the cycle of reciprocal violence on the basis of a consideration of real war. Clausewitz, in Book III, had indeed devoted a full chapter to "The Suspension of Action in War," and the idea that in real war the "frictions" generated by advancing, withdrawing, and hesitating momentarily "suspend" war is in line with Clausewitz's thought. And yet the theoretical origins of this double-move, in which mimesis is seen to function as both the poison and the remedy, do not lie in Clausewitz (who considers "suspension of action in war [a]s a contradiction in terms" [*OW* 152]). As the use of the French *différer* (to defer but also to differ) makes clear, they bear the traces of another intellectual figure who, while not explicitly acknowledged, looms large in the general economy of Girard's thought. In a silent theoretical move, Girard is in fact echoing his most formidable antipode and lifelong mimetic rival par excellence, a philosophical figure whose initial success in

literary studies he helped to promote: Jacques Derrida.²⁵ And this is where
yet another latent, but foundational, perhaps even originary arche-duel in
mimetic theory is added to this already densely layered scene of embattled
contestation. Since this scene informs my investigation of "The Duel" in
particular and Conrad's fictions in general, a brief confrontation between
two founding figures in contemporary mimetic theory is in order.

## The Pharmakon of Mimēsis

It is true that Derrida is usually recognized as a thinker of "difference" and
Girard as a thinker of "sameness," but this antithetical relation should not
blind us to the mimetic undercurrent that ties these two theoretical antagonists together. In fact, what Girard calls "the mimetic principle of reciprocity"
that both "provokes and suspends [defer and differ] the trend to extremes"
functions as both the problem and the solution to the problem, the poison
and the cure—what Derrida, echoing Plato, famously called a *pharmakon*.
As Derrida puts it in "Plato's Pharmacy," first published in 1968, the *pharmakon* "acts as both remedy and poison . . . can be—alternatively or simultaneously—beneficent or maleficent."²⁶ It is well known that the *pharmakon*
stands for the supplementary logic of *écriture* central to deconstruction; less
known is that since writing is a practice that, for better and worse, reproduces
speech, it also stands in for the paradoxical logic of mimesis central to mimetic
theory. This is why *mimēsis* and the *pharmakon*, for Derrida, are two faces of
the same coin. As he writes *mimēsis* "has no nature; nothing is properly its
own. Ambivalent, playing with itself by hollowing itself out, good and evil
at once—undecidably, *mimēsis* is akin to the *pharmakon*" (PP 139). Indeed,
animating Derrida's original reading of the *pharmakon* is the hollow figure
of the phantom of mimesis; Plato's pharmacological ambivalence rests on a
mimetic ambivalence. Thus Derrida specifies: "If the *pharmakon* is 'ambivalent,' it is because it constitutes the medium in which opposites are opposed,
the movement and the play that links them among themselves, reverses them
or makes one side cross over into the other (soul/body, good/evil, inside/
outside, memory/forgetfulness, speech/writing, etc.)" (127) and, we may
add, model/copy, idea/simulacrum, origin/phantom. This is a fundamental
theoretical insight that, were we to trace its genealogy, would lead us, via
Nietzsche, back to the origins of mimetic theory itself, in Plato's thought.²⁷

Girard is often antagonistic to intellectual father figures in mimetic theory such as Plato, Nietzsche, and Derrida. And in a romantic move that unveils a fundamental contradiction at the heart of his hypothesis, Girard often prefers to stress the originality of his mimetic thought. Yet familiarity with the mimetic tradition shows that Girard is one of the most recent, formidable, and incisive avatars of a long chain of thinkers who consider mimesis in its ambivalent, pharmacological manifestations. This is true of his take on the sacrificial "scapegoat" qua *pharmakos*, but it is still true for his recent take on mimetic reciprocity qua *pharmakon*, and other rivalrous, imitative subjects that traverse and in-*form* at the most fundamental level his entire corpus.[28] In an uncanny echo of Conrad's fiction, these two French intellectual antagonists—both Derrida and Girard are intensely abstract, theoretically ambitious, and care for academic honor—also turn out to be mimetic doubles qua rivalrous duelists.

With the echoes of this supplementary theoretical war in the background, the duel is escalating to a higher degree of theoretical intensity. We can in fact see that Girard implicitly aligns Clausewitz with a classical philosophical tradition that opens up a possible mimetic way out from the cycle of violence by making the poison the possible starting point of the cure itself. To put it in the diagnostic language we have ourselves inherited from this Platonic/Nietzschean tradition, we could specify this claim thus: if mimetic pathos (understood in its instinctual, automatic, psycho-physiological side) is responsible for the pathological escalation of violence characteristic of abstract war, mimetic distance (understood in its rational, identificatory, psychological side) is responsible for the patho-*logical* suspension of the violence of real war. And yet the distinctiveness of Girard's mimetic thought has always been to downplay the therapeutic side of mimesis and to emphasize its pathological side. Unsurprisingly, this tendency is even more accentuated in a book titled *Battling to the End*. Thus the late Girard, as a coda to a long career spent in a violent struggle with the contagious power of mimetic rivalries and the violence it generates, is primarily concerned with exploring the apocalyptic side of mimesis understood as poison, rather than developing its beneficial, therapeutic, and nonviolent side.

Caught up in the spell of his apocalyptic vision, Girard still sees a possible pharmacological way out left open by the mimetic tradition on which he relies. But after opening that door, he stops on the threshold, and, not without some oscillations and hesitations, he turns his back to it—and shuts it close. Thus a few pages below he says that reciprocal action "only suspends it [the escalation to extremes] in order to further accelerate it later" (*BE* 18). Indeed, for Girard, violence "always wins" (xvii) in the end. Consequently, in *Battling to the End* Girard's pharmacological observation remains at the level of a promising yet abstract hypothesis that requires closer empirical scrutiny in order to be finished. This is where Conrad, fictional duelist that he is, strikes back in order to pry open the door that leads to the end of the duel.

## The End of the Duel

In the final duel, Conrad offers a possible remedy for the problem of mimetic pathology and the mirroring reflex of violence it entails. We have seen that the previous duels that punctuate the narrative are based on the principle of mimetic reciprocity whereby the adversaries automatically strike back, mindlessly following the unconscious pathos of abstract war. The last duel, on the other hand, marks a sharp turn in Conrad's theorization of violence as it is predicated on a strategic logos characteristic of real war. This duel, in fact, no longer entails short-range weapons (such as swords, sabers, or horses) but, rather, takes place in a copse where the two duelists qua doubles, armed with pistols, stalk each other in order to put an end to the duel. A clear shift of emphasis in the dynamic of the duel has thus taken place: the proximity of the sword gives way to the distance of the gun; the immediacy of unconscious, mirroring reactions is replaced by the mediation of conscious, planned actions; single force gives way to strategic plan; abstract war to real war. It is thus on a firm, realistic ground that Conrad proposes a possible way out from the royal road of violence—opening up a short-cut to peace.

### Defensive Strategies

In his fictions in general, and in "The Duel" in particular, Conrad tends to posit the primacy of nature over culture, the darkness of affects over the light of reason; yet, in the final scene, the narrative unpredictably turns. And what emerges is a reciprocal, dynamic interplay between instinct and culture,

conscious rational actions and unconscious affective reactions whose interplay offers a way out from the determinism of mirror neurons. In a mimetic
reflection that will frame his entire final strategy, D'Hubert ponders: "'He
[Feraud] despises my shooting,' he thought, displaying that insight into the
mind of his antagonist which is of such great help in winning battles" (252).
And in light of this insight into the mind of the other, D'Hubert privileges
the defense over the attack, passivity over activity, reaction over action precisely in order to win and end the duel. This defensive strategy is still in line
with Clausewitz's famous realization that *the defensive form of warfare is
intrinsically stronger than the offensive*" (*OW* 160), but this is not only an
objective (or exterior) strategic realization. On the contrary, this passage
also suggests that D'Hubert relies on a subjective (or interior) insight into
the "mind" of the other in order to foresee what the other thinks and feels.
Put differently, thanks to a (mimetic) identification with the psychic life of
the other, D'Hubert momentarily suspends a direct (mirroring) confrontation with his double, keeps at a safe distance from the irresistible logic of
the reciprocal pathos characteristic of abstract war, and starts to think of a
possible solution to end this real war. Mimesis, in short, begins to work not
only as a contagious pathology but also as a possible patho-*logy*.

    And yet if Conrad agrees with the classical pharmacological thesis that
a mimetic identification functions as a possible solution to the problem of
mimetic reciprocity, he also adds important diagnostic supplements. For
instance, he makes us see that D'Hubert's strategy in real war entails a type
of conscious identification with the other that should not be too hastily
conflated with the unconscious mimesis characteristic of reciprocal actions
in abstract war. If the latter is based on an immediate bodily pathos, the
former is based on a reflective mental distance; if the latter entails an unconscious reaction, the former entails a conscious, reflective action. Mimesis, for
Conrad, has, indeed, pharmacological qualities; but one should not confuse
mimetic pathos with mimetic logos lest we muddle the distinction between
pathology and patho-logy that informs the mimetic unconscious. We should
thus specify our diagnostic by saying that because D'Hubert already finds
himself affected or, if you prefer, infected by Feraud's warlike pathos, he can
develop a privileged insight into his "mind" from a distance. An unconscious,
mimetic connection predicated on a mirroring mechanism we are now familiar with is thus paradoxically an essential condition for the development of a

conscious, mental, yet still mimetic insight into the psychic life of the other. This is how the poison turns into the remedy, pathology into patho-logy. And it is precisely from this dynamic interplay between body and mind, immediacy and mediation, consciousness and unconsciousness, pathos and logos, that Conrad opens up a theoretical way out from the escalating logic of violence. Let us look at it more closely.

At the climax of the last duel, the two antagonists confront each other in a "war to the death" (250) we have been tracing all along. But this time, the narrative articulates the complex interplay that ties instinctual actions to mental reactions. Since this is a dramatization of real, not abstract, war, it is important to picture the empirical details of the scene. D'Hubert is waiting for Feraud, lying flat on the ground, in a horizontal position of defense, so as to "draw his fire at the greatest possible range" (251); and thanks to this superior defensive strategy, he causes his adversary to miss the first of the two shots available. D'Hubert's strategic solution is not without analogies with the Chinese art of war. That is, he plans the battle in advance by exploiting the immanent potential offered by the situation and by relying on a form of action that is, in fact, a nonaction. This is how the strategist can "subdue the enemy's army without battle," says Sun Tzu in *The Art of War*.[29] But Conrad also adds a Western trope to this Chinese art. In fact, D'Hubert, in a rational move characteristic of his strategic side, exploits the position of the defender and maximizes his field of vision by relying on a classical, mimetic device that allows him, quite literally, to see double. A dandy always in possession of his "looking-glass," he turns into a Janus-faced figure that sees both ahead and behind. Thus we are told that "holding the little looking-glass just clear of his tree, he squinted into it with his left eye, while the right kept a direct watch on the rear of his position" (253). It seems then, that a conscious, visual representation introduces a rational distance that counters the unconscious immediacy of mimetic contagion; a specular mirror has the power to reframe the scene and prevent mirror neurons from firing.

And yet Conrad immediately complicates this specular scenario that privileges sight over affect, a conscious mental sense (I see) over an unconscious, bodily sense (I feel). In fact, D'Hubert's trick of the mirror (or mimetic representation) does not manage to fully frame, freeze, and contain the logic of instinctual mimesis (or mimetic reflex). As the shadow of his double enters D'Hubert's field of vision, it has the power to trigger, once again, his mirror neurons, causing them to fire, or better misfire. Hence, upon seeing that "the shadow of his enemy falling aslant on his outstretched legs" (255), the following unconscious reaction naturally ensues: "It was too much even for his coolness. He jumped up thoughtlessly, leaving the pistols on the ground" (255), exposing himself to Feraud's fire. This passage makes clear that, for Conrad, conscious mimetic reflections do not offer a bulletproof shield from instinctual, bodily reactions; an unconscious pathos is not, and will never be, under the full control of a conscious rational logos. It would be useless to deny that the shadow of mimesis has, once again, fallen upon D'Hubert's ego, turning him into a mimetic double that can easily be finished off.

Still, at the maximum moment of exposure and vulnerability, having dropped his weapons to the ground, D'Hubert, alias The Strategist, manages to turn his disadvantage into advantage, and radically inverts the final outcome of this duelist confrontation. Here is the final dramatic scene that puts an end to the duel:

> The irresistible instinct of an average man (unless totally paralyzed by discomfiture) would have been to stoop for his weapons, exposing himself to the risk of being shot down in that position . . . the fact is that General D'Hubert never attempted to stoop for them. Instead of going back on his mistake, he seized the rough trunk with both hands, and swung himself behind it with such impetuosity that, going right round in the very flash and report of the pistol-shot, he reappeared on the other side of the tree face to face with General Feraud. This last, completely unstrung by such a show of agility on the part of a dead man, was trembling yet. A very faint mist of smoke hung before his face which had an extraordinary aspect, as if the lower jaw had come unhinged. (255–56)

And so the legendary duel that mirrored the Napoleonic Wars eventually comes to an end. As the violent antagonist is finally "unhinged," the logic of violence can no longer swing the duelists back and forth, from violent action to mimetic reaction. Instead, restraining the "gust of homicidal fury, resuming in its violence the accumulated resentment of a lifetime" (256), D'

Hubert holds his fire and forces his disarmed antagonist to "fight no more duels" by dictating his conditions for peace, ultimately relegating his double's status to a man who, "as far as I am concerned, does not exist" (258). A true master of the art of war, D'Hubert finishes the duel—without finishing off his antagonist.

### First Bullet

How did this short-cut to peace open up? What is the patho-logy that puts an end to a pathological escalation of violence? D'Hubert does not fully know. But at this culminating turning point, Conrad—warlike writer that he is—intervenes to challenge this problem to a duel. And with a deft narrative move that cuts deep in the mimetic pathology of instinctual violence, he shoots this theoretical bullet: "Instinct, of course, is irreflective. It is its very definition" (255), he says. And then he adds: "But it may be an inquiry worth pursuing whether in reflective mankind the mechanical promptings of instinct are not affected by the customary mode of thought (255). In this striking oxymoronic passage imbued with affective and logical speculations concerning the relation between instinct and thought, nature and culture, pathos and logos, Conrad is opening up new patho-*logical* possibilities that not only challenge recent accounts of violence but also open up a short-cut to peace. In order to finish, let us watch the trajectory of Conrad's bullet in slow motion so as to flesh out its main theoretical implications.

At first sight, Conrad's emphasis on the primacy of "reflective mankind" over "irreflective instinct" seems to indicate a rationalist solution to the problem of violence that privileges reason over emotions, logos over pathos. But on a closer look, Conrad is careful not to fall into the rationalist trap that considers thought stronger than instinct, rationality more powerful than affects. As we have seen, despite the trick of the mirror, the shadow of the mimetic unconscious had triggered D'Hubert's mirror neurons to fire nonetheless, causing an instinctual and thoughtless reaction. That instincts can affect thoughts is well known. Clausewitz, for one, had already called attention to the importance of instinctual habits to make what he calls the "right decision" (*OW* 68).[30] But Conrad's bullet penetrates deeper. For him, what is essential is not simply that instincts turn into habits, or that nature forms culture. Rather, what is essential is that a "customary mode of thought" has the power to affect "instinct" itself. This is an unusual moment in Conrad's corpus. In his fictions Conrad usually represents thoughtful characters whose destiny is compromised by primal, basic, and quite mimetic instincts. In "The Duel," however, Conrad's diagnostic nuances the determinism of instinctual reactions that otherwise dominate his major works.[31] Thus he specifies that at the origin of D'Hubert's victorious move is not rational thought, nor natural instinct, but what he calls "*customary* mode of thought." This is an interesting oxymoronic phrase. It joins a rational, reflective activity ("thought") with something of the order of habit, repetition, and thus, of a certain degree irreflective automatism ("custom") in order to indicate that repeated thoughts can emotionally influence ("affect") certain patterns of behavior that, in turn, become instinctual. Thoughts, for Conrad, have the power to shape instincts in such a profound way that the distinction between emotion and reasons, pathos and logos, no longer holds—"An example this of training become instinct" (*SL* 73), as he says in another tale we shall later encounter. We could thus speak of instinctual thoughts, or rationalized instincts, as the key to making the right decisions at critical moments. Conrad in fact suggests that a repetition, or representation, of an "idea," which is the fruit of a "thought" sedimented into habit, has the power to "affect" in a nonrational, automatic, and thus unconscious way, instinct itself. A conscious action can generate an unconscious reaction; a bodily instinct (or mimetic pathos) is inflected by a representational thought (or mimetic logos)—but in a paradoxical rational-affective (or patho-*logical*) way. Clearly, in this complex passage neat distinctions between psyche and soma, consciousness and unconsciousness, reflex and idea, pathos and logos, culture and nature, break down insofar as Conrad articulates the dynamic interplay between the two.

But there is still a second bullet left to shoot.

## Second Bullet

Conrad's diagnostic is pushing patho-logical principles beyond a dualistic ontology, suggesting that when it comes to mimesis, clear-cut structural oppositions between mind and body, reason and unreason, consciousness and unconsciousness, and pathos and logos begin to interact and retroact, in a dynamic spiral that has a mimetic logic of its own. It is not simply rational

D'Hubert and instinctual Feraud who are caught in the logic of mimetic pathos. It is also the logic of Conrad's own thought on war that urges us to think through this complex interaction to the end. To put an end to this fictional duel, Conrad shoots a second theoretical bullet:

> In his young days, Armand D' Hubert, the reflecting, promising officer, had emitted the opinion that in warfare one should "never cast back on the lines of a mistake." *This idea, defended and developed in many discussions, had settled into one of the stock notions of his brain, had become a part of his mental individuality.* Whether *it had gone so inconceivably deep as to affect the dictates of his instinct,* or simply because, as he himself declared afterwards, he was "too scared to remember the confounded pistols," the fact is that General D'Hubert never attempted to stoop for them. (255–56; my emphasis)

Here we see that Conrad's mimetic "inquiry" was indeed worth pursuing to the end. With such a hypothesis, in fact, Conrad offers an alternative to the assumption that humans are naturally hardwired to battle to the end. While the royal road of violence is certainly a well-trodden road—especially in the age of global wars on terror whereby individuals and nations alike continue to automatically fire at the mere sight of others firing—for Conrad, it is not the only possible road. Thus, on the shoulders of Clausewitz, but with a longer mimetic tradition in mind, Conrad's untimely inquiry opens up a possible "short cut on the road to peace" (*OW* 35) for the future to pursue. Put in contemporary terms, he develops the hypothesis that the brain is not only driven by mirror neurons. It also has the power to generate "ideas" and "thoughts" that, through repetition, become "customary thoughts," "*settl[ing] into one of the stock notions of [our] brain, . . . becom[ing] a part of [our] mental individuality.*" For Conrad, then, custom, through the mediation of thought, has the power change instinct; culture, can reform nature itself, turning human nature into what Plato had already called "second nature."[32]

At the end of the duel, Conrad reminds us that the god Janus looked both ways because he presided both over the beginning and ending of wars, over battles to the end and end of the battles. Thus, if the fiercely Napoleonic Feraud "*won't* be reconciled" (*SoS* 265), his brain pathologically hardwired to the path of violence, D'Hubert steps out from the mindless logic of mimetic reciprocity and has the following, antimimetic response to what he calls Feraud's "stupid ferocity" (266): "I had the right to blow his brains out; but as I didn't, we can't let him starve." And he mercifully adds: "We must take care of him, secretly, to the end of his days" (266). After all, he reflects: "Don't I owe him the most ecstatic moment of my life?" (266). Rather than battling to the end, D'Hubert, The Strategist, overcomes the logic of mimetic violence. And in a grateful attitude toward his warlike antipode, he ends up taking care of him to the end of his days. At the end of "The Duel," ferocity has thus been replaced by sympathy, the logic of ressentiment by the logic of compassion, the laws of violence by the laws of imitation.

■     ■     ■

Recuperated in the context of global wars, international terrorism, genocides, revolutionary and counterrevolutionary movements that are literally driving entire nations to the end, the ancient realization that "man is the most thoroughly mimetic animal" (Aristotle) and thus is as vulnerable to both "good" and "bad" forms of imitation (Plato) is worth remembering. If it trickles down to our education system, which, for better and worse, has the power to mold, via the medium of cultural "impressions" what Plato famously called the "young and tender" characters of future generations,[33] it might even provide a possible theoretical and practical starting point to counter a mindless, mechanical escalation of violence that has, indeed, the potential to lead to "apocalyptic" ends (Girard). Girard usefully reminds us that the term "education" comes from *educatio*, leading out. The conclusion of "The Duel" takes this path a step further and suggests that education can lead us out of the spiral of violence as well. As William James put it in light of his account of the power of habit to form character, "The great thing, then, in all education, is to *make our nervous system our ally instead of our enemy*."[34] Conrad fundamentally agrees. He also specifies this claim by saying that customary thoughts allow fictional characters and, perhaps at an additional remove, customary readers as well to be in-formed by thoughts that counter mindless, instinctual, and violent reactions.

Having diagnosed the mimetic principles responsible for the mirroring violence that continues to cast a shadow on our contemporary times, and having offered a diagnostic alternative that would provide, at least in theory, a possible way out from the spiral of violence, we now turn our patho-logical lenses toward the ethics of catastrophe internal to Conrad's nautical fictions. As Girard also recognized, "A new ethic is required in this time of catastrophe; catastrophe urgently has to be integrated into rational thought" (*BE* 24). If we have seen that Conrad's account of the double helped us think through the mimetic principles responsible for both battles to the end and the end of battles, we now turn to see that his account of nautical storms offers us a possible starting point to develop an ethics of catastrophe that rests on mimetic foundations. It is thus no longer a question of mimetic duels to the end between singular doubles. It is rather a question of an entire crew being caught up in the same collective boat—as the shadow of a shared catastrophe looms on the horizon.

# CHAPTER 2

# Ethical Storms:
# *Typhoon* to "The Secret Sharer"

If your ship has been driven into these seas, very well! Now clench your teeth! Keep your eyes open! Keep a firm hand on the helm!—We sail straight over morality and *past* it.

—Friedrich Nietzsche, *Beyond Good and Evil*

It wasn't a heavy sea—it was a sea gone mad! . . . But you don't see me coming back to explain such things to an old fellow in a wig and twelve respectable tradesmen, do you?

—Joseph Conrad, "The Secret Sharer"

The mimetic affinities between Conrad and Nietzsche have been noticed before and have secretly animated our account of "The Duel," yet the nautical undercurrents that lead both philosopher and novelist to sail past moral norms in catastrophic scenarios is still in need of evaluation. So, taking our cue from these mirroring epigraphs, let us ask: What does it mean to sail over morality and past it? Does it mean that ethical questions should be left behind if a ship is caught in the midst of a storm? Or, more probably, that in perilous seas it might be necessary to sail beyond good and evil solutions in order to keep the ship floating? And if so, which seas have the power to generate "terrific" storms that seem to be as exterior as they are interior, as environmental as they are ethical? Nietzsche, the philosopher who went the farthest in reevaluating the value of our values, does not say. Instead, he looks back to a nautical image that is as old as the birth of ethical thought in order to invite what he calls "philosophers of the future"[1] to navigate storms yet to come.

## Perfect Storms

Independently of Nietzsche, recent developments in environmental theory have returned to nautical images to reflect on ethical concerns with anthropogenic catastrophes that increasingly haunt the contemporary world. In a book titled *A Perfect Moral Storm: The Ethical Tragedy of Climate Change* (2011), for instance, the ethical philosopher Stephen Gardiner relies on the image of a ship driven into a stormy ocean to rethink the basis of ethical decisions in the context of the impending threat of climate change. Drawing his source of inspiration neither from Nietzsche nor from Conrad but from a Hollywood blockbuster titled *The Perfect Storm* (2000), starring George Clooney as a skipper of a swordfishing boat called *Andrea Gail* caught in a hurricane, Gardiner says: "Like the Andrea Gail, we are beset by forces that are likely at least to throw us off course, and may even sink us into the bargain."[2] This catastrophic scenario may have appeared overly pessimistic, perhaps even apocalyptic, in the twentieth century. Less so in the twenty-first century. In the wake of the impending threat of climate change and the annual catastrophes that threaten to escalate in the future, René Girard is now no longer alone in ringing alarms bells. The recent turn to "environmental ethics" in philosophy, "ecocriticism" in literary studies, "climate change criticism" in critical theory, and the increasing theoretical focus on the fragility, precariousness, and vulnerability of life on earth testify to the vital urgency to address "an inconvenient truth"[3] that casts a shadow on the age of the Anthropocene.

In this new geological age, the image of a ship caught in a stormy ocean, forced to sail past old moral norms to confront new ethical problems that cast a shadow on contemporary and, especially, future generations, is timely and has recently regained new theoretical traction. But such a joint nautical and ethical problematic is, of course, not new to readers of Conrad, a writer who considered the ship as a "moral symbol of our lives" (*NLL* 149). From *The Nigger of the "Narcissus"* to *Youth, Lord Jim* to *Typhoon*, "The Secret Sharer" to *The Shadow-Line*, Conrad repeatedly represents ships caught in perilous waters, confronting characters and readers with ethical dilemmas that cannot be contained within prepackaged moral norms. To be sure, as a modernist writer who spent a good part of his life at sea and confronted firsthand catastrophic storms that put not only his own life at risk but also threatened to founder what he calls the "small planet" (*NN* 29) of the ship, Conrad is well positioned to use "the mirror of the sea" to reflect, and to help us reflect on, the new ethical riddles emerging from catastrophic scenarios that now threaten the planet as a whole. Still, despite Conrad's sustained critical and narrative engagement with catastrophes (such as the sinking of the *Titanic*)[4] and end-of-the world storms, his name is still surprisingly missing from contemporary discussions about environmental ethics and disaster narratives. This neglect is unfortunate, especially since contemporary cinematic representations of catastrophes that inform our apocalyptic imagination often lack the narrative complexity, phenomenological nuance, ethical sophistication, and philosophical density of Conrad's stormy fictions.[5] This chapter proposes a correction to this tendency by placing Conrad's name on the radar of disaster narratives. I suggest that a widely discussed tale such as "The Secret Sharer" (1912)—framed against the larger background of narratives of nautical catastrophe, such as *Lord Jim* (1900) and, especially, *Typhoon* (1903)—functions as an untimely case study to inaugurate a reading of Conrad in the age of the Anthropocene. In particular, it urges contemporary readers to move beyond ready-made good and evil moral distinctions in order to reevaluate the foundations of ethical decisions for times haunted by the shadow of catastrophe.

### Scylla and Charybdis

Of all Conradian narratives of the sea, "The Secret Sharer" is probably the clearest instance in which Conrad clenches his teeth and sails past conventional moral norms. One of his most controversial tales, it tells the story of Leggatt, a first mate who disobeys the captain's orders and kills a mutinous sailor in the midst of a storm, presumably to avoid shipwreck. A ship, a violent quarrel, and an ethical riddle: this is indeed a classical scene. Conrad, in fact, dramatizes Nietzsche's nautical imperative to sail past moral norms, and, in doing so, he mirrors a scenario that goes all the way back to the beginning of ethical theory. It is, in fact, Plato who first conceived of the ship—with its vertical social hierarchy, communal structure, and exposure to all kinds of unpredictable currents—as an ideal metaphor of the state. In particular, in Book VI of *Republic*, Socrates dramatizes a transgression whereby frenzied sailors take possession of the ship "after binding and stupefying the worthy shipmaster" (*R* 725) and put the life of the crew at risk along lines Plato morally condemns.[6] In "The Secret Sharer" Conrad mirrors and inverts this classical scene: Conrad, with Plato, dramatizes a sailor who goes against the captain's orders and transgresses moral norms; but contra Plato, Conrad stresses that this sailor does so in order save, not endanger, the ship along lines he ethically condones.

How should we reevaluate this ancient ethical riddle? Should we say, with Michel Serres, that "a single unwritten law thus reigns on board, the divine courtesy that defines the sailor, a nonaggressive pact among sea-goers, who are at the mercy of their fragility"?[7] Or should we rather say, with Nietzsche, that no such laws are set in stone and that human sailors know from immanent experiences that, in stormy scenarios, it might sometimes be necessary to sail beyond good and evil moral norms and rewrite the tables of ethical laws? And if both violent and nonviolent principles are at work in this tale of the double, what is the logic that connects them?

That Conrad, a master mariner turned writer who generally adheres to the maritime tradition, seems to take an anti-Platonic stance on a moral issue as serious as murder is a mystery that has troubled many critics. What the tale tells us is that after the storm is successfully weathered, Leggatt escapes imprisonment by jumping overboard and swimming toward another ship. Taken on board by a young, inexperienced, and uncannily similar captain, the two twin figures engage in a secret mimetic relation until the captain, having mysteriously absorbed some of Leggatt's authoritative qualities, sails toward to the coast, comes awfully close to running the ship aground, yet manages to steer, in the nick of time, so as to avert shipwreck and set his homo duplex free. In this tale of the double, then, not one but two ships are caught in dangerous seas, confronting characters and readers with decisions that go beyond good and evil solutions. Yet despite the impressive amount of commentary this text continues to generate, it is far from clear what its ethical destination is, or is meant to be. In fact, the homo duplex that casts an ethical shadow on the tale has been read both as a figure of justice and as an embodiment of evil, as an aristocratic hero and as a brutal murderer, as a manifestation of instinctual drives (or id) and as representation of an ideal ego (or superego).[8] Consequently, to this day, the controversy concerning this text's ethical status continues to oscillate between the moral polarity the narrative seeks to overcome.

In what follows, I would like to sail past the Scylla and Charybdis of good and evil moral evaluations in order to revisit the psychological, social, and environmental contexts against which the ethics of this complex text is framed. I suggest that the ethical dilemma that makes "The Secret Sharer" such a haunting, maddening, and, above all, urgent narrative to re-read today must be reframed against the catastrophic nautical contexts that—from beginning to middle and end—in-*form* the text in the first place. The shadow of mimesis, then, takes us from the escalating principles of total wars to the escalating threat of climate change, from a politics of violence to an ethics of survival; yet the basic diagnostic principles that orient our inquiry remain in place. Mimesis, in fact, remains a Janus-faced concept that is, quite literally, in the eye of Conrad's storms and is responsible for the contagious circulation of human and nonhuman actions and reactions. In the process of our diagnostic we shall confirm that mimesis turns out, once again, to be both the pathology that infects the body politic (as in panic) and the starting point for an ethics of catastrophe based on shared foundations (as in sympathy). As we sail past good and evil solutions, looking back to the ancient image of the ship will allow us to steer toward an ethics of sharing that looks ahead to the "shared catastrophe"[9] that now looms on our horizon as well.

## Storm Pieces

Catastrophes cast a long shadow on Conrad's nautical imagination. Time and again, he represents cataclysmic scenarios in which terrific storms threaten to overhaul the social microcosm of the ship. In *Youth*, for instance, Marlow opens his narrative with an account of the effects of "the famous October gale" (13) depicting a "world [that] was nothing but an immensity of great foaming waves rushing at us" (16). In *The Nigger of the "Narcissus"* Conrad frames the moral dilemma caused by the dying Jimmy against a physical storm in the following terms: "The ship tossed about, shaken furiously, like a toy in the hand of a lunatic" (53). And he adds, in apocalyptic overtones: "Nothing seem[ed] left of the whole universe but darkness, clamour, fury—and the ship. And like the last vestige of a shattered creation she drifts, bearing an anguished remnant of sinful mankind, through the distress, tumult, and pain of an avenging terror" (54). In *Lord Jim* we initially see a character imbued with heroic fantasies of "saving people from sinking ships, cutting away masts in a hurricane" (11), who miserably fails to live up to these ideal expectations in reality. Confronted with the possibility of a sinking ship in his role of first mate responsible for 800 passengers, Jim takes his infamous leap toward safety, forever compromising his ethical stance as a fictional character along lines real captains will not fail to reproduce in real life.[10] The ship does not sink, but Jim remains haunted by apocalyptic visions of a "crowd of bodies laid out for death" (84), a sign that "the end of the world had come through a deluge in a pitchy blackness" (89). Many years later, facing a different yet equally catastrophic situation, the captain-narrator of *The Shadow-Line* confronts the threat of an epidemic contagion while facing yet another storm, and, expanding the scope of this catastrophic scenario, compares his command to a "planet flying vertiginously on its appointed path" (62). The list could go on, but the general message should be clear. In Conrad's nautical fictions storms do not simply threaten individuals, or the microcosm of the ship; they also represent—via a synecdochal extension—a larger menace to the "planet" or "world" as a whole. As Marlow sums it up in *Lord Jim*, "When your ship fails you, your whole world seems to fail you" (95). For these reasons alone, there is significant theoretical potential in each of these nautical tales to help us rethink the ethical foundations in a world haunted by the shadow of perfect storms looming on the horizon.

## "A Running Wall of Water"

Still, as we are initially confronted with such apocalyptic, fictional possibilities, some amount of realistic suspicion is in order, especially given the skeptical nature of Conrad's fictions. This is also what Conrad seems to

initially suggest in *Typhoon*, an early novel that, perhaps more clearly than
any other Conradian tale, lays the foundations for the catastrophic scenarios that will continue to haunt his imagination. The captain responsible for
steering a steamer through a tropical cyclone in the Pacific Ocean, Captain
MacWhirr tends to be derided as a stupid, unimaginative, and even comic
figure. Such irony is certainly at play in the text, but Conrad also qualifies it.
In the "Author's Note," for instance, he says that MacWhirr is "the product
of twenty years of life" (viii); and he adds, in a mimetic mood, "My life"
(viii). When it comes to catastrophic scenarios, this character encourages
readers to think along skeptical, realistic, and down-to-earth lines many of
us would probably have found quite reasonable a few decades ago. We are
told that

> had he been informed by an indisputable authority that the end of the
> world was to be finally accomplished by a catastrophic disturbance of the
> atmosphere, he would have assimilated the information under the simple
> idea of dirty weather, and no other, for he had no experience of cataclysms,
> and belief does not necessarily imply comprehension. (20)

MacWhirr's perspective is neither comic nor unreasonable here. Instead,
he posits the test of "experience" over and against faith in "authority,"
"comprehension" over "belief," as the empirical foundation to evaluate
possible catastrophic scenarios. For an experienced sailor, then, it is not
a question of believing that the "end of the world" is at hand but, rather,
of "experiencing"—a term that has maritime origins, as Lacoue-Labarthe
reminds us (ex-perience, to traverse, sea passage)[11]—firsthand the danger of
cataclysmic situations. Lest such empirical evidence be provided, down-to-
earth characters like MacWhirr will dismiss such apocalyptic possibility as
"dirty weather."

But of course in a novella titled *Typhoon*, the experience of such an
end-of-the-world scenario is precisely what the text will eventually represent. Caught in the midst of a circular storm he refuses to circumnavigate,
Captain MacWhirr is confronted with the following sight: "a white line of
foam coming on at such a height that he couldn't believe his eyes—nobody
was to know the steepness of that sea and the awful depth of the hollow the
hurricane had scooped out behind the running wall of water" (74). Critics

have identified this scene as one of the worst storms of English literature, but when it comes to reflecting on its contemporary referents they have been slow in taking hold of its implications. True, not unlike MacWhirr, a few decades ago we still lacked "experience" of such scenarios. But can we still say the same today? When it comes to offering dramatic representations of the cataclysmic threat of natural catastrophes, Conrad is, indeed, ahead of his times. Well before contemporary representations in the media, documentaries, personal videos, and popular films, Conrad depicts "a white line of foam coming on at such a height that [we] couldn't believe [our] eyes." In the wake of the increasing number of annual disasters—from Hurricane Katrina to the Indian Ocean tsunami—we have become quite accustomed to believing our eyes. Unfortunately, images of "mountainous" waves resembling "a running wall of water" can no longer be restricted to fictional narratives; they roll over into the real world as well. To be sure, Conrad did not live to see the threats of global catastrophes caused by anthropogenic climate change. *Typhoon* is thus not mimetic in the sense that it realistically depicts a cyclone Conrad experienced; nor am I arguing that this text is mimetic in the futuristic sense that it magically reflects the effects of catastrophic disturbances of the atmosphere generated by climate change. What I suggest, instead, is that there is another, less visible and more theoretical sense in which *Typhoon* prompts mimetic reflections. Insofar as Conrad is dramatizing a storm that has the power to overturn not only a single ship but the social microcosm the ship represents—what he also calls a "planet"—he can help us reflect critically on the contagious and, in this sense, mimetic effects generated by what he calls end-of-the-world scenarios.

Storms, then, cast a shadow on Conrad's nautical imagination and deserve critical attention in the age of the Anthropocene. But what about "The Secret Sharer"? Isn't this tale primarily concerned with psychology rather than with the environment, inner experiences between secret sharers rather than exterior experiences with shared catastrophes? Judging from the critical commentary this seems indeed to be the only picture reflected by this tale. Yet some suspicion is in order for this is a tale of the double and has more than one side to it. Let us thus reframe "The Secret Sharer" so as take a look at both sides of the story.

## "The Secret Sharer" in the Anthropocene

Given its balanced formal structure, compressed style, symbolic density, unreliable narrative perspective, not to speak of the multilayered psychic, sexual, juridical, and ethical implications that in-form it, "The Secret Sharer" has been an ideal case study to try out a variety of new theoretical approaches: from new criticism to new historicism, psychoanalysis to feminism, deconstruction to queer theory.[12] These schools of criticism have successfully decentered unitary, homogeneous interpretations and have contributed enormously to our understanding of this heterogeneous tale, rendering it second only to *Heart of Darkness* in the amount of theoretical commentary it has generated in the past. And yet despite their differences, these theoretical approaches share a common anthropocentric bias that no longer holds for the future. That is, they tend to zoom in on the all-too-human actions in the foreground and to treat the shared environment in the background as a simple backdrop for deeper, more obscure, and humanly intriguing secrets. Consequently, no sufficient attention has been given to the fact that, despite the vertiginous number of indeterminacies that prevent unilateral interpretations, a narrative point remains rather stable throughout the whole narrative, an environmental, nonhuman point that allows us to anchor our reading and start uncovering what J. Hillis Miller calls "the most secret secret" of the tale: namely, "The basis of ethical decisions and acts."[13]

Anthropocentric approaches to the tale have insufficiently stressed that when it comes to the environmental context in which Leggatt's infamous murder takes place, Conrad is careful to univocally frame it against a narrative scenario that has explicit catastrophic implications. Even two antagonistic characters whose accounts of the events otherwise radically diverge (Leggatt and Captain Archbold of the *Sephora*) fundamentally agree on this central point. Leggatt says: "I tell you I was overdone with this terrific weather that seemed to have no end to it. Terrific I tell you—and a deep ship" (89). "It wasn't a heavy sea—it was a sea gone mad!" (105). And as Captain Archbold gives his own, otherwise antithetical version, he echoes: "terrible weather on the passage out—terrible—terrible" (99); the "mountainous seas . . . seemed ready every moment to swallow up the ship herself and the terrified lives on board of her" (101). Such "mountainous" waves, both perspectives agree, clearly threaten to "swallow up" the ship and the community of men on board. Now since in Conrad's fictional world the ship is representative of the social macrocosm, perhaps even the planet as a whole, this agreement should give us pause and make us wonder: could it be that at stake in this tale is not simply a representation of a local disaster, but an allegory of a global catastrophe? This, at least, is what Leggatt suggests as he says, in an apocalyptic mood: "I suppose the end of the world will be something like that" (105).

If we return to scrutinize the horizon of "The Secret Sharer" with this larger, environmental frame in mind, there are, once again, good reasons for critical suspicion—especially if we recall that, for Conrad, "The value of creative work of any kind is in the whole of it. Till that is seen no judgment is possible" (*CL*, II, 332). While a storm certainly looms in the middle of this tale, we have yet to prove that the shadow of catastrophe is cast over the whole tale, in-forming the telos of a carefully crafted narrative structure in which "every word fits" (*CL*, V, 128) from beginning to end. Only then is ethical judgment possible.

Let us thus start at the beginning.


### Janus-Faced Beginnings

The beginning of "The Secret Sharer," with its highly subjective perspective of the captain-narrator scrutinizing the horizon of the Gulf of Siam from his becalmed ship, not a breeze in sight, does not seem to support our catastrophic hypothesis. As many commentators have noticed, it is clear from the very first lines that this is a narrative intensely concerned with a private psyche of a split character rather than with catastrophic environmental conditions, with a journey within rather than with a journey without. As Albert Guerard trenchantly put it, influencing generations of critics, the captain's psychic relationship with his murderous homo duplex, Leggatt, is quite simply "the whole story."[14] Perhaps. Still, given what Cedric Watts calls "the Janiform symmetry of the tale,"[15] there might be more than one side to this story. And if one (psychological) side has been amply discussed, the other (ecological) side has been amply neglected. A careful reframing of the frame that is attentive to what William Connolly calls "an enlarged sense of the planetary entanglement of the species"[16] provides us with a fresh starting point to reevaluate the ethics of catastrophe that orients the tale as a whole.

In short, before attempting any ethical judgment, it is imperative to bring to the surface the side of the story that has so far remained submerged.

From the very first line, the narrative impeccably joins images of psychic division with images of collective catastrophes urging formally attentive readers to articulate the mirroring interplay between the two sides. We are told, for instance, that the fishing stakes the narrator initially sees from his ship are "half submerged" and "crazy of aspect" (*TLS* 81), and there is no need to repeat at this point that images of division reflect the narrator's splitting of the self. But then, in a surprising mental analogy that still requires explanation, the narrator specifies that these fishing stakes are "as if abandoned for ever by some nomad tribe of brown fishermen now removed to the other end of the earth" (91). This is, of course, not an objective mimetic representation. It is, rather, a subjective, internal association the narrator maps onto the landscape. Still, we are left to wonder about the mysterious narrative origins of this imaginary drama of departure whereby an entire community associated with a traditional mode of life now left behind (a "nomad tribe"), which is dependent on the sea for its survival ("fishermen"), is forced to definitively forsake their location (the stakes are "abandoned for ever") in order to relocate in a geographical environment that is as distant as possible from their original dwellings ("the other end of the earth"). The fact that "there was no sign of human habitation as far as the eye could reach" (81) is surely no sufficient narrative explanation for such drastic images of human dislocation.

If we follow the narrative eye and turn to the other side of the landscape, we see a similar intertwinement of environmental and psychic representations: "To my left a group of barren islets" (81), the captain-narrator says. And in another interior association that redoubles the first, he adds: "suggesting ruins of stone walls, towers and blockhouses" (81). A few lines into the text and we are already confronted with those "echo structures"[17] that resonate throughout the tale as a whole. But like an echo, this is a repetition with a difference. An external referent generates, for the second time, images of human abandonment. Yet this time the implications stretch from the nomadic tribe to an entire sedentary civilization; images of departure are replaced by images of violent destruction. Even the most enduring social structures are now reduced to mere "ruins." Again, the narrator does not dwell on the mysterious origins of his allusive and highly elliptical associations; yet the narrative keeps encouraging readers to unearth possible textual traces that would account for such destructive mental representations. For instance, we could notice that "stone walls," "blockhouses," and "towers" are metonymic of human civilization in general, and of military, political, and economic power in particular. The fact that these military structures are turned to "ruins," then, points toward the possibility of a violent anthropogenic destruction. The tale was written in 1909, and history will soon generate escalating horrors that will reduce European civilization to ruins. With the benefit of historical hindsight we can now see that there is an uncanny sense in which the narrator seems to be ominously looking ahead, toward horrors yet to come.

## Futuristic Ends

And yet, on a narrative level, it is actually the temporality of the tale itself that is Janus-faced and looks both ways. Despite the feeling of immediacy of these opening lines, the captain-narrator's use of the narrative past suggests a temporal splitting between the captain's perspective and the narrator's perspective. If the captain is located in the present, looking ahead to events to come, the narrator is actually looking back, via a retrospective first-person narrative that retells events that are already past.[18] As an eagled-eyed critic such as Cedric Watts recognized, there is indeed a "diachronic" element at play in this scene that needs to be considered in order to supplement the synchronic mirrorlike structure of the tale.[19] Could it be, then, that the imaginary destructions the divided figure of the captain-narrator projects onto the landscape a posteriori are generated by catastrophic events that may already have taken place or, since he is still alive to report them, were narrowly averted? If we adopt Janus's double lenses we see that in this imaginary, posthuman scenario, the narrator occupies the position of a futuristic observer who is confronted with the traces of a civilization that was once grand, but has now long been destroyed, leaving but scanty traces of a nomadic tribe behind who have themselves disappeared in order to relocate to the other end of the earth.

Now, if we join the two sides of the narrator's mental landscape, a second, more secret tale begins to emerge from the half-submerged system of imaginary associations the narrative encourages us to bring to the surface. Notice, in fact, that the archaeological layers of Conrad's apocalyptic imagination suggest an inversion of a deep-seated nineteenth-century evolutionary view on which he otherwise relies. If we consider the diachronic element in this scene, we notice that it does not follow the usual linear, nineteenth-century evolutionary pattern in which a nomadic stage is succeeded by a civilization, which, in turn, after a period of degeneration, is reduced to ruins. Rather, the nomadic tribe has only recently left (the fishing stakes are "still standing") whereas the sedentary civilization has long been destroyed (stone walls are "reduced to ruins"). We are thus encouraged to imagine, if only subliminally, that a violent anthropogenic cataclysm not only affected a single generation but also had what environmental philosophers now call an intergenerational impact, reducing what once was an organized, sedentary civilization back to the stage of nomadic tribes.

If an older generation of critics could still recognize such a scenario by turning back to H. G. Wells's *The Time Machine*, a new generation should be even more familiar with such futuristic images of catastrophe. A series of apocalyptic sci-fi movies obsessively show descendants of a civilization that, due to an anthropogenic cataclysmic event that has a geophysical impact on the earth, is now permanently gone, leaving behind nomadic tribes condemned to surviving among the destroyed walls of a human civilization reduced to ruins. To be sure, for a generation who has been welcomed to the desert of the real, these images of catastrophe are now timely. More untimely, however, is the observation that Conrad foreshadowed such images and perhaps even contributed to shaping them.[20] In any case, for future-oriented critics, there is now a term to designate Conrad's paradoxical temporality that leads us to revisit the present in view of a future perspective that has not yet happened. Climate change criticism alerts us to what Conrad seems to have been representing all along. Namely, that these images of catastrophe cannot be dismissed in terms of the old concept of anachronism; rather, they require a new understanding of what is now known as "catachronism."[21]

Whether you agree with Conrad's catachronistic imagination or consider such a reading a futuristic anachronism, one point should be clear. The beginning of "The Secret Sharer" does not only foreshadow a journey within the psyche of a split, individual self; it also joins images of psychic division with images of global destruction in order to foreshadow potentially catastrophic journeys. Thus reframed, the "terrific storm" in the middle of the tale can no longer be read only as an aesthetic achievement; nor can the images of destruction be dismissed as the product of the narrator's schizophrenic imagination.

Rather, we are encouraged to read these images of catastrophe in terms of an end-of-the world scenario that haunts Conrad's imagination in general, and the beginning of "The Secret Sharer" in particular. This beginning—not unlike the beginning of another apocalyptic text, *Apocalypse Now*—already foreshadows the end. It reminds us that a "terrific storm" can potentially drive people to the "other end of the earth" and reduce an entire civilization, with its "walls" and "towers," to "ruins"—leaving a deserted, posthuman world behind. It is as if Conrad may be whispering, between the cracks of carefully chosen words: welcome to the half-submerged ruins of the Anthropocene!

### Beginning, Middle, and End

But why should Conrad stress such an apocalyptic, posthuman scenario in the first place? What is the narrative source of this imaginary, end-of-the-world possibility? Textually based answers should be clearly in sight now. Given that an end-of-the-world storm haunts the middle of this tale, it is perhaps no wonder that the narrator begins by retrospectively projecting the possibility of such disastrous events onto the landscape. We can thus understand why after representing a departed "tribe" and a civilization in "ruins," the captain-narrator turns to describe a nautical image of catastrophe. Having turned East and West, he now looks into the background, toward the declining light of the "westering sun" and sees the following image: "the tug steaming right into the land became lost to my sight, hull and funnel and masts" (*TLS* 92). And in a third mental association that echoes—via what is not, strictly speaking, "delayed decoding" (Watt's term), but, rather, what I shall call Conrad's delay call forwarding narrative we're not in a position to decode—the previous two associations, he says: "as though the impassive earth had *swallowed her up* without an effort" (92; my emphasis). In this phrase, we have a key to solve the riddle of the narrator's catastrophic imagination. This image provides, in fact, the missing link that both foreshadows and backshadows the catastrophic possibilities that haunt the "whole"—from beginning to middle to end.

If we take a step back we are now in a position to see that this carefully crafted frame, in which every word matters indeed, firmly anchors the source of the narrator's catastrophic imagination at the beginning in two nautical events in which not one, but two ships are threatened to be "swallowed up," one in the middle, the other at the end: Leggatt's ship, as we have seen, is caught in an end-of-the-world storm that threatens to "swallow up" (101) the crew. And, at the end of the tale, as the narrator nearly sails his ship into the land of Koh-ring to free Leggatt, he echoes: "the shadow of the land," you will have guessed the verb, "already swallowed up" the ship (116). No wonder that the narrator, as he retrospectively relates his first experience as captain, is haunted by images of catastrophe! It is because two ships, with their nomadic tribes of sailors on board, and the social macrocosm the ship represents, come awfully close to being "swallowed up" by the sea that the shadow of catastrophe looms so large in this opening scene. In sum, at the beginning of his tale the narrator retrospectively projects an end-of-the-world scenario onto the landscape in order to alert readers—via a delayed call forwarding message we can now hear—to the possible disastrous implications that in-form the beginning, middle, and end of the tale. Quite literally, the secret shadow of catastrophe gives form to the narrative as a whole.

But there is a larger whole to be considered still. If we step farther back from this beginning, we notice that this shadow is not cast on a single narrative in isolation. This is the moment to see that the connection between *Typhoon* and "The Secret Sharer" is much more profound than it appears to be, and that an underlying mirroring structure joins these narratives of disaster. At the end of *Typhoon*, we are in fact left with an image of "the hurricane, with its power to madden the seas, to sink ships, to uproot trees, to overturn strong walls and dash the very birds of the air to the ground" (90). This environmental warning whereby the first novel ends is reflected at the beginning of "The Secret Sharer." We are in fact told that the soil is left "barren," there is "no sign of human habitation as far as the eye could reach" (81), and there is "not a bird in the air" (82). Indeed, "The Secret Sharer" starts where *Typhoon* ends. It re-presents a hypothetical end-of-the-world, posthuman scenario in which we are left to reflect on the devastating effects on humans, animals, and the environment of what Conrad calls "catastrophic disturbance of the atmosphere" (*TOS* 20).

This is an important aesthetic principle that, as we have already seen, informs Conrad's poetics. Repeatedly in his work mirror structures transgress the boundaries of individual texts, generating submerged mimetic continuities whereby Conrad picks up lines of inquiry left dangling in previous narratives in order to extend them toward unexplored fictional and theoretical territories in subsequent narratives. Such continuities generate aesthetic forms that need to be traced carefully across textual boundaries in order to be fully outlined. They also provide an underlying contextual homogeneity that serves as a bedrock to our heterogeneous textual mimetic investigations.

For the moment, however, suffice to say that the cataclysm that haunts both tales has a direct impact not only on the human world, nor solely on the institutions that define Western civilization, but also on the animal world, the ecosphere, and the geological sphere as a whole. Indeed, for contemporary readers living in the age of the Anthropocene, that is, a geological age in which humans play a determining role in changing the ecosystem of the earth, Conrad's images of catastrophe are particularly resonant. As he depicts not only "walls" and "towers" reduced to "ruins" but also "mountainous" waves, "abandoned" "habitations," and a "barren" soil deprived of animal life, this tale of the double acquires an ethico-political value that mirrors contemporary anxieties about what William Connolly calls "the fragility of things" and the dicey "entanglements" between human and nonhuman forces these things generate in the Anthropocene.[22] In a similar spirit, it is as if Conrad suggests a thought experiment that will have to wait the threat of climate change to be fully articulated. "Suppose that the worst has happened. Human extinction is a fait accompli. . . . Picture a world from which we all suddenly vanished," writes Alan Weisman in *The World without Us*.[23] Conrad had already sketched such a picture; we were simply not in a position to see it.

And yet unlike contemporary turns toward unavoidable apocalyptic destinations, Conrad also urges us to look for new theoretical beginnings in the hope that it is still possible to sail past such catastrophic ends. In this sense, Conrad offers a detailed, narrative-based case study for what the French philosopher Jean-Pierre Dupuy calls "enlightened doomsaying" (*catastrophisme éclairé*). That is, he "invites us to make an imaginative leap, to place ourselves by an act of mental projection in the moment following a future catastrophe and then, looking back toward the present time, to see catastrophe as our *fate*—only a fate that we may yet choose to avoid."[24] Dupuy, you will remember, observed that "there is no better preparation for acquiring this skill than a classical literary education."[25] This education, as I set out to demonstrate, is sharpened if the literary author under consideration not only had firsthand knowledge of catastrophic scenarios but also framed them within the paradoxical temporality of enlightened catastrophism.

Revisiting the ethical dilemma at the center of "The Secret Sharer" from the angle of catastrophes to be avoided allows us to reframe the very terms on which the ethical debate rests from a less anthropocentric, normative, and moralistic perspective. We are now ready to reopen the case. Insofar as this is a tale of the double, there shall be two parts to this case as there are two dossiers to examine: the case of Leggatt (or the *Sephora* Dossier) takes us through a physical storm that destabilizes the microcosm of the ship and generates ethical riddles from the outside-in; the case of the Double (or the Shared Dossier) takes us through a psychic storm that threatens to split the subject in two and generates an ethical riddle from the inside-out. Once both exterior and interior parts are joined we should have sufficient critical evidence to reevaluate Leggatt's actions, close the case, and open up new theoretical foundations to anchor Conrad's ethics of catastrophe.

Let the trial begin.


## The Case of Leggatt (The *Sephora* Dossier)

Leggatt's murder on the *Sephora* has been the source of numerous moral evaluations, juridical debates, and legal condemnations. Yet despite the critical ink that has been spilled on his case, no agreement has been reached that allowed the jury to pronounce a final verdict. Judged as a murderer and praised as a hero, condemned as an outlaw and taken as a model, diagnosed as the id and as the ideal ego, or, as a critic once simply put it, "good man or bad man?,"[26] Leggatt's case remains, to this day, open, unresolved, and passionate. His dossier continues to be filled with the most contradictory evaluations, but at least critics agree that the scene of the crime presents the following deceivingly simple ethical scenario: a first mate named Leggatt kills, or, better strangles, a sailor during a storm, and later claims that he did so in order to save the ship from shipwreck. Complications emerge less from the scene itself than from the narrative re-presentation of this scene. In fact, readers who are trying to impartially evaluate the case of Leggatt are not given an omniscient, third-person perspective. Instead, they are entangled in competing and highly subjective accounts originating from witnesses who are directly or indirectly implicated in the case and are thus notoriously unreliable in their testimony. In addition to Leggatt, who, while he is aware that he is not "an angel from heaven" (*TLS* 88), claims to be fundamentally innocent, Captain Archbold of the *Sephora* sees Leggatt as a murderous rival, whereas the captain-narrator sees Leggatt as an exemplary model. Given the lack of a stabilizing third-person narrative perspective, there seems to be no way out from this narrative double bind, especially since the captain-narrator who frames the events provides a hideout for Leggatt in his cabin, identifies with his "secret sharer," confuses himself with his "second self" (113), and, as a result of this "feeling of identity with the other" (102), which has strong homoerotic overtones, his mind gives signs of delusion, splitting, and madness. It seems, then, that no matter which perspective one adopts, the case of Leggatt frustrates any possibility of reaching a final verdict and is thus destined to remain an open case.

And yet as often in such cases, the discovery of secret evidence can urge private investigators to return to the scene of the crime and reframe the events in light of previously neglected facts that can provide the necessary evidence for closing the case. We have already taken an important step in that direction by stressing that the narrative testimony under scrutiny suggests that something much more radical than an individual murder is at stake. As we have seen, "The Secret Sharer" furthers a problematic internal to *Typhoon* by posing an ethical riddle in the context of the imaginative possibility of a catastrophe that is not simply local but has global, cataclysmic, environmental, and intergenerational implications. If Leggatt kills a sailor in the context of a storm that threatens to submerge not only a single ship but also, by symbolic association, the social order as a whole, having a lasting impact on the environment, we are thus encouraged to think about this global scenario first, before even attempting to proffer judgment on his individual actions. As Jane Bennett perceptively recognizes, "a politics devoted too exclusively to moral condemnation and not enough to a cultivated discernment of the web of agentic capacities can do little good." Bennett also specifies along lines that resonate with our aesthetic concerns: "The ethical task at hand here is to cultivate the ability to discern nonhuman vitality, to become perceptually open to it."[27] Conrad's tales provide a specific aesthetic context to articulate precisely such a type of "discernment" necessary for a politics and ethics to come.

Let us thus not let go of our modest contribution to opening the doors of perception via the mirroring lens of the literary case study at hand. Clearly, the ethical status of Leggatt's crime changes radically if we consider that his actions intend to prevent the possibility of a catastrophe that does not only "swallow up" a single ship but also has the potential to reduce an entire civilization to "ruins," leaving an "abandoned" and lifeless world behind. Put differently, if these images of global catastrophe narratively precede the images of local disasters, it follows that Conrad wants his readers to think global first, before turning to evaluate local ethical actions. This inversion of perspectives, as we now turn to see, overturns the entire ethical structure of the narrative and aligns Conrad's ethical thought experiment with contemporary theoretical debates about the implications of global catastrophe.

## Ethics of Catastrophe

In a book titled *L'Équivalence des catastrophes (Après Fukushima)*, the French philosopher Jean-Luc Nancy reminds us that the term "catastrophe" comes from the Greek *katastrophè* (overturning, inversion, foundering), and that this inversion is as physical as metaphysical, as material as epistemic. As he puts it: "What a catastrophe overturns is the distribution of substances, as well as the characters and registers throughout all modes of existence, of representation, of conception, and of imagination."[28] Writing in the aftermath of the nuclear disaster of Fukushima, but with a series of anthropogenic catastrophes in mind that go back to Hiroshima, Nancy cautions us against the temptation to look for ready-made "solutions" (*EC* 36) based on transcendental moral principles to evaluate ethical dilemmas generated in catastrophic contexts. These principles are themselves overturned by the *katasrophè* they are supposed to account for. Above all, for Nancy, ethical decisions made in a context of catastrophe cannot be judged in isolation or on the basis of given a priori norms. Rather, they must be evaluated against the larger system of "general interconnections" (15) that entangle such decisions in what he calls "tighter and ramified relations of interdependence" (49). And echoing a mimetic concern he shares with Lacoue-Labarthe, Nancy adds that interdependence in catastrophic contexts turns into a "generalized equivalence" (54) whereby "communication turns into contamination, transmission becomes contagion" (56). In this mimetic ecology, then, an ethics of catastrophe should not be restricted to individual actions in isolation. Rather, it should carefully consider the highly complex system of general mimetic relations in which ethical actions take place.

The ethicity of "The Secret Sharer" has long been considered problematic for its antidemocratic and violent implications, yet revisited in light of a contemporary ethics of catastrophe, this controversial tale can serve as an imaginative springboard to address, on a specific, situational, and complex narrative case, ethical riddles theorists are now also beginning to articulate. Like Nietzsche before him and theorists of catastrophe after him,[29] Conrad suggests that actions emerging from perfect storms cannot be evaluated a priori by applying existing juridical norms to events that threaten to overturn the very foundations of those norms. Instead, Conrad brackets traditional conceptions of morality (morality applied) and advocates a new ethics of catastrophe (ethics discovered). In what follows, it will thus not be a question of applying given moral norms to the text from the outside-in, but of discovering ethical principles that already inform the text from the inside-out.

Leggatt's account of the events on the *Sephora* is explicitly positioned up against normative a priori notions of justice and inaugurates a new chapter in our ethical education. After mentioning that his father is a "parson," this son of a preacher says to the captain-narrator in terms that already suggest an intimate complicity between the two: "You see me before a judge and a jury on that charge" (*TLS* 88). And later, he echoes: "But you don't see me coming back to explain such things to an old fellow in a wig and twelve respectable tradesmen. Do you? What can they know whether I am guilty or not—or of *what* I am guilty either?" (111). It is not only the captain-narrator who feels interpellated by such questions. The reader, or better, you do too, don't you? You might even have heard such critiques of the law in Conrad's fictions before. In *Lord Jim*, for instance, in a somewhat reversed ethical scenario, which concerns Jim's selfish preoccupation with his own life rather than the lives of his passengers, Marlow says: "These were issues beyond the competency of a court inquiry" (74). Instead of automatically condemning Leggatt's "contempt for the law,"[30] let us recognize that Leggatt—whose name, as J. Hillis Miller perceptively noted, bears the traces of "a legacy that has the force of the law" (Middle English *legat*, from Latin, *legare*, to appoint, ordain; from *lex*, law command)[31]—challenges not so much the law itself but traditional representatives of the law. More precisely, by linking parsons, judges, and tradesmen as part of the same juridical system, Leggatt unmasks the patriarchal, theological, and economic system of power/knowledge that informs normative approaches to justice. He not only calls attention to the human and thus fallible dimension of the law but also stresses the limitations of juridical norms to evaluate actions prompted by unprecedented catastrophic situations. Leggatt is not an "outlaw" simply because he operates outside the law. Rather, he is an outlaw because he is confronted with the limits of the law—limits he transgresses in the context of a storm in which, we are told, "there are no means of legal repression" (*TLS* 89). Conrad, like other modernists before him, may be representing an immoralist hero *de jure*, but this does not mean his character is *de facto* indifferent to ethical values. Rather, it is precisely his questioning of normative notions of morality that operate on a priori imperatives and his search for an alternative system of legal values to account for the "relations of interdependence" (Nancy's term) informing catastrophic scenarios that render his case timely to reevaluate. Leggatt may not be a moral figure in the sense that he follows the tables of the law. But he surely is an ethical figure in the sense that he questions the value of the values inscribed in the law.

Leggatt's challenge to the moral principles embodied by nautical figures such as Captain Archbold has tended to make critics uneasy as it undermines the maritime tradition Conrad otherwise adheres to. This historical concern is understandable. However, the traditional values of the past should not automatically be mistaken for universal, immutable, ahistorical truths to be applied to the present and future, especially since historically informed critics have noted that this tradition might have been less rigid than it has often thought to be.[32] Conrad, for one, is far from applying stringent maritime norms to this case. Thus he objects to Leggatt being called a "murderous ruffian" in the press by asking: "Who are those fellows who write in the Press? Where do they come from?" (*CL*, V, 121–22). I wonder too sometimes. What is sure is that if I have to choose between the Press and Conrad, I am inclined to side with Conrad here for reasons that are neither based on authorial intentions nor grounded on historical context (extrinsic reasons) but rather for ethical principles that emerge from within the text itself (intrinsic reasons).

From an ethical perspective that is attentive to both the underlying textual principles these characters embody and to the environmental context that surrounds them, Captain Archbold is, in fact, rejected as a figure of authority because of, not in spite of, his moral and legal principles. The captain of the *Sephora* may well represent the law on board, as he boldly claims: "I represent the law here" (*TLS* 93). But the fact that he is anxious to give Leggatt up "to the law" (101) suggests his subordination and dependency to the juridical system of the land. To be sure, Archbold's conception of morality rests on theological foundations rather than maritime foundations. We are told, for instance, that there is "something incomprehensible and a little awful; something, as it were, mystical" (101) in his commitment to the law. And if Leggatt claims that the reefed foresail he managed to set during the gale "saved the ship," Archbold dismisses this point with the following counterhypothesis: "'God's own hand in it. . . . Nothing less could have done it'" (101). The conflict between Archbold and Leggatt is not simply personal, psychological, or narratological. Nor is it a question of privileging one perspective over the other on the basis of a priori notions of good and evil. Rather, it is a question of recognizing two radically opposed ethical foundations these characters represent first, in order to subsequently reevaluate ethical problems in catastrophic situations that in-*form* the narrative itself.

## Immanence contra Transcendence

In the destabilizing scenario of a storm that threatens to overturn not only the stability of the ship but also the foundation of ethical decisions, the reader of "The Secret Sharer" is given two competing perspectives to evaluate Leggatt's action. On the one hand, Archbold's reassuring system of values is rooted in a normative juridical view that posits a priori, universalizing, and transcendental moral imperatives. If the origins of these imperatives ultimately rest on theological foundations, the narrative also exposes the all-too-human dimension of these foundations. On the other hand, Leggatt represents a problematic yet immanent approach to ethics that brackets universal commandments in favor of the specific relations of interdependence generated by the catastrophic event itself. If the former model claims to be universal and transcendental, the latter is singular and immanent; if the former claims divine origins, the latter avows its human origins; if the former is morality applied, the latter is ethics discovered. Archbold contra Leggatt, God as savior contra the sail as savoir, divine intervention contra human intervention:

this is the implicit agon upon which the ethicity of "The Secret Sharer" is anchored.

Readers have often wondered why the captain-narrator unconditionally sides with Leggatt's account, but we are now in a position to see that it is actually the underlying system of ethical values these characters represent that privileges one perspective over the other. In line with Nietzsche's untimely invitation to sail past conventional moral norms and anticipating contemporary theorists of the end times, Conrad proposes an ethics that counters transcendental, universal, and vertical notions of the law in order to advocate a more immanent, horizontal approach in which ethical responsibility is fundamentally redefined as a human, empirical, contextual, and systemic problem. This also means that, for Conrad, ethical evaluations in a situation of catastrophe cannot rely on a priori moral principles. Instead, they require a careful reexamination of the system of affective, human, and environmental interrelations that inform the complex ecology of the tale. And here is where the problematic of mimesis, in its good and bad effects, begins to circulate on the surface of Conrad's ecology of action.

## Good Affects/Bad Effects

"The Secret Sharer" is a narrative haunted by the shadow of the double. We should thus not be surprised that mimesis, understood not simply as realistic representation but as a form of psychic imitation that introduces secret continuities at the heart of seemingly discontinuous subjects, plays a decisive role in the ethical dilemma that haunts Conrad's ethics of catastrophe. In the absence of transcendental moral principles that guarantee the possibility of divine interventions, Conrad calls attention to the immanence of contagious affects—such as sympathy, panic, and madness—which, for better and worse, affect and infect the relations of interdependence on which the microcosm of the ship rests. I say for better and worse since Conrad's diagnostic continues to be double; both a source of irrational, contagious pathologies and of rational, diagnostic patho-logies, the problematic of mimesis opens up an interspace that goes beyond good and evil moral evaluations, while outlining alternative ethical foundations.

Take sympathy, for instance, a "good" mimetic affect characterized by a moral concern for the other so truly felt that the affect of the other becomes a shared pathos (*sym-pathos*). As a manifestation of this shared feeling, we are told that when the captain-narrator initially takes the anchor-watch himself to relieve his crew, he does so out of the "kindest of motives" (85). And yet as he realizes that the side ladder is left dangling as a consequence of his altruistic action, he is immediately faced with the systemic ethical consequences of his so-called good moral intention and wonders: "I asked myself whether it was wise to have interfered with the established routine of duties even from the kindest of motives" (85). Moral sympathy, for Conrad, does not translate into ethical wisdom. This incident urges both the captain and readers to reframe the value of personal feeling and intentions ("kindest motives") within the collective system of interdependent actions ("duties") on which the microcosm of the ship rests. Contrary to normative approaches to ethics, this passage suggests that it is neither the action considered in isolation nor the intentions motivating such actions that provide a reliable anchor for ethical judgment but, rather, the shared, systemic consequences of such actions. Technically put, for Conrad, as for Nietzsche and contemporary theorists after him, a conception of morality restricted to universal principles (deontology) or individual virtues (virtue ethics) must be extended in order to account for the general consequences of actions on the system of social interconnections (consequentialism). It is with this ethical principle in mind that we should approach the ethical dilemma at the heart of the catastrophic events that follow. In fact, if the narrative makes sure that the captain, and readers along with him, should evaluate individual "moral" actions (no matter how "good") in light of the consequences on the global context of the ship, it should follow that this ethical principle should apply to "immoral" actions as well (no matter how "bad").

This initial suspension of moral judgment is important to bring to the fore the general systemic implications of mimetic actions and reactions that inform Conrad's ethics of catastrophe. Despite its seemingly unconscious and instinctual nature, Leggatt's violence toward the mutinous sailor is in fact motivated by conscious, responsible, and above all informed concerns for the system of relations on which the entire ship depends. This is why Leggatt specifies that the sailor "wouldn't do his duty and wouldn't let anybody else do theirs" (88). Independently of the veracity of this subjective claim, we should notice that the word "duty" is objectively used for the second time in the context of an ethical problematic. And, for the second time, the narrative stresses that an individual departure from one's duties generates larger systemic consequences that need to be carefully evaluated before passing judgment. Significantly, it is only after this systemic reminder that we are given the full account of the "terrific storm" we have been expecting all along. With this frame in mind, let us listen to Leggatt's testimony, which I now restitute in its entirety:

> It was when setting a reefed foresail, at dusk. Reefed foresail—you understand the sort of weather—the only sail we had left to keep her running, so you may guess what it had been like for days. Anxious sort of job that. He gave me some of his cursed insolence at the sheet. I tell you I was overdone with this terrific weather that seemed to have no end to it. Terrific I tell you—and a deep ship. I believe the fellow himself was half crazed with funk. That was no time for gentlemanly reproof, so I turned around and felled him like an ox. He up and at me. We closed just as an awful sea made for the ship. All hands saw it and took to the rigging. I had him by the throat and went on shaking him like a rat, the men above us yelling "Look out! look out!" Then a crash as if the sky had fallen. They say that for ten minutes there was hardly anything to be seen of the ship—just the three masts and a bit of the forecastle head and of the poop all awash driving along wildly in a smother of foam. It was a miracle that they found us jammed together behind the forebits. Not a pretty miracle either. It's clear that I meant business because I was holding him by the throat still. He was black in the face. It was too much for them; it seems they rushed us aft together gripped as we were screaming Murder! Like a lot of lunatics and broke into the cuddy. And the ship running for her life, touch and go all the time, any minute her last in a sea fit to turn your hair grey only a-looking at it. (89)

This is clearly a catastrophic natural situation whose global consequences the narrative has been warning us against from the beginning. Yet, this time, the focus is not on an imaginary ecosystem that depicts a submerged posthuman world, but on the "ecology of action" (Edgar Morin's term)[33] that is meant to keep the boat floating. And what emerges from the eye of this storm, which is as ethical as it is natural, is a complex interplay between natural (physical) actions and human (affective) reactions that have both personal and systemic implications. Leggatt, for one, is clearly "anxious" because of the "terrific weather," and his duty is restricted to hoisting the storm-sail by hook or by crook. But the narrative implies a more general, systemic lesson as well. Namely, that the physical, exterior turmoil of "a sea gone mad" induces a psychological madness in a member of the crew, so that, we are told, "the fellow *himself* was half crazed with funk" (my emphasis). At the heart of this storm there is thus an infective madness that has the potential to spread—via what Conrad calls in *Lord Jim* "the contagion of example" (38)—that needs attentive diagnostic, if only because this mimetic contagion has larger pathological implications on the system of duties on which the ship relies to keep floating.

### "The Contagion of Example"

Notice that this is not the first time that Conrad articulates the complex interplay between environmental and human forces in the eye of a perfect storm. Once again, "The Secret Sharer" re-presents, for the second time, a scenario Conrad had already depicted in *Typhoon*. But Conrad's fictional repetitions, as we know, are never exact reproductions. Instead, they reframe such scenes in a new mimetic ecology that serves as a starting point for new ethical reflections. In this case, the repetition is at least double and generates mirroring effects between these twin narratives of catastrophe that bring our ethical riddle into sharper focus.

On one side, *Typhoon* also depicts the psychic effects of a physical catastrophe as the tale traces contagious continuities between the so-called madness of the typhoon and the madness of human behavior. Images of nonhuman, environmental storms in the exterior world are traditionally taken to reflect human, psychic storms waging in the interior world. And yet this anthropocentric perspective whereby the whole world is supposed to be a reflection of man can be reframed from a less anthropocentric view that considers the agentic force of nature on human behavior. Loaded with a cargo of 200 Chinese workers (or "coolies") who start a row in the midst of the typhoon, Conrad makes clear in the "Author's Note" that he is not interested in "bad weather" (vii) as such. Rather, he is interested in what he calls "the extraordinary complication brought into the ship's life at a moment of exceptional stress by the human element below her deck" (vii). In particular, he makes us see how "the wrath and fury of the passionate sea" (19) trigger a violent riot among the Chinese "coolies"—problematically redefined as "crazed men" (57)—that threatens the ship from within. And in order to reinforce the continuity between natural fury and human madness, exterior and interior infection, Conrad adds: "it seemed that an eddy of the hurricane, stealing through the iron sides of the ship, had set all these bodies whirling like dust" (77). Conrad is thus perfectly aware that in catastrophic scenarios a mimetic continuity exists between the physical violence, fury, and confusion of nature, on the one hand, and the psychosomatic disruption of human affects, on the other. This is why in *Lord Jim* Marlow speaks of the "shadow of madness" that falls on a ship in danger, and specifies: "Trust a boat on the high seas to bring out the Irrational that lurks at the bottom of every thought, sentiment, sensation, emotion" (95). Well before any theoretical turns to affect or catastrophe, Conrad joins these two sides of what is part of the same ethical problematic.

On the other side, in *Typhoon* Conrad equally justifies violent means to put an end to the irrational spread of mimetic affects that threaten the stability of the ship. The source of danger is, once again, located in a crazed individual, but this time the scenario is somewhat inversed as it is the captain who violently acts against the second mate. In the midst of the gale, the latter "lost his nerve," and the captain gives an account of what he calls an "awkward circumstance" in loose, disconnected sentences: "Gone crazy . . . Rushed at me . . . Just now. Had to knock him down" (68). This episode foreshadows the entire ethical problematic of "The Secret Sharer." Conrad is, in fact, painfully aware that the affective, contagious consequences of catastrophic natural forces on psychologically vulnerable subjects threaten the microcosm of the ship as a whole. Hence the need of extreme measures that transgress given moral norms in order to affirm collective survival. Interestingly, in the context of *Typhoon* such a violent action does not require additional explanations. It is tacitly accepted that given the seriousness of the nautical situation, knocking the second mate unconscious was the "good" thing for Captain MacWhirr to do. But in "The Secret Sharer" Conrad takes it a step further in order to pose a more complex ethical riddle. While continuing to locate the events in a situation of catastrophe in which one "crazed" individual threatens the already unstable social system, Conrad not only inverses the scenario by locating the moral transgression on the side of the first mate who, this time, contra the captain, attempts to save the ship; he also exacerbates the ethical dilemma by pushing Leggatt's moral transgression to the extreme case of murder. If the case of MacWhirr is easily solved, the case of Leggatt confronts us with a true ethical dilemma.

In "The Secret Sharer" Conrad dramatizes a perfect ethical storm with complex, spiraling effects that reframe individualistic conceptions of agency in the larger ecology of actions and reactions the tale minutely dramatizes. Natural and human elements mutually affect each other in a feedback loop whereby a catastrophic exterior event generates, by affective contagion, an effect of generalized madness, which, in turn, reinforces the possibility of catastrophe, along contextual lines Gregory Bateson would define as "systemic pathology."[34] Conrad offers a diagnostic insight in the circulating logic of the mimetic pathos informing this pathology. It is, in fact, no accident that the narrator speaks of the "*pestiferous* danger" of the "crazed" seaman. As a psychic pathology, madness is indeed pestiferous (from Latin, *pestiferus*, bearing plague). The plague is, indeed, "contagious" and generates a mimetic "crisis" that has the power to infect the entire body politic. This is why René Girard speaks of "the collective character of the disaster, its universally contagious nature."[35] Conrad, for one, insists on the semantic field of madness in order to trace the process of mimetic contagion that spreads from the catastrophic scenario to the entire social microcosm, reducing all members of the crew to a state of generalized hysteria: if the seaman is "himself . . . half crazed with funk," the other sailors are described as "lunatics"; and even the figure of the captain, who carries what Conrad calls in *Typhoon* "the prestige, the privilege, and the burden of command" (39) and upon whose sovereignty the fate of the ship depends, loses his head. Leggatt retrospectively says: "'I understand that the skipper too started raving, like the rest of them" (89). And he adds: he "whimpered about our last hope—positively whimpered about it and nothing else—and the night coming on. To hear your skipper go on like that in such weather was enough to drive any fellow out of his mind" (105). This loss of the leader's head is no minor matter for the social body, if only because it is such a head that holds the social body together. Once the head is lost, what Conrad calls the "the horrors of panic" (*LJ* 71) ensue.

## "The Horrors of Panic"

Panic is a mimetic reaction par excellence insofar as it spreads contagiously from subject to subject, overtaking like a wave the entire social body and generating a type of horror that introduces sameness where difference should be preserved. Panic was initially theorized by crowd psychologists in the early twentieth century in the context of the identificatory tie that binds the subjects to the (totalitarian) leader. But in the early twenty-first century this mimetic affect must be reframed within a less anthropocentric ecology. As Adriana Cavarero reminds us, "the term [panic] lends itself to designating those collective experiences in which terrorized masses flee from natural catastrophes like earthquakes, floods, or hurricanes."[36] Although theorists of panic argue that we should be careful not to automatically connect catastrophe and panic (many catastrophic scenarios fail to generate it),[37] it is indisputable that panic, when it occurs, cannot be disconnected from the problematic of affective contagion and the mimetic unconscious that spreads it. We are now in a position to understand why Jean-Luc Nancy, resuscitating a mimetic affect he had initially explored with Lacoue-Labarthe[38] in the context of catastrophe, stresses that due to mimetic forces of "terror" (or panic) "communication becomes contamination, transmission becomes contagion," generating a generalized "equivalence" (*EC* 56) where restricted differences should be maintained.

Panic is not a much-discussed affect in Conrad studies as yet, but Conrad repeatedly returns to diagnose its contagious effects along lines that anticipate contemporary theories of catastrophe. In *Nostromo*, for instance, we read that "there were a thousand ways in which a panic-stricken man could make himself dangerous" (274). In *Lord Jim* we are told that Jim's "confounded imagination had evoked for him all the horrors of panic, the trampling rush, the pitiful screams, boats swamped—all the appalling incidents of a disaster at sea he had ever heard of" (70–71). And in *Typhoon* Conrad describes the "the rage of a mob" (47) caused by the storm in terms of a "scramble of blind panic" (78), reminding us that in the equivalence generated by catastrophe, panic can trigger violence on the basis of the unconscious, mimetic, and thus mirroring principles I discussed in the previous chapter. But the mimetic unconscious also urges us to consider the spiraling movement of panic. Conrad's diagnostic, in fact, specifies that panic is not only a mimetic symptom of horror; it is also an unconscious cause of catastrophe. In particular, Conrad makes us see that even in the midst of so-called natural catastrophes the general circulation of mimetic affects transgresses structural binaries between "nature" and "culture," environmental actions and human reactions. Instead, a perfect storm generates a spiral of mutually reinforcing human and nonhuman forces, conscious and nonconscious actions that, together, contribute to the escalation of catastrophe. Catastrophes, then, for Conrad are never simply natural, but are anthropogenic instead. They are the consequence of an ecology of mimetic actions and reactions that introduce sameness in place of difference. In fact, nature not only has a physical effect on human lives; it also has a psychic effect on human affects, which disrupts the systemic structure of social "duties" and, in turn, accentuates the possibility of disaster. In sum, well before contemporary theorists of catastrophe, Conrad makes us see that the distinction between nature and culture no longer holds in catastrophic, posthuman scenarios.

Thus reframed, the case of Leggatt is not only a psycho-ethical case; it is an ethico-environmental case. We are in fact now in a position to see that it is only once the spiraling vortex of mimetic panic has already contaminated the entire social body—from the mutinous seaman to the captain, via the entire crew, threatening to affect Leggatt himself—dissolving the system of interrelated duties upon which survival of a ship depends that Leggatt, in an antimimetic move, intervenes. As he reports to the captain-narrator: "I just took it into my own hands and went away from him—boiling, and . . . But what's the use telling you? You know!"(*TLS* 124). Leggatt is assuming that a captain knows what theorists of panic know. Namely, that once the entire social body has lost its head, the "prestige" of the captain gone, a mimetic dissolution of relations ensues, and drastic measures are in order to contain the threat of a general catastrophic outcome. And since the narrative is very specific about the timing of Leggatt's intervention, it is clear that his action must be located in the general ecology of actions and reactions that threaten to swallow up the ship as a whole. Leggatt, for one, is perfectly aware of the kind of storm he is sailing through. He continues his testimony thus:

> Do you think that if I had not been pretty fierce with them I should have got the men to do anything? Not it. The boss'en perhaps? Perhaps! It wasn't a heavy sea—it was a sea gone mad. I suppose the end of the world will be something like that; and a man may have the heart to see it coming once and be done with it—but to have to face it day after day. . . . I don't blame anybody. I was precious little better than the rest. Only I was an officer of that old coal-wagon anyhow. (105)

Anyhow, reframing the actions in the foreground against the catastrophic background allows us to reevaluate the case of Leggatt along lines that supplement narrowly individualistic or anthropocentric approaches to ethics. Psychoanalytic critics are particularly vulnerable to such anthropocentric fallacies. Barbara Johnson and Marjorie Garber, for instance, are right to claim that "Conrad situates Leggatt at the vanishing point of moral (conscious) decidability"; yet as they stress that Leggatt was "*un*conscious at the moment of the murder" in order to zoom in on his "ongoing struggle with conflicting forces within the self,"[39] they restrict ethical evaluations to individual, solipsistic, or at best familial—that is, Oedipal (unconscious)—actions rather than opening them up to the general ecology of (conscious and unconscious) actions and reactions that the narrative attempts to make us see. Similarly, psychoanalytical evaluations of Leggatt in terms of the "id" or, alternatively, the "ideal ego" confine the discussion to a familial topography of the mind that is indifferent to the general ethico-politico-environmental context the narrative describes so minutely. This lack of attention to the larger contagious implications of affect is striking in a theory that, after all, originally had the ambition of theorizing the social bond; yet it might be diagnosed as a symptom of Freud's own tendency to reduce "group psychology" to the "analysis of the ego."[40]

Not so Conrad. As we have seen, for Conrad there is a path that leads from panic, by way of contagion, to hysterical pathologies that spread immediately across the body politic dissolving vital differences into a deadly equivalence. And it is because Leggatt is all too conscious of the power of panic to generate a form of mimetic madness that disrupts the system of relations upon which the ship—as a microcosm representative of a communal "tribe" and "civilization" that faces the possibility of being reduced to "ruins"—rests, that he acts violently in order to prevent this community of nomadic men to be swallowed up by a terrific sea in a scenario metonymic of the "end of the world."

## Verdict 1

So, then, after this lengthy circumnavigation that took us through and beyond this first storm, it is legitimate to ask: What's the verdict? Bluntly put, can killing another human being ever be justified as the last resort to avoid a situation of global catastrophe? The tale does not propose easy, transcendental answers that would be valid a priori in different contexts. The staggering amount of textual detail internal to the *Sephora* Dossier suggests that each case requires a close investigation of the ecology of actions and reactions that inform the transgression in question along interdisciplinary, systemic, and immanent principles I have outlined in some detail—part of a literary training in reading catastrophic scenarios. In this sense, "The Secret Sharer" provides an exemplary case study to reevaluate ethical principles in the context of catastrophic scenarios geared toward saving the maximum number of lives. It is thus a fundamental mistake to condemn Leggatt as "elitist," as many critics have done. His authoritarian stance is animated by a social imperative that privileges the common good based on a certain standard of fidelity to one's duty and communal solidarity—virtues Conrad consistently promotes.

All things considered, then, the inconvenient verdict that emerges from the case of Leggatt is the following. An unimaginable transgressive action in normal circumstances can be justified in extraordinary circumstances if, and only if, *all* of these conditions are fulfilled: such an action takes place in the context of a catastrophic situation that threatens the life of the entire social microcosm; it originates from an individual who, by training and profession, can read the systemic implications of such a threat, and is in a position to evaluate it and to effectively counter it; it counters systemically disruptive actions that actively contribute to bringing about a collective catastrophe; and it takes place in conditions in which there are no other means of legal repression. If all these conditions are met, "The Secret Sharer" suggests that even the moral imperative "thou shalt not to kill" can be transgressed, provided the ethical consequence of this transgression is to save the greatest number.[41] The captain-narrator, for one, brutally sums up his own understanding of the systemic implications of the ethical dilemma of the tale along the following, consequentialist principle: "It was all very simple. The same strung-up force which had given twenty-four men, a chance at least for their lives had, in a sort of recoil, crushed out an unworthy mutinous existence" (106).

And yet it is not so simple. If this claim is often quoted to justify Leggatt's action considered outside its catastrophic context, a series of additional diagnostic questions emerge precisely in light of the mimetic ecology I have just articulated. For instance, if mimesis is clearly part of the ecology of actions that generates a possible catastrophe, what kind of "strung-up force" is part of the solution? And why does the captain-narrator, at the end of the tale, seem to inverse the ethical principles outlined in the first dossier by sailing awfully close to a rocky shore to free Leggatt, while risking the lives of twenty-four men on board his own ship? In order to answer these mirroring questions we must remember that Leggatt has an identity that is not one but double; he is a Janus-faced figure who looks in two opposed ethical directions: if Leggatt is an antimimetic figure who counters mimetic contagion on the *Sephora*, he also turns into a homo duplex who is deeply implicated in the mimetic unconscious he initially countered as he is taken on board the captain-narrator's ship. Mimesis, once again, seems to be as much the source of catastrophic ends and final liberations. It is thus necessary to turn to the second side of this double case.

## The Case of the Double (The Shared Dossier)

It is a critical commonplace to say that in "The Secret Sharer" Conrad offers his most explicit representation of the homo duplex. Conrad is so insistent in his representation of Leggatt as "other self," "double," "secret sharer," and so on that, over the years, critics have tended to grow impatient with this reiteration of an old romantic trope, treating it with due modernist, critical, and, at times, ironic distance. Yet we can now see that this is a repetition with a difference. By joining the psychic trope of the double with the ethical dilemmas generated in a catastrophic scenario, Conrad manages, once again, to give the past figure of the doppelgänger a second life that resonates with contemporary psychic and ethical preoccupations, mimetic preoccupations concerning the relational foundation of an identity that is not one, in the sense that it is already shared. The case of the Double turns from exterior, environmental storms to interior, psychic storms; in the process, Conrad proposes shared intersubjective foundations to give an account of ethical relations. Ethics, in short, cannot easily be divided from psychology—if only because psychology and ethics are constitutive of the two faces of the same Janus-faced tale.

### Facing the Double

The captain-narrator's initial encounter with his alter ego neatly joins the ethical side of the story with its psychological counterpart, suggesting that this encounter must be framed within the dual perspective introduced at the beginning. Facing, for the second time, the sea, the captain is confronted with a mysterious apparition that emerges, shadowlike, from the water, along lines that are in a secret continuity with the half-submerged images of catastrophe he had initially foreseen. What he sees is a floating "naked body" initially mistaken for a "cadaveric" (85), "headless corpse" (86) who is eventually given a singular face: "he raised up his face, a dimly pale oval in the shadow of the ship's side" (86). And it is at this moment of face-to-face confrontation with a naked, vulnerable, and exposed other that the captain's ethical concern explicitly emerges. "'What's the matter?' I asked in my ordinary tone, speaking down to the face upturned exactly under mine" (86). And in an echo of this initial interrogation, Leggatt, turned homo duplex, connects the two sides of the case as follows:

> "There's a ship over there," he murmured.
> "Yes. I know. The *Sephora*. Did you know of us?"
> "Hadn't the slightest idea. I am the mate of her . . ." He paused and corrected himself: "I should say I *was*."
> "Aha! Something wrong?"
> "Yes. Very wrong indeed. I've killed a man."
> "What do you mean? Just now?"
> "No, on the passage. Weeks ago. Thirty nine south. When I say a man..."
> "Fit of temper," I suggested, confidently. (101)

We can confidently say that this is an enigmatic encounter that continues to be the source of much critical perplexity. It is usually approached from competing perspectives that consider Leggatt either as a realistic character or as an imaginary psychic projection. But perhaps it is not necessary to adjudicate between these competing sides since both are clearly part of the story. If the events of the *Sephora* rely on the assumption that Leggatt is a real character who opens up a legal and ethical case, the more secret events on the captain-narrator's ship—as an excessively self-conscious and insecure young captain hides his "secret sharer" in his cabin, feels progressively entangled with his "double self," and eventually, via a "mysterious communication," absorbs his qualities of command—play with the idea that Leggatt is an imaginary figure who offers a perfect case for a psychological investigation. Either way, considered from a double, psycho-ethical perspective that informs the text as a whole, we should notice that this initial scene of address not only posits an ethical problem in the context of a highly mimetic yet nonrealistic scene, confirming our intuition that mimesis and ethics, for Conrad, are two faces of the same coin (critical reasons). It also resonates with contemporary philosophical developments that ground ethics in intersubjective relations with singular others who are both external and interior to the self (theoretical reasons).

We have seen Conrad diagnose the catastrophic effects of mimetic contagion well before philosophers talked about the mimetic "equivalence" generated by panic. But this is the moment to recognize that he also returns to the individual face (and voice) of the other as a privileged starting point to rethink the foundations of ethical thought. Conrad is, in fact, no longer alone among ethical writers who emphasize a singular encounter with the face, voice, and timbre of the other in order to reframe ethical actions in catastrophic contexts. Jean-Luc Nancy, for instance, also suggests that in order to counter the forces of mimetic contagion and the equivalence of terror it entails, it is imperative to return to the shared rapports with singular others based on "esteem" as a viable starting point to reconstitute the social bond. Contrary to panic and the collective equivalence it generates, Nancy writes, "Esteem is addressed to the singular and to its singular way of coming to presence [*venir en présence*]—flower, face, timbre" (*EC* 66). If the mimetic power of panic dissolves the social bond, Nancy suggests that the singularity of the face and voice of the other solidifies these bonds. Thus he concludes his book on catastrophe by wishing for new forms of affective relations with singular others as starting points to rethink the foundations of community. These others, he says, are "neither individuals nor social groups" but "absolute singularities . . . emergences, arrivals and departures, voices, tonalities [*singuliers absolus . . . des surgissements, des venues et des départs, des voix, des tons*]" (*EC* 69). If you are wondering who these singular subjects could be, this is the moment to recall Lacoue-Labarthe's whisper to Nancy, a mimetic whisper he seems to have taken to heart given the poetic tone of his phrase:

namely, that we should "leave to 'literature' . . . the care of asking the question: 'who?'"[42]

In his fictions, Conrad certainly asked this question. Mysterious arrivals and departures punctuate his texts in general; and tonalities of shared voices that emerge from primal bonds between singularities that are neither individuals nor groups, but singular-plural souls, resonate strongly in "The Secret Sharer" in particular. Both Conrad and Nancy thus seem to agree that if the collective forces of panic (or "terror") generate the dissolution of the social bond (bad mimesis), a shared bond with a singular other (or "esteem") might serve as the starting point to build an ethics of catastrophe on alternative, intersubjective, relational foundations (good mimesis). They also agree that "the co-implication of existing [*l'exister*] is the sharing of the world,"[43] a sharing (*partage*) that rests on a conception of a "singular-plural" subject in which neat distinctions between self and other no longer hold. These are Nancy's terms but, as we shall presently confirm, they could as well have been Conrad's. Once again, there is no need to apply any theory to Conrad's writings, for these writings already generate mimetic reflections.

The figure of the doppelgänger, with its ambivalent status as an exterior other who is also part of the structure of the self, has long considered passé, yet this shared conception of subjectivity whereby the other is mysteriously part of the self is timelier than ever. It is not only central to Nancy's take on "esteem" based on the singularity of a *partage* or rapport with the face, tonality, and, I might add, whispers of a vulnerable, intimate, and precarious other. It is also at the foundation of Emmanuel Levinas's influential ethical turn in philosophy whose echoes are audible in Nancy's account of community as well, a turn away from universal imperatives inscribed in the ontology of the subject toward the singularity of the ethical encounter with the demand of the other. In addition to the initial confrontation with the vulnerable face of the homo duplex, so many of the reiterations about the captain-narrator's mimetic confusion of identity with his double seem to support Levinas's claim that the "*psychisme de l'âme*" is defined by the presence of the "other in the self [*l'autre en soi*]" and, consequently, "subjectivity is structured like the other in the same [*comme l'autre dans le même*]."[44] Again, literature seems to precede philosophy when it comes to the question, "who?" Forced to respond to the ethical address of a vulnerable and naked other, the narrator speaks of the "confused sensation of being in two places at once" (*TLS* 96), confesses that he "felt dual more than ever" (96), and claims of being "identified with [his] secret double" (107) to the point of madness, thereby approximating the ethical anxiety characteristic of Levinasian "insomnia."[45] Far from being an outmoded literary trope, the homo duplex assumes, once again, a second ethical life. A past-oriented trope looks ahead to recent ethical turns, and re-turns—via the shadow of mimesis—to haunt the critical and theoretical scene.

And yet what was true for Conrad and violence is equally true for Conrad and ethics. Conrad not only anticipates contemporary theories; he also supplements them by giving us an immanent, embodied, a-theological, and psycho-physiological insight in the shared structure of subjectivity. Both Levinas and Nancy, in fact, stress that the other is not external to the self but is somehow part of the self: Levinas speaks of the presence of the other in the self and defines the "subjectivity of the subject" in terms of "vulnerability" and "exposure to affection";[46] Nancy speaks of "inclination" of the self toward the other responsible for the emergence of a subjectivity that is neither singular nor plural but "singular-plural."[47] But both philosophers do not specify how, exactly, this affective, relational subject actually comes into being (*compears*); nor do they trace the immanent, psycho-physiological force that inclines the subject toward the other (*clinamen*). Instead, they rethink the foundations of subjectivity on principles that require either a leap of faith toward the *Tout-Autre* (Levinas), or shared metaphysical assumptions about what "Being," "Dasein," or "Mitsein" is or should be (Nancy).

Conrad is not a philosopher, but he has a literary lesson to share nonetheless. He suggests that the immanent experience of mimesis—rendered visible through the figure of the doppelgänger who is both interior and exterior to the self, both the same and different—inclines or swerves the subject toward the other, allowing for the emergence of a psychic subject that is not one, but is secretly shared instead. That the figure of the secret sharer cannot be dissociated from the experience of mimesis was already revealed in the specular reflection that frames the captain-narrator's initial encounter with his alter ego. Confronted with a mimetic image reflected in the mirror of the sea, the narrator says: Leggatt's face was "upturned exactly under mine" (86). And later, he adds: "The shadowy dark head, like mine, seemed to nod imperceptibly above the ghostly grey of my sleeping suit. It was, in the nights, as though I had been faced by my own reflection in the depths of a somber and immense mirror" (88). Here we see a confirmation that, for Conrad, mimesis and ethics are two faces of the same coin: it is because this is a scene of mimetic (mis)recognition that an ethical bond with an imaginary other who is not really other, but internal to the self, begins to emerge.

## Mirroring Reflections/Telepathic Connections

At first sight, this scene of specular misrecognition with an alter ego might seem reminiscent of Jacques Lacan's celebrated account of the "mirror stage." The mirroring effects are indeed suggestive, especially since the double is defined by stabilizing, ideal characteristics the ego still lacks in his turbulent, affective, and unconscious manifestations. And yet it would be a speculative misrecognition to align Conrad *avec* Lacan too closely. This scene, in fact, is less specular and unitary than it is auditory and relational. The main differences are visible, or better audible. Notice, in fact, that Conrad's account of identification, unlike Lacan's, is not confined within the static representation of a mirror image that frames the ego in an ideal, unitary form, *Gestalt* or *imago* (mimesis as visual form).[48] Rather, like many modernists attentive to bodily experiences of becoming, Conrad privileges an immanent, psycho-physiological, and turbulent mimetic communication that, via the medium of voice, breaks down the very ontological structure of what an ego is, or appears to be (mimesis as affective pathos). Thus, after the initial specular encounter with a seemingly dead *imago* reflected in the "glassy shimmer of the sea," the narrator repeatedly stresses the living *pathos* of a "good voice" to mysteriously "induce" the affect of the other into the very tissue of the self, generating a secretly shared ego that is inclined to become alter. For instance, the narrator says at the outset, in an enigmatic passage that reveals the mimetic foundations of his communicative intercourse with his alter ego: "[Leggatt's] voice was calm and resolute. A good voice. The self-possession of that man had somehow induced a corresponding state in myself." And then he adds: "A mysterious communication was established already between us two" (87). The "whispers" that bind these mimetic doubles—as they progressively share secrets while Leggatt lives a clandestine existence in the captain's cabin—transgress psychoanalytical accounts based on visual or Oedipal identifications and have intrigued fine-tuned readers before. J. Hillis Miller, for instance, suggests that a form of "telepathy" is at play in this mysterious communication.[49] This is a fine observation as this communication transmits affects (*pathos*) from a distance (*tele*) in ways that are not dependent on the reflection of an image (*imago*), but on the sound of a penetrating voice instead. What we must add is that this telepathy is not based on a mysterious, transcendental principle, but on an immanent, psycho-physiological, and unconscious principle that is constitutive of the modernist subject in general and Conrad's account of the homo duplex in particular.

We have encountered this principle before. Conrad is particularly attentive to unconscious forms of imitation that animate the psychic life of the ego. For him, involuntary reflexes that are not under the control of consciousness (such as anger) lead the subject to unconsciously reproduce the expression or gesture of the other, and thus to incorporate an affect that is proper to the other into the ego. What was true for violence in the case of an antagonistic double is now true for *all* shared affects in the case of communication with an admired model: via an unconscious mirroring reproduction of the gestures and expressions of the other, an exterior affect flows into the subject and becomes an interior affect, an individual quality becomes a shared quality. "The Secret Sharer" offers a precise reflection of this mimetic process. It is in fact no accident that we are repeatedly told that "the two strangers in the ship, faced each other in identical attitudes" (95). The strangers do not face each other because they are doubles (the narrator says that "he was not a bit like me really" [91]). The opposite is true: they become doubles because they face one another. This fundamental point is rendered visible in the following nonverbal, mirroring communication between the two mirroring figures on deck: "He rested a hand on the end of the skylight to steady himself with, and all that time did not stir a limb, so far as I could see." And then the narrator immediately adds: "One of my hands, too, rested on the end of the sky-light; neither did I stir a limb, so far as I knew" (90). The formal linguist symmetry could not be more balanced; the bodily communication could not be more symmetric. And not surprisingly so. The two characters find themselves in an unconscious rapport of shared mimetic communication in which they literally, and thus physically, and thus psychically, or better psycho-physiologically, mirror each other. Well before the discovery of mirror neurons, Conrad is once again providing a phenomenological description of the mimetic unconscious. For him, in fact, unconscious mimetic reflexes wire, as it were, the nervous system of the ego into the nervous system of the other (*socius*): not any other, but an admired, ideal, or exemplary other thereby establishing a secretly shared, nonverbal, yet deeply felt, communication with this *alter* (i.e., other)—ego.

Conrad is not alone in holding a mimetic view of the subject whereby a "corresponding state" is induced via a nonverbal communication. The centrality of unconscious forms of imitation was well known at the turn of the century. The social psychologist Gabriel Tarde, for instance, in his groundbreaking *The Laws of Imitation* (1890), makes this point succinctly as he compares the social man to a hypnotized subject who is vulnerable to the suggestion of others and "unconsciously imitates" what models do or feel. As Tarde writes, in a mirroring sentence Conrad would have appreciated: "everyone we imitate, we respect . . . everyone we respect we imitate."[50] And quoting the British psychiatrist Henry Maudsley, Tarde specifies that we "can perhaps read unconsciously in the spirit of the other, via an unconscious imitation (*imitation inconsciente*) of the attitude or expression of the person whose muscular contraction *he copies instinctively and with precision*" (*LI* 138). Tarde fundamentally agrees with Conrad that an unconscious mimesis can induce an affect proper to the other/model into the very physio-psychology of an ego that is not one for it is already double. This mimetic tendency, Tarde suggests, is even accentuated in the case of the psycho-social situations Conrad describes in his tale, that is, situations in which characters find themselves in a position of intimidation. Thus, speaking of a "profound perturbation of one's whole being, a dispossession of the self we call *intimidation*," Tarde gives an incisive diagnostic that perfectly captures the psychic state of the newly appointed captain-narrator, who, we should not forget, is the youngest man on board and who feels very much overwhelmed by his position of first-command: "The intimidated person who is under the gaze of the other escapes from himself and lends himself to being manipulated and molded (*devenir maniable et malléalbe*) by others" (*LI* 145). If the captain's excessively self-conscious behavior and psychic malleability have often been described in terms of a personal madness bordering on schizophrenia, Tarde offers a psychosocial diagnostic of this madness. And in order to give neurological substance to this malleability, he proposes the following mimetic hypothesis: "it is possible to conjecture that the relation of a cell to another cell within the same brain could be similar to the relation of two brains whereby one fascinates the other" (*LI* 148). Indeed, looking back to past laws of imitation casts new light not only on the captain-narrator's psychic suggestibility to his homo duplex; it also allows us to catch up with some of the most recent confirmations in the mimetic foundations of subjectivity.

In the past Freudian century the dominance of psychoanalysis in literary studies has intimidated critics with an interest in psychic life to open such pre-Freudian doors. Unsurprisingly, then, the critical emphasis in the clinical case of Leggatt qua double has tended to remain confined within a Freudian and Freudian-oriented metapsychology (the ego, the id, the ideal ego, Oedipal complexes, mirror stages, imagos, and so forth). Consequently, the specific psychosomatic concerns that directly inform Conrad's social psychology (the double, the model, psychic intimidation, social anxieties, mirroring reflexes, *sym-pathos*, and so forth) have remained in the critical background, or have simply been left unnoticed. But what was in the background in the past century is coming to the foreground in our post-Freudian century. In fact, key discoveries in the neurosciences, developmental psychology, and other immanent theoretical turns in line with Tarde's thought are currently generating a return of interest to the laws of the mimetic unconscious that equally fascinated modernists in general and Conrad in particular. Gilles Deleuze and Félix Guattari, for instance, were quick to recognize in Tarde a precursor of affect theory. As they put it: "Tarde was interested in the world of detail, or of the infinitesimal"; and, establishing bridge between affect theory and modernist mimetic theory, they usefully specify that, for Tarde, "microimitation . . . has to do not with an individual but with a flow or a wave. *Imitation is the propagation of a flow.*"[51]

And this flow is contagious. Why? As Vittorio Gallese, one of the discoverers of mirror neurons, explains, reframing the laws of imitation in contemporary terms: "mirroring mechanisms seem to be involved with our capacity to share emotions and sensations with others. When perceiving others expressing emotions by means of their facial mimicry, the observer's facial muscles activate in a congruent manner, with intensity proportional to their empathic nature."[52] This principle, first discovered in macaque monkeys, should not be dismissed as a monkey see, monkey do principle. Rather, it provides a confirmation that humans are indeed mimetic creatures and that it is through mimesis that, from birth onward, we can gain direct access to the psychic life of others, their intentions, feelings, and thoughts. Giving neurological substance to a mimetic principle that Conrad and other modernist writers had been tracing all along Gallese adds an anti-Oedipal point that challenges Girard's mimetic hypothesis but is in line with modernist accounts of the mimetic unconscious: "These results suggest that prior to any triangular mimetic relationship, the main object of infant's mimesis is the affective behavior of the 'other.' . . . I posit that mirroring mechanism and the functional mechanism they underpin—embodied simulation—are a crucial component of what makes our mind in the first place a *shared mind*."⁵³ Shared affects stem indeed from mirroring principles. But these principles are not imaginary or symbolic. They are rather based on the empirical realization that the human ability to share emotions is, from the very first hours of life, triggered by an embodied form of simulation that leads newborns, and later adults, to unconsciously reproduce the expressions of the other— not any others, but privileged others such as parents, friends, models, lovers, or, to use Pierre Janet's terminology, *socii*.⁵⁴ Hence, through this shadowlike reproduction, the ego mimes the other, feels the affect of the other, becomes other, via a form of unconscious communication that gives birth to the ego—out of the shared affects with the *socius*. This is perhaps the reason Marlow says in *Lord Jim*: "Besides the fellowship of the craft there is felt the strength of a wider feeling—the feeling that binds a man to a child" (101).

## The Secret Shared

Now, this detour via the intersubjective psychology of the mimetic unconscious that informs Conrad's obscure account of the captain's relation to his homo duplex allows us to understand the "mysterious communication" responsible for a telepathic feeling of shared identity that has troubled critics for so long. As the narrator says, "I saw it all going on as though I were myself inside that other sleeping suit" (*TLS* 89); when he tries to "clear [his] mind of the confused sensation of being in two places at once" (96), of feeling "dual more than ever" (96), of the "dual working of [his] mind" (97), of being "so identified with [his] secret double" (107), and so on, he is not simply going insane. Nor is he working through Oedipal anxieties (the crew is not a family but a social microcosm). Rather, he is dramatizing a "shared manifold of intersubjectivity"⁵⁵ that needed the advent of the neurosciences in order to be recognized but that Conrad had been secretly diagnosing all along. "The Secret Sharer," in fact, is an incisive diagnostic of the birth of a shared ego.

It makes us see the mimetic consequences of a secretly shared, neurological communication that leads the subject to unconsciously reproduce the gestures and affects of the *socius*, feel what the other feels, and integrate the other into the very tissue of the self so profoundly that the ego becomes a shared ego—or, if you prefer a phantom or a shadow of the ego.

Thus reframed, solutions to riddles that have cast such a long shadow on this tale prove to have been on the surface all along. Critics have been wondering: What, exactly, is shared in "The Secret Sharer"? What is the supposed "secret" that is hidden in this tale of the double? And how does this "mysterious communication" make an ethics of sharing possible? The mystery of mimetic communication does not point to any message. It is not a question of finding out the content of shared secrets, of unveiling the logos that secretly hides behind this shared pathos, no matter how intriguing these secrets may be. On the contrary, for Conrad, it is the medium of mimesis itself (the face, the body, the voice) that is the message. Or better, this mysterious communication is a mimetic communication in which mimesis is both the medium and the message. Thus, when the captain-narrator speaks of "the secret sharer of my cabin and of my thoughts," it is not only the cabin (or the bed) that is shared—though these are shared too. As he suggests, something much more intimate is at stake: it is the very structure of the ego that turns out to rest on shared, mimetic foundations. These mimetic doubles are thus not individuals in the etymological sense that they are indivisible. On the contrary, they are divided subjects who share an identity that is not singular in the sense that it is at least double, multiple, protean, or, as Conrad will later say, "composite." On the basis of this mimetic communication, then, a singular voice becomes a shared voice; a subjective quality becomes an intersubjective quality; a singular being becomes a shared, plural being. Nancy makes a similar point as he sums up what I take to be his answer to the question, "who comes after the subject? in the succinct phrase, 'you shares me' [*toi partage moi*]."[56] A Conradian literary voice might have whispered, even more simply, "you, secret sharer." In sum, with its undecidable mimetic status, suspended, as it were, in-between self and other, interior and exterior, sameness and difference, psychology and ontology, the doppelgänger serves as an ideal fictional trope to open up a mimetic conception of subjectivity that rests on shared affective foundations—fluid foundations in which the subject becomes oneself, while being someone other.

## Verdict 2

The psychological case of the double brings us back to the ethical case. There is in fact a subtle ethical lesson implicit in this psychological diagnostic that allows Conrad to supplement speculative accounts of ethical rapports with others. From an immanent perspective, mimesis quite physically—and thus psychically—inclines the subject toward the other in such a fundamental way that the distinction between self and other, interior and exterior, my affect and your affect, no longer holds—if only because this affect becomes a shared affect, my ego a shared ego. The captain's obsessive insistence that his so-called double or second self is a "secret sharer" not only of "my life" and of "my cabin" but also, and above all, of "my thoughts" (119) makes this psycho-ethical point clearly: this subject is a shared subject insofar as it emerges from an interior communication that generates a mimetic con-fusion between ego and alter ego, a first singular person (I) and a second person (you) that is as singular as it is already plural. In *Lord Jim* Conrad puts it even more succinctly as he makes clear that what matters in such exchanges is not the "I" nor the "you" considered separately, but the shared dash that both connects and disconnects the two. In a stuttering moment of self-recognition Jim tells his own alter ego, Marlow: "I—you—I" (*LJ* 140). "The Secret Sharer" is an untimely meditation on the "I—you—I" principle that reveals the shared affective foundations at the heart of ethical relations. This mimetic principle is thus not based on an egocentric psychology that reduces the other to the ego. Instead, it promotes a relational psychology that locates the ego in-between "I—you" relations, mimetic relations that do not generate rivalry but constitute the basis for an ethics of sharing instead. In fact, this diagnostic insight into the subject as *subjectum* gives an immanent, psychosomatic foundation to the contemporary realization that the subject is plural-singular. It also provides an immanent, affective, relational conception of subjectivity that emerges in-between the "I" and the "you," generating shared bonds of solidarity that incline the ego toward a subject that is not one—for it is already double in orientation and open to protean transformation.

What was true for the escalation of violence for the worse is thus also true for the ethics of sharing for the better. Ethical relations, for Conrad, rest on shared psychic foundations that transgress the boundaries of individuation, generating affective continuities in place of discontinuities. Giving psychic substance to the ethical turn to the other, Conrad considers that it is because the other is not simply external to the subject, nor simply interior to it, but constitutive of the shared, mimetic foundation of the subject, that ethical responsibility emerges from hypnotic communications or rapports with absolute singularities. The mimetic unconscious is thus at the foundation of Conrad's ethics. It accounts for both the reflex to respond to the demand of the other and for the principles that make this other a shared part of the ego. Bluntly, mimesis is the secret principle that informs Conrad's ethical care for secrets shared between divided subjects.

And yet this is the moment to remember that mimesis, just like the subject it gives birth to, remains a Janus-faced concept in need of reevaluation: if mimesis is the source of affective continuities that generate catastrophic pathologies on board Leggatt's first ship (bad mimesis), this affective continuity provides the source of ethical responsibility on board the second ship (good mimesis). Let us thus follow Conrad's nautical turn to the very end in order to see how the same mimetic force that inclines the self toward a privileged other can, in a sort of recoil, incline the ship as a whole and give "some twenty-four men, a chance" (106) to overturn the final catastrophe.

### Closing the Double Case

After having reopened the case of Leggatt qua Double, let us join the psychic and the ethical sides of this Janus-faced story in order to face the final catastrophe the tale has been preparing us from the very beginning, so as to close the case. Now that both sides are in place, the final turn should follow quite quickly.

We have seen that mimesis is a Janus-faced force that goes beyond good and evil evaluations that, in a "sort of recoil," turns pathologies into pathologies. On the one side, mimesis has pathological effects. As was already the case with sympathy, panic, and madness (the *Sephora* Dossier), the confusion of identity generated by a secretly shared communication in which the captain-narrator "identified with [his] secret double" (107) introduces sameness where difference should be preserved, generating a type of madness that threatens the mental stability of the captain as well as the stability of the ship as a whole (the Shared Dossier). The captain is the first to confess that "the dual working of [his] mind distracted [him] almost to the point of insanity" (97), and as a consequence he transgresses the system of duties upon which the stability of the ship rests. After spending more and more time "whispering" (105) with his secret sharer of his cabin, the captain becomes increasingly self-conscious, feels split in "two places at once" (96), alienates himself from the crew, and loses the "unconscious alertness" (106) necessary for successful navigations. On the other hand, the narrative trajectory of the tale suggests that this state of mimetic confusion, schizophrenic division, and nautical disorientation is but an intermediary, embryonic stage in which the structure of a unitary "I," in the secret, womblike space of the shared cabin, is momentarily dissolved so as to allow—in a sort of recoil in which the poison turns into the remedy—for a shared "I—you" personality to be born.

The conclusion of the tale, as the newborn captain sails close to the rocky shore of Koh-ring to set his double free, confirms the hypothesis that mimesis functions as the remedy that allows for the captain's successful nautical and ethical turn. Through an unconscious mimesis with his (Nietzschean) double, through a mirroring reproduction of his expressions and gestures, the captain becomes (the) double, assimilates the qualities of the double—from "self-possession" to a voice that is "calm and resolute" (87)—and, finally, occupies the position of authority necessary to successfully confront a catastrophic situation. The general lesson emerging at the end seems to be that in order to face and avoid the catastrophe foreseen at the beginning, a mimetic training with figures who have successfully avoided catastrophe is in order. If the captain has to sail so close to the shore, leading the ship to be "already swallowed up as it were, gone too close to be recalled" (116), it is perhaps because the final nautical turn puts this training to the test. How? By facing the catastrophe foreshadowed at the beginning and experienced in the middle.

That mimesis continues to be central to the risky nautical maneuver at the end is clear and loud. As the captain-narrator gives his order that leads the ship close to "the shadow of the land" (116) and calls all the men on deck, we are told that his "tone had a borrowed loudness" (117). As he continues: "My first order 'Hard a-lee' re-echoed ominously under the towering shadow of Koh-ring as if I had shouted in a mountain gorge" (117). Echoes and shadows are mimetic tropes. They have both an exterior and an interior side: Koh-ring provides the exterior echo, the double provides the inner voice. Both tropes suggest that the captain is not a subject but an echo of the subject; its identity is not singular but plural-singular; his ego is not an ego but a phantom of the ego. The narrator confirms this point as he says: "it was as if the ship had two captains to plan her course for her" (113). And as the possibility of shipwreck is nearing, the captain embodies Leggatt's qualities of authority by echoing his voice and reproducing his actions. Thus, if Leggatt on the *Sephora* "went on shaking him [the mutinous seaman]" (89), we are told that the captain "hadn't let go the mate's arm and went on shaking it" (117). In this mimetic reproduction of a potentially disastrous scene the final turn represents a psychic turn from passivity to activity, submission to command, strangeness to authority, intimidation to prestige. Conrad suggests that these qualities are essential to successfully string together the members of the crew in order to effectively face an impending catastrophe. And yet this is also a mimetic repetition with a difference, just like an echo or a shadow reproduces the original without fully copying it, altering and amplifying its reach. Remember that in his original action Leggatt still reacts mimetically to the violence of the crazed seaman, countering violence with more violence in an escalating move that unwittingly contributes to generating the madness and panic he sets out to counter. The captain-narrator's final turn, on the other hand, entails a mirroring inversion of perspectives. Thus, in his reproduction of Leggatt's gesture and voice, he strategically restrains the escalating reciprocity of violence. If the first mate echoes Captain Archbold's helpless panic and religious language ("O my God!" and "shook [his "poor devoted head"] violently" [117]), the newborn captain responds with a vigorous form of "shaking" that affirms his command in a firm yet controlled and measured way.

You will have noticed the mirroring structure. This is a repetition of an antimimetic turn I have already diagnosed in "The Duel" now reframed in a catastrophic nautical context. Not unlike D'Hubert's strategic final move, the captain's gesture is both mimetic and antimimetic; it entails both a mirroring repetition and inversion of perspectives. And what this mirroring gesture reveals is that mimesis is both part of the problem of catastrophe and of its solution, the poison and the remedy, the pathology that spreads contagiously and the patho-logy that keeps such contagion in check. In sum, in the sharing of identity that brings the subject into being, the captain mirrors the qualities of command he initially lacked but also supplements a nonviolent antimimetic touch Leggatt lacked. This is how he compears through the other, with the other, in a relation of secret "I—you" communication that generates a difference at the heart of sameness. And it is via this mimetic repetition with a difference that the captain is born as an (anti)mimetic subject endowed with the necessary will power to cast a spell over the crew, take control of the communal and nomadic tribe of sailors he is responsible for, and avoid the final catastrophe that has been the driving telos of the narrative from beginning, middle, to end.

Rather than being "swallowed up" the captain catches sight of the captain's hat Leggatt lost while swimming ashore (an obvious symbol of command but also of its shared birth), uses it as a reference point to feel the movement of the ship, gives the command, "'Shift the helm'... in a low voice" at the right moment, and after some suspense, offers "the quiet remark, 'She's round,' passed in a tone of intense relief between two seamen" (119). The narrator concludes the hero's journey thus: "already the ship was drawing ahead. And I was alone with her. Nothing! No one in the world should stand now between us, throwing a shadow on the way of silent knowledge and mute affection, the perfect communion of a seaman with his first command" (119).

·        ·        ·

And so the end brings us back to the beginning, turning the captain into a narrator with a tale to share. True, his secret is shared with a generation of readers who might no longer be familiar with life on board ship. Yet Conrad can still use the mirror of the sea to reflect on ethical riddles that emerge as the ship qua planet is driven toward potentially catastrophic destinations. The psycho-ethics of catastrophe that emerges from "The Secret Sharer" sailed past the Scylla of pathological forms of "bad" mimesis and the Charybdis of healthy forms of "good" mimetic power. For Conrad, in fact, actions during ethical storms cannot simply be based on the rational logos of an immutable maritime authority, no matter how much he respected such authority—since a captain must be receptive to the unpredictable systemic consequences of catastrophic scenarios that require adaptation, improvisation, and transformation. Nor is it simply a question of being mimetically receptive to the pathos of the other—since this pathos can have pathological systemic consequences that must be foreseen in advance. Rather, the diagnostic that emerges from the tale suggests that for subjects in a position of authority, responsibility, and command who are confronted, face-to-face, with the possibility of a general catastrophe, careful attention should be given to both sides of Janus-faced (anti-)mimetic principles. On the one hand, the authority of command is achieved via a mimetic reproduction of qualities, gestures, and actions of exemplary figures who may have transgressed moral laws in the past but only to successfully avoid catastrophic scenarios. Conrad suggests that it is not only by imitating their individual qualities from without but also by sharing in their singular being from within that a shared I-you subject able to face shared catastrophic situations that affect multiple singularities can possibly compear. On the other hand, this shared subject who is mimetically permeable to the pathos of chosen singularities should itself, by training and profession, be impermeable to the force of mimetic contagion that affects the singular-multiples. Conrad suggests, then, that in this joint (im)permeability to mimetic affects lies the possibility to avoid a global catastrophe. And it is because the captain's (anti-)mimetic tendencies can only be tested on board ship by facing the possibility of catastrophe that we are now "able to understand why" he says, in a confessional tone: "on my conscience, it had to be thus close—no less" (117). This is a perfect closure for a mimetic turn that comes thus close to touching ground, but no more—to keep her floating.

This is, indeed, a perilous final test for a newborn captain if there is one, yet it is one we had been prepared for from the beginning. There is in fact a secret sense in which having sailed beyond morality and past it, the captain has implicitly been following Nietzsche's ethical imperative all along. Since what Nietzsche says of the "independence of command" in *Beyond Good and Evil* could have served as an epigraph to "The Secret Sharer," I might as well use it to close the case of Leggatt qua double:

> One must test oneself to see whether one is destined for independence and command; and one must do so at the proper time. One should not avoid one's tests [*Proben*], although they are perhaps the most dangerous game one could play and are in the end tests which are taken before ourselves as only witnesses [*Zeugen*] and before no other judge [*Richter*].[57]

Since the possibility of catastrophe informs the beginning, middle, and end of this tale, serving as its driving telos, we should remember, as a coda to this complicated maneuver, that catastrophe is not only the designation of a disastrous physical overturning; it is also the Greek term that designates the dramatic reversal of events, or change of fortune, upon which a carefully crafted narrative (or *muthos*) turns. As Aristotle famously states in *Poetics*, this reversal is usually tragic, but not necessarily so. What is important, for him, is not so much the catastrophic dénouement itself but that the *katastrophè* (or "change of fortune") is in line with the events that in-*formed* (give form to) the *muthos* of the whole tale, beginning, middle, and end. I have tried to show at some length that Conrad, as a writer who affirmed that "the value of creative work of any kind is in the *whole* of it" (*CL*, II, 332), valued these ancient aesthetic principles. If the beginning introduces the possibility of catastrophe, the middle centers on an "end-of-the-world" scenario, and the conclusion brings the ship to the extremity of catastrophe—before turning to fulfill a classical *katastrophè*. This final turn is thus not only a nautical, psychological, or ethical turn; it is also, and above all, a narrative turn. And in a last mirroring reflection, it not only informs the message of the narrator turned captain; it also in-*forms* the medium of a captain turned master of English prose.

In the end, the case is secretly closed, but the secret sharer's destiny is left open, a "free man, a proud swimmer striking out for a new destiny" (*TLS* 119). Whether Conrad, the seaman whose destiny was to turn into a proud writer, can go farther and cross "the shadow-line" that marks a communion with his community as a whole is what we now turn to diagnose.

CHAPTER 3

# The Cooperative Community: Surviving Epidemics in *The Shadow-Line*

What there is in place of communication is neither the subject nor communal being, but community and sharing.

—Jean-Luc Nancy, *The Inoperative Community*

It seems now to have had a moral character . . . on the ground of that mysterious fellowship which unites in a community of hopes and fears all the dwellers of this earth.

—Joseph Conrad, *A Personal Record*

After the escalating violence of total wars and the threat of perfect storms, Conrad urges us to turn to yet another catastrophe that casts a shadow on the past, the modern, as well as the contemporary imagination: the spread of epidemic contagion. From the fever recorded in "The Congo Diary" to the little fever that renders Marlow scientifically interesting in *Heart of Darkness*, from the plague of tuberculosis that infects James Wait and affects the crew in *The Nigger of the "Narcissus"* to the epidemic of malaria that spreads to the community of sailors in *The Shadow-Line*, Conrad's fictions invite a diagnostic of different types of infectious pathologies.

It is worth noticing at the outset that these epidemics often occur in tales of the homo duplex, suggesting secret continuities between physical and psychic contagion. Conrad would thus have agreed wholeheartedly with René Girard's account of "the plague in literature" as a reflection of the affective dynamic of mimetic contagion central to "social phenomena."[1] As we move from mimetic doubles to escalating violence, emotional contagion to epidemic contagion, Girard's insights continue to find an important confirmation in Conrad's narratives of the homo duplex—if only because, for both authors, behind the shadow of contagious epidemics lurks the phantom of mimetic contagion.

And yet if Girard is particularly attentive to the metaphorical implications of the plague, Conrad also uses the "mirror of the sea" to reflect (on) the literal effects of epidemic diseases. Writing from the position of a still relatively immune nation-state, Girard, in the past, has in fact tended to downplay the medical side of contagion, treating it as a "disguise" of a more profound mimetic truth.[2] This hermeneutical choice is historically determined and can be dated to the post–World War II period, which shaped Girard's theoretical imagination. Equally dated is Girard's diagnostic that we now live in "a world less and less threatened by real bacterial epidemics."[3] Unfortunately, history taught us otherwise. From the plague of HIV that spread across the world in the 1980s and 1990s and continues to infect the "wretched of the earth" (Frantz Fanon's term) to the contemporary pandemics that, every year, threaten to contaminate an increasingly globalized, permeable, and precarious world, the shadow of epidemics looms large on the horizon. In his last book, however, Girard recognized this shadow and urged future mimetic theorists to develop a diagnostic of the immanent dynamic of contagion.[4] Hence the need to supplement Girard's hermeneutics in light of what epidemiologists call the threat of "the coming plague."[5] Hence the urgency to turn back to a writer like Conrad who, well before contemporary theorists, puts readers back in touch with the literal effects of pathological contagion.[6] Epidemic infections, in what follows, shall thus be treated à la lettre.

Time and again, we have seen that a nonhuman, often unrecognized, yet always menacing shadow lurks in the background of Conrad's fictions of the homo duplex. This shadow in the background constantly changes in its spectral manifestations and requires, each time, a different form of literary investigation; yet, once illuminated, it allows us to theorize mimetic shadows in the foreground. One of the diagnostic lessons that has emerged so far is that the ethical trajectory of Conrad's nautical fictions transgresses anthropocentric accounts of agency, is attentive to nonhuman forces, and thus cannot be considered in a contextual vacuum. Instead, a mimetic approach requires a specific foregrounding of environmental forces first, in order to subsequently trace the complex interplay of human and nonhuman forces. It is this spiraling interplay that also in-*forms* Conrad's diagnostic of catastrophic pathologies, a diagnostic that requires careful scrutiny of its clinical variations. As we steer our attention toward one of the best tales of his final period, *The Shadow-Line* (1917), we see that his concern is with a local epidemic of malaria on board ship in the Gulf of Siam. The context is thus familiar, but the patho(-)logy is different. For instance, contrary to the perfect storm depicted in "The Secret Sharer," *The Shadow-Line* dramatizes a menace that does not rock the ship from without but infects its community from within; it does not threaten to swallow up the ship in single moment, as in *Lord Jim*, but progressively contaminates each member of the community over a prolonged period of time. Consequently, the realization that things are "bound to end in some catastrophe" (*SL* 52) cannot be avoided with deft, immediate, and still somewhat romantic maneuvers that require authoritarian will power. Rather, it demands persistent and continuous endurance grounded on democratic and sympathetic interactions with the crew. As we sail from storm pieces to a calm water piece, we progressively realize that the possibility of survival does not rest on instinctual, individual reactions, but on prolonged communal actions.

If we want to do critical and theoretical justice to what Conrad calls "a fairly complex piece of work" (5) and sound the depth of his ethical thought for contemporary times characterized by a shared vulnerability to infections, a change of perspective is in order: a tale that is often simplistically depicted as a re-presentation of a linear process of personal maturation needs to be reframed against the collective shadow of epidemic contagion Conrad takes the trouble to represent. Furthering an ethico-environmental line of inquiry initiated in "The Secret Sharer" that considers the foundations of subjectivity in shared, relational terms, *The Shadow-Line* focuses on the threat of infective contagion in order to offer a diagnostic account of the shared vulnerability, collective responsibility, intergenerational relations, and ethical care that is not limited to two sovereign individuals but stretches

to include the community as a whole.[7] More precisely, *The Shadow-Line* calls
for the coming of a type of solidarity that cuts across distinctions between
self and others, high and low ranks, present and past generations, in order
to establish an ethos based on shared, intergenerational, and communal
cooperation. Once again, the experience of mimetic contagion is as poisonous as it is therapeutic, as dissociative as it is associative, as pathological as
patho-logical. It generates, for better and worse, an "inoperative community"
(Nancy's term) that can be turned into a cooperative community.

## Political (Con)Texts

Catastrophes, we are beginning to learn, come in successive waves. In "The
Duel" Conrad dealt with the escalation of violence that swept across Europe
during the Napoleonic Wars generating the years of "universal carnage" (165).
In *Typhoon* and "The Secret Sharer" he faced the psychic and ethical shadows
that emerged from the threat of "mountainous seas" (*TLS* 101) caused by a
"catastrophic disturbance of the atmosphere" (*TOS* 20). In *The Shadow-Line*
he confronts us with a less visible, less spectacular, but no less devastating scenario in which climatic, epidemiological, and sociopsychological factors all
contribute to generating an epidemic outbreak on the "small planet" of the
ship. This accumulation of multiple factors generates a spiral of affective and
infective pathologies that escape unitary diagnostics. Yet Conrad does not
give in to apocalyptic despair. Instead, he continues to advocate an ethics of
sharing, which is also a politics of shared, relational, intergenerational, and,
above all, communal cooperation. My hypothesis is that he does so in order
to affirm the possibility of collective survival—out of catastrophic situations.

### Grand Miroir

*The Shadow-Line* reflects psychological preoccupations with the process of
personal development we have already seen reflected in "The Secret Sharer."
The mirroring continuities are clear, the echoes loud: both texts deal with a
loosely autobiographical nautical experience set in the Gulf of Siam; both
texts give an account of the psychic anxieties of young, inexperienced, and
highly suggestible captains generated by the responsibility of "first command"

(this being also the first title of the novel); and, above all, both texts represent Conrad's obsessive fascination with mysterious forms of mimetic communication with exemplary alter egos responsible for formative, sometimes transgressive, but always transformative experiences of "initiation."[8] And yet the continuities between these "twin-stories" run deeper than critics previously realized. Both texts are, in fact, haunted by a shadow that is not simply personal and psychological but also collective and environmental. It is thus necessary to focus on a shadow that has so far remained in the background of critical discussions in order to cast new light on the process of psychic, political, and ethical maturation in the foreground.

Both personal and collective sides are already mirrored at the opening of the text. Subtitled "A Confession," *The Shadow-Line* opens with an epigraph by Charles Baudelaire, which reads: *"D'autres fois, calme plat, grand miroir / De mon désespoir"* (11). This mirror reflects an existential, romantic despair that casts a shadow on an individual ego. This is a central concern in the tale, yet Conrad also sets up a larger mirror for more general ethico-political shadows cast on the whole of Europe. Written in 1916, while the "universal carnage" of the Great War literally reduced a civilization to ruins, the novella opens with a deeply personal dedication that stretches to include an entire generation, thereby suggesting that personal and political despair cannot easily be dissociated: "To Borys and all others who like himself have crossed in early youth the shadow-line of their generation, with love." Conrad's son returned from the front; most of his generation did not. They crossed the "shadow-line" that divides not so much youth from maturity but, rather, the living from the dead. Retrospectively, we can see that this is probably one of the most intimately personal and, in the same breath, widely collective dedications in modern literature—if not literature tout court. More than 16 million people perished in the Great War. And this tragic number was soon amplified by the 1918 Spanish flu pandemic, which, one year after the publication of *The Shadow-Line*, spread around the world, generating a heartrending estimate of 50 to 100 million additional victims.[9] Conrad was, of course, not in a position to foresee how far his dedication would stretch; and within the text, the phrase "the shadow-line" is clearly taken to delineate a boundary that divides two periods in the life of a single, immature individual, a shady line in-between the youth/adulthood binary the captain-narrator needs to cross for personal maturation and successful collective navigation to occur. Still, Conrad's opening gesture toward what he also calls, in the "Author's Note," "the supreme trial of a whole generation" (6) testifies to his painful awareness that, during those dark years, a long shadow had been cast on the whole world. As Owen Knowles recently recognized, the dedication "actively invites the reader to attend to the story's wartime origins."[10] And as Martin Bock shows, Conrad was personally concerned with the Spanish flu pandemics, and his fictions gain from considering "germ theory" and its concern with "contagion" that were emerging at the time.[11] Hence *The Shadow-Line* invites us to open up a series of supplementary binaries that, at least in theory, and certainly in fiction, can potentially be crossed, binaries such as self/others, living/dead, fiction/history, sick/healthy, one generation/the next generation.

What, then, does this "*grand miroir*" reflect?

## Sovereign Head/Contagious Bodies

What is certain is that in light of such contextual historical horrors that press from the outside-in, the political metaphors that inform the text from the inside-out sound strikingly conservative, and in line with the authoritarian bent of "The Secret Sharer." In fact, the newly appointed captain relies on monarchic images of authority that inform his vision of what command is or should be. As he lands, somewhat unexpectedly, his first command, he confidently says: "In that community I stood, like a king in his country in a class all by myself. I mean a hereditary king, not a mere elected head of state" (54). This ship, we are given to think, is thus not simply a ship; it is representative of a "state." The crew is not simply a crew; it stands for a "community." The captain is not simply a captain; he is the embodiment of a "king"—a "hereditary" king whose power is guaranteed by his alignment with a dynastic, aristocratic tradition to which he claims to belong. The image of the king as head of the state, whose power is conveyed transcendentally by the "Grace of God" (54), alludes to the political topos of the two bodies of the king—one mortal, the other divine—a canonical, monarchic distinction the captain-narrator convokes in order to draw a line that divides him not only hierarchically but also affectively from his subjects. Thus he specifies: "My sensations could not be like those of any other man on board" (23–24). The captain might be in the same boat as the crew, yet his "sensations" should not be confused with communal sensations; the head is attached to the body, but should not be confused with the body. This, at least, is the theory.

And yet in practice boundaries are shadier than they appear to be, for the hierarchical line the human head sets up can easily be transgressed by non-human forces. Notice that already the organic analogy of the human body that informs this image of the body politic cuts both ways, and opens up the possibility of infectious continuities that cut across affective discontinuities. If the head/body dichotomy introduces a distance from communal "sensations," it also opens up channels for contagious infections that can potentially penetrate, contaminate, and, eventually, undermine the authoritarian power structure on which the body politic of the ship qua "state" rests. This, at least, is what the captain progressively realizes as his "abstract idea" (38) of what command is begins to give way to the empirical "experience" (3) of what command leads one to become. This tension between idea and experience, theory and practice, is central to Conrad's poetics in general and informs the immanent and transcendent sides of the Janus-faced shadow I am tracking. In the context of *The Shadow-Line* it generates a limit(ing) nautical experience that confronts the captain-narrator's idea of monarchic power with the reality of environmental forces that constrain the ability of the head to direct the social body.

## Epidemic Patho(-)logies

From the outset of his nautical journey, the captain realizes that the human head that controls the communal body is radically dependent on nonhuman factors beyond the control of his command. Trapped in a becalmed ship in a river, the captain finds himself unable to "get her out to sea" (55). If you recall, this is a repetition of a nautical situation that already haunted the beginning of "The Secret Sharer." But we should equally remember that Conrad never sails in the same river twice.[12] Instead, he echoes a previously explored scenario in order to add new narrative layers that complicate, alter, and ultimately reframe the shadow cast on board ship.

## Poisonous Infections

In *The Shadow-Line*, Conrad stresses that adverse meteorological conditions not only passively impede nautical action; they also actively generate new catastrophic possibilities. Thus, as a consequence of being stuck in what he calls a "pestilential river" (55), an epidemic of malaria breaks out on board ship. We are told that "the first member of the crew . . . [was] taken ashore (with choleric symptoms) and died there at the end of a week" (57). This is one of the slowest possible starts in the history of narratives of the sea (six weeks are spent in that poisonous river). And as the ship eventually reaches the Gulf of Siam, the epidemic, far from being cured, continues to determine the entire trajectory of the journey, eventually forcing a return to Singapore. As the captain-narrator retrospectively puts it, "the infection . . . clung to the ship. It obviously did cling to the ship. Two men. One burning, one shivering" (66).[13] Confronted with this epidemic infection, the captain's initial faith in his sovereign, monarchic power to be left unaffected begins to give way to a form of fatalistic, anxious, and rather desperate sensation, as he admits: "I felt a distinct reluctance to go and look at them. What was the good? Poison is poison. Tropical fever is tropical fever" (66). Poison is, indeed, poison. It affects the head as much as the body, rendering the head not only unable to direct the body but also as vulnerable as all the other members of the body politic. There is a subtle diagnostic lesson in this clinical realization. Indifferent to all-too-human hierarchical distinctions between (human and divine) bodies, the narrative alerts us that epidemic pathologies are mimetic in the sense that they are contagious and introduce (horizontal) sameness where there once was (vertical) difference, (shared) infection where there once was (divided) affection. Anticipating the possibility of a generalized contagion that poisons the entire body politic, the captain-narrator asks, in an apocalyptic mood: "Who hasn't heard of ships found floating, haphazard, with their crews all dead?" (74–75).

This is, indeed, the state of "undifferentiation" that Girard would consider "metaphorical" of the mimetic crisis that is hidden behind the mask of real epidemics. But while the shadow of mimetic doubles continues to haunt the tale, no violent crisis ensues. On the contrary, solidarity and sympathy follow. Moreover, Conrad's diagnostic of undifferentiation remains quite literal, and opens up a holistic, environmental, and nonanthropocentric perspective that is attentive to the complex ecological interplay between human and nonhuman contagion. As an ex-seaman, Conrad is, in fact, painfully aware that meteorological and epidemiological factors are intimately connected; conversely, as a seaman turned writer his narrative dramatizes the contagious pathologies that infect the bodies and souls of the entire body politic. This patho(-)logy, as we know, does not operate according to a billiard-ball causal logic, but according to a systemic feedback loop we have already encountered. The diagnostic, however, is different now. What Conrad calls the "double fight" of adverse weather and epidemic disease generates a spiral of contagious circulation that does not allow for any form of individual resistance à la Leggatt. The captain-narrator retrospectively diagnoses the logic of this poisonous pathology with incisive clinical precision:

> The fact was that disease played with us capriciously very much as the winds did. It would go from one man to another with a lighter or heavier touch, which always left its mark behind, staggering some, knocking others over for a time, leaving this one, returning to another, so that all of them had now an invalidish aspect and a hunted, apprehensive look in their eyes. . . . It was a double fight. The adverse weather held us in front; and the disease pressed on our rear. (70)[14]

This fight is at least double. It confronts both climatic and epidemic factors, which, in turn, retroact to affect and infect both the bodies and souls of the crew, generating a vortex of contagious actions and reactions. The mimetic ecology emerging from this widening spiral of climatic, epidemic, and anthropogenic forces generates what Gregory Bateson calls a "systemic pathology," making us realize, along with the captain, that "we are not by any means the captains of our soul."[15] It also opens up a diagnostic of the pathological effects of the immanent vibrations of matter that, as Jane Bennett aptly recognized—from viruses to wind, currents to storms—reframes human agency along lines that "are more emergent than efficient, more fractal than linear."[16]

The emerging spiraling logic of this vibrant pathology could be schematically diagnosed as follows. First, climatic factors deprive the captain (or head) of the power to effectively direct the ship (or body politic), leaving the entire crew (or community) exposed and vulnerable to additional threats that escape anthropogenic control. Second, viral, epidemic factors join hands with adverse weather conditions and cause a generalized physical pathology whereby one body infects another body, progressively knocking over subject after subject. And third, epidemic, environmental, and somatic factors affect the psyche of "all" the members of the crew, generating a haunting apprehension that, in yet another feedback loop, renders the bodies even more vulnerable to the circulating return of other waves of infection. Once caught in such a pathological spiral of environmental, epidemic, and anthropogenic infections, linear logic breaks down, preventing the possibility of effective antidotes to be applied.

There is, indeed, a thus far unrecognized monstrous shadow beyond human control haunting this tale, what the captain-narrator also calls "an invisible monster ambushed in the air, in the water, in the mud of the river-bank" (57). It is thus not surprising that even the captain's mind is infected by poisonous images of catastrophe. Once out of the pestilential river, but still followed by the infection, he says: "The intense loneliness of the sea acted like a poison on my brain. When I turned my eyes to the ship, I had a morbid vision of her as a floating grave" (74). This poisonous infection is as somatic as it is psychic, as personal as it is collective. And in an expansive narrative and theoretical gesture we are by now familiar with, Conrad does not limit such a vision to the microcosm of the ship and the community it sustains. Instead, by metonymic association, he extends the spiral of epidemic contagion to imaginatively infect what he calls "a planet flying vertiginously on its appointed path in a space of infinite silence" (62).

Confronted with this imminent possibility, the narrative posits a diagnostic problem to its captain: the problem of finding a remedy that would, if not magically cure, at least contain the contagious effects of epidemic infection.Much has been said about the episode of the missing quinine. Thrown overboard by the previous captain gone mad, this episode leaves the new captain without medical antidotes to counter the pathology on board. And as the phantom of the late captain continues to haunt the ship, this episode opens up the tale to supernatural, interpretative possibilities that have stimulated the critical imagination.[17] Conrad did not seem to be particularly fond of this line of inquiry: he stressed in a materialist mood his "invincible conviction that whatever falls under the dominion of our senses must be in nature" (5). While a transcendent touch unquestionably informs the tale, my focus here is less on supernatural ghosts than on natural shadows. There is, in fact, an environmental awareness internal to Conrad's work that still needs to be foregrounded for clinical reasons in line with the double principles of Janus-faced investigation. Thus, if we have seen that Conrad offers a precise diagnostic of the pestiferous spiral of infective contagion, we now turn to see how he provides a possible remedy to counter the equally poisonous dynamic of affective contagion.

## Affective Remedies

Let's face it. Still caught in the windless waters of the poisonous river, this adventure has not taken us physically far. And yet despite the paralysis generated by the becalmed ship, the epidemic infection, and the contagious demoralization that ensues, this experience of first command constitutes a decisive step ahead in the captain's psycho-ethical development. It leads to the realization that there is no second, divine body divided from the human body, no transcendental head of the state apart from the immanent body politic—if only because the head remains, for better and worse, attached to the body. Consequently, the captain experiences that the head is not only as vulnerable to the danger of infection as the body; it is also radically dependent on the social body for the survival of the "community" as a whole. To be sure, in a tale of maturation haunted by the shadow of catastrophe, a radical reform of the captain's psychology, politics, and ethics is urgently in order if he wants to navigate out of these poisonous waters. Before sailing ahead, however, it is necessary to cast a retrospective glance and retrace this process of psychic maturation from the very beginning of the tale by paying attention to the microlevel of intersubjective communications that tie the head to other bodies. This circumnavigation brings us back to mimetic currents we are by now familiar with and, I hope, shall give us the sufficient speed to navigate past the epidemic that infects the body politic on more relational, intergenerational, and communal foundations.

The first, incredibly slow chapters of *The Shadow-Line* are often considered to be marginal at best and totally dispensable at worst, but on closer inspection they reveal the push-pull of mimetic and antimimetic undercurrents that orients the tale as a whole. The beginning already makes clear that a mimetic anxiety casts a shadow on the captain-narrator's process of maturation. The novel starts with the narrator's complaint about the lack of originality provided on board his previous ship, where he served as first mate before giving up his berth. Invoking a romantic dissatisfaction characteristic of what he later diagnoses as "the green sickness of late youth" (12), he says: "one expects an uncommon or personal sensation—a bit of one's own" (11). And later, he echoes: "There was nothing original, nothing new . . . no opportunities to find out something about oneself" (25). Originality (something "one's own"), not imitative behavior (something "shared"), is what this romantic soul in search of adventure seeks as the cure to his youthful, existential despair. Interestingly, such a solipsistic self-sufficiency and narcissistic self-concern renders the newly appointed captain indifferent to catastrophic scenarios: "People might have been falling dead around me, houses crumbling, guns firing, I wouldn't have known" (35), he says. It is thus not surprising that his entire attitude at the Officers' Home in Singapore, as he is waiting demoralized, frustrated, and anxiously insecure, for a ship to take him on a passage home, is characterized by a fierce antimimetic stance toward kindly disposed, paternal figures who actively serve as helpers in his journey of maturation. This psychic anxiety of influence concerning "whiskered" father figures is not unusual in Conrad's nautical fictions, and the type of psychic rivalry it generates has traditionally been read in familial, psychoanalytical terms. This rivalry, and the ambivalences it generates, however, is not so much revealing of the subject's Oedipal complex (Freud)—though an anxiety of influence is at play; nor can it be fully understood within the triangular dynamic of "mimetic desire" (Girard)—though shadows have certainly been cast on his ego. Rather, it sets in motion the "influences" grounded on a mimetic unconscious that generates affective communal pathologies as much as critical patho-logies (Conrad).

Take, for instance, the captain-narrator's severe evaluation of Captain Giles, a calm, experienced, and benevolent figure he initially dismisses as a "churchwarden" from whom one could only expect "moral sentiments, with perhaps a platitude or two" (17). Especially revealing of the narrator's mental disposition is not so much what he says, but how he says it. As we tune in, pay particular attention to the captain's tonality of voice and its contrast with Captain Giles's tone. We are told, for instance, that Giles was a "low-voiced man," whereas the narrator "spoke a little louder" (18); if Giles asks questions in a "benevolent" voice, the narrator gets "angry all of a sudden" (19); if Giles "murmured" (19), the narrator "cried" (20), and so forth.[18] The Conradian subject is, once again, defined by how he sounds more than by what he says. The medium is the underlying message of these communications. For Conrad, in fact, tone is a defining feature of subjectivity in general and of authority in particular. It is a property that is attuned to the affective currents that traverse self and others, establishing both mimetic continuities and antimimetic discontinuities. The narrator's impulsive outbursts of "childish irritation" (22) take place prior to crossing the shadow-line, in a "twilight" zone (15) that has the power to turn sailors into shadows depriving them of a proper identity, as Giles's "deeper philosophy" suggests.[19] And what this philosophy reminds us of is that the refusal of imitation generates mirroring inversions that are imitative nonetheless and have the power to trigger affective reactions that are not under the control of consciousness and are, in this sense, unconscious. As it was already the case for the process of maturation in the other fictions of the homo duplex considered so far, it is via a mimetic, unconscious mechanism that the process of maturation takes place. And once again, it is in the other, not in the ego, that lies the mysterious source of one's originality.

## The Influence of Prestige

The mimetic unconscious continues to be central to Conrad's account of ethical maturation insofar as ethics, for him, rests on permeable, intersubjective, and thus relational foundations. Already at the moment of maximum antimimetic opposition to Captain Giles's paternal guidance, the captain-narrator is, in fact, caught in the hypnotic-suggestive-mimetic spell of the older man, acting in such a way that not his own will, but the will of the other directs his actions. Thus, as he sets out to chase the steward who is concealing the letter with the offer of his "first command," the narrator says: "To this day I don't know what made me call after him" (27). Retrospectively, however, he articulates the following hypothesis: "possibly I was yet under the influence of Captain Giles's mysterious earnestness. Well, it was an impulse of some sort; an effect of that force somewhere within our lives which shapes them this way or that" (23). And he concludes: "my will had nothing to do with that. . . . No. My will had nothing to do with it" (27). The psychic origins of the captain's personal "will" do not stem from the ego, but from the "influence" of another, more experienced, or, as he says, "exemplary" (104) figure whose "force" has mysteriously penetrated the ego in order to "shape" it from within. This is, indeed, a mimetic hypothesis. Diagnostically put, a nonverbal, affective, and suggestive communication creates a shared bond of solidarity with a more experienced alter ego, and thanks to an unconscious, mirroring mechanism we are by now familiar with, the thoughts of the other operate within the ego, influencing his own will. Drawing directly from the modernist tradition of the mimetic unconscious, Conrad calls this mysterious psychic will power, "influence," or, alternatively, "prestige"—qualities decisive for command in general and for navigating through catastrophic situations in particular. Indeed, authority in *The Shadow-Line* continues to have its foundations in the intersubjective, mimetic bonds with singular others central to "The Secret Sharer." It is on this initial mimetic influence that an alter ego (or *socius*) is anchored, so to speak, in the affective structure of the ego—generating a "feeling that binds a man to a child" (*LJ* 101), as Marlow puts it—and creating a subject that is already plural and thus, as we shall see, open to forms of cooperation with the community as a whole.

Contrary to contagious epidemics that are outside human control, Conrad's narrative suggests that contagious affects can be consciously transformed—by mimetic means. As the narrative gives an account of the "revolution in [the captain's] moral nature" (*SL* 35) that puts the head back in charge of the social body, we see a therapeutic transformation that turns the captain's impulsive (anti)mimetic behavior toward a more sympathetic stance that reproduces the qualities of restrained tonality initially located in the experienced other. Thus, as the narrator belatedly realizes Captain Giles's role in securing his first command, he addresses the older man by "assuming a detached tone" (36), a tone he manages to keep throughout the tale. To be sure, imitation often escapes conscious control and can generate violent, unconscious reactions. Yet Conrad is also aware that mimetic pathos can be consciously channeled by logical and detached reflections. Mimesis, as always, cuts both ways: it can lead to aggressive escalations that contribute to the spreading of pathologies but also to an increase of affective distance that can be put to patho-*logical* use.

If we now leap ahead so as to return on board the infected ship stuck in the poisonous river with the patho(-)logical lessons drawn from these seemingly dispensable chapters, we notice that they introduce secret steps for countering the epidemic that infects individual bodies as well as the body politic. In fact, by the time the captain-narrator confronts the choleric infection, he has not only learned to master his youthful desire for originality (his romantic "sickness") but also to control the infective provocation of others (his mimetic sickness). Take the captain's relation to the chief mate, Mr. Burns, for instance. If this relation initially generates the anxiety of influence he experienced with Captain Giles, it does so with a significant difference. Confronted with Burns's "red moustache" (47) attached to a "face" "several years ... older than [him]self" (48), the captain displays the usual symptoms of intimidation (that is, fear of "inexperience," "becoming self-conscious," and so forth [48]). This mimetic anxiety is understandable. Burns is, after all, openly antagonistic to the young captain, considers himself entitled to take up the position of command, and initially occupies the role of what Girard would call "mimetic rival." Thus Burns initially blurts out to the captain, in a "tone of forced restraint": "If I hadn't a wife and a child at home, you may be sure, sir, I would have asked you to let me go the very minute you came on board" (55). This is, of course, a contagious affective provocation that could easily escalate. But the captain has learned his antimimetic lesson from Giles, and no reciprocal violence ensues. Instead, he deftly avoids this mirroring contamination by "answer[ing] him with a matter-of-course calmness as though some remote third person were in question" (55). And later, he consistently responds to Burn's bitter accusations with what he calls a "systematic kindliness" (56) or "invariable kindliness" (59).

How can mimetic rivalry be avoided? This is a question that has not received sufficient attention in mimetic theory, but it is one Conrad helps us address. There is, in fact, a subtle psycho-ethical lesson at work in these seemingly marginal exchanges that is indicative of the captain's process of development and has larger therapeutic implications for the formation of communities—both imaginary and real. Mimesis, it should be noted, is central to both the message and the medium of Conrad's diagnostic. The message is that having assimilated, via the medium of mimesis, Giles's antimimetic qualities and refusing to automatically respond to a provocation with yet another provocation, the captain avoids generating contagious escalations on top of a contagious epidemic. Attention to the medium, on the other hand, tells us, exactly, how he avoids being caught in the spiral of mimetic reciprocity: by treating a first-person narrative speech (or mimesis) as if it was uttered in a "third-person" narrative speech (or *diegesis*). You want to avoid the contagion of an insulting provocation? Speak as if not you but a third person has been offended, and an antimimetic reply will naturally ensue. Such a shift of perspective indicates that a formal narrative distance is the necessary precondition not to be affected by the infective contagion of mimetic pathos; *diegesis* might be the antidote to mimesis; sympathetic distance functions as the best antidote to the pathos of poisonous feelings.

## The Ethos of Profession

I have traced this process of personal, psychic maturation in some detail because it signals an ethical reform in the captain's relation to the body politic as a whole. The case of Mr. Burns continues to be therapeutically instructive to diagnose the captain's shift from egocentric to we-centric concerns. One of the first victims of the contagious epidemic, Burns is taken to a hospital. Interestingly, as the captain regularly visits him, his cold distance characteristic of sovereign detachment that initially made him impermeable to the "sensations" of others gives way to affective proximity that makes him permeable to the pathos of the other, generating bonds of sympathy that cut across hierarchical barriers. Resting his case on their shared professional ethos in order to be taken back on board ship, Mr. Burns cries out with pathos, addressing the captain in mimetic speech: "You and I are sailors" (59). And confronted with this irresistible you-I ethical interpellation, the captain is forced to acknowledge that "he had happened to hit on the right words" (60). The words are right, but so is the medium: it is in fact the use of mimetic speech that introduces a flux of affects that blurs the line between you and me in the first place. Thus, echoing Mr. Burns, he repeats from a diegetic distance: "He and I were sailors. That was a claim, for I had no other family" (60). The linguistic repetition (*diegesis*) reflects the emergence of an affective "you-I" bond (*mimesis*). And as both pathos and distance are joined, Conrad opens up the possibility that sovereign forms of subjectivity are not self-contained but rest on shared bonds of sympathetic solidarity that begin to tie the head back to the social body to which he belongs.

As we move from "The Secret Sharer" to *The Shadow-Line*, the same shared feelings generated by a common training and profession continue to inform ethical relations with others. The mimetic foundations of the Conradian subject remain essentially the same. But now these foundations are no longer limited to two aristocratic individuals considered as "secret sharers." Instead, the you-I bond stretches from singular I to plural you to include the entire community of sailors considered as "family." Thus the captain immediately generalizes this familial feeling to the crew as a whole, making clear that a common sensation ties, for better and worse, the head back to the social body. As he puts it: "I could imagine no claim that would be stronger and more absorbing than the claim of that ship, of these men snared in the river . . . as if in some poisonous trap" (60). This passage marks an ethical turn that redirects the ship along communal lines I shall presently discuss. Yet it is important to recognize that its diagnostic lesson remains anchored in familiar structures. What these initial chapters suggest, in fact, is that the "poisonous trap" has a paradoxical double effect we have encountered before: it is not only responsible for a contagious pathology that infects the social structure of the ship from without; it also generates a psychic, intersubjective, and communal stimulus that can potentially serve as a cure from within. It is, in fact, because the ship is caught in a poisonous trap that generates a shared infection that the captain develops a shared bond of solidarity with the crew along communal lines that take Conrad's ethics of sharing a step beyond "The Secret Sharer." Put differently, the shared, contagious epidemic that infects the body politic is not only the problem but also contains, at least in embryo, a diagnostic solution; it contributes to generating an ethics of sharing that has the power to reanimate the entire social organism. The poisonous infection is new, but the diagnostic remains fundamentally the same: it reminds us that where the poison is, there also lies the remedy; where the danger of infection is, there also lies the cure.

We are indeed back to the Janus-faced diagnostic principle that orients this book. But as always Conrad gives a new spin to this ancient patho(-)logy that keeps our investigation on the move. Adding a new layer of complexity to the problematic of subject formation, Conrad suggests that this (horizontal) sympathetic bond with the community is itself dependent on a prior (vertical) identification with a leader figure that has the experience necessary for command. In this sense, *The Shadow-Line* relies on the same conception of the shared subject at work in "The Secret Sharer"; yet it also suggests that the range of identifications needs to be expanded in order to assimilate a plurality of "exemplary" figures that belong to both present and past generations. Thus, in this tale, Conrad multiplies models who contribute to in-*forming* the captain's still malleable character: from Captain Giles to Mr. Burns, from Captain Ellis to Ransom, the captain-narrator aligns himself with a chain of sovereign figures that belong to a fundamentally shared, maritime tradition. This also means that in *The Shadow-Line* sharing is no longer part of dyadic, private, and secret ethics, but a multiple, communal, and plural ethos; it not only concerns one generation but also links a multiplicity of generations; the shared soul, for Conrad, turns out to be not simply a split, or divided, soul, but a plural, or "composite," soul—homo duplex, in short, turns into homo multiplex.

## The Composite Soul

Confronting the shadow of catastrophe that haunts the community on board "the small planet" of the infected ship continues to require a Janus-faced approach, but Janus, as we know, leads to protean transformations. If Conrad repeatedly encouraged us to look back to the romantic trope of the doppelgänger to diagnose split souls, in *The Shadow-Line* he uses mirroring devices to look ahead to the formation of a protean or, as he says, "composite soul." Given the symbolic centrality of this transformative scene in the circumnavigation that will help bring the infected community back to where it started, it is necessary to look into this mirror in some detail—for we are only halfway home.

### Specular Identification

The theoretical foundations of Conrad's account of the "composite soul" are framed by a mimetic scene that seems to mirror narcissistic forms of specular identification. Having set foot on the deck of his "high-class vessel" for the first time (no epidemic in sight yet) and felt "the fine nerves of her rigging as though she had shuddered at the weight" with a "deep physical satisfaction" (48), the newborn captain descends into his cabin and is immediately confronted with a specular scene. Bodily satisfaction gives way to visual satisfaction as he looks around and sees "the sideboard, surmounted by a wide looking-glass in an ormoulu frame" (46). And as he looks again, in the direction of the looking glass, he finds himself face-to-face with a classical imaginary scene, which he retrospectively describes as follows: "Deep within the tarnished ormoulu frame, in the hot half light sifted through the awning I saw my own face propped between my hands. And I stared back at myself with the perfect detachment of distance, rather with curiosity than with any other feeling" (47). The scene is as specular as it is speculative and tickles our mimetic curiosity. Within this visual scenario, the narrator recognizes himself in his new role as captain from a visual "distance" that has the effect of splitting his ego in two, prompting the following mimetic reflection: "It struck me that this quietly staring man whom I was watching *both as if he were myself and somebody else*, was not exactly a lonely figure" (47; my emphasis). This is, indeed, a decisive affective and theoretical turning point in a narrative of psychic maturation; it also brings to light the shadow I have been tracing so far. This mimetic shadow confirms that, for Conrad, the ego is not a "lonely figure" that can be considered in isolation, no matter how introverted and isolated this subject feels—if only because "somebody else" is already at the heart of what the ego would like to become.

The specular scene of identification is, of course, a familiar one, for we have already faced it in "The Secret Sharer," but this time it fits more neatly speculative accounts of subject formation. If we put on our theoretical lenses—for this is, after all, what *theoria* means: seeing carefully, which is not very far from Conrad's view of what mimesis should do in praxis, that is, to "make you *see*"—the passage could be reframed as follows: in this specular scene of (mis)recognition, the subject realizes that this "figure" in the mirror is not simply constituted by his reflection but is itself constitutive of an ego that is not one, for it is already double. Faced with its own image (or imago) the newborn captain, who up to that stage has been animated by turbulent affective movements that render the ego formless, identifies with that ideal form (or Ideal-I), assumes that alienating shadow into its own ego. And, the story goes, this process of identification forms the ego, turning it into a shadow or phantom that "situates the agency of the ego, before its social determination, in a fictional direction [*ligne de fiction*]."[20] This, you will have recognized it, is Jacques Lacan's speculative hypothesis.

The similarities between both literary and theoretical accounts of subject formation are, indeed, uncanny. They are, in fact, at least double and blur the line that divides fictional and theoretical speculations. On the one hand, Conrad's account of an imaginary (visual) identification with a figure in a "looking-glass" who is "myself and somebody else" has speculative implications concerning the role of mimesis in the formation of the subject. On the other hand, Lacan's imaginary (identificatory ) account of the "mirage of maturation" via the medium of visual imago, or "phantom," is not far removed from imaginary (illusory), fictional, and romantic representations of the homo duplex Conrad equally relies on.[21] There is thus an interesting game of fictional/theoretical refractions and reflections at play in this mirroring scene of (mis)recognition that critics have not failed to recognize and analyze. And yet a long tradition that goes all the way back to Plato's *Republic* and is fully at play in modernist accounts of the unconscious has taught us to be suspicious of mirror tricks. The shadows they reflect, in fact, also invert the fundamental presuppositions they appear to simply reproduce. Hence the closer to reality the mirror-image appears, the farthest from the truth it may actually be. If we do not simply apply a theory to fiction but read fiction theoretically, this is the specular hypothesis that emerges from this scene.

In addition to the obvious fact that the newborn captain, while childish in his insecurity, is no longer at the infans stage, Conrad's narrative makes us see that this scene does not depict a solipsistic, narcissistic, and purely specular account of ego formation with an ideal imago considered from the angle of visual "representation."[22] We should in fact remember that this specular identification does not come "before" but after the ego's "social determination." For Conrad, in fact, the subject's social determination is mediated by oral communications whose affective, embodied, hypnotic, and suggestive "influences" orient his mimetic conception of the unconscious. It is thus not surprising that no matter how specular the scene appears at first sight, the subject is not really formed by what Lacan calls, rather hermetically, "the assumption of the armor of an alienating identity which will mark with its rigid structure [*structure rigide*] the subject's entire mental development."[23] Instead, this subject remains in-*formed* by the mimetic hypothesis of a "shared" soul that is open to the affect, or sensation, of the other. This is perhaps the underlying theoretical reason why, in my view, the novelist manages to go a step further than the psychoanalyst by leading the subject "to that point where the real journey [*veritable voyage*] begins."[24]

## From Homo Duplex to Homo Multiplex

To begin this journey—and beginnings, you will have noticed, are what this narrative is all about—it is important to recognize that already during the mirror stage, the Conradian subject does not linger too long on the surface of this specular "image" (or imago). Instead, he finds himself immediately in an affective communication based on a shared feeling of "sympathy" (*sym-pathos*) that ties what is "not exactly a lonely figure" to other imaginary, symbolic, and perhaps even real, all-too-real figures. After emphasizing the visual distance that divides him from this specular representation, the captain-narrator goes through the looking glass, as it were, and gets in touch with a mimetic feeling that is of the order of a lived, affective experience. Let me restitute this theoretically dense passage in its entirety:

> Deep within the tarnished ormolu frame, in the hot half-light sifted through the awning I saw my own face propped between my hands. And I stared back at myself with the perfect detachment of distance, rather with curiosity than with any other feeling *except of some sympathy* for this latest representative of what for all intents and purposes was a dynasty continuous not in blood indeed but in its experience, in its training, in its conception of duty and in the blessed simplicity of its traditional point of view on life. It struck me that that quietly staring man whom I was watching both as if he were myself and somebody else was not exactly a lonely figure. He had his place in a line of men whom he did not know, of whom he had never heard but who were *fashioned by the same influences*, whose souls in relation to their humble life's work had no secrets for him. (47; my emphasis)

The scene is more symbolic than it appeared to be; yet this symbolism goes beyond linguistic or narcissistic principles, for it is based on an affective, mimetic hypothesis that Lacan, as Mikkel Borch-Jacobsen has forcefully shown, foreclosed[25]—but Conrad, along with other modernists, explored. This hypothesis is affective rather than speculative, for it posits the primacy of sympathetic influences (or pathos) as the necessary condition for a visual recognition (or distance). Having opened up the door to an imaginary, specular identification with an ideal and static imago frozen in a mirror, the movement of Conrad's narrative immediately plunges into the turbulent zone of bodily affects and touches on an alternative, experiential source to ego formation along genealogical lines that are not deprived of mimetic yet embodied identifications. Conrad's diagnostic operation cuts deep: the captain recognizes, or better experiences, or better feels, from the depth of an experience that is as interior as it is exterior that a shared pathos ("sympathy") ties him, legates him, to an aristocratic genealogical tradition (or "dynasty"). Continuity, in this tradition, is no longer guaranteed by a transcendental or essentialist inheritance (or "blood"), but rather by an immanent training ("experience"). And it is the mimetic effect ("influence") of this experience that has the power to impress, form, or better in-*form*, an ego that is not one, nor simply double, but "composite" instead.

Now, it is on the basis of an inner experience based on a shared praxis and in line with a genealogy of leader figures that the captain's newborn ego begins to take hold of his symbolic position within the outer social structure of the ship. Significantly, already before catching a glimpse of his specular image in the looking glass, while he still lingers on the side of the bodily referent, the narrator had already testified to a truly felt, sympathetic bond with a series of dynastic figures. You have to picture the scene. The captain, we are told, sits down in "the armchair at the head of the table, the captain's chair with a small tell-tale compass swung above it, a mute reminder of unremitted vigilance" (46). And having adopted this position of vigilant orientation, a feeling of communal belonging creeps up to him from below, penetrating his self in ways that are not at all specular, but are speculative nonetheless: "A succession of men had sat in that chair" (47), he says. And in a moment of antinarcissistic jubilation, he adds: "I became aware of that thought suddenly, vividly as though each had left a little of himself between the four walls of these ornate bulkheads; as if a sort of *composite soul, the soul of command,* had whispered suddenly to mine of long days at sea and of anxious moments" (47; my emphasis).

This is, indeed, a sovereign experience. Secretly whispered, rather than visually impressed, it opens up the subject to the mimetic realization that the soul of command is neither singular nor double, but protean instead. If we trace the temporal movement of this specular scene, we realize that it is only after this sense of belonging to a wider tradition of "shared influences" has been intimately experienced that a visual image of his heterogeneous soul is represented. Conrad's theoretical insight is clear: a feeling of mimetic sympathy is the condition for a visual identification to be formed; the current of formless, transgenerational affects constitute the multiplicity of the "composite soul" (from Latin, *compositus*, placed together). What is theoretically at stake in this sensorial, bodily awareness that precedes the visual, mental identification is the realization that the soul of command is not the precipitate of a monadic, narcissistic, and idealized figure represented in a mirror—though this figure is physically isolated. Nor is it simply the product of a secretly shared mimetic communication with an ideal other—though secret identifications contribute to the captain's shared psychic foundations. Rather, this hypothesis opens up the possibility that the soul of command is a shared soul that is receptive to a multiplicity of voices, not images, but voices, nothing but voices that ring an echo within a composite soul, generating the affect necessary for command in catastrophic scenarios.

## The Affect of Command

We are now in a position to see, and perhaps also feel, that if this scene has both imaginary and symbolic connotations, we are no longer confined within the "ontological structure" of the mirror stage that frames the ego in an ideal form. Rather, Conrad's reflections on the composite soul invite us to go through the looking glass, as it were, and ground the soul in a more immanent, more social, yet no less mimetic hypothesis. Conrad is not alone in developing this hypothesis. He shares it with other modernists, most notably Nietzsche.[26] In a passage of *Beyond Good and Evil*, which, as we have already seen, has tremendous resonance with Conrad's nautical and stormy preoccupations, Nietzsche speaks of "the affect of command"[27] along lines that echo Conrad's diagnostic of the soul. Nietzsche, in fact, develops a "soul hypothesis" that opens the road to what he calls "'soul as a multiplicity of the subject' [*Seele als Subjekts-Vielheit*] and 'soul as social structure of the drives and emotions' [*Gesellschaftsbau der Triebe und Affekte*]" (*BGE* 12:43–44). For Nietzsche, as for Conrad after him, command is not understood as a solipsistic sovereign affair. Rather, it is predicated on a conception of the sovereign subject that is already plural, always social, for it is traversed by a community of mimetic affects that compose the soul of command. Composite soul, soul as multiplicity: indeed, these two literary/philosophical figures show two faces of the same captain.

Now, the politics of the soul structures this vision of command along lines that are relevant for the communal body as a whole. Conrad and Nietzsche, in fact, independently of each other but within a similar maritime concern with ethics, develop an immanent, psycho-sociological soul hypothesis that challenges an egocentric, narcissistic hypothesis that posits an ideal image as the ontological foundation of what the subject is, or should be. And what they reveal is that the soul of command is not simply a social soul because of its power to govern exterior subjects. Rather, it is social because it is already structured as a multiplicity subjected to the larger social body. The subject of command is thus a subject in the double sense of being a sovereign subject in command and being a sovereign subjected to the burden of command. Implicitly following up on the hypothesis opened up by Nietzsche, Conrad reveals, on a situational narrative basis, this process of subjection. He does so by articulating the multiplicity of heterogeneous "drives and emotions" that, far from being simply personal, or individualistic, are themselves already the product of "social structures" that orient the microcosm of the ship. The social—or to use a more specific concept, the *socius* (that is, privileged social others such as parents and models)—is thus already internal to the ego, constituting its body, generating a subject understood as a multiplicity of singular-composite souls. From homo duplex to homo multiplex, egocentric to we-centric experiences: this is the trajectory the captain's theoretical compass is pointing to.

But Conrad goes further. For him, the question of influence is not restricted to the living but cuts across generations in a process of mimetic formation that inscribes a living soul in a multiplicity of dead souls. And if the influence of noble figures in the maritime tradition is there to sustain the captain (good mimesis), the negative influence of figures who have departed from this tradition is there to prevent progress (bad mimesis). This is especially true of the captain-narrator insofar as his immediate predecessor, whose symbolic chair he is now occupying, marked a departure from the maritime principles of duties that are passed down from one generation to the next. Described by Mr. Burns as an "artist" and "lover," "ill in some mysterious manner" (52), the previous captain's behavior is symptomatic of a form of romantic individualism that is at odds with the communal structure of the ship and contributes to the creation of potentially catastrophic situations. Thus we are told that this captain initially kept the ship "for three

weeks in a pestilential hot harbor without air" (51) and then pushed the crew
to confront "a fierce monsoon" in an "insane project" that "was bound to
end in some catastrophe" (52). Epidemics and monsoons are environmental
catastrophes. But Conrad suggests that insofar as these nonhuman phenomena are entangled with human choices generating what William E. Connolly
calls "a cosmos composed of multiple, interacting force fields moving at different speeds,"[28] they are ultimately anthropogenic in nature. If the captain
is to cross the shadow-line that divides youth from maturity, then, it is not
sufficient to cross the latitude line where the late captain has been buried.
Rather, he must cross the shadow-line that divides a singular, individualistic
soul from the composite soul necessary to face catastrophic situations. This
entails shifting from personal, individualist concerns with originality that
still haunt the young captain's romantic imagination, to embrace a mimetic,
nonrivalrous, and composite social spirit vital to confronting situations of
shared catastrophe on a communal basis.

The captain-narrator is fundamentally aware that the qualities of command based on a genealogical notion of the composite soul can only be
tested on the basis of the individual, unique, and, in this sense, always new
experience of navigation. If the "compass" reminded the captain-narrator of
the importance of "vigilance," it is time for him to put his hands on the helm,
which he takes as "a symbol of mankind's claim to the direction of its own
fate" (63). And it is in the confrontation with a catastrophic situation that
affects and infects the social structure of the ship, and the "planet" it symbol-
izes, that the captain's composite soul and the social structures that compose
it come together as a cooperative community in which head and body are
finally joined to jointly steer—and affirm the possibility of survival.

## The Survival of Community

The affect of command that is formed by this speculative scene of mimetic
identification should not be read in terms of a solipsistic process of psychic
maturation confined to the inner space of the cabin. Rather, this inner
experience gives birth to a "composite soul" that opens up the sympathetic
channels of the sovereign experience of "command" to the wider, collective
and exterior question of what Conrad calls "community" (54). Critics have

noticed this concern before,[29] but the theoretical implications of Conrad's emphasis on community to sail past catastrophic situations still need to be articulated. In this concluding section, as "the feverish, enfeebled crew, in an additional turn of the racking screw" (91) is forced to face a storm that overshadows the "last gleam of light in the universe" (92), we turn to see that Conrad contributes to outlining the ethos of community by rendering it operative on the basis of affective forms of cooperation. This also entails supplementing past monocephalic or acephalic accounts of community that first emerged in a period haunted by the specter of Communism and the shadow of fascism (Georges Bataille) and were more recently reframed by continental philosophers who, on the shoulders of Bataille, rethought the question of the "in-common" on the basis of a relational ontology of the subject (Jean-Luc Nancy).[30] Building on this tradition, my aim is to propose some steps toward sovereign yet nontotalitarian forms of command based on sympathetic cooperation between the head and the social body, the composite soul and its social structure we have been tracing so far. For Conrad, in fact, it is only on an immanent, communal ground based on fundamentally shared infective and affective foundations that we can affirm the possibility of survival.

The slow beginning of the first part of the tale has the function of generating underlying currents that, in the second part, are instrumental to bringing the narrative to a speedy end. After spending seemingly useless yet fundamentally instructive time in the Officers' Home in Singapore and enduring an epidemic contamination that infects nearly all members of the crew stuck in windless waters, the ship, as well as the narrative, begins to pick up speed. And in a final nautical turn that faces, head on, the shadow of catastrophe, Conrad anchors the captain's composite soul (or head) in the social structure of the ship (or body) in order to fight for the survival of community via an experience of sovereign communication that is as interior as it is exterior, as individual as it is collective. Following a type of "training become instinct" through the formative influences of exemplary figures, the captain knows, or better feels, that "the difficulties, the dangers, the problems of a ship at sea must be met on deck" (73)—that is, from a position in which the "composite soul" of command can both animate and be animated by communal social bodies, on a sympathetic, we-centric, and nonviolent basis. And indeed, as the narrative unfolds, and the captain's mind is progressively haunted by "visions of a ship drifting in calms and swinging in light airs, with all her crew dying slowly about her decks" (82), he is led to abandon his solipsistic, aristocratic stance that initially characterized him in order to invest his soul—and thus his body—in the social structure, or "nerves," of the ship, so as to innervate—and thus reanimate—a feverish and moribund social body on "the common ground" of the deck.[31] A confrontation with a shared catastrophe leads the captain to open up the sympathetic channels that transect his already "composite soul." And on this affective basis emerges an ethics of communal cooperation that eventually allows the planet of the ship to sail past the Scylla of totalitarian command and the Charybdis of refusal of command, so as to return to a harbor with a community of infected yet still living subjects.

## Secret Sharers (Nietzsche to Nancy)

Plagued by a contagious "epidemic," afflicted by "windless" waters, driven by "mysterious currents" and, eventually, "beset by hurricanes," the narrative generates wave after wave of calamitous factors that "bewitched" (69) the ship, and require a type of strenuous, breathtaking, and continuous endurance to keep affirming the possibility of survival to the end. As Conrad had made clear from the beginning, it is via the systemic interplay of human interactions between the captain and the crew, the head and the body, which literally compose the composite soul of command, that this possibility can ultimately be affirmed. In particular, the concluding part of the journey, which takes the ship from the island of Koh-ring back to Singapore, suggests that the captain-narrator's ethico-political commitment to the body politic the ship represents stems from the juncture of two seemingly incompatible ethical traditions the narrative has been delineating all along—that is, a vertical, aristocratic tradition that inscribes the captain's soul in a "dynasty" of commanders (from Giles to Ellis, extending to the whole chain of past captain figures) whose "influences" are constitutive of his "composite soul," on the one hand, and a horizontal, social experience of "sympathy" (from Burns to Ransom, extending to the entire crew) that anchors this soul within a social "community" represented by the microcosm of the contaminated ship, on the other. I suggest that it is from this paradoxical conjunction of vertical, aristocratic bonds that tie the captain to an aristocratic past tradition and of the horizontal, democratic bonds that tie him to the present social relations that Conrad's communal ethics of survival emerges.

The bonds of shared solidarity that tie the captain to his fellow sailors are not opposed to the aristocratic soul of command. They rather, provide the living affects that transect the channels of what is already a composite soul. We could, in fact, say that "the composite soul of command" the captain inherits, in theory, from a past "dynastic" tradition of shared "influences," "training," and, above all, "conception of duty" is, in praxis, already organically connected to the horizontal bonds that tie this head, or, if you prefer, this soul, to the social duties that structure the "fine nerves" of the ship. For Conrad, in fact, it is because the soul of command is already informed by what Nietzsche calls, in a psycho-physiological mood, the "social structure of the drives and emotions" that the social duties that structure the ship can exercise such an absorbing affective "claim" on his composite soul, generating a bond so intense that he "could imagine no claim that would be stronger and more absorbing than the claim of that ship." The strength of this claim, in other words, stems from it being not simply an external claim addressed to a singular head. Rather, it is a claim coming from the entire social body on board, a communal body that is—via the ramified "nerves" of the ship—already neurologically connected to the head, part of an inner experience of a soul that is not singular but composite instead. Alternatively, the lived experience of command opens those sympathetic channels that already innervate, but do not yet irrigate, the composite structure of the soul. In his account of the soul as multiplicity, Nietzsche had already stressed that command is an affective affair, as he says: "will is not only a complex of feeling and thinking, but above all an *affect*: and in fact the affect of command" (*BGE* 19:48). Conrad furthers this affective view by putting the composite soul of command in touch with the nerves that tie the ship as social structure. That the head is back in touch with the social body is clear. The captain-narrator realizes, for instance, that "an order has a steadying influence upon him who has to give it" (*SL* 96). The notion of "influence" is thus used again to account for a process of nonverbal communication. Yet this time it does not designate a personal, psychological experience; nor does it have its origin in a totalitarian figure. Rather, it designates a collective, psychic-social dynamic whereby an order on the social body retroacts on the sovereign head, influencing him in return.

This mimetic circulation of reciprocal influences harmonizes the interior structure of the soul of command and the community on deck in a way that balances the microcosm of the social structure of the ship. We are in fact given to think that without these living, experiential bonds that tie the head to the social body and are constitutive of what the narrator calls "the strong magic" (30) of command, the latter is bound to remain what the captain calls "an abstract idea" (38)—a dead concept deprived of the living affects that reanimate this magical experience. In short, for Conrad, the hypothesis of a composite (mimetic) soul innervated by a shared (contagious) experience is necessary to bring a social organism (community) into being.

Conrad's rethinking of the problematic of command grounded on shared, communal foundations looks back to a past maritime tradition; but looking back allows him to anticipate recent developments in ethical theory that think of community in terms of a shared exposition to the limit experience of death. We have already seen that the French philosopher Jean-Luc Nancy develops an ethics of catastrophe based on a conception of intersubjectivity that resonates with Conrad's account of sharing. For both Conrad and Nancy, in fact, the ontological foundations of the self are shared, or, better, *partagés* (both shared and divided) with an other who is neither truly external nor fully internal to the self, but is in a relation of affective communication with the self. Conrad speaks of a "secret sharer" that generates a "mysterious communication" between two connected and disconnected bodies; Nancy speaks of the "sharing that divides and that puts in communication bodies."[32] For both novelist and philosopher, the subject is not a self-enclosed, self-sufficient monad but is born out of the intimate experience of sharing. What we must add now is that Conrad and Nancy also have in common an investment in rethinking the foundations of community on the basis of a shared exposure to finitude that threatens to render this community inoperative.

## From the Inoperative to the Cooperative Community

In *The Inoperative Community* Nancy engages with Georges Bataille's concept of "sovereign communication" to answer the question, "who comes after the subject?" His answer is not "no one," but, rather, everyone who is part of a community of subjects that are not singular because they are already plural, or better singular-plural. Nancy's conception of community, like Bataille's conception of communication, offers a challenge to the metaphysics of the subject; it is not simply understood as an assemblage of separate egos but is already constitutive of singularities whose being rests on shared communicative foundations. Nancy writes, for instance, that community "presupposes that we are brought into the world, each and every one of us, according to a dimension of 'in common' that is in no way 'added onto' the dimension of 'being itself,' but that is rather co-originary and coextensive with it" (*IC* xxxvii). For Nancy, as for Bataille, but also for Nietzsche and Conrad before him, community is predicated on a conception of subjectivity that is not based on unitary, monadic egos. Rather, community is predicated on a relational conception of the subject that is open to the outside and rests on shared foundations.

This experience of sharing (or *partage*), in which the subject is both connected and divided (*partagé*) with others, for Nancy, emerges from the common confrontation with the limit-experience of death. And this "exposure" to death is, for Nancy, "the essence of community" (29). This is a philosophical point in line with a number of figures who—from Socrates to Heidegger—think of death as the ontological horizon of subjectivity. But it is not only that. In an echo of Lacoue-Labarthe, in fact, Nancy gestures toward what he calls "literature" as an "inscription of the communitarian exposition" inscribed in what he calls "the instant of communication, in the sharing" (39) that philosophy cannot fully articulate via a rational logos. My sense is that he would have found in Conrad's fictions traces of a mimetic supplement to his account of shared community. For Conrad, too, in fact, sharing is the essential constituent of a subject that is not one, because she or he is already double, or better multiple, so intertwined with the other that the ontological distinction between you and me, singular soul and plural soul, no longer holds, giving way to a "shared" or "composite" soul. Similarly, for Conrad, this singular composite soul is part of a community that is not based on a fusion or confusion of identities, but on a shared exposition to the threat of finitude that allows the captain to compear as a singular-composite soul. Nancy's and Conrad's account of community could not be more intimately shared. And given the number of mimetic instances in which the soul, for Conrad, turns out to be double and composite, we are now in a position to say that Conrad, in his writings, goes furthest in his account of what we have seen Nancy call "you shares me" (*IC* 29). His tales of the homo duplex in particular reveal the immanent experience responsible for sovereign forms of communication that give birth to a community anchored on shared infective and affective foundations.

And yet as both Nancy and Conrad teach us, the experience of shared communication is as much based on conjunctions as on disjunctions, arrivals, and departures. Nancy puts it in Conradian terms as he speaks of "sharing [*partage*] that divides and puts in communication bodies, voices, and writings in general" (*IC* 6). If the shared foundations between Conrad and Nancy remain profound, it is in what divides them perhaps more than in what unites them that lies Conrad's originality. Notice, in fact, that Nancy's philosophical model of "community" is grounded on an ontological exposition of *ipse* restricted to the inner experience of death. Consequently, he does not explicitly address a community exposed to the general equivalence of catastrophe that will preoccupy him later in his career. This is perhaps why he claims that "I recognize that in the death of the other there is nothing recognizable" (33). Yet in Conrad's tales the experience of a shared catastrophe seems to force precisely such a mimetic recognition, perhaps based on the lived affective experience that "you and I are sailors," as Burns puts it while he is exposed to the possibility of his death (*SL* 59). It is thus not surprising that important theoretical shifts of emphasis in their conception of a shared community need to be signaled. Conrad is, in fact, less preoccupied with the impossible confrontation with the limit-experience of finitude and more with the possibility of surviving the limit-experience of catastrophe, less with an ontology of the inoperative community and more with the psychophysiology necessary to render the community operative. There is, indeed, a Nietzschean, life-affirming side in Conrad's writings that supplements contemporary philosophical accounts of death as community by affirming the survival of catastrophe.

The communal ethics that emerges from Conrad's tale, then, suggests that in catastrophic situations haunted by the real possibility of catastrophe, the composition rather than dissolution of community should be at the center of literary and philosophical thought, a community that, with its social body innervated by the head (and vice versa), has all the characteristics of what Conrad also calls a "living organism" (*TOS* 69). To be sure, models of social cohesion based on an organicist view of society in which the head governs, by "influence," the body politic have not been popular in the second half of the twentieth century, unsurprisingly given the poisonous effects of popular *Gemeinshaften* predicated on fascist forms of will to power. Nancy is thus right to be "suspicious" of what he calls an "organic communion . . . constituted . . . by a fair distribution of tasks and goods, or by a happy equilibrium of forces and authorities" (*IC* 10, 9), for this community can easily turn into an organism in which a totalitarian head generates fusions or confusions that, in the past, led to unspeakable political horrors (I will return to this). Still, the horrors of the past should not prevent us from looking ahead to the horrors of the future. While the dangers of authoritarian will to power should always be kept in mind for political reasons, and self-contained notions of organic unity have become suspicious for aesthetic reasons, the ancient metaphor of the organism is currently regaining traction for ethical and ecological reasons, especially concerning contemporary preoccupations with epidemic infections and contagious pathologies.[33] Conrad contributes to these debates by adding a diagnostic that shows how a social organism is vulnerable to forms of infection that have the potential to affect equally— and in this sense "democratically"—the head and the body. He also dramatizes nonauthoritarian, democratic solutions in which the head cooperates with the entire social organism in order to fight off pathologies and jointly affirm the possibility of collective survival. As he succinctly puts it in *Lord Jim*: "We exist only insofar as we hang together" (170).

Time and again, what emerges from Conrad's communal ethos is that the pathology that infects the social body also generates the possible remedy to cure it. A catastrophic situation that infects the social organism and confronts the community with the specter of death has, paradoxically, the power to generate the collective efforts necessary to keep the organism living. There is an immanent, life-affirming tendency at work in Conrad's communal ethos that cannot afford to think of sharing only as an individual exposure to death. Instead it uses the shadow of death to affirm communal life. This is, indeed, what happens in the end. The ship is hit by a storm, which is not terrific in itself yet, given the pathological state of the crew, has catastrophic implications nonetheless. Enfeebled by the epidemic, crew and captain have to join forces to hoist a sail necessary to keep the ship floating. Here is how Conrad pictures the scene:

The shadows swayed away from me without a word. Those men were the ghosts of themselves and their weight on a rope could be no more than the weight of a bunch of ghosts. Indeed, if ever a sail was hauled up by sheer spiritual strength it must have been that sail for, properly speaking, there was no muscle enough for the task in the whole ship, let alone the miserable lot of us on deck. (88)

These subjects are reduced to mere "shadows" or "ghosts"; yet these living ghosts cooperate in order to affirm life. They are animated by a "spiritual strength" that is not singular (the head), nor plural (the body), but is generated by the communal work of a composite crew in which the head works in organic communion with the social body. Spiritual strength, just as communal work, can be perceived as oxymoronic concepts. Nancy, for instance, drawing on Bataille's ontological distinction between work and play, slavery and sovereignty, claims that "community cannot arise from the domain of *work*" since "one does not produce it, one experiences or one is constituted by it as the experience of finitude" (*IC* 31). The secret continuities between Conrad and Bataille, especially when it comes to the experience of the sacred, are profound, and I shall return to them later. And yet in *The Shadow-Line* Conrad transgresses this venerable Bataillean distinction between work and play, slavery and sovereignty, the sacred and the profane. He makes us see that in a catastrophic scenario, work has the power to generate the flow of affect that keeps the infected organism together. For Conrad, in fact, this type of communal work cannot be reduced to a materialistic and servile conception of life, if only because the "strength" involved is not simply physical but "spiritual," an indication that the type of work required to affirm survival in a catastrophic scenario does not belong to the sphere of the profane but of the sacred, not to servile but to sovereign experiences. In short, catastrophe, for Conrad, renders work a sacred, sovereign, and spiritual experience.

It is perhaps no accident that at the final turning point in the narrative, of all affects, Conrad privileges a social, contagious, and, as Bataille would say, sovereign effusion such as "laughter" in order to strengthen the communal bonds of solidarity that ties self to others, while at the same time exorcising supernatural fears. "Well, then—laugh! Laugh—I tell you" (95), Mr. Burns shouts insanely and somewhat comically. And in an attempt to spread this laughter by mimetic contagion to the whole crew, he adds: "Now then—all together. One, two, three—laugh!" (95). This insane laughter is only slightly comic and does not make the crew burst out in communal laughter, yet the narrative suggests that it is not deprived of magical efficacy. In fact, it marks the end of the storm and the crossing of a "barrier" the captain had been trying to cross all along, a shadow-line that could not be crossed individually but required communal affective cooperation. We are thus given to think that laughter is not only cathartic; it also opens up those sympathetic channels that tie self to others via sacred forms of communication based on joyful, mimetic effusions that generate what I have called elsewhere "the laughter of community."[34] The mimetic experience of sovereign communication gives birth to the communal desire of survival, and out of this desire the possibility of cooperative communities to come is at last affirmed. Thus the captain-narrator makes clear to his crew that "the best chance for the ship and the men was in the efforts all of us, sick and well, must make to get her along out of this" (78). The shift from a diegetic perspective that speaks of "the men" from a position of temporal distance, to an immanent, mimetic perspective that includes the pathos of the narrator ("all of us") is indicative of the affective investment, sharing, and cooperation between the head and the social body necessary to overcome a catastrophic conclusion.

                                  .          .          .

We were wondering: What is the possible antidote that allows the crew to affirm survival once it has reached the shadow-line that divides the living and the dead? Which principle animates these half-living shadows of disease and starvation? What *The Shadow-Line* suggests, between the lines, is that the strength necessary to affirm survival as individual bodies are infected by a shared pathology stems from a sovereign communication of souls who are not singular (the head) nor solely plural (the body). They are, rather, composite souls in the sense that each soul is mimetically entangled with another, composing an affective chain of solidarity that holds subjects together forming a social and cooperative organism (the community). Thus understood, the Conradian emphasis on the notion of "composite soul" and the "spiritual" strength it generates stems from the immanent realization that the soul is a living breath that animates a collective organism. Hence the individual, far from being indivisible, is fundamentally interconnected in a web of other souls in such a fundamental way that one soul feels, responds to and supplements the failings of another soul in a shared feeling of solidarity that, at the microlevel of the ship, is constitutive of a community. Thus understood, the ship becomes "a symbol of mankind's claim to the direction of its own fate" (63). This, at least, is what emerges during moments of maximum vulnerability in which precarious lives take hold of the realization that their soul is a composite soul, their destiny is a shared destiny, their community a shared community. The ship as a microcosm of a social world threatened by the possibility of catastrophe becomes a privileged space to explore what Conrad calls in *A Personal Record* "that mysterious fellowship which unites in a community of hopes and fears all the dwellers on this earth" (23–24).

The image of the ship as a metaphor of the body politic goes back to the origins of ethical theory and is currently being recuperated by theorists concerned with the precariousness of life. It is equally central to Conrad's ethical imagination. As we are sailing our planet into the age of the Anthropocene, the picture of the ship effectively reflects our exposure to the changes of climate, our vulnerability to the turbulence of currents, our openness to epidemic contagion, and, more generally, the fragility of our all too human foundations. Meanwhile, Conrad already suggested that as we continue to navigate—compass and helm at hand—the rapid changes that are currently reorienting "a planet flying vertiginously on its appointed path in a space of infinite silence" (*SL* 62), we should start developing those shared bonds of "solidarity" vital to sailing through turbulent waters that both sustain and threaten to dissolve the small planet we ultimately share. As the future of our children looks increasingly uncertain, turning back to Conrad's nautical experiences also reminds us that what is needed to affirm the survival of community is a type of "solidarity" that, as he so presciently put it, "binds men to each other, which binds together all humanity—the dead to the living," but above all—"the living to the unborn" (*NN* xii).

PART 2

# Anthropology of Frenzy

CHAPTER 4

# A Picture of Europe: Possession Trance in *Heart of Darkness*

Africa is to Europe as the picture is to Dorian Gray.
> —Chinua Achebe, "An Image of Africa"

It is the same picture . . . and there is a bond between us and that humanity so far away.
> —Joseph Conrad, "The Congo Diary"

The title of this chapter might appear slightly provocative. It mirrors what is probably one of the most famous, most often quoted, and, above all, most controversial essays in Conrad studies, and by doing so inverses some of its terms, suggesting that Conrad's *Heart of Darkness* does not function as "an image of Africa" but as "a picture of Europe" instead. Much has been said about the race debate since the appearance of Chinua Achebe's "An Image of Africa: Racism in *Heart of Darkness*" in 1977,[1] so much that one may wonder about the need to add yet another chapter to what appears to be, if not a closed, at least an excessively discussed case. If initial responses to Achebe's critique of Conrad as a "bloody racist" emphasized how *Heart of Darkness* functions as a thoroughgoing critique of imperialism, subsequent critics informed by the bourgeoning field of postcolonial studies have done much to further this line of inquiry, unpacking the historical, political, narratological, psychic, and discursive forces that transect Conrad's problematic and highly ambivalent account of racial "otherness."[2] And yet, as we had occasion to see, when it comes to intriguing, complex, and passionate cases, the unexpected discovery of a new perspective to revisit central evidence to the case cannot only justify a reopening of the dossier; it can also reframe the very terms upon which the debate rests. Part 2 is concerned with such a reframing.

In what follows I reconsider the textual evidence in Conrad's problematic image of Africa, which, in Achebe's view, functions as the smoking gun that proved Conrad to be "guilty" of racism: namely, his dehumanizing representations of rituals whereby African people dance, collectively, to the sound of drums in a state of intoxicating "frenzy" (IA 338).[3] It is true that in the wake of Achebe's virulent critique of Conrad as a "purveyor of comforting myths" (339) that set up Africa as the "antithesis of Europe and therefore of civilization" (338) the anthropological meaning of these rituals have tended to remain unexplored. But it is equally true that such enthusiastic outbreaks of ritual dances cannot simply be dismissed as the product of Conrad's so-called mythical imagination whose purpose, as Achebe puts it, is to induce "hypnotic stupor in his readers" via "fake ritualistic repetition" of images of "frenzy" (338). These images of Africa are, by now, known outside literary studies. They are especially well known among anthropologists of religion specialized in collective rituals in sub-Saharan Africa, which have the function to induce altered states of consciousness for religious, social, and communal purposes. Extending an anthropological line of inquiry in Conrad studies,[4] I argue that this realization does not simply provide us with a new referent to approach Conrad's enigmatic tale; it also gives us an insight into the driving telos of Marlow's experience, a ritual experience that in-*forms*—from beginning, middle, to end—the narrative as a whole.

As we shall see, Conrad's representations of frenzy cannot simply be dismissed as a distorting "image" of Africa. Rather, they emerge out of a carefully crafted artistic "picture," a dark, opaque, yet nonetheless mimetic picture that looks back to the past in order to make us "see," in a self-reflexive turn we are by now familiar with, the horrors that ensue when massive forms of ritual frenzy break out, not so much at the heart of Africa but at the heart of Europe instead. It is my contention that the terms of the race debate, as well as the uncanny picture of Western horrors that emerges from Conrad's tale, need to be radically reframed in the light of this mimetic hypothesis.[5]

## Reframing the Picture

If we approach Conrad's *Heart of Darkness* from an anthropological perspective, Achebe's affirmation that "Africa is to Europe as the picture is to Dorian Gray" (IA 348) will ring true at some point—perhaps even truer than Achebe originally intended. Marlow, in fact, seems to share the past-oriented evolutionary belief that Africa represents an earlier stage in human development, a primitive, barbaric, and thus inferior stage supposed to represent the hidden, "prehistoric" side of the modern, "civilized" self. We can thus understand why Achebe denounces the distorting effects of Conrad's image of Africa, a past-oriented image that reduces the other to an atavistic version of the self. According to Achebe, in fact, Conrad's image of Africa is representative of a wider European projection of its "physical and moral deformities" onto the African "other" whereby the "civilized" European subject "unloads his physical and moral deformities so that he may go forward, erect and immaculate" (348), leaving Africa behind once the cathartic projection has taken place. It is no wonder that in his view, Conrad's image of Africa is like the picture of Dorian Gray—at least in the narrow sense that this artistic picture involves a distortion of African features in order to reassure the evolutionary superiority of the European "self." Hence the conclusion Achebe draws from Conrad's tale is that "Africa is something to be avoided just as the picture has to be hidden away" (348).

And yet the exact opposite has taken place. In the wake of Achebe's critique, readers have continued to be haunted by *Heart of Darkness*, feeling compelled to return repeatedly and unveil this disquieting image of Africa in order to find out what, exactly, it reveals about the horror at the heart of European souls. As Edward Said perceptively puts it in *Culture and Imperialism*, there are "two visions in *Heart of Darkness*," and if Achebe stresses the imperialistic side, Said balances this perspective by outlining a contrapuntal, anti-imperialistic counterpart.[6] In order to further this Janus-faced line of inquiry, we should notice that even from this antithetical, forward-looking perspective, Conrad's representation of Africa continues to function like

Oscar Wilde's picture of the homo duplex. In fact, *Heart of Darkness* not only entails an unfaithful "deformation" of the "other" but also, and more important, serves as a faithful, yet not narrowly realistic, mirror that reveals the horror lurking behind "civilized" souls. Not surprisingly then, scholars interested in the critical dimension of *Heart of Darkness* have tended to emphasize Conrad's untimely critique of imperialism in order to reveal the horrors so-called civilizing missions tend to produce in the name of a blind faith in progress and evolution. This shift of perspective entails a radical shift of focus that modifies the perception of what critics see, analyze, and theorize. We move from Conrad's image of Africa to his account of what Europe was doing in Africa, from Conrad's uncritical portrait of African subjects to his critical account of the ethical blindness of European subjects, from the racist horrors of the text to the horrors of colonialism the text denounces. Figuratively put, we move from Marlow's picture of the African "frenzy" to Kurtz's picture of the blindfolded woman with a "sinister" face—a sexist representation of the blindness that informs the Western project of *Aufklärung*.

This critical shift from a racist image of Africa to a critical image of Europe has been immensely effective in unmasking the moral and political "darkness" that continues to inform the ideology of progress once it is put into practice; it has also had the benefit of placing the horrors of colonialism in Africa at the center of critical debates. Thanks to Conrad's tale, as well as Achebe's reading of it, Africa is no longer "something to be avoided" but something to be explored instead—at least in the burgeoning field of postcolonial studies. And yet in this dialectical inversion of perspectives, the terms of Achebe's pictorial equation have been somewhat altered, and the strength of his critique avoided. Notice, in fact, that it is no longer Africa that is to Europe as the picture is to Dorian Gray, but Europe itself that turns out to have a self-referential, mirroring function. Hence the moral degradation of the European colonists in Africa is seen to mirror the moral degradation of European souls in Europe. Clearly, in this shift of perspective something fundamental is left out of the picture: namely, Conrad's problematic representation of Africans as irrational, savage, and potentially violent people. Or, better, what is left out of the picture is the disturbing self-referential mirroring function of the "primitive" other as an image of the "civilized" self, an image that, like the picture for Dorian Gray, is supposed to reveal something true and fundamental about the ethical horrors of modern souls.

In short, if we take Achebe's simile concerning the picture of Dorian Gray seriously (and I think we should), it seems that neither Achebe nor his critics have fully explored the theoretical implications of this provocative pictorial reflection—the former too busy denouncing the painter, the latter too busy defending the painting.

Though it does not offer the promise of a grand synthesis, this chapter articulates such competing perspectives by focusing on Conrad's picture of Africa (and not of Europe) in order to see what this picture reveals about the horrors of Europe (and not of Africa). I argue that no matter how problematic the picture, there is something fundamental to learn about the horrors of Europe and Europeans from Conrad's representation of Africa and Africans. In particular, I approach *Heart of Darkness* through the filter of both evolutionary and contemporary anthropology in order to cast new light on the religious rituals responsible for generating the notorious states of "frenzy" that infuriated Achebe. An approach informed by contemporary anthropological developments demonstrates that the much-discussed notion of "frenzy" cannot simply be dismissed as an expression of Conrad's "racism" (Achebe), nor can it be left in the background in order to foreground Conrad's "critique" of imperialism (Achebe's critics). Instead, we shall have to re-read Conrad's representation of the ritual "frenzy" in light of an anthropological phenomenon that appears to be quite common in Africa: a ritual, contagious and thus mimetic phenomenon Conrad was probably among the first to give aesthetic form to in Western literature: Conrad called this state "frenzy"; modern anthropologists now call it "possession trance."

Despite its evolutionary assumptions, *Heart of Darkness* moves beyond past ethnocentric accounts based on a hierarchical distinction between "us" and "them," the modern subject and its denigrating picture, in order to make us see—in a "self-reflexive" turn that, for James Clifford, characterizes the modern anthropological project itself[7]—the mimetic frenzy at the heart of European souls. Like Wilde's picture of Dorian Gray, then, Conrad's picture of Africa is not an aesthetic end in itself; nor is it only a distorted representation. Rather, it is a picture that unveils the horrific aspects of Europe the latter tends to disavow and project onto "others" in the name of civilization and progress. More precisely, Conrad's anthropological sketch of rituals of possession trance in Africa reveals how sacrificial forms of ritual "frenzy" continue to take possession of modern souls in post-Napoleonic Europe and are responsible for the ethico-political horrors that ensue as this collective escalation of frenzy reaches massive proportions of universal carnage. My wager in this chapter is that Conrad's specific brand of mimetic anthropology is ahead of its times not only because of its self-reflexive epistemic premises. It is equally untimely because it allows him to anticipate the murderous frenzy generated by charismatic leader figures who will soon reenact religious rituals in order to take possession of the modern masses at the heart of the European body politic. This anthropological realization supports René Girard's thesis concerning the sacrificial foundations of mimetic violence. It is also directly in line with what Philippe Lacoue-Labarthe has recently called "the horror of the West."[8] In a characteristic double-faced gesture that orients our approach, Conrad looks back to horrors of the past and, by doing so, helps us cast light on mimetic horrors of the present.

As we now unveil Conrad's disquieting picture of Europe we shall progressively realize how untimely his artistic representation actually is—a self-reflexive, mimetic representation that makes us see, with uncanny clarity, the horrors of ritualized forms of possession trance we so often fail to confront, in the name of what Achebe would probably call an "immaculate" image of Europe.

## The Two Faces of Evolutionary Theory

In order to adequately frame the two faces of evolutionary theory, it is useful to situate Conrad's picture of Africa within a broader theoretical landscape. The evolutionary account of racial otherness that emerges from Charles Darwin's *The Descent of Man* (1871) is particularly revealing of a tension that is central to evolutionary thinking in general, and helps us reframe the Janus-faced perspective internal to Conrad's representation of the "primitive" other in particular.[9]

### Darwin's Image of Frenzy

Darwin's image of racial otherness is shot through with contradictory imperatives we shall equally see represented in Conrad's picture. In fact, Darwin relies on what we would now call a racist representation of the primitive other that introduces a cultural discontinuity between "civilization" and "savagery" in order to convince his readers that a fundamental biological continuity exists among species and, by extension, human groups. This fundamental tension is most clearly expressed in the concluding lines of *The Descent of Man*. There Darwin succinctly sums up his evolutionary discovery in the following, denigrating terms: "there can hardly be a doubt that we are descended from barbarians."[10] And then, in a more personal, narrative mood, he gives an account of the anthropological experience that contributed to this evolutionary realization:

> The astonishment which I felt on first seeing a party of Fuegians on a wild and broken shore will never be forgotten by me, for the reflection at once rushed into my mind—such were our ancestors. These men were absolutely naked and bedaubed with paint, their long hair was tangled, their mouths, frothed with excitement, and their expression was wild, startled, and distrustful. They possessed hardly any arts, and like wild animals lived on what they could catch. (*DM* 208)

Commenting on these lines, Hunt Hawkins notices that Darwin is contributing to spreading the view that "non-Europeans were children and primitive" and persuasively argues that the racial hierarchy introduced by the theory of evolution is, to a certain degree, complicit with the imperialist project.[11] This is certainly true with respect to the content of this problematic passage, and Hawkins is right to emphasize the regressive cultural and ideological implications of Darwinian and post-Darwinian evolutionary theory, as well as their damaging impact on Conrad's racial beliefs. And yet if we pay close attention to the rhetoric that informs this passage, it is no longer clear whether Darwin's denigrating affirmations are simply the product of his conservative cultural ideology or, alternatively, if they are also—and in the same breath—part of a rhetorical strategy to convey his (r)evolutionary biological theory to a conservative Victorian readership.

## The Rhetoric of Evolution

Darwin is, indeed, painfully aware that his theory of evolution will be, as he says, "distasteful to the many" (*DM* 208). And as the end of the book is approaching, he attempts, one last time, to present his controversial idea concerning "the descent of man" to his reluctant Victorian readers. Consider the rhetorical movements that frame the above-quoted passage. After his denigrating account of the Fuegians as "barbarians" akin to "animals," Darwin addresses the reader thus: "He who has seen a savage in his native land will not feel much shame, if forced to acknowledge that the blood of some more humble creature flows in his veins" (208). And then, in a confessional tone, he adds: "For my own part I would as soon be descended from that heroic little monkey, who braved his dreaded enemy in order to save the life of his keeper . . . as from a savage who delights to torture his enemies, offers up bloody sacrifices" (208). With the benefit of hindsight it is now easy to see that Darwin's cultural denigration of the Fuegians is, indeed, predicated on a racist cultural move that sets up a discontinuity between "self" and "other."

Somewhat less readily perceptible is the hypothesis that this racism does not seem to be an end in itself. Rather, it serves at least two related rhetorical functions, which are directly in line with Darwin's fundamental thesis. First, by setting up a (racist) evolutionary distance between "modern" man and "primitive" man, Darwin confirms the (racist) cultural expectations of his readers. This move is strategically important insofar as it strengthens the bonds of cultural identification with his Victorian audience, making clear that, despite his geographical and intellectual explorations, culturally speaking, he is still one of them. And, second, this cultural discontinuity predicated on a racist representation of the "primitive" other serves, in turn, as a rhetorical lever to promote the main idea of his book: namely, the biological continuity with the animal world, a world now represented by the positive anthropomorphic representation of a "heroic little monkey," which strikingly contrasts with the "savage" Fuegians. The ideology that informs his rhetoric is, indeed, crude: it is better to be a "heroic" little monkey than a "bloody" primitive. Yet this ideology is set to work in order to drive home the theoretical point that has been the driving telos of an intellectual career devoted to proving the continuity between the human and the animal world. In short, it is as if Darwin confirms the evolutionary expectations of his listeners concerning cultural evolution in order to better subvert their expectation concerning biological evolution.

To be sure, this rhetorical double bind does not excuse Darwin for promoting a racist image that other, less sophisticated thinkers will later reproduce in the sphere of cultural, rather than biological, evolution. Yet Darwin's image immediately alerts us to the fact that in matters of race and evolution we need to pay careful consideration to the rhetorical situation of the telling if we want to fully account for the theoretical implications of what is told. This point is especially important for reevaluating Conrad's equally ambivalent and paradoxical evolutionary representation of the Africans on the shore of the Congo River. More generally, Darwin's account of cultural otherness puts us in a position to see that evolutionary theory is Janus-faced and looks in opposed directions. On one side, this monogenist theory affirms a fundamental biological continuity between human groups, stresses that we all share the same human nature, and considers the "primitive" other as our "ancestor." On the other side, it establishes a violent division based on a hierarchical cultural discontinuity between different social groups, relegating "primitive" man (from Latin, *primus*, that comes first) to an earlier and thus inferior stage of evolution, which modern man has supposedly long outgrown. If the first side is theoretically progressive and promotes unity and kinship, the second is theoretically regressive and undermines the first by setting up a distance that deprives "primitive" subjects of their culture and thus, by extension, of their humanity as well.

## An Image of Africa Redux

If we now return to *Heart of Darkness* with this evolutionary frame in mind we notice that Conrad's image of Africa is informed by similar rhetorical and theoretical double-movements that are both complicit with and subversive of racist expectations about racial otherness. From the outset, in fact, Conrad explicitly relies on an evolutionary frame in order to set up a temporal distance between "modern" and "prehistoric" subjects that is in line with the denigrating, ethnocentric tendencies of evolutionary theory. For Marlow, as for Darwin before him, traveling in space brings modern man back in time, to an earlier stage of evolution. Thus he infamously states that "going up that river was like travelling back to the earliest beginnings of the world" (*YOS* 77) and that the "prehistoric men" Marlow encounters belong to what he calls the "night of first ages" (79). Moreover, in order to make clear that he considers this temporal distance in terms that are informed by Darwin's biological theory of evolution, he establishes a direct and rather crude continuity between African people and the animal world. Thus Marlow repeatedly links the Africans he meets to dogs, hyenas, bees, and ants, and goes as far as saying that the "short ends [of their rags] behind wagged to and fro like tails" (56), a distorting projection of monkeylike features onto subaltern African bodies who are not given a voice to speak. Needless to say, such a racist representation of the racial other does not allow for any form of self-recognition to take place. As Achebe forcefully pointed out, it only reinforces the distance between a "civilized" image of Europe and a "primitive" image of Africa.

That said, we should also notice that Conrad implicitly grants African people a cultural, religious tradition that situates the "primitive" other in a paradoxical relation of distant proximity with the "modern" self. This double-movement extends the implications of Darwin's theory of evolution toward the field of evolutionary anthropology, a field that, as John Griffith has persuasively shown, informs the "anthropological dilemma" at work in *Heart of Darkness*.[12] If we want to further this line of investigation, we should notice that in order to frame his encounter with the ritual practices of "primitive cultures," Marlow repeatedly relies on E. B. Tylor's theory of "animism" (from Latin, *anima*, soul), which informed his evolutionary account of religious practices.[13] In *Primitive Culture* (1873) Tylor, in fact, considered "animism" a rudimentary form of religion that leads people who have not yet achieved the status of "civilization" to attribute life (or a soul) to inanimate, natural elements. Animism, thus understood, is based on the anthropocentric belief that man can influence the spirit of nature through mimetic incantations and magical rituals, a mimetic belief prominent among other anthropologically oriented modernists, such as D. H. Lawrence and Georges Bataille.

References to the language of animism are pervasive in *Heart of Darkness*. They account for Marlow's multiple personifications of nature, as well as for his consistent reliance on the language of magic, witchcraft, and "weird incantations" (113). As a ritual practice, however, animism is perhaps most clearly exemplified by Marlow's description of the "fireman." We are told that this member of the crew relies on a "charm" in order to magically influence the "evil spirit inside the boiler" (80) of the steamer Marlow and his crew use to navigate up the Congo River, a clear expression of the "primitive" belief that inanimate objects—especially objects that are invested with religious affects—are living, spiritual entities that have the power to possess a soul.

Marlow's characterization of the bond that ties him to this animistic figure in terms of "distant kinship" (96), then, confirms the contradictory double movement toward/away from the primitive other and the prereligious, magical practices he enacts. Conrad's account of both Africa and Africans remains, thus, in line with cultural forms of evolutionary theory and the paradoxes they entail. And yet it also supplements them. If nineteenth-century anthropologists of religion like Tylor were primarily interested in offering a general evolutionary account of different cultural stages in the system of beliefs of primitive cultures, Conrad is much more fascinated by the specific affective impact of animistic practices on the members who partake in rituals. I suggest that in this diagnostic exploration of the affective effects of ritual on the psychic life of the subject lies Conrad's anthropological and theoretical originality.

The first, most memorable, and, above all, most problematic encounter with the affective life of African people is worth reconsidering in light of this hypothesis. The scene not only informs all the subsequent descriptions of African rituals but also brings us very quickly to what I take to be the beating heart of Conrad's anthropological dilemma. After restating the evolutionary assumption that they were "wanderers on a prehistoric earth," Marlow offers the following, notorious description of "prehistoric man":

> suddenly as we struggled round a bend there would be a glimpse of rush walls, of peaked grass-roofs, a burst of yells, a whirl of black limbs, a mass of hands clapping, of feet stamping, of bodies swaying, of eyes rolling, under the droop of heavy and motionless foliage. The steamer toiled along slowly on the edge of a black and incomprehensible frenzy. (79)

It is an understatement to say that in the wake of the racism/antiracism debate, these lines have been at the center of considerable critical and theoretical attention. And not surprisingly so. In fact, Conrad's representation of African rituals triggered by the repetitive rhythm of the drum whereby subjects dance in an enthused state of "frenzy," mindlessly clapping their hands and rolling their eyes to the sound of tom-toms, involves an account of the Fang people, and, by extension, African people, as savage, irrational, and potentially violent creatures. This is indeed the "mindless frenzy of the first beginning" that Achebe denounced in "An Image of Africa" as an expression of Conrad's personal "racism," as well as of a larger Western anxiety to set up a distance between Europe and Africa, "civilized" modern souls and their "primitive" degenerate image (338).

What has not been sufficiently noticed is that Achebe's critique of Conrad implicitly challenges the double movement that informs Conrad's evolutionary representation of the racial other in particular and evolutionary theory in general. On the one hand, Achebe makes clear that the distance Conrad initially sets up between Europe and Africa reveals an evolutionary representation of the racial other as temporally distant or, as he calls it, mimicking evolutionary parlance, as a "primordial relative" (IA 338) representative of "primordial barbarity" (347)—evolution as temporal discontinuity. On the other hand, Achebe's diagnosis of the fundamental reasons that inform Conrad's racism suggests that the anxious need to set up an evolutionary distance betrays wider cultural and psychic anxieties about the "lurking hint of kinship" that ties "primitive" and "modern" men (338)— evolution as biological continuity.[14] There is thus a sense in which the race debate continues to be implicitly informed by the paradoxical evaluation of racial otherness as radically different yet fundamentally the same, as representative of a primitive humanity yet still our contemporary—a paradoxical evaluation that despite its different inflections continues to be in line with nineteenth-century evolutionary accounts of racial difference.

Achebe's reading of Conrad marked a watershed in modernist and postcolonial studies. It has also been much critiqued and his one-sided evaluation corrected. Still, when it comes to this particular passage, even Achebe's most severe critics tend to agree that Marlow's account of "frenzy" is problematic and should not be taken as a faithful representation of African people when they dance. An exception to this tendency can be found in one of the earliest and most incisive responses to Achebe. Toward the beginning of the race debate, Cedric Watts made the controversial point that "the passage is patently justified on realistic grounds."[15] Twenty years and many articles later, Nicholas Harrison, in his informed *Postcolonial Criticism*, returns to this passage to challenge Watts's realistic (mimetic) point. Drawing on Gérard Genette's (antimimetic) narratology, Harrison suggests that we should not simply consider what these words represent, but rather "how these words *work*, or *how* they *make sense* and what sort of sense they make, for the narrative as such and for the reader."[16] Now, if we want to reconsider Conrad's specific account of ritual "frenzy" from a mimetic perspective that is not naively realistic, but is attentive to the formal structure of Conrad's self-reflexive narrative, perhaps we do not need to choose between Watts's and Harrison's competing theoretical perspectives. In fact, it is only if we consider *both* the anthropological referent of these words *and* their formal arrangement in the texture of the text that we can begin to reveal the aesthetic, ethical, and political function of these rituals as they are prefigured in Conrad's narrative picture.

If we return to reconsider Conrad's account of ritual frenzy and the psychic dispossession it entails from the perspective of more contemporary anthropological developments, we notice that a fundamental point concerning this scene has been surprisingly missed, both by Achebe and his critics. No matter how problematic the picture, Marlow's account of frenzy is not as decontextualized as it initially appears to be. Marlow, in fact, begins to frame his picture of Africa against the background of a ritual context that endows this mysterious outbreak of frenzy with a cultural and religious meaning. Right before telling us what he saw in the foreground, he refers to what he heard in the background; and what he heard is a ritual phenomenon that seems to be in a relation of proximity to the hidden meaning of the "heart of darkness." Thus he says:

> We penetrated deeper and deeper into the heart of darkness. It was very
> quiet there. At night sometimes the roll of drums behind the curtain of
> trees would run up the river and remain sustained faintly, as if hovering in
> the air over our heads till the first break of day. Whether this meant war,
> peace or prayer we could not tell. (79)

This is, to be sure, just a passing reference to a ritual context in the background that remains, for the moment, "incomprehensible" (79). Yet it also suggests that, if not for Marlow, at least for Conrad, this "frenzy" is not simply a spontaneous expression of primitive savagery. It is, rather, the direct outcome of collective, religious rituals in which subjects dance, from night till dawn, to the intoxicating rhythm of drums, to the point of exhaustion. This is not an isolated concern in Conrad's work. In his other Congo story, "An Outpost

of Progress," he had already dramatized a similar musical ritual. Speaking of
the two hapless protagonists and mimetic doubles of the tale, Kayerts and
Carlier, at a turning point in the narrative, he writes: "All night they were disturbed by a lot of drumming in the villages. A deep, rapid roll near by would
be followed by another far off—then all ceased. . . . And through the deep
and tremendous noise sudden yells that resembled snatches of songs from a
madhouse darted shrill and high in discordant jets of sound" (*TH* 99). As
always, Conrad picks up a motif sketched in an earlier narrative in order to
further elaborate on it. And this time, framed within a more densely layered
picture, the narrative suggests that the "frenzy" in the foreground must be
understood in light of the ritual drumming in the background, a drumming
that, as we shall repeatedly confirm, haunts the tale and perhaps Conrad's
African experience as a whole.

Over the past decades, we have become so accustomed to reading
Conrad's account of the primitive "frenzy" through Achebe's perspective
that critics have failed to notice the potential anthropological implications
of such a problematic representation. In fact, the religious, musical ritual
Conrad describes has the power to induce a mysterious, psychosocial phenomenon that remains obscure to Marlow, yet is well known in contemporary anthropological literature: clapping hands, rhythmic music, collective
dancing, ritual "frenzy," "enthusiasm" (from Greek, *entheos*, possessed by a
God), "rolling eyes," and the psychic dispossession that ensues from nightlong, communal effervescence. Indeed, if we consider these lines in the
light of contemporary anthropology we notice that in addition to its rather
obvious evolutionary bias they also entail an attempt to describe in clumsy,
ethnocentric terms a widespread ritual phenomenon: namely, an irrational,
contagious, and thus essentially mimetic ritual phenomenon that is common
in Africa and is known in anthropological literature under the names of "possession," "trance," or, most often, "possession trance."[17]

Has too much been said about Conrad's racist images in *Heart of Darkness*? Perhaps. But here is a new hypothesis: *Heart of Darkness* is not only
a backward-oriented text predicated on evolutionary anthropology. It also
offers one of the first novelistic accounts of possession trance in British literature, and account that is forward-looking and anticipates contemporary
developments in religious anthropology and mimetic theory in intriguing
and complex ways.

## The Frenzy of Possession

Despite the elusive dimension of trance, the multiplicity of its ethnographic manifestations, and the controversies it has generated among different schools of anthropology of religion, specialists in the field tend to agree that this ritual phenomenon is found across different cultures, is "frequent" in Africa, and is "widely prevalent in the entirety of sub-Saharan Africa."[18] As the ethnomusicologist Gilbert Rouget explains in his authoritative *Music and Trance*, this state is usually "obtained by means of noise, agitation, and in the presence of others," and is often "considered to be the direct result of music and dance," and he adds: "In this way, savagery and aggression are externalized by means of scant gesticulation that makes use above all of movements expressing agitation and frenzy."[19] Characteristic symptoms of "possession trance" (from Latin, *transire*, to pass), he adds, are "convulsions, foaming at the mouth, protruding eyes, large extrusions of the tongue."[20] This might not be a pretty, politically correct image of the subaltern, I agree. Yet this does not mean that it is deprived of an anthropological meaning we can now attempt to comprehend. Anthropologists make clear that in order to understand the "frothing and wild stare" that had already caught the attention of Darwin, we need to place this disconcerting phenomenon in its proper ritual context. If we read Marlow's account of "frenzy" against the background of contemporary anthropological accounts of "possession trance," we begin to notice that his representation of participants, dancing to the rhythm of the drum in a state of enthusiasm, rolling their eyes, clapping their hands, and stamping their feet, may have a referent in the African world he represents after all.

### Distant Observation

This does not mean that Conrad's mimetic text can simply be reduced to a transparently realistic picture of Africa. We should in fact take seriously Said's antimimetic warning not to misread *Heart of Darkness* as "just a photographic literary 'reflection.'"[21] If reflection there is, it shall not be photographic but pictorial, not fully realistic but impressionistic. Nor do I believe that an account of the "enthusiastic outbreak" that Marlow witnesses on the shore of the Congo River through the contemporary anthropological terms

of "trance" or "possession trance" diminishes the problematic dimension of
Conrad's picture. On the contrary. At this stage, Marlow's account of ritual
is predicated on ethnocentric, evolutionary assumptions that set up a multilayered hierarchical and thus still racist distance between "modern" and
"primitive" people, sane and mad subjects. Here is how Marlow reacts to the
"enthusiastic outbreak" on the shore:

> The prehistoric man was curing us, praying to us, welcoming us—who
> could tell? We were cut off from the comprehension of our surroundings;
> we glided past like phantoms, wondering and secretly appalled as sane men
> would be before an enthusiastic outbreak in a madhouse. We could not
> understand because we were too far and could not remember because we
> were travelling in the night of the first ages, of these ages that are gone,
> leaving hardly a sign—and no memories. (79)

Marlow's distance from the ritual phenomenon of possession trance he witnesses is not only physical but also temporal. Consequently, he considers this
disconcerting phenomenon as being too far removed in time to be "remem-
bered." Evolution, for Marlow, seems to have erased all the traces of memory
of such irrational, affective responses within the psychic life of modern man.
Further, following a trend that is characteristic of the first European encounters with rituals of possession trance, Marlow attempts to translate the unfamiliar anthropological phenomenon to his "modern" Victorian listeners via
the familiar medical analogy of mental pathology.[22] Thus Marlow says that
they were "secretly appalled, as sane men would be before an enthusiastic
outbreak in a madhouse." This patho-logical connection begins to establish a link between primitive man and modern man, including possession
trance within the boundaries of Europe, as it were. Yet since the mad subject
has traditionally been seen as the "other" of the subject of *Aufklärung*, this
pseudo-medical analogy rests on yet another exclusion, an internal exclusion
that ultimately maintains a distance from the primitive frenzy of the first
beginnings represented in Conrad's image of Africa.

Clearly, at this stage, Marlow's anthropology is still based on naive,
ethnocentric assumptions insofar as it does not attempt to approximate
the perspective of the other but, rather, judges the other from the point of
view of his own cultural stereotypes. We can thus understand why Conrad

scholars interested in anthropology have pointed out that Marlow's external and distant position is eventually responsible for his lack of anthropological "understanding" and "touristic" apprehension of the other.[23] These critiques are, indeed, justified and equally apply to Marlow's initial account of possession trance. At this stage, Marlow's emphasis is clearly less on proximity than on distance, less on affective participation than on distant observation. His evolutionary brand of anthropology sets up a distance from the other that is temporal, physical, psychological, as well as epistemic, a multilayered distance that seems to preclude any possibility of understanding the enigmatic ritual phenomenon he witnesses.

## Affective Participation

Let us not forget, however, that prominent anthropologists, from Malinowski to Lévi-Strauss and beyond, expressed their admiration for Conrad. And if we look closer, this admiration turns out to be justified. If we frame this description within the general structure of Marlow's narrative picture, we notice that already at this early stage the evolutionary distance Marlow initially establishes between "modern" man and "prehistoric" man turns out to be less stable than it first appears to be. That Marlow's emphasis begins to turn from visual distance to affective proximity, discontinuity to continuity, is already indicated by his reliance on the ambivalent notion of "remote kinship"—an oxymoronic notion that economically points to the Janus-faced perspective characteristic of evolutionary theory. But now Marlow is beginning to feel that the madness generated by the ritual frenzy is contagious too and can no longer be relegated to the jungle alone. For instance, the "mad helmsman" (45) on the steamer, who was receptive to animistic beliefs and practices, is particularly responsive to the "outbreak" in the background, mediating its psychosomatic effects for the other men to see in the foreground. As Marlow puts it, upon hearing the clamor of the drums, "That fool-helmsman with his hands on the spokes was lifting his knees high, stamping his feet, champing his mouth" (89). And in order to dispel any doubts that this is a mimetic response that reproduces the bodily effects triggered by the ritual of possession trance, we are told that "his eyes rolled, he kept on lifting and setting down his feet gently, his mouth foamed a little" (89–90). The helmsman is thus making visible on board the steamer in the Congo River a theoretical principle Marlow is trying to make intelligible to the Victorian listeners on board the *Nellie* in the Thames River—stretching to include modern readers as well. The narrative telos of his argument, in fact, has already begun to swing from distance to proximity, from affective discontinuity to affective continuity.[24] Changing his tonality of voice and challenging his modern listeners to acknowledge their own vulnerability to "the wild and passionate uproar" triggered by the "primitive" uproar of the first beginnings, Marlow quips to his "civil" audience:

> if you were man enough you would admit to yourself that there was in you just the faintest trace of a response to the terrible frankness of that noise, a dim suspicion of there being a meaning in it which you—you so remote from the night of the first ages—could comprehend. And why not? The mind of man is capable of anything—because everything is in it, all the past as well as all the future. (79–80)

I return to the neurological reasons why "the mind of man is capable of anything" at the end of this book. For the moment, suffice to say that this Janus-faced passage marks a radical turn in Marlow's anthropology. After setting up a racist distance from the ritual "frenzy" of "prehistoric" times, Marlow sets his evolutionary rhetoric to work in order to bring the modern "civilized" self back in touch with the mysterious affective phenomenon of possession trance he initially disavowed as an expression of savagery.[25]

Does this sound familiar? It should, for we have seen a similar rhetorical move before. The formal movement of Marlow's account of the Fang ritual of possession is strikingly reminiscent of a movement we have already encountered in Darwin's evolutionary account of the Fuegians with their "frothed" mouths. Like Darwin before him, Marlow is perfectly aware of the cultural expectations of a Victorian audience that is horrified at the thought that a possible connection may exist between their "civil" behavior and the ritual "frenzy." No wonder that Marlow is forced to deploy considerable rhetorical efforts in order to convey his counterintuitive evolutionary point: namely, that an underlying continuity does indeed exist between "us" and "them," the "civil" self-possessed listeners and the "primitive" dispossessed dancers. Further, and again like Darwin, Marlow initially emphasizes the evolutionary distance between "modern" and "primitive" subjects—a racist move that makes clear to his Victorian listeners that he is still one of them, after all—in order to better subvert, in a second moment, their theoretical expectations.

Marlow's rhetorical shift is still in line with the double movement we have seen at work in evolutionary theory. But if Darwin was concerned with establishing a *biological* continuity between primitive and modern man, and Tylor was invested in establishing a *cultural* continuity between different stages of religious practices, Conrad, via the medium of Marlow, insists on the *affective* continuity generated by the power of this ritual phenomenon, a contagious, and thus mimetic power that animates rituals of possession trance on the shore in Africa and that need to be recognized by contemporary people in Europe as well. This is an important point for Conrad, and he will return to it in other novels. In *Nostromo*, for instance, in the context of a fictional South American revolution, he speaks of "the barbarous and imposing noise of the big drum, that can madden a crowd, and that even Europeans cannot hear without a strange emotion" (126). The point is clear: the affective continuity drumming music generates transgresses the evolutionary distinctions between past and future, primitive and civilized. Unsurprisingly so. Since evolutionary theory, despite its violent hierarchy, postulates a biological unity and cultural continuity between "primitive" and "modern" man, the latter should be in a position to both respond to (biologically) and comprehend (culturally) the emotional frenzy generated (affectively) by the phenomenon of possession trance. "And why not?" asks Marlow, rhetorically, since "all the past as well as all the future" is in the mind of human beings.

Marlow is here beginning to draw the antievolutionary implications internal to his evolutionary account of mimetic frenzy. Namely, that with respect to strong affective reactions generated by the irrational ritual phenomenon that leads subjects to dance in a state of trance, so-called modern humans might not be radically different from so-called primitive humans, after all—if only because affective responses generated by the ritual "frenzy" of the African "ancestors" continue to inform the mind of modern "descendants." Such a past-oriented evolutionary view of mental development has, of course, long been cast into disrepute. And quite rightly so, for it is complicit with ethnocentric and racist accounts of "primitive cultures" I have been critiquing all along. And yet we are now in a position to see that this passage looks both ways, to the past as well as to the future.

Once again, what is true in Conrad's fiction is also true in theory. Recent discoveries in the neurosciences have in fact warned us that discarding evolutionary accounts of culture should not necessarily lead to a rejection of evolutionary accounts of the brain. Antonio Damasio, for instance, in *Descartes' Error*, writes that "it is intriguing to find the shadow of our evolutionary path at the most distinctly human level of mental function."[26] The shadow of evolution, it seems, continues to leave traces on our brain. Later in the book Damasio confirms that this shadow cannot easily be detached from mimetic reactions that are not under the volitional control of consciousness, thereby providing empirical support for the hypothesis of the mimetic unconscious. As he puts it: "At a nonconscious level, networks in the prefrontal cortex automatically and involuntarily respond to signals arising from the processing of the above images. . . . much perception and thinking is prior to consciousness, even without introducing a repression hypothesis to make that point."[27] To be sure, Victorian listeners/readers are not inclined to follow Marlow/Conrad down this (r)evolutionary path. And in an ironic turn, which is perfectly in line with the (anti-)evolutionary implications of Marlow's/Conrad's affirmations, they express their rejection of such an anthropological hypothesis with a "grunt." In a characteristic, ironic twist, Conrad turns an animal-like expression to diagnostic use: such civil grunts, in fact, perfectly confirm the power of the mimetic unconscious to respond automatically, thereby showing how "sedimented 'memory traces' . . . can affect thinking and judgment without themselves being articulable."[28] What is clear, then, is that the unflattering picture of the ritual of possession trance Conrad has been sketching thus far—with Marlow as a brush as it were—begins to function in a disturbing, self-referential way. And what we begin to see is that looking back to evolutionary theory with a critical eye attentive to its racist bias allows us to look ahead to mimetic traces of evolution that, whether we like it or not, are still very much with us.

Now, if we do not let go of Conrad's anthropological account of rituals we notice that as Marlow's journey progresses toward Kurtz, into what is enigmatically called the "heart of darkness," he continues to rely on evolutionary assumptions in order to frame his representation of racial difference. But if his initial emphasis was on temporal and cultural distance and this distance subsequently shifted toward a more ambivalent double-movement toward/away from the primitive other, in the final section the narrative radically turns, implicating the "civilized" subject into the "primordial" frenzy of the "first beginnings" Marlow initially seemed to disavow. In fact, it becomes progressively clear that the question of possession trance—and the dispossession of the self that ensues—cannot be limited to archaic, "primitive" people representative of "prehistoric times." Rather, it stretches in order to affect modern European souls as well—and in horrifying ways.

Too much has been said about Conrad's image of Africa, yes. But this image is actually a carefully crafted artistic picture. We are now beginning to see that Conrad's picture of Africa, not unlike Wilde's picture of Dorian, is not without effects of self-recognition, a mimetic recognition that continues to blur the hierarchical difference between "primitive" and "civilized," the picture of African frenzy and its uncanny European referent.

## The Music of Trance

Despite the impressive amount of critical commentary that *Heart of Darkness* continued to generate in the twentieth century, there are shadows that have been left for the twenty-first century to illuminate. Crucial to this illumination is the following structural point: Conrad is careful to frame Marlow's final encounter with Kurtz against the background of the ritual frenzy we have already encountered, suggesting that the culminating events of his tale must be understood in a relation of formal continuity with the religious anthropology that informs the tale from beginning to end. This continuity is especially clear if we consider the passage that immediately precedes Marlow's final confrontation with Kurtz and the "culminating point of his experience" it entails. The passage should now ring a bell:

> The monotonous beating of a big drum filled the air with muffled shocks
> and a lingering vibration. A steady droning sound of many men chanting
> each to himself some weird incantation came out from the black flat wall
> of the woods as the humming of bees comes out of a hive, and had a strange
> narcotic effect upon my half-awake senses. I believe I dozed off leaning
> over the rail till an abrupt burst of yells, and overwhelming outbreak of a
> pent up and a mysterious frenzy, woke me up in a bewildered wonder. (111)

That we are confronted with a structural repetition is clear. The same biological and cultural evolutionary assumptions are in place; the same rhythmic instrument is in the background; the same terminology ("outbreak," "burst of yells," "frenzy," and so forth) emerges in order to account for this mysterious ritual phenomenon. This repetition calls attention to itself and strongly suggests that the two accounts of ritual "frenzy" must be read as part of the same narrative sequence, a sequence that is continuously haunted by the ritual "clamour" in the background. Further, this passage indicates that Marlow's fascination with the ritual phenomenon of possession trance was not an isolated, punctual instance but, rather, punctuates the climax and driving telos of his tale: namely, his encounter with his atavistic homo duplex, Mr. Kurtz—an indication that the anthropology of possession trance frames not only Marlow's encounter with the other but also his encounter with a picture of the self.

## Ritual Echoes

What, then, is the function of this structural repetition? And why does Conrad take the trouble to establish a ritual continuity in the background of his already densely textured picture of Africa? We could say that via this echo, Marlow offers his listeners, and Conrad his readers (and occasional listeners),[29] a second chance to get an insight into that "incomprehensible" ritual phenomenon his civil audience initially disavowed with a not-so-civil "grunt." Yet this is a repetition with a difference, for Marlow radically diminishes the evolutionary layers of distance he had previously set up. The enthusiastic frenzy Marlow had initially perceived from a physical, temporal, moral, and methodological distance, as a vestige of the "prehistoric" past, is now experienced, felt by the modern subject himself, a subject who, we are told, "responds" to the affective "frankness" of this ritual "noise." And why not? After all, this affective response is perfectly in line with Marlow's evolutionary assumption that "everything" is in the mind of modern men. Conversely, if we have seen that evolutionary theory frames Marlow's picture of the other, we are now in a position to see that the opposite is also true and that an affective, inner experience informs his particular brand of religious anthropology—a paradoxical kind of evolutionary anthropology that no longer emphasizes temporal distance, but affective proximity instead.

Marlow's affective implication in the ritual phenomenon he describes does not diminish the anthropological interest of his picture of Africa. On the contrary, it marks a theoretical progress in his understanding of the slippery ritual phenomenon in the background. The internal narrator, in fact, no longer occupies the position of the external "observer," the "tourist" who considers the primitive other from a "distance," but, rather, approximates, if not the position of the participant anthropologist, at least the one of the moved bystander who is affectively—with his whole body, and thus with his whole soul—involved in the phenomenon he describes. Marlow's perspective is, indeed, in line with James Clifford's account of "new ethnographic subjectivity" characterized by what he calls "a state of being in culture while looking at culture."[30] And as contemporary anthropologists often point out, this shift of emphasis from an exterior to an interior perspective is crucial to take hold of an elusive phenomenon like possession trance whose meaning, by definition, cannot be fully comprehended from without.[31]

We should thus not be surprised to see that Marlow's affective response gives him a new insight into the ritual frenzy he had previously defined as "incomprehensible," sharpening his anthropological understanding of the complex relation that exists between music and trance. Marlow had already insisted on the importance of nightlong ritual drumming that would last "till the first break of day" (79), as well as of collective dancing and singing for the ritual frenzy to ensue.[32] But this time he demonstrates a much more nuanced, sensorial awareness of the psychosomatic effects of what I later call Dionysian music on his sensorium. Thus he stresses the "monotonous" beat, the "shocks," the "lingering vibration," as well as the association between "the throb of drums" and the "drone of weird incantations," deliberately selecting a lexical field that attempts to translate on the page the affective "response" to what he had previously called "the frankness of that noise." Marlow's affective participation, then, allows him, if not to fully understand, at least to feel that the ritual music is endowed with a psychosomatic power to induce an altered state of consciousness akin to trance. As he admits, this "weird incantation . . . had a strange narcotic effect upon [his] half-awake senses." Moreover, the passage makes clear that it is precisely in a state of half-sleep (or hypnotic trance), triggered by his proximity to the "narcotic" rhythm of the drum, that Marlow responds to the mysterious "frenzy" (or possession trance) he had previously described from a visual distance. This association suggests that the ritual "noise," whose meaning he could not communicate to his listeners through language, can be communicated quite directly to him—through mimetic contagion. In sum, Conrad, via Marlow, gestures toward the anthropological realization that in matters of possession trance, no clear-cut distinctions can be made between the medium of communication (trance) and the message to be communicated (trance)—perhaps because the (mimetic) medium *is* the (mimetic) message.

Could it be, then, that the elusive message *Heart of Darkness* is trying to mediate is inextricably intertwined with the experience of possession trance generated by the ritual drums in the background? What is sure at this stage is that the affective communication implicates the narrator himself and goes, quite literally, to the heart of the inner experience he is trying to communicate. After acknowledging his affective response to the intoxicating noise of the drums, Marlow specifies: "And I remember I confounded the beat of the drum with the beating of my heart and was pleased at its calm regularity" (112). The drum that is beating in the heart of darkness and is responsible for the ritual trance in the background is now literally confounded with the heart of the protagonist in the foreground; an experience that is initially projected onto the African other is now located at the heart of the European protagonist. This is, indeed, an interesting avowal in a text titled *Heart of Darkness*.

What are the origins of this primal fascination for this rhythmic beat, and wherein lies its power of affection? Marlow's inner experience points toward an anthropological hypothesis concerning the musical power of drums to induce an altered state of consciousness. There might even be a theory of the origins of music, embryonic in this scene. The analogy between the beat of the drum and the beat of the heart indicates that the former's affective power derives from its reproduction of the rhythmic sound of the heart: namely, a sound that is familiar to humans even before birth and must have a tranquilizing, hypnotic, suggestive effect on the psychic life of the (unborn) subject due to its rhythmic "regularity." This is perhaps the reason why the rhythm of drums beating continues to affect the subject after birth so profoundly, inducing different psychosomatic effects that are in tune, so to speak, with this beat.

A mimetic theorist can be convoked to sound this hypothesis. In a fascinating lecture on the origins of music addressed to children, Lacoue-Labarthe develops an embryonic hypothesis of the birth of music out of the "echo" of the maternal voice heard already in her womb. "And so," he says, in a characteristically oral tone, "like all arts according to the Greeks, music attempts to imitate something heard *before* [birth]:" namely the voice of the mother. "Music, then, would attempt to find this thing, to become its echo. . . . What I want to say is that if music exists, it is in order to re-find [*retrouver*] this first, very first, emotion."[33] Conrad's *Heart of Darkness* is in tune with this embryonic hypothesis; it even contributes to giving it a push. How? By making us hear that it is not only the maternal voice that gives birth to music, but something darker, rhythmic, and impenetrably profound: the beating of her heart. This hypothesis helps us understand why rhythmic music has such a deep effect on Marlow's sensorium, generating an affect (*émotion*) that dispossesses the subject of its ego (*moi*), that is, an é-*moi*, to echo Lacoue-Labarthe. Hence we are told that a regular, monotonous rhythm generates a "narcotic" effect on Marlow's senses, while a stimulating, intoxicating beat generates a state of enthusiastic "frenzy." This is perhaps also the reason why the hypnotic power of the drum not only affects Marlow's "senses" and "heart" but also serves to frame what he calls "the culminating point of [his] experience" (47), that is, his final encounter with Kurtz and the enigmatic horror he attempts to make us see.[34] In sum, the inner experience of possession trance serves not only as a leitmotif in Conrad's tale but goes quite literally to the "heart" of the protagonist's experience and of the story he is trying to communicate. It even offers a more general thesis on the dark origins of music that accounts for resounding effects that, to this day, continue to go beyond good and evil: birth of music out of the power of the maternal heart—a feminist Nietzschean hypothesis for fine-tuned readers to both register and amplify.[35]

We are, indeed, getting closer to unveiling Conrad's picture of Africa, an enigmatic, obscure picture that ultimately urges us to reflect back on Europe—if only because the mimetic frenzy in Africa cannot be dissociated from Marlow's enigmatic encounter with his mimetic double who casts a shadow on "all Europe."

## Anthropology of the Double

Traditionally, critics interested in exploring the affective relation between Marlow and his double, Mr. Kurtz, have tended to rely on psychology in order to account for the multiple ways in which the two characters function as mirror images of each other. As Albert Guerard famously put it, this self-reflexive line of inquiry considers *Heart of Darkness* as "the night journey into the unconscious, and confrontation of an entity within the self."[36] This psychological approach helped to cast some light on both the impressionistic dimension of the tale and the disquieting mirroring effects with which we are concerned. Accordingly, Kurtz is reframed as a manifestation of Marlow's psychic life, a homo duplex who, like the picture of Dorian Gray, unveils the atavistic tendencies at the heart of the modern, "civilized" self. More recently, however, critics interested in the anthropological and political implications of Conrad's image of Africa have tended to be suspicious of such a psychological approach. Marianna Torgovnick, for instance, finds the critical emphasis on Conrad's impressionistic style and the "'psychological complexity'" it is supposed to represent problematic.[37] As she puts it, this conjunction of formalist and psychological approaches "veils not only what Kurtz was doing in Africa but also what Conrad is doing in *Heart of Darkness*."[38]

In order to unveil further the disquieting implications of Conrad's impressionistic picture one should not choose between these competing perspectives but articulate the complex interplay between the two. The complexity of *Heart of Darkness* requires an approach that is as attentive to psychological and formal matters as to the anthropological, ethical, and political questions that are already internal to the structure of the narrative. Let us thus reconsider Marlow's psychological confrontation with his European double in the foreground in light of the anthropological account of the African trance in the background, while at the same time paying careful attention to the aesthetic form of Conrad's picture. F. R. Leavis was in fact right to stress, many years ago, that Conrad was "an innovator in form and method."[39] But Conrad was not typical, and his formal method transgresses national ideas about so-called "great" Western traditions. It is only if we reframe Marlow's moment of psychic self-recognition within the religious anthropology of possession trance that in-*forms* the narrative as a whole—beginning, middle, and end—that we can unveil both what Marlow/Kurtz was doing in Africa and what Conrad is doing in *Heart of Darkness*.

## Ritual Leaps

We have seen that it is precisely at the moment Marlow is emotionally affected by the ritual drums and the "frenzy" (or trance) in the background that he enters an altered state of consciousness similar to a narcotic "half-sleep" (or trance) in the foreground of the narrative, and then realizes that his mimetic double (or shadow), Kurtz, vanishes in the background. This disappearance, we are told, has an inexplicable psychological and moral effect on Marlow's soul and senses. He experiences it as a "moral shock," "something monstrous, intolerable to the thought, odious to the soul" (111). Importantly, it is in this state of psychic anguish that he decides to do what he had previously refused to do—namely to "[leap] ashore" (111). The final confrontation with his (psychic) shadow, then, is not only directly triggered by the noise of the drum and the (anthropological) frenzy in the background but also takes place "behind the curtain of trees" (114) in a textual topography that is (formally) linked to the ritual mysteries of possession trance that have been animating this mythic tale all along.[40]

What, then, does this curtain veil? Anthropologists interested in "possession trance" tell us that this ritual phenomenon is traditionally conceived in terms of a loss of the soul, a soul that is possessed by another (usually a god or a spirit), as well as with an attempt to regain this soul in a ritualized, religious context. It is thus perhaps no accident that Marlow consistently associates Kurtz with the notion of "soul." We are told that Kurtz was an "unlawful soul" (113), that his "soul was mad," that "he pronounced judgment upon the adventures of his soul" (117), that he was "a mystery of a soul that knew no restraint" (114). And Marlow exclaims, in a confessional mood: "Soul! If anybody had ever struggled with a soul I am the man" (113). Could it be, then, that Marlow's enigmatic confrontation with his mimetic double, not unlike Dorian's encounter with his uncanny picture, actually entails a confrontation with his own perverted, degenerate, atavistic soul? That is, a soul that he has lost—perhaps by taking part in "ceremonies of some devilish initiation" (93) or "midnight dances ending with unspeakable rites" (95)—and that he is now struggling to regain, via another initiatory ritual that generates a state of possession trance at the very culminating point of his journey? The shape of the protean shadow I am outlining constantly changes, yet Conrad's diagnostic of mimetic pathos remains double: it is in an engagement with possession trance that we find both the problem and the solution to the problem; the pathology and the patho(-)logy are two sides of the same (dis)possession.

## (Dis)Possession

To confirm this mimetic hypothesis, let us take a closer look at Marlow's impressionistic and notoriously opaque account of his homo duplex. This enigmatic figure is not only consistently linked to the animistic concept of "soul" but is also described in ethereal, ghostly terms that do not apply to a realistic character. Kurtz is consistently defined as a "shadow" or "phantom." He is compared to "an initiated wraith" (95), "something altogether without a substance" (92), "hollow at the core" (104), and Marlow goes as far as comparing him to "a vapour exhaled by the earth" (112). These are, indeed, opaque, impressionistic, perhaps even surreal descriptions, and, over the years, they have not failed to spark controversy in Conrad studies. Famously conceived as representative of Conrad's stylistic failure (F. R. Leavis), they are most often read in terms of his impressionistic achievement (Watt), and, more recently, they have been dismissed, once again, as an expression of "vaporish posturings" (Torgovnick). Now, rather than going around in circles, we could adopt a different perspective. If we reconsider these descriptions from the angle of Conrad's religious anthropology in the background that gives *form* to the representations in the foreground, we notice that *style* is perhaps not the only issue here.

These vague descriptions acquire a more transparent cultural meaning if we read them in the light of what anthropologists of religion have been saying all along. James Frazer, for instance, in his chapter titled "The Nature of the Soul" in *The Golden Bough*, which builds on Tylor's account of animism, already insisted that the savage mind often "regards his shadow or reflection as his soul."[41] Along similar lines, Émile Durkheim, in his account of Tylor in *The Elementary Forms of Religious Life*, specifies that "in each of us there is a double, another self, which under certain conditions has the power to leave the body it lives in and to go wandering. . . . This double is the soul."[42] And here is how E. B. Tylor himself, in *Primitive Culture*, describes the "ghost-soul" among "primitive cultures" that practice animism. The soul, Tylor writes, is conceived as "a thin unsubstantial human image, in its nature a sort of vapour, film, or shadow." And he adds: "mostly impalpable and invisible, yet also manifesting physical power, and especially appearing to men waking or asleep as a phantasm separate from the body of which it bears the likeness; able to enter into, possess, and act in the bodies of other men, of animals and even of things."[43] A "vapour," "shadow," or "phantom," a "thin" figure endowed with "physical power" to "posses" others. Far from being an expression of the "vagueness of Marlow's style," this sounds like a literal description of the soul traditionally conceived by native societies that rely on animistic rituals of possession trance: namely, rituals that are constitutive of the formal structure of *Heart of Darkness* and that Conrad has been sketching in the background from the very beginning of his tale. The picture of the homo duplex is beginning to take the following form: Kurtz neither as a real character nor simply as psychic characterization of Marlow's double but, rather, Kurtz as an anthropomorphic manifestation of Marlow's soul, a soul that has been lost by participating in mysterious rituals of possession trance and that he tries to recuperate via an initiatory journey that culminates in possession trance. We are beginning to sense it: trance, just like mimesis, has patho(-)logical properties, if only because the remedy for dispossession can be found in reenactment of a ritual of possession.

From an anthropological perspective that is as attentive to the rituals of possession trance in the background as to their psychic effects on Marlow's mind in the foreground, this realization should not come as a surprise. The culminating point of Marlow's experience is, in fact, shot through narrative elements that are notoriously obscure, yet acquire a much clearer meaning if considered against the background of the anthropology of music and trance that Conrad has been sketching all along. We are told that Kurtz vanishes precisely at the moment Marlow is under the "narcotic" effect of the drum responsible for a ritual "frenzy" that takes possession of the "crowd of obedient worshippers" (121). We are also told that Marlow, this time, "[leaps] ashore," perhaps for a dance and a howl, he does not say. What he does say is that he is "acutely conscious all the time" (114) of the ritual drumming in the background and the frenzy it generates. He finds himself in an altered state of consciousness in which he is "strangely cocksure of everything"; "chuckles to himself"; has enigmatic, hallucinatory flashbacks; and, during a musical

inner experience that sounds the unspeakable, but quite audible, musical origins of *Heart of Darkness*, goes as far as confounding the "beat of the drum
with the beating of [his] heart" (112). And in order to make absolutely clear
that this culminating scene should be understood in the context of a ritual
of possession trance, Conrad even inserts a direct allusion to a shamanistic
figure who presides over Marlow's ritual confrontation with Kurtz: "A black
figure stood up . . . it had horns—antelope horns, I think, on its head. Some
sorcerer, some witch man, no doubt" (112).[44] Finally, as Marlow finally takes
possession of (t)his soul, we are told that he tries to "break the spell" that ties
his double, Kurtz (or the "soul" he struggles with), to—what? Neither to
"his ivory" nor to "his station" or "his career" foregrounded in the narrative
but, rather, to his "less material aspirations" linked to what Marlow has been
hearing all along: namely, the "throb of the drums" and the ritual "frenzy"
characteristic of possession trance in the background. Rhythmic music, ritual
dances, altered state of consciousness, hypnotic spells, shamanic sorcerers,
and the (dis)possession of the soul triggered by the throb of the drums—
everything framed by ritual "mysteries" that "fought for the possession of
that soul" (115–16): Conrad's style might be misty at the edges, and this mist
has led many critics astray. But his formal delineation of the heart of the tale
is illuminating nonetheless. We are now in a position to see that Conrad has,
in fact, been carefully framing Marlow's final encounter with Kurtz against
the background of religious anthropology he has been preparing his listeners
for from the very beginning of his tale, that is, an anthropology resting on a
mimetic patho(-)logy that informs his oeuvre as a whole.

   With this general frame in mind, this dark picture is now getting clearer.
If we scrutinize this impressionistic tableau in the light of the anthropology
of possession trance that is already internal to the text, Conrad's "vaporish"
descriptions do not so much veil as unveil both what Marlow/Kurtz was
doing in Africa and what Conrad is doing in *Heart of Darkness*. What this
text reveals is a fundamental vulnerability at the heart of the modern "civilized" self to violent states of entranced (dis)possession the West disavows
and projects onto "primitive others." Speaking of the "spell" responsible for
the awakening of Kurtz's "monstrous passions," Marlow diagnoses: "This
alone, I was convinced, had driven him out to the edge of the forest, to the
bush, towards the gleam of fires, the throb of drums, the drone of weird
incantations; this alone had beguiled his unlawful soul beyond the bounds of

permitted aspirations" (113). We can now understand why Marlow had previously warned his listeners against the power of "primitive" forms of ritual frenzy to affect the mind of modern, "civilized" man.[45] What he discovers at the heart of darkness is not only that the evolutionary line dividing "modern" man from "primitive" man is actually a shadow-line permeable to the power of mimetic (dis)possession. He also finds out that the exposure to "primitive" forms of ritual possession that generate pathos entails a dispossession of the soul responsible for a regression to European "savagery" and moral "degradation." Indeed, the culminating point of Marlow's experience emerges from a causal connection between the much-discussed sacrificial horrors at the heart of the tale, on the one hand, and the so far unnoticed experience of possession trance that frames such a tale, on the other. The formal connection is direct, Conrad's diagnosis precise. It is, in fact, because Kurtz—and Marlow through him—is, quite literally, spellbound by musical rituals that have the power to induce an altered state of consciousness (or trance) that sacrificial horrors generated in the context of "midnight dances" ensue. It is thus no accident that back in Europe, Marlow, thinking of Kurtz, will recall—and now the echo should be loud and clear—"the beat of the drum regular and muffled like the beating of a heart, the heart of a conquering darkness" (121). Having registered the palpitating beat of *Heart of Darkness*, it is now time to formulate a preliminary critical diagnostic. At the center of *Heart of Darkness* is the experience of possession trance; the loss of the soul that ensues from such a mimetic (dis)possession is the beating heart of what Conrad calls "the horror."

And yet this picture of Africa is not without mirroring inversions of perspectives that have broader theoretical implications that have their origins in the text but cast a shadow on the real world as well. Let us in fact recall that while the experience of possession trance is set at the heart of Africa, the horrors that the texts reveals are not the horrors of "primitive" subjects— "restraint" rather than savagery defines them. Instead, the horrors are embedded in "civilized" European souls—savagery rather than progress defines them. As Marlow puts it, it is Kurtz himself who is endowed with the "power to charm or frighten rudimentary souls into an aggravated witch-dance in his honour" (50), not vice versa. In other words, the self-reflexive turn in Marlow's particular brand of evolutionary anthropology is concerned with exposing the fragility of the moral and psychic foundations of the modern soul once the boundaries of culture (with its police, neighbors, and public opinion) are stripped away. And what we find at the heart of modern, civilized man is a "hollow" man, a subject "without a substance," a secret "shadow" who is responsible for staging "midnight dances" that culminate in sacrificial bloodshed. This picture is thus not only personal and psychological but also collective and anthropological; it is not only about the violence of racist representations but also about the violence of the sacred itself.

## The Violence of the Sacred

We have seen that our understanding of Conrad's tales benefits from critically engaging with Girard's thought, just as mimetic theory gains from Conrad's diagnostic insights into the Janus-faced patho(-)logies of mimetic processes. This is equally true for *Heart of Darkness*, a text that dramatizes many of the anthropological insights that are central to Girard's mimetic theory: from mimetic doubles to ritual violence, the crisis of difference to sacrificial scapegoats, it is indeed possible to frame the trajectory of Marlow's evolutionary account of sacred rituals within Girard's structural model of mimesis. This connection has been noticed and explored before,[46] but it has not been sufficiently stressed that both Conrad's and Girard's anthropology of religion rests on shared theoretical foundations. Not only is Girard's theory of mimesis in line with anthropological figures such as E. B. Tylor and James Frazer, which we have seen animating Conrad's tale, but he also considers his approach as a cultural offshoot of Darwin's evolutionary theory, which equally informs Conrad's anthropology. As Girard puts it, he "always tried to think within an evolutionary framework," for the driving ambition of mimetic theory is to provide what Girard calls an "evolutionary interpretation to human culture."[47] But the evolutionary connection between Conrad and Girard cuts even deeper. It touches on the very rituals of possession trance, which, I am arguing, serve as the driving telos of *Heart of Darkness*. Girard's evolutionary approach to trance, not unlike Conrad's, is Janus-faced and has both progressive and regressive implications. A mirroring confrontation between these two advocates of mimetic theory is thus in order to articulate the continuities and discontinuities between their respective approaches to mimetic forms of (dis)possession.

## From Mimetic Doubles to Monstrous Possession

Girard's short but penetrating account of possession trance appears in *Violence and the Sacred* in a chapter titled "From Mimetic Desire to the Monstrous Double."[48] As this title suggests, this chapter joins Girard's previous literary investigations in the mimetic structure of human desire with his anthropological analyses of monstrous rituals whose social function is to channel the frenzy of mimetic violence against a sacrificial victim or scapegoat. Less visibly, but equally fundamentally, this chapter also joins the synchronic and diachronic sides of Girard's theory. There are thus two sides to Girard's mimetic hypothesis that need to be briefly and schematically disentangled.

On the one hand, Girard sets out to reframe classical anthropological accounts of possession within the alienating structure of mimetic desire and the monstrous doubling of identity it entails. As he puts it, "The condition called 'possession' is in fact but one particular interpretation of the monstrous double. . . . The [possessed] subject feels that the most intimate regions of his being have been invaded by a supernatural creature who also besieges him without" (*VS* 165). Girard's logic is associative and comparative rather than empirical and ethnographic. It could be summarized as follows: just as the mimetic subject who is under the influence of a model is alienated in his desire, the mimetic logic goes, so the possessed subject who is under the influence of a god is alienated in his soul. Hence Girard says: "Possession, then, is an extreme form of alienation in which the subject totally absorbs the desires of another" (165). This is an elegant theoretical solution to the riddle of possession. Structural in its analogical orientation, this hypothesis allows Girard to capture a slippery collective phenomenon of possession trance within the familiar intersubjective structure of mimetic desire. For Girard, then, the "hysterical mimesis" (165), or frenzy, characteristic of ritual possession is not primarily a ritual, musical, or group phenomenon, as Conrad suggested. Rather, it can be brought back to an analysis of the ego, the double, and the alienation of desire that entails. Thus the crowd becomes a triangle; the pathos of (dis)possession becomes an hysterical identification. This is a move that departs, in original ways, from the standard anthropology of trance, but is not without psychological antecedents. It is actually strikingly reminiscent of Sigmund Freud's account of "group psychology"— which Girard will discuss in detail in a following chapter—in the sense that in both cases a collective, hysterical ritual phenomenon is framed within a familial, rivalrous dynamic; irrational fluxes of mimetic frenzy that tend to vary historically are thus channeled within a rational synchronic triangular structure.[49] The comparison is intriguing and suggestive, but as they say in France, *comparaison n'est pas raison.*[50]

On the other hand, Girard turns to consider the ritual origins of possession by adding a diachronic, evolutionary layer to his structural hypothesis. Thus he specifies: "The existence of a ritual form of possession implies that something in the nature of an intense case of collective possession took place *initially* [la première fois]," and adds that "ritual possession is inseparable at first from the sacrificial rituals that serves as its culmination" (166; trans. modified). This is once again an original hypothesis in the sense that it goes against contemporary anthropological accounts of possession by positing an unverifiable sacrificial murder at the origins of culture, a murder that is subsequently reproduced for its cathartic effects. But again, this hypothesis is not without mimetic precedents. As Girard readily acknowledges later on, Freud, this time in *Totem and Taboo*, builds on anthropological figures such as James Frazer to posit the hypothesis that an initial and unverifiable murder of the father generated the rivalrous logic of desire. It would be useless to deny it: Girard's theory of possession, in both its synchronic and diachronic dimensions, is of Freudian and, thus, Oedipal inspiration. The underlying parallels could be extended further, especially since specialists of ritual studies have now situated Girard's theory of sacrifice within a wider nineteenth-century genealogy of anthropologists of religion that goes from Frazer to Freud.[51] I return to this tradition in part 3. For the moment, suffice to say that on the shoulders of Freud, much more than of Darwin, Girard's account of possession trance looks back to the hypothesis of the violent, sacrificial "origins" of culture, and, by doing so, he looks ahead to forms of mimetic violence that are present across cultures, are still with us, and, as we have seen, might lead to apocalyptic ends. *Comparaison n'est pas raison*, yet it reveals a mimetic logic of its own.

Now, there is much in this Janus-faced hypothesis that finds a fictional confirmation in *Heart of Darkness*, unsurprisingly since the links between Conrad and psychoanalysis, as so many have noticed, can be uncanny. Conrad's insistence on Marlow's mimetic identification with his monstrous double, Kurtz; their rivalrous confrontation; Marlow's strange infatuation with

Kurtz's girlfriend, and, closer to our anthropological preoccupations, the presence of sacrificial victims, collective rituals, and the possession trance at the culminating point of his experience fit Girard's mimetic hypothesis concerning the homo duplex qua scapegoat. This hypothesis is confirmed if we recall that there is in fact a "murder-plot"[52] at the heart of the tale. The Manager, in fact, slows down Marlow's efforts to repair the steamer by not delivering the rivets he needs, a calculated move intended to eliminate Kurtz, who is already sick, and take his much-desired place in an outpost of regress. As the Manager says, speaking of the Harlequin but with Kurtz as the ultimate sacrificial victim in mind: "We will not be free from the unfair competition till one of these fellows is hanged for an example" (*YOS* 75). And his uncle replies: "Get him hanged! Why not? Anything—anything can be done in this country" (75). In this sense, Kurtz occupies simultaneously the role of "monstrous double" and of "sacrificial scapegoat," thereby embodying the ambivalence of the *pharmakos*. Marlow's dispossession of his soul would thus be a consequence of his mimetic identification with his rivalrous double and the alienation of desire it entails. Hence the ritual of possession at the heart of his inner experience becomes inseparable from the sacrificial rituals at the heart of Kurtz's anthropological experience. Thus reframed, *Heart of Darkness* culminates in a mimetic experience of dispossession that can be inscribed within a sacrificial trajectory that goes from the violent horror of our origins to the violence of our possible destination.[53] In this general sense, Girard's mimetic theory and Conrad's mimetic fiction look in the same direction.

## Conrad's Secular Difference

But in another, more specific sense, Conrad also looks in a different direction and offers a possibility for further theoretical reflections. As I have been arguing so far, Conrad remains important for us today not simply because his fictions confirm mimetic hypotheses about our past but also, and more important, because mimetic theory finds in Conrad's fictions further insights for the future. If we do not let go of Girard's major insight that great novelists tell us more about mimesis than theorists themselves, then we should take seriously the theoretical potential of Conrad's (anti-)evolutionary assumptions, especially since the goal of Conrad's dark narrative is to "make us *see*," which is, of course, also the original meaning of theory itself—*theorein* from Greek, to see.

Let us thus not lose sight of Conrad's picture of Europe and the mirroring inversions it generates. As we have seen, Conrad's narrative trajectory emphasizes the collective and nonviolent dimension of African rituals from the outset (musical dances, not sacrifice, define them), suggesting that the violent sacrificial culmination is a product of European (not African) mimetic desires that are violently imported on colonial soil to carry out mimetic forms of dispossession on a massive scale. From this perspective, Kurtz is less a sacrificial victim (or scapegoat) than an authoritarian oppressor and perpetrator of sacrificial horrors—as the decapitated heads on the stakes in front of his hut clearly make visible. But it is not only Conrad's critique of colonial politics that complicates evolutionary accounts of (dis)possession. The religion used to justify such "civilizing missions" is subjected to a similar critique, too. Conrad's "dislike" of Christian religion is well known.[54] In this sense, Conrad's anthropology of religion firmly parts ways from Girard's view that "archaic religions [function] as a prior moment in a progressive revelation that culminates in Christ."[55] Instead, in *Heart of Darkness* Conrad offers an a-theological perspective that inverses the telos of Christian metanarratives of progress. Marlow not only speaks of the "dustbin of progress" (*YOS* 96). He also speaks ironically of Kurtz as "an emissary of pity and science, and progress, and devil knows what else" (67). Similarly, the enthusiastic aunt who is responsible for securing Marlow's colonial position and considers him an "emissary of light, something like a lower sort of apostle," is also a faithful proponent of "weaning those ignorant millions from their horrid ways" (53). Conrad is, of course, painfully aware that ideological appropriations of Christianity are at the heart of "civilizing missions." King Leopold II of Belgium had in fact infamously stated that the goal of his invasion of the Congo was to "open to civilization the only part of our globe where Christianity has not yet penetrated and to pierce the darkness which envelops the entire population."[56] As Conrad sets out, in a mirroring move, to envelop his tale with light, darkness turns out to be as religious as it is political, as sacred as it is profane—two sides of the same mission, so to speak. In sum, the driving telos of *Heart of Darkness* makes strikingly clear that both sacrifice and Christianity are part of the problem of violence rather than its solution; they do not lead to cultural evolution, but serve as an ideological mask to cover up the horrors generated by the ideologies of progress.

And yet this does not mean that Conrad's theoretical insights into possession trance are inimical to mimetic theory, as I understand it. Girard, for one, has not been silent on the historical process that led the Christian world to turn disempowered "minorities" into sacrificial scapegoats—from the burning of witches to colonial exploitations to the massacre of Jews.[57] In this antievolutionary sense, Girard's lesson about the violence of the sacred and the horrors that ensue has not lost any of its timeliness. If it foreshadows the "horrorism" of contemporary terrorism I discuss later, it also resonates with another profound thinker of mimesis who has tended to remain in the shadow of mimetic theory so far and deserves to be brought into the foreground. After a career spent ruminating on the problematic of mimesis, Philippe Lacoue-Labarthe also recognized that at the heart of the West is the horror of sacrificial dispossession. Conrad's *Heart of Darkness* played a crucial role in this philosophical realization. For Lacoue-Labarthe, in fact, Kurtz is not only a scapegoat or a sacrificial victim but a symbol of Europe, for he takes seriously the claim that "all Europe contributed to the making of Kurtz" (*YOS* 95). This also means that Conrad's image of Africa is not simply a reflection of what Achebe calls the "break-up of one pretty European mind" (IA 344). It is also a critical reflection of Europe that urges us to reflect on the larger political horrors that are ultimately of the West.

## Reflecting (on) the West

In a groundbreaking article titled "The Horror of the West" ["*L'horreur occidentale*"], that already received an echo of critical responses,[58] Lacoue-Labarthe offers us a last mimetic insight into *Heart of Darkness* that allows us to complete our reflection on Conrad's picture of Europe. The French philosopher implicitly agrees with Achebe that *Heart of Darkness* is a mythic text, but, contrary to Achebe, he does not question the theoretical value of Conrad's mythic imagination. On the contrary, he calls Conrad's mythic tale "one of the greatest texts of Western literature" (HW 111). Nor does he suggest that this "myth" is about Africa. On the contrary, he says that what is at stake in Conrad's myth is nothing less than the "entire destiny of the

West" (113). As he puts it, in a dense theoretical passage that sums up his philosophical thesis:

> The myth of the West, which this narrative [*récit*] recapitulates (but only in order to signify that the West is a myth), *is*, literally, the thought of the West, is that which the West "narrates" about what it must necessarily think of itself, namely—though you know this already, you have read these pages—that the West is the *horror*. (112)

For Lacoue-Labarthe, then, what Conrad's mythic tale reveals is not the horror of primitive images of Africa but "the horror of the West" instead. What does this striking phrase mean? I have already offered a preliminary explanation elsewhere, but since this thesis remains untimely, not only for the politics it entails but also, and above all, for the ontology that informs it, let me reiterate a fundamental point. When Lacoue-Labarthe speaks of "the West," he certainly does not mean to designate a geographical location commonly restricted to the political boundaries of Europe and the United States in whose name horrors are routinely carried out—though Conrad's insight that "all Europe contributed to the making of Kurtz" is constitutive of what Lacoue-Labarthe calls "the horror of the West." Rather, as a formidable commentator of Plato, Aristotle, Diderot, Nietzsche, Heidegger, and many other figures in Western philosophy, Lacoue-Labarthe has something quite specific in mind as he speaks of "*the thought* of the West": namely, a Western philosophical tradition that starts with the ancient Greeks, is recuperated by the moderns, and, via the imitation of the modernists, continues to inform contemporary thought, art, and politics along lines that go well beyond the political boundaries of the West, yet generates horrors nonetheless. Consequently, any critical engagement with Lacoue-Labarthe's concept of "the West" needs to start by reinscribing this concept in the philosophical tradition of thought from which this concept emerges.[59]

Once this is done, we are better placed to hear Lacoue-Labarthe's thesis and to provide an anthropological echo to it. This thesis states, in a nutshell, that *Heart of Darkness* reveals the horror of mimetic forms of (dis)possession that generate a "void" at the heart of the subject, a mimetic subject who is so dispossessed of proper identity that, for Lacoue-Labarthe, he is quite literally "no one [*personne*]" (116). This, you will remember, is also Lacoue-Labarthe's answer to the question, "who comes after the subject?" Kurtz, a "shadow" or "phantom" who is "hollow at the core," is, for Lacoue-Labarthe, a mimetic avatar of the figure who comes after the subject. But we are now in a position to hear echoes of larger ethico-political preoccupations that go beyond, or better "beneath," the metaphysics of the subject. Lacoue-Labarthe's fundamental claim, in fact, is that as the modern, depersonalized subject of the crowd participates in collective rituals and capitulates to the power of charismatic leader figures à la Kurtz endowed with a charismatic "voice" whose intention is to "exterminate all the brutes" (*YOS* 50), the horror of the West is not far from being enacted. More precisely, according to Lacoue-Labarthe, "through the example of colonization" (HW 117) this tale makes us see the horror of genocidal practices in the Congo; and conversely, it allows us to reflect on another genocide that relied on mythic, collective rituals to generate entranced states of dispossession at the sacrificial heart of Europe: namely, the horror of fascist and Nazi politics and the Holocaust that ensues. With a nod to Girard, Lacoue-Labarthe defines this mimetic horror as "a sort of gigantic sacrificial politics with reformative aims" (*RU* 90). And with a nod to Conrad, he echoes once again: "This is, to my eyes, the horror itself [*l'horreur même*]" (90).

## Facing the Horror

I have already commented on the psychological and philosophical implications of such horrors, but an anthropological supplement to this mimetic hypothesis is still in order. For Lacoue-Labarthe, in fact, "European imperialism" should remind us that "we go to the other in order to recognize ourselves" (*RU* 110). What we must add is that the same mirroring logic is, for better and worse, reflected in Conrad's picture of Africa. In fact, Conrad's theoretical recognition concerning forms of mimetic dispossession that culminate in "unspeakable rites" in Europe emerges from the religious anthropology that serves as the driving telos of *Heart of Darkness*. As the end of the tale is approaching, it becomes progressively clear that Conrad's anthropology concentrates on ritual forms of possession trance in Africa only in order to better reveal—in a mimetic reflection that is both specular and speculative—how such collective (mimetic) rituals continue to operate at the heart of Europe. This cross-cultural connection implies that, for Conrad, Western politics, far from representing an "outpost of progress," continues to be haunted by frenzied rituals that have traditionally been linked to archaic forms of religious practices, practices that originally had a cohesive rather than a disruptive social function. Marlow had already hinted at the political dimension of Kurtz's mimetic will to power in Africa as he focused on his charismatic voice, a voice that he described as being "loud like a hail through a speaking trumpet" (112) and is disturbingly reminiscent of a totalitarian leader figure. And as the narrative speeds toward its conclusion, it is clear that Kurtz's hypnotic power to take possession of the masses is not confined to Africa but stretches in order to include entire crowds in Europe. Once back in Europe, Marlow finds out from a journalist that "Kurtz's proper sphere ought to have been politics 'on the popular side'" (120). And he adds, "heavens! how that man could talk! He electrified large meetings. He had the faith—don't you see—he had the faith. He could get himself to believe anything—anything. He would have been a splendid leader of an extreme party'" (120).

The (anti-)evolutionary implications inherent in Conrad's religious anthropology are now clear, the echoes loud. The narrative, in fact, introduces a direct continuity between Kurtz's anthropological rituals in Africa and his political rituals in Europe, suggesting that rituals of possession can be reenacted at the heart of modern, political organization that cast a long shadow on the West. The lesson that emerges from Conrad's anthropological tale remains in line with the Janus-faced perspective that guides my investigation. In particular, it makes us see that the type of "faith" that leads someone to be possessed by an idea so profoundly to "get himself to believe anything" is not only a source of potential progress but also of possible regress.

Not a flattering picture, for sure, but can we seriously blame the painter? At this stage, Conrad's mimetic anthropology has reached a degree of self-reflexive sophistication that, as Clifford also noticed, aligns his literary project with the contemporary understanding of anthropology as a discipline that studies distant traditional societies in order to cast light on the workings of the more familiar (and thus less visible) modern societies. No wonder that anthropologists of the caliber of Malinowski and Lévi-Strauss would have liked to have written Conrad's books. A distinctive mimetic perspective offers a literary/theoretical justification for this admiration. What Conrad's anthroplogy reveals is that modern politics reenacts massive phenomena of ritual dispossession that should be thought in a relation of mimetic continuty with archaic phenomena of possession trance and thus studied through the filter of religious anthropology. This is a crucial theoretical insight. It not only anticipates the contemporary understanding of anthropology in terms of "translation of cultures" but also more recent developments in the anthropology of possession trance. Luc de Heusch, for instance, one of the leading authorities on the question of trance, concludes a recent book devoted to this subject thus: "The behaviour of the charismatic leader on the political scene is related to it [possession trance]: those who contemplate his image and listen to his voice find themselves in a state close to possession."[60] That Conrad had foreseen this fundamental connection between possession trance and totalitarian politics already at the dawn of the discipline, without the benefit of historical hindsight, testifies to the sharpness of his anthropological lenses as well as to the untimeliness of his diagnostic approach. His specific brand of mimetic theory allows him, well before the coming of fascism and Nazism, their use of mythic figures as instruments of dispossession, and the horrors that ensued, to picture Kurtz as a political "leader of an extreme party," "on the popular side," endowed with a voice "loud like a hail through a speaking trumpet" that "electrified large meetings" (*YOS* 110) in Europe and, as he says in a passage that was not included in the final version of *Heart of Darkness* but haunts the entire text nonetheless, has the power to induce the "joy of killing" in otherwise "pacific fathers."

> You know how it is when we hear the band of a regiment. A martial noise—and you pacific father, mild guardian of a domestic heart-stone [*sic*] suddenly find yourself thinking of carnage. The joy of killing—hey? Or did you never, when listening to another kind of music, did you never dream yourself capable of becoming a saint—if—if. Aha! Another noise, another appeal, another response. All there—in you.[61]

Music, we now know why, has a tremendous power of (dis)possession that cuts both ways: it not only triggers both good mimesis (saintly sympathy) and bad mimesis (sacrificial frenzy), but can easily go beyond good an evil in turning compassionate behavior into the justification for sacrificial frenzy. We are now also in a position to see that Achebe was right in claiming that poetry should be "for the brotherhood and unity of all mankind and against the doctrines of Hitler's master races" (IA 344n2). What he did not see, however, is that even on this ethico-political point, Conrad was on his side. Having lifted the veil that covers the picture, I think it is not an exaggeration to say that Conrad's prophetic picture of Europe revealed mimetic horrors that not even the most forward-looking of his contemporaries could imagine.

Has the medium managed to convey his message to his listeners? Is this picture of Europe successful in revealing to the future the horrors of mimetic dispossession that he senses coming? His repeated interrogations at the opening of the tale mask his theoretical frustration: "Do you see him? Do you see the story? Do you see anything?" (*YOS* 70). Marlow's disillusionment is justified. At crucial moments in the narrative the listeners on the *Nellie*, bureaucrats holding position of power in the colonial administration, manifest their refusal to recognize and acknowledge their own vulnerability to the experience of possession trance and to violent forms of sacrificial frenzy that ensue as the modern subject capitulates to the intoxicating power of mimesis. For Lacoue-Labarthe, this refusal to acknowledge our own implications in the horrors we continue to generate is the real horror of the West. As he succinctly puts it: "To recoil from the horror is Western *barbarity* itself" (HW 118). The horror, thus understood, is not only a reference to the political carnages that ensue from massive forms of mimetic dispossession in Europe but also to the human, all too human, disavowal of such horrors once they already have taken place. In short, the inability of Western *thought* to confront the atrocities that continue to be committed in the name of progress, freedom, religious beliefs, and democratic ideals—a rhetoric so often still used to mask regressive forms of (dis)possessing practices—*is* the horror *Heart of Darkness* attempts to render visible.

To conclude, let us cast a retrospective glance at the picture with which we started. This theoretical insight, we are now in a position to see, is already revealed by Kurtz's "sketch in oils, . . . representing a woman draped and blindfolded carrying a lighted torch" (*YOS* 67). Critics often notice that this painting is part of Conrad's suspicion of the ideology of progress embodied by the subject of *Aufklärung*, since this woman cannot see where she is going and thus understand what she is doing. After this inquiry into Conrad's mimetic anthropology, I should add that the painting, while complicit with the "mimetic sexism" I have denounced elsewhere, is also revelatory of the invisible logic informing the blindness hypnotically induced by dominant forms of ideological indoctrination. Namely, that as we bow down to either old or new beliefs that aim to confirm our cultural and moral superiority

over and against other cultures, the veil of progress and the spiritual idea(l)s
that go with it might, quite literally, blind us to our own implication in the
horrors such ideas continue to generate—for others.

.    .    .

Achebe's comparison between Conrad's "image of Africa" and Wilde's "picture of Dorian Gray" was well taken. And yet the problem with this analogy
is that it is more ambivalent than Achebe actually realized, and, as often with
mirroring tricks, it ultimately inverses what it is supposed to simply represent. Conrad's picture is, in fact, not merely an "image" (from Latin, *imago*,
copy, related to Latin *imitari*, imitate). That is, a distorted copy, or imitation
far removed from the "true" "original" reality. Rather, Conrad's literary text
is an artistically crafted picture (from Latin, *pictura*, painting, from *pingere*,
to paint), which also means that it is a product of a poetic praxis implying
the formal mastery of an art, or *techne*. In this specific Wildean sense, Conrad
sets his artistic craft to work not so much to hide but rather to reveal, via
the power of artistic *re*-presentation, the truth about the horrific side Europe
has tended to disavow and project onto others in the past. Whether we will
continue to do so in the future remains to be seen.

What we do see is that mimesis is clearly at the heart of this postcolonial quarrel, but the quarrel is not as original as postcolonial theory suggests.
There is even a secret sense in which Achebe's moral, aesthetic, and epistemic
excommunication of Conrad's mimetic "image of Africa" replicates an ancient
antimimetic gesture. Achebe's attempt to ban *Heart of Darkness* from the ideal
Western canon on the assumption that Conrad does not represent reality as
such, but a deceiving "image" of reality with mirroring effects reminiscent of
Wilde's picture of Dorian Gray, is surely not a Wildean move. Unlike Achebe,
Oscar Wilde never denounced aesthetic pictures for distorting reality or mis-
representing life. On the contrary, he considered that "Life imitates Art far
more than Art imitates Life."[62] If one were to trace the origins of this suspicion
of mimetic images based on moral grounds, other ancient (not modern) can-
didates come to mind. Given Achebe's denunciation of Conrad (or Marlow's
alter ego) as a "purveyor of comforting myths" (IA 339), one could do worse
than tracing this quarrel back to the condemnation of mimetic images at the
very origins of mimetic theory. Let us not forget that in Book X of *Republic*,
Plato (or Socrates's alter ego) attempted to ban his mimetic rival (Homer)

from the ideal republic on the assumption that "mimetic" art, and the "myths" it conveys, does not represent reality as such, but a false image, "shadow," or "imitation" (mimesis) of reality. Moreover, in Books II and III of *Republic*, in the context of a discussion of the pedagogical effects of myths, "Plato" makes clear that he wants to ban the makers of myths from the ideal polis for their damaging effects on the body politic. Myths, he says in substance, have problematic moral consequences for education (*paideia*) insofar as they offer bad examples (or types) that form the impressionable characters of children. And as he specifies in *Ion*, myths also have the power to hypnotically affect the emotions of poets, rhapsodes, and spectators alike, taking them out of themselves in an enthusiastic transport, which Plato compares to the Maenads dancing in a state of frenzy when they "launch into harmony and rhythm . . . are seized with the Bacchic transport and are possessed."[63]

Achebe's concern with mimesis is set in a radically different historical and political context, yet the rhetoric, tropes, and arguments he mobilizes become familiar when we set them under Western eyes, eyes that, like Achebe's, are familiar with Western thought. His critique of Conrad's "image" (or "myth") of Africa as far removed from reality; his diagnostic that this myth is designed to induce what he calls "hypnotic stupor" via images of "frenzy"; and his realization that this ritual frenzy leads to "reflex action" rather than critical thought is strikingly reminiscent of Plato's critique of the damaging pedagogical effects of myths in general and mimetic (dis)possessions in particular.[64] There is, indeed, a sense in which Achebe the critic offers a postcolonial twist to an ancient suspicion of images of frenzy, going as far as suggesting an exclusion of such a mythic image of Africa from the ideal canon. The analogies are so profound, the echoes so loud, that, once revealed, one cannot help but wonder: is Achebe's critique of Conrad's mythic image of Africa a Platonism for postcolonial theory?

Perhaps. Yet as both the ancients and the moderns taught us, beyond straightforward oppositions and exclusions often lies the phantom of imitation. Achebe is, in fact, not simply a critic of mimesis; he is above all an artist who is himself engaged in mimetic re-presentations. I thus let go of Conrad's picture of Europe in order to turn our gaze to Achebe's picture of Africa. And when these two opposed pictures are joined, we shall see how profoundly they both inverse and mirror each other.

# CHAPTER 5

# A Picture of Africa:
# Postcolonial Mimesis in Achebe's
# *Things Fall Apart*

The steamer toiled along slowly on the edge of a black and incomprehensible frenzy.

—Joseph Conrad, *Heart of Darkness*

Drums beat violently and men leaped up and down in frenzy.

—Chinua Achebe, *Things Fall Apart*

What is the difference between a picture of Africa and an image of Africa? Are the two the same, as their referent implies, or not quite, as their medium suggests? These are tricky questions when asked in the context of postcolonial studies. They immediately conjure two modernist artists who always tend to be considered as opponents, perhaps even rivals, certainly as antipodes: Joseph Conrad and Chinua Achebe. Despite Achebe's explicit opposition to Conrad as a critic, as an artist he might actually turn out to represent a different face of the same picture. If the previous chapter focused on critical differences, this chapter focuses on their artistic similarities. In the process, I move beyond the polarization that continues to routinely pit Conrad's image of Africa in *Heart of Darkness* (1899) against Achebe's picture of Africa in *Things Fall Apart* (1958)[1] in order to offer a less antagonistic and rivalrous, but nonetheless, mimetic reflection on the anthropological, narrative, and discursive forces that give form to Achebe's postcolonial picture of Africa—out of Conrad's colonial image.

## The Race Quarrel Revisited

As Achebe's mirroring observations on the relation between Conrad's *Heart of Darkness* and Wilde's *The Picture of Dorian Gray* had already suggested, with mirror images it is often difficult to tell the difference between the original and the copy, the referent on the side of life and its reversed counterpart on the side of art. These are, indeed, old mimetic riddles that have haunted literary theory form its very beginning, have generated virulent disciplinary quarrels, and continue to cast a shadow on the contemporary imagination. This shadow is particularly haunting in the fields of modernist studies and postcolonial studies, fields of force in constant tension whereby "mimesis," understood not as realistic "imitation" but rather as a form of narrative "mimicry" that ironically inverses what it appears to simply represent, continues to be the source of critical and theoretical disputes. Having considered Conrad's picture of Europe from an anthropological perspective, I now invite readers to go through the looking glass in order to reconsider the quarrel about images of African rituals from the other side of the spectrum. That is, from the perspective of the ritual outbreaks of mimetic "frenzy" that follow, shadowlike, Achebe's first and most influential picture of Africa, *Things Fall Apart*.

### Mirroring Reflections

In order to initiate this delicate reflection, let us begin with the mirrorlike dimension of the two epigraphs that preface this chapter. The uncanny redoubling of images of "frenzy" taken from a colonial narrative and a postcolonial counternarrative indicates that even with respect to the notion at the very heart of the race quarrel, the opposition may not always be as clear-cut as it initially appears to be; a shadowy continuity may actually exist between Conrad's image of Africa and Achebe's picture of Africa. This continuity has been recognized before, most notably by Edward Said, who, in his last interview on Conrad, suggested that "*Things Fall Apart* is unintelligible without *Heart of Darkness*."[2] In what follows, I explore this thought-provoking suggestion and take it a step further. I argue that underneath the first layer of straightforward opposition and narrative inversion, we find an underlying continuity between Conrad's colonial image of Africa and Achebe's postcolonial representation—a mimetic continuity that is especially visible when it comes to the notorious rituals of frenzied (dis)possession.

Given the loaded terms of the race debate, a focus on Achebe's novelist reproduction of the Conradian notion of "frenzy" in *Things Fall Apart* may initially appear as a provocation meant to generate even more animosity, polemics, and accusations across the postcolonial fence. I thus want to make clear at the outset that my aim is not to add more fire to what is already an incendiary debate. Nor do I intend to utter battle cries for either side, perpetuating what Said calls a "rhetoric and politics of blame."[3] Instead, I suggest that in our globalized, hybrid, and plural world, taking sides may no longer be the most productive way to approach such burning issues. I thus propose a more nuanced and, hopefully, more balanced approach to the race quarrel that considers both the inversions and continuities between Conrad's and Achebe's mirroring pictures. The relation between these two authors is, in fact, not only one of opposition and rivalry; it is also revealing of a mimetic logic that transgresses a dichotomizing system of representation based on neat distinctions between dominant and subordinate, colonial and postcolonial pictures. The goal, then, is not to mimetically reproduce ad hominem accusations but, rather, to better understand the complex textual, contextual, and theoretical logic that informs such virulent accusations in the first place. Above all, my hope is that such an approach will unmask the theoretical implications of this exemplary mimetic quarrel for our contemporary, postcolonial, globalized, and transnational times.

In what follows, then, Achebe may not only be considered as Conrad's fierce rival and opponent but also as Conrad's postcolonial counterpart, perhaps even as his anthropological and theoretical supplement. The Girardian concept of "mimetic rivalry" will help me partially explain the quarrel between the two competing authors, yet this concept remains too much anchored in romantic anxieties of influence. Adding a characteristic modernist twist to this concept, I turn to supplement imitative rivalry from a more impersonal, postcolonial perspective attentive to both the reproductive and productive dimension of such quarrels.[4] As Said recognizes, "in some of his novels he [Achebe] rewrites—painstakingly and with originality—Conrad" (*CI* 76). This rewriting is especially visible when it comes to the notion that triggered the race debate in the first place. In fact, a specific focus on Achebe's repeated narrative use of the notion of "frenzy" in *Things Fall Apart* reveals that the Nigerian novelist furthers an anthropological insight into the functions of rituals of possession trance that had already caught Conrad's attention in *Heart of Darkness*, mimetic rituals that Conrad's European perspective could not fully account for. Achebe not only as a critic who challenges the racist implications of Conrad's colonial image of Africa, but, rather, Achebe as a novelist who pursues Conrad's anthropological investigation into African rituals generating a state of mimetic "frenzy" along lines that call for a new understanding of mimesis in postcolonial studies. I shall call this form of mimesis "postcolonial mimesis" to distinguish it from its mirroring counterpart, that is, "colonial mimicry" (Bhabha's term). If superficial similarities exist between "colonial mimicry" and "postcolonial mimesis" in terms of the ambivalences and menaces they entail, fundamental differences remain, if only because "postcolonial mimesis" is rooted in the perspective of the postcolonial author who, far from submitting to colonial power, uses the language of the dominant to actively reframe colonial narratives—in a mimetic way. Whether Achebe's counternarrative is really the opposite, or not quite, is what we now turn to see.

Indeed, the secret shadow of mimesis can take many forms. It does not only operate at the psychological, anthropological, and narrative levels but also at the wider and more capillary discursive level, a level that is difficult to see, but if brought to the fore complicates the antagonistic relation between Africa and Europe, the picture and what it is supposed to represent. Tracking this shadow will allow us to make visible the mimetic, impersonal, and paradoxical logic that informs the discursive circulation that both opposes and connects colonial narratives to postcolonial counternarratives. It will also encourage postcolonial critics and theorists to reframe wider issues on power, subjection, and narrative agency along mimetic lines that go beyond conscious authorial intention. In the end, a productive, forward-looking dialogue, perhaps even a friendly reconciliation between these two antagonistic authors, will take place, paradoxically, via the past-oriented question that started the quarrel in the first place.

## The Quarrel Reloaded

As noted in the preceding chapter, since the publication of his influential lecture "An Image of Africa" (1977), Achebe has been routinely considered Conrad's most formidable critic in matters of race; and Conrad scholars, while often disagreeing with the Nigerian novelist's evaluation of *Heart of Darkness*, have tended to accept an image of Achebe as Conrad's antipode par excellence. And quite rightly so. In fact, the Nigerian novelist as critic points out, with moving pathos and insightful logos, what had escaped Western critics before. Namely, that *Heart of Darkness* is a fundamentally racist text, not only because it deprives African people of a narrative perspective but also because it constantly represents them as irrational, mad, and backward creatures, jumping up and down the shore in a delirious state of "frenzy" (from Latin, *phrēnēsis*, madness), a pathology that strips them of reason, self-control, and their humanity as such.

What I must stress now is that, for Achebe, the Conradian notion of "frenzy" is not a signifier among others, but functions as one of the main targets and leitmotifs of his critique. Using this notion as leverage for his debunking critical operation, he considers that, for Conrad, it functions as a marker of a radical difference between Europeans and Africans that deprives the latter of essential human attributes such as reason, language, and culture, ultimately relegating the subaltern subject to madness, bodily instincts, and the bush. Consequently, Achebe the critic insists on Conrad's "fake-ritualistic repetition" (IA 338) of images of "frenzy." Placing what he calls, mimicking Conrad, "the mindless frenzy of the first beginnings" (338) at the center of his argument and repeating, echolike, this notion more often than Conrad himself,[5] Achebe shows that Conrad's masterpiece functions as a self-reflecting mirror that reveals more about European "myths," disavowals, and fictional projections than about African reality itself. Achebe's patho-*logical* perspective, then, presents itself as the very antithesis to Conrad's, a necessary dialectical inversion of perspectives that passionately denounces the racist implications inherent in Conrad's representation of African subjects "clapping their hands and stamping their feet" (340), "too busy with their frenzy" (341). This, at least, is the official story that emerges if we limit ourselves to Achebe's critical evaluation of *Heart of Darkness*.

If we now briefly recall Conrad's side of the story that deals with enthusiastic outbreaks of ritual "frenzy," we notice that Marlow's narrative perspective is more ambivalent than Achebe suggests. While clearly problematic and
diminishing, what is at stake in subjects dancing collectively to the sound of
drums, clapping their hands, stamping their feet, and rolling their eyes is not
only an expression of barbarism and savagery; nor can it be only dismissed
as a ritual phenomenon characteristic of "prehistoric" people—though it is
both. As we have seen, Conrad's account of African "frenzy" is also one of the
first novelistic attempts to represent a mysterious anthropological phenomenon that is found across different cultures, is widespread in sub-Saharan
Africa, and is known in the anthropological literature under the rubric of
"possession trance." Accompanied by the rhythmic music of the drums that
are constantly in the background of the tale, rituals of possession trance
affect both Africans and European subjects alike, informing mimetic scenes
that go, quite literally, to the heart of the novel and are constitutive of a type
of horror that is not African but European in origins.

Furthermore, from the very beginning of his tale, Marlow suggests that
the musical rituals responsible for generating collective states of "frenzy"
are part of a religious, cultural phenomenon that should still be intelligible
to a modern audience. Reflecting back on his Congo experience, he says:
"Perhaps on some quiet night the tremor of far off drums, sinking, swelling,
a tremor vast, faint; a sound weird, appealing, suggestive, and wild" (*YOS*
61). And then, in a more relativist and comparative mood he immediately
specifies: "and perhaps with as profound a meaning as the sound of bells in a
Christian country" (61). This is a punctual yet important moment in Conrad's religious anthropology. Rather than automatically relegating this ritual
phenomenon at the heart of Africa to the sphere of savagery, barbarity, and
pathology, Marlow runs against reflex racist reactions in order to establish a
direct cultural continuity between "modern" man and "primitive" man, the
religion of the self and the religion of the other, the sound of "bells" and the
sound of "drums."

Scholars interested in Conrad's anthropology have tended to be critical of his reduction of otherness to selfhood. And quite rightly so, since
in *Heart of Darkness* Conrad does not consider cultural otherness in its
own terms, but tends to subordinate it to the larger picture of Europe he is
attempting to sketch. And yet, in this particular instance, Conrad's religious

anthropology may not be as ethnocentric as it initially sounds. The point of the comparison is, in fact, not to subordinate a "primitive" ritual to a "modern" religious practice, thereby reducing the difference of the "other" to the sameness of the "self." Rather, the point is to establish a cross-cultural echo between an unknown religious ritual in Africa and a known religious ritual in Europe, without necessarily advocating the superiority of one over the other. This initial analogy serves as a reminder that, if not for Marlow, at least for Conrad, there is a fundamental continuity between self and other, religious practices in Africa and religious practices in Europe. We can thus better understand why, later on, Marlow will repeat that there is a "meaning" in rituals triggered by the "roll of drums" that his listeners "could comprehend" (*YOS* 79). Thus understood, the drums in the background and the ritual "frenzy" in the foreground are not deemed a priori barbaric and incomprehensible. They are rather implicitly endowed with the dignity of a culturally accepted, Western religious practice. The African other, then, is first pictured via a religious, cultural comparison that is not only intelligible to the Victorian listeners on the *Nellie* but also has the power to challenge hierarchical distinctions between "savagery" and "civilization," Africa and Europe, for contemporary readers.

And yet it must be acknowledged: Marlow's anthropological insights into the specific cultural meaning of African rituals based on the hypnotic rhythm of drums remain limited—at least, as far as his picture of Africa is concerned. Conrad, for one, seems perfectly aware of Marlow's limitations when it comes to religious rituals that generate a state of "frenzy" and collective outbreaks of "enthusiasm," anthropological limitations that do not allow his ethnocentric narrator to fully grasp the cultural significance of the rituals he describes. Thus, falling back on the evolutionary language we are by now familiar with, Marlow asks, in a disconcerted mood: "The prehistoric man was cursing us, praying to us, welcoming us—who could tell?" (79). If the narrative gestures toward the possibility of an anthropological understanding of the other, it ultimately fails to fully take hold of it, leaving this narrative possibility open for others to explore. In fact, by insisting that the religious meaning internal to these rituals is "profound" (61), Conrad indirectly invites a more informed, interior perspective to supplement Marlow's distanced and ethnographically limited account of African rituals in general and religious frenzy in particular.

If we now want to pursue this anthropological line of inquiry, we need to shift our perspective from what is ultimately still a picture of Europe to a picture of Africa Conrad was not in position to fully sketch. This is precisely the kind of picture a writer like Chinua Achebe sets out to represent in *Things Fall Apart*, a narrative picture told from the perspective of a postcolonial author whose intention is to reframe dominant images of Africa in a more positive and informed light.[6] As Conrad's postcolonial mirror image, Achebe deserves a central place in a book titled *Conrad's Shadow*.

## Anthropology of Mimesis

*Things Fall Apart* is Achebe's first and most influential novel; it occupies an exemplary position in African literature that can hardly be underestimated. Hailed as the "archetypal modern African novel in English" (Appiah),[7] this text is exemplary both in terms of its opposition to colonial representations of Africa and as an alternative, postcolonial picture of precolonial African culture. Achebe, in fact, positions himself in a relation of dialectical tension up against the colonial heritage in order to develop a picture of precolonial Igbo culture that counters dominant images of Africa. As he puts it: "I would be quite satisfied if my novels (especially the ones I set in the past) did no more than teach my readers that their past—with all its imperfections—was not one long night of savagery from which the first Europeans acting on God's behalf delivered them."[8] It is thus understandable that critics, following the author, routinely define *Things Fall Apart* as the postcolonial "counter-narrative" or "counter-weapon" par excellence (Pandurang), whose goal is to "negate the prior European negation of indigenous society" (JanMohamed) and advocate an "oppositional discourse to *Heart of Darkness*" (Nwosu).[9] It is clearly not my intention to dispute the validity of these readings. Nor do I question the status of *Things Fall Apart* as a foundational counternarrative that inaugurates "the institution of African literature" (Gikandi).[10] Achebe's first picture of Africa remains the masterpiece that it is and deserves to be. What I would like to suggest is that the relation between colonial narrative and postcolonial counternarrative is much more complex than previously realized and that striking mimetic continuities exist between the two pictures of Africa—continuities that pertain to anthropological rituals in general and rituals of possession trance in particular.

## Good and Evil (Dis)possession

One of the ambitions of *Things Fall Apart* is to provide those anonymous subjects we have seen in *Heart of Darkness*, dancing enthusiastically on the shore in a state of incomprehensible "frenzy" with a culturally informed narrative perspective that had been denied by European counterparts, such as Joyce Cary and, especially, Conrad.[11] From the very first lines, the narrative voice frames his protagonist's ritual actions within the larger symbolic order of Igbo precolonial culture, making clear that Okonkwo, a wrestling champion and leader who serves as the protagonist of the novel, with his individual successes and failures in the narrative foreground acquire meaning only insofar as they are read against the background of the larger anthropological picture of Africa Achebe is about to sketch. This contextual reframing is important to situate all the rituals described in part 1 of the novel—from wrestling matches to public debates, harvesting to storytelling, festivals to funerals—but is essential to take hold of a slippery mimetic phenomenon that blurs the shadow-line between self and other(s). Mimesis is, in fact, as central to the textual economy of *Things Fall Apart* as it was to *Heart of Darkness*, and neither its doubling nor its protean meanings have so far received the critical attention they deserve.

Among the variety of sacred ritual practices that pervade Achebe's picture of Igbo culture, a number of them are strikingly reminiscent of the rituals that had already caught Conrad's attention: collective, musical rituals that generate states of affective effervescence, bodily motions, and psychic (dis)possession that spread contagiously—via the medium of the mimetic unconscious—among the crowd of participants. Achebe confirms the mimetic dimension of such rituals as he says, for instance, that during a traditional Igbo masquerade, "You must *imitate* its motion. The kinetic energy of the masquerade's art is thus instantly transmitted to a whole arena of spectators."[12] This imitation is not based on a static aesthetic, and thus visual, representation characteristic of Western art; it is rather based on a kinetic ritual, and thus bodily, impersonation characteristic of African rituals. If the former tradition tends to understand mimesis as a representation to be seen (or read) from a distance, the latter experience mimesis in terms of a bodily participation in a pathos that spreads contagiously among the community. And in part 1, Achebe depicts mimetic rites whereby members of the Igbo community, stimulated by the "kinetic energy" of the drum, are invested or, as he repeatedly says, "possessed" by another personality (such as a god, spirit, ancestor, or demon) and enter an altered state of consciousness whereby they are no longer themselves but become other instead. These rituals of possession are thus mimetic not in the simple sense that the mask is an imitation of a god. Rather, they are mimetic in the anthropological sense that the ritual mask enables a (dis)possession by a god, which, in turn, troubles the distinction between self and other, transgresses the line that divides the sacred from the profane, and generates outbreaks of affect that are transmitted contagiously across the social body.

If we put on our diagnostic lenses we see that, generally, in *Things Fall Apart*, rituals of possession are not symptomatic of a pathology but occupy a positive, therapeutic function; they are linked to sacred figures that sustain the Igbo order of things. Such figures, you will recall, make a small appearance in *Heart of Darkness*. Marlow, in fact, catches a glimpse of a masked "sorcerer" with "horns" suggesting its centrality for rituals of possession trance, yet he has nothing specific to say about his shamanic powers. Achebe, on the other hand, is in a position to give anthropological substance to this European narrative perspective. His account of Chielo, the priestess of the Hills and Caves, is particularly revelatory of the entranced states of (dis) possession that interest us. We are told that via a divinatory trance, Chielo is no longer herself but becomes "possessed" (*TFA* 60) by the god Agbala and speaks mimetically, in the god's name, as she starts "prophesying" (60). This is a ritual phenomenon that is not particular to Africa. Under a different ethnographic mask, it has been known since ancient Greece under the rubric of *mantic mania* (or divinatory trance).[13] Just as the prophetess at Delphi (or Pythia) was possessed by Apollo, entered an altered state of consciousness, and prophesized the future, so, we are told, the priestess of the Hills and Caves is possessed by Agbala: "There was nothing new in that. Once in a while Chielo was possessed by the spirit of her god and she began to prophesy" (60). This divinatory practice is mimetic in a dual yet related sense: on the one hand, it leads the oracle to speak in the name of the god, as if she were the god (mimetic *lexis*); on the other hand, it entails a confusion of identities so profound that it breaks down all distinctions between self and other, priest and god, human and divine (mimetic *mania*). This double mimesis comes to the fore as we read that it is a "different Chielo" (61) who gives expression to "possessed chanting" (64), and as she is *plena deo*, so to speak, she warns Okonkwo thus: "Beware of exchanging words with Agbala. Does a man speak when a god speaks?" (60). Clearly, the woman Chielo is not in communication *with* the god Agbala. She *is*, quite literally, the god. Or, better, she is the medium through which the voice of the god speaks.[14] Her mimetic speech, in fact, signals that she is no longer herself but someone other, a sacred figure who bridges the gap between the human world and the underworld, the community of men and the spiritual world. While feared, the narrative makes clear that this is a manifestation of a "good" form of mimetic possession, a therapeutic mimesis that has the potential to heal both individual and social pathologies.

And yet what was true for Conrad's picture of lost European souls still holds true for Achebe's picture of lost African souls. As we have come to expect, there is always a pathological counterpart to forms of mimetic (dis)possession. *Things Falls Apart* confirms this Janus-faced diagnostic. For instance, the possession of newborns by the spirit of a dead child— what Igbos call "*ogbanje*" (47)—entails a loss of the self that functions as a mimetic symptom of what mimetic rituals are supposed to heal. The case of Okonkwo's daughter, Ezinma, whom Chielo/Agbala abducts in order to cure, illustrates precisely such a case of possession by another, which is also a dispossession of the self. We are told that "everybody knew that she was an *ogbanje*" (49). And an entire chapter is devoted to the ritual practices Igbos use to bring this confusion of identities to an end.[15] This is, once again, a case of mimetic indistinction between self and other, human and nonhuman. And as the narrative progresses, it becomes clear that such a pathological form of mimetic (dis)possession can only be cured via rituals based on what the narrator calls "possessed chanting" (64), whereby the god speaks through the voice of the oracle. At work in Achebe's text is thus an anthropological confirmation of a diagnostic principle we have already seen at work in Conrad's texts. Namely, that the cure of a pathological possession (or *ogbanje*) is to be found in another, patho-logical form of possession trance (or divinatory trance). The ethnographic context has changed, yet the diagnostic remains the same: (dis)possession is both the source of the disease and its potential remedy—a clear indication that mimetic trance in *Things Fall Apart* operates according to a Janus-faced patho(-)logy that exceeds binary oppositions such as good and evil, health and sickness, poison and cure.

These examples already suggest that, though rarely discussed, trance, and the mimetic confusion it generates is, quite literally, at the center of *Things Fall Apart*. It generates different forms of indistinction between "self" and "others" that are as pathological as patho-logical, and supplements Conrad's anthropological perspective by giving us an insight into the Igbo order of things. What we must add now is that among these outbreaks of individual forms of mimetic possession we equally find collective outbreaks of (dis)possession that require a more careful diagnostic, for at least two reasons: first, because they are predicated on the very conception of "frenzy" that triggered the quarrel between Achebe and Conrad in the first place; second, because they are symptomatic of a type of narrative mimesis that is as reproductive as it is productive and requires a new form of textual investigation to be fully understood. If we want to reframe this mimetic quarrel from an Africanist perspective informed by anthropological accounts of frenzied possession, we now need to take a closer look at the images of frenzy that cast a shadow on Achebe's counternarrative.

## A Picture of Frenzy Redux

Given Achebe's authorial intention to both counter and rectify what he perceives to be Conrad's ethnocentric representation of African people as irrational, nonverbal, bodily creatures who are easily swept away by the contagious power of affects, we should expect his own picture of African rituals to be antithetical to dominant images of Africa—or at least that it would not reproduce "the mindless frenzy of the first beginnings" (IA 338) he so virulently denounces in *Heart of Darkness*. We are thus surprised to find out that the Conradian notion of "frenzy," which horrified Achebe *the critic*, is central to Achebe *the novelist*. Equally striking is the fact that Conrad's representation of Africans as irrational creatures who are possessed, body and soul, by the intoxicating rhythm of drums resonates throughout the entirety of *Things Fall Apart*. Here are a few close-ups of Achebe's own picture Africa:

The wrestlers were not there yet and the drummers held the field. . . . Three men beat them [the drums] with sticks, working feverishly from one drum to another. They were possessed by the spirit of the drums . . . the crowd roared and clapped. The drums rose to a frenzy. The people surged forward. . . . The crowd roared and clapped and for a while drowned the frenzied drums. (*TFA* 29)

Does this passage sound untypical? This is actually by no means an isolated or unusual passage in Achebe's counternarrative. The drums resonate throughout the text, generating a disconcerting psychosomatic effect on the masses of Igbos. For instance, we read that "the drums went mad and the crowds also" (31). At another moment we are informed that the "drums beat violently and men leaped up and down in frenzy" (73). And during a funeral ceremony, we find the following representation of the Igbos: "The ancient drums of death beat, . . . men dashed about in frenzy, cutting down every tree or animal they saw, jumping over walls and dancing on the roof" (72). Roaring crowds, clapping hands, stamping feet, rhythmic tom-toms, collective madness, ritual violence, possession trance, and, yes—ritual frenzy. Not only is the same mimetic phenomenon Achebe violently objected to in "An Image of Africa" fully at work in his own representation of Igbo rituals but also his account of the frenzy of possession trance seems to mimetically echo, ad verbum, Conrad's denigrating terminology.

   In the wake of Achebe's critique of *Heart of Darkness*, the output of criticism that addresses the problem of race in Conrad and Achebe studies has been impressive. Yet this striking mimetic tension at the heart of such a loaded debate has not received the critical attention it deserves.[16] Consequently, the terms of the racism/antiracism debate have tended to remain polarized around a dichotomy that considers Achebe's take on race and ritual as antithetical to Conrad's. Now, since the question of "frenzy" is the hinge upon which this mimetic quarrel turns, we need to carefully reconsider the anthropological and narrative implications of these disputed images of Africa first, before proceeding to offer a more nuanced critical evaluation of what, exactly, is at stake in such (mimetic) reproductions of (mimetic) rituals at the heart of a celebrated counternarrative. This also involves looking past ideological blinders that prevent critics from seeing images of frenzy in postcolonial narratives, suspending the quarrel, and looking at both sides of the picture in order to bring to light the mimetic logic that both opposes and joins two Janus-faced pictures of Africa.

Taken out of context, it would be difficult, even for an experienced reader, to discriminate between Conrad's and Achebe's respective images of ritual "frenzy." The same hysterical states of dispossession seem to be in place, the same musical tom-toms are in the background, even the same terminology—from "madness" to "frenzy" via hands "clapping," bodies "jumping," "crowds" roaring, and so on—animates this postcolonial image of Africa. But of course it would be a gross misreading to place the two accounts of African "frenzy" on the same anthropological and narrative level, treating the latter as mere repetition, shadow, or mimicry of the former. Contrary to Conrad's image of Africa, Achebe's narrative picture re-presents these scenes of "frenzy" within the wider cultural context of Igbo traditions, and frames outbreaks of mimetic madness within an informed and sympathetic narrative perspective that gives these actions a specific cultural, religious, and sociohistorical meaning. The images of frenzy might be similar, but the narrative context in which they are set radically reframes their meaning.

## The Order of Trance

Achebe's representations of the mimetic frenzy generated by the intoxicating rhythm of drums take place within carefully organized, ritual festivals that punctuate the rhythm of Igbo communal life. If we restitute some of the passages quoted above in their proper context, we learn that it is always during sacred festivals and "communal ceremonies" (53) that images of frenzy emerge in *Things Fall Apart*. For instance, in the context of a description of a wrestling match, the narrative shifts from the individual wrestlers in the center to the enthusiastic crowd of spectators and musicians that surround them. And it is only afterward that we read: "The drums went mad and the crowds also. They surged forward as the two young men danced into the circle" (31). An intoxicating, contagious, and mimetic madness is thus part of Achebe's picture of Africa. Yet this madness does not spin out of control, affecting the irrational part of the soul and threatening the social order, as Plato already suggested in *Republic*.[17] Rather, this outbreak is framed by a carefully organized and codified ritual with a unifying social function, as Émile Durkheim suggested in *The Elementary Forms of Religious Life*.[18] Ritual frenzy is thus not a manifestation of savage disorder; it is constitutive of the Igbo social order. Further, in Achebe's narrative reevaluation of mimetic contagion, the function of such a ritual frenzy is clearly revealed. The narrative continues: "The crowd had surrounded and swallowed up the drummers, whose frantic rhythm was no longer a mere disembodied sound but the very heart-beat of the people" (31). This passage confirms that frenzy, as it operates in Achebe's narrative economy, has a fundamentally central and, above all, vitalizing social function. The very "heart" of the Igbo community lies in those palpitating musical rituals, mimetic rituals whose throbbing rhythm of frenzy galvanize the entire social body.

Let us recall that this is not the first time that the frenzied rhythm of the drum is placed at the heart of a collective ritual. Already in *Heart of Darkness*, the "beat of the drum" among the ritual crowd in the background is confounded with what Marlow calls "the beating of [his] heart" (112) in the foreground. Yet, in Achebe's mimetic representation, it is not the figure of the European colonist who is affected by the ritual frenzy but the entire African community instead. Moreover, in this narrative context, the mimetic frenzy does not lead to the murderous horror of Kurtz's sacrificial rituals. Rather, it is at the origins of a revitalization, unification, and solidification of the social bonds that gives birth to a communal organism. From this alternative anthropological perspective, then, the notion of "frenzy" can no longer be read as an expression of natural "savagery," or as an evolutionary remnant of "pre-historic" times (Conrad's terms). Rather, this narrative representation of frenzy illustrates the anthropological role of mimetic rituals in the formation of those "bonds of kinship" that are at the "heart" of the precolonial African community itself (Achebe's terms). If Achebe's critique of Conrad's image of Africa is still in line with a Platonic denunciation of mimetic myths (bad mimesis), his novelistic practice reveals a positive, anti-Platonic reevaluation of mimetic rituals as the centralizing social force that keeps people together (good mimesis).

Despite the structural similarity between the colonial text and its postcolonial counterpart, a deft inversion of perspectives has thus taken place as we move from Conrad's image of Africa to Achebe's picture of Africa. The focus has shifted from the heart of a European subject in Africa (Europe as subject) to what happens at the heart of African people (Africa as subject). The collective "frenzy" understood as an expression of the primordial savagery of the first beginnings turns into an expression of the living heart that gives life to the entire social body. The "bad mimesis" that threatens the stability of the social bond in Conrad's picture of Europe turns into a "good mimesis" that strengthens communal bonds in Achebe's picture of Africa. Mimetic rituals are, in fact, responsible for generating those enigmatic "invisible forces" that have intrigued critics for a while and that bind single individuals (intersubjective bond), the individuals and the community (communal bonds), as well as humans and the spirits/gods (spiritual bonds). In short, rituals of frenzied (dis)possession are, quite literally, at the center of *Things Fall Apart*. They generate the bonds that hold Igbo things together. The mimetic "frenzy" is thus no longer identified with the "heart of darkness" but with the "heartbeat of the people."

There are some general theoretical lessons that emerge from this pictorial reproduction. Achebe's narrative reevaluation of frenzy not only offers a counterpart to Conrad's mimetic fictions by giving us an insight into the social function of Igbo rituals; it also supplements mimetic theory by giving us an account of the positive, communal, and vitalizing side of ritual mimesis. René Girard, for one, is of course aware of the festive side of rituals and engages with some of its most important advocates. Nonetheless, he consistently privileges the violent face of mimesis over its joyful counterpart. Thus he argues that "the fundamental purpose of the festival is to set the stage for a sacrificial act that marks at once the climax and the termination of the festivities" (*VS* 119). These sacrificial acts, as we have seen, were fully at work in the culmination of Kurtz's rituals, and we shall return to them in the context of *Apocalypse Now*. But Achebe has a different mimetic hypothesis in mind. For Achebe, in fact, affective contagion and the ritual frenzy that ensues is not the source of a violent mimesis that would generate a collective loss of identity (or "crisis of difference") that threatens to disrupt the social body. Rather, Achebe considers the sacred, mimetic frenzy and the transgression of boundaries that ensues as a positive, regenerative, and vital event in Igbo culture, a mimetic event responsible for the social cohesion and solidarity among the members of the community. Much closer to the founder of French anthropology, Émile Durkheim, in sensibility, Achebe stresses the forms of collective "effervescence," contagion, and mimetic communications that must be understood as the living source of the "moral unity" (Durkheim's term) of society and is responsible for the cohesion among members of the same village. Put in more contemporary terms, his vision of precolonial Igbo culture is one of a sacred community that has been rendered inoperative in the West, yet offers an imaginative starting point to affirm bonds of communal solidarity necessary to counter the forces that cause things to fall apart.[19] In sum, for Achebe, ritualized forms of mimetic frenzy are not the problem of social cohesion but its organic solution; they do not wrest people violently apart but bring them together—in a communal dance.

This anthropological reading emphasizes the positive, vitalizing, and cohesive aspect of rituals of possession trance and makes clear that if Achebe apparently mimics the Conradian language of frenzy, he does so not in order to repeat it but in order to re-present it in a new, positive, communal light. The general picture that emerges from the rituals of frenzy depicted in part 1, devoted to precolonial Africa, offers a much-needed corrective to Conrad's colonial images. And yet despite the mirrorlike reversal of anthropological perspectives, Achebe's quarrel with Conrad is not altogether deprived of mimetic ambivalence. In fact, his account of ritual frenzy does not always fit this narrative countermovement. At times, Achebe even seems to run counter to an organic representation of good mimesis, coming awfully close to the bad images of frenzy he denounces in Conrad.

The clearest and most striking example of possession trance in *Things Fall Apart* takes place during a ritual context that is, indeed, extremely violent and is characterized by dangerous forms of collective frenzy that seem to threaten, rather than sustain, the Igbo social order. The chapter in question starts with a ritual summons that resonates throughout the community and has the function of bringing people together: "Go-di-di-go-go-di-go. Di-go-go-di-go" (71). And then we find this striking passage:

> The ancient drums of death beat, guns and cannon were fired, and men dashed about in frenzy, cutting down every tree or animal they saw, jumping over walls and dancing on the roof. . . . Now and again an ancestral spirit or *egwugwu* appeared from the underworld, speaking in a tremulous unearthly voice and completely covered in raffia. Some of them were very violent, and there had been a mad rush for shelter earlier in the day when one appeared with a sharp matchet and was only prevented from doing serious harm by two men who restrained him with the help of a strong rope tied around his waist. Sometimes he turned round and chased those men,

and they ran for their lives. . . . He sang, in a terrifying voice, that Ekwenzu, or Evil Spirit, had entered his eye. (72)

That this is a case of possession trance is clear. The account recapitulates trance's most prominent ritual characteristics: rhythmic music, collective movement, emotional contagion, and, above all, possession by ancestral spirits that penetrate the subject and dispossess it of its proper identity.[20] Achebe provides readers with the anthropological reasons behind this outbreak of collective madness and violence (that is, the possession of men by the *egwugwu*). Still, it is unclear why he should risk anachronism by representing what Henry Staten calls "the savage core of culture (where 'savage' does not necessarily mean 'primitive')."[21] Above all, we wonder: why should Achebe reproduce some of the narrative stereotypes he so eloquently denounces in dominant images of Africa, from irrationality to madness, violence to unearthly voices?

## Mimetic Differences

In order to account for this counterintuitive narrative move it is, once again, crucial to place Achebe's representation of possession trance in its proper narrative and anthropological context. No matter how violent, irrational, and disruptive, this mimetic outbreak of frenzy is not a random expression of "savagery," but takes place in the context of a highly organized religious ritual: that is, the funeral of Ezeudu, one of the oldest men in the village who had once been a noble warrior and had won many titles. This time, the chaos and violence generated by the ritual of possession are reminiscent of what Girard calls "mimetic crisis," and his account of "ritual possession," as we have seen, casts some light on the "hysterical trance" (*VS* 165–66) that is at the heart of this scene. As with Conrad's image of Africa, so with Achebe's postcolonial picture, rituals of possession trance bring us very close to a savage heart of culture. This Dionysian core, as Staten also noticed, has been veiled by the Apollonian tendencies that dominate postcolonial studies, yet is very familiar to theorists of the sacred who—from Nietzsche to Rohde, Bataille to Girard, as we shall see in Part 3—have taken it upon themselves to bring us back in touch with violent Dionysian transgressions that constitute the palpitating heart of the sacred.

Achebe, then, can be productively aligned with this anthropological tradition for he frames such a savage frenzy within the specific context of the Igbo order of things, providing a cultural, ethnographic, and narrative specificity that is often missing in European accounts of other cultures, such as Conrad's. In this particular case, the narrative voice gives readers an insight into the religious implications of the death of a great warrior. Thus the narrator makes clear that the transgression of boundaries generated by that disruptive and tragic event, which is death, entails a wider, cosmological transgression of boundaries. We are told, for instance, that during these sacred times, "The land of the living was not far removed from the domain of the ancestors. There was coming and going between them, especially at festivals and also when an old men died, because an old man was very close to the ancestors" (*TFA* 73). We can thus better understand why the ritual of possession trance, whereby the *egwugwu* transgress the frontier between the land of the dead and the land of the living, takes place during a funeral rite. The function of the rites of possession trance is, in fact, to help regain—via an organized, collective ritual—the equilibrium that has been momentarily lost so as to recompose the disrupted social order. How? By engendering a collective state of violent frenzy that reenacts the violent transgression of the frontier that divides life and death, the human and the divine, the world of men and the underworld, a transgression caused by that sacred event par excellence, which is death.

For Achebe, this mimetic reproduction of the phenomenon of possession trance—and the frenzy that ensues—functions as the ritualized solution to the problem of the momentary disruption of the communal social order. Or, better, it entails a ritualized reenactment of the violence and transgression death introduces in the Igbo order of things—a mimetic reenactment with a cathartic social function, as it were. Needless to say that this is an anthropological insight into rituals of possession trance that external visitors like Conrad were not in a position to fully sketch. It also anticipates recent anthropological accounts of possession trance that emphasize the cathartic social function of chaotic, mimetic rituals. This diagnostic point has been made by a number of anthropologically oriented theorists. Girard writes, for instance: "In principle, the religious practices [around possession] follow the order of the cycle of violence they are attempting to imitate." And adopting pharmacological lenses, he specifies: "The phenomenon

of possession . . . can appear as sickness, cure, or both at once" (*VS* 166).
More recently, Bertrand Hell writes that the aim of these rituals "is clearly
to discharge a destructive potential rather than nullify it stricto sensu," and
then he goes on to speak of the "social cathartic function" of such rituals as
well as of "the importance of disorder as a factor of regeneration of order,
as a force which brings new creative forces."[22] And François Warin, speaking of possession trance in a funeral rite among African (Dagara) people he
and Lacoue-Labarthe witnessed, via the filter of both Conrad and Bataille,
describes this inner experience thus: "The Africans had turned death into
a holy day; they could also dance in front of this 'dark sun,' as Georges
Bataille would have put it. . . . But along with its violence, what we were also
given to think and feel was the great wisdom of this ceremony, a cathartic
or purgative ceremony."[23] In sum, these anthropological insights stem from
different perspectives; they make us see that Achebe does not simply mimic
stereotypical accounts of "frenzy." Rather, he re-presents them, presents
them again, in a new light, in order to clarify the cathartic function of those
religious rites Conrad had glimpsed but not fully managed to account for.
Possession trance, for Achebe, provides a catharsis of mimesis via mimesis in
which mimetic (dis)possession is both the problem of violence and its therapeutic solution. Such rituals are no longer at the center of culture, yet their
mimetic efficacy should not be underestimated. If Achebe's novel continues
to remain important it is perhaps also because it helps new generations of
African subjects—in postindependence, "neocolonial" nation-states that
are engaged in an ongoing process of decolonization that is as material as
it is psychic—to imagine communities that rely on positive, unifying, and
therapeutic functions of mimetic rituals. This, at least, is the anthropological lesson that emerges from the rituals of possession trance dramatized in
*Things Fall Apart.*

But what about the literary and narrative implications of Achebe's aesthetic picture? After all, Achebe himself has cautioned readers not to read
his text solely through anthropological lenses. And quite rightly so, since the
rituals he dramatizes in his novel are themselves framed within a carefully
crafted narrative structure, a structure that, in turn, adds an additional layer
of complexity to the phenomenon of possession trance and the narrative
inversions that are at the heart of Achebe's picture of Africa.

## Narrative Mimesis

Rituals of possession trance have been kept at the margins of postcolonial studies so far but are, quite literally, at the center of Achebe's narrative project. This is confirmed if we do not let go of the mimetic undercurrent that runs through the entire texture of *Things Fall Apart*. After the in-depth account of the intoxicating effects of the drums on the dancers during the funeral scene we have just considered follows what I take to be the culminating narrative point of the entire novel. And, once again, images of "frenzy" are center stage in Achebe's dramatization:

> Drums beat violently and men leaped up and down in frenzy. . . . The drums
> and the dancing began again and reached fever-heat. Darkness was around
> the corner, and the burial was near. Guns fired the last salute and the cannon
> rent the sky. And then from the centre of the delirious fury came a cry of
> agony and shouts of horror. It was as if a spell had been cast. All was silent.
> In the center of the crowd a boy lay in a pool of blood. . . . Okonkwo's gun
> had exploded and a piece of iron had pierced the boy's heart. (*TFA* 73–74)

This scene dramatizes Okonkwo's accidental killing of Ezeudu's son (a structural repetition of his voluntary killing of Ikemefuna) and determines the hero's tragic fate, marking his exclusion from Umuofia and prefiguring his subsequent downfall. But as the narrative structure suggests, this is not only a personal tragedy. It also marks a decisive turning point in the narrative as a whole. In fact, this dramatic scene occurs in the chapter that concludes part I, the section devoted to precolonial Igbo life, during one of those climactic moments in which not only the destiny of the tragic hero but also of Igbo culture and, by metonymic extension, of African culture at large turns—and things begin to fall apart.

What is perhaps most surprising here is not that Achebe situates the culminating point of the protagonist's experience in direct relation to rituals of possession trance. Conrad had already done so. What is surprising is rather that in this passage Achebe condenses most of the terms that were already central to *Heart of Darkness* in order to account for the narrative turning point (or *katastrophé*) of *Things Fall Apart*, terms like "drums," "spell," and "frenzy" but also "darkness," "horror," and "heart." We can, indeed, begin to understand why Edward Said, in his last interview, affirms that "some of [Achebe's] early work, like *Things Fall Apart* is unintelligible without *Heart of Darkness*."[24] Perhaps, then, in order to continue to highlight the underlying implications of Achebe's mimetic counternarrative we should start asking ourselves Conradian questions after all—questions like: What kind of "darkness" is at the heart of Achebe's narrative? What, exactly, is "the horror" in *Things Fall Apart*? And if this horror is tied to the "frenzy" of possession trance, what is Achebe's mimetic *différend*?

## "The Heart-Beat of the People"

It is easy to see that Achebe sets out to denounce the devastating consequences of the colonization of Africa, thereby adding a new layer to Conrad's critique of Europe. Somewhat less readily perceptible is that he does so via the very question of mimetic frenzy he will later denounce in Conrad's image of Africa. A perspective that is as attentive to the anthropological as to the narrative implications of this central scene suggests that what Achebe calls the "horror" is inextricably intertwined with the experience of possession trance that was also at the heart of Conrad's picture of Europe. And yet if Achebe's emphasis on the language of "frenzy," "spells," and the "darkness" that ensues may still be implicitly Conradian in narrative inspiration, important differences need to be signaled. For Conrad, as we have seen, the experience of possession trance was identified with the "heart of darkness" and with the mimetic forces responsible for what Lacoue-Labarthe calls "the horror of the West." Achebe, writing from the other side of the mirror, has something quite different in mind. In fact, in *Things Fall Apart* he identifies rituals of possession with the "heart-beat of the people" and with those invisible forces that keep Igbo society together. The "horror," in this text, is thus not the horror of mimetic frenzy; the "spell" cast by rituals of possession trance is not a spell that ties the protagonist to sacrificial rituals. On the contrary, the horror and the spell that ensues are generated by the violent interruption of a communal ceremony based on the frenzy of possession trance—a mimetic frenzy whose goal was not to disrupt but to reestablish the traditional order of things.

The chapter in which Achebe's version of the horror appears is a transitory chapter that marks a historical shift from precolonial Igbo society characterized by traditional communal values whereby the mimetic bond is identified with the heart of the people (Part I) to a colonial Igbo society where this mimetic bond begins to give way, and things start to fall apart (Parts II and III). It is thus significant that the "shouts of horror" stem from what the narrator calls the "*center* of the delirious fury." That is, a fury generated by the mimetic frenzy whose ritual function, as we have seen, was to guarantee the social cohesion and moral unity of the community. If we situate the ritual frenzy within the general narrative economy of *Things Fall Apart*, it is clear that the source of the horror does not stem from the "fury" of the mimetic crowd itself, nor from the "frenzy" generated by the rituals of possession trance. Rather, the "shouts of horror" and the "spell" that ensues are the effects of the realization that at the "center of the delirious fury" (74) is the body of an innocent, sacrificial victim, as Girard would call it—albeit one that does not bring about social cohesion but social dissolution instead. Figuratively put, at the center of the dancing, mimetic crowd are no longer the beating drums that constituted the "heart-beat of the people" but are now a "pool of blood" (90) and a "pierced . . . heart" (74).

Clearly, Achebe's deft rearticulation of mythic images that were present in *Heart of Darkness* supplements Conrad's perspective and mediates a revelation that is central to *Things Fall Apart*. It makes clear that the blood spilled at the center of the crowd is, by metonymic extension, the blood of the heartbeat of the African people itself, that is, the living blood, or vital energy, generated by the rituals of mimetic trance whose function was to keep the precolonial Igbo community together as a living, palpitating organism.[25] More precisely, if Conrad dramatizes the horror of the ritual frenzy in Africa in order to critique hollow leader figures whose voices take possession of the masses in Europe (bad mimesis), Achebe dramatizes the horror of the loss of religious forms of ritual frenzy in order to critique the loss of communal bonds that were once at the heart of Africa (good mimesis). Already at the heart of Africa, then, sacrifice is not the restricted, precolonial cultural solution to mimetic violence. Rather, it is metonymic of a generalized, colonial, civilizationist savagery that will soon bring about the horror of communal dissolution. Indeed, the subsequent development of narrative events in parts 2 and 3, with the progressive fragmentation of Umuofia at the hands of missionary and colonists—that is, the Bible and the sword—dramatizes the historical consequences of what is already implicit

in this dramatic turning point of this African tragedy: the shift from a precolonial to a colonial society entails not only the external subjugation of
Igbo people to British colonialism and Christianity; it also triggers a much
more insidious manifestation of colonial power that operates from within
the community itself and spreads contagiously, like a sickness, across the
communal body politic. Such an infiltration of the colonial "other" into
the precolonial community has the effect of dissolving the ritual frenzy
responsible for the "bond of kinship" that allows Igbos to speak with "one
voice" (96) and guarantees the social cohesion of Umuofia. Possession is
not only of the Igbo precolonial spirits; the colonial Western demons also
(dis)possess African bodies and souls.

It is thus no accident that at the end of the novel Okonkwo's last, tragic,
and futile attempt to stand up against the colonial invasion does not stem
from the center of the mimetic crowd, where the narrative initially positions
him, but from its margins instead, where the narrative finally relegates him.
In one of the final scenes of the book, we are told that during a communal
gathering, whose function is to attempt, one last time, to bring the Igbo community back together in order to counter the colonial invader, "Okonkwo
was sitting at the edge [of the crowd]" (115). Such a dramatic displacement of
the hero from the center of things to its edge is indicative of the cultural and
historical turn of events the book traces as a whole: it prefigures the fall of the
tragic hero and, more generally, the falling apart of a communal, precolonial
Igbo society. Furthermore, it indicates that heroic forms of individual action
can only succeed if they are supported by the collective energy emanating
from the palpitating center of the community—a mimetic center that, as we
have seen, functions as "the heart-beat of the people" (31) that animates the
communal organism. In sum, as we move from Conrad's picture of Europe
to Achebe's picture of Africa, the horror is no longer the horror of mimesis.
Rather, the horror stems from the death of the living heart that held the
organic community together. The heart of darkness is no longer identified
with massive sacrificial atrocities. Rather, the heart of darkness is that tipping
point when the center no longer holds—and things fall apart. This, at least,
is the picture of Africa that emerges if we consider both the anthropological
and narrative implications of mimetic representations of possession trance at
work in these mirroring, and thus doubling, texts.

And yet in a postcolonial narrative that is so inextricably intertwined with the colonial narrative it sets out to counter, we now need to pay closer attention to the larger discursive logic that ties the subaltern African text to the dominant European text—in a mimetic way. In fact, if we turn to diagnose Achebe's aggressive take on the Conradian notion of "frenzy" once we have realized that Achebe himself relies quite heavily on this notion in order to describe anthropological phenomena of possession trance, his critique of Conrad, while providing a badly needed anthropological supplement and narrative correction, begins to sound not only excessive but also strangely paradoxical. This paradox, as we now turn to see, is the paradox of what I call "postcolonial mimesis."

## Postcolonial Mimesis

It is crucial to remember that Achebe delivered his influential lecture on *Heart of Darkness* in 1975, seventeen years after the publication of his own representation of African frenzied rituals in *Things Fall Apart* (1958). Nearly two decades separate these two texts, and during this lapse of time, the author radically shifted subject positions. If Achebe the novelist is an unknown writer in his late twenties freshly subjected to colonial education, still living in Africa, and progressively rediscovering his cultural roots, Achebe the critic is a mature and well-established postcolonial author in his midforties with an international reputation, occupying an honorific professorial position at the heart of the empire. The divergence in his evaluation of the notion of "frenzy"—generously used at first, violently rejected later—could thus be explained by saying that Achebe, the mature author and critic, is in a position to articulate a critical reflection on images of frenzy that was not yet fully in place at the time of writing his first novel. According to this perspective, Achebe's critique of Conrad's image of Africa would stem from a belated realization of the racist implications inherent in the notion of "frenzy," a realization somewhat disconnected from his own youthful novelistic practice. The advantage of this authorial line of inquiry is clear: no "contradiction," as Michel Foucault would say,[26] ensues between Achebe the novelist and Achebe the critic, and the distinction between narrative and counternarrative, Conrad's image of Africa and Achebe's picture of Africa, remains firmly in place. And yet, as we had multiple occasions to see, one could extract from *Things Fall Apart* an entire zone throughout which accounts of rituals remain in-*formed* by Conradian images, metaphors, and narrative structures. If we take seriously the realization that Achebe the novelist is himself quite busy with the images of "frenzy" he will later violently reject as a critic, a clear-cut distinction between dominant and subaltern narrative, the center and the periphery, begins, if not to fall apart, at least to sound less stable than it first appeared to be.[27]

## Can the Subaltern Imitate?

This second, less-reassuring hypothesis is in line with recent developments in postcolonial studies that urge critics to move beyond binary distinctions between colonizer and colonized and, by extension, narratives and counter-narratives in order to explore the underlying complicities and ambivalences that tie these structural polarities. Homi Bhabha, for instance, in *The Location of Culture*, argues that "the place of difference and otherness, or the space of the adversarial . . . is never entirely on the outside or implacably oppositional."[28] Along similar lines, in *A Critique of Postcolonial Reason* Gayatri Spivak writes: "I repeatedly attempt to undo the often unexamined opposition between colonizer and colonized implicit in much colonial and postcolonial discourse study."[29] Within the field of Conrad studies, Edward Said is probably the critic who saw this ambivalence and structural complicity most clearly. Thus in *Culture and Imperialism* he states: "Between classical nineteenth-century imperialism and what it gave rise to in resistant native cultures, there is . . . *both* a stubborn confrontation *and* a crossing over in discussion, borrowing back and forth, debate" (*CI* 30; my emphasis). And then, in a flash of critical insight that joins the two strands of discourse we have been following all along, he adds: "Many of the most interesting postcolonial writers bear their past within them—as scars of humiliating wounds, as instigation for different practices, as potentially revised visions of the past tending toward a new future" (30–31). These illuminating comments appear in the context of a discussion of *Heart of Darkness*, and since the name of Achebe surfaces as a representative of such "interesting post-colonial writers," we can see how they pave the way for Said's late affirmation that "*Things Fall Apart* is unintelligible without *Heart of Darkness*."[30] Indeed, as we had multiple occasions to confirm, *Things Fall Apart* is not only a text that, *contra*

Conrad, advocates a "revision of the past" but also a text that, *with* Conrad, bears the traces of the colonial language of "frenzy" and the wounding stereotypical representations it entails.

If we now want to further Said's innovative line of inquiry and continue to move beyond the authorial disciplinary dichotomies that—for forty years now—have informed the race quarrel, I suggest that we must not let go of the intrinsic, impersonal discursive logic that motivates the re-presentation of a frenzied conception of the subaltern subject at the heart of a celebrated counternarrative. A consideration of the "crossing over" between Conrad's and Achebe's ambivalent take on the scarring issue of mimetic frenzy opens up a productive, intermediate space to interrogate the more general network of discursive logic that ties—in a mimetic double bind—the subaltern counternarrative to the dominant narrative. In the process, the question of mimesis can no longer be restricted to the cultural meaning and social function of ritual frenzy (anthropological mimesis), nor to the narrative implications of this aesthetic representation (narrative mimesis). Rather, it needs to be supplemented by an approach that considers mimesis from a new postcolonial perspective (postcolonial mimesis).

The most influential starting point to think about questions of mimesis in postcolonial studies is probably still Homi Bhabha's chapter titled "Of Mimicry and Man: The Ambivalence of Colonial Discourse" in *The Location of Culture* (85–92).[31] Let us recall that Bhabha defines colonial mimicry as a "strategy of colonial power and knowledge" (*LC* 85) that has its origin in the colonizer's "desire for a reformed, recognizable Other, *as a subject of a difference that is almost the same but not quite*" (86). His paradigmatic example of "colonial mimicry" is "a class of persons Indian in blood and colour, but English in tastes, in opinions, in morals and in intellect" (87)—subjects, in other words, who embody, via mimicry, a "repetition of a *partial presence*" (86). And as Bhabha famously suggests, at work in this repetition with a difference is both an "ambivalence" and a "menace" (86) insofar as this uncanny mimetic redoubling is not simply generative of passive subaltern copies but, in a mirroring move, also threatens the sense of "identity" of the dominant subject who sees itself reflected in a copy that is not one. Can the subaltern mime? Yes, of course we can. But imitation has more than one meaning, and it is important to be attentive to the different shades of this chameleon concept.

Achebe, as Conrad's homo duplex, specifies what some of the meanings are. His narrative and critical practice equally render visible the ambivalence and menace of mimicry, yet they do so from an opposed perspective, which changes the type of imitation altogether. In fact, despite the similarities between Bhabha's and Achebe's postcolonial take on mimesis, *Things Fall Apart* does not simply repeat stereotypical images of Africa in order to conform to the discourse of the colonizer, but rather re-*presents* them with a difference. And what emerges from this re-presentation is not at all a "partial [European] presence" but an impartial African presence instead. Hence, insofar as Achebe's narrative is far from complying with colonial representations of the colonized as "almost the same but not quite" (86), we cannot rely on Bhabha's account of colonial repetition that considers the colonized from the perspective of the colonizer (colonial mimicry). Instead, we need to develop an alternative perspective that takes into consideration the point of view of the postcolonial subject itself. I thus call this form of "mimicry," which is in fact not mimicry at all, "postcolonial mimesis."[32]

## From Mimicry to Mimesis

In order to articulate the logic that informs postcolonial mimesis, I extend a Foucauldian line of inquiry in postcolonial studies inaugurated by Edward Said, and treat this exemplary debate as a micro example to conduct what Foucault calls "an *ascending* analysis of power."[33] That is, a microanalysis on a specific narrative paradox that brings to the fore a thus far neglected, yet no less general mimetic logic that informs narrative subjection in both its disciplining and productive dimension. More precisely, as Foucault's searching diagnostic of the insidious and often paradoxical dynamic of power has taught us, subjection is not only disruptive but also potentially productive; it is not only repressive, but it is also constitutive.[34] What Foucault does not say is that mimesis is central to this type of subjection, if only because mimesis is the double-edged sword that power uses to bring subjects into being in the first place. And since there is no reason to believe that this is not true for narrative forms of subjection, we could say that counternarratives are at least partially initiated through a primary mimetic submission to the power at work in the dominant narratives they set out to counter.

The case of Achebe's ambivalent take on frenzy suggests that subjection to power operates according to a paradoxical mimetic logic that is as potentially regressive as it is empowering. We have seen that Achebe's novelistic reproduction of Conrad's images of Africa bring him close to the very frenzy of the first beginnings he severely condemns as a critic. And yet we have equally seen that Achebe's mimetic *différend* not only denounces the power of colonial subjection but also reveals, via a subversive counternarrative, how the language of the colonizer can effectively be used against itself, and set to productive narrative, critical, and theoretical uses. Thus Achebe the novelist reveals how the dissolution of rituals of mimetic "frenzy" at the heart of a precolonial African community is associated with the horror of colonialism. Postcolonial mimesis, then, is a double-edged sword. On the one side, it cuts against Achebe (with Conrad) insofar as it partially implicates Achebe in the images of Africa he critiques. In this regressive, past-oriented sense, postcolonial mimesis reveals what Said calls the "scars of humiliating wounds" inflicted by the colonial past. On the other side, it cuts against Conrad (with Achebe) insofar as it is one of the conditions for the emergence of an exemplary counternarrative that reframes dominant images of Africa within a nonracist picture. In this second, more empowering and future-oriented sense, postcolonial mimesis functions as an effective medium to articulate what Said calls "revised visions of the past tending towards a new future" (*CI* 34).

If we now turn to Achebe the critic with this Janus-faced insight in mind, we should be in a position to resolve a problem that continues to be the source of much controversy and to uncover the underlying mimetic patho-*logy* that informs the quarrel between these two exemplary authors. Having granted the recognition Achebe's critique of Conrad deserves, critics have continued to wonder at the stridency of his tone; his one-sided rejection of a narrative that is, after all, critical of colonialism; his denigration of an author who demonstrates a "special regard for the rights of the unprivileged of this earth" (*PR* 6); his baffling comparison between Conrad's racism and Nazism; his diagnostic of Conrad as a "physician who poisons his patients" (IA 344n2)[35]; and, we may add, his acute sensitivity to the notion of frenzy. Sympathetic critics as artists who, in an imitation of Marlow, went on a journey in the hope that a chat with Achebe would unveil this riddle have tended to return disappointed,[36] perhaps because the reasons of such critical violence lie deep below the surface, are not fully conscious, and belong to the paradoxical sphere of the mimetic unconscious. This is, in fact, the moment to realize that some of the rhetorical excesses, critical tendentiousness, and interpretative violence Achebe mobilizes in order to launch his attack on Conrad acquire a new meaning if we take into consideration the complicities, ambivalences, and crossings overs that tie, in a mimetic double bind, Achebe's picture of Africa to Conrad's image of Africa.

In order to do so we should remember a few facts and summarize the key mimetic paradoxes we have encountered thus far. We are all familiar with Achebe's mature dislike of Conrad, but we should not forget that Conrad is one of the authors the young Achebe, as he himself puts, "liked particularly."[37] Given the lack of national African authors who could serve as models to develop his counternarrative, it is perhaps not surprising that the young novelist, writing in the language of the colonizer, turned to the authors he admired most for inspiration. Nor is it surprising that a still romantic form of "anxiety of influence" (Bloom's term) developed over time in a "mimetic rivalry" (Girard's term), a rivalry exacerbated by the violent cultural hierarchy that, in the 1970s, still divided these two authors. What I find surprising, however, concerns critical and theoretical practices more than personal artistic anxieties. We all know that as a critic Achebe violently rejects the notion of "frenzy" in *Heart of Darkness*, and, following the author, we have become quite accustomed to this image of Achebe. Hence the fact that in *Things Fall Apart* Achebe multiplies references to the notion of "frenzy" has largely gone unnoticed. This lack of critical awareness concerning such a loud and overly discussed controversy is disquieting and is symptomatic of the way ideological blinders interfere with the art of reading. Despite the equally loud proclamations of the death of the author in theory, an implicit ongoing tendency to trust the author more than the text in practice might also have played a role. In his essays on Conrad, in fact, Achebe never mentions his own novelistic usages of images of frenzy, not even to address how they differ from colonial images of Africa, while at the same time continuing to be very outspoken about what he calls Conrad's "images of gyrating and babbling savages."[38] Conversely, and somewhat revealingly, in his subsequent novels, Achebe is very careful not to reproduce such images, relegating them to the side of Conrad's narrative instead.[39]

Now, if we consider postcolonial power not in simple oppositional terms but in its complex process of opposition and connection (the hyphen that was once visible in "post-colonial" both opposes and connects the two terms), these paradoxical loops lead to the following mirroring interrogations: Could it be that the interpretative violence and intolerance that informs Achebe's mature postcolonial critique of Conrad in general and of the notion of "frenzy" in particular is at least partially motivated by the belated realization that he himself, in his youth, had uncritically assimilated such colonial images, reproducing them in his own postcolonial picture of Africa? More positively framed: What if the diagnostic sharpness of Achebe's postcolonial insights into the racist implications of images of frenzy stems partly from the belated realization that he himself had unwittingly been caught in the network of colonial discourses and their wounding representations? In short, what if Achebe's postcolonial critique of power stems, at least partially, from his mimetic implication in colonial power?

To be sure, such an avowal would not necessarily have been strategically productive for Achebe to make at the time he was writing "An Image of Africa," if only because it complicates the distinctions between dominant and subordinate, colonizer and colonized, he was working to set up. And given the foundational dimension of this distinction, we can understand why a theorist like Terry Eagleton cautions critics that there is a political risk in recent postcolonial developments that stress the "mutual implications" between colonizer and colonized.[40] The dominant is not the subaltern. Granted. Yet the point of an analysis that unmasks at the microlevel how power circulates freely from narratives to counternarratives is not necessarily meant to "blunt the political cutting-edge of anti-colonialist critique."[41] On the contrary, making visible this mimetic entanglement between the dominant and the subordinate allows us to sharpen our understanding of both the oppressive and productive dimensions of postcolonial mimesis for a series of theoretical reasons, which I now flesh out as concisely as possible—as arrows for future readers to pick up.

First, Achebe's youthful assimilation of the dominant language of frenzy in his narrative practice illustrates what theorists of power have been arguing for a while now. Namely, that there is no safe position outside of power to launch a critique of power, no simple antagonistic oppositional strategy to critique the network of power relations in which we operate. Informed, nolens volens, by dominant forms of discourse, the postcolonial novelist and critic who turns the language of the oppressor against itself is always confronted with the risk of reproducing some of the images she or he sets out to counter. We are, of course, not immune to this risk. As Said reminds us, "the power of discourse is that it is at once the object of struggle and the tool by which the struggle is conducted."[42] The case of Achebe the novelist suggests that the risk is, of course, worth taking. Mimetic re-*productions* like *Things Fall Apart* have the power to counter oppressive images of Africa, inverse some of their presuppositions, and, more generally, open up new fields of studies that allow for new pictures of Africa to emerge.

Second, Achebe's narrative reproduction of the language of frenzy in the context of his counternarrative indicates that discursive power is more insidious than initially realized. It transgresses the frontiers between the dominant and the subordinate, affects and infects its most outspoken and original critics, and continues to be operative in the interstices where the "post" in "postcolonial" both opposes and connects its "colonial" counterpart. Unmasking operations, then, require a higher degree of critical and theoretical vigilance that has been exercised so far in order to diagnose the paradoxical logic of mimetic patho(-)logies that destabilize unilateral evaluations. This logic does not hesitate to make visible the mechanisms whereby power, and the racist images it conveys, can continue to partially speak through the pen of the most astute and insightful critics of colonial power, rendering counternarratives both complicit with and subversive of dominant representations of the other.

Third, the realization that power crosses disciplinary and political boundaries should alert critics not to polarize debates on the basis of given disciplinary, ideological, and authorial intentions. If mimetic rivalries continue to generate quarrels between competing fields of study, which often reproduce at the level of theoretical discourse the very violence they critique in practice, less rivalrous postcolonial alternatives are now in view. For instance, taking our clue from Foucault's affirmation that power "must be analyzed as something that circulates,"[43] we could turn our diagnostic lenses to the impersonal movement of power and its process of spiraling circulation from dominant to subaltern narratives, and vice versa. This should allow us to continue exposing and critiquing the less visible, but not less damaging pathologies of racist discourse in a postcolonial world where the cultural barrier between the dominant and the subordinate is not always easy to locate—which does not mean that it fails to operate in covert and no less oppressive ways.

Finally, this exemplary debate teaches us that forms of narrative subjection to dominant images of Africa can be productive of sharp critical discourses that effectively counter power through the very realization that one has been subjected to power. If Said was quick to recognize that the "most interesting post-colonial writers bear their [colonial] past with them," both in the form of "humiliating wounds" and of "revised visions of the past tending towards a new future" (*CI* 34), an account of postcolonial mimesis furthers this insight by articulating a patho-logical connection between these apparently competing claims. Namely, that subjection to humiliating forms of wounding can potentially serve as a catalyst for the (anti-)mimetic emergence of powerful critiques of the narratives that have inflicted such wounds in the first place. In fact, it is not unlikely that Achebe's assimilation and reproduction of some of the images of frenzy in his fiction (mimetic pathology) enabled him, in due time, to think through the full implications of such images of Africa and to effectively turn this realization to productive diagnostic use in order to make visible what exactly is wounding in such images (mimetic patho-logy). Critical lenses and analytical insights can thus be sharpened by the belated realization that the speaking subject whose intention is to write back to the empire can, at the same time, be subjected to the power she or he denounces.

The subaltern can, indeed, mime, and original creations emerge from this form of postcolonial imitation. After all, if we inverse an old Christian saying, we could say that after receiving a speck of sawdust in our eye, we can better the see the beam in our brother's eye. Or, to echo an Igbo proverbial counterpart Achebe is fond of quoting, "when one thing falls, another stands in its place."

           ·      ·      ·

The ideological fence that divided narrative and counternarrative in the past falls, but a new theoretical bridge stands in its place for the future. My point is not, of course, that Achebe would not have been in a position to write *Things Fall Apart* had he not been subjected to European narratives such as *Heart of Darkness*—though we probably would have had a quite different counternarrative. Nor that he would have failed to see the racist implications of Conrad's image of Africa had he not himself reproduced similar images of mimetic frenzy in his first novel—though we probably would have had a less tendentious and virulent critique. Rather, my point is that the specific case of Achebe's mimetic quarrel with Conrad offers us a productive case study to radically rethink a fierce personal, disciplinary, and cultural debate that has generated quarrels in the past from a more impersonal, transdisciplinary, and, hopefully, less quarrelsome perspective for the future. This new Janus-faced perspective on postcolonial mimesis sets out to unmask, critique, and diagnose the workings of power—rather than of authors—for a globalized age that can no longer rely on neat conceptual boundaries that divide "colonizer" from "colonized," "dominant" from "subordinate"—yet continues to generate insidious, wounding, and powerful forms of oppression nonetheless. So, is Achebe's critique of Conrad a postcolonial Platonism? Yes and no. If the critical side of postcolonial mimesis is not without echoes of an old Platonic suspicion of mimetic images of reality, its novelistic side is part of a patho(-)logical form of discursive "subjection" that should be critiqued for its power of subordination, but should above all be considered in its productive role in the formation of counternarratives that, while in-*formed* by power, fight against power.

The case of Achebe's narrative and critical relation with Conrad is encouraging and forward oriented. It demonstrates that postcolonial mimesis is not only the site of disciplinary rivalries and vicious quarrels; it can also be the site of potential narrative reconciliations that can be set to productive critical and theoretical use. Mimetic re-productions of dominant racial stereotypes do not preclude innovative productions of new pictures of Africa; partial complicity with forms of colonial discourse does not preclude agency, least of all, narrative agency. On the contrary, the different forms of mimesis I have been tracking—anthropological, narrative, postcolonial—offer a starting point for the development of a critique of discursive stereotypes that goes beyond prepackaged distinctions between colonial and postcolonial texts, original and copy, bad and good mimesis, dominant pictures of Europe and subaltern pictures of Africa. It also looks forward to a mass-mediatized, hybrid, and globalized age in which neat distinctions between national, religious, cultural, and political boundaries no longer seem to hold, leaving the possibility open for liberating forms of cultural revolutions to emerge— mimetic revolutions that critique totalitarian messages through the effective use of the very same mimetic mass-media that were used as an instrument of subjection.[44]

Achebe's multilayered take on mimesis allows him not only to unveil the racist implications of Conrad's image of Africa but also to supplement Conrad's limited insight into the Janus-faced sides of mimetic frenzy. Above all, I find Achebe's postcolonial mimesis an enabling device instrumental in sketching an admirably complex and illuminating representation of Africa, a pictorial re-*presentation* that, in its firm oppositions, deft inversions, and covert reproductions of dominant images of Africa, turns out to be almost the opposite—but not quite.

# PART 3

# Metaphysics of Tragedy

# CHAPTER 6

# Surrealist Mimetism: Fear of the Dark in *The Nigger of the "Narcissus"*

No one could tell what was the meaning of that black man.

—Joseph Conrad, *The Nigger of the "Narcissus"*

From forbidden darkness emerges a second world (which is proper surreality).

—Roger Caillois, "Le surréalisme comme univers de signes"

The Preface of *The Nigger of the "Narcissus"* (1897) is Conrad's most concise attempt to give voice to his poetics. It is also a poetic statement that expresses the deeply felt aesthetic principles informing his artistic practice, modernist principles that challenge long-standing assumptions about the relation between art and philosophy, appearance and essence, reality and truth. Going against a long and venerable philosophical tradition that has its origins in Plato's *Republic*, Conrad counters ancient devaluations of art as a mere imitation, reproduction, or shadow of an ideal, transcendental reality in order to advocate the creative, productive, and above all illuminating power of artistic creation. He also champions the artist—over and against the philosopher and the scientist—as the main figure on the

modernist scene endowed with the gift to unveil what he considers "enduring and essential" (*NN* xi). Thus Conrad opens the Preface by affirming that
"art itself may be defined as a single-minded attempt to render the highest
kind of justice to the visible universe, by bringing to light the truth, manifold
and one, underlying its every aspect" (xi). The task of the artist, as Conrad
famously puts it in an enigmatic passage that continues to require meditation, is thus "to make you hear, to make you feel—it is, before all, to make
you *see*" (xiv). And thanks to this artistic insight into the essence of things,
he concludes that readers might perhaps even catch "that glimpse of truth for
which [they] have forgotten to ask" (xiv).

### Artistic Truth, Philosophical Lies

This celebration of artistic truth is, indeed, a bold opening move for a
new artist on the modernist scene. It reopens ancient quarrels long fought
between art and philosophy, specialists of affects and specialists of concepts,
and redresses the balance in favor of art. The Preface, in fact, stresses that
the philosophical focus on abstract "ideas," as well as the scientific take on
hard "facts," does not come anywhere near what Conrad considers "the very
truth of [human] existence" (xi). For him, as for his romantic predecessors,
literature is clearly not the ancilla of philosophy; nor can it simply be considered as antithetical to philosophy. Rather, literature turns out to be, once
again, the feared double or shadow of philosophy, a mimetic shadow that, in
a deft move of (re)appropriation, turns the traditional object of philosophy
("truth manifold and one") into its own subject of representation. Given the
far-reaching implications of this overturning gesture, the old questions that
go along with this literary-philosophical quarrel over the reality of shadows
immediately resurface for the modernist artist and critic to resolve. For
instance, the reader is made to wonder: How can the artist bring to light
a truth that, we are told, "underlies" the visible and is thus, by definition,
invisible? What exactly is the missing link between the visible world of manifold phenomena and its underlying, unitary "truth," the apparent ephemeral
world and what is "enduring and essential"? And if Conrad's early modernist
poetics joins art and truth, aesthetics and ontology, appearance and essence,
what, then, is the logical relation that connects these competing spheres?

## Metaphysical Riddles

Over the past several decades, critics have confronted these theoretical problems by addressing the philosophical underpinnings of Conrad's poetics of darkness. Ian Watt, for instance, in his illuminating and now canonical *Conrad in the Nineteenth Century*, says that in the Preface Conrad provides "a view of 'how we go'" from pluralism to truth, the singular to the universal.[1] Watt acknowledges that this is already a lot to be grateful for. But when it comes to the fundamental question as to "how to rescue the universal meaning from the evanescent concrete particular," he is much less positive in his evaluation. And in a provocative affirmation he concludes his incisive account by ironically saying: "three-quarters of a century and many foundations grants later, we still await reliable information."[2] Despite the impressive amount of criticism Conrad continues to generate in general, and the careful readings generated by the Preface in particular,[3] we are still awaiting an answer to this fundamental question. This chapter proposes a solution to this literary/philosophical riddle by revisiting the metaphysical fear of the dark that informs Conrad's poetics of darkness. After psychology and anthropology it is now the turn of ontology to give us a supplementary patho-logical insight into the mimetic and, as we shall see, tragic foundations of Conrad's shadow.

Modernist writers from Friedrich Nietzsche to D. H. Lawrence, Thomas Mann to Virginia Woolf, have relentlessly addressed the metaphysical mystery of the dissolution of the modern subject. But it is arguably Joseph Conrad who has taken it upon himself to explore the dissolution of individuation in an ocean of darkness with most tenacity, persistence, and illuminating power. Conrad's emphasis on an abyssal darkness that emerges, shadowlike, from introspective analyses, affective turbulences, and dissolution of boundaries that are *tremendus et fascinas* continues to be deeply "rooted" in romantic preoccupations with the expressive power of the imagination that breaks with theories of imitation.[4] And yet, if Conrad's message is romantic in metaphysical inspiration, his medium is modernist in its aesthetic representation. As we shall confirm in the next chapter, *Heart of Darkness* continues to be his most ambitious, influential, and philosophically dense modernist text in this respect. However, I would like to suggest that in *The Nigger of the "Narcissus"* Conrad is doing something no less ambitious and equally radical, both at the level of thematic and aesthetic experimentation. Given the anti-Platonic overtones of Conrad's poetics, we should not be surprised to see that his artistic solution to the metaphysical riddles he posits in the Preface shall not be straightforwardly Platonic. The modernist artist, in other words, does not rely on a classical philosophical view of art understood as a simple copy, or imitation far removed from the true, essential, and enduring world, for reasons that are as ontological as they are aesthetical. Ontological because Conrad does not partake in a hierarchical metaphysics that considers the immanent, phenomenal world as a mere "shadow" of ideal, transcendental forms. Thus in the Preface he immediately specifies that, unlike the (idealist) philosopher and the (realist) scientist, the (modernist) artist does not turn his illuminating gaze upward, toward the transcendental world of "ideas," but inward, toward the immanent world of the "senses" (xiii). And aesthetic because his artistic practice is not predicated on a realist poetics that considers art as a mirroring reflection of phenomenal reality (the many), let alone an ideal, intelligible, and abstract reality (the one). Hence he makes clear that in order to represent a truth that is both manifold and one, he must abandon the still mimetic language of "Realism, Romanticism, Naturalism" (xiv–xv).

## Mimetic Answers

And yet this does not mean that the classical answer to the riddle of mediation between art and truth, the physical and the metaphysical—that is, mimesis understood in its protean manifestations—is left out of Conrad's narrative picture. As we have had numerous occasions to see, this protean principle traverses, chameleon-like, Conrad's entire corpus. Like a secret shadow, mimesis in-*forms* the doubles and double binds, possessions and dispossessions, identifications and reconciliations at the heart of Conrad's poetics. As we now turn to consider some of the darkest of Conrad's tales, the presence of this shadow not only intensifies; it also reveals the metaphysics of tragedy animating his antirealistic view of artistic creation. This also means that the pervasiveness of images of "darkness" that haunt texts like *The Nigger of the "Narcissus," Almayer's Folly, Heart of Darkness*, and *The Secret Agent* cannot be confined to the riddles informing the ethics of catastrophe we have encountered in part 1; nor to the anthropological quarrels I examined in part

2—though they continue to be part of Conrad's preoccupations. As we turn to see in part 3, for Conrad, images of darkness acquire a larger, metaphysical dimension insofar as they are inextricably connected to the tragedy of death and the dissolution of individuation it entails.

This dark side has been relegated to the background by critics concerned with identity politics in the last decades of the twentieth century, but it resurfaces again in the twenty-first century.[5] As a preliminary gesture to foreground this metaphysical re-turn in Conrad studies, I suggest that it is precisely this type of darkness in the background that goes beyond the physical and which both sustains and dissolves the human shadows in the foreground that Conrad's artistic praxis attempts to "make us see"—via the illuminating medium of mimesis. There is, in fact, a sense in which, for Conrad, the *Sturm und Drang* that is at the heart of humans mirrors, in an enigmatic, nonrealistic, shadowy way, the larger "stress and strife" (xii) that is at the heart not only of the modern subject but also of the physical and metaphysical world that surrounds it. Hence the need for the modernist artist to do justice to the visible world by turning his gaze toward that dark, shadowy region within himself first, in order to subsequently account for metaphysics of darkness that follows, shadowlike, this physical self.

In his poetics, Conrad does not fully spell out the principles of his mode of aesthetic re-presentation in the language of criticism (or *logos*), but this does not mean that his poetic principles fail to give form to his artistic craft (or *praxis*). As we turn our attention from the Preface to *The Nigger of the "Narcissus,"* we shall see that this early modernist text, with its insistent emphasis on images of darkness, is not only looking back to an "impressionistic" aesthetics; nor can it simply be dismissed because of its "racist," ideological implications—though these principles continue to inform it. Rather, in a characteristic Janus-faced gesture, Conrad looks back to a mimetic metaphysics of darkness that is romantic in its original inspiration but will have to wait the coming of surrealism in the 1930s and 1940s in order to be explicitly articulated. Instead of relying on an old-fashioned understanding of mimetic realism to mediate between appearance and reality, the many and the one, Conrad's poetics of darkness continues to make our understanding of mimesis new. It does so by advocating a nonrealist, self-consciously modernist and, above all, surrealist fascination for images of darkness that blur the boundaries of individuation in order to reveal an intimately felt fear of the dark that is perhaps less physical than metaphysical, less anchored in reality than in what the surrealist writer and mimetic theorist avant la lettre Roger Caillois will call "surreality" (*la surréalité*). As we shall see, the detour via the problematic of mimesis and the kaleidoscopic shadows it generates, allows us to tackle, and perhaps resolve, the "metaphysical puzzle" Ian Watt urges us to reconsider.

## Mimetic Ontology

First published in 1897, *The Nigger of the "Narcissus"* occupies a privileged place in Conrad's corpus: it is not only the novel that marks his transition from a life at sea to a life at a writing desk but is also "the book by which, not as a novelist perhaps, but as an artist striving for the utmost sincerity of expression, [Conrad is] willing to stand or fall" (ix). This is, indeed, a perilous claim for an artist to make; especially since this text, even more explicitly than *Heart of Darkness*, seems to scandalously operate within the racist assumptions that have continued to haunt, perhaps even rock, the world of Conrad studies. The "N-word" is certainly shocking for contemporary readers to see, so shocking that in a recent edition of the tale, the editor goes as far as substituting "N-word" for every occurrence of the word "nigger" in the tale, now retitled *The N-word of the "Narcissus."* Alternatively, and on more serious scholarly grounds, critics have argued that the darkness that pervades the tale represents "our human blackness," and is "epistemologically rather than morally significant."[6] Still, even from this critical perspective, we are far from having answered what, exactly, this episteme of blackness reveals, and why this insight should be so central to Conrad's artistic vision. A possible clue, however, is already suggested by the title of the novel itself. We should in fact not forget that there is another "N-word" in the title: that is, "Narcissus." This reference to a mythic figure enthralled with its mirror image to the point of death in a narrative that turns around the ambivalent feelings generated by a dying protagonist should make us wonder as to which forms of mimetic reflections, affective echoes, and, perhaps, even tragic recognitions this novel ultimately attempts to make us see.

This turn to the specular question of mimesis to address the fundamental relation between art and truth, appearance and essence, and, by doing so,

cast new light on the images of darkness that pervade this particular tale—
and, by extension, Conrad's poetics as a whole—might initially surprise.
After all, *The Nigger of the "Narcissus"* is not a mimetic text in the sense that
it does not represent a transparent, fully realistic, mirrorlike image of reality. Even though the events narrated are grounded in reality, and external
referents are never out of sight for Conrad, the text is impressionistically
opaque, modernist in its obscurity, perhaps even surrealist in its suggestiveness. Hence the images of darkness that pervade it do not simply re-present
(present again) a physical, nautical reality, but re-create (create anew) a
metaphysical sphere beyond reality. This point is suggested repeatedly in
the text, and is especially visible at moments of potential catastrophe, when
the microcosm of the ship is threatened by the macrocosm of the ocean
that surrounds it. For instance, consider the description of the *Narcissus* as
it is approaching Cape Horn, at a decisive turning point in the narrative on
which the entire destiny of the crew depends. "Out of the abysmal darkness of the black cloud overhead white hail streamed on her" (*NN* 53), says
the narrator. He continues: "Nothing seems left of the whole universe but
darkness, clamor, fury—and the ship" (54). And he adds: "Soon the clouds
closed up and the world again became a raging, blind darkness that howled,
flinging at the lonely ship salt sprays and sleet" (55). Such dark, ominous
descriptions pervade the novel, enveloping it from beginning to end. They
inform its atmosphere, tonality, and mood, indicating that this is not simply
a realistic narrative about a perilous physical journey from the Indian to the
Atlantic Ocean; it is also a metaphysical journey that exposes readers to the
invisible, underlying darkness associated with the direct, and quite literal,
threat of annihilation. Could it be, then, that the darkness that pervades
Conrad's poetic praxis is there to reflect, in an obscure, enigmatic way, the
abyssal dissolution of the boundaries of individuation in a more "enduring
and essential" sphere that had, thus far, been mainly the domain of philosophers and metaphysicians?

We have seen that in the Preface, Conrad addresses classical aesthetic
questions concerning the relation between ideas and phenomena, essence
and appearance, light and shadows, structuring his poetics on the classical
metaphysical distinction between the "manifold" and the "one," the "visible"
and the "invisible." What we must add now is that this artistic metaphysics
has not only classical but also modern philosophical antecedents. In fact,

as Conrad posits "pity" at the center of what he calls "the latent feeling of fellowship with all creation," stresses "the warlike conditions of existence" (xii), and defines music as the "art of arts" (xiii), he is implicitly revealing his debt to a philosophical figure who also considered truth as something that needs to be "brought to light from darkness"[7] via artistic media. That is, the German romantic philosopher Arthur Schopenhauer.

## Philosophical Surfaces (Conrad and Schopenhauer)

Critics have rightly noticed that Schopenhauer is a pessimist philosopher Conrad had many elective affinities with, but these affinities might run deeper than previously realized, for they rest on common nautical and metaphysical foundations. Schopenhauer, in fact, like Nietzsche after him, also relied on the image of a ship in stormy waters in order to account for the metaphysical relation between the manifold world of phenomena (what he called "representation," or *Vorstellung*) and the unitary and essential world that sustains these phenomena (what he called "will," or *Wille*). Here is how the philosopher puts it in the *World as Will and Idea*: "Just as in a stormy sea that, unbounded in all directions, raises and drops mountainous waves, howling, a sailor sits in a boat and trusts in his frail bark: so in the midst of a world of torments the individual human being sits quietly, supported by and trusting in the *principium individuationis*."[8] A sailor, a ship, and a stormy metaphysical ocean that threatens to engulf the fragile boat of individuation. The relevance of such a conceptual image for a pessimistic writer with metaphysical inclinations who spent good part of his life at sea and had firsthand knowledge of such "mountainous waves" is clear. Schopenhauer's nautical image also provides us with a useful metaphysical frame to reframe the fundamental polarity that Conrad's novel attempts to represent: if the *Narcissus* stands for the world of passing phenomena linked to individuation (the many), the ocean of darkness stands for an impersonal, immortal sphere linked to what is "enduring and essential" (the one). Conrad's metaphysical riddle could then be rephrased thus: how can the image of a dark, impersonal sea, mirror, represent, and thus render visible the fundamental reality that both sustains and threatens to founder the personal boat of individuation?

Schopenhauer's answer to this question is as anti-Platonic as it is Platonic. Anti-Platonic because he privileges art as a medium to approach what is enduring and essential, most notably, the less representative of all the arts (that is, music) influencing thus a strain of literary-philosophical figures from Nietzsche to Pater, Wilde to Conrad. Platonic because his definition of music as a "transparent mirror of the essence of things" indicates that he continues to rely on the understanding of art as representation, or "mirror" (*WWI* 274), to think through the relation between the world of phenomena and the world of Being, the manifold and the One. The romantic philosopher, as Nietzsche will also notice, is thus caught within the Platonic ontology he seeks to overturn. But what about the modernist artist?

If we return to *The Nigger of the "Narcissus"* with this philosophical frame in mind, it is clear that in order to account for the process of mediation between the essence of things and their phenomenal apparition, we can no longer consider the dark, metaphysical ocean in the background in isolation. Rather, we need to see it in relation to the physical foreground: that is, the ship (the *Narcissus*) with its shadowy crew in general, and the physically dark protagonist (the "Nigger") in particular. In fact, the enigmatic presence of a black character onto whom much of the metaphysical anxiety of the tale is projected gains from being read in a relation of continuity with the ocean of darkness that surrounds and threatens to dissolve what Schopenhauer calls "the frail bark" of individuation. It is thus no accident that from the very beginning of the tale, and repeatedly so thereafter, James Wait is represented as being quite literally indistinguishable from this darkness in the background. As he initially appears on board the *Narcissus*, we are informed that "the face was indistinguishable" (*NN* 17) in the darkness. Later, the narrator says that "in the blackness of the doorway a pair of eyes glimmered white, and big, and staring" (34). And as his illness worsens, and the shadow of death— what Conrad also calls "the very shadows of Eternity" (*PR* 30)—approaches, we are told that he is lying, with his "black face . . . blinded and invisible in the midst of an intense darkness" (*NN* 104).

These are unusually obscure visual representations, no matter how dark-skinned the protagonist actually is, and over the years critics have often wondered about their narrative function in the general economy of Conrad's tale and poetics at large. A common observation is that the figure of Jimmy embodies the binaries upon which the tale is structured, binaries such as white and darkness but also, by symbolic extension, life and death, truth and lies, solidarity and selfishness, good and evil, and so on. This is certainly possible at a deep, allegorical level. And yet, if we remain for a moment still on the surface of the visual phenomena Conrad takes the trouble to represent, we have to stress that what is most apparent in these images of darkness are not so much the binary conceptual oppositions as such but, rather, the binary aesthetic conjunctions these dark images form. On a closer look, these binaries are no longer, strictly speaking, opposed: a visual continuum blends the physical darkness of the tragic figure in the foreground and the metaphysical darkness in the background. Thus, as the narrator describes Jimmy's "black face" as being "*invisible* in the midst of an intense darkness" or, alternatively, when he says that the "face was *indistinguishable*" (my emphasis), it is no longer clear where the dark human figure ends and the dark background begins. The repeated definition of Wait as a "phantom" or "shadow"—terms that loom large in Conrad's metaphysics of the subject—is thus most apt to indicate his intermediary ontological status: he is suspended on the shadow-line in-between foreground and background, the mortal men on the ship and the "immortal sea" old Singleton sees, "unchanged, black and foaming under the eternal scrutiny of the stars" (99). Consequently, if Wait has to be read symbolically at all (as a symbol of death, for instance), we should be extremely careful not to read this symbol in clear-cut binary terms, as if death were simply antithetical to life, the metaphysical darkness in the background simply antithetical to the physical darkness in the foreground. The visual universe Conrad depicts suggests that the opposite is true: as a "shadow" cast against a dark background, Jimmy is a figure that consistently transgresses the "shadow-line" between light and darkness, foreground and background, the physical world and the metaphysical world, what is ephemeral and what is "enduring and essential."

Jimmy is, indeed, a mimetic figure, just as a shadow is a mimetic image; and like every figure, or image, he needs to be framed in his proper aesthetic context in order to be properly seen. It should be clear by now that if aesthetic mimesis remains at the center of Conrad's single-minded artistic attempt to mediate between the (visible) "universe" and (invisible) "truth," *The Nigger of the "Narcissus"* goes beyond a realistic principle in order to make us see a deeper, evanescent, and, above all, more obscure metaphysical principle. It does so by showing how the dark protagonist of the tale in the foreground merges, mimetically—that is, chameleon-like—against an impersonal ocean of "darkness" in the background. As we shall repeatedly confirm, this blurring

of the shadow-line that structures the ontology of the tale *is* the central principle of Conrad's tragic metaphysics. It allows him to establish that "perfect
blending of form and substance" (xiii) he strives to achieve, a blending generated by a mimetic continuity that mediates between the personal physical
darkness of the protagonist and the impersonal metaphysical darkness of
the ocean, the ephemeral phenomenal subject and the enduring, essential
reality that both sustains it and threatens to dissolve it. What we must add
now is that this mimetic principle has not only ontological implications (the
sphere of the "philosopher"); it is also fundamentally in line with Conrad's
affective and aesthetic preoccupations that inform his poetics (the sphere of
the "artist").

## Artistic Depth (Conrad and Breton)

So far we have been floating on the formal surface of the text in order to
render visible the principle of mimetic continuity that gives aesthetic form
to Conrad's poetics of darkness from without. Let us now plunge deeper into
that "lonely region of stress and strife" (xii) characteristic of the deeply felt
affective sources that inform his literary shadows from within.

Much has been said about Conrad's impressionism, understandably
so given the neat fit between impressionism and Conrad's opaque images
of darkness.[9] This venerable association should, however, not preclude the
exploration of alternative artistic affiliations. Here is a new aesthetic association: the "secret spring" of Conrad's "responsive emotions" (xiii) emerges as
the tragic figure of the tale is progressively haunted by what the founder of
surrealism, André Breton, would later call, in the "Manifesto of Surrealism"
(1924), "the surrealist voice." That is, a voice that "continues to preach on
the eve of death and above storms" functioning as "an invisible ray" on the
most obscure realities of the imagination.[10] In this sense, Conrad is perhaps
a surrealist writer avant la lettre, for his Preface echoes, in an uncanny way,
principles internal to the surrealist poetics.

This does not mean that Conrad follows *à la lettre* surrealist techniques
such as automatic writing, dream analysis, and collage, nor that he is a direct
influence on surrealism. Rather, this means that Conrad's poetics foreshadows what André Breton, in his *Second Manifesto*, calls the surrealist "idea."
Breton writes:

Let us not lose sight of the fact that the idea of Surrealism aims quite simply at the total recovery of our psychic force by a means which is nothing
other than the dizzying descent into ourselves, the systematic illumination of hidden places and the progressive darkening of other territory (*la
descente vertigineuse en nous, l'illumination systématique des lieux cachés et
l'obscurcissement progressif des autres lieux*).[11]

The echoes with Conrad's Preface—with its emphasis on the artist's
"descen[t] within himself" in order to make us see an "episode in the obscure
lives of a few individuals" in a "dark corner of the earth" (xii)—are loud and
clear. For both Breton and Conrad, the goal of the artist is to put his or her
introverted psychic faculties to work in order to explore the mysterious,
affective darkness at the heart of the subject and, in a second moment, to use
artistic surfaces to give aesthetic form to illuminating and surreal pictures.
The context is different, but the Janus-faced principles remain the same. It
is as if turning back to a romantic ontology allows Conrad to foreshadow
fundamental principles that animate Breton's surrealist aesthetics.

But Conrad gives a mimetic twist to this surrealist turn. If Breton
was content with magical, supernatural, and thus transcendental forms of
inspiration, Conrad does not let go of natural, human, and thus immanent principles. In fact, Conrad's luminous ray into the horror beyond the
threshold of life gives narrative voice to an anxiety of dissolution of identity
that has so far gone unnoticed in Conrad studies and modernist studies, but
that is well known in the transdisciplinary field of mimetic theory. More
precisely, Conrad's representation of a figure that merges against a dark,
homogeneous, chromatic background entails an assimilation to space that
matches, this time *à la lettre*, what the French anthropologist, avant-garde
theorist, and surrealist writer Roger Caillois famously called "mimetism" (*le
mimétisme*).

## The Mimetism of Psychasthenia

Unlike his closest early collaborator and dissident surrealist thinker George
Bataille, Roger Caillois is not as yet a well-known figure in new modernist studies. However, the recent edition of *The Edge of Surrealism: A Roger*

*Caillois Reader*, as well as other literary and anthropological explorations, testifies to the growing interest in the heterogeneous work of a writer Georges Dumézil did not hesitate to call "the genius of our time."[12] An insight into Caillois's transdisciplinary take on mimesis (a take that straddles biology, anthropology, and psychology) not only offers us a precious key to continue unfolding the invisible logic that gives form to Conrad's images of darkness; it also reveals Conrad's untimely anticipation of fundamental mimetic principles that will have to wait the 1930s and 1940s in order to be explicitly formulated. As usual, mimetic theory shall not simply be applied to Conrad. On the contrary, it is Conrad who anticipates and furthers mimetic theory.

## Caillois's Diagnostic

In a chapter titled "Mimétisme et psychasthénie légéndaire" collected in *Le Mythe et l'homme* and originally published in 1938, Roger Caillois considers mimetic phenomena of physical camouflage in the animal world in order to cast light on a mimetic phenomenon of psychic depersonalization in the human world.[13] Taking as his starting point certain lower animals (such as spiders or lizards), Caillois observes that they are mimetic in the physical sense that they have a tendency to visually disappear, chameleon-like, in order to blend with the homogenous background against which they are situated. Caillois notices that in such a state, the mimetic figure in the foreground is, quite literally, indistinguishable from the background, and wonders about the origin of this disquieting mimetic phenomenon. The classical answer, of course, is that mimetism is a defense mechanism perfected through evolution meant to guarantee the survival of the species. This is certainly a realistic, positivist hypothesis in line with scientific and philosophical principles Caillois is familiar with. But Caillois, surrealist writer that he is, has a different, more artistic hypothesis in mind.[14] In his view, "what is essential about this phenomenon" is that the blending between living organism and background entails what he calls a "return to an inorganic state" (*MH* 116). In fact, he notices that the static insect nested on inorganic matter is not simply invisible, but enters in a state of "catalepsy" whereby "life," as he says, "steps back a degree [*recule d'un degree*]" (113). Caillois's hypothesis, then, is that rather than being a strategy for survival, this mimetic principle is associated with a drive that pulls the animate, organic being toward inanimate, inorganic matter. Coming close to the Freudian conception of Thanatos, but echoing philosophical principles that go back to Schopenhauer and Spinoza, Caillois infers from these phenomena a mimetic death drive that induces a dissolution of the boundaries of individuation. As he puts it: "the being's will to persevere in *its* being [*la volonté de l'être de perséverer dans* son *être*] consumes itself to excess and secretly attracts it toward the uniformity that scandalizes its imperfect autonomy" (122). In sum, for Caillois, this disquieting form of mimesis whereby a figure disappears against the homogeneous background that surrounds it is not simply a *visual*, external phenomenon. It is rather an *affective*, interior phenomenon that pulls a living being on the side of death, while leaving it on the side of life, or better, on the shadow-line that both connects and divides life and death.

Now, as an anthropologist of surrealist inspiration, Caillois is clearly much more interested in the human than in the natural world. If he focuses on natural, mimetic phenomena it is because, in his view, this mechanism reveals a fundamental psychic principle at the heart of humans. His thesis rests on the "psychological analysis," not of Freud, but of the long-neglected French philosopher and psychologist Pierre Janet. Janet, it should be recalled, invented the term *analyse psychologique* in the first place to account for phenomena of automatism, hypnotic dissociation, and double personality, among other mimetic pathologies; was a major source of inspiration for the surrealist generation; paved the way for a Freudian discovery of the unconscious, which, as historians of psychology have now demonstrated, was not a discovery at all;[15] and, as critics are beginning to realize, is a key figure in new modernist studies and mimetic theory as well. On Janet's broad shoulders, Caillois establishes a connection between animal mimesis and human mimesis, a physical blurring of forms and a psychic dissolution of individuation, or, as he puts it, "mimetism" and "legendary psychasthenia." Janet had devoted a lengthy study to "psychasthenia," a personality trouble that affects people's relation to their environment and affects the unity of the ego, generating shadows, or phantoms of egos.[16] Building on Janet's case studies, Caillois explains that "for these dispossessed spirits, space seems to be endowed with a devouring capacity. . . . The body, then, dissociates itself from thought so that the individual crosses the frontier of its skin and lives on the other side of its senses" (111). These subjects are vulnerable to affects that trouble the boundaries of individuation and establish a continuity between the human inside and the nonhuman outside. This is why, in a phrase Conrad would probably have liked to see, he concludes: "The subject itself feels that it is becoming space, *black space*" (111). Caillois is not simply describing individuals who are physically invisible in the darkness here, but something much more disquieting and fundamental. This process of becoming black space is disconcerting because it is not only something seen; it is above all something felt. Conrad would say that it reaches "the secret spring of responsive emotions" (*NN* xiii). It does so because it entails a feeling of psychic permeability to darkness that blurs the boundaries of individuation. Following the phenomenological and psychological work of Eugène Minkowski, Caillois explains the effects of darkness in clinical terms:

> Obscurity is not the simple absence of light; there is something positive in it. While clear space disappears in front of the materiality of objects, obscurity is "substantial" ["*étoffée*"]; it touches directly the individual, envelops, penetrates, and even traverses him/her. Hence, writes Minkowski, "the ego is *permeable* to obscurity whereas it is not so to light." (*MH* 112)

Does this experience sound too surreal? Go back in time and think of that all-too-real fear of the dark you experienced as a child. Why were you afraid? After all, as we now say in our role as parents, there is nothing to be afraid of. But the child in us might still reply that it is precisely this nothing that is frightening! This is, in a sense, also Caillois's reply. For him, children are afraid of the dark because their egos are still permeable and not yet fully formed. Caillois specifies that they do not fear darkness as such. Rather, what they fear is a loss of selfhood generated by the dissolution of boundaries between the figure and the background, the human organism and the nonhuman environment: "The magical hold . . . of night and obscurity, *the fear of the dark*, has unquestionably its roots in the threat it generates with respect to the opposition between the organism and the environment" (112). Caillois is not alone in suggesting this mimetic hypothesis. As that other theoretical chameleon of surrealist inspiration Jacques Lacan will also claim, children fear darkness for its affective power to dissolve the boundaries of the ego, just as they jubilate to see their own mirror-image for its power to delineate and give form to the ego.

Lacan, just like Freud, has received much critical attention, whereas other figures like Janet and Caillois have not. It has thus not been sufficiently stressed that Caillois's Janetian psychological analysis of mimesis and psychasthenia informs, quite directly, Lacan's celebrated "mirror stage" and provides the latter with a mimetic model of the unconscious for his own account of ego formation. Janet's influence on Lacan's "analysis of the ego" has been characteristically erased, but the theoretical shadow Caillois casts is still clearly visible in "The Mirror Stage." Lacan writes: "But the facts of mimicry (*mimétisme*) are no less instructive when conceived as cases of heteromorphic identification, in as much as they raise the problem of the significance of space for the living organism."[17] And he specifies:

> We have only to recall how Roger Caillois (still young, his thought still fresh from his break with the sociological school that had formed it) illuminated the subject by using the term "*legendary psychasthenia*" to classify morphological mimicry (*mimétisme morphologique*) as an obsession with space in its derealizing effects.[18]

This is a revealing genealogical connection for mimetic theory. There is, in fact, a fundamental sense in which the mythical "mirror stage," with its celebrated account of the birth of the ego out of the subject's identification with a bright, heterogeneous, and ideal form (or *Gestalt*), is nothing less and nothing more than a mirroring inversion of what Caillois, following Janet, called legendary psychasthenia: that is, an intimately felt experience of the death of the ego out of the subject's nonspecular identification with a dark, homogeneous, and formless space. The Lacanian ego is thus the positive imprint of Caillois's negative configuration; the exterior form of the ego is what appears in the foreground once the inner experience of formlessness is left in the background. This is how the mirror stage became a legend, while psychasthenia was actually dissolved. But a theoretical lesson remains nonetheless: seemingly original theories, we should not be surprised to find out, have mimetic origins, which does not mean that mimetic pathologies can be easily cured.

Caillois is, in fact, careful not to dismiss this personality trouble as an anomalous, mimetic pathology that affects only children or neurotic cases. Rather, he considers both the animal (physical) mimesis and the human (psychic) pathology as revealing of a more generalized (metaphysical) anxiety of dissolution of the boundaries of individuation in "black space" that affects humanity in general. Moreover, his mimetic hypothesis has nothing to do with a fully visible, mirrorlike realistic representation of the self but, rather, designates an intimately felt, yet truly invisible, psychic dissolution of the boundaries of selfhood in spatial darkness, a dissolution that is most intimately and obscurely connected to the horror of death. In sum, unlike Lacan, Caillois stresses the importance of affect over vision, turbulent bodily senses over unitary images, becoming space rather than being an imago. This is why he provides us with a more direct access to Conrad's shadow and the unconscious, mimetic symptoms it generates.

## Psychasthenic Symptoms

If we now return to *The Nigger of the "Narcissus"* with these speculative considerations in mind, the specular image of the dying Jimmy, a black "shadow" consistently represented against a background of "darkness" that literally blurs the boundaries of his personal figure, begins to appear less impenetrable than it initially seemed to be. Over the years, critics have often wondered at Conrad's obsessive fascination with tropes of darkness in general and representations of Jimmy's darkness in particular, arguing whether this fascination should be read in realistic or symbolic terms. From a mimetic perspective attentive to the surrealist principles that inform this darkly textured tale, it is perhaps not necessary to advocate between these competing evaluations. As the narrator describes Jimmy as a "shadow of a man," a "black phantom" (*NN* 151) who is practically indistinguishable from the "the impenetrable darkness of earth and heaven" (104), he is representing on the page a mimetic fear of the dark that will later haunt the surrealist imagination as well. He is also giving aesthetic form to one of the most invisible affective manifestations of the mimetic unconscious, thereby diagnosing fears of dissolution of the ego that haunted the mind of modernism. Above all, Conrad is fulfilling the aesthetic promise made in the Preface that has troubled critics for so long. In fact, the artist is appealing to his "less obvious" emotional capacities within himself, in order to make visible and re-present a deeply felt mimetic anxiety of dissolution that haunts the heart of human beings in general and the narrator's imagination in particular. This is a secretly shared mimetic anxiety that, as

Conrad had put it in the Preface, "binds together all humanity—the dead to the living and the living to the unborn" (xii). In sum, Conrad's images of darkness, and the mimetic indifferentiation between figure and background they entail, function as a stylistic-surrealist-mimetic strategy to render visible an anxiety of a loss of individuation that is neither of the order of the factual (the sphere of the "scientist") nor of the ideal (the sphere of the "philosopher"), but of the affective instead (the sphere of the "artist").

To be sure, this is neither the first nor the last time that Conrad gives artistic form to an unconscious fear of mimetic dissolution that is as spatial as it is psychic. His tales are obsessively animated by insubstantial human and nonhuman figures that tend to disappear against a homogeneous, shady background. From Marlow's steamer whose "outlines blurred as if on the point of dissolving" (*YOS* 84) to the "shade of Mr. Kurtz" (95) that haunts *Heart of Darkness*, from the "shadows" of the crew affirming their survival in *The Shadow-Line* to the "shadow" that follows Razumov in *Under Western Eyes*, from Decoud's "doubt about his own individuality [that] had merged into the world of cloud and water" (497) in *Nostromo* to Heyst's passionate cry to Lena, "Here I am on a Shadow inhabited by Shades" in *Victory* (350), from the "gloom that seemed to envelop him [Jim] from head to foot like the shadow of a passing cloud" (176) in *Lord Jim* to Verloc's blending in the streets of London "as if he too were part of inorganic nature" (17) in *The Secret Agent*, Conrad's characters repeatedly find themselves wandering in a twilight zone in which the shadow-line that divides figure from background, human organism from nonhuman matter, is blurred along lines that are not simply visual or physical but also, and above all, psychic and metaphysical.

What Caillois called *le mimétisme* literally casts a long shadow on Conrad's physical figurations and metaphysical disfigurations. It equally stretches to inform Francis Ford Coppola's *Apocalypse Now*, an innovative cinematic interpretation of *Heart of Darkness* that is faithful to the underlying metaphysics of Conrad's surrealist poetics. Coppola, as we shall see in more detail later on, not only reproduces surreal landscapes that blur neat contours dividing human figures from natural backgrounds but also reveals the psycho-mimetic anxieties that inform such images. Hence when the most psychologically fragile member of Willard's crew, the surfer Lance (Sam Bottoms), covers his face with green camouflage paint, cries out to a

misty landscape, and progressively merges with ritual crowds of natives, he does so not so much for military, strategic, or survival purposes. Rather, he does so for artistic, psychic, and ontological purposes, mimetic purposes that are revealing a characteristic Conradian anxiety of dissolution Coppola's surrealist Vietnam War film manages to effectively represent.

Such a mimetic anxiety of dissolution is perhaps not surprising if we consider the types of subjects that tend to suffer from this psychic pathology. In *Les Névroses*, Pierre Janet specifies that "psychasthenia" tends to affect imaginative characters, such as artists and philosophers prone to shyness, social intimidation, and introversion. He also adds that it is often triggered by sudden and repeated changes of context, and the need for adaptation to new social environments.[19] This is an interesting patho-logical diagnostic for a study titled *Conrad's Shadow* dealing with a chameleon-like conceptual protagonist. It not only applies to that "phantom of man" who is James Wait, an alienated, anxious, and withdrawn black subject among a foreign, intimidating, and racist white crew. Nor does it solely concern so many Conradian characters who are confronted with imaginary, exotic journeys around the world whose culminating experiences challenge the very ontological foundations of their identity, generating fluttering shadows in place of stable egos. The shadow of psychasthenia also seems to stretch to affect Conrad himself, an imaginative, introverted, self-conscious artist who was, incidentally, also a foreign, transnational, multilingual subject shaped by a constant process of adaptation to the most strikingly different natural, social, cultural, and linguistic backgrounds, and who—let us not forget it—repeatedly suffered from different forms of psychosomatic anxieties that lead to depression and repeated mental breakdowns.[20] Could this be the reason why the shadow of mimetic psychasthenia haunts the entirety of Conrad's corpus?

*Peut-être.* What is certain is that in *The Nigger of the "Narcissus,"* the binary between symbolic and realistic reading is nonexistent, in the sense that the tale expresses a psychological reality that mirrors, in a surreal way, an all-too-human anxiety vis-à-vis the metaphysical darkness of death—a tragic reality that, throughout Conrad's writings, is "fundamental . . . , enduring and essential" (xi). This mimetic hypothesis is supported by the fact that these two dimensions of darkness (the psychic and the metaphysical) are constantly associated with the (physical) presence of the dying Jimmy along terms that are strikingly isomorphic with Caillois's account of mimetism and psychasthenia.

Take, for instance, the long description of the rescue after the storm, as Jimmy is trapped in the submerged cabin, enveloped in a palpable darkness that literally threatens to swallow up his life in the impersonality of death. Jimmy's fear of the dark is intimately linked to a literal fear of death and has a strong affective and infective impact on all the members of the crew. The narrator says: "The agony of his fear wrung our hearts so terribly that we longed to abandon him. . . . Probably he heard his own clamour but faintly. We could picture him crouching on the edge of the upper berth . . . in the dark, and with his mouth wide open for that unceasing cry" (67). This "picture" is obviously not mimetic in a realist sense; yet it is mimetic in the surreal sense that it reveals an interior and intimately felt fear of the dark: that is, a fear of self-dissolution in the darkness of space whereby, as Caillois clearly puts it, the subject "is not *in* space, he *is* this space" (*MH* 122). While fundamentally agreeing with Hillis Miller that Conrad's concern with images of darkness is essentially a concern with a "return to eternal rest,"[21] we are now in a position to see that Caillois's emphasis on "space," perhaps more than Heideggerian concerns with "time," is the key to access Conrad's metaphysics of darkness. From the beginning of the tale, in fact, the narrator links images of spatial darkness to a real enough fear of dissolution, of being trapped in dark, homogeneous space, such as the berths that, as the narrative had initially made ominously clear, "yawned black, like graves tenanted by uneasy corpses" (*NN* 22). In sum, at such moments it is not simply darkness as such that is associated with the horror of death, but the mimetic continuity between the black figure and the darkness that envelops him, the visible phenomenal subject and the invisible enduring essence all around him.

## From Restricted to General Mimetism

That said, it is important to stress that this struggle with the shadow of death at the heart of a human being cannot be restricted to a personal, existential, or minoritarian anxiety. Darkness, as it operates in the general economy of the tale (and Conrad's corpus in general), is not only linked to the dying black subject onto whom the metaphysical anxiety of the tale is projected; nor is it simply the product of the narrator's overheated imagination. Rather, from the very beginning of the journey, darkness stretches in order to envelop all the subjects on the frail bark of individuation, shadowy subjects whose "responsive emotions" render them affectively vulnerable to the psycho-metaphysical fear of the dark Jimmy physically embodies. In other words, the shadow of psychasthenia concerns not only what Conrad calls "the center of this ship's collective psychology" (ix) but also stretches to include all the characters that surround him. We are told, for instance, that his presence "overshadowed the ship" (47). As Jimmy is first introduced, we see him coming to the fore by "detaching himself from the shadowy mob of heads visible above the blackness" (15). And in an enigmatic yet for us revealing passage we read: "He seemed to hasten the retreat of departing light by his very presence; . . . a black mist emanated from him; a subtle and dismal influence; a something cold and gloomy that floated out and settled on all the faces *like a mourning veil*" (34; my emphasis). Clearly it is not only black Jimmy who is dark. The white mob is shadowy too. Consistently, the other members of the crew are defined as "heavy shadows" (145), "black clusters of human forms" (123), or, as the narrator says at the very opening of the tale, "silhouettes . . . very black, without relief, like figures cut out of sheet tin" (3). In *The Nigger of the "Narcissus,"* blackness is clearly not restricted to racial blackness. On the contrary, it mirrors in a nonrealistic reflection, a more generalized metaphysical fear of the dark (and the dissolution of boundaries it entails) that haunts the crew in general and, as we shall soon see, the narrator's imagination in particular. These shadows are mimetic in the surreal sense that they generate forms without boundaries, subjects without relief, appearances without substance. These figures that emerge from the darkness are not men but shadows of men, not egos but phantoms of egos.

We can now see that these two shades of blackness (racial and metaphysical) do not simply operate independently, side by side. They are rather two sides of the same picture, a Janus-faced picture that urges readers to adopt a chameleon-like form of double-vision and look, simultaneously, both to the physical and to the metaphysical sides of darkness. In fact, if we put on our metaphysical lenses we see that the shadow of mimesis represented in the novel is instrumental in bringing together the (anti-)Platonic, Schopenahuerian, and surrealist threads that inform Conrad's poetics of darkness. Toward the end of the tale, while Wait is really waiting to die, Conrad's mimetic rhetoric takes us through an impressive tour de force that has the power to inverse ontological relations between truth and illusion, shadows and reality:

> In the magnificence of the phantom rays the ship appeared pure like a vision of ideal beauty, illusive like a tender dream of serene peace. And nothing in her was real, nothing was distinct and solid but the heavy shadows that filled her decks with their unceasing and noiseless stir: the shadows darker than the night and more restless than the thoughts of men. (145)

Conrad's lyrical ascension to the high spheres of "ideal beauty" appears to be Platonic in initial orientation. And yet the artist ironically undermines Platonism by linking a seemingly ideal, transcendental "vision" to the mimetic, immanent sphere of "phantom[s]." Thus, he suggests, this time with Schopenhauer, that what appears to be "real" is but a "dream" or "illusion." Finally, in a surrealist mood in line with Caillois, he locates what is real and essential in the mimetic sphere of "shadows darker than the night," surrealist shadows that mirror the secret "thoughts of men" concerned with the looming shadow of death. Indeed, the shadow of mimesis has fallen on more than one ego. But what is revealed is not a unitary, ideal form. On the contrary. As Caillois puts it, "from forbidden darkness emerges a second world (which is proper surreality)."[22]

Seen in this light, then, the crew's deeply ambivalent feelings that swing them toward "Jimmy" and away from the "Nigger" continue to be related to the issue of moral solidarity generated by the secretly shared threat of annihilation I discussed in part 1. They also reveal the racist and antiracist evolutionary moves I diagnosed in part 2. But above all, they mirror the little-discussed ambivalence of the crew's mimetic fear of the dark and the dissolution in the physical and metaphysical darkness it foreshadows that is central to part 3. In the middle of a violent storm that threatens to disrupt their "small planet" (29) in the "black turmoil of the waves" along catastrophic lines we have previously considered, we read that "their thoughts floated vaguely between the desire to rest and the desire of life" (92). This is a revealing remark if we read it against the mimetic background Conrad has been sketching. It allows us to see that the sailor's external battle with the sea functions as a surrealist mirror of an interior battle confronting two oppositional tendencies: one toward life and antimimetic differentiation, the other toward death and mimetic indifferentiation; one toward the discontinuity of form, the other toward the continuity of darkness; one toward real images of light, the other toward the surreal shadows of the night. Accordingly, the crew's ambivalence toward Jimmy/the Nigger can be read not only in moral or ideological terms but also, and perhaps more fundamentally, in terms of the surrealist fear of the dark generated by the "center of the ship's collective psychology" (ix). That is, a darkness that threatens to disrupt the boundaries of subjectivity from both within (tuberculosis) and from without (the storm), and is rendered visible by dark human figures cast against a dark nonhuman background (mimetism). This mimetic dissolution is feared for the threat to life it presents; yet its "light of magic suggestiveness" (xiii) is also attractive for the promise of liberation from the burden of differentiation it entails.

What we must add is that this psychic ambivalence does not only operate at the level of the mimetic message of Conrad's tale diagnosed thus far; it is also mediated at the level of its mimetic medium that informs this tale. It is to this medium we must now turn to in order to complete this Janus-faced account of Conrad's "perfect blending of form and substance" (xiii).

## Mimetic Narratology

*The Nigger of the "Narcissus"* does not explicitly rely on the modernist narrative devices characteristic of *Lord Jim* or *Heart of Darkness*. Still, the tale is now aptly recognized as "one of the decisive moments in the emergence of modernism."[23] This is true for its emphasis on irony, ambivalence, and radical epistemological uncertainty but also, and for us more importantly, because its narrative form mirrors, in a self-reflecting (rather than realistic) turn, the double movement of attraction and repulsion generated by the shadow of death and the fear of the dark that ensues. This mimetic fear, we must now add, is not only inscribed in the content but also in the form of the novel—unsurprisingly so, since Conrad's poetics aims for the "perfect blending" between the two.

As commentators have long recognized, this novel is not predicated on a unitary (homogeneous) narrative perspective. Instead, it relies on a participant narrator who oscillates between two competing (heterogeneous) narrative voices: a third-person singular narrative voice that considers events from a position of critical distance (or "they-narration"), and a more empathic, first-person plural narrative voice that affectively involves the narrator in the darkness he represents ("we-narration"). If early critics have tended to dismiss this oscillation as a formal inconsistency, or technical failure, more recent developments have been less evaluative and more explicative in their approach, recognizing the modernist (even postmodernist) implications of this narrative choice. And in order to account for the logic that informs such oscillating shifts of perspective, critics themselves have oscillated between mimetic and nonmimetic tendencies, reproducing shadowlike the movement they set out to account for.[24] In order to continue clarifying the invisible logic of these narrative oscillations, I suggest that we should move beyond mimetic/antimimetic principles (understood in terms of realist representation) in order to consider these shifts from an alternative, yet still deeply mimetic perspective (understood in terms of surrealist narration). This perspective considers mimesis both as the medium and the message of the tale.

## The Message in the Medium

We have become so accustomed to considering mimesis from the angle of realism that it is easy to forget that an alternative, narratological sense of mimesis operates in the Western tradition, from the very origins of mimetic theory onward. Let us recall, in fact, that as the concept of mimesis initially appears in Book III of Plato's *Republic*, it does not so much designate a mimetic message (logos), or a realistic narrative strategy. Rather, Socrates initially introduces this concept in order to distinguish between different modes of poetic diction (*lexis*) associated with a reciter of poetry on the theatrical stage: what he calls mimesis, *diegesis*, and mixed style.[25] Introducing these Platonic narratological distinctions in Conrad studies, Philippe Lacoue-Labarthe grounds his philosophical reading of *Heart of Darkness* on what he calls a "'mimetic' device" (*dispositif 'mimétique'*).[26] For Lacoue-Labarthe, this narrative device whereby Conrad's multiple narrators oscillate between mimesis and diegesis is instrumental in rendering Kurtz's experience of "the horror," if not fully visible, at least emotionally audible. In order to further this ancient, yet also contemporary line of inquiry, we must add that such an oscillating "mimetic device" is equally at work in *The Nigger of the "Narcissus,"* albeit within a singular-plural narrative voice that blends the philosophical message with the artistic medium.

In *The Nigger of the "Narcissus"* Conrad's poetic practice oscillates, pendulum-like, between two modes of narrative lexis as he moves from a diegetic third-person singular voice to a mimetic first-person plural. This is no accidental or clumsy narrative move. On the contrary, it makes possible what Hillis Miller calls "a double motion of descent into the darkness and return from it."[27] In our language, this narrative oscillation mirrors, at the level of the medium, the fundamental affective ambivalence toward the mimetic fear of the dark, at the level of the message. Let us dissociate these two narrative vectors that inform a single, pendular movement.

On the one hand, the first-person plural mimetic narrative ("we-narration") is predicated on a mimetic lexis that gives voice to feelings of empathy and solidarity with the crew. This narrative mode involves the narrator in an experience of shared communion that puts him—and, at an additional remove, us with him—affectively in touch with the mimetic pathos generated by the shadow of death. For instance, here is how Jimmy is addressed after his rescue: "We pressed round him, bothered and dismayed; sheltering him we swung here and there in a body; and on the very brink of eternity we tottered all together with concealing and absurd gestures, like a lot of drunken men embarrassed with a stolen corpse" (71). The narrative voice plunges, via a mimetic device, into the "lonely region of stress and strife" (xii) centered around the black subject and represented by the *Sturm und Drang* of the metaphysics of darkness that surrounds the ship. In this sense, this narrative choice allows the narrator and, at an additional remove, us with him, to participate in the mimetic pathos of that phantom who is closest to the shadow of death, to partake in the communal feelings of solidarity that emerge from this shared experience, and even to come as close as possible to the "brink of eternity"—while remaining on the side of life. The mimetic narrative is also instrumental in merging the narrator's singular, heterogeneous voice with the collective, homogeneous voice of the crew and the "clamour" they experience. There is thus a sense in which the formal side of the mimetic medium (or *lexis*) replicates the mimetic dissolution that is at work on the affective side of the message (or *logos*). And as we press round him, at an additional remove, bothered and dismayed, we might feel something of this affect (or *pathos*) too.

On the other hand, the third-person diegetic narrative ("they-narration") tends to be voiced in imagistic, visual, poetic, at times ironic language that distinguishes the narrator—and us with him—from the rest of the crew, introducing a distance from the contagious pathos that affects them. This voice often has the characteristics of omniscience and encourages a cold, speculative, even clinical attitude toward the affective experience that emerges as the crew of the *Narcissus* sails through a storm and is confronted with the shadow of death. For instance, in the midst of the gale, the narrator addresses the emotional oscillation between life and death that affects the crew in precise, detached, visual terms: "their thoughts floated vaguely between the desire of rest and the desire of life" (92); "they worked like men driven by a merciless dream to toil in an atmosphere of ice or flame" (93). And when it comes to confronting that "shadow of a man" (151) who is Jimmy, dying in the darkness, the same oscillating movement is reproduced and the same clinical distance preserved: "In the shadows of the fore rigging a dark mass stamped eddied, advanced, retreated. . . . They clustered round that moribund carcass, the fit emblem of their aspirations" (122).

Now follow the pendular movement: if a narrative mimesis puts us in a position of affective proximity to Wait's inner experience of dissolution, a narrative diegesis is necessary to make readers see this mimetic pathos from a critical distance. Put differently, a diegetic "they-narrative" that sets itself aside from this mimetic "we" is instrumental in re-presenting the internal (invisible) feelings of dissolution in an ocean of darkness via external (visible) images of darkness. We are told, for instance, that "the shadows of high waves swept with a running darkness the faces of men" (75). Or: "The black cluster of human forms reeled against the bulwark, back again towards the house . . . and some one's shadowy body scuttled rapidly across the main hatch before the shadow of a kick" (123–24). In sum, if making us *feel* requires a degree of mimetic participation in the affect of the other, making us *see* requires a degree of diegetic distance in order to turn the interior language of felt affects into the exterior one of visible forms. The surrealist (mimetic) shadows that we are made to see from the outside are thus a representation of a (mimetic) fear of the dark experienced from the inside.

Now, since Conrad in the Preface insists on the centrality of both affect and sight, making us "feel" and making us "see," we should not be surprised that, in the novel that follows, in order to move from the "interior" to the "exterior," the "invisible" to the "visible," the "one" to the "manifold," Conrad oscillates between mimetic and diegetic speech, affective participation and visual representation. We could thus say that on board that rocking narrative that is *The Nigger of the "Narcissus"* recognition of the self in that metaphysical ocean of darkness that surrounds it is predicated on an in-*sight* into the affective foundations of being, mimetic foundations that are intimately felt, to be sure, but are also aptly rendered visible through the language of surrealist shadows. Far from being representative of an aesthetic failure or indecision, this formal shift from diegesis to mimesis, distance to pathos, pathology to patho-logy, mirrors, at the level of the medium, the Janus-faced patho(-)logy generated by the message. Mimesis, once again, in-forms both the medium and the message of the tale; it is the formal hinge on which this oscillation from seeing to feeling, pathos to logos, turns.

We were wondering how Conrad's poetics mediates from the many to the one, from the visible to the invisible. We wanted to know what is at stake in the pervasive images of darkness in a novel ominously titled *The Nigger of the "Narcissus."* My hope is that a surrealist account of mimesis attentive to both the medium and the message of the tale offers, if not a transparent reflection, at least a textually based solution to reflect on these fictional and metaphysical riddles. Schematically put, my mimetic hypothesis addressed three interrelated levels of experience: ontological, psychological, and aesthetic. First, the emphasis on surrealist images of darkness expresses the narrative concern with a meta-physical (beyond the physical) anxiety of mimetic dissolution generated by the threat of physical annihilation. If Jimmy's actual death is in question throughout the narrative, the images of darkness that envelop him reveal what old Singleton has been seeing all along: namely, that Wait is a paradigmatic case, for, not unlike all of us, he is just waiting to die—"Why, of course he will die" (42). Second, this anxiety is not simply personal and rooted in the metaphysical threat of death, but is revealing of the wider psychic anxiety of dissolution of individuation that Caillois, following Janet, called psychasthenia, a fear of loss of identity that envelops everyone on board the *Narcissus*, and that the tale, like many other of Conrad's narratives, attempts to reflect—via the surreal mirror of the sea. Finally, by stressing the mimetic continuity between figure and background, the shadow and the essence, at the level of the message (mimetic logos), and by oscillating between mimetic and diegetic speech at the level of the medium (mimetic lexis), Conrad manages to give aesthetic form to an intimately felt, perhaps even secretly shared, experience—a tragic inner experience that scientists, philosophers, and psychologists can only represent from without, but that artists who are masters of their medium have the power to animate from within.

■        ■        ■

In his "Manifesto of Surrealism," André Breton famously offered a genealogy of writers who anticipated some of the major insights of surrealism. He proclaimed, for instance, that "Sade is surrealist in sadism," "Swift is surrealist in malice," "Poe is surrealist in his adventures," "Baudelaire is surrealist in morality," and so on.[28] In an uncharacteristic generous mood, Breton left the list open, for future theorists to complete. After this detour through the secret shadows that haunt *The Nigger of the "Narcissus,"* we can perhaps propose a new candidate to supplement this genealogy of surrealist precursors. This might be a timely moment for doing so, especially since the time of racialized/politicized readings of what lies at the "heart of darkness" has somewhat exhausted the controversial dimension characteristic of its initial impetus, and the shadow-line dividing pictures of Africa and pictures of Europe is no longer as clear-cut as it initially appeared to be. Let us dare to look ahead, then, to future, imaginative theoretical readings of these darkly textured modernist tales and affirm that Conrad is a writer who is surrealist in his images of darkness.

"Realism, Romanticism, Naturalism, even unofficial Sentimentalism," writes Conrad in the Preface, "all these gods must, after a short period of fellowship, abandon him" (xiv–xv), the artist who has taken it upon himself to supplement the scientist and the philosopher in the eternal quest for "what is enduring and essential" (xi). Indeed, Conrad's picture of darkness makes us see, with mimesis as a magical mirror, a metaphysical anxiety that is deeply rooted in the immanence of the physical "senses" and "responsive emotions"—dark, tumultuous, and often conflicting emotions that emerge from the subject's confrontation with the haunting shadow of death. As we have seen, and perhaps even felt, mimesis continues to be an effective device that allows Conrad to deftly move from the physical to the metaphysical, the particular to the universal, appearance to essence, and back. It may even have allowed us to catch something of that "glimpse of truth" for which—thanks to Conrad's poetics of darkness—at least we didn't forget to ask.

Let us thus keep interrogating these darkly textured tales. The density of Conrad's metaphysics of darkness is indeed such that other questions remain to be answered in light of the tragic images that in-*form* his artistic metaphysics—from beginning to end.

# CHAPTER 7

# Rebirth of Tragedy: *Almayer's Folly* to *Apocalypse Now*

Every artist is an "imitator," that is to say, either an Apollinian artist in dreams, or a Dionysian artist in ecstasies, or finally—as for example in Greek Tragedy—at once artist in both dreams and ecstasies.

—Friedrich Nietzsche, *The Birth of Tragedy*

And the multitude feels it obscurely too; since the demand of the individual to the artist is, in effect, the cry "take me out of myself!" meaning really, out of my perishable activity into the light of imperishable consciousness.

—Joseph Conrad, *Notes on Life and Letters*

M etaphysical speculations have not been fashionable in Conrad studies during the last decades of the twentieth century; unsurprisingly so, given the contemporary urgency to revisit horrors that are immanent rather than transcendental, physical rather than metaphysical.[1] With the emergence of cultural interests in identity politics in the 1980s and 1990s, earlier concerns with Conrad's "metaphysics of darkness"[2] have been relegated to the back of the critical and theoretical scene in order to foreground the more tangible, material, and referential side of what Conrad called "the horror." And as the darkness pervading Conrad's texts became progressively synonymous with moral, ethical, and political horrors, readers were encouraged to reflect on the tragedies of colonialism, racism, sexism, and other ideological/material subjugations. This shift of emphasis from transcendental shadows intrinsic to the texts to immanent referents that have an extrinsic realty outside the texts has been immensely productive. It opened up Conrad studies to political concerns with the formative power of ideology, the deformation of the mass media, the docile conformation of public opinion, contributing to forming an image of Conrad as a writer who "holds great and plural interest in the contemporary moment."[3] We can thus understand why Hillis Miller's contrapuntal appeal that readers should not lose sight of the "Metaphysical language" that permeates Conrad's tales was, at the dawn of the twenty-first century, still an "untimely observation."[4]

## Ontological Turns

And yet meditations that appear untimely and past-oriented from one perspective may turn out to be timely and future-oriented when considered from a more contemporary perspective. If we have seen in the previous chapter that Conrad's poetics of darkness is informed by a forward-looking surrealist aesthetics that rests on metaphysical foundations, a recent philosophical turn in Conrad studies has now confirmed Miller's imperative to take seriously the metaphysical dimension of his fictions in general and of his most discussed tale, *Heart of Darkness*, in particular. Thus the French philosopher Philippe Lacoue-Labarthe argues that what characterizes the horror that stretches from the Roman Empire to colonialism and Nazism is a type of "excess or transgression" that "echoes" a typical "Western *hybris*" defined by what he calls "the metaphysical will to pass through death" (HW 116, 119). Echoing this though-provoking claim, philosophically oriented representatives of contemporary thought, such as Hillis Miller, Avital Ronell, Jonathan Dollimore, Martine Hennard Dutheil de la Rochère, François Warin, and Henry Staten, among others, have supplemented this account from an immanent perspective that makes metaphysical reflections central again to Conrad studies.[5] On another philosophical front, but with similar ontological preoccupations in mind, the Italian philosopher Adriana Cavarero concludes a book with the Conradian title *Horrorism* with a consideration of *Heart of Darkness* as a "classic of horrorism" that reflects what she calls the "ontological crime in which the West cannot avoid seeing itself mirrored."[6] As we know, "mirrors" and "echoes," just like phantoms and shadows, are mimetic tropes. They also make us see that ontology is not opposed to politics; it already informs the fundamental presuppositions of political discussions. As such, this philosophical turn adds an additional twist to our Janus-faced investigation and urges us to continue unearthing the metaphysics of tragedy in-*forming* Conrad's insights into what he enigmatically calls "the horror."

These final chapters build on this new ontological turn in Conrad studies to pursue our diagnostic of the mimetic patho(-)logies that underlie Conrad's persistent fascination with tragic images of disfiguration that disrupt the boundaries of the metaphysical category of the subject. Taking my clue from that "untimely" figure par excellence whose thought on tragedy has been recently considered "newly timely," namely Friedrich Nietzsche,[7] read in the company of some of his contemporary philosophical avatars—from Lacoue-Labarthe to Girard to Bataille—I take some additional steps to unveil the "formless" metaphysics that—at the obscurest level of Conrad's poetics of darkness—gives birth to his tragic fictions. Turning back to the origins of Conrad's literary career articulated in his first novel, *Almayer's Folly* (1895), allows us to revisit in a new light the Dionysian horrors that pervade the most secret and obscure side of Conrad's most influential tale, *Heart of Darkness* (1899). It also allows us to look ahead to the Apollonian images of sacrificial disfiguration that are at the heart of Francis Ford Coppola's *Apocalypse Now* (1979). Indeed, multiple images of disfiguration run like an undercurrent, connecting these tragic texts and cinematic intertext. They reveal an underlying continuity that is constitutive of Conrad's metaphysics of tragedy but also stretch, via cinema, into the present. These images are the product of a will to see at the center of Conrad's poetics. They also reveal a formless ontological ground underneath seemingly discontinuous psychic, ethical, and political preoccupations that have dominated theoretical debates in the second half of the twentieth century.

If we want to fully move Conrad studies into the twenty-first century, we need to recognize that, for Conrad, politics and metaphysics are not opposed but are two sides of the same reality. Behind the veil of cultural difference lies, in fact, the tragic core of ontological sameness. More precisely, Conrad's modernist tragedies are truly modernist in the sense that

they foreground framing aesthetic devices that stress the necessity for formal mediation to make us see the horror of tragic disfigurations. In this
sense, his tragic poetics is born out of the reconciliation of Apollonian and
Dionysian mimesis along lines that are resonant with Nietzsche's artistic
metaphysics. And yet if Conrad's modernist, sacrificial tragedies look back
to sacred, Dionysian horrors reserved for a few initiates, doubles, and aco-
lytes, they also look ahead to a profane, Apollonian horrorism that is now
mediated—via the mass media—for all the world to see. I argue that in this
Janus-faced will to see that looks back to the birth of tragedy in order to
better unmask the sacrificial horrors of the present lies the originality of
Conrad's artistic metaphysics.


## Tragic Confessions

It is unfashionable to say that tragedy, for Conrad, was not only an aesthetic
concern but also a matter of personal experience. And rightly so, for such a
claim risks confining the general scope of his poetics to private, biographical,
and rather intimate matters of little philosophical or artistic relevance for the
present moment. And yet if we take seriously Nietzsche's untimely insight
that "every great philosophy has hitherto been . . . a personal confession on
the part of its author and a part of involuntary and unconscious memoir,"[8]
there are reasons to believe that this principle applies to every great artist
as well—especially if the artist in question admits that he "stands confessed
in his works" (*PR* 89). Let us thus not forget that Conrad lost his mother
in early childhood and his father soon thereafter in circumstances that—as
his pragmatic maternal uncle and substitute father figure will make clear
to him—implicated the idealism of the father in the material causes of the
mother's death.[9] There is thus a structuring experiential conflict (or *agon*)
between romantic idealism and rational pragmatism, the idea and the reality,
in Conrad's biographical memories that continues to in-*form*, perhaps even
animate (in the sense of giving a soul to) the tragic figures that haunt his
confessional fictions and the narrative oscillations they generate. In many
ways, Conrad's persistent representation of the downfall of romantic, idealist figures (or phantoms), and their equally tragic female counterparts (or
shadows), via the medium of participant narrators who are both attracted to
and horrified by such shady figures can be seen as an attempt to conjure dead

shadows—which, as Conrad confesses, grow "more precious as the years pass" (*CL*, III, 491)—back to life, via the medium of tragic fictions. There is perhaps a secret sense in which writing, for Conrad, is a ritual, at times pathological, at other times patho-logical practice. And what this practice represents are tragic, sacrificial scenes generative of pity and horror, which, since the origins of literary theory, have been considered as the locus classicus of mimetic identifications and cathartic purifications.

And yet what was true of ancient tragedies is equally true of Conrad's modernist imagination: tragic falls must be framed against a wider onto-logical background that informs, deforms, and sometimes disrupts artistic representations in the foreground. In particular, Conrad's artistic meta-physics supplements the surrealist images of psychic dissolution we have explored in the preceding chapter with images of physical disfiguration that consistently transgress the metaphysical boundaries of individuation: bodies pierced by arrows, traversed by spears, stabbed to death, hit by bul-lets, penetrated by grass, exploded by bombs, sunk in rivers, rotten in mud, torn to pieces by love, shattered by grief, disfigured by pain—I think it is no exaggeration to say that there is hardly a major Conradian text that does not attempt to catch a glimpse of that state of deadly undifferentiation that hides behind the veil of representation, lies beyond the reach of a realist aesthetics, yet in-forms Conrad's tragic poetics nonetheless. Despite the notorious obscurity of Conrad's linguistic formulations, one thing is clear: persistently in his fictions, Conrad dramatizes a fundamental concern with inner, sacrificial experiences that, as *Heart of Darkness* and Francis Ford Coppola's *Apocalypse Now* equally confirm, can be rooted back to the very origins of tragedy itself. There is thus a secret continuity between ancient, modernist, and postmodern tragedies. But let us proceed in order and move from the roots of Conrad's view of tragedy to its heart and finally to the darkness of its apocalyptic revelations.

## The Roots of Tragedy: *Almayer's Folly*

The most striking visual representation of the artistic metaphysics that underlies Conrad's philosophical fictions already surfaces in the novel that marks his unpredictable entry into the world of literature. Started in his paternal home, carried with him at sea, taken up the Congo River and back, *Almayer's Folly* (1895) foregrounds the personal misadventures of a dream-like, inefficient, mediocre, yet nonetheless tragic Dutch merchant, Kaspar Almayer, living on the shore of the Berau River in a Borneo village called Sambir with his Malay wife and his beloved half-caste daughter, Nina.[10] While Almayer has delusional hopes of finding gold and of returning rich and prosperous to Europe with Nina, the latter abandons him for a Malay rajah named Dain Maroola with whom she elopes, leaving her father behind to become fatally addicted to opium in an unfinished mansion on the banks of a muddy river, which is taken as an image of the "folly" that gives the title to the novel.

At the level of the plot, the novel foregrounds an exotic, colonial adventure with touches of romance depicting a tragic downfall that follows a rather classical telos. An ambitious individual in a position of relative good fortune aims to complete an action of some magnitude, but in the process discovers that fortune has turned; his goals turn out to be beyond his reach; he fails to recognize his tragic flaw (an excess of parental love); and he is eventually driven mad by circumstances that prove to be totally beyond his control. To adopt Aristotle's canonical categories from *Poetics*, these events are framed in a narrative "structure" (*muthos*) based on an "imitation" (*mimesis*) of an action that culminates in a conflict (*agon*). This conflict, in turn, leads to a tragic error and to a reversion of fortune whose effect is to generate pity and horror for this flawed (anti-)hero.[11] To be sure, as the plot unfolds, it does not lead to tragic recognitions for the protagonist himself. Nor does this pity and horror guarantee cathartic purifications for the readers so far removed from this dramatic fictional action. And yet, as we shall see, this plot does not preclude the possibility of disconcerting identifications for both protagonist and readers alike. These identifications are mimetic not only in the narrative sense that they are based on an "imitation of an action" (Aristotle), nor solely in the psychological sense that they generate a psychic desire "to be the other" (Freud), or to desire the "desire of the other" (Girard). Rather, they are mimetic in the deeper, philosophical sense that they establish an ontological continuity between individual human figures in the foreground and a formless subject matter in the background (Conrad). I suggest that it is out of such metaphysical mimesis—in both its loving and horrific configurations—that Conrad's modernist tragedy is born.

## Metaphysics of Love

Not unlike Jimmy's fear of the dark, Almayer's tragic folly in the foreground must be framed against the metaphysical background that informs the aesthetics of the tale, generating formless images that are as surreal as they are transgressive. If influential critics have had trouble locating this novel's "center of interest"[12] in the past, it is perhaps because this center requires a careful articulation between foreground and background along Janus-faced lines we are by now familiar with. Already in this first novel, in fact, we find traces of the surrealist metaphysics that dissolve unitary images along lines Conrad will continue to explore in subsequent tales. In *Almayer's Folly* heterogeneous human figures repeatedly merge against the homogeneous background of "misty" fogs, "dark" waters, and "shadowy" trees, generating blurry images that introduce secret continuities where discontinuities should be preserved. For instance, at a moment of crisis that marks Nina's romantic departure with Dain and the start of Almayer's fall, we read that behind the tragic protagonist, "Every outline had disappeared in the intense blackness that seemed to have destroyed everything but space" (136). Darkness is once again identified with black space that has the power to dissolve individual outlines, yet the shadow that appears is not the shadow of death but of love. Even more explicitly, earlier in this scene we had been told that the two lovers' "forms melted in the play of light and shadow at the root of the big trees" (130). The shadow of mimesis, in its surrealist manifestation, is thus present from the very origins of Conrad's writings, lending metaphysical support to inner experiences that blur the boundaries of individuation along lines that establish secret continuities between fearful dissolutions and desired fusions.

And yet this time Conrad also adds a material, chthonic dimension to the fear of the dark we have explored above. Thus, in a key scene that marks the two lovers' departure, foreshadows their subsequent reunion, and prefigures the protagonist's downfall, we are given a metaphysical image of the wilderness in the background that mirrors the physical power animating the lovers in the foreground:

> the intense work of tropical nature went on: plants shooting upward, entwined, interlaced in inextricable confusion, climbing madly and brutally over each other in the terrible silence of a desperate struggle towards

the life-giving sunshine above—as if struck with sudden horror at the seething mass of corruption below; at the death and decay from which they sprang. (55)

This scene is often read in evolutionary terms that emphasize nature's "struggle" for physical survival, and, as we have seen, Conrad remains in line with this Darwinian, evolutionary perspective. Yet the conflicting dynamic at play in this landscape also reflects a "confusion" that is as physical as it is metaphysical in nature. This natural nonhuman background, in fact, represents contradictory principles that reflect the all-too-human metaphysics of love in the foreground. Notice, for instance, that in this image of "tropical nature" the distinction between light and darkness, life and decay, the rotting mass below and the shining sun above is far from stable, and a violent dynamic polarizes these contradictory forces generating an image of life as "will to power" that is as deadly as it is vital.

The reference to will to power is not accidental. This is what Nietzsche also suggests, as he had identified will to power with the *sipo matador*, a liana that grows in tropical forests in general and is found in Indonesia in particular, which is also the setting of *Almayer's Folly*. In *Beyond Good and Evil*, Nietzsche speaks of "those sun-seeking climbing plants of Java—they are named *sipo matador*—which clasp an oak-tree with their tendrils so long and often that at last, high above it but supported by it, they can unfold their crowns in the open light and display their happiness."[13] Will to power not as a human, personal, often exclusively masculinist force. But will to power as a nonhuman, materialist, and impersonal energy that illustrates the vitalist, brutal, yet life-affirmative power of nature itself. Attracted by this image, the French philosopher Michel Onfray in *Cosmos* recently elaborated on Nietzsche's take on the *sipo matador* from the point of view of a materialist ontology that I take to be at the heart of Conrad's metaphysics as well. Echoing Nietzsche, Onfray offers the following image of the jungle: "All these species, all these individuals so tightly intertwined, disturb and damage each other reciprocally. Their apparent tranquility is deceiving. In reality they are engaged in an ongoing and implacable battle against each other."[14] This is, indeed, the very image of will to power that also caught Conrad's attention. But the artist's diagnostic is actually more precise than the philosopher's as he traces the material *movement* of will to power. In particular, he makes us see that the abject, chthonic foundations that root nature, and with it human nature, in the homogeneous "mass" of deadly "corruption" below are also the very source that generate a life-affirming force striving toward the light above. Or better, the "life-giving" forces above spring from the very "horror" this deadly "corruption" generates below. Either way, this picture of will to power is not only physical; it is also, and above all, metaphysical. And this metaphysics generates a spiral of mimetic "confusion" indicating that Conrad's vision of life cannot be dissociated from the horror of death—if only because it is from this horrific and formless mass that life stems, sprouts, and blossoms.

There is thus a fertile, light-oriented, and life-affirmative side to Conrad's metaphysics that supplements his darker mimetic preoccupations along Janus-faced lines that orient this study. The image of the two lovers, dancing "with a rhythmical swing of their bodies . . . towards the outlying shadows of the forests that seemed to guard their happiness in solemn immobility" (129–30), for instance, testify that, for Conrad, mimetic dissolutions are not only the source of tragic destinies but also the living source of new beginnings. They not only melt the forms of the ego in an ocean of darkness but also fertilize the ground upon which loving relations sprout and grow. Hence, as Conrad paints a vitalizing picture of Nina's and Dain's "forms melted in the play of light and shadow at the foot of the big trees" (130), he is not giving aesthetic form to a fear of the dark concerned with the horror of death. Rather, he is representing a mimetic dissolution of shadows born out of a metaphysical ground out of which new forms spring.

This Janus-faced lesson is of course not original. Its foundations can be traced back to ancient Greece and are embodied in the tragic figure of Dionysus, the god of vine and sex, but, as James Frazer reminds, also of "trees in general."[15] Celebrated in the context of fertility rites, Dionysus, as Frazer puts it, "was believed to have died a violent death, but to have been brought to life again."[16] Frazer is here framing the motif of a violent dismemberment and subsequent rebirth that will continue to animate Western accounts of tragedy concerned with what Nietzsche calls "an overwhelming feeling of unity leading back to the very heart of nature [*Hertz der Natur*]."[17] Conrad's view of tragedy, we shall have numerous occasions to confirm, rests precisely on such a Dionysian ground. For the moment, however, suffice to say that this "feeling of unity" in the lovers' hearts mirrored at the heart of the jungle is precisely what this scene represents. Hence the palpitating heart of nature in the background and the palpitating hearts of the lovers in the foreground are intimately connected, along mimetic lines that blur the distinction between foreground and background. Similarly, at the culminating point of Dain and Nina's romantic experience—which, in my view, is also one of the most romantic passages in Conrad's corpus as a whole—we are told that Nina has not only the power to generate ecstatic flights that propel Dain's "soul out of the body" along vertical, ideal trajectories familiar to us from classical antiquity. She also brings his body down on its knees in a demiurgic gesture that endows her with the imaginative, material power of "moulding a god from the clay at her feet" (129). This double movement is ontologically significant. Just as the abject, chthonic, and formless matter (or "mass") at the ground of the forest nourishes the metaphysical will to power at the heart of trees, so the metaphysics of love can generate inner experiences that turn impure formless matter (or "clay") into an ideal, pure, and somewhat divine form (or "god"). Forests, trees, and lovers alike indicate that, for Conrad, transcendent flights toward the sun are firmly rooted in the darkness of Dionysian foundations. And since one of Dionysus's secret titles was "'bursting (as of sap or blossoms),'"[18] we could say that such a fertilizing, metaphysical ground nourishes the living sap flowing through the artistic arteries of Conrad's metaphysics of love.

## Metaphysics of Death

And yet, as always, the shadow of mimesis has two sides, and this certainly applies to a Janus-faced god such as Dionysus that is as much oriented toward regeneration as toward disintegration. If one side looks upward, toward light, life, and the emergence of powerful loving forms that generate ecstatic flights, the other side looks downward, toward dark, chthonic, and tragic disfigurations that generate pity and horror instead. This duality is fully represented in *Almayer's Folly*. For instance, early on in the narrative, in a scene that prefigures Almayer's tragic fall, a drowned body is found on the shore of the river causing a "long and piercing shriek" that fills Almayer "with astonishment and horror" (72). The face of the drowned man, we are told, is covered by a "veil" and cannot be seen directly. Yet the third-person diegetic voice gives us a disconcerting insight into what Almayer sees as he looks down to the formless mass below: "at last [he] arrested his fascinated gaze on the body lying on the mud, with covered face in a grotesquely unnatural contortion of mangled and broken limbs, one twisted and lacerated arm—with white bones protruding in many places through the torn flesh—stretched out" (74). Such visual images of disfiguration and confusion have been read as part of an "impressionist" aesthetics. Art historian Michael Fried, for instance, perceptively argues they are part of an "aesthetic of erasure" understood "both as the disfiguring of a prior representation, and a restoration of an originary blankness" that informs Conrad's relation to writing.[19] This is certainly a hypothesis worth considering, especially given Conrad's complaints about the slowness of his artistic creation. What we must add is that the muddy intertwinement of formless physicality informing these images of disfiguration also points—through the medium of writing—to something beyond the limits of representation, touching on a Dionysian metaphysics that is not only impressionist but continues to be in line with the surrealist principles we are familiar with.

If we read such images against the picture sketched so far, we are in a position to see that they also give material substance to the fear of mimetic dissolution that inform Conrad's metaphysical representation of shady, formless bodies. This image of a body torn to pieces is but one of a long series we shall soon encounter. It already suggests that Conrad is indeed a "Dionysian artist [*dionysischer Künstler*]" in the Nietzschean sense that he "has identified himself with the primal unity [*Ur-Einen*], its pain and contradiction" (*BT* 49). Consequently, if we want to touch on the most obscure side of the secret shadow we have been tracing, it is important not to turn our faces away from such abject metaphysical matters—out of which Conrad's tragedies grow. In a distant echo of the Aristotelian realization that art allows us to contemplate, even take pleasure from, abject figures, such as "corpses,"[20] time and again, Conrad zooms in on images of human disfiguration in order to point to a dissolution of individuation that opens up the possibility of horrific, yet disturbingly fascinating continuities at the heart of discontinuities. The motif of the body torn to pieces is not only present in Conrad's fictions but has a long genealogy for it is an early modernist rendering of a type of "dismemberment" characteristic of what Nietzsche calls "Dionysian insight" into "the shattering of the individual and his fusion with primal being" (*BT* 65). The question for a "Dionysian artist," then, is how to mediate this insight artistically. How to render a

metaphysical reality that is perceived as radically other yet is at the foundation of very physical experiences recognizable for others to see, and perhaps
feel.

Recognition is the key problem of this tragic scene—and perhaps also
its solution. Notice, in fact, that this body torn to pieces disrupts the internal
unity of the human figure, rendering it indistinguishable from others, easily
confused with others, and thus difficult to recognize. Here is a description of
this disfiguration as it is reported to Almayer:

> "Look Tuan; the logs came together so,"—and here he pressed the palms
> of his hands together—"and his head must have been between them, and
> now there is no face for you to look at. There are his flesh and his bones;
> the nose, and the lips, and maybe his eyes, but nobody could tell one from
> the other." (*AF* 75)

Nobody can identify this impersonal body. Hence this is a body that is, in
a sense, nobody, and can thus pass for being virtually anybody, opening up
mimetic confusions that blur the line between self and others, individu-
ated bodies and impersonal bodies. This is precisely what happens at the
narrative level: we will later find out, via a characteristically Conradian use
of "delayed decoding" (Ian Watt's term), that this mutilated body whom
Almayer, and we with him, believe to be Dain, was actually disfigured
by Mrs. Almayer—so that it could be confused with Dain—in view of
facilitating the latter's plan to elope with her daughter, Nina. For the tragic
protagonist, this physical disfiguration may prevent the identification
(or visual recognition) of the body itself; yet it opens up a series of psychic identifications (or affective recognitions) that blur the line not only
between self and others but also between the living and the dead and, by
extension, the physical and the metaphysical. Let us look at these affective
ties more closely.

As the first of a long series of mimetic protagonists that will continue
to animate Conrad's fictions, Almayer is, of course, easy prey to such tragic
identifications. We are in fact told that upon seeing this body torn to pieces,

> a strange fancy had taken possession of Almayer's brain distracted by this
> new misfortune. It seemed to him that for many years he had been falling

into a deep precipice. Day after day, month after month, year after year, he had been falling, falling, falling. . . . A dead Malay: he had seen many dead Malays without any emotion; and now he felt inclined to weep, but it was over the fate of a man he knew; a man that fell over a precipice and did not die. (75–76)

Almayer's pity is not for the dead other but for the living self, a self-pity that stems from a tragic recognition of his own fate in the fate of the other. And in a psychological turn that already foreshadows the motif of the homo duplex and prefigures the entire problematic of affective mimesis that casts such a long shadow on Conrad's tragic fictions, the narrator adds:

He [Almayer] seemed somehow to himself to be standing on one side, a little way off, looking at a certain Almayer who was in great trouble. Poor, poor fellow! Why doesn't he cut his throat? He wished to encouraged him; he was very anxious to see him lying dead over that other corpse. Why does he not do it and end his suffering?—He groaned aloud unconsciously and started with affright at the sound of his own voice. Was he going mad? (76)

The mimetic unconscious continues to be a cause of maddening identifications that look both ways. On the one hand, this madness entails a form of "possession" whose primary psychic effect is to generate an unconscious identification of the self with the other, a living being with a dead being, a formed subject with a formless subject. This is a carefully crafted narrative move that fits within the trajectory of the hero's tragic destiny. It is thus no accident that once abandoned by Nina, Almayer's face is later described as a "blank wall" (143) while "inwardly he felt torn to pieces" (146)—an inner experience of proper Dionysian suffering. More precisely, the disfigured face functions as an exterior physical representation that mirrors the protagonist's interior psychic disfiguration masked behind the "wall" that both hides and reveals the Dionysian horror of death—at the palpitating heart of life. On the other hand, the effect of this inner experience is to split the self in two, generating an alter ego (or shadow) "standing aside" this body, who is both nobody and anybody. And it is this fictional other that is not one—for he is, and he is not Almayer—who becomes the medium that allows for the feeling of pity and horror to emerge, a self-pity induced by this mimetic confusion between the living ego and the dead alter ego. Prefiguring Marlow's identification with Kurtz's tragic destiny ("It is his extremity that I seem to have lived through" [*YOS* 118]), as well as other tragic confusions we shall soon encounter, Conrad's first novel already suggests that it is via a mimetic identification that "takes possession" of the "brain" that the protagonist can get close to death—while remaining on the side of the living.

There is an important tragic lesson buried in this scene, a mimetic lesson that applies not only to the fictional protagonist but to readers of tragedies as well. Mimesis is not only part of the message represented in this plot (*muthos*); it is also, and perhaps more important, the very medium of tragic suffering (or *pathos*). It is in fact because mimesis, in its Dionysian, ecstatic, and affective manifestations, makes possible a transgression of the Apollonian boundaries that divide self and other, the living and the dead, that a tragic feeling of pity and horror can emerge in the first place. These mimetic affects put Almayer in touch with a kind of suffering that is not simply personal or psychological, generating cathartic purifications that, in theory we are told should have good, therapeutic effects; it also offers an insight into a suffering that is physical and metaphysical and functions as the very womb out of which tragedy is born. Further, the novelistic use of free-indirect speech ("Poor, poor fellow!"), a speech whereby mimetic pathos infiltrates a diegetic narrative mode, brings this subject's inner experience closer to the reader, for you to feel as well, at an additional remove. Mimesis is thus both the message and the medium of tragedy; or better, mimesis is the very medium that mediates the contagious affects of pity and horror that animate the message of this tragedy. We begin to sense that, for Conrad, mimesis breathes suffering (or *pathos*) into tragedy and is, therefore, the very soul (or *psyche*) of tragedy.

But how is this tragedy rendered visible for others to see and feel? What is the aesthetic medium that allows Conrad to mediate Dionysian horrors? This is the moment to turn to professional philosophers who have asked the same question. Lacoue-Labarthe answers this question with characteristic succinctness: "The Ancients invoked the gods, Conrad invents Marlow" (HW 114). In this narrative invention, modernist tragedy is reborn.

## Modernist Tragedy: *Heart of Darkness* Redux

If we return to "The Horror of the West" with this tragic frame in mind, we notice that Lacoue-Labarthe provides a new and stimulating starting point to revisit Conrad's insights into the metaphysics of darkness at the heart of his most famous tale. We have already seen that for the French philosopher, Conrad's insights into Western horrors in *Heart of Darkness* concern not only the horror of colonialism but also foreshadow the horror of the Holocaust. There is thus an unquestionably political side to the horror. For a philosopher schooled in classical antiquity, politics and metaphysics have, in fact, never been in opposition. On the contrary, for Lacoue-Labarthe, Conrad's "mythic" tale looks ahead to the physical horrors of modern politics because this tragic text looks back to metaphysical foundations in classical antiquity. This, at least, is what Lacoue-Labarthe whispers between the lines—waiting for an echo to make it audible.

### Dionysian Chorus

The fundamental *agon* that structures Lacoue-Labarthe's philosophical reading of *Heart of Darkness* is summed up early in his essay when he says: in this tale "everything is deliberately constructed around an opposition between two voices: that of the indistinct 'clamour' of the savages (the chorus) and that, obviously (and audibly), of Kurtz" (HW 114). For Lacoue-Labarthe, two voices structure Conrad's tragic "tale" qua "*muthos*." One of them is in the background, is collective, musical, rooted in nature (*phusis*), and belongs to what he calls "the chorus"; the other is in the foreground, is individual, poetic, in control of both technology and art (*techne*), and belongs to what he calls the "hero." To be sure, Lacoue-Labarthe does not say it loudly, but this is a mimetic hypothesis in a sense that is at least double: it echoes Nietzsche's accounts of the birth of Greek tragedy and, by doing so, foreshadows mimetic principles at the heart of modern tragedies. Let us recall that in a famous section of *The Birth of Tragedy*—a text Lacoue-Labarthe knew intimately, for he translated it into French and analyzed it in *The Subject of Philosophy*[21]—Nietzsche sums up the metaphysical polarity that structures his own hypothesis concerning the origins of Western tragedy as he considers the "duality" between what he calls "the chorus and the tragic hero of that tragedy . . . as the origin and essence of Greek tragedy, as the expression of two interwoven artistic impulses, the Apollonian and the Dionysian" (*BT* 81).²² The echoes are thus loud, the symmetry clear, and Lacoue-Labarthe will later enlist the name of Nietzsche to account for Conrad's insights into horrors yet to come (HW 117). There is, thus, an unstated, more general embryonic thesis in the background of Lacoue-Labarthe's "The Horror of the West," I take the liberty (and risk) to summarize as follows: *Heart of Darkness* is not only structured around "two voices"; it also emerges out of the same metaphysical ground out of which Greek tragedy stems. This also means that *Heart of Darkness* is a Dionysian tragedy—born out of the halo of Apollonian mediations.

That the Dionysian continues to animate the darkest, ritualistic side of Conrad's most famous tale was already implicit in the musical rituals that are constantly in the background of the tale. From rhythmic music to collective dance, frenzied intoxication to ecstatic communion, enthusiastic dispossession to sacrificial disfigurations, it is clear by the time we reach Kurtz's mysterious "ceremonies" that Conrad is not only offering an anthropological account of possession trance that concerns "prehistoric" people. He is also grounding his modernist text in what Nietzsche considers the ritualistic, musical, and ontological foundations of Western tragedy itself, thereby adding both a metaphysical and aesthetic dimension to the ethico-political and anthropological horrors of frenzied (dis)possession we have considered in part 2. Let us now situate Conrad's artistic metaphysics in a wider ontological landscape in order to see what distinguishes his modernist account of the rebirth of tragedy.

The link between the anthropology of possession trance and the aesthetic phenomenon of Greek tragedy was not unfashionable in fin de siècle Europe. Nietzsche, for one, in *The Birth of Tragedy* claims that a Dionysian form of "pantomime" about which "the song of all primitive men and peoples speak" continues to resonate in the "Bacchic choruses of the Greeks" (*BT* 36). Along similar lines, Nietzsche's friend and colleague, the classicist Erwin Rhode, in his monumental *Psyche* (1890–94)—a book Girard praises for its "profound intuitive grasp or reality" (*VS* 134)—also establishes an anthropological-philological bridge between rituals of frenzied dispossession among traditional people and ancient Greek people along lines that resonate with both Lacoue-Labarthe's hypothesis about the chorus and my anthropological hypothesis about rituals of possession. As he speaks of the "Dionysian frenzy" characteristic of the ritual mysteries at Eleusis, Rohde specifies: "The means most commonly adopted by such [traditional] peoples to produce the desired intensity and stimulation of feeling is a violently excited dance prolonged to the point of exhaustion, in the darkness of night, to the accompaniment of tumultuous music."[23] And with Euripides's *The Bacchae* clearly at the back of his mind, Rohde paints the following picture of frenzied rituals in the darkness:

> The festival was held on the mountain tops in the darkness of night amid the flickering and uncertain light of torches. The loud and troubled sound of music was heard. . . . Excited by this wild music, the chorus of worshippers dance with shrill crying and jubilation . . . they even had horns fixed to their heads. . . . In this fashion they raged wildly until every sense was wrought to the highest pitched of excitement, and in the "sacred frenzy" they fell upon the beast selected as their victim and tore their capture prey limb from limb. . . . A strange rapture came over them in which they seemed to themselves and others "frenzied and possessed."[24]

Reframed in this classical tragic context, we can see that Conrad's picture of frenzied possession in *Heart of Darkness* is not only based on anthropological principles at the heart of African rituals; it is also in line with aesthetic principles at the foundations of Western tragedy.[25] Put differently, Conrad is not only dramatizing a ritual phenomenon that is central to African culture, as Achebe confirmed; he is equally representing an artistic proto-phenomenon that is at the very origins of Western culture, as Lacoue-Labarthe implies. Perhaps, then, the sacred frenzy in *Heart of Darkness*, with its notorious musical chorus, horned sorcerer, states of frenzied possession, and sacrificial horrors, can tell us something about the aesthetic and ontological foundations of the birth of tragic art itself that supplements our Dionysian reading of *Almayer's Folly*.

This hypothesis finds textual support if we consider that Marlow also adds a metaphysical dimension to images of physical depersonalization that disrupt the boundaries of individuation. We should not forget, in fact, that Marlow is on board a frail bark, which from Schopenhauer to Nietzsche serves as a privileged metaphor to depict the fragility of the *principium individuationis* as it rests on an impersonal, fluid, metaphysical ground. And as Marlow insistently speaks of a type of "truth" or "essence" that is hidden "deep under the surface" (*YOS* 82), of "drums behind the curtain of trees" (79), something "like evil or truth" (65), a "mystery of the wilderness" (78), which like the "mud" from which it grows, introduces a disturbing continuity at the heart of discontinuity, the echoes with Nietzsche's artistic metaphysics get louder and louder. Nietzsche speaks of this truth in terms of "ecstasy," Conrad in terms of "frenzy"; Nietzsche links this state with sacrificial bodies torn to pieces, Conrad dramatizes acephalic bodies; Nietzsche says that this truth offers an insight into "the horror of existence [*Entsetzlichkeiten des Daseins*]" (*BT* 42), Conrad says that it forces us to confront the "horror"; Nietzsche calls this metaphysical essence "heart of nature [*Hertz der Natur*]" (59), Conrad calls it "heart of darkness"; and so on.[26] Given such striking connections it is thus not surprising that contemporary critics of *Heart of Darkness* who have taken up the task to respond critically to the metaphysical implications of Lacoue-Labarthe's reading confirm the latter's hypothesis that the "clamor," for Conrad, is ultimately "Dionysian" in nature and gives voice to the "metaphysics of oblivion" (Dollimore) and the "Dionysian cry" (Staten) that ensue.[27] Indeed, no matter how past-oriented and "untimely" Hillis Miller's observation was at the dawn of the twenty-first century, some of the most incisive readers of *Heart of Darkness* I know of agree that the connection between Conrad and a Dionysian metaphysics is now timely again and calls for future-oriented investigations.

Now, if Lacoue-Labarthe's Nietzschean hypothesis about the birth of tragedy is correct—and René Girard agrees that it is[28]—then a mimetic supplement concerning the underlying aesthetic principles that give birth to this tragic text is in order. Lacoue-Labarthe structures his reading of this "mythic" tale on the opposition between the voice of the clamor (or "chorus") and the voice of Kurtz (or "hero"), thereby reproducing the Dionysian/Apollonian opposition Nietzsche convokes. But there is, of course, an additional voice that needs to be foregrounded if we want to read this tale as a "tragic" modernist tale. You will recall that, for Nietzsche, tragedy is not simply born from the opposition but, rather, from the "reconciliation" of Apollonian and Dionysian principles.[29] If we rigorously follow Nietzsche's artistic metaphysics, we should thus say that it is not so much Kurtz—a figure who, as we have seen, is up to his neck in Dionysian rituals—but, rather, Marlow who, while coming close to his Dionysian homo duplex, embodies Apollonian principles that give aesthetic form to Conrad's tragic text in general and to disfiguring experiences behind the veil of representation in particular. Marlow is, in fact, a narrative medium who is somewhat removed from the dark experience of the horror itself; yet, precisely because of this distance, he can give aesthetic form to formless, metaphysical matters. There is thus a deeper mimetic polarity that in-*forms* this modernist tragedy and that leads us to reframe Lacoue-Labarthe's Nietzschean hypothesis as follows. In *Heart of Darkness* everything is deliberately structured around the opposition between two mimetic principles: the principle of mimetic intoxication (or Dionysian) embodied by a chain of tragic figures that are attuned to the metaphysics of darkness in the background, on the one hand, and the principle of mimetic representation (or Apollonian) that mediates such experience for listeners and readers to hear, and above all to see, in the foreground, on the other. The dark, Dionysian message of *Heart of Darkness* is thus illuminated via an Apollonian medium that is as much based on voice as it is on vision, on affect as it is on thought. This is, in a nutshell, the mimetic *agon* out of which Conrad's modernist tragedy is reborn.

## Apollonian Halos

From the outset of Marlow's journey, it is clear that Conrad's artistic metaphysics is structured on the dynamic interplay between antagonistic mimetic principles that equally inform Nietzsche's view of tragedy. Marlow, in fact, sets up a tension between the sphere of "dreams" that remain on the "surface" of things and are thus illusory (or Apollonian), and a type of "sensation" that is hidden "below the surface," yet is constantly in touch with an impersonal musical, ontological ground he considers "true" and "essential" (or Dionysian). Reconciling these two antagonistic mimetic principles is seemingly impossible without dissolving unspeakable affects in illusory dreams. Hence Marlow exclaims: "It seems to me I am trying to tell you a dream—making a vain attempt—because no relation of a dream can convey the dream-sensation" (*YOS* 70). And he adds: "it is impossible to convey the life-sensation of any given epoch of one's existence—that which makes its truth, its meaning—its subtle and penetrating essence" (70). Marlow senses that giving aesthetic form to inner sensations is like using light to reveal shadows—an impossible operation that is bound to generate the retreat of the secret shadow we have been following via the very medium used to illuminate it. This is why Marlow says: "No, it is impossible. . . . We live, as we dream—alone." (70).

This is a typical modernist riddle that reveals the limits of a realistic aesthetics to represent essential, dreamlike, affective experiences with metaphysical implications for others to see, and perhaps feel. But, as we know, Marlow was "not typical" in his narrative figurations. Take the notion of "dream-sensation," for instance. It already points to a possible reconciliation between dreamlike, Apollonian figurations geared toward making us see and affective Dionysian intoxications intended to make us feel. But Conrad goes further in his pictorial attempt to mediate the relation between inside and outside, affect and vision. The frame narrator, who is even further removed from the metaphysical "essence" Marlow is trying to mediate, offers us a key to get closer to the hidden "meaning" of this uneasy reconciliation. In a passage that frames Marlow's artistic practice as a storyteller and casts light on the type of lenses one should adopt to read this tale, the frame narrator famously says:

> The yarns of seamen have an effective simplicity, the whole meaning of which lies within the shell of a cracked nut. But, as has been said, Marlow was not typical (if his propensity to spin yarns be excepted) and to him the meaning of an episode was not inside like a kernel but outside, enveloping the tale which brought it out only as a glow brings out a haze, in the likeness of one of these misty halos that, sometimes, are made visible by the spectral illumination of moonshine. (45)

This dense image is "impressionistic" in its misty visual implications, but as Hillis Miller has perceptively pointed out, it is also "parabolic" in the way it urges us to reflect on the tropological "correspondence" between form and content.[30] In order to further Miller's penetrating rhetorical analysis of this central and much-discussed passage in Conrad's poetics, we should add that mimesis continues to cast light on this magical correspondence between form and substance along lines that structure Marlow's mythic tale in particular and Conrad's artistic metaphysics in general. Let us take a closer

look at this obscurely illuminating passage by framing it within the broader
aesthetic/ontological tradition from which it emerges—shadowlike.

The theoretical sources that in-*form* this impressionistic image are old
and go to the heart of the quarrel between moderns and the ancients. Invert-
ing the Platonic image of the artist as a maker of "shadows" twice removed
from reality, Conrad conjures a romantic image of artistic representations
as a source of "illumination." Thus reframed, the artistic representation is
no longer a shadow far removed from the original source of light, as in a
Platonic mythic cave, but a source of light generative of insights into the
darkness, as in Conrad's mythic tale. To use M. H. Abrams's aesthetic categories from *The Mirror and the Lamp*, Conrad's image is visibly indebted to
a romantic, "expressive," and thus fundamentally antimimetic theory of art,
for it suggests that the tale does not simply "mirror" the world outside but
casts an illuminating halo all around.[31] This modern inversion of perspectives reenacts what Plato called in Book X of *Republic* an "ancient quarrel"
(*R* 832) between philosophy and art and, in the process, redresses the balance
in favor of art. Hence, as we move from the ancient Platonic trope of the
mirror to the modern romantic trope of the lamp, mimetic shadows turn
into expressive moonshines.

And yet the transition from a mimetic to an antimimetic theory is
not clear-cut, for every illuminating image, for Conrad, continues to cast a
shadow. Notice, in fact, that the kind of artistic light emerging from Conrad's
mythic tale is not the direct and blinding light of the sun, which, in Plato's
own original mythic figuration, is the source of true, intelligible, and original
Forms enlightened philosophers can sometimes see as they free themselves
from the spectral "shadows cast from the fire on the wall of the cave," (*R*
747) as Socrates says in Book VII of *Republic*. Rather, it is what Hillis Miller
aptly calls the "twice-reflected light"[32] of the moon that serves as the illuminating source necessary to have an in-sight into the darkness all around.
This luminous image is getting shady, misty, and enveloped in a thick layer
of mimetic mediation. While the image of a light twice removed from the
origin is still of Platonic derivation, it also finds an important modern rearticulation in romantic theories of poetry, antimimetic theories that seem to
have cast some indirect light on Conrad's poetics as well. The romantic critic,
writer, and philosopher William Hazlitt, for instance, in an essay titled "On
Poetry in General," complicates the analogy of the mimetic mirror and the

antimimetic lamp along lines that cast a surprising new light on Conrad's famous passage: "'The light of poetry is not only a direct but also a reflected light, that while it shews us the object, throws a sparkling radiance on all around it."[33] The mirroring reflection with Conrad's passage is striking and illuminating. It suggests that even seemingly antimimetic images, and the theories they entail, might have their secret origins in twice-refracted mirroring reflections that generate a fascinating game of artistic, critical, and theoretical re-presentations.

Be it ancient or modern, Platonic or romantic, mimetic or antimimetic, this celebrated passage makes strikingly clear that a re-presentation twice removed from the origin functions as the artistic medium to reflect on Conrad's poetics and the metaphysics it entails. The conflict between the artist and the philosopher we have encountered in the Preface is truly made explicit here. On one side, the philosopher leaves immanent mimetic shadows behind in order to privilege transcendental speculation on a type of illuminating truth that comes from staring at the sunlight directly—to the risk of blindness. On the other side, the artist favors insights that emerge in the darkness by relying on the mediation of a light that has already been mimetically reproduced by the twice-reflected light of the moon. The ontological inversion is clear: for the artist, mimesis is not the source of shadowy illusions but, rather, of illuminating insights into what Conrad considers "enduring and essential" (*NN* xi).[34]

But there is still more to see. In fact, this image is also mimetic in a more self-consciously modernist sense, insofar as it implicates the artistic medium in this game of mirroring refractions and reflections. The framing device Conrad uses to reflect on Marlow's experience envelops the tale, just as the mist envelops the moon, bringing out its meaning as "a glow brings out a haze." Structurally speaking, what envelops the tale is the exterior layer of framing narrators (external and internal) who rely on layers of dreamlike Apollonian halos to bring out the obscure Dionysian "sensation" that would otherwise remain in the darkness. The tale Marlow tells is the source of light or glow. Hence he says later on that this experience, which leads him to confront Kurtz's Dionysian horrors, seemed "to throw a kind of light" (*YOS* 48). Yet it is actually the frame narrator's echo of this voice, or re-presentation of this moonshine, that brings this light to bear on the darkness and haze of misty London, rendering visible a type of "truth" at the "heart of an immense darkness" (126) for listeners to hear and readers to see in the final scene. Once again, the horror may be Dionysian in "sensation," yet it requires an Apollonian, dreamlike, and somewhat dense layer of mediation that blurs clear boundaries between origin and copy, frame and content, light and darkness in order to make the tale, if not fully intelligible, at least atmospherically suggestive.

We may not have cracked this image open, yet it seems to throw a new kind of light. Mimesis is the locus of metaphysical refractions that have their mirroring counterpart in formal reflections at the level of the telling, yet this modernist tale also adds an additional layer of reproduction at the level of what is told. Within the tale, this misty moonlike atmosphere is, in fact, pervasive and surrounds Marlow as he continues his mysterious ritual initiation, suggesting a permeable continuity between outside and inside, the formal Apollonian structure and the formless Dionysian content. For instance, Marlow insists on "the smell of mud, of primeval mud" (69), which, as we have seen, is the formless chthonic ground on which Conrad's metaphysics rests. But he also stresses that this mud is rendered visible through the light of the moon. We are in fact told that "the moon had spread over everything a thin layer of silver—over the rank grass, over the mud, upon the wall of matted vegetation" (69). Marlow's focus is as much on abject "sensation" as on dreamlike illuminations. And given Conrad's imperative to both make us "feel" and "see," we should not be surprised to find out that it is the dynamic interplay between visual and affective mimesis that structures his final tragic recognitions.

## Tragic Recognitions

This point is confirmed if we zoom in on a misty part of the journey that condenses the Dionysian and Apollonian layers we have been peeling off and foreshadows sacrificial horrors soon to be seen. Just prior to the meeting with Kurtz, Marlow and his crew find themselves surrounded by an impenetrable white fog that prevents them from seeing behind the surface of things, yet allows them to feel the vibration of what Henry Staten aptly calls, in a different voice from Lacoue-Labarthe but with similar Nietzschean ontological foundations, the "Dionysian cry" at the heart of the tale.[35] It is in fact at this moment that Marlow hears "a cry, a very loud cry as of infinite desolation

[that] soared slowly in the opaque air. . . . It ceased. . . . A complaining clamour, modulated in savage discords" (83). And a bit later, he adds that there was an "inexplicable note of desperate grief in this savage clamour that had swept by us on the river-bank behind the blind whiteness of a fog" (86). Not unlike the "wall" of the jungle, or the "curtain of trees," the "fog" serves as a misty "veil" that prevents Marlow from seeing the source of what "lay[s] deep under the surface" (82). But as the frame narrator had foreshadowed via his misty image of the moon halo, the fog also brings out the palpable mimetic effect of dark Dionysian experiences. In a ghostly atmosphere that generates "not sleep" but, we are told, a "state of trance" (83), Marlow depicts the surreal image of the steamer with "outlines blurred as if on the point of dissolving, and a misty strip of water" (84). This misty atmosphere may not be illuminating in realistic terms. We are in fact told that "the world" is rendered out of sight in such a fundamental way that there is not even "a shadow behind" it (84). Yet it brings out blurred forms rendered formless along surrealist, metaphysical lines that perfectly capture the dissolution of the *principium individuationis* that is the beating heart of Conrad's tragic insights. Surrealist, Apollonian aesthetic principles in the foreground, then, provide just the right atmosphere to reveal the horror of Dionysian metaphysical principles in the background.

That we are confronted with a mediation of a Dionysian sensation via Apollonian dreamlike representation is confirmed if we continue exploring the misty interplay between surface and depth, affect and vision, light and darkness, physical intoxication and metaphysical disfiguration condensed in this surreal scene. Marlow's narrative makes clear that the clamor in the background is Dionysian in nature, for it induces frenzied human reactions in the foreground. This is the moment to recall that the helmsman, who had previously shown restraint when confronted with images of frenzy on the shore, started "lifting his knees high, stamping his feet, champing his mouth" (89). And then Marlow specifies: "his eyes rolled, he kept on lifting and setting down his feet gently, his mouth foamed a little" (89–90). This is a physiological, contagious reaction characteristic of possession trance among rituals in sub-Saharan Africa, but this is the moment to notice that it is also characteristic of Western tragedies in classical antiquity. In the culminating scene of Euripides's *The Bacchae*—arguably the paradigmatic text on Dionysian tragedy—as Pentheus, who has been spying on the enthused and frenzied Maenads, is about to be discovered, we are given the following picture of his mother, Agave: "she was foaming at the mouth, and her crazed eyes rolling with frenzy."[36] And it is in this state of "frenzy" that Agave sets out to tear her son's body to pieces, in a bloodcurdling sacrificial scene that entails "wrenching away the arm at the shoulder," playing "ball with scraps of Pentheus' body," and "picking up his head, impal[ing] it on her wand" (*B* 592). Since Agave is possessed by Dionysian frenzy, we can understand why Nietzsche, in *The Birth of Tragedy*, stresses that via the "analogy of intoxication" (36) and the "frenzy" it entails, we catch a glimpse of that ritual proto-phenomenon that culminates in the "dismemberment" characteristic of "properly Dionysian *suffering*" (73). The metaphysical insight Nietzsche derives from a Greek tragedy can be explicitly derived from a modernist tragedy as well. Namely, that tragic insights into Dionysian horrors require the mediation of Apollonian veils that both hide and reveal a type of violent reconciliation with nature characteristic of the horror of sacrificial death.

It is thus no accident that it is precisely at the moment the helmsman enters into a state of Dionysian frenzy that his body is traversed by a spear, leaving Marlow facing what he calls a "death-mask" that will fill him with horror and will make him (as narrator) think ahead to Kurtz's death. Nor is it accidental that at this moment Marlow (as protagonist) catches a glimpse of the "true," "essential" reality below the surface of things. Here is what he sees: "then suddenly as though a veil had been removed from my eyes I made out deep in the tangled gloom, naked breasts, arms, legs, glaring eyes—the bush was swarming with human limbs in movement" (*YOS* 89). This is a decisive insight into the metaphysical ground on which the narrative rests. If it is reminiscent of the type of disfiguration we have already seen in *Almayer's Folly*, as Almayer lifts the "veil" that covers the disfigured body, this revelatory scene also complicates the mimetic schema of the first novel. In particular, it condenses the interplay of Apollonian mediation and Dionysian disfiguration necessary for tragic insights to appear. And what we see is a picture of fragmentation of human body parts set against the impersonal bush as a swarming being that cuts both ways. On one side, this image calls attention to the disruption of the boundaries of individuation characteristic of sacrificial death. As such, it anticipates the Dionysian horrors that culminate with "heads on the stakes" adorning Kurtz's "ceremonies." In this confused intermixture of bodies and nature we have an insight into what Girard calls "crisis of difference," which

foreshadows the anthropology of sacrifice based on scapegoating of innocent victims. On the other side, this passage also offers an insight into the
impersonal, metaphysical ground of which these bodies are a living part. In
this sense, this confusion is not so much physical but metaphysical, and is in
line with the Dionysian account of the "clamour" characteristic of tragedies as
Nietzsche and Lacoue-Labarthe understand them.

Furthermore, this metaphysical picture makes us see the role of aesthetics not only in representing bodies torn to pieces but also in contributing
to tearing them apart, if not physically and literally, at least aesthetically
and linguistically. There is, in fact, something selectively perspectival, fragmented, and incongruent in the way the narrative joins disjointed body parts
to recompose an image of "tangled gloom, naked breasts, arms, legs, glaring
eyes." In such a modernist, primitivist, protocubist picture, clean distinctions
between the violence of Dionysian sensation and the mediation of Apollonian images no longer hold. And what we begin to see is that the Apollonian is fully implicated in the violence of the Dionysian. It is not simply a
question of mediating a deep metaphysical horror that is on the side of the
Dionysian, which the Apollonian medium transparently re-presents on the
surface for us to see, nor simply of reconciling two opposed principles, one
luminous and formal, the other dark and formless. Rather, in this modernist
tragedy, the Dionysian is constitutive of the Apollonian—if only because it
is an artistic medium that does violence to language in order to paint such
an ontological image of disfiguration. If Conrad's take on tragedy is rooted
in metaphysical foundations, then, this tragedy is truly modernist for it is
born out of what we could call, oxymoronically, a Dionysian representation;
conversely, Conrad's tragedy is a metaphysical tragedy reborn out of the light
of Apollonian disfiguration.

Is there a politics buried in Conrad's metaphysics of darkness? Yes, there
is, and it is double. The tragic lesson that emerges from Conrad's artistic
metaphysics is Janus-faced and can be put to both regressive and progressive
political uses: if this tragic insight can easily lead to an aestheticization and
celebration of Dionysian violence, it can also lead to the Apollonian self-
recognition that this violence is at the very heart of Western civilization—
including the very practice of artistic representation. Terry Eagleton is thus
right to mention that the polarity of Nietzsche's metaphysics of which Conrad is, as he says, an "acolyte," can be "dismantled" as the Apollonian "shares

in the very [Dionysian] forces it strives to contain."³⁷ This dismantling is
certainly exemplified by Kurtz, a "universal genius" who is also a "painter,"
"poet," and "musician" whose mastery of *Apollonian* artistic forms leads him
to the bloodcurdling *Dionysian* imperative to "exterminate all the brutes."
The disruption of the boundary that divides Apollonian from Dionysian
practices, "civilization" from "savagery," can thus be recuperated for a moral
and political critique of the horror of civilizing missions. And quite rightly
so since, as we have seen, "All Europe contributed to the making of Kurtz"
(*YOS* 95) and will soon be implicated in unprecedented sacrificial practices.

But this critique is not radical enough. What we must add is that *Heart
of Darkness* implicates artistic Apollonian practices into Dionysian horrors
along lines that have been constitutive of the origins of tragic art and, as
Jonathan Dollimore powerfully argued, are constitutive of *"the history of
civilization."*³⁸ In this deeper sense, the birth of tragic art is constitutive of
mimetic violence, part of the violence it sets out to represent. This is, again,
far from being an original insight. Mimesis has long been recognized to have
both therapeutic and poisonous effects. Yet it allows us to correct dominant
accounts of what mimesis, or tragedy is, or should be. For instance, we should
not conclude, with Terry Eagleton, that tragic art "is the enemy of mimesis,
since the role of art is to transfigure rather than reflect"³⁹—if only because
mimesis is Janus-faced and has the power to reflect as much as to transfigure.
Nor should we state, with Walter Kaufmann, that no novel "*could* approximate a Greek or Shakespearean tragedy"⁴⁰—if only because the line that
divides ancient tragedies and modernist tragedies is permeable at best when
considered from the angle of mimesis. Let us say instead, with Conrad, that
*Heart of Darkness* is a modernist tragedy with a tremendous power of illumination into the horror of what is enduring and essential. It also makes us see
how mimetic reflections and transfigurations are not in stable opposition,
at least if we consider mimesis in both its Apollonian and Dionysian manifestations. This creative and destabilizing interplay gives aesthetic form to
modernist tragedy—out of a formless, metaphysical ground.

Conrad's modernist emphasis on Apollonian images in the foreground
serves as a medium that both veils and unveils the Dionysian essence in the
background. The narrative is consistent in emphasizing images of mediation that look both ways: one side looks toward formal representation, the
other toward formless undifferentiation; one toward the surface, the other

toward the truth below it. For instance, as the dying helmsman is lying on the deck, his body traversed by a spear, face-to-face with the horror of death, he is represented as a "death-mask" (91)—an indication that the surface of the mask and the horror of death beneath are not simply opposed, as light is opposed to darkness. Rather, the "inconceivably somber" sensation of death lurks on the surface of a tragic mask, which both reveals and veils the horror underneath.[41] This is also what Kurtz suggests, as he utters his famous insight at the "supreme moment of complete knowledge" (117). In fact, he cries out not at the horror itself, nor at death, but at "some image at some vision" (117). If a "veil has been rent," this apocalyptic revelation does not confront us with any transcendental truth; rather it opens onto another image for yet another figure—or medium—to reproduce.

Marlow is, of course, this medium. He mediates between ritual horrors he felt as protagonist and Apollonian representations he depicts as narrator. His face is thus Janus-faced: he looks both inside to horrors he *feels* and outside to horrors he wants others to *see*. On the affective side, he identifies with his homo duplex, Kurtz, and lives through "his extremity," thereby catching a glimpse beyond the abyss, along lines that echo Almayer's identification with the disfigured corpse underneath the veil. The essence of tragedy, Conrad suggests, is part of a Dionysian experience that must be felt first, albeit at one remove from reality. In this sense, the tragic female figures qua doubles—the African mistress and the Intended—come much closer to the Dionysian. These opposed figures are indeed mirror images of each other; they both "cry out" tragically—one echoing the other—giving a distinctive feminine voice to a metaphysical pain Marlow can only represent from a distance. They are, in this sense, the secret soul of tragedy. No wonder Marlow comes close to being torn to pieces by such Dionysian cries.

And yet on the side of Apollonian mediation, Conrad, via the frame narrator, via Marlow, can bring layer after layer of tragic reality to the surface of the text for listeners to hear and readers to see, via a multilayered narrative structure characteristic of what I dub modernist tragedy. Put differently, this tragedy is truly modernist for it touches the heart of Dionysian pathos along lines familiar from classical antiquity, yet also realizes that in order to convey the feeling of horror a multiplication of Apollonian frames is needed. These frames are based on mimesis understood as representation, in the sense that each narrative filter re-presents, halolike, the experience of a more interior, more secret and intimate perspective, in a regress that goes from the frame narrator, to Marlow, to the tragic Dionysian figures at the heart of the narrative. But it is only because the link between each perspective is based on mimesis understood as affective identification that tragic pathos can flow through the layers of modernist mediation and reach readers from a distance. The tremendous tragic effect of *Heart of Darkness* relies on a paradoxical logic Lacoue-Labarthe called "hyperbologic." It could be adapted as follows: the more distant the reader is from the events she or he is given to see, the closer to the palpitating heart of the tragic pathos; Apollonian distance intensifies the pathos of Dionysian tragedy—because the Apollonian medium is a constitutive part of the Dionysian message it sets out to represent.

To conclude with a Janus-faced image that sums up the interplay between Dionysian and Apollonian principles I take to be the beating heart of this modernist tragedy, let us picture Marlow, one last time, sitting in "the pose of a Buddha" (47), telling his tale. Picture him in detail: his "lean face," "worn, hollow" (92), appearing and disappearing in a flickering interplay of light and darkness. And then remember that this figure is the medium that mediates the horror of death; his voice is the voice that echoes "The horror! The horror!" (107) Should we then take it as a simple coincidence that Marlow, a figure described with "sunken cheeks" (43), as well as with "dropped eyelids" (92), finds himself face-to-face with the horror of a decapitated head on the stake and sees an image that—lo and behold!—is also "sunken—with closed lids—smiling continuously at some endless and jocose dream of that eternal slumber" (103–4)? A dream, only a jocose dream; yet what a pathos of recognition it can generate. This is, so to speak, the face of tragedy. And in a striking mirroring reflection, this face is not deprived of ironic inversions. It rests on a metaphysical form of delayed decoding based on what I have renamed a delayed call forwarding technique that, even for Conrad, is unusually allusive yet reflects the horror of mimesis nonetheless. What this image suggests, in fact, is that the face of tragedy may be more intimate than previously realized; the line dividing a living (sunken) face and a dead (sunken) face is not real but illusory—unsurprisingly so since Conrad's metaphysics constantly transgresses the shadow-line between appearance and reality. Marlow's greatest irony might thus actually be a self-irony. This final mirroring image reflects a horror not only outside, in sacrificial experiences of the "other," but also, and at the same time, inside, at the heart of an inner experience of the "ego."

Has Marlow managed to convey his dreamlike sensation? Do you see the image? Do you feel anything? What is certain is that in this mirroring reflection the distinction between a Buddha image and a sacrificial image, Apollonian narrators and Dionysian practices no longer holds. And as this modernist narrative ends with an image of tragicomic self-recognition, it also paints the surreal landscape—for another tragedy to begin.

## Sacrificial Revelations: *Apocalypse Now Redux*

Can you picture a human face mirrored by a Buddha statue? Frame it against a surreal image of wilderness and pain exploding into flames that burn down boundaries between human figures and divine figures to the rhythmic sound of Jim Morrison's mesmerizing voice singing, "This is the end, my friend, the end," and you'll realize that Francis Ford Coppola's *Apocalypse Now*[42] begins where Conrad's *Heart of Darkness* ends.

In both original and redux versions, *Apocalypse Now* is not a faithful cinematic adaptation of *Heart of Darkness* that mimetically represents Conrad's masterpiece on the screen for us to see. Rather, it reframes colonial abominations in the context of the horrors of the Vietnam War in an original and innovative movie that brings Conrad's political critique to bear on the present. The referential dimension of the establishing shot whereby the film begins, opening on a wall of green and lush vegetation in the background, dark helicopters in the foreground, accompanied by the sound of the extradiegetic music of The Doors, makes immediately clear that we have shifted from the horrors of Belgian colonialism in the 1890s to the horrors of Vietnam in the 1960s and 1970s. Given the contemporary reenactment of such horrors, it is thus no wonder that the cinematic text is often used as a pre-text to foreground ethico-political principles already internal to Conrad's critique of civilizing missions, past and present.

And yet the aesthetic and philosophical continuities between these two tragic fictions run much deeper than previously noted and inform—from beginning to end—the texture of this cinematic text. There is, in fact, much in the formal structure of this opening scene that re-*produces* the surreal atmosphere characteristic of Conrad's tale, adding yet another Apollonian layer of mediation to the Dionysian experiences beating at its palpitating heart. For instance, this image of the jungle set on fire by napalm already reveals that the source of the horror does not lie behind the wall of vegetation. On the contrary, it originates from new technologies of death used in the name of the idea that "the West is the best," as Morrison ironically sings. Shot in slow motion, shrouded in a mist of yellowish dust that mixes wilderness with human pain to the sound of hypnotizing music, these oneiric frames of horror do not offer a direct window onto an exterior, realistic referent. Rather, they are the product of a carefully crafted cinematic frame that calls attention to itself and reminds us that we are witnessing an aesthetic re-presentation of a "desperate land" filtered by the imagination of the protagonist of this film, a military officer called Captain Willard (Martin Sheen) stuck in a hotel in Saigon, waiting for a mission. We do not need to wait long, in fact, to realize that the Conradian effect of "delayed decoding" can be effectively transferred to another medium as well, opening alternative doors of perception based on cinematic, and no less haunting visions. As we see a close-up of Willard's face staring at a rotating overhead fan that recalls, by metonymic association, the helicopter blades, we belatedly realize that this image of "wilderness and pain" does not directly depict a natural landscape but a mental landscape, not an exterior experience but an inner experience mediated by Willard's dreamlike, surreal, and perhaps even hyperreal imagination. But does this mean that this cinematic simulation has nothing to do with the reality of war itself?

## Hyperreal Simulation / Surreal Imagination

This is what media theorist Jean Baudrillard suggests. In his account of *Apocalypse Now* in *Simulacres et simulation* (1981), Baudrillard zeroes in on such surreal images of napalm exploding in the jungle in order to make the controversial claim that "the Vietnam War 'in itself' perhaps never took place."[43] The philosophical qualification "in itself" is important here. It is in fact ontology rather than politics that is at stake in his account of postmodern forms of simulation. *Apocalypse Now*, for Baudrillard, is but one symptom of a "hyperreal" world in which the ontological distinction between reality and copy, truth and appearance no longer holds, for signs of the real are substituted for reality itself. Conrad, as we shall see, already gave artistic form to this dissolution of reality in *The Secret Agent*; Coppola makes it visible in

*Apocalypse Now.* For Baudrillard, in fact, Coppola "makes his film like the Americans made war" (*SS* 89). That is, in a spectacular, hypermediatized way that, in a mirroring gesture, turns the reality of war into a colossal movie. In both cases, argues Baudrillard, war seems to have lost touch with its solid, material, referential ground—no matter how bloody this war was. What we have, instead, is an image of war as "technological and psychedelic fantasy, the war as a succession of special effects" (89).

Baudrillard is alluding to the opening scene of *Apocalypse Now* with which we started, but this hyperreal hypothesis finds support in the surreal atmosphere that pervades the film in general, and in the mirroring effects generated by a scene of cinematic mise en abyme in particular. At one point in the midst of a combat scene, in fact, the camera pans and we see Coppola himself and his crew filming, in a journalistic mode, Willard advancing, while repeatedly shouting at him, "Don't look at the camera! Just go by, like you're fighting. Don't look at the camera! It's the television." It's the television, to be sure, but the meaning of tele-vision is no longer clear. In fact, this is a "realistic" testimony of the cinematic nature of war that blurs the ontological barrier dividing "reality" and "fiction" along simulated principles that cut both ways. On the one hand, this scene is seemingly "realistic" and calls attention to the *message* of Coppola's directions. Namely, that soldiers fighting in real, contemporary, mass-mediatized wars are not different from actors; they follow a script in order to fictionalize "real" fighting for the tele-vision—that is, for spectators to see (vision) at a distance (tele). Not breaking the fourth wall, in this sense, is a real rule of acting necessary to sustain the "realty" of a war that is already fictionalized as it unfolds. Paradoxically, then, it takes a real actor like Martin Sheen to effectively represent the fictional reality of war real soldiers engage in.[44] On the other hand, this scene is "cinematic" and calls attention to the *medium* of cinema. The camera Coppola uses in his fictional role as TV journalist is a camera really used for shooting a close-up of Willard's face that is an integral part of this cinematic fiction. In an additional turn, Coppola's "journalistic" TV camera within the diegesis faces the "cinematic" camera, thereby generating endless games of mirrors in which the boundary between "reality" and "fiction" no longer holds, marvelously illustrating Baudrillard's hyperreal principle whereby "the film became war, the war becomes film" (*SS* 89). We could thus say, with Baudrillard, that in *Apocalypse Now* it is not only the jungle that explodes; it is the entire metaphysical distinction between reality and fiction that is burning down. Gone is the ancient and modernist world of real, sacrificial horrors. Welcome to the burning jungle of the hyperreal!

And yet such images are not as clear-cut as they appear to be, and the cinematic logic of surreality cannot fully be contained within the postmodern ontology of hyperreality. Already the opening scene of the film suggests that this landscape is not solely a mental representation or a mediatized simulation—though it is clearly both. Rather, this scene is surreal in the sense that while clearly oneiric, the relation to the referential world is not completely lost, only distorted, inverted, and modified. It is important to look at the opening scene closely. Notice that the close-up of Willard's face in the foreground does not replace, or wipe out, the fire in the jungle in the background, as simulation replaces, or wipes out, reality. On the contrary, it lingers upside down, superimposed on it, generating a multilayered image that suggests as much continuity as discontinuity between foreground and background. More precisely, Willard's upside-down face in the foreground suggests that his perspective will not simply filter the exterior events "objectively" but, rather, will be in a relation of subjective opposition with the ethical and political horrors of the war in the background. Further, his blurred face indicates that we cannot easily detach a subjective dreamlike imagination from the exterior violent referent—perhaps because it is a double inner/outer experience that generates the horror at heart of this tragic film. What is sure is that by the time Willard's face on the left of the screen is juxtaposed to

a Buddha statue on the right and confused in the mist of a fiery sky that blurs the distinction between foreground and background, human figure and divine figure, we begin to suspect that what is re-presented is not simply a political horror but an aesthetic and tragic recognition of a sacred horror. It is as if Coppola opens surrealist doors of perception to access Conrad's insights into the metaphysical violence of dissolution. In this sense, his description of *Apocalypse Now* as "the first $30 million surrealist movie" might have been more illuminating than he actually realized.[45]

Critics have long recognized that in *Apocalypse Now*, Coppola remains faithful to Conrad's political message and the critique of the real horrors of colonialism and imperialism it entails. And in the wake of Baudrillard's critique we have also learned to pay attention to the medium and the ontology of simulation it generates. Somewhat less readily perceptible is that Coppola's surreal film visually dramatizes the underlying surreal ontology I have been tracing in this chapter, supplementing real images of formless disfiguration (the message) with sacrificial horrors for readers to see via the artistic mediation of a cinematic screen (the medium). As the protagonist embarks on yet another muddy river, he is in fact progressively exposed to mimetic experiences that introduce Dionysian continuities at the heart of Apollonian discontinuities. The echoes are loud, the mirroring reflections numerous. From the clamor of Wagner's Valkyries scene and the enthusiastic outbreaks it generates to tigers leaping out from the jungle threatening to devour soldiers, from psychedelic hallucinogenic drugs that dissolve interior boundaries to surreal representation of foggy landscapes that blur formal boundaries, from camouflaged human faces to sacrificial animal bodies, from kinky sex in muddy camps to explosions that tear bodies to pieces, from acephalic bodies to bodiless heads—indeed, as we shift from *Heart of Darkness* to *Apocalypse Now* the Apollonian medium of representation may have changed, but the Dionysian message is fundamentally the same.

## Dionysian Sacrifice (Euripides to Girard)

That an underlying metaphysical continuity runs, like an undercurrent, between the two literary-cinematic texts is confirmed by the culminating part of the journey, which brings Willard face-to-face not only with his homo duplex, Kurtz (Marlon Brando), but also with a sacrificial horror that was already central to *Heart of Darkness*. Following the imperative, "never get out of the boat!," lest human figures find themselves torn to pieces by tigers, the final scene represents Willard emerging, chameleon-like, from a muddy, misty, surreal river with his face mimetically covered in camouflage paint and mud—a picture that makes clear he is now, quite literally, fully immersed in the formless, Dionysian reality he had previously tried to keep at bay. Having initially heard the echo of Kurtz's voice recorded on a tape, and seen his youthful image reproduced on a picture shown to him with the imperative to "terminate the Colonel's command," Willard now realizes that there are wider metaphysical forces that animate and trigger his seemingly political

actions. His voice-over, which punctuates the narrative and reminds us that the events that unfold on the screen have actually already taken place and are re-presented, for a second time for us to see, retrospectively comments: "even the jungle wanted him dead." And what the culminating scene reveals is an image of sacrifice that is, of course, double: we see two shadows (or mimetic doubles) dueling to the end in the chiaroscuro of the background, while in the foreground we see a ritual clamor of dancing and singing that culminates in the sacrificial killing of a caribou (or sacrificial victim).[46]

What, then, is the theoretical lesson we can draw from these images of sacrifice redux? What is the horror *Apocalypse Now* attempts to reveal in this enigmatic and bloodcurdling scene? Commentators, reviewers, and the public alike have often been baffled by the final sacrificial scene in which Coppola apparently "*deviates* most decisively from Conrad" in order to embrace a modernist aesthetics informed by mythic structures.[47] And yet a closer look reveals that there is no deviation at all. This scene is in fact perfectly in line with the tragic, Dionysian ontology that concerns us and brings this account of the rebirth of tragedy to an end.

This horrifying scene is, indeed, past-oriented. It offers a contemporary cinematic re-presentation of sacrificial ceremonies that are internal to Conrad's African tale, are familiar to the West as well, and stretch back to our mythic and tragic past. Particularly noteworthy is the legend of the sacrificial killing of the King of the Wood reported in James Frazer's *The Golden Bough*. The connection is all the more direct as we see a copy of *The Golden Bough* on Kurtz's desk—a theoretical manual for the sacrificial ritual Marlow is about to reenact. As Frazer explains in his section of *The Golden Bough* titled "Dionysus," "At his festivals, Dionysus was believed to appear in the bull form," and he adds: "According to the myth, it was in the shape of a bull that he was torn to pieces by the Titans."[48] We are thus back to the Dionysian ritual ground that equally informed Conrad's metaphysics. But this time the Dionysian returns with the vengeance of a physical supplement. The sacrificial violence is, in fact, explicitly shown on the cinematic screen for everyone to see, bringing not only Kurtz's homo duplex but all spectators face-to-face with Dionysian horrors that had so far remained hidden behind a veil. In this revelatory gesture, *Apocalypse Now* urges us to look back to the origins of these Dionysian scenes in order to better face a type of horror that,

as the title suggests, is occurring now. Let us thus cast a glance further back at the ancients, before returning to the (post)moderns.

In many ways, Euripides's *The Bacchae* (405 BC) provides the most influential dramatization of tragic, Dionysian horrors that are at the origins of Western culture. Though unnoticed so far, these horrors continue to secretly inform Conrad's and Coppola's modern literary and cinematic representations respectively. The confrontation between the two first cousins, Pentheus king of Thebes and the god Dionysus returning from the East, stages two antagonists who embody opposed principles: human power versus divine power, political norms versus religious rites, profane principles versus sacred principles. According to a pattern we have learned to recognize, these doubles progressively turn out to be mirror images of each other, "twin brothers" whose difference masks an underlying mimetic sameness: they are both rivalrous, concerned with honor, and ready to engage in escalation of violence. Thus, at a decisive turning point Pentheus's vision doubles, and here is what he sees:

> I seem to see two suns blazing in the heavens.
> And now two Thebes, two cities, and each
> with seven gates. And you—you are a bull
> who walks before me there. Horns have sprouted
> from your head. Have you always been a beast?
> But now I see a bull. (*B* 583–84)

Mimesis, in this play, is on the side of true revelations, not shadowy illusions. By doubling his vision Pentheus not only sees, for the first time, Dionysus's true, divine nature; he is also set on the path to experiencing the deeper metaphysical truth of tragic Dionysian disfigurations. In *The Bacchae* it is in fact not a bull or Dionysus that is torn to pieces, but Pentheus instead. The moral lesson of the play is that this is actually Dionysus's punishment for a human, all-too-human hubris that led Pentheus and his mother, Agave, not to recognize him as a god. But there is also a metaphysical lesson that makes us see that "Dionysian suffering," as Nietzsche calls it, requires an artistic mediation.

Importantly, at the culminating point of the play we do not see the horror of the Dionysian *sparagmos* directly. Rather, it is via the theatrical medium of a *diegesis* far removed from the mimetic message, in which a witness reports the events, that we, spectators, are given to see, or better imagine, Pentheus's body torn to pieces, decapitated, and impaled by the Maenads in a state of frenzy along lines that are intimated but not fully revealed in *Heart of Darkness*. Here is an image of sacrifice generating the horror that, so far, has remained behind the veil of representation:

> One tore off an arm,
> another a foot still warm in its shoe. His ribs
> were clawed clean of flesh and every hand
> was smeared with blood as they played ball with scraps
> of Pentheus' body.
> The pitiful remains lie scattered,
> one piece among the sharp rocks, others
> lying lost among the leaves in the depths
> of the forest. His mother, picking up his head,
> impaled it on her wand. (*B* 592)

This harrowing scene has been subjected to different readings and perspectives, but the tragic ontology that concerns us is fundamentally the same as the one we have been unearthing. As we move from an ancient play to a modernist novella to a postmodern film, the medium changes, but the metaphysics of violence doesn't. And what this ancient medium makes us see is that

Pentheus, as he is torn to pieces by the Maenads, literally embodies the suffering of the Dionysian *sparagmos*. The identification between Pentheus and Dionysus is thus not only psychological but ontological. Insofar as Pentheus offers us an image of Dionysus torn to pieces, he is the perfect embodiment of Dionysian ontology. Initially depicted as physical and psychic doubles, these two cousins turn out to represent the same metaphysical principle. At the same time, with the sacrifice of Pentheus the play reminds us that metaphysical suffering is always first and foremost human, all-too-human suffering; Dionysian tragedies reveal human tragedies. And as Nietzsche was quick to recognize, these tragedies require an Apollonian distance that gives aesthetic form to the Dionysian frenzy it appears to simply re-present. In sum, this theatrical frame makes us see that *Apocalypse Now* is far from deviating from *Heart of Darkness*. On the contrary, the detour via the *Bacchae* (ancient tragedy) helps us confirm that what was true for *Heart of Darkness* (modernist tragedy) continues to remain valid for *Apocalypse Now* (postmodern tragedy).

In a sense, then, these rituals look back to the origins of tragedy and the metaphysical horror it entails. But this is the moment to recognize that in another sense they also look ahead to what René Girard calls a "crisis of difference" and the anthropological violence it reveals.[49] What was true for *Heart of Darkness* is even more apparent in *Apocalypse Now*: from mimetic doubles to ritual sacrifice, from a crisis of difference to the killing of a scapegoat, from the horror of human sacrifice to the catharsis of violent emotions, all the elements of Girard's account of "Dionysus" in *Violence and the Sacred* are in place in this contemporary cinematic text. This is indeed a confirmation of Girard's claim that "genuine artists can still sense that tragedy lurks somewhere behind the bland festival" (*VS* 125). Coppola, just like Conrad, is precisely such a genuine Dionysian artist who confronts us with the tragic horrors of modernity. In particular, he confirms the theoretical connection Girard traces between mimetic crisis, mimetic violence, and the sacrificial scapegoat that puts an end to this violence. As Girard puts it, "The ritual *sparagmos* reenacts and imitates with a scrupulous exactitude the scene of lynching that brought riot and disorder to an end" (131; trans. modified). Framed within this ritual model that leads collective violence (or crisis) to be discharged on an innocent victim (or scapegoat), we can better understand the ritual function of the final scene, a cathartic function that "strives

to achieve violence only in order to eliminate it" (132). We could thus say, with Girard, that just as the mimetic rivalry between Pentheus and Diony-sus in the *Bacchae* mirrors a wider escalation of ritual violence with tragic and cathartic implications, so the duel to the end between the two mimetic doubles in *Apocalypse Now* mirrors a wider sacrificial crisis with both tragic and cathartic effects. If Willard, just like Marlow, is Kurtz's double, *Apoca-lypse Now* specifies that Kurtz is the sacrificial animal's double, an association that signals both his divine nature as Dionysus and his sacrificial nature as scapegoat.

This mimetic hypothesis finds ample confirmations in the message of the sacrificial scene, which cuts both ways. Coppola, in fact, stages an under-lying cinematic continuity generated by the loss of differentiation between Willard and Kurtz as doubles that leads to the sacrificial killing of Kurtz qua pharmakos in the background on the one hand, and the loss of differentia-tion at work in the ritual sacrifice that leads to the killing of the caribou as *sparagmos* in the foreground, on the other. The sacrifice of the tragic hero thus coincides with the sacrifice of the animal, unsurprisingly so since both human and animal figures are embodiments of the same Dionysian principle. This mimetic continuity at the end had been carefully prepared from the beginning. Early on in the film we had already seen an image of Kurtz as a sacrificial scapegoat. When Willard receives the order to "terminate the Col-onel's command" he is having lunch with Intelligence Corps, surrounded by stuffed animals while listening to Kurtz's voice playing on a tape and looking at his picture against the background of slices of veal on a plate, ready to be consumed. This picture already makes us see that Kurtz is the scapegoat that will be sacrificed. He is a sacrificial victim who is far from innocent, and thus makes possible the *méconnaissance* of a violence that is internal to the military officers and, by metonymic extension, Western imperialism as a whole. The purifying rain after the ritual sacrifice of Kurtz would then suggest that the ritual has, indeed, succeeded. Violence has been discharged on the scapegoat, social cohesion has been reestablished, and the sacrificial blood on Willard's body—and by metonymic extension the blood of war tout court—washed away. The pharmakos is thus truly a *pharmakon* in the sense that it functions as a cure that, as Girard says, "prevents the spread of violence [*empêche les germes de violence de se développer*]" (*VS* 18). This critical alignment is, once again, informed by the shared anthropological influences at work in both theory and fiction. Coppola's theoretical inspiration from Frazer's *Golden Bough* automatically aligns him with Girard's theory, if only because Frazer's chapter on the "scapegoat" is a decisive influence on Girard. Despite its title, then, *Apocalypse Now* may not be as apocalyptic as it appears to be after all. It does not culminate in an apocalyptic revelation that "this is the end," but in a cathartic purification that opens up the possibility for new beginnings.

And yet we have not read the text to the end. Coppola's anthropological debt to Frazer's account of the scapegoat aligns him with Girard, but his direct ethnographic source of inspiration also allows him to confirm and supplement mimetic theory. This is the moment to recognize that Coppola's sacrificial scene is actually based on a cinematic reenactment of a ritual performed by Ifugao Indians, a local tribe he had initially hired to lend realistic credibility to Kurtz's surroundings but who also ended up providing the ritual context for the culminating scene of the movie. As Eleanor Coppola shows in her documentary of the making of *Apocalypse Now*, aptly titled *Hearts of Darkness*, the Ifugao ritual takes place in a spirit of ritual communion, peace, and solidarity whereby the entire community partakes in a ritual involving singing, drinking, dancing, and storytelling—which lasts the whole night— giving us an insight into the mysterious ceremonies that, in a different ethnographic context, interested both Conrad and Achebe. The following day we are told, for instance, that sacrificial animals like hens and pigs are killed "in a very sacrificial way," says Eleanor Coppola, to indicate a structured and organized ritual. And the ceremony culminates in the sacrificial killing of a caribou that is violently cut to pieces, ritually cooked, and eaten collectively during a "festival like Thanksgiving."[50] This ritual is thus Dionysian in the violence of the sacrificial killing. It also provides a confirmation, if not of an originary "mimetic crisis" that Girard hypothetically posits in *illo tempore*, at least of the efficacy of ritual in "promoting harmony between the members of the community" (*VS* 137). As Jane Harrison had already pointed out, such Dionysian rituals that culminate by eating the sacrificed animals (such as pigs and bulls) are geared toward partaking in the qualities of the animal-god, assimilating its strength, and revitalizing both the powers of nature and of the community.[51] What we must add is that this violence is not only Dionysian in nature. It is also measured by an Apollonian ritual frame that harmoniously and ritually contains it—a Nietzschean point also emphasized by Joseph Campbell in his comparative account of the sacrifice in Eastern Asia.[52] The frame of art is particularly important in the account of ritual under scrutiny. For Francis Ford Coppola, in fact, just as for Achebe before him, sacrifice is far from being predicated on an outbreak of mad "frenzy." Rather, this ritual confirms the festive, joyful, and above all communal framework that anthropologists find central in maintaining social harmony and social cohesion during sacred, religious times. Tragic plays, modernist tragedies, and postcolonial tragedies, we should not forget, belong to this sacred tradition too. They might be bloody and Dionysian in their sacrificial messages, but they always frame such violence via an Apollonian medium that keeps mimetic contagion in check, and generate experiences of imaginary communion instead.

### The Apollonian Medium (Bataille to Coppola)

If we return to *Apocalypse Now* with this larger cultural and theoretical frame in mind we are now in a better position to recognize that the culminating scene not only represents a ritual sacrifice steeped in sacred practices geared toward maintaining the stability of the social order during sacred times via the ritual killing of a scapegoat. It is also, and above all, a cinematic representation of a traditional religious sacrifice reframed via an aesthetic Apollonian medium that mediates Dionysian horrors for spectators to see from a cinematic distance. From this perspective, *Apocalypse Now* reminds us of the Nietzschean hypothesis that the type of "dismemberment" characteristic of what Nietzsche calls Dionysian mimesis is radically dependent on an Apollonian mimesis in order for tragedy to be born. This is an important aesthetic lesson we have already seen at work in *Heart of Darkness*. But we are now in a position to specify the complex interplay between ritual (Dionysian) message and tragic (Apollonian) medium along lines suggested by another thinker of Nietzschean inspiration who was a direct influence on the mimetic theorists considered so far—from Derrida to Girard, Lacoue-Labarthe to Baudrillard—and will allow us to read this sacrificial scene to the end: Georges Bataille.

As a student of the French school of anthropology, Bataille was interested in sacrifice throughout his entire career. But it is probably in a late text titled "Hegel, la mort, le sacrifice"[53] that he confronts the philosophical stakes of sacrifice most directly. Let us briefly recall that like other Dionysian practices, such as eroticism and drunkenness, laughter and play, sacrifice, for Bataille, reveals the power of affective forms of communication to introduce sacred continuities at the heart of profane discontinuities. Bataille is here following Alexandre Kojève's anthropomorphic reading of Hegel's master and slave dialectic in claiming that humans are truly humans, or better sovereign, only insofar as they are ready to look at the horror of death *bien en face*. Still, he remains fundamentally Nietzschean in his emphasis on Dionysian sacrifice as the paradigmatic example of this horror. The function of sacrifice, as well as of tragedy, for Bataille, is thus to make us both see and feel what he often calls the impossible—that is, the horror of our

death, while remaining on the side of life. How? By generating an inter-play between visual representation and affective identification, seeing and feeling, distance and pathos, a mimetic interplay that is central to Conrad's modernist accounts of tragedy.

In a passage that has tremendous resonance with the culminating scene of *Apocalypse Now* and condenses the metaphysics of tragedy I have been articulating, Bataille sums up the function of sacrifice as follows: "during sacrifice, the sacrificer identifies with the animal hit by death. Thus, in way, he dies by watching himself die" (HM 336). A mimetic identification with the sacrificial victim, for Bataille, is thus at the origin of sacred horrors that put humans in touch with the universal tragedy of death. Put in his language, ritual sacrifice establishes a sovereign communication between sacrificer and victim, human and animal, that transgresses the distinction between life and death, the discontinuity of human beings (the profane) and the continuity of Being (the sacred). Bataille's diagnostic is steeped in a Janus-faced concep-tion of mimesis we are by now familiar with. In fact, a sacrificial transgression mediates the Dionysian experience of the other ("he dies") via the filter of Apollonian representation in the self ("watching himself die"). The tragic horror of death, for Bataille as for Conrad before him, cannot be known or experienced immediately; it needs the mediation of what Conrad called an "image" and Bataille calls a "subterfuge." Thus Bataille continues by saying that "knowledge of death cannot avoid the mediation of a subterfuge [*ne peut se passer d'un subterfuge*]: the spectacle" (337).

The emphasis on representation is important here, for it is the subterfuge of the spectacle that allows Bataille to shift his account of sacrifice from ritual to art and articulate the sacred core of the metaphysics of tragedy that con-cerns us. Thus, thinking of tragic spectacles as an offshoot of sacrificial spec-tacles, Bataille specifies: "It is a question, at least in tragedy, of identification with a character that dies and of believing that we die, while remaining alive" (HM 337). This is the metaphysical function of what Bataille calls tragedy or, more generally, "sovereign literature" (337): namely, to "extend the obsessive magic" (337) of sacrificial rituals and tragic spectacles so as to make us see and feel what Conrad would have probably called the horror of what is "enduring and essential" or, alternatively, the "heart of darkness," while at the same time remaining on the side of light and representation, Conrad, in this specific Bataillean sense, is one of the most incisive and sophisticated advocates of sovereign literature. And so is Coppola. They both give expression to what Mircea Eliade calls "the purest poetic act," whose goal is to "to re-create language from an inner experience that, like the ecstasy or the religious inspiration of 'primitives,' reveals the essence of things."[54]

In a theoretical tour de force that captures the metaphysics of tragedy we have been tracing, Bataille roots literature back to its tragic ritual foundations, while at the same time emphasizing the medium of Apollonian representation. For Bataille—as for Nietzsche or Harrison before him and Conrad or Coppola after him—tragedy is thus an Apollonian subterfuge to mediate what used to be a Dionysian ritual in which people originally participated. This spectacle also brings spectators and readers face-to-face with an image of ecstatic (*ek-statsis*, to stand outside) transgression that partakes in the horror of death, while remaining on the side of life. And Bataille adds, in a sovereign mood that, for an instant, breaks the spell of tragedy: "But it's a comedy!" (HM 337). Perhaps. But this comedy doesn't make us laugh. The efficacy of this ritual-artistic connection for us is a different one and consists of mediating a tragic pathos from antiquity to (post)modernity. Ancient plays are temporally closer to the ritual origins of tragedy, yet if we rewatch the culminating scene of *Apocalypse Now* the impression is that cinematic simulations are far from being disconnected from referential horrors. On the contrary, *Apocalypse Now* stages and reenacts probably one of the clearest representations of what an entire school of anthropology—from Frazer to Girard, Nietzsche to Bataille—considers the sacrificial origins of tragedy. The aesthetic surface of the final scene of *Apocalypse Now* reminds us that even in postmodern tragedies that harken back to the Dionysian origins of art, we cannot do without what Bataille calls the "subterfuge" of Apollonian "representation" to mediate tragic horrors that continue—pace Baudrillard—to have a material referent.

*Apocalypse Now* cuts through the heart of tragedy for at least two reasons. On one side, this bloody scene directly connects a sacrificial ritual killing of an animal with the sacrificial killing of the Dionysian hero, suggesting that a mimetic continuity exists between a "primitive" ritual and contemporary art. In this sense, modernist, even postmodern, cinematic tragedies continue to be rooted in the horror of sacrifice. On the other side, the cinematic spectacle re-presents Dionysian pathos that was felt inside by ritual participants, on the Apollonian surface outside of representation for spectators to see from a distance. In this sense, tragedy is revealed, or better unmasked, as a spectacular subterfuge. Either way, there is much in this horrifying final scene that lends support to the Girardian hypothesis that the cult of Dionysus is pervasive in primitive societies, as well as to the Nietzschean hypothesis that tragedy is born out of a mimetic continuity with Dionysian rituals. But above all, *Apocalypse Now* reveals the function of Apollonian representation to generate identifications that transgress the boundaries of individuation introducing bloody continuities at the heart of discontinuities. And in this modernist inversion of perspectives that foregrounds the role of Apollonian representation for Dionysian identifications to take place lies this scene's cinematic efficacy. Let us rewind the scene and watch this tragic spectacle in slow motion to tease out a few last insights into sacred, metaphysical horrors.

## The Horror Is the Medium

The end of *Apocalypse Now* is set in a ritual context dominated by both the Buddha statue and the Dionysian music we have seen/heard at the beginning. It suggests that the tragic revelation we have been promised in the title (apocalypse, from *apokaluptein*, uncover, reveal) will be reflected in an ending that brings home the realization that tragedy takes place now—that is, as we watch sacrificial spectacles. This game of mirrors is central to the subterfuge represented in the final scene. We are back to ritual dancing to the sound of Dionysian, intoxicating, and entrancing music as the Ifugao Indians prepare for a sacrificial ceremony, which is, of course, double. The ritual sacrifice of the caribou in the foreground is framed against the sacrifice of Kurtz in the background, suggesting a direct mimetic continuity between the death of the sacrificial animal and the death of the tragic hero—a confirmation of Bataille's thesis that tragedy is rooted in sacrificial rituals. And this double sacrifice makes clear that the tribe's identification with the sacrificial animal is mirrored by the protagonist's identification with the tragic hero, and, at an additional remove, by spectators watching this double sacrifice, or sacrifice of the double—in the movie theaters, an indication that contemporary spectators continue to partake in tragic spectacles. Put in Bataillean terms, tragic representations in which a character dies in our place operate as a contemporary subterfuge to mediate what used to be a ritual, communal experience for spectators to see and feel. And to follow up in Nietzschean

terms, Dionysian music is, once again, the palpitating heart of this inner experience for it generates an echo that breaks through the Apollonian wall of the cinematic screen. In fact, the frenzied, intradiegetic musical crescendo does not simply register the Ifugao's ritual music (drumming, bells ringing) in the background used by the participants to enter into a state of trance (the chorus). It is also mashed up, so to speak, with the extradiegetic entrancing and equally intoxicating music of The Doors, used to both express and perform the killing of the homo duplex in the foreground (the tragic hero). That we are equally implicated in this ritual is clear for Morrison's lyrics encourage us to affectively join in: "Come on baby take a chance with us." But as we take this chance we should not forget the general theoretical lesson that emerges from this dance of shadows and the double sacrifice that ensues; namely, that identification with the sacrificial victim generates not only pity and fear (Aristotle) but also puts us back in touch with the Dionysian ground of being (Nietzsche)—while at the same time retaining us at a safe Apollonian distance from the pathos of death (Bataille).

As a tragic text, then, *Apocalypse Now* truly begins where *Heart of Darkness* ends. It makes us see that Apollonian images do not simply represent sacrificial rituals, but contribute to generating aesthetic spectacles that are constitutive of what Conrad called "the horror." This sacrificial scene is, in fact, highly cinematic, and calls attention to the role the medium plays in configuring the images of dismemberment that generate tragic pathos. No matter how horrifying the message, let us follow Bataille's injunction not to turn away from

such images to the end. Coppola, just like Conrad before him, makes us see a dark side of humanity we do not like to recognize, by zooming in on the violent, sacrificial core of this tragic spectacle. The parallel editing (or cross-cutting) alternates between scenes that focus on Kurtz's killing in the shadow and on the killing of the caribou in the firelight. And in this interplay between shadow and light, the camera focuses on the sacrificial animal, now in the foreground, framing it from different perspectives, in a series of sharp, abrupt, cinematic cuts that re-present, at the level of the (Apollonian) medium, the same, horrifying detail of the sacrificial blade repeatedly cutting into the flesh of the caribou's neck, at the level of the (Dionysian) message. And what we see in this image of dismemberment is the living, palpitating flesh of the animal body cut to pieces and framed from an increasing cinematic proximity—from extreme long shots to medium shots—which brings spectators awfully close to the Dionysian suffering that is constitutive of the sacred source of tragic horrors—while sitting comfortably on the side of life.

The Apollonian frame is thus a subterfuge to convey a Dionysian message, but it is also more than that. There is in fact a striking mimetic continuity between the medium and the message that transgresses the distinction between presentation and re-presentation. It is as if the cinematic shots and cuts do not simply re-present but actually re-enact the ritual sacrifice, cutting through the flesh of the sacrificial victim itself. It is as if the camera, in its Apollonian mediation, cuts as deep as the machete does in its Dionysian dismemberment; it brings us closer to the *sparagmos* than any other medium (poetic, theatrical, literary) could ever do before, and ultimately makes us see what I call a hypermimetic "image" (Conrad's term) of carnage that is far from being only visually simulated or cathartic, but actively generates a real, all-too-real feeling of horror. The cinematic screen here does not so much function as a protection from tragedy but as a medium of its actualization; cinematic images do not simply represent horrors, but bring these horrors into being; the Apollonian medium *is* the Dionysian message of *Apocalypse Now*.

The mimetic originality of *Apocalypse Now* consists in an incisive use of a cinematic subterfuge to bring the experience of the horror back home, on the side of spectators. Its culminating point implicates contemporary viewers in horrors that can no longer be confined to the side of ("primitive") Dionysian rituals, nor to the side of the tragic (Greek) hero but, rather, bleed over into Apollonian representation for (contemporary) viewers to see and feel.[55] Speaking of "the horror," there is an important point that, as far as I know, has eluded commentators so far and allows us to confirm our Janus-faced diagnostic. Let us recall that in *Heart of Darkness* Kurtz's last famous lines, "The horror! The horror!," are directed at what *he* sees as he "cried out at an image" before crossing the veil that divides life from death. This in-sight opens up the possibility of a tragic identification for Kurtz's double, Marlow, who later on, as he is facing the shadow of his own possible death, says, in a confessional mood reminiscent of Almayer: "It is his extremity I seemed to have lived through." The listeners on the *Nellie*, and even more so, the readers of the novella, on the other hand, remain protected from this "complete knowledge" by a multilayered screen of framing narrative devices that set up a distance from the horrifying pathos of death.

Not so in *Apocalypse Now*. This cinematic tragedy not only culminates in Willard's sacrifice of Kurtz along mythical lines that confirms the mimetic status of these doubles. It also brings the spectators into play along cinematic lines that indicate our mimetic participation in the experience of the horror. In fact, the enigmatic meaning of what the horror is, or may be, in this film must be read in light of the images of sacrifice that both frame it and cut through it *for us as spectators to see*. Could it be, then, that Coppola's Kurtz, as he echoes his famous words, "The horror! The horror!" is giving voice to an extremity *we* (not he) have just seen on a cinematic image? Is Kurtz crying out at an image to express a horror that is not his but ours?

There is a striking mirroring operation at work in this sacrificial scene, which brings tragic recognition home from a dual perspective. As we see a close-up of Kurtz's face whispering "the horror, the horror" just after we have seen the horror of the ritual sacrifice, it is no longer clear who identifies with whom. The scene cuts both ways. On one side, spectators identify with the tragic hero as he is about to die and feel the mimetic pathos of the (Dionysian) horror of death via the medium of an image of sacrifice. In this sense, Kurtz gives voice to the horror he himself feels directly, whereas we are given to see something of this horror via an (Apollonian) mediation, at one remove. This is a view of mimetic identification that, despite radical changes in the medium, remains fundamentally the same—from ancient tragedy to the modern novel to contemporary films. On the other side, there is something more deeply cinematic and self-reflexive in this scene that cuts deeper into the modernist metaphysics of tragedy we have been tracing. The subterfuge of the cinematic medium complicates the classical view that ties the experience of the horror to the tragic protagonist first, in order to be mediated to the audience afterward. Instead, we, spectators, see the horror in a specular image of sacrifice *first*, and it is only *afterward* that Kurtz gives voice to "The horror! The horror!"

There is a subtle lesson at work in this scene of horror redux: it is as if the tragic hero echoes the horror we (not he) experience as we watch this image, a mirror image that reflects the horror of our (not his) visual and affective participation in such bloody rituals. In this deeper sense, the line between Kurtz, who, we should never forget, participates in "inconceivable ceremonies" (*YOS* 93) at the ritual level, on the one hand, and us watching a representation of such ceremonies at the artistic level, on the other, has never been thinner. Ritual and artistic horrors are indeed intimately connected in this scene of abomination, and we are meant to both feel and see its fascination. It is as if Kurtz identifies with the spectator's point of view riveted on the carnage on the screen, lives through our extremity, and gives voice to the horror emerging from the (Apollonian) vision of cinematic images of (Dionysian) sacrifice. In short, the message of the Dionysian hero springs from the contemplation of an Apollonian medium because the Dionysian message *is* in the Apollonian medium itself. And what the medium makes us see and feel is that the horror is not the horror of Dionysian rituals Kurtz cannot see; rather, it is the horror of Apollonian spectacles we have just witnessed.

This is a crucial point that inverses the tragic metaphysics we have been tracing in this chapter. It flips the horror of tragedy from the inner sensation of Dionysian disintegration to the exterior vision of Apollonian representation. Thus, if the message of *Apocalypse Now* continues to be in line with a sacrificial ontology we have been unearthing all along, formal attention to the medium suggests that in this scene, the Apollonian image is at the source of such tragic in-*sights* into the horror of art—not of ritual. It is thus no accident that repeatedly in the film the camera breaks the fourth wall and urges spectators to reflect on what one of the intelligence agents, addressing Willard, calls the "the dark side" of our nature, while Willard, facing the camera, reflects the question back to us. Nor is it a coincidence that Willard faces us once again after the killing of Kurtz, just before we see an image of Ifugao Indians dancing and eating from the sacrificial carcass in ways that depart from realistic representations of sacrificial rituals, yet might well be metaphorical of us feasting on such spectacles. Finally, as the phrase "The horror! The horror!" is echoed by the voice-over, for the last time, at the very end of the movie, we see a close-up of Willard's face dissolve against the background of the Buddha statue whereby the film had begun—Willard's eye intensely watching us watching *Apocalypse Now* ties, one last time, the horror of Dionysian dissolution to the Apollonian eyes that contemplate it. Indeed, *Apocalypse Now* continues to be in line with an ancient view of tragedy, but the emphasis is on a modernist tragedy that foregrounds the horror of Apollonian re-presentation: an image of tragedy reborn—now. In the modernist and postmodern period, the horror of the Dionysian message

already in-*forms* the Apollonian medium. Modernist tragedy is born out of Apollonian images of carnage.

·       ·       ·

At the end of this literary and cinematic journey, we are left with no metaphysical comfort or cathartic resolutions. Tragedies that were once confined to the side of ritual or artistic mediation are now bleeding over in real life via the very medium that was used to keep the horror at bay. Conrad's and Coppola's images of the heart of tragedy coincide in their Janus-faced orientation. On one side, they articulate the metaphysical foundations of tragedy back to a mimetic violence that can be traced back to the origins of culture; on the other side, they make us see that ancient rituals are now aestheticized along Apollonian lines that implicate the readers and viewers in the Dionysian horrors we are so quick to denounce—yet eagerly consume. The ontological message of tragedy, in this sense, continues to remain rooted in ancient sacrificial rituals. But the medium though which this message is conveyed gives new form to our understanding of tragic pathos as well. What *Apocalypse Now* ultimately reveals is a type of human, all-too-human fascination for sacrificial horrors that, far from being limited to archaic rituals, continue to determine our contemporary fascination for artistic images of disfiguration. This is, indeed, the "fascination of the abomination" (*YOS* 46) that is already internal to Conrad's Dionysian message. The culminating point of Coppola's images of sacrifice brings this message back home to reflect on the power of the medium itself to generate the pathos of tragedy.

Should we denounce these images of horror for the ontological violation of human boundaries they entail? Or should we rather consider them as mirrors that allow us to reflect on new forms of tragic disfigurations? Despite its title, *Apocalypse Now* does not really offer a final revelation on this point. Still, it reminds us that the horror of sacrifice remains central to Western tragedy, from antiquity to modernity. As we turn to see, Conrad helps us address such timely questions as he urges us to consider the horrorism of contemporary terrorism from modernity to now.

# CHAPTER 8

# Hypermimesis: Horrorism Redux in *The Secret Agent*

Tell me, what is it really—this horror?

—Joseph Conrad, *The Secret Agent*

Among the victims of the carnage—dismembered corpses, limbs oozing blood, hands blown off—the greatest number were children.

—Adriana Cavarero, *Horrorism*

*he Secret Agent* (1907) adds a final mimetic twist to Conrad's tragic metaphysical turn by representing the horror of sacrificial explosions generated by the dismembering violence of modern terrorism. Loosely based on an actual historical attempt to blow up the Greenwich Observatory in 1894, this "Simple Tale" (Conrad's subtitle) vividly shows how sacrificial horrors that tear bodies to pieces can no longer be confined to Dionysian rituals of past, "primitive," or ancient origins. Nor can they fully be contained within Apollonian frames representing tragic spectacles from a modernist or postmodern distance. Rather, *The Secret Agent* suggests that such horrors now literally explode at "the very center of the Empire" (*SA* 162) and form the horrorist core of what Conrad calls a "civilization always so tragically eager for self-destruction" (5). As we turn to see, a type of violence that in the past used to be directed toward sacrificial victims outside the boundaries of the West now literally explodes at its center, generating what Italian philosopher Adriana Cavarero, echoing Conrad, calls the "horrorism" of contemporary terrorism.[1]

We are thus back to the Janus-faced perspective that orients our investigation. In one sense, as Conrad explains in the "Author's Note," this tale focuses on the "dynamite outrages in London" (6) during the last decades of the nineteenth century in order to represent the "violence of tragic passion" (160) surrounding an innocent sacrificial victim, a child named Stevie, who is "blown to bits for nothing even most remotely resembling an idea" (9). In another sense, *The Secret Agent*, with its emphasis on a bomb outrage, a symbolic target, and a body "blown to fragments in a state of innocence and in the conviction of being engaged in a humanitarian enterprise" (200), also seems to offer forward-oriented readers a diagnostic prefiguration of terrorist attacks that will continue to haunt the twentieth and, above all, the twenty-first century. This double orientation allows us to conclude our diagnostic of the horrors that inform Conrad's metaphysics of tragedy. Far from being a mere shadow cast by our sacrificial anthropological past, the horror of (Dionysian) dismemberment continues to be reframed via (Apollonian) media that generate images of horrorism redux. As we now turn to see, with *The Secret Agent* the message of these media (of which a modernist novel is a particularly self-reflective manifestation) is that they do not simply reproduce real events (imitation) or generate hyperreal effects disconnected from reality (simulation)—though they might do both things. Rather, and for us more importantly, horrorism redux joins the real laws of imitation with the virtual laws of simulation in order to bring real, material horrors into being. That is, violent, disfiguring horrors that are not simply mimetic or hyperreal, but hypermimetic instead. As an initial welcome to the world of hypermimesis, let us briefly consider how fictions can become reality.

### How a Fiction Became Reality

Contemporary readers who approach *The Secret Agent* for the first time in the twenty-first century are immediately confronted with a strange feeling of déjà vu. This fiction is clearly about the past, but it resonates so strongly

with the present that the echoes cannot be ignored. If we place the text in
a broader context, the ontological distinction between a fictionalized representation of late nineteenth-century terrorism in the textual foreground
and the referential reality of contemporary terrorism in the contextual
background begins to give way, generating disturbing mimetic continuities
that cut across discontinuities between fiction and reality. This interplay
between art and life does not follow the traditional laws of realistic imitation whereby the fictional shadow follows the real referent. Instead, it
inverses perspectives in order to suggest that the shadow comes first, and
reality secretly imitates it. Such a perspectivist turn whereby fictional media
serve as models for reality to mimic informs the final message of Conrad's
text. But its underlying laws can be made initially visible if we briefly retrace,
in broad brushstrokes, *The Secret Agent*'s critical and not-so-critical contextual reception in the mass media.

## From the Unabomber to 9/11

For a good part of the twentieth century, outside specialized circles, *The
Secret Agent* has tended to be overshadowed by more influential Conradian
tales that directly, ambivalently, and profoundly represent Western horrors.[2]
Somewhat paradoxically, a sense of the timeliness of this tale was triggered
in the last decades of the twentieth century by the very mass media Conrad
denounces within the text for being complicit with, rather than subversive
of, the contagious logic of terrorism. Worthy of mention is the case of Ted
Kaczynski, aka the Unabomber, a professor of mathematics turned anarchist
who, in a series of bombings that haunted the American imagination from
1978 to 1995, turned, yes, to *The Secret Agent* as a source of inspiration for
his anarchic and terroristic opposition to technology, going as far as adopting
the alias of "Conrad" as one of his mimetic masks. In a sense, the Unabomber
succeeded in reality where Conrad's protagonist failed in fiction. His case not
only managed to catch the attention of the mass media but also to steer public
opinion toward *The Secret Agent*. The success of this operation can be gauged
by the fact that this case led FBI agents to read Conrad's tale for potential
clues as to the terrorist's location, to consult Conrad scholars for critical indi-
cations, and to use this fiction of anarchism as a realistic map to track down
this anarchic figure.[3] Critics may be right in theory as they suggest that the

novel as a genre is "beside the point" with respect to "plotting" contemporary terror;[4] yet the specific case of Conrad's novel proves them wrong in practice. Transplanted from the fictionalized reality of an actual terrorist explosion in the late nineteenth century to the historical reality of anarchic bombings of the late twentieth century, *The Secret Agent* had, in a sense, come full circle. Caught in the same loop, both FBI agents and terrorist seemingly agreed in considering *The Secret Agent* not only as a fictional representation of the horrors of the past but also as a possible re-*productive* model for real terrorist acts in the future. As the line dividing representations and reality was becoming fictional, this fiction was becoming real, so real that it was vaguely felt, it was not simply imitating reality but actually in-*forming*—in the double sense of giving form through fictional information to—reality itself.

Little did the police, the anarchist, and the public know at the end of the twentieth century that an unexpected confirmation of this mimetic principle was soon to come at the dawn of the twenty-first century. As two planes hit the Twin Towers of the World Trade Center on September 11, 2001, the West entered the dark and tragic age of terrorism Conrad seemed to have foreseen. The attacks on the Twin Towers were anything but fictional; their tragic effects were all too real for relatives, friends to feel—and for all the world to see. And yet theorists who were reflecting on these images did not fail to notice that this real horror seemed to uncannily reproduce terrors that had already been seen in the sphere of fiction. Reframing the horror of 9/11 in light of, not so much Conrad's tale but catastrophe movies depicting the bombings and collapse of central administrative buildings in New York, philosopher Slavoj Žižek controversially claimed that "America got what it fantasized about."[5] Along similar and not less controversial lines, media theorist Jean Baudrillard argued that "we have dreamt of this event"; and he specifies: "The countless disaster movies bear witness to this fantasy."[6] That fantasies, just like dreams or nightmares, can have real effects we all know. But these philosophers went further in suggesting that fantasies can give birth to physical horrors that are not only real, but have the power to tear the metaphysical veil of reality in order to reveal "the horror" of the Real itself. Reframed in our mimetic language, the horror of 9/11 made us see that the Apollonian filter of apocalyptic media could serve as the fictional origin of the real Dionysian horror at the heart of this terroristic message. This mimetic, or as I shall rather call it, hypermimetic hypothesis, lurks in the background of both Žižek's and Baudrillard's accounts of "the desert of the Real." But concerned with a different (Lacanian, postmodern) ontology, neither philosopher explicitly brings this hypothesis to the foreground.[7]

This is somewhat surprising. After all, the idea that a fictional copy, fantasy, or dream precedes and has the power to give form to real life scenarios is far from being a postmodern invention. As that philologist of (anti-)Platonic inspiration, Oscar Wilde, had already foreseen at the dawn of modernism, "Life imitates Art far more than Art imitates Life."[8] What Wilde means is that human actions are less original than they appear to be; they are mimetic in the sense that they take inspiration from models that first appear in fictions. Fictions, thus, do not simply imitate reality. Rather, fictional representations bring into being simulations of reality that have nothing to do with the real world, yet have the power to retroact onto the real in order to generate fully embodied, mimetic, or as I call them, hypermimetic effects. Hypermimesis, then, cannot be contained within the realist logic of representation, or the postmodern logic of simulation. Instead, it urges us to diagnose the spiraling patho(-)logical effects of mediatized simulations in the formation and deformation of mimetic subjects. Be that as it may, while philosophers were speculating on the desert of the Real in theory, hypermimetic principles were being put to pragmatic preventive practices in real life. Thus the Pentagon appointed Hollywood directors specialized in catastrophe movies that might unwittingly have contributed to generating models of terrorism in the past to help anticipate possible terrorist attacks in the future.[9] This hypermimetic logic is disquieting but not unfamiliar. New horrors awaken old phantoms; old pathologies can be turned into new patho-logies; tragic realities bring horrific fictions back to life (and vice versa), generating a spiraling patho(-)logy whereby it is no longer clear if the fictional shadow comes after or before the horror of reality.

It is thus not surprising that in the aftermath of 9/11, journalists old enough not to have forgotten the case of the Unabomber were once again quick to return to Conrad. And since *The Secret Agent* had been ominously published the day after September 11, 1907, and dealt with the attempted explosion of a symbolically central Western institution, the mass media turned the limelight, once again, back to Conrad's so-called "Simple Tale." In an enthusiastic outbreak of mimetic contagion Conrad would probably have been the first to deplore, this relatively neglected novel quickly became "one

of the three works of literature most frequently cited in the American media"
(Schulevitz), was revered as the "classic novel for the post-9/11 age" (Reiss),
and, on a more serious scholarly ground, has been reframed as "the first
suicide-bomber novel of English literature" (Eagleton).[10] Indeed, given the
long shadow cast by the attacks of 9/11 on the twenty-first century, *The Secret
Agent* returned to the forefront of the mediatic scene—with a vengeance. It
recaptured the imagination of journalists, public opinion, the secret police,
all the way up to critics and theorists who are now reevaluating this fiction
of terrorism in light of the real, all-too-real horrors it mysteriously seemed to
foreshadow.

### Frames of Reading

*The Secret Agent* is a fictional story loosely based on a historical fact. And in
an inversion of perspectives worthy of Nietzsche (a strong presence in the
novel), this brief account of its contextual reception tells the story of how a
fiction became reality. But, we may wonder, is the story true? Or is it rather
the history of an error?

There are different answers to these questions, which vary depending
on the ontology that informs the questioner. Peter Mallios, for instance, the
literary critic who has taken up the challenge to respond contrapuntally to
the view of Conrad as visionary "prophet" popularized by the media, offers a
searching demonstration of the way the news operate within the novel itself.
Drawing on Jean Baudrillard's take on simulation as producing "models of
a real without origin or reality: a hyperreal," Mallios deftly turns Conrad's
story against the media accounts that celebrated it. Thus he argues that these
mediatized interpretations are but a "simulation of the interpretive act."[11]
For Mallios, then, Conrad is our contemporary not because the terroristic
message of the tale predicts real effects, but rather because this tale calls attention to the interpretative terrorism of mass media, which hijack the reality
of literary texts creating a "hyper-Conrad" that has nothing whatsoever to do
with the real Conrad.[12] Mallios's answer to my question would thus probably
be that the simulated version of *The Secret Agent* emerging shadowlike from
the media is symptomatic of the history of a critical error (literary pathology). On the other side of the ontological spectrum, and with a long philosophical tradition in mind, the Italian philosopher Adriana Cavarero takes

Conrad's fictional naming of the horror as an occasion to seriously reflect on the historical reality of the violence of terrorism.[13] What this story makes us see, in Cavarero's incisive account, is a tragic, physical, and metaphysical reality characterized by an "ontological dismemberment" that does not simply generate fear, but what she calls "horrorism" instead. For Cavarero, then, Conrad's novel in general, and the case of Stevie in particular, become "paradigmatic" models for a philosophical logos on a type of dismembering pathos, which is not only physical but metaphysical as well. Cavarero thus considers the metaphysics internal to Conrad's fictional account of terrorism as revelatory of the true ontology of horrorism (philosophical patho-*logy*).

There is a striking mirroring inversion of perspectives at play in these equally compelling readings. Considered together, they make us see that the responses to this story's entanglement with the history of terrorism vary radically depending on whether the focus is on Conrad's aesthetic fiction (critical reasons) or on the metaphysical reality this fiction represents (theoretical reasons). Schematically put, if the focus is on the mediatized critical simulation that distorts Conrad's fiction, we have the history of an error—a pathology that should be left behind. Conversely, if the focus is on the material explosion of physical reality constitutive of Conrad's metaphysical message of disfiguration, the story reveals an ontological truth that allows us to look ahead. Both sides are, indeed, true to one side of the story—a patho-*logy* that should be explored. They also elevate the discussions surrounding a text that was previously considered "short in intellectual substance and coherence"[14] to an unprecedented degree of critical and theoretical sophistication, and, in what follows, both perspectives continue to inform my approach. And yet Conrad also taught us to be attentive to *both* critical *and* theoretical sides of his fictions. From our Janus-faced perspective, we are already in a position to see that these two competing sides both belong to the same tale—if only because the problematic of mimesis finds itself at the palpitating heart of both the fictional medium of simulation and the real metaphysical message of disfiguration of Apollonian pathologies and Dionysian patho-logies.

Perhaps, then, as we set out to answer our ontological riddle about the truth and lies of this metaphysical fiction, we do not need to sharply advocate between these fictional/ontological perspectives, but we can supplement them by confronting both sides of the story. That is, both the

ontology of horrorism rooted in tragic fictions and the fictional simulations
of horrorism with real "contagious" effects.¹⁵ The diagnostic that emerges
from this tale—which, it should be clear by now, is far from simple—is
that in the age of terrorism there is no easy way to disentangle the material
reality of bodily explosions from the mediatized effects of such explosions,
the tragic horrors of the past from the political horrorism of the present,
the physics of terrorism from the metaphysics of horrorism, the abomination of human disfiguration and its disturbing power of fascination. If *The
Secret Agent* remains an untimely text today, then, it is because it continues
to require a type of reflection that is both attentive to metaphysical horrors
rooted in material reality and to hyperreal simulations represented by the
media. It does so by articulating a surreal logic that is neither simply realistic (mimesis) nor only hyperreal (simulation), but—as this brief history
of a metaphysical fiction turned real already suggests—emerges from the
generative interplay between the reality of terrorism and simulated images
of horrorism redux (hypermimesis).

## Metaphysics of Terrorism

From the opening pages of *The Secret Agent* it is clear that as we move from
the Napoleonic Wars whereby we started to the terroristic wars whereby
we end, we find ourselves far removed from an image of war framed via the
romantic paradigm of the duel in its escalating, face-to-face, mimetic confrontation. And yet we remain close to what Gabriel Tarde called "the laws
of imitation," understood in their heterogeneous, formless, and transgressive
manifestations. The contagious sickness changes, but the secret patho(-)
logies continue to operate according to Janus-faced principles.

### The Secret Sickness

While the novel pullulates with a number of grotesque and hopelessly inef-
fective anarchic characters who infect, viruslike, the streets of London and
the body politic at large, it is the figure of "the secret agent," a mediocre spy
named Adolf Verloc who, we are told at the outset, "arrived in London (like
the influenza) from the Continent" (11), that is responsible for the tragic

explosion at the center of the novel. Pressured into blowing up a symbolically central institution representative of Western values of scientific progress by the First Secretary of the Russian embassy, for whom he works, the secret agent turned *agent provocateur* manipulates his mentally disabled brother-in-law into depositing a bomb in the Greenwich Observatory. The objective: creating a scandal that would spread contagiously (like the influenza) across the media, would generate panic and terror, and would serve as a "cure" (25) to British liberal immigration policies. The plan grotesquely misfires: Stevie trips before reaching the observatory, and, as a consequence, we are belatedly told, he is "blown to fragments in a state of innocence and in the conviction of being engaged in a humanitarian enterprise" (200). The cure, once again, turns out to be a poison; the political logic turns into a pathology that triggers the metaphysical tragedy at the heart of this tale.

Explosive attacks, symbolic buildings, bodies torn to pieces, terrorist epidemics, mass-mediatized contamination, all this framed within a body politic torn by anxieties of immigration and cultural assimilation, which implicate antiterrorist forces in the terrorism they are supposed to cure. Indeed, given the exponential number of suicide bombers' attacks that turn subjects into human weapons to strike at symbolically central institutions, generating images of carnages that are subsequently reproduced by the media, and, in turn, trigger wars on terrors that reproduce the violence of the terrorist wars they set out to oppose, it is not surprising that the case of Stevie has regained new critical traction in the first decades of the twenty-first century, giving yet another twist to Conrad's critical fortune, and turning him into "the first great novelist of the 21st Century."[16] This regaining of attention is welcome but is not without dangers. It would in fact be a gross mistake to map contemporary passions triggered by the media of the present back onto the tale. Such a critical move would not only reproduce the mimetic logic Conrad denounces in his fiction; it would also impede a critical reflection on Conrad's own insights into the violence of terrorism, metaphysical insights that emerge from the tale itself.

As Conrad sets out to dissect the horror of such an explosion it is, in fact, clear that his main concern is not primarily with the politics of terrorism, which he ridicules, nor with the psychology of anarchism, which he diagnoses elsewhere, most notably in *Under Western Eyes*. Rather, his most penetrating insights remain consistent with the tragic metaphysics

that concerns us. It consists in dissecting a type of metaphysical violence
that tragically shatters the boundaries of individuation, disfigures a single
human body, cuts into the flesh and bones of its being, and catches a glimpse
of that true, essential, and formless reality that, for Conrad, lies behind
the veil of representation and is the horror of Being itself. Chief Inspector
Heat, the character who lifts the veil covering Stevie's body torn to pieces, is
confronted with what he calls the "inexplicable mysteries" (*SA* 71) revealed
by those "mangled remains of a human being" (70). Such images of abject,
formless disfiguration, as we have seen, inform Conrad's tragic metaphysics,
from the origins of his career with *Almayer's Folly* onward. But in *The Secret
Agent* the diagnostic cuts deeper in this abject subject matter. We are in
fact told that "the shattering violence of destruction which had made of
that body a heap of nameless fragments affected his feelings with a sense of
ruthless cruelty" (71). And later, as Heat coldly breaks the news to Winnie
Verloc, Stevie's sister and mother figure, he gives the following concise but
telling report: "Blown to small bits: limbs, gravel, clothing, bones, splin-
ters—all mixed up together. I tell you they had to fetch a shovel to gather
him up with" (159). Conrad is, indeed, turning back to represent the physical effects of terrorism characteristic of the last decades of the nineteenth
century.[17] Yet his linguistic emphasis on the dismemberment of the body,
the radical innocence of the victim, and the nameless, abject horror that
ensues looks ahead to a metaphysical disfiguration that is constitutive of the
"horrorism" of contemporary violence. This, at least, is Adriana Cavarero's
thesis.

### Narratives of Horrorism: Cavarero *Racconta* Conrad

As the title of Cavarero's penetrating book *Horrorism: Naming Contemporary
Violence* indicates, the Italian philosopher is not concerned with the fashionable, mediatized image of Conrad as an inspired prophet of terrorist politics.
Rather, she considers Conrad an untimely writer who can help us rename the
ontology of terrorist violence characteristic of contemporary times. As it was
already the case for Lacoue-Labarthe, but from a different ontological perspective, Cavarero argues that Conrad's tragic narratives should be reframed
against a larger philosophical background than has hitherto been provided.
Spanning key figures in the Western tradition—from Homer to Euripides,

Hobbes to Schmitt, Bataille to Arendt—Cavarero makes clear that Conrad not only fully belongs to this tradition; he also provides an illuminating and culminating perspective to retrace the outlines of the metaphysics of disfiguration that inform contemporary horrorism. Thus Cavarero turns to fictions such as *Heart of Darkness*, *Under Western Eyes*, and, especially, *The Secret Agent*, to outline her groundbreaking effort to think through a type of human, all-too-human violence that, while constitutive of what she calls the "physics" of terrorism, has deeper metaphysical foundations. Here is Cavarero's diagnostic:

> As its corporeal symptoms testify, the physics of horror has nothing to do with the instinctive reaction to the threat of death [fear or terror]. It has rather to do with instinctive disgust [*disgusto*] for a violence that, not content merely to kill because killing would be too little, aims to destroy the uniqueness of the body, tearing [*si accanisce*] at its constitutive vulnerability. (*H* 8)

And in order to make clear that this physics has metaphysical implications, Cavarero adds: "The human being, as an incarnated being, is here offended in the ontological dignity of its being as body, more precisely in its being as singular body" (8).[18] From the case of Ajza, a Chechen girl whose only remains left for her father to pick up after the explosion consisted in her decapitated head, "five or six kilos no more," to the two sixteen-year-old girls, the Palestinian Ayat and the Israeli Rachel, both "brunette, with long hair," whose bodily fragments, due to the girls' resemblance, were mistakenly thought to belong to one body—victim and victimizer tragically intermixed together in a blood of mimetic confusion—each individual story would require a singular narrative of its own. Still, if Cavarero considers Stevie's case as "paradigmatic" and "exemplary", it is because it contains, in a nutshell, the essential characteristics of horrorism that, in her view, haunts, in a plurality of forms, our contemporary world. As she puts it, as an innocent, mentally impaired child, the death of Stevie "becomes the paradigm of the ontological insult inherent in the dismemberment of a helpless person [*un inerme*]. . . . In this sense, he is the exemplary vehicle of the narrative process that will reveal the horrorist nucleus of the supposedly terrorist basis of the bombing" (121).

In a move that lends metaphysical support to Conrad's fiction and flies
in the face of antimetaphysical readings of Conrad that dominated the past
three decades, the Italian philosopher turns the chilling representation of
Stevie's body torn to pieces in a mirroring figure to reflect (on) the ontology
of disfiguration that underscores the contemporary (meta-)physics of
terrorism. And what Conrad makes us see, in Cavarero's diagnostic, is
nothing less than the "nucleus" of terrorist violence, that is, a metaphysical
violence that generates "horror" (rather than fear or terror) insofar as
it "undoes" (in the Italian sense of *disfare*, a violent undoing that cannot
easily be redone and is characteristic of defeat, *disfatta*) the very ontology
of the individual (in the etymological sense of indivisible), tearing what
she calls its "figural unity" (8) to pieces. For Cavarero, then, the horror
Conrad describes in *The Secret Agent* is generated by the terroristic power
of physical disfiguration. Yet it is clearly at the level of what the subject
is, or should be, in its unitary metaphysical figuration that Cavarero sets
out to interrogate the ontology of contemporary violence. And what this
horrorism names is a type of "disgust" (*dis-gusto*, literally, dis-taste, an
unpleasant taste) generated by a body that is no longer one, for its unity
is "undone" and reduced to a multiplicity of disfigured, abject fragments.
Disgust, defeat, and, above all, an ontological disfiguration that obliterates
the boundaries of individuation: these are the defining features of Conrad's
horrorist ontology Cavarero encourages us to unearth. Let us now turn to
hear Conrad's side of the story.

### Conrad, *Tu Che Mi Racconti*?

In order to answer the narrative question Cavarero encourages us to pursue,
let us reframe Conrad's "picture of massacre" against the larger metaphysical
background I have been sketching so far. The paradigmatic case of Stevie
alerts us to a characteristically Conradian form of double vision that, as
we know, cuts both ways, toward the present violence Cavarero outlines
but also toward the sacrificial origins Conrad unearths. On the one hand,
the disfiguring violence of Stevie's body torn to pieces by the explosion is
future-oriented and looks ahead to the emergence of a new physics of terror
that haunts an increasingly vulnerable, precarious, and some would even
say declining West. On the other hand, the underlying metaphysics that

underscores Cavarero's account of this paradigmatic case, and the ontology of horrorism it reveals, is past-oriented and re-presents tragic myths constitutive of Western origins.

Cavarero's ontological account of horrorism already implicitly points in this past-oriented direction, a tragic direction that becomes fully apparent if we reframe her contemporary terminology in more classical terms. The emphasis on the subject's unitary figure or image (*imago*), the killing of an innocent sacrificable being (*pharmakos*), a body violently torn to pieces (*sparagmos*), the disruption of the boundaries of individuation (*principium individuationis*)—indeed, Cavarero, a political philosopher trained in classical antiquity, is fully informed by past mythic and philosophical precursors of horrorism. Thus she foregrounds feminine figures such Euripides's Medea, who notoriously kills her children, as well as Medusa, with her severed head whose look freezes the onlooker in an image of horror, in order to call attention to a Western patriarchal bias that projects horrorism on the side of a monstrous femininity. This feminist move is particularly resonant with the kind of horrorism at play in *The Secret Agent*. In a distant echo of these classical tragic figures, we discover the "maternal and violent" (*SA* 182) side of Winnie, Stevie's loving sister, as she stabs her husband with a knife in a Maenad-like state of frenzy that renders her "raving mad—murdering mad" (197). There is thus a gender politics at work in Conrad's account of horrorism that Cavarero will certainly help future critics to unmask.

And yet, at the same time, when it comes to the underlying metaphysics that informs these scenes of horrorism, we should notice that there is another tragic figure that casts a long shadow on the disfiguring ontology of horrorism as both Cavarero and Conrad understand it. Frenzied madness, sacrificial violence, a body torn to pieces, and a formless ontology of disfiguration that blurs the boundaries of individuation: indeed, Conrad makes us see that the physics of contemporary terrorism continues to rest on a tragic, chthonic metaphysics, which as we have seen, finds a most powerful initial configuration in Euripides's *The Bacchae*. Consequently, if we continue to be interested in Conrad's exemplary account of horrorism because he helps us rename contemporary violence, we should qualify Cavarero's claim as follows: for Conrad, the horror of physical disfiguration is tragic horror because it rests on metaphysical foundations that are deeply rooted on the chthonic ground of Dionysian horrorism.

## The Birth of Horrorism

Not unlike Nietzsche before him, Conrad's tragic representations are often based on an aristocratic tendency that privileges artistic, enthusiastically inspired, often tragic, and sometimes genial characters. As we have seen, these characters mediate between the physical and the metaphysical, tear the veil of representation, have an insight into images of disfiguration, and sum it all up in memorable phrases that continue to provide the source of inspiration to name the horror of a metaphysical reality. Echoing Nietzsche, and with a longer philosophical tradition in mind, I have grouped this horror under the rubric of the Dionysian *sparagmos*. The centrality of the Dionysian in understanding the violent psychology and politics of terrorism has been noticed by other theorists before. Terry Eagleton, for instance, reads Euripides's account of the Dionysian in *The Bacchae* in terms of violent "unconscious" drives that, if "repressed" by rational forces, return with a vengeance and require sacrificial "scapegoats" for cathartic purifications to take place.[19] This Freudian/Girardian lesson captures the mimetic psychology and anthropology of the Dionysian violence qua death drive at work in *The Secret Agent* along subjective lines resonant with the authoritarian politics I discussed in part 2. Yet it misses the impersonal, presubjective, metaphysical foundations, which for Nietzsche, Conrad, and, later, Cavarero, are the essential starting point to frame the materialist ontology of horrorism. It is this Dionysian background that I continue to unearth in order to provide an alternative metaphysical foundation to horrorism.

### Dionysian "Blood and Dirt"

When it comes to the Apollonian filtering of images of Dionysian horrorism, *The Secret Agent* seemingly breaks with a philosophical tradition that requires artistic insights, ritual initiations, or metaphysical depth in order to catch a glimpse of what is true and essential. Take Chief Inspector Heat, for instance, the character who comes closest to touching the reality of Dionysian horrorism. While his insights below the veil of representation are sufficiently incisive to prompt professional philosophers to turn Stevie's body into a paradigmatic example of horrorist metaphysics, Conrad stresses that he is "no physiologist, and still less a metaphysician" (*SA* 71). Along similar lines, the other privileged filter of Dionysian violence in the novel, Mrs. Verloc, is characterized by a "philosophy" that, we are repeatedly told, consists in "not taking notice of the inside of facts" (120). Clearly, in the novels we have considered so far, such characters would have remained on the surface of things, safely protected by an illusory veil and by the reassuring presence of the butcher, the policeman, and kind neighbors around the corner. Hence, for them, the horror remains mostly hidden below the surface. Not so in *The Secret Agent*. In this novel, in fact, the Apollonian veil, screen, or wall seems to have lost its protective power. Thus we repeatedly see how easy it is for the disfiguring reality of Dionysian horrorism to surface, so that the horror becomes visible even to characters whose very philosophy is to stay on the very surface of facts. It is as if metaphysical mysteries are rendered, if not less bloody and horrific, more visible and accessible—perhaps even superficial in their formal manifestations. There might be a political lesson at work in this metaphysical principle. Terrorism, in fact, makes everyone equally vulnerable to the experience of the horror. It does not require "universal geniuses" to be unveiled; it is seen and felt by even the most superficially inclined characters.

The horrorism of terrorism requires no philosophical depth to be perceived, yet it does not fail to trigger profound metaphysical reflections in line with the Dionysian undercurrents we have been following. That the physics of terrorist violence continues to rest on a tragic metaphysics is confirmed by the very figure that, while "disinclined to look under the surface of things" (141), brings Dionysian horrors to the surface for readers to see as well. As Inspector Heat reports, from a diegetic narrative distance, to Winnie the metaphysical horror of Stevie's body torn to pieces, the narrator mediates mimetically, via free indirect speech, the following image for us to picture: "Greenwich Park. A park! That's where the boy was killed. A park—smashed branches, torn leaves, gravel, bits of brotherly flesh and bone" (195). The setting has changed from the African jungle to a European park; the techne of death has "evolved" from sacrificial machetes to explosive bombs; characters have lost philosophical depth and move to the surface of things. Yet the underlying metaphysics remains essentially the same. Hence Winnie's face is compared to a "mask which she was ready to tear off violently" (160). And the narrator specifies: "The perfect immobility of her pose expressed the agitation of rage and despair, all the potential violence of tragic passions"

(160). The tragedy of death is once again covered by a tragic mask; but
this time the mask can easily be torn off. And what we are given to see is a
picture of Dionysian pathos: a materially abject, fragmented, and formless
body, whose "flesh and bone" are torn to pieces, is enmeshed in nature in
such a fundamental way that the distinction between human and natural
fragments, the wilderness and the heart of wild (wo)men, no longer holds,
introducing tragic continuities at the heart of discontinuities. "Blood and
dirt. Blood and dirt" (217), Winnie compulsively repeats upon realizing that
what her husband did was "taking [her] very heart out of [her] along with
the boy to smash in the dirt" (217). And as Winnie enters a Maenad-like state
of frenzy that leads her to reproduce the violence her brother was subjected
to, we are told that she becomes "raving mad—murdering mad," and conjures
"all the inheritance of her immemorial and obscure descent, the simple ferocity of the age of caverns" (197) to stab Verloc in the chest with a knife—in a
scene that surely impressed Alfred Hitchcock—it is clear that, for Conrad,
Dionysian impulses can easily resurface at the heart of the most innocent,
loving, maternal, and surface-oriented creatures—an indication that the age
of terrorism entails a democratization of horrorist impulses that cuts across
gender barriers.

Furthermore, such images reveal that both the politics and the psychology of terrorism continue to be firmly rooted in a Dionysian ontology in
which individual figures return to an undifferentiated, abject, unformed,
and muddy ground that, for Conrad, is the ground of Being itself. It is thus
no accident that upon waking from her Dionysian "frenzy" (208), Winnie
realizes that "she was alone in London," and catches another glimpse under
the surface of things as she realizes that "the whole town of marvels and mud,
with its maze of streets and its mass of lights, was sunk in a hopeless night,
rested at the bottom of a great abyss" (203). Similarly, Comrade Ossipon,
one of the anarchist cronies who remains on the surface of events, especially
media events, confirms Winnie's revelation into the underlying foundations
of civilization by picturing an image of London "slumbering monstrously on
a carpet of mud under a veil of raw mist" (224). The same type of Dionysian
"frenzy" that affected degenerate Europeans in Africa now affects ordinary
people in domestic England; the same disgusting "mud" or enveloping "mist"
surrounding the Congo River that penetrated Marlow's sensorium and
generated surrealist images of dissolution is now revealed to be part of the

bedrock and atmosphere of London itself; the same visionary insights below the "surface of things" once reserved to exceptionally gifted individuals qua romantic geniuses are now accessible to characters qua modern passersby with no metaphysical inclination whatsoever. Indeed, the surreal metaphysics of darkness Conrad had initially projected at the margins of an expanding colonial Europe is now revealed to have been underneath the West all along. And as the violence of terrorism makes us see, this horrorist ontology is not only breaking through but also breaking up individual bodies subjected to the violence of the Dionysian *sparagmos*.[20] In sum, as the confusion between "flesh," "blood," "dirt," "mist," and "mud" points toward a progressive mimetic dissolution of individual forms against a homogenous and abject ground, we continue to sense and see that the shadow of mimesis—with its confusion between human foreground and natural foreground, dissolution of boundaries, and merging of forms—returns to haunt, perhaps even in-form, the metaphysics of terrorism.

With this general reminder of Conrad's artistic metaphysics in mind, let us now return to Cavarero's specific philosophical account of horrorism in view of supplementing it with some Conradian narrative insights. Given the different layers of abjection that can be peeled off from Conrad's tragic representations of bodies penetrated by knives, torn to shreds, mingled with dirt, and driven into mud, Cavarero is fundamentally right in making "disgust" the primary instinctual reaction generated by the metaphysics of horrorism. This is, indeed, the feeling these images provoke: "Confronted with the mangled remains of human beings," we are told that Captain Heat "had been shocked by the sight disclosed to his view" (70) and "fought down the unpleasant sensation in his throat" (71). And as Conrad's naming of the horror lingers on "the gruesome detail of that heap of mixed things" (71), comparing Stevie's remains to "an accumulation of raw material for a cannibal feast" (70), or alternatively, "by-products of a butcher's shop with a view to an inexpensive Sunday dinner" (71), it would be difficult to disagree with Cavarero's claim that this "physics of horror" generates an "instinctive disgust" (*H* 8) that renders such scenes "unwatchable" (9), "driv[ing] some to avert their gaze altogether" (55).[21] Still, Conrad's narrative imagination continues to linger, with an obsessive clinical precision, on such disgusting scenes of ontological disfiguration in order to make us gaze at the horror. I wonder why.

If we reinscribe Conrad's picture of massacre within the general artistic metaphysics that informs his tragic fictions, we notice that responses to scenes of horrorism may not be as clear-cut as they initially appear to be. Physical forms of "abomination," for Conrad, may not be without generating perverse forms of visual "fascination." That tragic spectacles are the source of aesthetic pleasure is, of course, not an original observation. On the contrary. It is a lesson as old as Aristotle. In *Poetics*, Aristotle inaugurates a theory of tragedy on the premise that "we take pleasure in contemplating the most precise images of things whose sight in itself causes pain," including "corpses."[22] This disturbing lesson harkens back to what Fredric Jameson calls the "classic problem of the aesthetic pleasurability of tragedy," and has been much discussed.[23] But if this problem could be framed within a classical view of cathartic purgation of the emotions of pity and fear such images generated in the past, Conrad's modernist poetics of tragedy already looks ahead to a society of the spectacle that thrives, cannibalistically, on such images in the present. Cavarero, only once, briefly stops to consider this problematic fascination for the horror internal to a genre that we have been taught to consider the culmination of Western art, namely tragedy. Yet she does not follow through it, relegating this fascination for the accursed share to *poètes maudits* such as Georges Bataille. The only problem is that Bataille and Conrad are not as far apart as they appear to be in their ontological tastes. Eroticism, for Bataille, is not simply synonymous with sexuality but consists in "assenting to life to the point of death,"[24] which is also the culminating point of Conrad's tragic insights. And, as we have seen, when it comes to the formless metaphysics that in-forms images of communal sharing, sacrificial death, abject subject matter—from mud to blood, sacrifice to acephalic bodies—Conrad's metaphysics is very much in line with the currents of "attraction and repulsion" at the heart of Bataille's account of "heterology" and the ontological "homology" it entails. We should thus be careful not to turn away from this chthonic side of Conrad's metaphysics lest we miss the palpitating core of what Conrad calls the horror. It is, in fact, in this Dionysian excess, mediated by Apollonian images, that lies Conrad's most disturbing, penetrating, and perhaps even "revolutionary" insight into the mimetic logic of Dionysian horrorism.

In *The Secret Agent* the double movement generated by scenes of horror is rendered visible by that mimetic phenomenon par excellence, which is the crowd as it assembles around bloody spectacle in the streets. Take, for instance, the "dramas of fallen horses" (13), a tragic drama that triggers as much Stevie's heartfelt compassion as mad enthusiasm in the crowd. In a characteristically ironic turn, Conrad tells us that its "pathos and violence induced him [Stevie] sometimes to shriek piercingly in a crowd, which disliked to be disturbed by sounds of distress in its quiet enjoyment of the national spectacle" (13). The "pathos" of violence inflicted on other living creatures, Conrad suggests, is far from generating a generalized *sym-pathos* for this spectacle of cruelty. On the contrary, Conrad's clinical distance unmasks the crowd's spellbound fascination for tragic sacrificial representations that are part of what Conrad bitingly calls a "spectacle." The fact that this "enjoyment" is "quiet" and that the crowd "disliked to be disturbed" suggests that this is a type of entertainment in which the subject of the lonely crowd is hypnotically absorbed. Tragic Dionysian suffering, for Conrad, as for Nietzsche before him—and the Nietzschean echoes in this text are so loud that they do not need to be stressed—generates pity for a few tragic individuals who, in the age of the crowd, are more often turned into a dramatic representation to be "enjoyed" from a safe Apollonian distance for the many.

Conrad is particularly attentive to the contagious movement and countermovement of terror and fascination that affects subjects in a crowd exposed to the violence of terrorism. In *Under Western Eyes*, for instance, another tale based on anarchism and terrorist attacks, we see the double-movement generated by the crowd's fascination for images of abomination. As the first explosion kills the horses and mortally wounds the coachman who transports an oppressive minister of state at the heart of St. Petersburg, we are told that "a lot of people [were] surging up on all sides of him in the falling snow and all running towards the scene of explosion. . . . In an incredibly short time an excited crowd assembled round the sledge" (*UWE* 15). The initial impulse triggered by scenes of terrorism witnessed from a distance is thus to generate an excitement that pulls the mimetic crowd toward the horror. And yet as the second bomb is flung over, and the masses feel personally at risk, the opposite reaction ensues: "With a yell of horror the crowd broke up and fled in all directions" (16), "panic-struck people flying away from the spot after the second explosion" (21). And the narrator retrospectively comments on this double movement: "The first explosion had brought together a crowd as if by enchantment, the second made as swiftly a solitude in the street for hundreds of yards in each direction" (15). Conrad's diagnostic is not unilateral. What the crowd renders visible on the surface of its physical movement is not only the disgust generated by horrorism. Rather, we see a polarized, contagious, and thus mimetic metaphysical double movement of attraction and repulsion, "enchanted" fascination and panic-struck "horror," that, for Conrad, constitutes the culminating point of the metaphysics of terrorism. Conrad's picture of the crowd, in short, turns physical motion into a seismograph that registers the contradictory affective movements that constitute the palpitating heart of metaphysical horrors.

### Apollonian Spectacles (Winnie to Hitchcock)

Time and again, Conrad's pictures of massacre cut through the initial layer of disgusting abomination in order to reveal something of the human, all-too-human fascination for bloody sacrificial spectacles. That Dionysian horrorism exerts a power of Apollonian fascination in *The Secret Agent* is already indicated by the obsessive narrative focus on Stevie's fragmented body, a focus that does not stop at Conrad's act of naming the horror, but stretches to infect the reader as well, including perhaps the contemporary scholar of horrorism that turns such images into a privileged focus of philosophical investigation. What is certain is that within the text itself, even the figure that is most painfully affected by Stevie's explosion is not immune to its disturbing power of fascination. Here is how Winnie Verloc's mimetic imagination—mediated by the narrator's diegesis—reframes this picture of horrorism in a key passage that I now restitute in its entirety:

> Greenwich Park. A park! That's where the boy was killed. A park— smashed branches, torn leaves, gravel, bits of brotherly flesh and bone, all sprouting up together in the manner of a firework. She remembered now what she had heard, and she remembered it pictorially. They had to gather him up with the shovel. Trembling all over with irrepressible shudders, she saw before her the very implement of its ghastly load scraped up from the ground. Mrs. Verloc closed her eyes desperately, throwing upon that vision the night of her eyelids, where after a rainlike fall of mangled limbs the decapitated head of Stevie lingered suspended alone, and *fading out slowly*

*like the last star of a pyrotechnic display.* Mrs Verloc opened her eyes. (*SA*
195–96; my emphasis)[25]

This is a picture of horrorism redux. It replays the explosion in the character's imagination and shows us two faces of horrorism. In a physical sense,
this scene is part of the "accumulation of disgust" that, for Cavarero, marks
"a decisive turn in the story" (*H* 121). But in a deeper—or perhaps more
superficial—metaphysical sense, it also traces a decisive turn in the concep-
tualization of the horrorism of terrorism. In particular, this picture of horrorism condenses all the layers of Conrad's metaphysics we have been peeling
off (from the formless ground of nature to a body torn to pieces to a visual
surreal representation) by rooting terroristic images back to a Dionysian,
sacrificial ground—and tracing its ascending Apollonian countermovement.
Let us now replay this scene in slow motion in order to capture the ascending
theoretical movement of this visual re-presentation sprouting, once again,
from the soil of a bloody sacrifice.

Horrorism redux is revealing of a metaphysical shift of emphasis from
the violence of an abject bodily fragmentation to the spectacle of visual representation not deprived of spellbound fascination. What we see, as we trace
the movement of Winnie's imagination, is a cultural location representative
of scientific progress at the heart of the empire ("Greenwich Park"), which is
immediately stripped of its cultural status and rooted back in the context of
a generic image of civilized nature ("a park"). It is thus within an imaginary
landscape that Winnie, a person "disinclined to look under the surface of
things" (141), brings what Conrad likes to call the "essence," "truth," or "reality" to the surface—for readers to see. And what we see is a violent image of
disfiguration in which the distinction between nature ("smashed branches")
and human nature ("flesh and bone") no longer holds. This is, indeed, the
abject metaphysical "horror" we are now accustomed to seeing in the background of Conrad's modernist tragedies. But this time, this horrific image of
death is no longer hidden in the depth of a natural (Dionysian) background.
On the contrary, it is brought to the surface of an imagined (Apollonian)
foreground. Moreover, it does not direct our gaze downward, toward obscure,
bloody, and chthonic destinations; rather, it shoots upward, toward luminous,
organic, and celestial ramifications. Thus images of deadly, violent fragmentation ("torn leaves" and "flesh") are transplanted in a picture of living and

organic growth ("sprouting"). It is as if Conrad's metaphysics of horrorism is the ground out of which an Apollonian display grows, sprouts, and explodes, generating a squandering and spectacular picture ("fireworks").[26] Finally, at the culmination of this scene, the line between tragedy and comedy no longer holds. And in a surreal image of tragicomic horror we see "the decapitated head of Stevie lingered suspended alone, and fading out slowly like the last star of pyrotechnic display." This scene is strikingly cinematic. It also makes us wonder if behind the last layer of a dark, sacrificial tragedy lurks the shadow of a grotesque, illuminating, and surrealist comedy.

This is, in a way, what Alfred Hitchcock, in his 1936 cinematic adaptation of *The Secret Agent*, *Sabotage*, suggests. Picking up on the cinematic potential of the novel in general and its scenes of horror in particular, Hitchcock complicates the distinction between tragedy and comedy, disgust and fascination, by implicating the medium (cinema) as well as the spectators (viewers) in a picture of horrorism redux represented from a distance. The scene that leads to Stevie's explosion is a classic scene of suspense, not horrorism, for spectators know what the character does not know. Namely, that while Stevie is caught up by various spectacles that attract the fascination of the crowd (a salesman's show, a military parade) and slow down his journey to the observatory, he is getting closer to his tragic death. It is thus no surprise to the viewers that as Stevie finally hops on a streetcar carrying the deadly package—the ticking of clocks matching the ticking of the bomb in an increasing crescendo of suspense—the bomb finally goes off, the streetcar is blown to pieces, and so is Stevie. What is surprising and shocking is not the body torn to pieces, which we don't get to see. Rather, what is shocking is that immediately after the detonation, Hitchcock cuts to a frontal scene in which we see Verloc, Inspector Heat, and Winnie merrily laughing. Indeed, as Mark Wollaeger rightly stresses, in this move "Hitchcock both foregrounds its status as spectacle and implicates the viewers in the horror they have witnessed."[27] Further, and more problematically, Hitchcock also reveals, in a self-referential move, an underlying affective continuity between the tragedy of horrorism and spectacular forms of entertainment by calling attention to the way aesthetic pleasure rests on images of tragic pathos in which someone dies in our place. "Everything seems to be all right," says Verloc laughing, after the explosion kills Stevie, giving voice to a relief that is ours too. Is this tragedy a comedy then!

Identification with a tragic victim, as Georges Bataille taught us to recognize, allows us to participate in the pathos of the dying other. Yet since we experience this pathos from a safe representational distance, this mimetic identification leaves us "all right" in the end—for he died in our place. While not culminating in spectacular fireworks, the scene confirms the link between terrorism and mediatized spectacles nonetheless. The medium is here clearly part of the message; or better, the medium is the terroristic message of horrorism redux. This fundamental point is confirmed in a later scene, as Winnie realizes Stevie is actually dead by reading a newspaper article; Hitchcock re-presents Conrad's picture of horrorism redux in cinematic terms. Thus the newspaper article reports that the bomb was hidden in a "cinema film tin" intended to blow up a movie theater, not the observatory. Cinema is thus the terroristic medium used for the explosion represented at the level of the horrorist message. If we add to this that the scene takes place outside a movie theater, and Winnie's cinematic vision of Stevie's head fading against the crowd culminates with a medium frontal shot of Winnie in the crowd breaking the fourth wall, facing away from the crowd and interpellating the

public, we cannot help but feel implicated in this picture of horrorism redux culminating with the death of an innocent child. It's as if Winnie were asking, and you, spectator, are you not also partially complicit in turning pictures of terror into an entertaining spectacle to watch from a distance?

Hitchcock is indeed a careful reader of *The Secret Agent*, for this diagnostic is also present within Conrad's novel itself. Conrad's detailed attention to the surface of horrorism makes us see that Cavarero's insight that at the heart of images of massacres is a point of "affinity between horror and vision" (*H* 8) is correct. Yet it also makes us feel that this affinity goes beyond "disgust" by reframing such "unwatchable" images in terms of a general economy of visual spectacles. For Conrad, in fact, such Apollonian images reveal the excessive, explosive, and, above all, grotesquely fascinating side of Dionysian horrorism that continues to inform ancient, modern, and contemporary spectacles. This ontological message looks back to the origins of Western poetics in Greek tragedy, yet the aesthetic media that represent such horrors in modern and postmodern culture—from novel to film, newspapers to news—point to a fascination for the abomination we are far from having overcome. In the wake of the attacks on 9/11, for instance, Jean Baudrillard made the provocative claim that the "impact of the images, and their fascination, are necessarily what we retain," and—establishing a bridge between Debord's critique of (Apollonian) spectacles and Artaud's celebration of (Dionysian) cruelty—he specifies: "The Spectacle of terrorism forces the terrorism of spectacle upon us. . . . This is *our* theater of cruelty, the only one we have left."[28] Along similar lines, Terry Eagleton even suggests that this postmodern aesthetic fascination has modernist foundations. Thus he compares terrorism to "a Dadaist or Surrealist 'happening' pressed to an unthinkable extreme. It is spectacle as well as slaughter."[29] And he provocatively adds: "one can still see some forms of suicide bombing as a murderous version of the artistic avant-garde."[30] Eagleton's proposition may sound shocking to contemporary ears; it might also partially fall prey to the same anesthetization of Dionysian violence we have seen him previously critique. Yet a Conradian perspective suggests that he may be more right than he actually intended—if only because Conrad's images of dissolution are rooted in a mimetic metaphysics of darkness, which, as we have seen, anticipates surrealist aesthetics.

Conrad stretches modernist aesthetic categories to include the horrific message of terrorism; yet he also contributes to our aesthetic education by directing our attention to both the fascinating and horrific side of the medium itself. As *The Secret Agent* repeatedly suggests, the medium of such an imaginary happening might no longer be the one of avant-garde works of art exposed in salons reserved for the privileged few. Rather, Conrad has in mind an aesthetic medium far more popular and accessible to the many, a mass medium whose telos is to generate "national spectacles" that not only affect the crowd of spectators in the streets of London but also that emerging "virtual crowd" that, as French sociologist Gabriel Tarde noted, goes under the rubric of the "public."[31] As Verloc's cover for his secret activities suggests (a shop specialized in pornographic magazines) and the pervasive presence of newspapers in the novel confirms, the excessive logic of Dionysian horrorism is no longer mediated by the aesthetic sphere of surrealist modernist art. Rather, it is framed by the spectacular, seemingly informative, but often grossly entertaining, perhaps even pornographic, domain of the daily news.

Conrad's tragic insights into Dionysian horrorism have taken us deep into the ontology of disfiguration that lurks in the background of this tale. But as we reach the bottom of such muddy, chthonic, and formless ground, the tale also encourages us to resurface to the foreground and reflect on the Apollonian media that give form to images of disfiguration—in-*forming* the very type of formless, malleable, and thus mimetic subjectivity on our operating table. This loop in which an aesthetic medium retroacts on the terrorist message brings us back to the riddle whereby we started, making us see it from the other end of the spectrum. If we started by considering how the mediatized context frames our understanding of Conrad's text, we must now add that Conrad's text helps us critically reflect on the media that framed it in the first place. These media, as we turn to see, do not represent the world as it really is, but bring into being a hypermimetic simulation that is not even based on any attempt at realistic imitation.

## The Typing Machine

The specter of mass media was already in the background of Conrad's colonial narratives concerned with the formation of egos that turn out to be mere phantoms; but it is only recently that critics have noted that this mimetic theme is foregrounded in *The Secret Agent*. Peter Mallios rightly observes that the media serve as "a vital ground and *terra mirabila* from which the novel extends," generating a new type of subjectivity "penetrated by the press."[32] Along similar lines, Mark Wollaeger stresses that "Conrad understood new media as a defining feature of modernity," and offers a searching analysis of the role of propaganda in *The Secret Agent* as well as in Hitchcock's *Sabotage*.[33] Furthering this innovative line of inquiry in light of a formless metaphysics we should specify that it is because Conrad's account of the public, as it was already the case with the crowd, rests on malleable, mimetic foundations that this subject is emotionally vulnerable to the mass media's power of penetration. Mass, as Raymond Williams reminds us, comes from Latin, *massa*—that is, "a body of material that can be moulded or cast (the root sense was probably of kneading dough)."[34] It is precisely in this plastic or, as I later call it, neuroplastic sense that Conrad understands the masses. Take Comrade Ossipon, for instance, one of the anarchist cronies, a former medical student "nicknamed the Doctor" and an enthusiastic supporter of Cesare Lombroso's notorious craniological theories. Like the Belgian doctor in *Heart of Darkness*, we are confronted with a "fool"; yet foolish characters in Conrad's fictions are not deprived of mimetic insights. Thus the Doctor offers the following diagnostic concerning the centrality of emotions in the manipulation of public opinion: "The only thing that matters to us is the emotional state of the masses. Without emotion there is no action" (*SA* 44). Along similar lines, but speaking from an opposed political front, Chief Inspector Heat expresses a similar concern for the power of the press to generate emotions, as he says: "It was impossible to say yet whether [the public] would roar or not. That in the last instance depended, of course, on the newspaper press" (90). And later, Heat evaluates the potential effect of Mr. Verloc's confession, in case he would go public, as follows: it would "make no end of a row in the papers, which, from that point of view, appeared to him by a sudden illumination as invariably written by fools for the reading of imbeciles" (159). Such biting critiques of the power of mass media to trigger mimetic effects in the public are voiced by antagonistic characters who represent opposed ideological positions. Yet, since they appear repeatedly in Conrad's fictions, they point to a single diagnostic that is central to Conrad's critique of modernity and can be summed up as follows: if the crowd had the streets as its paradigmatic mimetic medium to generate brutal national spectacles for otherwise quiet individuals, the public has the newspaper to turn otherwise intelligent readers into what Conrad often calls—with no regard whatsoever for public opinion—"imbeciles." Mimesis is central to this pitiless diagnostic. As I have shown elsewhere, if the crowd operates according to the physical laws of contagion, the public follows the virtual laws of imitation.[35]

But in *The Secret Agent* Conrad takes these mimetic laws a step further so as to generate a loop that problematizes the very relation between copy and origin, fiction and reality "itself." Writing at the dawn of the age of the public, Conrad furthers the laws of imitation by showing the impressive power of the media not only to affect the opinions of the masses (imitation) but also to bring into being a new simulated reality that has nothing to do with reality itself (simulation). What the Assistant Commissioner says of the spy perfectly applies to the journalist as well: that he "will fabricate his information is a mere commonplace," but he also "has every facility to fabricate very facts themselves" (108). We have encountered this modern, or better postmodern, fabrication of facts before. And we are not alone in adopting future-oriented lenses. Peter Mallios, for instance, aptly recognized

that Conrad welcomes us in a world of "simulation" understood in the Bau-
drillaridan sense of a "fabrication by models of a real without origins and
reality: hyperreality."³⁶ As we have seen in our reading of *Apocalypse Now*,
simulation, for Baudrillard, should not be confused with imitation. It does
not copy or reproduce referential reality but, rather, involves the dissolution
of a materialist ontology rooted in reality. Let us thus ground the simulations internal to the text, which Mallios calls "the ultimate sign of *The Secret
Agent*'s contemporaneity,"³⁷ at the ontological level that concerns us.

## Hyperreal Simulosis: The Shortest Shadow

The hyperreal ontology that seemingly informs the tale is already introduced
early on in the novel in one of those striking Conradian images that prompt
metaphysical reflection for their power of illumination. Picture the scene:
the Secret Agent is framed strolling the streets of London, surrounded by
a luminous, golden atmosphere that generates a disquieting pictorial effect.
The "London sun," we are told, generates a "diffused light, in which neither
wall, nor tree, nor beast, nor man cast a shadow" (*SA* 15). In many ways, this
sunny image of London deprived of shadows in *The Secret Agent* entails a
mirroring inversion of Marlow's account of London in the moonshine surrounded by shadows in *Heart of Darkness*. The atmosphere has radically
changed: we move from night to day, the moon to the sun, twice-reflected
light to an original source of light, haunting phantoms to the dissolution of
all shadows: bright day, late morning, close to noon, moment of the shortest
shadow.

    And yet a "town without shadows" (15) is no less spectral and surreal
than a town haunted by shadows. As always with Conrad, there is a subtle
metaphysical lesson to be drawn from such pictorial images. This surreal
world without shadows indicates that we have moved beyond the laws of
imitation and the dualist ontology they entail. Gone are the chains that
imprisoned subjects at the bottom of the cave; free are the prisoners to
contemplate the golden source of light. Still, it is not so simple. With the
disappearance of shadows, in fact, we can no longer rely on neat ontological
distinctions between the original and the copy, the true world and the apparent one, which, from Plato to Nietzsche, have structured Western metaphys-
ics.³⁸ Echoing this philosophical tradition, Baudrillard says: "It's the whole

of metaphysics that disappears: no more mirror of being and appearances, of the real and its concept" (*SA* 22). Once the shadows are abolished, then, what remains? The true world perhaps? Not really. With the loss of shadows it is also the reality of referents that is dissolved, evaporated in a hyperreal world without substance. Thus Conrad vividly depicts this world in a metaphysical image of London without shadows, surrounded by "an atmosphere of powered gold" (*SA* 15).

This hyperreal picture of London without shadows frames a type of human, all-too-human simulation that equally troubles the distinction between copy and original. It is thus no accident that this description occurs as Verloc is on the way to the Russian embassy to meet his employer, Mr. Vladimir, a Russian diplomat who, we are told, speaks "idiomatic English without the slightest trace of a foreign accent" (21). We have shifted from a landscape to people, images to sounds; yet the absence of original traces points to the same metaphysics. Accents, in fact, make us hear through the medium of voice what shadows make us see through vision. Their function is dual and cuts both ways. On the one hand, foreign accents initially sound as mere imperfect copies of the native language and are symptomatic of an imitation far removed from the original. Hence they deprive the subject of native originality. On the other hand, an accent actually makes us hear the traces of another, original language underneath the foreign language spoken. Hence it doubles one's speech, supplementing the second language with the presence of an original.

Now, Conrad, as a trilingual subject who spoke English with a strong Polish accent, was in a good position to diagnose the double effects of multi-lingualism in a predominantly nationalist—and thus ethnocentric—cultural environment. His clinically cold ironic distance from Vladimir might thus be tainted by an affective ressentiment against British linguistic national-ism, itself doubled by his well-known anti-Russian political stance. And yet his fundamental ontological point is consistent with the hyperreal image of London without the slightest trace of shadows. The absence of an accent in a foreign speaker is a confirmation that we have entered a world of "simulation" in which the distinction between the original and the copy no longer holds: "It is no longer a question of imitation, nor of parody," writes Baudrillard, but rather the "double ends up confusing itself with the real" (*SS* 9, 11). And in the process of this hyperreal confusion, the ontological reality of national identity itself is ultimately dissolved. More generally, Vladimir's "idiomatic English" is symptomatic of a dissolution of national identity markers that affects and infects the entire body politic, introducing a generalized simulation without originals. Gone is the real world of copies and originals restricted by the laws of imitation. What is left is a type of hyperreal simulation, which, given its contagious, pathological, and somewhat excessively mimetic character, I cannot help but diagnose as *simulosis*.

Hyperreal simulosis in *The Secret Agent* affects all the senses. After the loss of shadows and of accents, the loss of taste and of national individuality reveals how pervasive this pathological atmosphere actually is. Waiting in "a little Italian restaurant … baited with a perspective of mirrors" that reproduce simulacra of men in an "atmosphere of fraudulent cookery mocking an abject mankind," the Assistant Commissioner offers the following diagnostic:

> On going out the Assistant Commissioner made to himself the observation that the patrons of the place had lost in the frequentation of fraudulent cookery all their national and private characteristics. And this was strange, since the Italian restaurant is such a peculiarly British institution. But those people were as denationalized as the dishes set before them with every circumstance of unstamped respectability. Neither was their personality stamped in any way, professionally, socially or racially. They seemed created for the Italian restaurant, unless the Italian restaurant had been perchance created for them. But that last hypothesis was unthinkable, since one could not place them anywhere outside those special establishments. (*SA* 115)

This is, indeed, a sharp diagnostic of the hyperreality of simulosis that envelops a multicultural city. It suggests that the modernist, denationalized, depersonalized subject is not only deprived of original cultural traces but is fabricated so as to fit a model without origins or reality. In this form of fraudulent cultural simulation it is in fact not simply a question of a type of cookery losing its distinctive national taste in order to become a debased copy of what it originally was (imitation), nor solely a question of a cultural assimilation so profound that an originally foreign cuisine reaches the authentic status of national food (assimilation)—though it is both. Rather, and more disturbingly, we are told that it is the very "personality" (from Latin, *persona*, mask worn in the theater) that has lost any proper qualities in their "frequentation of the place," turning them into men without distinctive, national, cultural, and social qualities (simulosis). These men are no longer typical, for they are left "unstamped"; they no longer bear the traces of any cultural imprints, stamps, or forms. Being no one, they can become everyone: seals without stamps, phantoms without substance, shadows without origins—simulosis is worse than neurosis, for it deprives the subject of an ego to be cured!

This rather severe diagnostic is not only about "the other"; it is also about the self. It is in fact not without moments of mirroring reflections that concern the identity of "original" British subjects as well. Not only the Italian patrons but also the Assistant Commissioner is affected by simulosis. Thus we read that "reflecting upon his enterprise, [he] seemed to lose some more of his identity . . . he saw himself in the sheet of glass, and was struck by his foreign appearance" (115). In this world of generalized simulation, a reflection in a "perspective of mirrors" does not restitute an original singular figure, nor does it cause the recognition of a personal, individual identity. Rather, it dissolves the boundaries of selfhood in a chain of unstamped and formless personality that bears the symptomatic stamp of a hyperreal, (post) modernist: simulosis. In *The Secret Agent* Conrad foreshadows a postmodern metaphysics that dissolves physical realty, introducing a world of simulation where previously there was simple imitation. In this sense, this novel is indeed a welcome into a world without shadows!

And yet in another, perhaps more disturbing sense, the chilling image of the Professor whereby the novel concludes, ready to blow himself up while "walking on unsuspected and deadly, like a pest in the street full of men" (231), reminds us that this world without shadows generates pathologies that make lasting impressions on the materiality of life. These impressions, as we now turn to see, are not simply mimetic, nor solely simulated, but are hypermimetic instead.

## Hypermimesis: The Longest Impressions

If we take a step back to reinscribe Conrad's diagnostic of simulation within the larger ontological picture I have been sketching, we notice that his modernist metaphysics cannot easily be dissolved in the hyperreal spheres of postmodern simulations, for it rests on real, immanent, material foundations.

Like other modernist writers, Conrad has, in fact, not lost sight of the ground of referentiality. This ground is no longer solid, for it has turned muddy, but it can help us give ontological substance to a postmodern dissolution of reality. We have seen that Baudrillard posits the logic of simulation beyond the laws of imitation understood as simple representation. Still the examples of hyperreality that emerge from *The Secret Agent* make us wonder if mimesis, understood as embodied, behavioral, and contagious imitation, may not be tacitly informing this hyperreal world without origins. For instance, if Mr. Vladimir's perfect idiomatic English without an accent is not original, it still betrays what René Girard would call a "mimetic desire" to conform to dominant linguistic models. Conversely, the emotional effects of "emulation" and "panic" triggered by simulated facts diffused by the media continue to reveal how the public responds to what Gabriel Tarde calls the "laws of imitation." But Conrad's fundamental supplement to simulation is not only psychic or social; it emerges at the level of the metaphysics of terrorism that casts a shadow on his tale and on the contemporary world as well. Conrad, like Nietzsche before him and Bataille after him, never lets go of the referential ground the hyperreal pretends to dissolve. On the contrary, he roots subjectivity in an ontology of horrorism that rests on formless, malleable, but still material foundations. If we peel off the golden layers of hyperreal simulation that pervade the tale, the formless and muddy ground is still materially there for critics and theorists to read. It emerges, shadowlike, from the very texture of the picture of hyperreal simulosis we have just considered—exploding the very ontology of hyperreality itself.

That Conrad's modernist tragedy may be throwing a bomb into the postmodern ontology of hyperreality "itself" is suggested repeatedly in the tale. Time and again, fragments of reality emerge from the very images of simulations so seemingly dissociated from reality. Take the Italian restaurant, for instance, with its reflection of "unstamped" (115) personalities who have lost all traces of an original national identity. On a closer diagnostic look, Conrad is actually diagnosing an "abject mankind" (115) that is still in a material relation of mimetic continuity with the abject ground he urges critics to unearth. Here is a depiction of the Assistant Commissioner, as his identity is no longer framed within the "perspective of mirrors" he faces, but is sustained from the muddy ground underneath him: "He advanced at once into an immensity of greasy slime, and damp plaster interspersed with lamps, and enveloped, oppressed, penetrated, choked, and suffocated by the blackness of a wet London night, which is composed of soot and drops of water" (116). Baudrillard argues that simulation cannot operate according to the laws of imitation for it entails the "liquidation of all referents." Not so Conrad. In fact, this image does not represent the liquidation of all referents, but rather a liquid material that serves as the formless, ontological mold for a malleable, abject subject to be formed, deformed, and conformed.

*The Secret Agent* may be more forward-oriented than previously realized, for it brings the pure, transcendental sphere of simulation back in touch with the immanent, material foundations of Dionysian horrorism, revealing not simply mimetic, nor solely simulated, but rather hypermimetic continuities at the heart of hyperreal discontinuities. For Conrad, in fact, the type of fictional reality the media represent goes beyond the laws of imitation understood as realistic representation (mimesis); nor is it simply disconnected from real referents in a hyperreal sphere without origins and reality (simulation). Rather, and for Conrad more importantly, these simulated fictions continue to have real, all-too-real effects because they are rooted in the same materialist, abject, ontological ground that introduces disturbing material continuities at the heart of discontinuities (hypermimesis). Hypermimesis thus designates a third space beyond the Scylla of mimetic realism and the Charybdis of antimimetic simulations that emerges from the material encounter between virtual shadows (or copies) and material reality (or origins). This is a strange world in which the shadow does not follow the original forms but, rather, contributes to materially bringing these forms into being. It is thus no longer a question of unmasking how media simulate reality, generating copies of facts, or shadows without real substance. It is rather a question of realizing that the mask has material effects and in-*forms* the subject it covers in its very ontological substance, along lines that transgress the distinction between surface and depth, copy and original, ideas and matter, surreal shadows and real figures.

Conrad repeatedly diagnoses the media's hypermimetic power not only to form but also to in-form and, above all, deform and conform a type of malleable "subject" (understood as the Latin *subjectum* or the Greek *hupokeimenon*—that is, the support qua substratum that lies beneath, which is also the underlying matter from which we are made) that, like the muddy ground on which it rests, has lost all proper qualities. That Conrad's image of human

nature continues to rest on a materialist ontology is confirmed if we trace the
hypermimetic continuities between the mass media and the subjects in the
mass he carefully depicts. Here is a picture that goes to the foundations of the
ontology I have been tracking all along:

> In front of the great doorway a dismal row of newspaper sellers standing
> clear of the pavement dealt out their wares from the gutter. It was a raw,
> gloomy day of the early spring; and the grimy sky, the mud of the streets,
> the rags of the dirty men, *harmonised excellently* with the eruption of the
> damp, rubbishy sheets of paper soiled with printers' ink. (65; my emphasis)

This passage takes place in the aftermath of Stevie's failed terrorist attack and
is usually read in terms of the media's psychic and political power, or lack of
power, to control the movement of the masses.[39] And yet underneath the first
layer of ideological and political control lies a more obscure and primordial
form of hypermimetic ontological interpenetration between mass media and
the subject in a mass. The semantic field Conrad mobilizes clearly echoes
the formless metaphysics we are by now familiar with—from the horrific
"gloom" and "mud" of monstrous towns to the "rags" and "dirt" of sacrificial
horrorism, now stamped with a working-class connotation. And yet Conrad
also supplements this metaphysics with a mass medium that serves as the
hypermimetic interface that "harmonise[s]" the formless ontology in the
background with the formless subjects in the foreground. What this grim
picture of London suggests, in fact, is that the modern, abject subject of
the crowd ("dirty men") is no longer directly rooted in the formless darkness of nature ("the mud of the street") but is con-formed by the dark and
typographic background of the gutter press ("rubbishy sheets"). And it is this
multilayered harmonization between nature, human nature, and mediatized
simulations introducing hypermimetic continuities at the heart of discontinuities that, for Conrad, constitutes the ontological horizon of modern
subjectivity. Welcome to the mud pool of hypermimesis!

## Typing the Subject

We are thus back to the surrealist metaphysics in which the formless subjects in the foreground are homologous with the muddy substance in the

background. But this time it is the printing press that, far from transgressing the laws of imitation, brings these surreal laws to the extreme. It does so by generating a hypermimetic image of (dis)figuration that, quite literally, presses into the very ontological substance of the modern subject, subjecting it to the violent power of the typographic press to "stamp" the "unstamped" contours of an identity that is no longer one—for it is open to the hypermimetic experience of becoming everyone. Conrad's most famous metaphysical image of the universe comes to mind here and helps us cast light on the hypermimetic ontology that has emerged from his surreal picture of the world: "let us say that—there is—a machine." The echo is faint and difficult to reproduce correctly, but it sounds like a typographic machine. It evolved out of scraps of iron of the printing press, and behold!—it types. I am horrified at the horrible work and stand appalled. I feel it ought to embroider—but it goes on typing. You come and say: "This is all right; it's only a question of the right kind of medium. Let us use this—for instance—a digital medium and the machine shall embroider the most beautiful design in purple and gold." Will it? Alas no. You cannot by any special digitation make embroidery with a typographic machine.[40] Do you hear the echo? Do you see the image? It's far from clear, but the point seems to be that this machine types us in and it types us out. And in this typographic production and reproduction that goes on without thought, without conscience, without foresight, without eyes, without heart, lies the horrorism of hypermimesis.

If we take a few steps back in order to look ahead, what emerges from this embroidered picture of modernity is that Conrad's metaphysics can no longer be dissociated from the medium that is supposed to convey the horrorist message. This mass medium is so constitutive of the message that the distinction between the stamp and what it imprints no longer holds; yet it continues to have real, material, and immanent effects nonetheless. What this picture suggests, then, is that the modern subject has so mimetically harmonized with the sensationalistic typography of the gutter press that it has not only been informed by it but also formed, deformed, and conformed. It does not sound nice to say it, but one cannot avoid thinking that the subject of the crowd or public, for Conrad, is but a typographic stamp impressed on a rubbishy newspaper. If he would have been horrified by the mass-mediatized reception of *The Secret Agent* whereby we started, he would have probably carefully diagnosed the real, hypermimetic effects of his fictions whereby we conclude. This, at least, is what he suggests in a final diagnostic of the hypermimetic effects of the printing press on the human brain, which, this time, I faithfully reproduce:

> There must be something subtly noxious to the human brain in the composition of newspaper ink; or else it is that the large page, the columns of words, the leaded headings exalt the mind into a state of feverish credulity. The printed voice of the press makes a sort of still uproar taking from men both the power to reflect and the faculty of genuine feeling; leaving them only the artificially created need of having something exciting to talk about. (*NLL* 76)

                    ▪          ▪          ▪

In light of this rather severe diagnostic, we may finally wonder: What is the significance of this hypermimetic turn that reveals a disquieting harmonization between human subjects and the printing press that informs them? Do representations of scenes of horrorism trigger ethical responsibility "regarding the pain of others" as cultural critics such as Susan Sontag suggest?[41] Or is "the universal attraction" such images exert "on a par with pornography," as postmodern philosophers such as Baudrillard suspect?[42] In a general philosophical sense, *The Secret Agent* paves the way for both possibilities. It all depends on whether the focus is on the Dionysian dismemberment of a tragic, innocent figure in the referential background—as the realist logic of mimesis suggests, or on the Apollonian images of disfiguration offered up for a cannibalistic and pornographic consumption foregrounded in the media—as the postmodern logic of simulation implies. But in a more specific, narrative sense, the media are eventually turned into the very typological substance on which the tragic metaphysics of this tale rests—as the ontology of hypermimesis indicates.

What is certain is that in a universe in which the very materiality of the modern subject, down to the formation of its "brain," is shaped, molded, and stamped by the power of impression of the media, there is not much hope at the level of Conrad's political message. Thus, in *The Secret Agent*, the pathos of tragedy gives way to the irony of critique. The general indifference that emerges from this scene of hypermimetic harmonization between media and men is disconcerting but real. For Conrad, the diagnostic is clear and points to the hypermimetic effects of "newspaper ink" on what he calls the human brain." It indicates that the press has generated a type of subjectivity made out of the very abject matter on which it feeds cannibalistically. More generally, the fact that scenes of horrorism in *The Secret Agent* are framed by superficial characters concerned with the sensationalistic effects of the press, reframed by images shot through by the spectacular side of terrorism, and covered under the facade of a cheap pornographic newspaper shop, alerts us to the reality that the tragedy of Dionysian horrorism is wrapped up in Apollonian layers of mediation that surround it. These layers are not simply representing scenes outside the subject. Rather, they have been typographically impressed inside, on a type of hypermimetic malleable and thus plastic subject that is not only informed but formed, deformed, and horribly conformed by the stamp of the gutter press.

The concluding lines of *The Secret Agent* are particularly efficacious in reminding us that horrorism entails not only a physics or metaphysics that explodes real bodies. It is also the product of hypermimetic media that poisons the material structure of the brain. It is thus no wonder that in a novel so concerned with the power of the press, the very character who is most abjectly dependent on the media turns out to have his brain permanently impressed by them. By the end of the novel, Ossipon (alias the Doctor) is in fact no longer in a position of diagnosing any case. Rather, he has himself turned into a clinical case study that illustrates a final "impenetrable mystery": namely, "the mystery of a human brain pulsating wrongfully to the rhythm of journalistic phrases" (231). The conclusion, in a sense, brings us back to the beginning and confirms the diagnostic of the media with which we started, from the other end of the spectrum. We have in fact moved from the terroristic horrors the mass media represent outside to a diagnostic of the psychic terror they contribute to generating inside, from the ontological explosion of real bodies to a mysterious psycho-physiology that explodes the human brain.

If Conrad's diagnostic leaves no doubts about the pathological effects of "newspaper ink," can novelistic ink still suggest possible patho-logies? Conrad does not say. What is certain is that by the end of this "Simple Tale," the diagnostic has been doubled and redoubled. On one side, a terrorist explosion ultimately failed to generate simulations of reality within the fiction—which does not mean that the fiction did not have explosive effects in reality.

On the other side, the media have themselves made a lasting impression on the brain of formless characters—which does not mean that Conrad fails to inscribe incisive clinical diagnostics. Whether the mystery of such a plastic brain lies in its vulnerability to be formed or deformed by external impressions, or in its power to form and reform itself via artistic impressions is what we now still need to diagnose.

# Conrad's Neuroplasticity

The brain is a work, and we do not know it. We are its subjects—authors
and products at once—and we do not know it.

—Catherine Malabou, *What Should We Do with Our Brain?*

It is only through an unremitting, never-discouraged care for the shape
and ring of sentences that an approach can be made to plasticity.

—Joseph Conrad, Preface to *The Nigger of the "Narcissus"*

The driving telos of my Janus-faced approach has been to look back to
the ancient concept of mimesis in order to open up new approaches
to Conrad's shady fiction and, by doing so, reflect (on) mimetic shadows that are looming on our horizon as well. As this study is drawing to an
end, we are in a position to confirm that the homo duplex, for Conrad, has
indeed more meanings than previously realized, and that a double critical/
theoretical approach was necessary to reveal its protean manifestations. As
we moved from Conrad's take on the escalation of violence to his images of
catastrophe, passing from the quarrels generated by (post)colonial counternarratives in order to plunge into his tragic metaphysics, we have repeatedly
seen that mimesis not only animates the problematic of the homo duplex but

secretly in-*forms* Conrad's poetics. From mimetic doubles to the reciprocity of violence, contagious affects to infectious epidemics, ethical storms to shared communities, colonial quarrels to postcolonial reconciliations, surrealist aesthetics to tragic insights, sacrificial horrors to mediatized horrorism, I think it is safe to say that some of the most timely problems in Conrad's corpus have been illuminated by the untimely filter of mimesis.

In the process of following this conceptual protagonist without stable identity, this book's ambition was not to dissipate the secret shadows that pervade Conrad's fictions—though the filter of mimesis allowed us to solve riddles that have haunted critics for a while, nor to identify what the meaning of the homo duplex is, or should be, once and for all—though mimesis is the elusive soul that animates its protean transformations. Rather, its ambition was to use Conrad's shady fictions as surreal mirrors to reflect on some of the most pressing shadows that haunt our contemporary world. Adding layer after layer of mimetic insights to Conrad's aesthetic pictures, I set out to progressively reveal the ethical, anthropological, and metaphysical principles that inform the heterogeneous layers of darkness internal to Conrad's poetics. In guise of conclusion, I do not intend to add yet another layer to this already densely textured picture of Conrad. Instead, I would like to use this Coda to turn our gaze back, in a sort of recoil, to the malleable foundations of the Conradian subject itself that made possible such protean transformations in the first place.

We have seen in the Introduction that this malleability is grounded in what Conrad called the "plasticity" of his "character," but this is the moment to stress that this plasticity is constitutive of impressions that go as far as giving form to what he also calls "the brain." This also means that in order to look ahead to plastic transformations Conrad is already configuring in his fictions, an engagement with the neurosciences can no longer be postponed.

## The Neuro Turn

Nothing seems to escape the neuro turn. Not content with scientific disciplines such as neurology, neuropsychology, and neuropsychiatry, the neurosciences are now infiltrating the humanities as well. There is now talk of neurophilosophy, neuroanthropology, neuroethics—even God is approached from the angle of neurotheology. It is thus not surprising that an adaptable and malleable field such as literary studies is currently being revisited from what goes under the rubric of neuoraesthetics. This enthusiastic outbreak of neuromania is contagious and seductive, but it can also be perceived as maddening and reductive. And rightly so. The oxymoronic connection between aesthetics and the neurons that fire in our brain risks not only to infect the art of interpretation but also to kill the very soul of the subject matter it sets out to dissect. After a lengthy hermeneutical engagement with the soul of Conrad's poetics my allegiance should be clear: I am certainly not going to suggest that knowing which part of the brain lights up when we penetrate deeper into the "heart of darkness" can help us grasp the ethical, anthropological, and philosophical shades of what Conrad enigmatically called "the horror."

And yet on a closer diagnostic look, the binary that divides these competing cultural and scientific perspectives might not be as polarized as it first appears to be, and a productive dialogue can emerge as these "two cultures" face, confront, and reflect on each other—provided they do not attempt to mirror one another.[1] As Paul Armstrong puts it in *How Literature Plays with the Brain*, "What the humanities have most to gain from . . . taking up conversations with the neuroscientific community about matters of mutual interest" is nothing less "than a rediscovery of our disciplinary identity."[2] In this Coda, I would like to play in favor of this hypothesis by tracing Conrad's mimetic faculties back to the question of subject formation with which we started. Paradoxically, in fact, the neurosciences can support a point the humanities have been making all along, albeit from the other end of the spectrum. Namely, they also emphasize the dominant role played by culture—not nature—in the formation, deformation, and transformation of subjectivity. This, at least, is what the emerging field of neuroplasticity is currently demonstrating.

Discoveries in the neurosciences have established that the human brain is far more malleable than previously realized and, as a consequence, is continuously molded by different forms of environmental and cultural impressions throughout our entire lives. It is not simply that our mind is shaped by external, social influences that inform the content of what we think—that we long knew. Rather, it is the structure of the brain itself, in its synaptic, neuronal connections that changes over time, re-forming the very medium through which we think. As Norman Doidge puts it in *The Brain That Changes Itself*, "the brain can change its own structure and function through thought and activity."[3] This is good news for patients suffering from brain-damage conditions that were previously thought to be irreversible, such as poststroke paralysis and phantom limbs. It is also good news for fields like the humanities that are going through precarious and vulnerable times. If talk of plasticity, adaptability, resilience, and self-improvement is now spreading quickly through the media, forming—while not always informing—public opinion, scholars in the humanities in general, and in literary studies in particular, are well positioned to critically absorb the impressive theoretical implications of this revolutionary discovery. Far from wiring subjectivity in a fixed, immutable, biological essence, the neuroplastic revolution paradoxically contributes to moving us away from essentialist assumptions about what human nature "is," or should "be." It also encourages unreconstructed humanists to take an active stance in the formation of who we would like to become. If we used to think there was not much we could actively do with our brain, we'd better think again. This is, at least, is what the French philosopher Catherine Malabou suggests at the opening of a book titled *What Should We Do with Our Brain?*, as she provocatively states: "The brain is a work, and we do not know it. We are its subjects—authors and products at once—and we do not know it."[4]

My contention, in what follows, is that Conrad knew it. And as the author—subject and product at once—of impressionistic fictions that represent plastic characters, he wanted his readers to know it too. An orphan driven into a continuous process of cultural adaptation that took him across different continents, languages, and professional identities, Conrad was particularly well placed to feel the power of cultural impressions on his brain. And as an artist concerned with malleable fictional characters embarked on a journey of self-transformation, he could give artistic form to these impressions in his literary fictions. How? By converting "nervous force into phrases" (*CL*, III, 85), as Conrad clinically observed in a letter to H. G. Wells. Not unlike mimesis, plasticity, for Conrad, has a double, paradoxical function: it is both the source of good and bad impressions, psychic formations and of aesthetic representations, subjection to cultural models and creation of fictional types, passive adaptation and active transformation. Furthering the recent insight that plasticity, for better and worse, is central to the (de)formation of the modernist subject,[5] I argue that Conrad's fictions in general, and *Under Western Eyes* (1911) as well as *A Personal Record* (1912) in particular, are inscribed in a philosophical tradition that—from Plato to Rousseau, Derrida to Lacoue-Labarthe—helps us productively reframe the new scientific concept of "neuroplasticity" against the general philosophical background of the ancient artistic concept of mimesis.

My wager is that this protean concept understood not as simple homogeneous imitation but in its heterogeneous, hypermimetic manifestations— including aesthetic re-presentation, psychic adaptation, and neurological transformation—continues to in-*form* Conrad's impressionistic poetics (critical thesis).[6] And, in a mirroring move, Conrad's neuroplasticity casts light on some of the paradoxes the neurosciences are currently confronting as well (theoretical thesis). A diagnostic account of the plasticity of mimesis is sharpened by adopting philosophical, psychological, and aesthetic lenses that are attentive to the complex, spiraling patho(-)logical effects that turn psychosomatic (dis)figurations into aesthetic re-presentations, and vice versa. In the process, a hypermimetic approach to plasticity goes beyond structural oppositions that have dominated the past century in order to think through the dynamic relation that connects nature and culture, the mind and the brain, psyche and soma, subject formation and artistic formation, along lines relevant for the twenty-first century.

To be sure, Conrad, as an artist, does not provide us with hard scientific facts or immutable philosophical ideas that answer, once and for all, the question, "what should we do with our brain?" Yet his reliance on what he calls, in his Preface to *The Nigger of the "Narcissus,"* his "less obvious," but not less accurate, artistic "capacities" (xii) provides a neuroaesthetic foundation to the mimetic patho(-)logies we have been diagnosing throughout this book. In the process, this diagnostic also contributes to the ongoing dialogue between literature and science.

## A Record of Plasticity

For Conrad, plasticity was not an abstract idea but a matter of lived experience, not a philosophical or scientific hypothesis but a cultural and artistic practice. It is thus useful to recall a biographical point I made at the beginning to provide a preliminary theoretical indication as to where we are going to end. What is true for all subjects is particularly true for Conrad: since he was not imprinted with a stable identity at the outset, he could give it a protean form throughout his life. Thus, as Conrad moved from Poland to France, in his teens, switching from Polish to French, while embarking on an improbable sailing career that took him across the world, while switching to English midroute, and working his way up from steward to captain, only to switch, once again, in his midthirties to start an even more improbable literary career in a new country, in his third language—as he struggled through these perilous maneuvers—Conrad did not simply wonder about what he should do with his brain. He actually relied on its plasticity to do something with it.

This, at least, is what Conrad is ready to avow in his autobiographical memoir, *A Personal Record*. In what he considers "a bit of a psychological document" (18), Conrad retrospectively turns to meditate on his improbable navigation from master-mariner to master of English prose in order to diagnose a journey that is as exterior as it is interior. It is, in fact, in the context of a discussion of his linguistic, professional, and subjective transformations that Conrad, in the "Author's Note," speculates about what he calls his "still plastic character" (5). This is an incisive, self-diagnostic phrase whose psychic, aesthetic, and philosophical contours I will be delineating in what follows. Taken out of context, it already encapsulates what is essential. Namely, that the "still plastic" disposition of what Conrad calls here "character" functions as the material base, the malleable substance, perhaps even as the very medium to navigate this delicate transition from a life at sea to one at a writing desk.[7] Conrad is talking about his own personal plasticity here, and I return to *A Personal Record* in the second part of the Coda. But since this claim appears in the context of his linguistic adoption of the English language he will use as a "medium of expression" (5), it is important to immediately stress that in his works, in which, admittedly, "he stands confessed" (89), he also represents figures who are not in possession of fixed, hardwired identities, but are always open to transformative experiences that render them pliable to external impressions.

This lesson is now familiar to us. Consistently in his novels, Conrad thinks of his literary characters as malleable, adaptable figures that are relational in nature, affective in disposition, and ready to be formed, or deformed, by external impressions. In *Heart of Darkness*, for instance, we have seen a charismatic leader such as Kurtz endowed with the will power to impress not only malleable figures like the Harlequin but also more sharply delineated characters like Marlow, not to speak of the "crowd" of worshippers both in Africa and at "large meetings" in Europe. Along similar lines, in *The Secret Agent* we have seen Conrad speak of the power of the printing press to literally impress the subject of the mass so profoundly as to "stamp" its "personality" and "brain." And indeed, from the malleable, muddy origins of subjectivity in *Almayer's Folly* to its tragic destinations in *Apocalypse Now*, from the crowd psychology at the center of *The Nigger of the "Narcissus"* to the crowd behavior in *Typhoon*, from the protean identifications that inform *Lord Jim* to the figure of the *homo duplex* animating "The Secret Sharer" and *The Shadow-Line*, we have repeatedly seen that the shadow of mimesis falls on Conrad's fictions, outlining a subject that is continuously shaped by impressions that are as physical as they are psychic, as exterior as they are interior. Plasticity, just like mimesis, is a principle that runs through the entirety of Conrad's corpus. But it is perhaps in *Under Western Eyes*—a novel whose writing literally made a serious dent in the author's neurological system, causing severe psychosomatic symptoms that threatened to dissolve his own plastic character—that Conrad goes furthest in his diagnostic of plasticity.[8]

## The Case of Razumov: *Under Western Eyes*

That plasticity is central to the affective and conceptual delineation of *Under Western Eyes*' protagonist is clear from the outset of the novel. Kirylo Sidorovitch Razumov, the tragic hero of this Russian tale—a student of philosophy unwittingly implicated in a revolutionary bombing that literally explodes an oppressive minister of state—is immediately defined in terms of a disarming malleability that, in both a figurative and material way, already seals his tragic destiny. The narrator, a teacher of English language who frames and reports the events, introduces him as a "tall, well proportioned young man" whose "good looks would have been unquestionable if it had not been for a peculiar lack of fineness in the features" (*UWE* 12). And going below the aesthetic surface of his physical appearance—this English teacher is a bit of a psychologist—he cuts deep into the psychosomatic substance of Razumov's character as he outlines his figure as follows: "It was as if a face modelled vigorously in wax (with some approach even to a classical correctness of type) had been held close to a fire till all sharpness of line had been lost in the softening of the material" (13). What Conrad represents, or better sculpts—with the narrator as a chisel—is not only an impressionistic picture of the protagonists' malleable face; it is above all a diagnostic delineation of the plastic foundations of an impressionable, waxlike character whose process of psychic (dis)figuration the novel will subsequently trace.

We shall soon confirm that this picture of a malleable subject, which is the soul this novel diagnoses, should be taken literally, for it looks ahead to new accounts of the plasticity of the human brain. But let us first recall that it also looks back to an ancient philosophical account of character—at least if we understand character in its classical definition (character from Greek, *kharassein*, to be stamped or engraved). This picture of Razumov, in fact, reminds us that plasticity is far from being a new concept. And as Conrad sets out to delineate the process of figuration and disfiguration of a waxlike character who, by the way, is also a "third year's student in philosophy" (13), strolling up and down a famous road at the heart of Geneva called Boulevard des Philosophes, he implicitly encourages readers to slow down and look back to the philosophical foundations of plasticity first—before leaping ahead to contemporary scientific discoveries.

## Plasticity and Mimesis

In his representation of fictional characters in general and of Razumov's psychic life in particular, Conrad is relying on an ancient conception of human character qua *kharassein* in order to outline the double effects of mimetic impressions. This passage in particular reveals that plasticity, like mimesis, is a Janus-faced concept that cuts both ways: on one side, plasticity provides a malleable, material base that can potentially be fashioned in a beautiful form or "classical type"; on the other side, it also characterizes a soft material that can be "melted" in a formless figure. A plastic character can thus simultaneously be the subject of an artistic figuration and the object of a psychic disfiguration. Good and bad impressions, active and passive imprints, artistic formation and psychic deformation: Conrad's view of human plasticity could, indeed, not be more classical. Lest we hastily proclaim as a revolutionary discovery what a third year's student of philosophy with some aspirations should recognize as a revolutionary confirmation of well-known philosophical and literary principles that look back to the very foundation of the humanities, a philosophical reminder is in order.

In his delineation of Razumov's plastic character, Conrad is providing a classical literary diagnostic of the ups and downs of mimetic configurations. On the one hand, Conrad's aesthetic emphasis on appearance, proportion, delineation, and the language of sculpture that informs this initial character-ization is, indeed, "classical" in the literal sense that it goes all the way back to Ancient Greece, to that locus classicus of mimetic theory that is Plato's *Republic*. In particular, Conrad echoes an idealist view of beauty that val-ues aesthetic figures on the basis of an imitation (mimesis) of ideal "types," "models," or "forms." As Socrates puts it, in Book X of *Republic*, where the question of mimetic representation is outlined, the craftsman "fixes his eyes on the idea or form"[9] so as to reproduce a phenomenal copy of such a form, an ideal type that mimetic artists such as painters, poets, but also sculptors, will, in turn, reproduce, generating shadows of shadows. As Conrad speaks of modeling a material so as to "approach even to a classical correctness of type," he is thus not only convoking a classical conception of beauty based on ideal forms; he is also relying on a classical view of artistic creation that considers human characters to be modeled on such ideal types. This is per-haps why Conrad says in his Preface to *The Nigger of the "Narcissus"* that art should aspire to "the plasticity of sculpture" (xiii). In a sense, then, Conrad's impressionistic delineation of Razumov's character already suggests that mimesis continues to be the medium through which ideal, artistic types can be formally impressed.

And yet mimesis is not only implicitly part of the impressionistic medium of Conrad's characterization; it also explicitly informs the psychological mes-sage of the tale itself along hypermimetic lines that cut across the boundaries between aesthetic representation and behavioral imitation. Razumov, in fact, is both an object of ideal aesthetic representation and a subject in the process of deep psycho-physiological, and thus material, transfiguration. As the language of "model[ling] vigorously in wax" indicates, and the content of a novel dealing with what Conrad calls, oxymoronically, the "labours of the soul" (24) confirms, *Under Western Eyes* outlines the "plastic shape" (87) of malleable characters and diagnoses the impressions they both produce on others and receive from others. Notice that even, or perhaps especially, from this materialist, psychosomatic perspective, Conrad's view of plasticity

continues to remain in line with a classical view of character (de)forma-
tion. As the father of mimetic theory had made clear in Books II and III of
*Republic*, ideal forms, or types, do not only serve as reproductions of what
Socrates calls mere "phantoms" or "shadows" of reality to be seen from the
outside. Rather, for Plato, literary characters, as they appear in Homer's *The
Iliad* or *The Odyssey*, are constitutive of a classical education (*paideia*) insofar as they function as exemplary models that form real human characters
via impressions to be felt from the inside. It is, in fact, in the context of a
discussion of the educational role of these fictional types, which inaugurates
Plato's critique of mimesis in *Republic*, that Socrates speaks of children's
mimetic dispositions in terms of malleable, waxlike characters that are, as
he says, "best molded [*plattetai*] and takes the impression [*tupos*] that one
wishes to stamp upon it" (*R* 624). Plato, fine psychologist that he is, is fully
aware of the waxlike plasticity of children's character and of their vulnerability to cultural impressions. Hence he fears the power of cultural types to
form it or, more often, deform it. This plastic realization, in his view, is far
from being limited to childhood, but continues to inform adulthood as well,
generating mere shadows or phantoms in place of egos. This is why Conrad, speaking of the masses' vulnerability to the "intoxication" generated by
emotional impressions, says, "the ancient Greeks understood that very well"
(*UWE* 226). This is clearly a lesson that is as old as *Republic*, a philosophical
dialogue that is not only an ideal picture or representation (mimesis) of what
the ideal polis should be but also, and perhaps more important, a dramatic
dialogue in which characters speak mimetically, in *prima persona* (mimetic
*lexis*) in order to outline—via dialectical twists and turns designed to leave
traces on the brains of readers—what future characters impressed by this
new philosophical form could possibly become.[10]

Closer to the moderns, this ancient pedagogical awareness of human
plasticity is equally central to Jean-Jacques Rousseau, an educator of Platonic
inspiration who, in *Émile*, called *Republic* "the most beautiful treaty on
education that has ever been written."[11] Like other modernists before him,
Conrad tends to be notoriously critical of his literary models, and his critique increases in direct proportion to the models' power of impression. This
applies most notably to Dostoevsky (*Crime and Punishment*, as many have
noticed, is a major influence in *Under Western Eyes*) but also to what he calls
"confessions *à la* Jean Jacques Rousseau" (*PR* 273). And yet these confessions

cast a long shadow in a confessional novel set in Geneva, literally under the shadow of "the effigy of Jean-Jacques Rousseau seated on its pedestal" (*UWE* 226). Conrad is thus, nolens volens, impressed by Rousseau, an author who, echoing Plato, claimed that "nature endows the child's brain with a malleability [*souplesse*] which renders him able to receive all kinds of impressions [*toutes sortes d'impressions*]."[12] Hence Rousseau's alternative outline of that treaty on education for adults to read such as *Émile*, a text that, not unlike *Republic*, not only offers a representation of what education should be in theory but also offers a pedagogical exemplum of how education could be enacted in practice.

More recently, Philippe Lacoue-Labarthe extends this long-neglected Platonic view of plasticity from the other end of metaphysics in order to account for the imitation of the moderns. The Platonic language Lacoue-Labarthe mobilizes in *Typography* is not without Conradian echoes, unsurprisingly so since, as we have already seen, their shared affinities run deep. The French philosopher puts it in a philosophical language that would have caught Conrad's attention: "Things, begin then—and this is what mimesis is all about—with the 'plastic' (fashioning, modelling, fictioning) with the impression of the *type* and the imposition of the *sign*, with the mark that language, 'mythic' discourses . . . originally inscribe in the malleable—plastic—material of the infant soul."[13] For Lacoue-Labarthe and Conrad, just as for Rousseau and Plato before them, mimesis and plasticity are two sides of the same coin. And once these sides are joined they give form to a Janus-faced "soul." Far from having only a spiritual, disembodied, transcendental side, within this Platonic tradition, the soul also has a plastic, material, and thus immanent side, which is best molded by the typographic power of hypermimetic impressions. Thus Lacoue-Labarthe, on the shoulders of Plato, speaks of subjectivity in terms of a "pure and disquieting plasticity . . . which doubtless requires a 'subjective base'—a 'wax'—but without any other property than an infinite malleability."[14] A plastic view of the subject understood in its classical philosophical sense of *subjectum* (what is underlying or subjacent), it would be useless to deny, is indeed internal to a most classical literary and philosophical definition of mimesis. And Conrad knew it. The human character, or soul, has been defined from the beginning of mimetic theory in terms of a waxlike material base that is formed by culture and formative of culture. And Conrad equally knew it.

Razumov is an exemplary case study to diagnose the symptomatic effects of neuroplasticity. His character, in fact, allows us to outline both the formative and deformative sides of this Janus-faced concept. An impressionable youth "without a family" (*UWE* 16), this orphan's identity is not hardwired in firm, hereditary, and familial dispositions, for "no home influences," we are told, "had shaped his opinions or his feelings" (16). Hence he is not only "impressionable" (174) but also relies on his malleable disposition to actively give form to his character. In particular, Razumov aspires—via the medium of philosophy—to write a "prize essay" that would gain him a "silver medal" (17), attract the attention of the aristocratic father who orphaned him, and eventually approximate a "classical correctness of type" potentially present in his plastic character. And yet, as the narrative unfolds, his philosophical plan backfires. Razumov finds himself implicated in a revolutionary bombing in St. Petersburg that explodes not only an oppressive minister but also his academic future. In turn, Razumov is subjected by the Russian authorities to playing the role of a double agent in Geneva, and, in the process, falls hopelessly in love with the beautiful and trusting Natalia Haldin, the "divine" sister of Victor Haldin, namely, the revolutionary student responsible for the bombing Razumov had betrayed who now haunts, like a "phantom" or "shadow," Razumov's divided conscience. Unsurprisingly, then, the impossible double binds generated by these political, cultural, and, above all, affective impressions eventually lead to the material disfiguration of Razumov's malleable character along lines the beginning of the novel had initially foreshadowed.

And yet precisely for this reason, Razumov's tragic case provides clinical readers with an exemplary case study to diagnose both the idealist and material sides of Conrad's Janus-faced account of plasticity. As the events of this ex-student of philosophy unfold in Boulevard des Philosophes, under the shadow of a long philosophical tradition attentive to the formative and, above all, deformative power of mimesis, Conrad gives dramatic form to a classical philosophical concern with the plastic foundations of subjectivity. Thus the teacher of English language who frames and narrates the events by reporting, at one remove, the confessions Razumov wrote down in his diary, speculates, in an idealist mood: "Life is a thing of form. It has its plastic shape and a definite intellectual aspect" (87). But then as a "man who believes in the psychological values of facts" (225), the narrator immediately adds, in a more down-to-earth, materialist mood: "The most idealistic conceptions of love and forbearance must be clothed in flesh as it were before they can be made understandable" (87–88). For Conrad, then, the "shape" of psychic life needs to be anchored in the materiality of the "flesh" in order to be properly configured. No matter how ideal the "plastic shape" may be in its philosophical aspirations, a diagnostic of the soul cannot escape the dissection of the materiality of flesh in its plastic transformations. The diagnostic is, of course, double-faced.

## A Pharmacy for Plasticity

Looking back to the classical origins of mimetic theory in its idealist foundations allows us to better see how Conrad outlines plastic paradoxes that are now at the forefront of contemporary discussions in the neurosciences. Neither scientists, nor historians, nor even philosophers have yet recognized that plasticity follows, shadowlike, mimesis in its power to generate both good and bad impressions. And yet this old philosophical lesson casts a long shadow on the paradox that structures contemporary accounts of neuroplasticity. Norman Doidge, for instance, drawing the implications of a number of contemporary clinical case studies, writes that "neuroplasticity isn't all good news; it renders our brains not only more resourceful but also more vulnerable to outside influences."[15] Along similar lines, Nikolas Rose and Joelle Abi-Rached articulate from a historical perspective the duplicity of neuroplasticity along quasi-Platonic lines as they remind us that "by the close of the twentieth century, the brain had come to be envisioned as mutable across the whole of life, open to environmental influences, damaged by insults, and nourished and even reshaped by stimulation—in a word *plastic*."[16] And Catherine Malabou, the most outspoken philosopher on the neuroplastic revolution, speaks of plasticity in terms of active, revolutionary power to "give form" to one's brain, on one side, and in terms of a passive, "docile" submission "to receive a form or impression," on the other (*WSW* 6, 12). Scientists, historians, and philosophers, then, tend to agree that this is a foundational realization that forces us to rethink what the human subject is—or can possibly become. And quite rightly so, for this realization opens up new, mind-boggling possibilities concerning human evolution, flexibility, free will, and adaptation, generating life-negating or life-affirming transformations.

And yet the case of this third-year student of philosophy also warns scholars in the humanities not to jump on the latest neurological bandwagon without considering first the philosophical tradition that informs the double pharmacological effects of the plasticity of the subject. While the traces of this tradition have been generally erased, they are still partially visible in Malabou's philosophical diagnostic. Thus the French philosopher aptly convokes the Greek etymology of plasticity "*plassein*, to mold" (*WSW* 5) and the "sculpture molding" (6) it entails in order to subsequently trace the double effects of what she calls the "power of *impression*" (6) or "formation" through submission (or refusal to submit) to a "pre-established form" or "original model" (6). Plasticity is, indeed, not a new conceptual protagonist on the philosophical scene—and Malabou knows it. Thus she writes: "Flexibility is a vague notion, without tradition, *without history*, while plasticity is a *concept*, which is to say: a form of quite precise meanings that bring together and structure particular cases" (13). And she adds: "This concept has a long philosophical past, which has itself remained too long in the shadows [*dans l'ombre*]" (13). Too long, indeed. But then why not bring these mimetic shadows that tacitly inform Malabou's incisive account of plasticity into the foreground, or at least mention it in the background in one of those dense footnotes her mentor, Jacques Derrida, taught her to trace?[17] You will have guessed the diagnosis: just as there was a patho(-)logical dimension to mimesis as both sickness and therapy in the past, there is now a pharmacological side of plasticity as the source of revolutionary transformations and docile adaptations in the present. If these scientific discoveries are empirically new in their neurological findings, they are not new in their conceptual delineation. To put it boldly, I am even tempted to say that the paradoxical diagnostic of neuroplasticity is nothing less and nothing more than the contemporary translation of an ancient mimetic pharmacology into the new language of contemporary neurology.

Having traced the structural contours of the double effects of plasticity against a general philosophical account of good and bad mimetic impressions, let us take a closer look at the psychosomatic side of this Janus-faced concept. An objection lingering in the reader's mind can no longer be postponed. Plasticity may well be constitutive of the Conradian account of "character," or "soul," but it does not yet follow that this waxlike "material" actually concerns the brain itself. After all, psychology, not neurology, is the focus of Conrad's diagnostic of a "Russian soul" representative of what he calls, in the "Author's Note," "the psychology of Russia itself" (*UWE* 5). Indeed, as I have argued throughout this book, Conrad's insights into the foundations of subjectivity are precious for their psychological, anthropological, ontological, and thus fundamentally humanistic implications, not for their scientific, factual, and cognitive observations. These principles remain valid and continue to inform my diagnostic of mimetic patho(-)logies. But we are now in a position to provide a new empirical supplement to these ancient humanistic claims. In fact, Conrad's attention to plasticity allows him to sail past the Scylla of an idealist tradition that thinks of the soul in opposition to the brain and the Charybdis of a materialist tradition that reduces the soul to the mere activity of the brain. When it comes to the plasticity of characters, in fact, clear-cut structural oppositions between psyche and soma, matter and spirit, nature and nurture no longer hold, and fluid, psychosomatic continuities spill over the conceptual divide that opposes the soul to the brain. Conrad is, of course, no scientist. We should thus be careful not to frame his artistic account of human character within the confines of a reductionistic view that identifies subjectivity with the materiality of the brain alone, if only because he clearly defines the soul as "that part of Razumov which was not his body" (224). But we would do Conrad's artistic sensibility a literary injustice were we not to recognize that as he looks back to a philosophical account of the typographic impressions on the "soul," which, by the way, he uses "not in the theological sense" (224), he does so on a materialist basis that for him is rooted in what he calls the "brain."

## The Soul and the Brain

For Conrad, the soul-brain divide is not as watertight as a Cartesian tradition thought it to be. Characters' *mouvements d'âme* affect the fleshy, neurological base of the brain repeatedly in *Under Western Eyes*. For instance, after Razumov's brutal beating of a drunk coach-driver called Ziemianitch in a "shadowy" "cavernous place" reminiscent of a Platonic cave, we are given the following materialist insight into the psychosomatic effects of the "terrible fury" (30) that is unexpectedly triggered within the protagonist's otherwise "silent soul" (26) as we read: "Something seemed to turn over in his head bringing upper-most a singularly hard clear facet of his brain" (36). A primary psychic affect (or *pathos*), such as anger, has the power to turn the structure

of the "brain" so as to reveal a previously concealed "facet." This is a preliminary indication that affects, for Conrad, have not only psychological but also
psycho-physiological, or as we now say, neurological foundations. And in
order to make clear that the brain is not only affected by primitive pathos
(such as anger) but also by more complex and psychologically obscure affects
(such as horror), the narrator wonders in a patho-*logical* mood: "What
vision of all the horrors that can be seen in his hopeless country had come
suddenly to haunt his brain?" (153). Horror, then, for Conrad, is a pathos
that affects the soul as much as the brain. Again, this does not mean that
the obscure meaning of what Conrad enigmatically calls "the horror" can
be illuminated by seeing which parts of the brain light up as we read *Under
Western Eyes* or *Heart of Darkness*. Nor should we give Conrad's use of
two different signifiers—one spiritual and psychological (soul), the other
material and physiological (brain)—a scientific value per se. Rather, what
is significant is that Conrad uses these signifiers interchangeably, suggesting
that the distinction between psyche and soma, the soul and the brain, the
mental facet and its material base, breaks down in his diagnostic of the power
of impressions on his waxlike material, introducing a continuity between
psychic (mental) and physiological (neuronal) functions. Psychology and
neurology, the study of the soul and the study of the brain, for Conrad, cannot be considered in isolation but must be revisited in a relation of (hyper)
mimetic communication.

Repeatedly, Conrad makes clear that affective impressions that leave a
trace on characters' souls and brains continue to be intimately connected
with the problematic of mimesis as we understand it. Thus Conrad peppers
his diagnostic of Razumov's character with passages like these: "coming to
himself as though his brain had been awakened from a trance" (156). Or:
"Some brains can not resist the suggestion of irresistible power and of
headlong motion" (154). And again: "A false suggestion enters one's brain
and then fear is born" (287). To be sure, altered states symptomatic of the
mimetic unconscious such as trance, suggestion, and automatic reflexes animate not only the ego or soul of Conrad's characters; they are also constitutive of what he repeatedly calls the "brain." This is, in a way, not surprising.
As we have repeatedly seen, the trancelike, hypnotic, suggestive, and thus
mimetic states that pervade Conrad's novels are not simply psychological
but rather psycho-physiological states that—from body to soul, neurological

reflexes to contagions affects—open up the subject to external influences. In such altered states the subject's rational guard is lowered, the boundary that divides self and other(s) is no longer impermeable, and, as a consequence, affective, unconscious communicative relations with others qua *socii* become more intense, immediate, and instinctual, rendering the ego quite literally impressionable. The mimetic unconscious designates impersonal, psychosomatic states, contagious intersubjective influences, affective responses, non-verbal communications, and covers a wide range of psychic awareness, from waking consciousness to trancelike states that can be fully un-conscious, and are in any case not under the full control of consciousness, rendering the human subject materially receptive to psychosomatic impressions that affect the soul as much as the brain. Hence, for Conrad, mimetic pathoi—such as fear, panic, or horror—spread contagiously from self to other, induce pathological states of (dis)possession, and in this liminal unconscious state especially, though not only, make a direct hypermimetic impression on the waxlike foundations of a soul that is not ideal or winged, but is firmly rooted in the plasticity of the brain.

If a long-standing Cartesian tradition has influenced us to think of concepts such as brain and soul in terms of dualistic opposition, and a scientific tradition has suggested to think of the brain as fixed and hardwired, Conrad encourages us to think again. His Janus-faced approach to the patho(-)logies of plasticity destabilizes the distinction between brain and soul, suggesting not only that they are two facets of the same subject but that the interface that divides these seemingly opposed facets also connects them, generating a dynamic interplay that requires more fluid interrogations. This is also what Paul Armstrong suggests as he questions the "mind-brain divide" on the basis of a neurophenomenology concerned with "establishing dynamic constraints between subjective experience and neurobiology."[18] And as Catherine Malabou puts it, drawing the philosophical lesson that was already implicit in classical waxlike representations of the malleable soul, "the difference between the brain and psychism is shrinking considerably, and we do not know it" (*WSW* 8). Conrad, once again, not only knew it; he also gave artistic form to this connection.

As the case of Razumov makes clear, and so many Conradian characters repeatedly confirm, Conrad is fundamentally aware that brain plasticity cuts both ways: just like wax it can be both molded and melted, formed and deformed, before being re-formed or conformed in an endless process of (de-re-con-)formation that can be as enabling as disabling, as empowering as disempowering. While not discussed so far, this is far from being a minor theme in Conrad's corpus. It is perhaps even the underlying mimetic principle that gave form to his work as a whole. Time and again, we have seen Conrad constantly returning to diagnosing the double patho(-)logical effects of mimetic impressions. On the one hand, he repeatedly represents malleable characters who aspire to ideal types. Be it in the form of duelist ("The Duel"), captain ("The Secret Sharer," *The Shadow-Line*), adventurer (*Lord Jim*), leader (*Nostromo*), moral center (*The Nigger of the "Narcissus"*), universal genius (*Heart of Darkness*), or compassionate creature (*The Secret Agent*), Conrad's literary characters are constantly striving toward ideal and exemplary standards of conduct that require plastic qualities of adaptation. On the other hand, precisely because of their plasticity, indeterminacy, and openness to impressions, these characters also prove to be disarmingly vulnerable to the material effects of interpersonal, cultural, political, and environmental deformations. Thus the honorable duelist turns into a swashbuckler, the promising captain into a schizophrenic self, the heroic adventurer proves to be a coward, the noble leader a traitor, the universal genius a degenerate, and the compassionate, plastic subject is, quite literally, exploded—without revolutionary outcomes whatsoever, except those hypermimetic principles articulated in Conrad's fiction.

Stamped by the press, modeled on types, graven by words and events, the soul-brain binary, for Conrad, is both the locus of grotesque psychic, moral, and political deformations, and the starting point for new artistic configurations. Both principles, in their ideal and material configurations, are central to Conrad's diagnostic of the plastic symptoms internal to the case of Razumov. The teacher of languages, speaking of the events following the explosion, articulates this paradoxical process that turns a character subjected to formative impressions into a subject who gives form to such impressions clearly as he speculates: "The words and events of that evening must have been graven as if with a steel tool on Mr. Razumov's brain since he was able to write his relation with such fullness and precision a good many months afterwards" (*UWE* 26). Critics attentive to the novel's narrative structure have tended to be suspicious of mimesis understood in terms of old realistic representation; and rightly so, given the obvious, unreliable status of this participant narrator. But if this narrative "has not lost all its interest" (5), as Conrad hopes to be the case, it is perhaps also because it converts the ancient paradox of mimesis into the new language of plasticity. As the case of Razumov's indicates, and Conrad's writing career confirms, brain plasticity is not only the site of violent pathological disfigurations; it is also the basis of a confessional type of logos that gives full and precise artistic form to traces left on the brain by "converting nervous force into phrases" (*CL*, III 85), as Conrad suggests. It is, in fact, because the impressions generated by "words and events" are "graven as if with a steel tool" in the plastic materiality of the "brain" that they are permanently inscribed in his memory and can, in turn, in-form that "labour of the soul" par excellence, which, for Conrad, is "writing," or, as they say in Geneva—*écriture*.

## Brain Inscriptions

We are now in a position to fully trace the contours of a conceptual loop that gives form to the paradoxical structure of plasticity. For Conrad, brain plasticity renders the subject both passive and active, both vulnerable to the power of impressions that leave memory traces on the brain and endowed with impressive force to turn these traces into a type of writing that gives form to a waxlike character. This Janus-faced diagnostic is, once again, not original. It is but an echo of a pharmacological principle that can be traced from Rousseau back to Plato. As Jacques Derrida famously suggests in "Plato's Pharmacy," mimesis and writing operate according to the same pharmacological principles that leave, for better and worse, traces on memory. On one side, "the *pharmakon* of writing is good for *hypomnēsis* (re-memoration, recollection, consignation)" (91), for it traces mimetic reproductions for the future to read. On the other side, writing only "plays with the simulacrum. It is in its type the mime of memory, of knowledge, of truth" (105), which is to say that it is not an original memory, knowledge, or truth. Either way, writes Derrida, "The imprints (*tupoi*) of writing," for Plato, have the power to "inscribe themselves . . . in the wax of the soul *in intaglio*, thus corresponding to the spontaneous, autochthonous motions of psychic life" (104). It would be useless to deny it: mimesis, writing, and plasticity cannot easily be disentangled, if only because it is the pharmakon of mimesis that gives conceptual form to the paradoxical structure of plasticity, while plasticity gives material substance to writing. From time immemorial, plasticity has indeed been a Janus-faced concept that transgresses the line between active and passive, nature and culture, interior and exterior, poisonous effects and therapeutic cures. Consequently, plasticity renders the subject both passive and active, both vulnerable to the power of impressions that leave traces on the brain and endowed with impressive force to turn these traces into a type of writing that gives form to the soul. The difficulty of grasping the dual, ever-changing, and above all malleable implications of this chameleon -concept is that, like mimesis, plasticity transgresses the line between active and passive, nature and culture, interior and exterior, pathology and patho-logy.

Inscribed in a classical philosophical tradition, Conrad's conception of plasticity cannot be dissociated from the practice of that pharmakon par excellence that is writing. This connection is all the more clear since, as Derrida reminds us, "the specificity of writing" is "intimately bound to the absence of the father" generating the "distress of the orphan" (77), which, of course, is precisely Razumov's distress. An orphan in search of a father, by the end of the novel that errant "phantom" who is Razumov may not have won his silver medal, or discovered a stable, original identity. Yet he is metamorphosed into a hypermimetic embodiment of the Janus-faced sides of plasticity itself. The final diagnostic is thus double in its patho(-)logical manifestations: on one side, Razumov's ends his adventure in Geneva with a violent and traumatic operation that leaves profound and permanent traces on his brain. After his "confession" (278) that reveals his identity as a double agent, the revolutionaries pierce his eardrums, a horrifying punitive operation that "seemed to split his head in two" leaving him permanently deaf and crippled, "staggering down a long empty street . . . like a lost mortal in a phantom world" (280).[19] On the other side, due to the violent impressions stamped on his brain, this phantom is in a position to convert these traces into nervous phrases left in his diary along confessional lines that are not deprived of self-diagnostic insights into the patho(-)logies of plasticity. Initially addressed to his beloved Natalia, this confession is subsequently reframed and translated by the narrator for others to read and further diagnose. The case of Razumov, I have tried to argue, is thus not only a pathological illustration of the poisonous effects of plasticity; it also provides an incisive diagnostic of the double principles inscribed in his personal confession.

But this confession is not only the one of a fictional character; it spills over, hypermimetically, to affect a real character as well. As Conrad's personal breakdown in the writing process of *Under Western Eyes* suggests, these traces also point toward another distressed, yet adventurous orphan who, admittedly, "stands confessed in his works" (*PR* 89). This shadow, we are told, operates as the "figure behind the veil, a suspected rather than a seen presence—a movement and a voice behind the draperies of fiction" (12). "I" thus let go of the plasticity of a fictional character (the case of Razumov) in order to diagnose the plasticity of the orphan as artist (the case of Conrad).

## The Orphan as Artist: *A Personal Record*

We have already outlined the mimetic underpinnings of Conrad's poetics as they appear in his famous "Preface" at the level of his surrealist message, yet in his autobiographical memoir, *A Personal Record*, Conrad supplements this account as he turns to consider his plastic medium. So far, this text has been treated mainly as a source of the author's personal information, understandably so given its explicit autobiographical intention.[20] Yet this "psychological document," as Conrad calls it, is not deprived of larger diagnostic insights into plastic principles that inform his impressionistic poetics.

### Plastic Birth / Artistic Adoption

In support of the hypermimetic hypothesis that, for Conrad, writing and plasticity, fiction and life are intimately connected, in the "Author's Note" of *A Personal Record* Conrad frames his account of his "still plastic character" within a larger discussion concerning the linguistic adoption that eventually led to his identity as a writer. Denying any "act of deliberate volition" as well as any conscious "choice" in the "adoption" of English as a medium, Conrad qualifies his linguistic, and thus aesthetic, adoption as follows: "well yes, there was adoption; but it was I who was adopted by the genious of the language" (5). The language of adoption is pregnant with meaning. Conrad, the son of anti-Russian revolutionaries who died early in his youth, puts himself in a position of an orphaned child when it comes to his linguistic adoption necessary for his artistic birth. That is, a vulnerable, passive position that seemingly deprives him of agency, volition, and conscious control over the choice of his artistic medium. Just as an orphaned child cannot choose his adoptive parents, the analogy suggests, so the multilingual artist cannot choose his adoptive language. Instead, as Geoffrey Harpham puts it, adoption "requires assent,"[21] in the sense that the orphan must make himself receptive, *disponible* to the possibility of such an adoption. This is, to be sure, a humble rhetorical move that reduces the subject of speech (subjective genitive) to a subject of speech (objective genitive). Hence, in this process of linguistic adoption, the virtues of artistic activity are reduced to the dependency of childish passivity. And yet this move of (dis)possession is not without ironies that cut both ways. The orphan may be dispossessed of what is proper to him, for his character is not definitively impressed by formative "influences" hardwired in the brain. Yet, for this very reason, he can also be possessed by superior linguistic forces that are not deprived of what he calls "genius."

Now, if the case of Razumov suggested that plasticity at the level of the brain is necessary to record the traces of personal impressions inscribed in his memory, the case of the artist as orphan implies that plasticity at the level of language is essential to render these impressions in aesthetic terms. In this double sense, the choice between French and English is particularly revealing of the underlying linguistic foundations that literally in-form Conrad's impressionistic aesthetics. As he explains, familiarity with the language from infancy is not necessarily an advantage if one aspires to plasticity: "though I knew French fairly well and was familiar with it from infancy," writes Conrad, "I would have been afraid to attempt *expression* in a language so *perfectly 'crystallized'*" (*PR* 4; my emphasis). This is an interesting phrase. It suggests that Conrad's objection to French is deep and fundamental: it does not concern sound or lexicon, but structure and form. Since French syntactical and grammatical rules—*dixit* the *Académie Française*—tend to remain perfectly rigid over time, Conrad's artistic impression seems to be that these beautiful forms, precisely because of their perfect crystallization, do not allow him to capture the fluidity of the "responsive emotions" (*NN* xiii) so central to his impressionistic poetics. Despite his admiration for French masters of style, such as Flaubert and Maupassant, Conrad considers French crystallized (formal) structures inimical to the plasticity of the emotional (formless) force he aims to "convert into phrases." More precisely, Conrad stresses that artistic creation is not a question of expressing thoughts or emotions so as to fit preexisting linguistic structures—no matter how perfect and luminous these forms are—for such a move would freeze the plastic material he is trying to mold. Rather, for Conrad, it is a question of rendering sense-impressions through a medium fluid enough to capture the flux of "responsive emotions"—no matter how dark and murky these emotions are—for it is on such malleability that the plasticity of his art rests. This is perhaps why Conrad says that art should aspire to "the plasticity of sculpture" in order to achieve the "perfect blending of form and substance" (*NN* xiii). The conflict between French and English is thus not simply linguistic or cultural, but aesthetic and ontological. The former entails the ideal expression through the medium of "crystallized" forms; the latter is based on a material impression through the medium of "plastic" forms. French presupposes a formed subject who can express himself through the structure of language; English presupposes a formless subject who can be impressed by the power of affects. The former rests on an ontology of being; the latter promotes an ontology of becoming. In short, the impressionistic medium is mimetic in the sense that it blends in—chameleon-like—with the psychosomatic impressions that inform Conrad's view of artistic creation at the level of the message.[22]

Conversely, plasticity, for Conrad, is not only formative of aesthetic impressions represented in his fictions but also of real psychic impressions felt on his plastic character, generating an interplay between feeling and seeing that is the palpitating heart of his poetics. That Conrad's linguistic formation and his personal transformation are deeply interconnected was already indicated by the language of "adoption" he convokes. But an orphan is not only in search of a language; he is also in search of an identity. And it is precisely this lack of restricted familial influences that renders him open to more general cultural adoptions. Conrad, in fact, anchors his view of artistic creation in material, natural dispositions, along hypermimetic lines that complicate structural binaries that oppose nature to nurture, biological birth to artistic birth, fiction to reality. Here is how his discussion of linguistic adoption continues: "The truth of the matter," Conrad says, "is that my faculty to write in English is as natural as any other aptitude with which I might have been born. I have a strange and overpowering feeling that it had always been an inherent part of myself" (*PR* 4–5). Despite his cultural "adoption," Conrad now suggests that an acquisition as sophisticated as literary expression in a language twice removed from his linguistic origins is rooted in aptitudes that he considers "natural," present at "birth," and thus "inherent" to the subject. This seemingly contradictory passage has puzzled Conrad's commentators, but it can be easily resolved if we notice that Conrad is not speaking of English itself, but of his "*faculty* to write in English" (my emphasis). Above all, he specifies that this natural faculty not only informs his writerly abilities but stretches in order to make possible what he calls "any other aptitude with which [he] might have been born." That plasticity plays a decisive role in this so-called natural faculty present from birth and constitutive of all of Conrad's protean "aptitudes" is suggested a few lines below, as he clarifies that this belated linguistic adoption was made possible thanks to what he calls his "still plastic character."

## An Impression of Plasticity

We were wondering about the philosophical, psychological, and aesthetic contours of Conrad's insights into neuroplasticity. I have traced them in some detail for reasons that are double. On the one hand, they help us reframe Conrad's impressionistic account of plastic characters (literary reasons); on the other hand, they outline Conrad's artistic contribution to our understanding of the implications of neuroplasticity (theoretical reasons). In fact, the preposition "still" indicates that Conrad considers that his character was not only born plastic but remained plastic throughout—and quite naturally so. And it is this plastic malleability in his nature that, Conrad suggests, allowed him to successfully be adopted and impressed, formed and transformed by a language that, though he will always speak with a thick accent (voice, more than writing, registers the limits of plasticity), he will master in writing in such a way few native speakers born directly into it will ever do. Conrad's neuroplasticity may account for what Ford Madox Ford called Conrad's "marvelous resilience,"[23] but, more important, it indicates that, for Conrad, a type of plasticity, which is natural, present from birth, and, above all, ongoing, is the very medium that made possible his belated artistic transformation. In this sense, the genius of the language does not precede Conrad's natural plasticity. Rather, it is plasticity that makes a genial assimilation of the language possible.

What was true for Razumov in fiction, then, is equally true for Conrad in real life. In his account of the interplay between linguistic formation and character transformation, the distinction between nature and nurture, birth and adoption, activity and passivity no longer holds, and a complex, spiraling, hypermimetic joins natural and cultural sides to form a Janus-faced figure. Conrad's so-called plasticity was decisive in the formation of his artistic character, providing the natural base for the growth of this cultural faculty. But Conrad also specifies that this cultural faculty retroacts, via a feedback loop, on the material, subjective base, re-forming its still plastic brain. Having traced all the elements of this artistic transformation, let us step back and re-read this most (in)formative paragraph in its complete form:

> The truth of the matter is that my faculty to write in English is as natural as any other aptitude with which I might have been born. I have a strange and overpowering feeling that it had always been an inherent part of myself. English was for me neither a matter of choice nor adoption. The merest idea of choice had never entered my head. And as to adoption—well, yes, there was adoption; but it was I who was adopted by the genius of the language, which directly I came out of the stammering stage made me its own so completely that its very idioms I truly believe had a direct action on my temperament and fashioned my still plastic character. (*PR* 4–5)

Conrad's artistic delineation of plasticity has deep theoretical implications. It is not simply a question of realizing that the genius of the language speaks through him, in a mimetic way, that is, by divine inspiration or enthusiasm—as Plato or the romantics thought. Nor is this a reenactment of the myth that language speaks to us, *ça parle*, in an imaginary way—as some French (post)-structuralists thought. Rather, Conrad has a more materialist, duplicitous, and ultimately hypermimetic hypothesis in mind. Namely, that "plasticity" is both the medium of his artistic formation and of his character's transformation, part of a spiraling process that is both active and passive, natural and cultural, conscious and unconscious, fictive and real.

If we were to stop the circulation of this process so as to individuate the two sides simultaneously at play in this hypermimetic interface, two faces appear. On the one hand, plasticity is a natural, neurological base responsible for Conrad's penchant for chameleon-like adaptations, cultural adoptions, and professional transformations, including the aptitude to write in English. In this sense, plasticity is not only responsible for bringing a linguistic subject into being; it also provides the material source of inspiration for what we used to call Conrad's linguistic genius. On the other hand, in his genial use of the language in his fictions, this mimetic faculty turns upon itself and retroacts on the speaking subject, "fashioning"—or as Conrad will also say throughout his fictions, "stamping," "molding," "impressing"—its "still plastic character" qua *kharassein* in a process of hypermimetic transformation that keeps this artistic chameleon on the move. In sum, Conrad's diagnostic of the traces of plasticity continues to have double, pharmacological properties. And yet his patho-logical diagnostic also differs on a fundamental point: if only because for the orphan as artist typographic impressions do not originate in a linguistic play still too much concerned with a transcendental logos but from a mimetic pathos that remains firmly and tenaciously rooted in the immanent malleability of a still plastic character, brain, or, to use an ancient yet no less material concept, soul. In this sense we could perhaps say that plasticity is the material soul of the orphan as artist.

To be sure, this artistic account may not be based on solid facts or crystal-clear ideas; yet it delineates the reciprocal interplay between natural and cultural formation that informs contemporary accounts of neuroplasticity nonetheless. Plasticity, for Conrad, is both what gives form to his artistic faculty and what is being formed by it; it is the natural base that makes cultural formation possible, and the cultural subject matter that engenders biologically transformations. As Catherine Malabou reminds us, in a passage we can now hear echoing a long literary and philosophical tradition that, from Derrida to Lacoue-Labarthe, Conrad to Rousseau, can be traced all the way back to Plato:

> According to its etymology—from the Greek *plassein*, to mold—the word *plasticity* has two basic senses: it means at once the capacity to *receive form* (clay is called 'plastic,' for example) and the capacity to *give form* (as in the plastic arts or in plastic surgery). Talking about the plasticity of the brain thus amounts to thinking of the brain as something modifiable, 'formable,' and 'formative' at the same time. (*WSW* 5)

Conrad, the orphan as artist who, in his fictions, aspired to the "plasticity of sculpture," could not have agreed more. He would probably have added that artists are privileged figures who can trace this paradoxical process of formation in general. Orphans as artists who had to struggle to master a protean foreign language are particularly privileged. They remind us that "it is only through an unremitting never-discouraged care for the shape and ring of sentences that an approach can be made to plasticity" (*NN* xiii). Either way, in his impressionistic fictions, the figure of the artist supplements the scientist and the philosopher by sculpting possible configurations of what human characters could potentially become.

Plasticity is not a minor topic in Conrad's corpus. It is the very medium of its formation. If I have left its discussion for the end of this study it also brings us back to the mimetic principles I have been outlining from the very beginning. Plasticity is, in fact, but the most contemporary manifestation of the secret shadow I have been tracing all along. It is thus not surprising that throughout this book we have seen Conrad repeatedly pushing mimetic, or better hypermimetic, principles beyond clear-cut oppositions between mind and brain, thought and body, reason and instinct, culture and nature, in order to diagnose the power of impressions to form, deform, and re-form characters. Be it in the context of political wars or ethical storms, psychic identifications or communal solidarity, colonial rivalries or postcolonial reconciliations, metaphysical dissolutions or tragic rebirths, terrorist explosions or media transformations, we have consistently seen that the plasticity of hypermimetic characters cuts both ways: it is both the source of violent deformations that lead to death and of successful adaptations necessary for survival, pathologies that infect the subject and patho-logies that propose cures, battles to the end and end of battles.

Conrad's diagnostic attention to the power of language and culture to mold the very structure of the brain explodes some of the assumptions concerning the stability of human "nature." It also troubles the shadow-line that divides the mind and the brain, nurture and nature, being oneself and becoming other. Let us thus look back, in a final Janus-faced gesture, to the tale with which we started in order to see how Conrad outlines this revolutionary hypothesis to the very end.

## Mimetic Ends, Plastic Beginnings

Having started with a fictional "Duel," let us end with a theoretical duel, which, in a sort of recoil, opens up the possibility for new beginnings. Of all the tales we have considered, "The Duel" is probably the text that appears most inimical to the possibility of plastic transformations. You remember the story. Set in the context of the "universal carnage" generated by the Napoleonic Wars, the two seemingly opposed officers qua duelists are hardwired to respond to violence, mimetically, that is, with more violence. This is a picture of opposed yet mirroring characters qua doubles, but we are now in a position to add a diagnostic supplement to this Janus-faced image. One side is rational and the other emotional, one is cognitive and the other is instinctual, one is verbal and strategic and the other nonverbal and impulsive. Doesn't this look like one of those popular pictures of the two hemispheres of the brain, one cognitive the other affective, one prone to reason (logos) the other to affect (pathos)? Could it be, then, that these mimetic doubles mirror the duality of the human brain itself?

Since both sides literally stem from the same brain, this sounds like a plausible hypothesis. But if Conrad's understanding of the homo duplex benefits from considering not only psychological but also neurological tendencies, the point for him is that the division between these two sides is far from clear-cut. Both characters, in fact, operate according to the same mimetic principle, which leads them to fire at the sight of the other firing. Conrad's picture of the brain, it seems, is interested in the mirroring continuities that underlie structural discontinuities along lines that find current empirical support. As we have seen, mirror neurons, which operate on both hemispheres of the brain, are automatically triggered by the sight of gestures and expressions that originate in others and are responsible for the type of mirroring escalation that, for Conrad, as for Girard after him, can go on *usque ad finem*. Interestingly, Girard's mimetic hypothesis also rests on a certain image of the brain. If humans, unlike animals, can go on battling to the end, in his view, it is in fact because "an increased mimetic drive, corresponding to the enlarged human brain, must escalate mimetic rivalry beyond the point of no return."[24] This picture of human "evolution" is of course not flattering. Bluntly, it suggests that the bigger the brain, the stupider the animal. Conrad is not more optimistic. In most of his fictions he shows us the pathological effects of what has been known, since classical antiquity, as the most mimetic animal. But then Conrad also adds a second, patho-logial side. Thus in "The Duel" he suggests that it is more productive to affirm survival on assumptions that are not driven by the determinism of mirror neurons but are nonetheless in line with new hypermimetic insights on the plastic potential of our enlarged brain. There is thus a last duel I have kept for the very end.

## Mirror Neurons contra Neuroplasticity

We are now in a position to see that the final duel in "The Duel" has more than one meaning. In fact, the fictional duel between the homo duplex mirrors a theoretical duel between two opposed yet related conceptions of the brain. The conflict is thus as exterior as it is interior, as physical as it is neurological. In particular, it stages the determinism of mirror neurons that informs duels to the end on one side, and the adaptability of plasticity that opens up possibilities for ending the duel, on the other. Mirror neurons, as we have seen, have been driving the entire trajectory of the tale from the beginning and continue to determine the end. They cause the rational D'Hubert to jump up at the sight of his double's shadow, thus exposing himself to Feraud's fire. But then something more mysterious and unpredictable happens. Acting against the instinctual reflex to stoop for the gun he had left on the ground, D'Hubert counters a natural instinct on the basis of a more mysterious, yet nonetheless effective "instinct" that allows him to swing around a tree, cause his double to misfire, and put an end to the duel—without violence.

What we must add now is that Conrad's hypothesis about the end of violence was a hypermimetic hypothesis that finds its source of inspiration in the plasticity of the human brain. Let us revisit the "inquiry" he urged us to pursue in light of this plastic hypothesis: "it may be an inquiry worth pursuing whether in reflective mankind the mechanical promptings of instinct are not affected by the customary mode of thought." And then he specifies: "an idea, defended and developed in many discussions, had settled into one of the stock notions of his brain, had become a part of his mental individuality" possibly going "so inconceivably deep as to affect the dictates of his instinct" (255). There is considerable theoretical potential in this line of inquiry that deserves to be traced to the end. Despite Conrad's awareness of the difficulty to break out from mirroring patterns of human violence, the conclusion of "The Duel" suggests that the plasticity of the brain offers a way out from the determinism of mirror neurons. If thoughts have been repeated in the mind, Conrad's inquiry suggests, they can change instincts, including violent instincts. How? By becoming inscribed in the "brain" and operating on an automatic, instinctual, and unconscious basis. You will have noticed that Conrad's inquiry breaks down the mind-brain, nature-nurture divide generating a transformative feedback loop, which is constitutive of the hypermimetic structure of plasticity. Thus, for Conrad, ideas, which used to be confined to the side of the mind (or culture), have the power to retroact on the plasticity of the brain (or nature) and reform characters so profoundly that they transform human instincts (or second nature). It is thus not a question of asking what the brain can do, but of asking what the mind can do to the brain, through the medium of the brain, in relation of unconscious communication with the brain. In short, for Conrad, the mind is not opposed to the brain, just as culture is not opposed to instinct. Rather, thoughts can change instincts; the mind can change the brain.

This is no minor hypothesis to venture at the dawn of the twentieth century. A century later, most scientists were still not quite ready for it. As Jeffrey Schwartz puts it in *The Mind and the Brain*: "Since I was arguing that the mind can change the brain, persuading the scientific community that I was right required that scientists accept an even more basic fact: that the adult brain can change at all."[25] Over time, however, brains do change, and new hypotheses reach receptive minds. The reality of neuroplasticity has in fact been repeatedly confirmed; the scientific community is now ready to accept it; and Conrad's inquiry is being widely pursued, informing not only neuroscientists but also philosophers, psychologists, historians, literary critics, stretching to the general public as well. Thus, bringing together a number of case studies from different areas of neuroplastic investigation, Norman Doidge, in *The Brain That Changes Itself*, reminds us "how truly integrated imagination and action are, despite the fact that we tend to think of imagination and action as completely different and subject to different rules," and concludes by saying that "our 'immaterial' thoughts have a physical signature."[26] This is a signature that, as Conrad traces with his incisive steel, has "gone so inconceivably deep as to affect the dictates of his instinct." Conrad called this an inquiry "worth pursuing." Doidge does not hesitate to call it "one of the most extraordinary discoveries of the twentieth century."[27] It is precisely this neurological possibility, which Conrad—an author deeply impressed, formed, and transformed by the experience of the plasticity of the human brain—read in light of mimetic theory, urged us to consider. This is just a final indication that the artist's appeal to his so-called less obvious capacities might still be worth considering, after all. As he diagnosed the patho(-)logical effects of plasticity in specific sociohistorical contexts, he would probably have specified that the brain does not "change itself." It is changed by culture.

.     ■     ■

This is a fictional happy ending, to be sure, but by ending "The Duel" Conrad also opens up new theoretical beginnings. His hypermimetic hypothesis not only looks back to the ancient lesson that literary fictions, if read closely, foreground new theoretical principles; it also looks through mirror neurons, toward neuroplasticity, in order to find alternative, nonviolent models to shape the still plastic behavior of the living and the unborn. Whether the humanities will be in a position to continue promoting cultural models, interdisciplinary reflections, and critical reevaluations to face the challenges future generations will have to face is something that remains to be seen. What we have seen is that reading and re-reading an impressively plastic writer like Conrad reminds us of the hypermimetic power of artistic shadows to contribute to original diagnostic reflections.

Over time, via education and other formative practices, different models might become customary one day—at least if we take it upon ourselves not only to inform the brains of future generations but also to form them and, perhaps, transform them. This plastic transformation is now certainly possible in theory. As for turning mimetic theory into practice, Conrad leaves it up to each one of us.

# Notes

## Introduction: The Secret Shadow

1. Plato, "Ion," in *The Collected Dialogues of Plato*, ed. Edith Hamilton and Huntington Cairns, tr. Lane Cooper et al. (Princeton, NJ: Princeton University Press, 1963), 215–28, 227. Eric Havelock calls mimesis the "most baffling of all words in [Plato's] vocabulary," and provides an informed account of its different meanings in Eric A. Havelock, *Preface to Plato* (Cambridge, MA: Harvard University Press, 1963), chap. 2.

2. Recent developments in "mimetic theory" have given new life to the ancient realization that man is a most thoroughly mimetic animal by confirming the centrality of behavioral imitation in the formation of subjectivity, desire, the unconscious, and the brain. On mimesis and desire, see René Girard, *Deceit, Desire, and the Novel*, tr. Yvonne Freccero (Baltimore: Johns Hopkins University Press, 1965); René Girard, *To Double Business Bound: Essays on Literature, Mimesis, and Anthropology* (Baltimore: Johns Hopkins University Press, 1978). On mimesis and the subject, see Mikkel Borch-Jacobsen, *The Emotional Tie: Psychoanalysis, Affect, Mimesis*, tr. Douglass Brick et al. (Stanford, CA: Stanford University Press, 1992); Philippe Lacoue-Labarthe, *Typography: Mimesis, Philosophy, Politics*, ed. Christopher Fynsk (Cambridge, MA: Harvard University Press, 1989). On mimesis and the unconscious, see Nidesh Lawtoo, *The Phantom of the Ego: Modernism and the Mimetic Unconscious* (East Lansing: Michigan State University Press, 2013). One mimesis and modernism, see William A. Johnson, *Violence and Modernism: Ibsen, Joyce, and Woolf* (Gainesville: University Press of Florida, 2003). On mimesis and the neurosciences, see Scott R. Garrels, ed., *Mimesis and Science: Empirical Research on Imitation and the Mimetic Theory of Culture and Religion* (East Lansing: Michigan State University Press, 2011). For general surveys of the protean ramifications of mimesis in contemporary theory, see Mihai Spariosu, ed., *Mimesis in Contemporary Theory: An Interdisciplinary Approach*, vol. 1, *The Literary and Philosophical Debate* (Philadelphia: John Benjamin Publishing Company, 1984); and Matthew Potolsky, *Mimesis* (London: Routledge, 2006). For an informed account of the history of mimesis as an "'impure'

concept," see Gunter Gebauer and Christopher Wulf, *Mimesis: Culture-Art-Society*, tr. Don Reneau (Berkeley: University of California Press, 1995).

3. See Nidesh Lawtoo, ed., *Conrad's* Heart of Darkness *and Contemporary Thought: Revisiting the Horror with Lacoue-Labarthe*, ed. Nidesh Lawtoo (London: Bloomsbury, 2013), chap. 4, 12; Lawtoo, *The Phantom of the Ego*, chap. 2.

4. Virginia Woolf, "Joseph Conrad," in *The Essays of Virginia Woolf*, vol. 4, *1925–1928*, ed. Andrew McNeillie (London: Hogarth Press, 1994), 227–33, 229.

5. Woolf, "Joseph Conrad," 229.

6. Albert Guerard, *Conrad the Novelist* (Cambridge, MA: Harvard University Press, 1958), 2; Zdzisław Najder, *Joseph Conrad: A Chronicle* (Cambridge: Cambridge University Press, 1983), xi; Cedric Watts, *A Preface to Conrad* (London: Longman, 1993), 7; Edward Said, *Joseph Conrad and the Fiction of Autobiography* (Cambridge, MA: Harvard University Press, 1966), 9; Ian Watt, *Conrad in the Nineteenth Century* (London: Chatto, 1980), 32; Geoffrey Galt Harpham, "Beyond Mastery: Future of Conrad's Beginnings," in *Conrad in the Twenty-First Century: Contemporary Approaches and Perspectives*, ed. Carola M. Kaplan, Peter Mallios, and Andrea White (New York: Routledge, 2005), 17–37, 19. For readers interested in the continuities between Conrad's life and his art, see Robert Hampson, *Conrad's Secrets* (London: Palgrave Macmillan, 2012). My Janus-faced focus on mimesis is not historical or biographical but hermeneutical and theoretical.

7. Guerard, *Conrad the Novelist*, 108.

8. See Lawtoo, *Phantom of the Ego*, chap. 2; Nidesh Lawtoo, ed., *Conrad's* Heart of Darkness *and Contemporary Thought*, chaps. 4, 12.

9. Friedrich Nietzsche, *Beyond Good and Evil: Prelude to a Philosophy of the Future*, tr. R. J. Hollingdale (London: Penguin Books, 2003), 192.

10. Cedric Watts, *Conrad's* Heart of Darkness: *A Critical and Contextual Discussion* (New York: Rodopi, 2012), ix. See also Watts, *Preface to Conrad*, 7–8, 114–18.

11. Harpham, *Beyond Mastery*, 20.

12. Girard, *Double Business Bound*, 36.

13. On the concept of mimetic "patho(-)logy," see Lawtoo, *Phantom of the Ego*, 3–8.

14. Marc Fumaroli, *Les abeilles et les araignées*, in *La querelle des Anciens et des Modernes*, ed. Anne-Marie Lecoq (Paris: Gallimard, 2001), 7–218, 37 (my translation).

15. Philippe Lacoue-Labarthe, *L'imitation des modernes (Typographie 2)* (Paris: Galilée, 1986), 282 (my translation).

16. The most influential discussion of mimesis as *pharmakon*, which had an impressive impact on mimetic theorists from Girard to Lacoue-Labarthe, is still Jacques Derrida's "Plato's Pharmacy," in *Dissemination*, tr. Barbara Johnson (Chicago: University of Chicago Press, 1981), 61–171.

17. Benjamin writes in his famous essay: "Nature creates similarities. One need only think of mimicry. The highest capacity for producing similarities, however, is man's. His gift of seeing resemblances is nothing other than a rudiment of the powerful compulsion in former times to become and behave like something else. Perhaps there is none of his higher functions in which his mimetic faculty does not play a decisive role." Walter Benjamin, "The Mimetic Faculty," in *Reflections: Essays Aphorisms, Autobiographical Writings*, tr. Edmund Jephcott, ed. Peter Demetz (New York:

Schocken Books, 1978), 333–36. This compulsion to become something else, Conrad might have added, continues to animate present times.

18. Vincent B. Leitch, *Literary Criticism in the 21st Century: Theory Renaissance* (London: Bloomsbury, 2014).

19. E. M. Forster, *Abinger Harvest* (London: Edward Arnold, 1936), 138; Guerard, *Conrad the Novelist*, 15; F. R. Leavis, *The Great Tradition: George Eliot, Henry James, Joseph Conrad* (New York: New York University Press, 1964), 177; Watt, *Conrad in the Nineteenth Century*, 169; Chinua Achebe, "An Image of Africa: Racism in Conrad's *Heart of Darkness*," in Joseph Conrad, *Heart of Darkness*, 4th ed., ed. Paul B. Armstrong (New York: Norton, 2006), 336–49, 343; Bronislaw Malinowski quoted in Christina A. Thompson, "Anthropology's Conrad: Malinowski's in the Tropics and What He Read," *The Journal of Pacific History* 30.1 (1995): 53–75, 68; Claude Lévi-Strauss and Didier Eribon, *Conversations with Claude Lévi-Strauss*, tr. Paula Wissing (Chicago: University of Chicago Press, 1991), 91; James Clifford, *The Predicament of Culture: Twentieth-Century Ethnography, Literature, and Art* (Cambridge, MA: Harvard University Press, 1988), 96; J. Hillis Miller, *Poets of Reality: Six Twentieth-Century Writers* (Cambridge, MA: Harvard University Press, 1965), 28; Fredric Jameson, *The Political Unconscious: Narrative as a Socially Symbolic Act* (Ithaca, NY: Cornell University Press, 1981); Terry Eagleton, *Exiles and Émigrés: Studies in Modern Literature* (New York: Schocken Books, 1970); Edward Said, *Culture and Imperialism* (New York: Vintage Books, 1994); Adriana Cavarero, *Horrorism: Naming Contemporary Violence*, tr. William McCuaig (New York: Columbia University Press, 2011), 116; Philippe Lacoue-Labarthe, "The Horror of The West," tr. Nidesh Lawtoo and Hannes Opelz, in Lawtoo, *Conrad's* Heart of Darkness *and Contemporary Thought*, 111–22, 111. For an exhaustive account of Conrad's critical reception, see John Peters, *Joseph Conrad's Critical Reception* (Cambridge: Cambridge University Press, 2013).

20. Carola M. Kaplan, Peter Mallios, and Andrea White, introduction to *Conrad in the Twenty-First Century*, xiii–xxii, xv; Lawtoo, *Conrad's* Heart of Darkness *and Contemporary Thought*, a collection that includes essays by prominent theorists such as J. Hillis Miller, Philippe Lacoue-Labarthe, Jonathan Dollimore, Henry Staten, and Avital Ronell.

21. Gebauer and Wulf, *Mimesis*, 2.

22. Girard, *Deceit, Desire, and the Novel*, 38.

23. Girard, *Double Business Bound*, ix.

24. In a pioneering article that brings Girard's mimetic theory in dialogue with Conrad's poetics, William Johnsen articulates a methodological principle that I fundamentally share: "The best way to keep company with Girard is to take up seriously his regard for the greatest writers as antecedents and fellow researchers of human behavior. If we simply 'apply' Girard, transcoding Conrad into Girardian terms, we have learned nothing more than Girard has already accomplished, and we have wasted Conrad." William A. Johnsen, "'To My Readers of America': Conrad's 1914 Preface to *The Nigger of the 'Narcissus*,'" *Conradiana* 35.1–2 (2003): 105–22, 106.

25. Philippe Lacoue-Labarthe, "The Response of Ulysses," in *Who Comes after the Subject*, ed. Eduardo Cadava, Peter Connor, and Jean-Luc Nancy (New York: Routledge, 1991), 198–205, 198.

26. Philippe Lacoue-Labarthe, *La Réponse d'Ulysse: Et autres textes sur L'Occident*, ed. Aristide Bianchi and Leonid Kharlamov (Lignes/Imec, 2012), 21 (my translation).

27. J. Hillis Miller, foreword to Kaplan, Mallios, and White, *Conrad in the Twenty-First Century*, 1–14, 2.

28. This tendency to dismiss the environment as simple background can be traced back to early commentators like F. R. Leavis, who considered images of "exotic seas and the last plunge of flaming wrecks" as material for "compliers of Prose anthologies." Leavis, *Great Tradition*, 188.

29. Paul J. Crutzen and Eugene F. Stoermer, "The Anthropocene," *IGBP [International Geosphere-Biosphere Programme] Newsletter* 41 (2000): 18. See also Dipesh Chakrabarty, "The Climate of History: Four Theses," *Critical Inquiry* 35.2 (2009): 197–222.

30. Michel Serres, *The Natural Contract*, tr. Elizabeth MacArthur and William Paulson (Ann Arbor: University of Michigan Press, 1995), 31.

31. Jane Bennett, *Vibrant Matter: A Political Ecology of Things* (Durham, NC: Duke University Press, 2010), 14. I am very grateful to Jane for numerous stimulating conversations during my stay at Hopkins. Her vibrant receptivity to mimetic matters and the sympathy that animates it created Promethean bonds of solidarity vital for my Conradian navigations.

32. Jean-Pierre Dupuy, *The Mark of the Sacred*, tr. M. B. Debevoise (Stanford, CA: Stanford University Press, 2013), 33.

33. Dupuy, *Mark of the Sacred*, 47.

34. René Girard, *Battling to the End: Conversations with Benoît Chantre*, tr. Mary Baker (East Lansing: Michigan State University Press, 2010), xiv.

35. In a section of *Beyond Good and Evil* titled "On the Prejudices of Philosophers," Nietzsche sides with the artist, contra the philosopher, as he argues that "a higher and more fundamental value for all life might have to be ascribed to appearances." Nietzsche, *Beyond Good and Evil*, 34.

36. Borch-Jacobsen, *Emotional Tie*, 16; Lawtoo, *Phantom of the Ego*, 282. On psychoanalysis and the mimetic/hypnotic subject, see Mikkel Borch-Jacobsen, *The Freudian Subject*, tr. Catherine Porter (Stanford, CA: Stanford University Press, 1988). On the origins of this genealogical connection between mimetic theory and psychoanalysis, see René Girard, *Violence and the Sacred*, tr. Patrick Gregory (Baltimore: Johns Hopkins University Press, 1977), chap. 7; Philippe Lacoue-Labarthe and Jean-Luc Nancy, "The Unconscious Is Destructed Like an Affect (Part I of The Jewish People Do Not Dream)," *Stanford Literature Review* 6.2 (1989): 191–209; Philippe Lacoue-Labarthe and Jean-Luc Nancy, "From Where Is Psychoanalysis Possible (Part II of The Jewish People Do Not Dream)," *Stanford Literature Review* 8.1–2 (1991): 19–55.

37. Deleuze and Guattari put it aptly in their sequel to *Anti-Oedipus*, *A Thousand Plateaus*, as they write: "Freud tried to approach crowd phenomena from the point of view of the unconscious, but he did not see clearly, he did not see that the unconscious itself was fundamentally a crowd." Gilles Deleuze and Félix Guattari, *A Thousand Plateaus: Capitalism and Schizophrenia*, tr. Brian Massumi (London: Continuum, 2004), 33. Conrad, not less than other modernists on which Deleuze and Guattari rely (such as D. H. Lawrence), will help Freud(ians) see more clearly on this point.

38. Miller, foreword to Kaplan, Mallios, and White, *Conrad in the Twenty-First Century*, 6.

39. Roger Caillois, "Mimétisme et Psychasthenie légendaire," in *Le Mythe et l'homme* (Paris: Gallimard, 1938), 86–122.

40. Peters, *Conrad's Critical Reception*, 245.

## Chapter 1. Dueling to the End/Ending "The Duel": Clausewitz *avec* Girard

1. Carl von Clausewitz, *Vom Kriege* (Bonn: Dummler, 1973); Carl von Clausewitz, *On War*, tr. Michael Howard and Peter Paret (Oxford: Oxford University Press, 2008).

2. René Girard, *Achever Clausewitz: Entretiens avec Benoît Chantre* (Paris: Carnet Nord, 2007); René Girard, *Battling to the End: Conversations with Benoît Chantre*, tr. Mary Baker (East Lansing: Michigan State University Press, 2010).

3. Noam Chomsky reminds us that "nuclear war has come unpleasantly close many times since 1945." And he adds: "That's a low-probability event, but with low-probability events over a long period, the probability is not low." Noam Chomsky and Laray Polok, *Nuclear War and Environmental Catastrophe* (New York: Seven Stories Press, 2013), 41–42. Philosophers and theorists as diverse as Jean-Pierre Dupuy, William E. Connolly, and Jean-Luc Nancy, among others, have confirmed this point.

4. Conrad writes in the "Author's Note" that the story found its source of inspiration in a newspaper article about "two officers in Napoleon's Grand Army having fought a series of duels in the midst of great wars and on some futile pretext" (x). On the historical sources of Conrad's "The Duel," see J. H. Stape, "Conrad's 'The Duel': A Reconsideration," *The Conradian* 11.1 (1986): 42–46.

5. For a contextualization of Conrad's tale within fictions of the duels, see Jeffrey Meyers, "The Duel in Fiction," *North Dakota Quarterly* 51.4 (1983): 129–50.

6. John Herdman defines the doppelgänger as "a second self, or alter ego, which appears as a distinct and separate being apprehensible by the physical senses (or at least, by some of them), but exists in a dependent relation to the original." John Herdman, *The Double in Nineteenth-Century Fiction* (London: Macmillan, 1990), 14. More recently, Dimitris Vardoulakis reframes this romantic trope from a philosophical perspective that emphasizes resistance to presence, decentering, relationality, and transformation along lines that mimic poststructuralist critiques of the subject. See Dimitris Vardoulakis, *The Doppelgänger: Literature's Philosophy* (New York: Fordham University Press, 2010). My approach supplements such literary, philosophical perspectives by reinscribing the doppelgänger in a wider, interdisciplinary mimetic tradition that accounts for such immanent transformations in the first place. In so doing, it multiplies the protean meanings of the double by establishing new bridges with theories of war, catastrophe, rituals, and other areas of investigation.

7. What René Girard says of doubles in general applies to Conrad's characters in particular: "*from the inside you must always believe in your difference*, and respond more and more quickly and forcefully. From the outside, the adversaries look like what they are: simple doubles" (*BE* 14). Jacques Derrida makes a similar point in his account of the *pharmakon*: "In distinguishing himself from his opposite, Toth also imitates it, becomes its sign and representative, obeys it and conforms to it, replaces it, by violence if need be." Jacques Derrida, "Plato's Pharmacy," in *Dissemination*, tr. Barbara Johnson (Chicago: University of Chicago Press, 1981), 93. As the sociologist Gabriel Tarde had already realized, roughly at the same time as Conrad: "There are two modalities of imitation: doing all the model does or doing the exact opposite." Gabriel Tarde, *Les lois de l'imitation* (Paris: Seuil, 2001), 49 (my translation). On Tarde's illuminating comparison of a logical fight with a duel, see also 213–31.

8. Meyers, "Duel in Fiction," 130.

9. René Girard, *Violence and the Sacred*, tr. Patrick Gregory (Baltimore: Johns Hopkins University Press, 1977), 8 (trans. modified).

10. What Deleuze and Guattari say of Kleist's take on the war machine equally applies to Conrad's: "feelings become uprooted from the interiority of a 'subject,' to be projected violently into a milieu

of pure exteriority that lends them an incredible velocity, a catapulting force: love or hate, they are no longer feelings but affects. . . . Affects transpierce the body like arrows, they are weapons of war." Gilles Deleuze and Félix Guattari, *A Thousand Plateaus: Capitalism and Schizophrenia*, tr. Brian Massumi (London: Continuum, 2004), 392–93. On the distinction between "emotion" as based on "subjective content" and "affect" as "unqualified" pre-subjective force, see also Brian Massumi, *Parables for the Virtual: Movement, Affect, Sensation* (Durham, NC: Duke University Press, 2002), 28. What contemporary theorists of Deleuzian inspiration group under the category of affect, a Nietzschean tradition of thought considered this capacity to be affected in terms of the Greek concept of *pathos*: "The will to power not a being, not a becoming but a pathos—the most elemental fact from which a becoming and effecting first emerges." Friedrich Nietzsche, *The Will to Power*, tr. Walter Kaufmann and R. J. Hollingdale (New York: Vintage Books, 1968), 339.

11. Along similar lines, Clausewitz writes: "If he [the enemy] were to seek the decision through a major battle, *his choice would force us against our will to do likewise*" (*OW* 41).

12. As Raymond Aron also recognized, for Clausewitz, "passion and reason (*Vernunft*) are not opposed. It is passion that provokes the escalation of violence to extremes and, in the same stroke, bestows upon it its internal unity, its necessity, and its pure form." Raymond Aron, *Sur Clausewitz* (Paris: Editions Complexe, 1987), 59–60 (my translation).

13. Aron, *Sur Clausewitz*, 34.

14. Among different emotions central to the art of war, Clausewitz specifies that none "is so powerful and so constant as the longing for honour and renown"—what he also calls "the essential breath of life that animates the inert mass" (*OW* 50).

15. See Nidesh Lawtoo, *The Phantom of the Ego: Modernism and the Mimetic Unconscious* (East Lansing: Michigan State University Press, 2013), 52–68.

16. See Andrew Meltzoff and Keith Moore, "Persons and Representation: Why Infant Imitation Is Important for Theories of Human Development," in *Imitation in Infancy*, ed. Jacqueline Nadel and George Butterworth (Cambridge: Cambridge University Press, 1999), 9–35.

17. Marco Iacoboni, *Mirroring People: The New Science of How We Connect with Others* (New York: Farrar, Straus and Giroux, 2008), 146.

18. Iacoboni, *Mirroring People*, 258.

19. For a collection of essays that initiates a productive dialogue between the neurosciences and mimetic theory, see Scott R. Garrels, ed., *Mimesis and Science: Empirical Research on Imitation and the Mimetic Theory of Culture and Religion* (East Lansing: Michigan State University Press, 2011).

20. Giacomo Rizzolatti and Corrado Sinigaglia, *Mirrors in the Brain: How Our Minds Share Actions and Emotions*, tr. Frances Anderson (Oxford: Oxford University Press, 2008), 124.

21. Girard's idea of escalation to extremes predates his reading of Clausewitz. See, for instance, Girard, *Violence and the Sacred*, 27; René Girard, *To Double Business Bound: Essays on Literature, Mimesis, and Anthropology* (Baltimore: Johns Hopkins University Press, 1978), 201, 204, 227.

22. As the historian Christopher Bassford also recognized, for Clausewitz, "reality (experience) always took precedence over the kind of abstract 'truth' that can be transmitted by mere writing." Christopher Bassford, *Clausewitz in English: The Reception of Clausewitz in Britain and America* (Oxford: Oxford University Press, 1994), 11. Similarly, writing in the midst of the Cold War, Raymond Aron acknowledges that "in our times, the escalation to extremes means the escalation toward nuclear threat," but specifies that "this threat was never executed" insofar as politics

managed to contain this escalation. Aron, *Sur Clausewitz*, 106, 111. See also Raymond Aron, *Penser la guerre, Clausewitz*, vols. 1 and 2 (Paris: Gallimard, 1976), esp. vol. 2, part 2, "L'Age Nucléair."

23. As Nietzsche diagnoses: "The strength of one who attacks has in the opposition he needs a kind of *gauge*; every growth reveals itself in the seeking out of a powerful opponent: for a philosopher who is warlike also challenges problems to a duel." Friedrich Nietzsche, *Ecce Homo*, tr. R. J. Hollingdale (New York: Penguin Books, 1980), 47.

24. As Daphna Erdinast-Vulcan recognized, "unlike Dostoevsky, whose work, even at its most polyphonic, ultimately bows down before the need for the Word, Conrad is already far beyond the consolations of metaphysics." Daphna Erdinast-Vulcan, *The Strange Short Fiction of Joseph Conrad: Writing, Culture, and Subjectivity* (Oxford: Oxford University Press, 1999), 16.

25. Girard helped organize the famous 1966 conferences at Johns Hopkins University that sparked interest in (post-)structuralism in general, and Derrida in particular, in the United States. See Richard Macksey and Eugenio Donato, eds., *The Structuralist Controversy* (Baltimore: Johns Hopkins University Press, 1970). I'm grateful to Dick Macksey for sharing his memories of this legendary conference in his impressive home library close to Homewood Campus.

26. Derrida, "Plato's Pharmacy," 70.

27. See Lawtoo, *Phantom of the Ego*, 8–12, chap. 1.

28. In "Plato's Pharmacy," Derrida offers the following definition of the *pharmakos*: "The character of the *pharmakos* has been compared to a scapegoat. The *evil* and the *outside*, the expulsion of the evil, its exclusion out of the body (and out of) the city—these are the two major senses of the character of the ritual" (130). A lengthy footnote follows where Derrida relies on the work of James Frazer, Jane Harrison, and other anthropologists in order to stress the "necessity of bringing together the figures of Oedipus and the *pharmakos*" in a discourse that "is not in a strict sense a psychoanalytical one" (130–31n56). In a subsequent note, Derrida makes the link with literature explicit as he says: "In his *Anatomy of Criticism* (New York: Atheneum, 1970), Northrop Frye sees in the figure of the pharmakos a permanent archetypal structure in Western literature. The exclusion of the pharmakos, who is, says Frye, 'neither innocent nor guilty' (41), is repeated from Aristophanes to Shakespeare" (132n59). Indeed, if one is looking for the hidden "origins" of Girard's mimetic theory, one could do worse than pointing to "Plato's Pharmacy" in general and pages 130–32 in particular. Girard's theory of the scapegoat qua pharmakos, his emphasis on a dual literary/anthropological tradition, his reliance on the model of Oedipus, his instance that his reading of Oedipus is not a psychoanalytical one, the privilege accorded to literary figures from Sophocles to Shakespeare, and so forth are neatly summed up there. On the continuities between deconstruction and mimetic theory, see also Andrew McKenna, *Violence and Difference: Girard, Derrida, and Deconstruction* (Urbana: University of Illinois Press, 1991).

29. Sun Tzu, *The Art of War*, tr. Yuan Shibing (Ware, UK: Wordsworth Editions, 1998), 25. On the differences between the Chinese art of war and Clausewitz's Western principles, see François Jullien, *Traité de l'efficacité* (Paris: Grasset, 1996), 24–36.

30. In a section devoted to the "frictions" characteristic of real war, Clausewitz draws the following analogy: "As with a man of the world instinct becomes almost habit so that he always acts, speaks, and moves appropriately, so only the experienced officer will make the right decision in major and minor matters—at every pulse-beat of war" (*OW* 67–68).

31. It may be an inquiry worth pursuing whether Jim's infamous leap from the *Patna* at the opening of *Lord Jim*, which occurs despite his heroic representation of himself "saving people from sinking

ships, cutting away masts in a hurricane" (*LJ* 11), is an example of the mind's inability to shape certain deep-seated instincts such as fear or panic in catastrophic scenarios. I will return to this.

32. As Socrates famously asks in Book III of *Republic*, "have you not observed that imitations, if continued from youth far into life, settle down into habits and second nature in the body, the speech, and the thought?" Plato, *Republic*, in *The Collected Dialogues of Plato*, ed. E. Hamilton and H. Cairns (New York: Pantheon Books), 575–844, 640.

33. In his discussion of children's education (*paidea*) in Book II of *Republic*, Socrates says: "Do you know, then, that the beginning in every task is the chief thing, especially for any creature that is young and tender? For it is then that it is best molded and takes the impression that one wishes to stamp upon it" (*R* 624). For an impressive philosophical commentary of this book of *Republic*, see Philippe Lacoue-Labarthe, *Typography: Mimesis, Philosophy, Politics*, ed. Christopher Fynsk (Cambridge, MA: Harvard University Press, 1989), 43–138.

34. William James, *Psychology: The Briefer Course*, ed. Gordon Allport (Notre Dame, IN: University of Notre Dame, 1985), 11. See also chap. 1.

## Chapter 2. Ethical Storms: *Typhoon* to "The Secret Sharer"

1. Friedrich Nietzsche, *Beyond Good and Evil: Prelude to a Philosophy of the Future*, tr. R. J. Hollingdale (London: Penguin Books, 2003), 71.

2. Stephen Gardiner, *A Perfect Moral Storm: The Ethical Tragedy of Climate Change* (Oxford: Oxford University Press, 2011), 7.

3. Al Gore, *An Inconvenient Truth*, directed by Davis Guggenheim, 2006. For a pioneering account of the fragility of the environment, see Michel Serres, *The Natural Contract*, tr. Elizabeth MacArthur and William Paulson (Ann Arbor: University of Michigan Press, 1995), 40–41. For more recent, materialist turns to the fragility of the environment and the power of human and nonhuman agency, see especially William Connolly, *The Fragility of Things: Self-Organizing Processes, Neoliberal Fantasies, and Democratic Activism* (Durham, NC: Duke University Press, 2013); Jane Bennett, *Vibrant Matter: A Political Ecology of Things* (Durham, NC: Duke University Press, 2010).

4. See also Joseph Conrad, "Some Reflections on the Loss of the *Titanic*" and "Certain Aspects of the Admirable Inquiry into the Loss of the *Titanic*" (*NLL* 213–28, 229–48).

5. The tendency to focus on the individual, the couple, or the nuclear family in contemporary disaster films is symptomatic of a culture that has lost the capacity to think about the communal and thus shared implications of global catastrophe. Conrad's tales provide a communal supplement to this individualistic perspective.

6. In Plato's foundational account of the state qua ship in *Republic*, the shipmaster in possession of the art of sailing (read the philosopher) is a victim of the sailors' irrational and violent behavior (read politicians). Thus Socrates says that sometimes frenzied sailors run amok "put the others to death or cast them out from the ship, and then, after binding and stupefying the worthy shipmaster with mandragora or intoxication or otherwise, they take command of the ship, consume its stores and, drinking and feasting, make such a voyage as it is to be expected." Plato, *Republic*, in *The Collected Dialogues of Plato*, ed. E. Hamilton and H. Cairns (New York: Pantheon Books, 1963), 575–844, 725.

7. Echoing Plato, Serres continues: "Since the remotest antiquity, sailors (and doubtless they alone) have been familiar with the proximity and connection between subjective wars and objective

violence, because they know that, if they come to fight among themselves, they will condemn their craft to shipwreck before they can defeat their internal adversary. They get the social contract directly from nature." Serres, *Natural Contract*, 40.

8. For an account of the reception of "The Secret Sharer" in the twentieth century, see Daniel R. Schwarz, "A Critical History of 'The Secret Sharer,'" in *The Secret Sharer: Case Studies in Contemporary Criticism*, ed. Daniel R. Schwarz (Boston: Bedford Books, 1997), 63–78.

9. Dipesh Chakrabarty, "The Climate of History: Four Theses," *Critical Inquiry* 35.2 (2009): 218.

10. As I write this chapter, the arrest of the captain of the tragic case of the MV *Sewol*, a South Korean ferry that capsized in April 2014 with mostly secondary school children on board, is currently under way; one could mention a number of examples of captains who have jumped. More important than the moral, mass-mediatized condemnation of the jump itself (a condemnation obviously justified but easy with a solid pavement under one's feet, Marlow would say) is Conrad's analysis of the complex ecology of action whereby environmental and human factors contribute to generating such catastrophes—understanding such ecology would be a first step to avoid such horrors in the future.

11. Thinking of the *Odyssey* but with Conrad not too far from his preoccupations, Lacoue-Labarthe specifies that the term "experience is a nautical term": "ex-perience: to traverse, in the maritime sense of a sea passage [*traversée maritime*]." Philippe Lacoue-Labarthe, *La Réponse d'Ulysse: Et autres textes sur L'Occident,* ed. Aristide Bianchi and Leonid Kharlamov (Lignes/Imec, 2012), 110 (my translation).

12. See Hunt Hawkins and Brian W. Shaffer, eds., *Approaches to Teaching Conrad's "Heart of Darkness" and "The Secret Sharer"* (New York: Modern Language Association of America, 2002); Schwarz, *The Secret Sharer*. On the biographical and historical sources of this tale, see the introduction to the Cambridge edition of *TLS*, xxxiii–xlii.

13. J. Hillis Miller, "Sharing Secrets," in Schwarz, *The Secret Sharer*, 232–52, 249.

14. Albert Guerard, *Conrad the Novelist* (Cambridge, MA: Harvard University Press, 1958), 22.

15. Cedric Watts, *The Deceptive Text: An Introduction to Cover Plots* (Sussex, UK: Harvester Press, 1984), 88.

16. Connolly, *Fragility of Things*, 13. I am very grateful to Bill for our ritual Wednesday conversations at Hopkins in the fall of 2015, and for inviting me to present my recent work on Conrad in a terrific course on left-Nietzschean in the Anthropocene—*agencements* that continue to generate life-affirmative entanglements.

17. Louis H. Leiter, "Echo Structures: Conrad's 'The Secret Sharer,'" *Twentieth Century Literature* 5.4 (1960): 159–75.

18. Guerard's claims that "The Secret Sharer" "is Conrad's most successful experiment by far with the method of nonretrospective first person narration," and proceeds to say that the "nominal past is, actually, a harrowing present which the reader too must explore and survive." Guerard, *Conrad the Novelist*, 27. This is a narrative possibility that held sway in the past but should be corrected for the future. In fact, it is only if we consider the retrospective temporal dimension secretly at play in this nominal past that the catastrophic symbolism informing the tale as a whole can be fully illuminated.

19. Cedric Watts, "The Mirror-Tale: An Ethico Structural' Analysis of Conrad's 'The Secret Sharer,'" *Critical Quarterly* 19.3 (1977): 25–37, 31.

20. Fredric Jameson recognized that "the intergalactic spaceship is . . . an avatar of Conrad's merchant vessel." Fredric Jameson, *The Political Unconscious: Narrative as a Socially Symbolic Act* (Ithaca, NY: Cornell University Press, 1981), 218. For a Conradian reading of such futuristic avatars, see Nidesh Lawtoo, "*Avatar* Simulation in 3Ts: Techne, Trance, Transformation," *Science Fiction Studies* 125.42 (2015): 132–50.

21. As Srinivas Aravamudan puts it, "catachronism re-characterizes the past and the present in terms of a future proclaimed as determinate but that is of course not fully realized." Srinivas Aravamudan, "The Catachronism of Climate Change," *Diacritics* 41.3 (2013): 6–31, 8.

22. Connolly, *The Fragility of Things,* 7.

23. Alan Weisman, *The World without Us* (New York: St. Martin's Press, 2007), 3.

24. Jean-Pierre Dupuy, *The Mark of the Sacred*, tr. M. B. Debevoise (Stanford, CA: Stanford University Press, 2013), 33. See also Jean-Pierre Dupuy, *Pour un catastrophisme éclairé: Quand l'impossible est certain* (Paris: Seuil, 2002).

25. Dupuy, *Mark of the Sacred*, 47.

26. Daniel Curley, "The Writer and His Use of Material: The Case of 'The Secret Sharer,'" *Modern Fiction Studies* 13.2 (1967): 179–94, 179.

27. Bennett, *Vibrant Matter*, 38, 14.

28. Nancy adds: "Whereas, from the beginning of humanity onwards, we have had an ordered world, configured around its regimes, its hierarchies, its roles, we now see the unfolding of what is more than a simple transformation: a generalized transformability that does not offer the unity of a principle or law of transformation but, rather, keeps changing, diversifying the modalities, directions, causalities of every form of transformation, transposition, or transmutation." Jean-Luc Nancy, *L'Équivalence des catastrophes (Après Fukushima)* (Paris: Galilée, 2012), 48 (my translation).

29. Malcom Bull writes that an ethics of catastrophe "is not morality applied but morality discovered, a new chapter in the moral education of mankind." And he adds: this new chapter "may tell us things we do not wish to know (about democracy perhaps), but the future development of humanity may depend on what, if anything, it can teach us." Malcom Bull, "What Is the Rational Response?," *London Review of Books* 34.10 (2012): 6.

30. Guerard, *Conrad the Novelist,* 23.

31. Miller, "Sharing Secrets," 233.

32. As Steve Ressler also stresses, "there is for a captain a critical area of initiative and personal decision beyond rulebook procedure and conventional thinking." Steve Ressler, "Conrad's 'The Secret Sharer': Affirmation of Action," *Conradiana* 16.3 (1984): 195–214, 203. For a historical account of "maritime ethics" that complicates neat distinctions between "just" and "unjust" actions, see Eugene Davis, "The Structure of Justice in 'The Secret Sharer,'" *Conradiana* 27.1 (1995): 64–73.

33. The French sociologist Edgar Morin uses the term "ecology of action" to designate the fact that "every human action, from the moment that is undertaken, escapes the control of its initiator and enters a game of complex interactions that can deviate from its goal and, at times, give it a destination that is opposed to the original intention." Hence Morin specifies that "the consequences of an act with moral intention can be immoral. Conversely, the consequences of an

immoral act can be moral." Edgar Morin, *La méthode 6: Éthique* (Paris: Seuil 2004), 89, 45 (my translation).

34. Gregory Bateson, *Steps to an Ecology of Mind: A Revolutionary Approach to Man's Understanding of Himself* (New York: Ballantine Books, 1972), 438.

35. René Girard, *Violence and the Sacred*, tr. Patrick Gregory (Baltimore: Johns Hopkins University Press, 1977), 77. An orthodox Girardian reading might want to consider Leggatt's murder in terms of a "sacrificial crisis" that discharges violence on an innocent "scapegoat." While this structure is evocative, especially in light of the biblical allusions in the tale, the driving telos of Conrad's narrative does not follow this pattern *à la lettre*. The differences are numerous and fundamental: it is "panic" and "madness" rather than violence that are contagious; the crew resists rather than triggers Leggatt's violence; the victim is not innocent but "crazed"; Leggatt's action is not irrational but informed by a sense of "duty"; and so forth. In such narrative choices, Conrad supplements mimetic theory from the new angle of an ethics of catastrophe.

36. Adriana Cavarero, *Horrorism: Naming Contemporary Violence*, tr. William McCuaig (New York: Columbia University Press, 2011), 5.

37. Jean-Pirre Dupuy, *La Panique* (Paris: Seuil, 1991), 20–22.

38. Jean-Luc Nancy and Philippe Lacoue-Labarthe, "La Panique Politique," in *Retreating the Political*, ed. Simon Sparks (New York: Routledge, 1977), 1–28.

39. Marjorie Garber and Barbara Johnson, "Secret Sharing: Reading Conrad Psychoanalytically," *College English* 49.6 (1987): 628–40, 631.

40. Sigmund Freud, *Group Psychology and the Analysis of the Ego*, tr. James Strachey (New York: W. W. Norton, 1959). I have discussed Freud's model of the social bond in detail in Nidesh Lawtoo, *The Phantom of the Ego: Modernism and the Mimetic Unconscious* (East Lansing: Michigan State University Press, 2013), 233–47.

41. Conrad is consistent on this point. Thus in *Lord Jim* the very character who fails to live up to such ethical standards also says: "'Eight hundred living people, and they were yelling after the one dead man to come down and be saved'" (*LJ* 87). Compare this claim to Jean-Pierre Dupuy's recent account of consequentialist ethics: "The aim is to increase good and diminish evil *globally* in the world. Consequently, it so happens that in exceptional cases, which constitute a dilemma for ethical reflection, the maximization of global good, prescribes a transgression of moral prohibitions." And he specifies: "What if, by killing an innocent, I avoid that other twenty-two innocents are killed? If I really think that the murder of an innocent is an abominable action, then the prohibition of murder, in this case, appears contrary to reason." Hence he concludes: "Traditional morality (Christian, Kantian, deontological) seems guilty of irrationalism." Dupuy, *Pour un catastrophisme*, 42 (my translation).

42. Lacoue-Labarthe, *Réponse d'Ulysse*, 21.

43. Jean Luc Nancy, *Being Singular Plural*, tr. Robert D. Richardson (Stanford, CA: Stanford University Press, 2000), 29.

44. Emmanuel Levinas, *Autrement qu'être ou au delà de l'essence* (Paris: Seuil, 1990), 46, 111 (my translation). Levinas claims, for instance, that "the responsibility for the Other [*Autri*] ... orders me to the other, to the first person who comes, and renders him near to me, renders him my neighbor [*m'approche de lui, me le rend prochain*]." This other may be a stranger or even a "persecutor," an embodiment of what Levinas qualifies in terms of "anarchic passivity," but his ethical address is irrevocable. Above all, for Levinas, it is the "vulnerability of the other"

rendered visible by the "face" addressing me, a vulnerable surface he defines in terms of nakedness: "denudation of denudation, . . . expression of exposition—hyperbole of a passivity that disturbs dormant waters [*dénudation de la dénudation, . . . expression de l'exposition—hyperbole de la passivité qui dérange l'eau qui dort*]." Levinas, *Autrement qu'être,* 26, 83. This passage could be taken as a critical commentary of "The Secret Sharer."

45. This presence of the other at the very heart of the self is by no means reassuring. Levinas thinks of it in terms of hostage and possession that have the most disquieting psychic consequences: these generate an anxious psychological state he qualifies as "insomnia"; it is akin to "madness" and is responsible for the rupture of identity and the suspension of being in what he calls a "*non-lieu de la subjectivté.*" Levinas, *Autrement qu'être,* 104, 85, 24.

46. Levinas, *Autrement qu'être,* 85.

47. Nancy's account of the "primal, ontological condition of being with or being-together" based on the principles of "sharing [*partage*]" is especially suggestive in this respect. See Nancy, *Being Singular Plural,* 28–41.

48. Jacques Lacan, "Le Stade du miroir comme formateur de la function du Je," in *Écrits* (Paris: Seuil, 1966), 89–97.

49. Miller, "Sharing Secrets," 233.

50. Gabriel Tarde, *Les lois de l'imitation* (Paris: Seuil, 2001), 157 (my translation).

51. Gilles Deleuze and Félix Guattari, *A Thousand Plateaus: Capitalism and Schizophrenia,* tr. Brian Massumi (London: Continuum, 2004), 241. Deleuze and Guattari are very critical of mimesis understood in its stabilizing function of visual representation (for it promotes a transcendental ontology of Being); and yet as heirs of Nietzsche and Tarde, they are very receptive to mimetic experiences understood in their deterritorializing function of affective contagion (for it generates an immanent ontology of becoming). Given that Conrad's take on mimesis extends this Nietzschean and Tardian line of flight from an anti-Oedipal perspective attentive to intersubjectivity, collective states, multilingualism, and processes of becoming that cut across the human/nonhuman divide, he lends support to this minor fictional/theoretical tradition.

52. Vittorio Gallese, "The Two Sides of Mimesis: Mimetic Theory, Embodied Simulation, and Social Identification," in *Mimesis and Science: Empirical Research on Imitation and the Mimetic Theory of Culture and Religion,* ed. Scott R. Garrels (East Lansing: Michigan State University Press, 2011), 87–108, 95. For mirroring reflex in newborns, see Andrew N. Meltzoff, "Out of the Mouths of Babes: Imitation, Gaze, and Intentions in Infant Research—the 'Like Me' Framework," in Garrels, *Mimesis and Science* 55–74.

53. Gallese, "Two Sides of Mimesis," 97.

54. Lawtoo, *Phantom of the Ego,* 274–80.

55. Gallese, "Two Sides of Mimesis," 97.

56. Jean-Luc Nancy, *The Inoperative Community,* tr. Peter Connor (Minneapolis: University of Minnesota Press, 1991), 29.

57. Nietzsche, *Beyond Good and Evil,* 70 (trans. modified).

## Chapter 3. The Cooperative Community: Surviving Epidemics
## in *The Shadow-Line*

1. For Girard, "an analysis of significant texts . . . reveals definite analogies between the plague, or rather all great epidemics, and social phenomena." René Girard, "The Plague in Literature and Myth," in *To Double Business Bound: Essays on Literature, Mimesis, and Anthropology* (Baltimore: Johns Hopkins University Press, 1978), 136–54, 138.

2. Girard writes that contagious epidemics work as a "transparent metaphor for a certain reciprocal violence that spreads, literally, like the plague." Later, he specifies that "the properly medical aspects of the plague never were essential; in themselves they always played a minor role, serving mostly as disguise for an even more terrible threat no science has ever been able to conquer [that is, mimetic violence]." Girard, "Plague," 139, 148.

3. Girard, "Plague," 148.

4. As his comments on the spread of bird flu H5N1 indicate, Girard no longer maintains the purely metaphorical interpretation of the plague but takes it quite literally as he says that this "is a pandemic that could cause hundreds of thousands of deaths in a few days and is a phenomenon typical of the undifferentiation now coursing across the planet." René Girard, *Battling to the End: Conversations with Benoît Chantre*, tr. Mary Baker (East Lansing: Michigan State University Press, 2010), 24.

5. Laurie Garrett, *The Coming Plague: Newly Emerging Diseases in a World Out of Balance* (London: Penguin, 1995). See also Bruce Magnusson and Zahi Zalloua, eds., *Contagion: Health, Fear, Sovereignty* (Seattle: University of Washington Press, 2012).

6. Bruce Magnusson and Zahi Zalloua write that "over many decades, contagion has been a metaphor of choice for everything from global terrorism, suicide bombings, poverty, immigration, global financial crises." The goal of their collection is to interrogate "what happens to the concept of contagion when it exceeds its original epidemiological context and starts contaminating other discourses in the social sciences and the humanities?" Bruce Magnusson and Zahi Zalloua, "The Hydra of Contagion," in Magnusson and Zalloua, *Contagion*, 3–24, 4.

7. Ian Watt influentially framed Conrad's narrative trajectory in literary history as follows: "Old-fashioned because Conrad's movement towards the ageless solidarities of human experience was much commoner among the Romantics and Victorians. But the first half of his life had forced Conrad to see that his problematic dependence on others was a necessary condition for the very existence of the individual self; and so during the second half of his life his imagination was impelled, in many different ways, to confront a more contemporary question, and one which was not to be of any particular concern to the other great figures of modern literature: 'Alienation, of course; but how do we get out of it'"? Ian Watt, *Conrad in the Nineteenth Century* (London: Chatto, 1980), 33. This dependency on others, as we turn to see, is accentuated as Conrad confronts an even more contemporary and, perhaps, less anthropocentric question: Catastrophe, of course; but how do we survive it?

8. Carl Benson, "Two Stories of Initiation," *PMLA* 69.1 (1954): 46–56, 46. See also Barbara Handke, *First Command: A Psychological Reading of Joseph Conrad's "The Secret Sharer" and* The Shadow-Line (Berlin: Galda Verlag, 2010).

9. See Mike Davis, *The Monster at Our Door: The Global Threat of Avian Flu* (New York: Owl Books, 2005) 124–25.

10. Knowles's introductory essay provides an informed historical reframing of "catastrophic effects of

the war throughout Europe" on Conrad's creative imagination. Owen Knowles, "Introduction," *SL* xxvi, xviii; see also xxvi–xxxv.

11. Martin Bock, "Joseph Conrad and Germ Theory: Why Captain Allistoun Smiles Thoughtfully," *The Conradian* 31.2 (2006): 1–14.

12. This is a lesson that is as old as Heraclitus, yet has tended to escape acute psychological readers of Conrad who consider the tales as "truly analogous." Albert Guerard, *Conrad the Novelist* (Cambridge, MA: Harvard University Press, 1958), 30.

13. Martin Bock reminds us that "malaria was thought at the time to inhere in the environment" (miasmic theory) and reads this passage in *The Shadow-Line* as evidence of Conrad's "miasmic" (as opposed to the contagious) "view of the disease"; but later he also adds that Conrad "may have known" about "germ theory" and makes a strong case for Conrad's concern with the dynamic of contagion in *The Nigger of the "Narcissus."* Bock, "Joseph Conrad and Germ Theory," 4, 5, 6. I argue that the dynamic, if not the theory, of contagion is equally central to *The Shadow-Line*.

14. In order to make sure that the epidemic is inextricably tied to the weather, Conrad adds: "There is something going on in the sky like a decomposition, like a corruption of the air" (*SL* 85).

15. Gregory Bateson, *Steps to an Ecology of Mind: A Revolutionary Approach to Man's Understanding of Himself* (New York: Ballantine Books, 1972), 438.

16. Jane Bennett, *Vibrant Matter: A Political Ecology of Things* (Durham, NC: Duke University Press, 2010), 33.

17. See, for instance, Cedric Watts, *The Deceptive Text: An Introduction to Cover Plots* (Sussex, UK: The Harvester Press, 1984), 90–99.

18. The captain-narrator is obsessively attentive to Captain Giles's voice. He registers his "quiet, thick tone" (*SL* 36), "complacent low tones" (39), "conciliating tone" (39), "unanswerable tone" (40), and, at their last meeting, as the captain-narrator is "irritated by his tone," Captain Giles responds "in a musing tone" (105), and so on.

19. Captain Giles's "deeper philosophy" is concerned with a type of dissolution of identity with characteristic mimetic symptoms. He says: "The difficulty [for Western sailors in the East] was to go on keeping white, and some of these nice boys did not know how" (19). This statement initially sounds predicated on an essentialist view of racial identity. But on a closer look this turns out not to be the case: it is precisely because whiteness is not an essence that it is difficult to "keep white." Put in more contemporary terms, for Giles, Western identity is not based on essentialist features rooted in nature and thus can easily be lost once the subject is exposed to foreign cultural influences. As often in Conrad, couched behind a racist-sounding language lies also a profound understanding of the constructed, plastic, and mimetic dimension of identity formation.

20. Jacques Lacan, "Le Stade du miroir comme formateur de la function du Je," in *Écrits* (Paris: Seuil, 1966), 91.

21. Lacan is attentive to "the role of the mirror apparatus of the *double*, in which psychical realities, however heterogeneous, are manifested"; and echoes of Edgar Allen Poe's "William Wilson" in particular can be heard in his account of the ego in terms of an "interior castle" where the id is confined. Lacan, "Miroir," 92, 94.

22. The most solid philosophical critique of the problematic of representation in the mirror stage I know of is Mikkel Borch-Jacobsen, *Lacan: The Absolute Master*, tr. Douglas Brick (Stanford, CA: Stanford University Press, 1991), chap. 2. Building on the mimetic work of Jean-Luc Nancy and, especially, Philippe Lacoue-Labarthe, Borch-Jacobsen usefully reminds us that "Lacan's account

of the mirror stage is far from being truly original" and remains fundamentally in line with a speculative "onto-photo-logical" tradition of the moderns that conceive of the subject in terms of "representation." As Borch-Jacobsen puts it, "The Lacanian ego is the ego as it theorizes itself, never as it feels 'itself' or experiences 'itself.'" Mikkel Borch-Jacobsen, *Lacan: The Absolute Master*, tr. Douglas Brick (Stanford, CA: Stanford University Press, 1991), 47, 57.

23. Lacan, "Miroir," 94.

24. Lacan, "Miroir," 97.

25. As Mikkel Borch-Jacobsen puts it in his affective reframing of the mirror stage: "before knowing (*connaître*) another and the world as objects, the human ego . . . is born with them (*co-naît*)— immediately, prior to any language and representation, according to a 'sym-pathy' in which any resolvable separation between the 'ego' and the 'other,' the 'subject and the 'object,' is totally scrambled. This is a truly decisive hypothesis, one that could have led Lacan a long way toward a non-theoretical (affective) problematic of the 'ego' and identification." Borch-Jacobsen, *Lacan*, 58. For an extension on this mimetic hypothesis in modernism, Nidesh Lawtoo, *The Phantom of the Ego: Modernism and the Mimetic Unconscious* (East Lansing: Michigan State University Press, 2013), esp. 175–81, 272–80.

26. A note for the wise: here or elsewhere, I am not arguing that Conrad was directly influenced by Nietzsche, or that he is a card-carrying Nietzschean writer, for he clearly posits himself at a distance from Nietzsche, just as he does with Dostoevsky, which does not mean that mimetic continuities are not operative at a deeper, theoretical, or, to use an old-fashioned term, philosophical level. It is this level that concerns me here.

27. Friedrich Nietzsche, *Beyond Good and Evil: Prelude to a Philosophy of the Future*, tr. R. J. Hollingdale (London: Penguin Books, 2003), 48.

28. William E. Connolly, *The Fragility of Things: Self-Organizing Processes, Neoliberal Fantasies, and Democratic Activism* (Durham, NC: Duke University Press, 2013), 7.

29. For critics who have recognized that "community" is a key concept in Conrad's ethics and provides a foundation for his account of solidarity, see, for instance, Watt, *Conrad in the Nineteenth Century*, 3–21; Daphna Erdinast-Vulcan, *Joseph Conrad and the Modern Temper* (Oxford: Clarendon Press, 1991), 25; Mark A. Wollaeger, *Joseph Conrad and the Fictions of Skepticism* (Stanford, CA: Stanford University Press, 1990), 14–15. In what follows, I supplement this *literary* concern in light of recent *philosophical* accounts of community.

30. In recent decades, the concept of community has received much attention from a number of theorists, from Maurice Blanchot to Jean-Luc Nancy and Giorgio Agamben. Despite their different theoretical and political orientation, these accounts share a line of inquiry initiated by Georges Bataille that is attentive to sovereign confrontations with the limit-experience of death. Informed by this Bataillean tradition, but attentive to a life-affirming side of "sovereign communication" Bataille inherits from Nietzsche, I have proposed the foundation of a more joyful account of community that has its origin in laughter in Lawtoo, *Phantom of the Ego*, 295–304. This last section furthers this line of inquiry by considering Conrad's life-affirmative account of a shared community in light of the threat of a shared catastrophe.

31. As Debra Romanick Baldwin aptly puts it, "the deck is a social place, a common ground; and going on deck takes him out of the isolation of an individual cabin, and puts him in the company of others in his capacity as captain." Debra Romanick Baldwin, "*Victory* (1916) and *The Shadow-Line* (1916)," in *A Joseph Conrad Companion*, ed. Leonard Orr and Ted Billy (London: Greenwood Press, 1999), 231–51, 241.

32. Jean-Luc Nancy, *The Inoperative Community*, tr. Peter Connor (Minneapolis: University of Minnesota Press, 1991), 6.

33. Magnusson and Zalloua, "Hydra of Contagion," 3–24, 10.

34. Lawtoo, *Phantom of the Ego*, 295–304.

### Chapter 4. A Picture of Europe: Possession Trance in *Heart of Darkness*

1. Chinua Achebe, "An Image of Africa: Racism in Conrad's *Heart of Darkness*," in Joseph Conrad, *Heart of Darkness*, ed. Paul B. Armstrong, 4th ed (New York, London: Norton, 2006), 336–49.

2. For informed accounts of the theoretical stakes of this much-discussed debate, see, for instance, Padmini Mongia, "The Rescue: Conrad, Achebe, and the Critics," *Conradiana* 33.2 (2001): 153–63; Inga Clendinnen, "Preempting Postcolonial Critique: Europeans in *Heart of Darkness*," *Common Knowledge* 13.1 (2007): 1–17. For books that frame the race debate in the larger context of postcolonial studies, see Terry Collits, *Postcolonial Conrad: Paradoxes of Empire* (New York: Routledge, 2005); Nicholas Harrison, *Postcolonial Criticism: History, Theory and the Work of Fiction* (Malden, MA: Polity Press, 2003).

3. As Achebe puts it, the problem with Conrad's mythic "method" is that it "amounts to no more than a steady, ponderous, fake-ritualistic repetition of two antithetical sentences, one about silence and the other about frenzy" (IA 338).

4. See John W. Griffith, *Joseph Conrad and the Anthropological Dilemma* (Oxford: Clarendon Press, 1995); Paul B. Armstrong, "Reading, Race and Representing Others," in Armstrong, *Heart of Darkness*, 429–44.

5. This chapter supplements a mimetic line of inquiry initiated in Nidesh Lawtoo, *The Phantom of the Ego: Modernism and the Mimetic Unconscious* (East Lansing: Michigan State University Press, 2013), chap. 2.

6. Edward Said, *Culture and Imperialism* (New York: Vintage Books, 1994), 19–31.

7. James Clifford, *The Predicament of Culture: Twentieth-Century Ethnography, Literature, and Art* (Cambridge, MA: Harvard University Press, 1988), 113.

8. Philippe Lacoue-Labarthe, "The Horror of the West," in *Conrad's* Heart of Darkness *and Contemporary Thought: Revisiting the Horror with Lacoue-Labarthe*, ed. Nidesh Lawtoo (London: Bloomsbury, 2012), 111–222.

9. Cedric Watts rightly affirms that "*Heart of Darkness* has a more potentially Darwininan atmosphere than any other major work of fiction." Cedric Watts, *Conrad's* Heart of Darkness: *A Critical and Contextual Discussion* (New York: Rodopi, 2012), 73. What follows uses mimetic and anthropological lenses to bring out the theoretical implications of this atmosphere.

10. Charles Darwin, *The Descent of Man*, in *Darwin: A Norton Critical Edition*, 2nd ed., ed. Philip Appelman (London: W. W. Norton, 1970), 208.

11. Hunt Hawkins, "*Heart of Darkness* and Racism," in Armstrong, *Heart of Darkness*, 365–75, 368.

12. Griffith, *Joseph Conrad and the Anthropological Dilemma*, 76–80.

13. Tylor argued in favor of an evolutionary approach to culture that considered man as passing through different stages, moving from "savagery" and "barbarism" to "civilization." His evolutionary cultural model introduces a hierarchical, racist distance between modern man and

primitive man, but it also presupposes an underlying unity and continuity between cultures, as well as a "general likeness of human nature." E. B. Tylor, *Primitive Culture*, vol. 1 (London, 1871), 108.

14. Subsequent critics more sympathetic to Conrad have taken care to nuance Achebe's critique by emphasizing Marlow's affective proximity that ties Africans and Europeans. See, for instance, C. P. Sarvan, "Racism and the *Heart of Darkness*," in Joseph Conrad, *Heart of Darkness*, ed. Robert Kimbrough, 3rd ed. (New York: Norton, 1988), 280–84, 283; Olusegun Adekoya, "Criticising the Critic: Achebe on Conrad," in Chinua Achebe, *Things Fall Apart*, ed. Francis Abiola Irele (New York: Norton, 2009), 189–99, 191.

15. Cedric Watts, "'A Bloody Racist': About Achebe's View of Conrad," *The Yearbook of English Studies* 13 (1983): 196–209, 199.

16. Harrison, *Postcolonial Criticism*, 27.

17. The cults of possession trance most studied by anthropologists are those of the Yoruba of Nigeria, the cult of the *zar* of Ethiopia, and the Holey of Niger. Despite the ethnographic specificity of each group, anthropologists recognized common features of trance and possession phenomena. It is on these general characteristics that I rely in order to account for the form of ritual frenzy at work in Conrad's tale. On the question of "possession" and/or "trance," I have found the French school of anthropology particularly useful. See Georges Lapassade, *La transe* (Paris: Presses Universitaires de France, 1990); Georges Lapassade, *Les rites de possession* (Paris: Anthropos, 1997); Bertrand Hell, *Possession et chamanisme: Les maîtres du désordre* (Paris: Flammarion, 1999); Luc de Heusch, *La transe et ses entours* (Paris: Éditions complexe, 2006). On the relation between music and trance, see Gilbert Rouget, *Music and Trance: A Theory of the Relations between Music and Possession*, tr. Brunhilde Biebuyck (Chicago: University of Chicago Press, 1985). On the question of trance in sub-Saharan Africa, see Marie-Claude Dupré, ed., *Familiarité avec les dieux: Transe et possession (Afrique Noire, Madagascar, La Réunion)* (Clermont-Ferrand, France: Presses Universitaires Blaise Pascal, 2001). Unless specified otherwise, all translations are the author's.

18. Lapassade, *Transe*, 45. Bertrand Hell confirms this point as he writes that "Black Africa appears as the true land of possession" and "is presented as being the *domaine par excellence* of possession cults." Hell, *Possession*, 26, 42.

19. Rouget, *Music and Trance*, 7, 62, 209. Along similar lines, Hell writes that trance "involves the group, noise and music, movement and sensorial overstimulation" and specifies that "the clapping hands of the chorus of musicians" is an additional source of stimulation. Hell, *Possession*, 37.

20. Rouget, *Music and Trance*, 13, 39. Rouget also observes that one of the functions of music is to bring about a state of exhaustion in order to facilitate trance and confirms a point equally observed by Marlow: namely, that "participants can sing for days and nights on end without a break." Rouget, *Music and Trance*, 14. Similarly, speaking of trance in African cultures in particular, Marie-Claude Dupré writes: "This altered state of consciousness generates remarkable manifestations: hebetude, ecstasy, crisis, enthusiasm, mania, madness, delirium, convulsions." Dupré, *Familiarité avec les dieux*, 8. For a visual representation of possession trance in West Africa (Ghana), see Jean Rouch, *Les maîtres fous* (1956), in *Jean Rouch*, DVD. Edition Montparnasse, 2004.

21. Said, *Culture and Imperialism*, 67.

22. The link between possession trance and madness is at least as old as Plato, but the connection

to mental pathology is particularly present at the turn of the twentieth century, a period that witnesses the birth of psychology. See Lapassade, *Transe*, 7–6; Lapassade, *Rites*, 14.

23. Griffith, *Joseph Conrad and the Anthropological Dilemma*, 62, 64; Armstrong, "Reading, Race and Representing Others," 432.

24. It is useful to recall that earlier Marlow, upon believing that he shall finally get the rivets necessary to repair the steamer, had already given in to little dances in the company of the foreman, as he admits: "we behaved like lunatics . . . [he] snapped his fingers above his head, lifting one foot. I tried a jig" (72).

25. I have given a more detailed account of the complex rhetoric of this passage in Lawtoo, *Phantom of the Ego*, 117–25.

26. Antonio Damasio, *Descartes' Error: Emotion, Reason, and the Human Brain* (New York: Penguin Books, 2005), xvii.

27. Damasio, *Descartes' Error*, 136, 8; see also 159–60.

28. Damasio, *Descartes' Error*, 17.

29. Conrad's friend and collaborator, Ford Madox Ford says, for instance, that "the scenes of Conrad's life as afterwards rendered, say in 'Heart of Darkness,' are really as vivid in the writer's mind from what Conrad's [*sic*] said as from what Conrad wrote." And to confirm that the mimetic qualities of Marlow are a fictional projection of mimetic tendencies in Conrad's mimetic faculties, Ford specifies: "For it was not possible to be taken imperiously through Conrad's life . . . and not to feel—even believe—that one had had, oneself, that experience." Ford Madox Ford, *Joseph Conrad: A Personal Remembrance* (New York: Octagon Books, 1971), 102, 103.

30. Clifford, *Predicament of Culture*, 93.

31. As Lapassade puts it, "the trance described in behavioral terms from the outside, without participating in it, is not the trance described from the inside, by the actors themselves, that is, by those who actually experienced it." Georges Lapassde, *Les états modifiés de conscience* (Paris: Presses Universitaires de France, 1987), 24.

32. Gilbert Rouget argues that possession is associated everywhere with music and dance, and specifies: "Sometimes, then, trance is triggered by the constant acceleration of tempo, at other times, on the contrary, by an alternation of acceleration and deceleration. It seems, too, that whatever its rhythmic form may be, the sound of the drum is thought to possess within itself the power to call upon spirits." Rouget, *Music and Trance*, 128.

33. Philippe Lacoue-Labarthe, "Le Chant des Muses" in *Pour n'en pas finir: écrits sur la musique*, eds. A. Bianchi, L. Kharlamov (Paris: Christian Bourgeois Éditeur, 2015), 27–54, 36, 43, (my translation).

34. In the "Author's Note" Conrad explicitly states his intention to convey this vibration in writing for readers of *Heart of Darkness* to register, as he says: "That sombre theme had to be given a sinister resonance, a tonality of its own, a continued vibration that, I hoped, would hang in the air and dwell on the ear after the last note had been struck" (*YOS* 6). I thank Bill Johnsen for reminding me of this passage.

35. The connection between Nietzsche and feminism might sound oxymoronic given the philosopher's notorious misogynist comments, but there is an entire feminine side to Nietzsche (and Nietzschean philosophers) that is concerned with maternal forms of will to power that have

birth as their paradigmatic example. For an account of this maternal side, see Lawtoo, *Phantom of the Ego*, 38–43, 253–57.

36. Albert Guerard, *Conrad the Novelist* (Cambridge, MA: Harvard University Press, 1958), 329.

37. Marianna Torgovnick, *Gone Primitive: Savage Intellects, Modern Lives* (Chicago: University of Chicago Press, 1990) 146.

38. Torgovnick, *Gone Primitive*, 146.

39. F. R. Leavis, *The Great Tradition: George Eliot, Henry James, Joseph Conrad* (New York: New York University Press, 1964), 18.

40. In a passage of *Nostromo* that has tremendous resonance with Marlow's altered state of consciousness, we read that Decoud, the ironic and detached skeptic, as he is left stranded on an island, finds himself affected "by a powerful drug," and enters a state of hypnotic slumber that causes him to doubt "whether he were asleep or awake" (262), and as he regains consciousness we read: "He had the strangest sensation of his soul having just returned into his body from the circumambient darkness" (262). Similarly, as Nostromo himself wakes up from the swim that leaves Decoud and the treasure behind, his coming to consciousness is described "as if an outcast soul, a quiet, brooding soul, finding that untenanted body in its way, had come in stealthily to take possession." (493)

41. James G. Frazer, *The Golden Bough* (New York: Gramercy Books, 1981), 141. Frazer specifies: "the shadow, if not equivalent to the soul, is at least regarded as a living part of the man or the animal, so that injury done to the shadow is felt by the person or animal as if it were done to his body" (143).

42. Émile Durkheim, *The Elementary Forms of Religious Life*, tr. Carol Cosman (Oxford: Oxford University Press, 2001), 49.

43. Tylor, *Primitive Culture*, vol. 1, 387.

44. It has been common to read *Heart of Darkness* in terms of an epic journey in the underworld that, from Dante to Goethe, entails spiritual initiations for the soul or Faustian pacts whereby the soul is lost. Such literary allusions are certainly at play in this scene, but Conrad also frames Western epics within a ritual context predicated on what the historian of religion Mircea Eliade calls a "shamanic structure." As Eliade suggests, "shamanic experiences," characterized by ritual drumming, descent into the underworld, ecstatic dispossession, loss and recuperation of a soul, and so on, "contributed toward crystallizing the first great epic themes." Mircea Eliade, *Shamanism: Archaic Techniques of Ecstasy*, tr. Willard R. Trask (Princeton, NJ: Princeton University Press, 1974), 214.

45. My reading is intrinsic, yet the reader inclined to look for extrinsic confirmations might find it interesting to know that Conrad in *A Personal Record* says, in a confessional mood, that he has "an instinctive horror of losing [his] sense of full self-possession" (101).

46. For a reading of Conrad's take on sacrifice that relies on Girard's mimetic theory, see Andrew Mozina, *Joseph Conrad and the Art of Sacrifice: The Evolution of the Scapegoat Theme in Joseph Conrad's Fiction* (New York: Routledge, 2001).

47. René Girard, Pierpaolo Antonello, and João Cezar de Castro Rocha, *Evolution and Conversion: Dialogues on the Origins of Culture* (London: Continuum, 2007), 97, 184.

48. See René Girard, *Violence and the Sacred*, tr. Patrick Gregory (Baltimore: Johns Hopkins University Press, 1977), 164–66.

49. I have discussed Freud's recuperation of hysterical/mimetic bonds within a triangular structure in more detail in Lawtoo, *Phantom of the Ego*, 233–46.

50. "Comparison is not reason."

51. Catherine Bell, *Ritual Perspectives and Dimensions* (Oxford: Oxford University Press, 1997), chap. 1.

52. Watts, *Conrad's* Heart of Darkness, 72.

53. See Pierpaolo Antonello and Paul Gifford, eds., *Can We Survive Our Origins? Readings in René Girard's Theory of Violence and the Sacred* (East Lansing: Michigan State University Press, 2015).

54. Conrad's critical view of Christianity is clearly summarized in his letters to Garnett where he says: "It's strange how I always, from the age of fourteen, disliked the Christian religion, its doctrines, ceremonies and festivals." And in another letter he adds a Nietzschean twist to his critique as he specifies that Christianity is "the only religion which, with its impossible standards, has brought an infinity of anguish to innumerable souls—on this earth." Conrad, quoted in Zdzisław Najder, *Joseph Conrad: A Chronicle* (Cambridge: Cambridge University Press, 1983), 287, 392.

55. Girard, Antonello, and de Castro Rocha, *Evolution and Conversion*, 217.

56. King Leopold II, quoted in Joseph Conrad, *Heart of Darkness: Case Studies in Contemporary Criticism*, ed. Ross C. Murfin, 3rd ed. (Boston: Bedford/St. Martin's, 2011), 5.

57. René Girard, *Le Bouc émissaire* (Paris: Éditions Grasset et Fasquelle, 1982), chap. 1.

58. Lacoue-Labarthe, "Horror of the West," 111–22. This article is unique in its kind and escapes easy summaries. For general theoretical introductions to this essay, see J. Hillis Miller, "Prologue: Revisiting '*Heart of Darkness* Revisited' (in the Company of Philippe Lacoue-Labarthe)," in *Conrad's* Heart of Darkness *and Contemporary Thought: Revisiting the Horror with Lacoue-Labarthe*, ed. Nidesh Lawtoo (London: Bloomsbury, 2012), 39–54; Nidesh Lawtoo, "A Frame for 'The Horror of the West,'" in Lawtoo, *Conrad's* Heart of Darkness, 89–108. All the essays in this collection—which includes interventions by Michael Bell, Jonathan Dollimore, François Warin, Stephen Ross, Claude Maisonnat, Beth Ash, Henry Staten, Martine Hennard Dutheil de la Rochère, Nidesh Lawtoo, and Avital Ronell—offer different perspectives on "The Horror of the West." For a study completely devoted to Conrad's take on the West, see also Christopher GoGwilt, *The Invention of the West: Joseph Conrad and the Double-Mapping of Europe and Empire* (Stanford, CA: Stanford University Press, 1995).

59. As I tried to make clear in "A Frame for the Horror of the West," all of Lacoue-Labarthe's texts revolve around preoccupations concerning mimesis, techne, will to power, and the Holocaust, among other themes, which inform his account of Western thought. Good places to start engaging with this thought are the following: Philippe Lacoue-Labarthe, *Typography: Mimesis, Philosophy, Politics*, ed. Christopher Fynsk (Cambridge, MA: Harvard University Press, 1989); Philippe Lacoue-Labarthe and Jean-Luc Nancy, "The Nazi Myth," tr. B. Holmes, *Critical Inquiry* 16.2 (1990): 291–312; Philippe Lacoue-Labarthe, *Heidegger, Art and Politics: the Fiction of the Political*, tr. C. Turner (New York: Blackwell, 1990). Readers of French will find a collection of essays by Lacoue-Labarthe specifically devoted to the "West" in Philippe Lacoue-Labarthe, *La Réponse d'Ulysse: Et autres textes sur L'Occident*, ed. Aristide Bianchi and Leonid Kharlamov (Lignes/Imec, 2012), which includes the French version "Horror" along with other texts on "the West." For a philosophical contextualization of Lacoue-Labarthe's writings on "the West," see also Aristide Bianchi and Leonid Kharlamov, "Les Écrits sur l'Occident de Philippe Lacoue-Labarthe," in Lacoue-Labarthe, *La Réponse d'Ulysse*, 145–83. I am grateful to Leonid and Aristide for inviting me to present my edited volume on Conrad and Lacoue-Labarthe in conjunction to their presentation of *La Réponse d'Ulysse* at the IMEC in Paris in the fall of 2012.

60. Luc De Heusch, *La transe et ses entours* (Paris: Éditions complexe, 2006), 216.

61. Joseph Conrad, *Heart of Darkness: A Norton Critical Edition*, 4th ed., ed. Paul B. Armstrong (New York: W. W. Norton & Company, 2006), 91.

62. Oscar Wilde, "The Decay of Lying," in *The Complete Works of Oscar Wilde*, vol. 4, ed. Josephine M. Guy (Oxford: Oxford University Press, 2007), 90.

63. Plato, "Ion," in *The Collected Dialogues of Plato*, ed. Edith Hamilton and Huntington Cairns, tr. Lane Cooper et al. (Princeton, NJ: Princeton University Press, 1963), 216–28, 220.

64. See Plato, *Ion* and books II and III of *Republic*.

## Chapter 5. A Picture of Africa: Postcolonial Mimesis in Achebe's *Things Fall Apart*

1. Chinua Achebe, *Things Fall Apart*, ed. Francis Abiola Irele (New York: W. W. Norton, 2009).

2. Edward Said and Peter Mallios, "An Interview with Edward Said," in *Conrad in the Twenty-First Century: Contemporary Approaches and Perspectives*, ed. Carola M. Kaplan, Peter Mallios, and Andrea White (New York: Routledge, 2005), 283–303, 288.

3. Edward Said, *Culture and Imperialism* (New York: Vintage, 1994), 18.

4. On the productive side of mimetic rivalry, see Nidesh Lawtoo, *The Phantom of the Ego: Modernism and the Mimetic Unconscious* (East Lansing: Michigan State University Press, 2013), 45–52.

5. In *Heart of Darkness* the notion of "frenzy" appears twice in the whole novel. In "An Image of Africa" it appears twice in a single page, and references to this ritual scene punctuate the whole essay. See Chinua Achebe, "An Image of Africa: Racism in Conrad's *Heart of Darkness*," in Joseph Conrad, *Heart of Darkness*, 4th ed., ed. Paul B. Armstrong (New York: Norton, 2006), 338, 339, 340, 341.

6. For postcolonial studies that complicate the opposition between *Heart of Darkness* and *Things Fall Apart*, see, for instance, Michael Valdez Moses, *The Novel and the Globalization of Culture* (Oxford: Oxford University Press, 1995), 110–12; Byron Caminero-Santangelo, *African Fiction and Joseph Conrad: Reading Postcolonial Intertextuality* (Albany: State University of New York Press, 2005). What follows builds on these developments to reframe the race controversy via the filter of frenzied images critics have avoided so far.

7. Anthony Kwame Appiah, introduction to Chinua Achebe, *Things Fall Apart* (New York: Knopf, 1992), ix–xvii, ix.

8. Chinua Achebe, *Hopes and Impediments: Selected Essays 1965–1987* (Oxford: Heinemann, 1988), 30.

9. Mala Pandurang, "Chinua Achebe and the 'African Experience': A Socio-Literary Perspective," in Achebe, *Things Fall Apart*, 343–58, 344, 347; Abdul JanMohamed, "Sophisticated Primitivism: The Syncretism of Oral and Literate Modes in Achebe's *Things Fall Apart*," in Achebe, *Things Fall Apart*, 571–86, 571; Maik Nwosu, "The River, the Earth and the Spirit of the World: Joseph Conrad, Chinua Achebe, Ben Okri and the Novel in Africa," *Matatu Journal for African Culture and Society* 35 (2007): 93–109, 97.

10. Simon Gikandi, "Foreword: Chinua Achebe and the Institution of African Literature," in *The Chinua Achebe Encyclopedia*, ed. M. Keith Booker (Westport, CT: Greenwood Press, 2003), vii.

11. *Heart of Darkness* is not the only image of frenzied Africa Achebe is rewriting. For other images

of frenzy linked to entranced states, see also Joyce Cary, *Mister Johnson* (London: Michael Joseph, 1975), 29, 32, 40, 133, 159, 161.

12. Achebe, *Hopes and Impediments*, 44 (my emphasis).

13. See Plato, *Phaedrus*, in *The Collected Dialogues of Plato*, ed. Edith Hamilton and Huntington Cairns (Princeton, NJ: Princeton University Press, 1963), 475–525, 491.

14. For Rouget, this mimetic indistinction defines "possession in the strict sense of the word." Gilbert Rouget, *Music and Trance: A Theory of the Relations between Music and Possession*, tr. Brunhilde Biebuyck (Chicago: University of Chicago Press, 1985), 26.

15. Another case of mimetic confusion concerns "twins," which "were put in earthenware pots and thrown away in the forest" (38), a phenomenon also discussed by Girard; see René Girard, *Violence and the Sacred*, tr. Patrick Gregory (Baltimore: Johns Hopkins University Press, 1977), 56–63.

16. When faced with Achebe's dramatization of ritual frenzy, critics tend to praise Achebe's "artistic objectivity" and "coherent anatomy of standards" and do not invoke Achebe's critique of Conrad on this very notion. Oladele Taiwo, "Things Fall Apart," in Achebe, *Things Fall Apart*, 359–69, 361. Abiola Irele is an important exception to this tendency. As he recognizes, "The omnipresence of the drum in Achebe's image of Igbo tribal life seems at times on the verge of betraying him into the kind of unmediated stereotyping of the African by Western writers to which he himself has vehemently objected." Irele's point is well taken, and is perfectly in line with his affirmation that "the drum functions so obviously as a leitmotif in the novel." Abiola Irele, "The Crisis of Cultural Memory in Chinua Achebe's *Things Fall Apart*," in Achebe, *Things Fall Apart*, 453–91, 459. Yet after having noticed this homology, Irele does not stop to account for this narrative move at the heart of a postcolonial counternarrative meant to counter, not promote, representations of "frenzy" in dominant narratives—leaving this striking contradiction for others to explore.

17. Plato, *Republic*, 640–42, 830.

18. Émile Durkheim's account of religious force in the context of Australian totemism, while still couched within an evolutionary frame, resonates with Achebe's account of frenzy. Durkheim writes: "Once the individuals are assembled, their proximity generates a kind of electricity that quickly transports them to an extraordinary degree of exaltation. . . . And as passions so strong and uncontrolled are bound to seek outward expression, there are violent gestures, shouts, even howls, deafening noises of all sorts from all sides. . . . It is not difficult to imagine that a man in such a state of exaltation no longer knows himself. Feeling possessed and led by some external power that makes him think and act differently from normal times he naturally feels he is no longer himself." Durkheim's conclusion is that this "religious force is nothing but the collective and anonymous force of the clan." Émile Durkheim, *The Elementary Forms of Religious Life*, tr. Carol Cosman (Oxford: Oxford University Press, 2001), 162–64, 164, 166.

19. Benedict Anderson writes that "all communities larger than primordial villages of face-to-face contact (and perhaps even these) are imagined. Communities are to be distinguished, not by their falsity/genuineness, but by the style in which they are imagined." Benedict Anderson, *Imagined Communities: Reflections on the Origins and Spread of Nationalism* (New York: Verso, 1991), 6. The style of community Achebe imagines and represents, at the narrative level, is one based on rituals of mimetic communion whereby the imagined social bond emerges from a collective, bodily experience.

20. The description matches most of the anthropological accounts of this enigmatic ritual phenomenon in western Africa. For instance, the missionary G. T. Basden, despite his

ethnocentric bias, gives an account of an Igbo funeral that approximates Achebe's description: "There is a terrific ding from the beating of tom-toms (egwu-olu) and the shouts of the assembled company, and the whole proceeding grows into a noisy drinking carousal. . . . To the excited audience there are verily believed to be figures animated by spirits from the underworld . . . The noise and excitement reaches the utmost pitch . . . suddenly firearms are discharged." And a bit later he adds: "The dancers work themselves into a veritable frenzy. . . . I have watched such dances and can testify to the extraordinary manner in which the dancers, for the time being, lose consciousness of their surroundings." G. T. Basden, *Among the Ibos of Nigeria* (London: Frank Cass, 1966) 124, 132–33. See also Rouget, *Music and Trance*, 40; Bertrand Hell, *Possession et chamanisme: Les maîtres du désordre* (Paris: Flammarion, 1999), 37.

21. Writing against the dominant stream, Staten argues that *Things Fall Apart* challenges a "civlizationist prejudice" in postcolonial studies that draws a veil over bloody, sacrificial images at the heart of subaltern narratives. Henry Staten, "Tracking the 'Native Informant': Cultural Translation as the Horizon of Literary Translation," in *Nation, Language, and the Ethics of Translation*, ed. Sandra Bermann and Michael Wood (Princeton, NJ: Princeton University Press, 2005), 111–26, esp. 123–26.

22. Hell, *Possession*, 333, 334, 337.

23. François Warin, "Philippe's Lessons of Darkness," in *Conrad's* Heart of Darkness *and Contemporary Thought: Revisiting the Horror with Lacoue-Labarthe*, ed. Nidesh Lawtoo (London: Bloomsbury, 2012), 123–42, 130.

24. Said and Mallios, "Interview," 288.

25. Joyce Cary in *Mister Johnson* offers a crudely limited account of the functions of ritual frenzy. Still, he seems to glimpse at, without taking hold of, such an organic insight as he stresses that the members of a ritual of possession "are like parts of one being and now every part is mad with the same frenzy." Cary, *Mister Johnson*, 155.

26. Foucault influentially argued that the name of the author "serves to neutralize the contradictions that are found in a series of texts." Michel Foucault, "What Is an Author," in *Critical Theory since 1965*, ed. Hazard Adams and Leroy Searle (Tallahassee: Florida State University Press, 1989) 138–47, 144.

27. Let me admit that the thesis concerning images of frenzy in *Things Fall Apart* has not been an easy sell. An anonymous external reviewer of a prestigious journal in modern literature even assured me in his report that he or she was "not convinced there are images of frenzy in *Things Fall Apart*." I mention this incident not for *ad hominem* accusations but because it reveals, at the microlevel, the power of ideology to blind (professional) readers of the ability to read the words on the page, especially as we take sides in political quarrels. Western pre-Achebe critics were unable to see the problematic implications of frenzy in *Heart of Darkness*; postcolonial post-Achebe critics did not see the images of frenzy in *Things Fall Apart*. The ideology is different—or, rather, opposed—yet the mimetic mechanism that generates this blindness is fundamentally the same.

28. Homi K. Bhabha, *The Location of Culture* (London: Routledge, 1994), 109.

29. Gayatri Chakravorty Spivak, *A Critique of Postcolonial Reason: Towards a History of the Vanishing Present* (Cambridge, MA: Harvard University Press, 1999), 46.

30. Said and Mallios, "Interview," 288. Influenced by Said, Byron Caminero-Santangelo usefully suggests that postcolonial authors "create their own voices through a process of parodic absorption and transformation of Western classics and the colonial discourse they represent." Caminero-Santangelo, *African Fiction*, 11.

31. For an informed account of Bhabha's take on mimicry, see also Robert Young, *White Mythologies: Writing History and the West* (London: Routledge, 1990), 145–49.

32. Simon Gikandi also uses the concept of "postcolonial mimesis" in order to counter antimimetic trends in postcolonial studies, but we develop different sides of this concept. For Gikandi, "postcolonial mimesis" designates a representational aesthetics that reinscribes a concern for the "reality effects invoked in postcolonial texts" under the signature of "irony" and "empty time." Simon Gikandi, "Theory after Postcolonial Theory: Rethinking the Work of Mimesis," in *Theory after Theory*, ed. Jane Elliott and Derek Attridge (New York: Routledge, 2011), 163–78, 173, 176. I refer to "postcolonial mimesis" to designate a form of nonrealistic imitation that connects postcolonial counternarratives to colonial narratives and is responsible for the circulation of power in its repressive and productive forms. These two sides of postcolonial mimesis are, in my view, not antagonistic but supplement each other.

33. Michel Foucault, "Two Lectures," in *Power/Knowledge: Selected Interviews & Other Writings 1972-1977*, ed. Colin Gordon (New York: Pantheon Books, 1980), 78–108, 99.

34. See Foucault, "Two Lectures," 93–108. For a Foucauldian account of the paradoxical logic of subjection, see also Judith Butler, *The Psychic Life of Power: Theories in Subjection* (Stanford, CA: Stanford University Press, 1997), 1–18.

35. Achebe's references to Nazism and the poisonous physician, which he mobilizes to deprive Conrad of the status of "artist," appeared in the original version only; critical editions still reproduce them in a footnote.

36. See Caryl Phillips, "Was Joseph Conrad Really a Racist?," *Philosophia Africana* 10.1 (2007): 59–66.

37. Achebe said: "I don't really think that there's any one I can say I admire all that much. I used to like Hemingway; and I used to like Conrad. I used to like Conrad particularly." Chinua Achebe, *Conversations with Chinua Achebe*, ed. Bernth Lindfors (Jackson: University Press of Mississippi, 1997), 6. Despite Achebe's and Conrad's seemingly opposed perspectives, a series of underlying continuities connect them: like Achebe, Conrad is also writing in a language that is not his own (English) at a time in which the Polish novel (like the African novel), as Zdzisław Najder points out, "was practically nonexistent." Zdzisław Najder, *Joseph Conrad: A Chronicle* (Cambridge: Cambridge University Press, 1983), 117.

38. Chinua Achebe, "Africa's Tarnished Image," in Achebe, *Things Fall Apart*, 209–20, 216.

39. In *No Longer at Ease*, for instance, the narrator explicitly refers to *Heart of Darkness* as he describes Mr. Green, a colonial administrator, in the following Conradian terms: "He must have come originally with an ideal—to bring light to the heart of darkness, to tribal headhunters performing weird ceremonies and unspeakable rites. But when he arrived, Africa played him false. Where was his beloved bush full of human sacrifices?" Chinua Achebe, *The African Trilogy: Things Fall Apart, No Longer at Ease, Arrow of God* (New York: Everyman's Library, 2010), 235. Both the language and the content of this passage suggest an explicit attack against the image of Africa portrayed by Conrad; yet we should also notice that human sacrifices are central to the picture of Africa portrayed in *Things Fall Apart*. For an account of the echoes between *No Longer at Ease* and *Heart of Darkness*, see Caminero-Santangelo, *African Fiction*, chap. 1.

40. Terry Eagleton, *Literary Theory: An Introduction* (Oxford: Blackwell, 2008), 205.

41. Eagleton, *Literary Theory*, 205–6.

42. Edward Said, "The Problem of Textuality: Two Exemplary Traditions," *Critical Inquiry* 4.4 (1978): 673–714, 705.

43. Foucault, "Two Lectures," 98.

44. The revolutionary movements in Northern Africa (or "Arab Spring") testify to the contemporary political relevance of postcolonial mimesis understood both as visual representations and as emotional contagion to counter oppressive, totalitarian regimes. What these movements teach us is that a complex, spiraling effect can emerge from these two forms of mimesis: if collective protests in the social sphere generate a "local" revolutionary effervescence that, in turn, serves as the message to be communicated "globally" by the mass media, new social media (from mobile phones to Facebook and other modes of virtual communication) and the images of Africa they convey have the power to retroact, via a back-looping effect, on the immanent social sphere and to amplify the effervescence they are supposed to merely represent across national barriers. These mimetic revolutions illustrate how inadequate distinctions such as copy and original, active and passive, reality and imitation of reality actually are to think about mimesis today. They also show how urgent it is to think and rethink both the damaging and productive power of mimesis for our contemporary, mass-mediatized times.

### Chapter 6. Surrealist Mimetism: Fear of the Dark
### in *The Nigger of the "Narcissus"*

1. Ian Watt, *Conrad in the Nineteenth Century* (London: Chatto, 1980), 79.

2. Watt, *Conrad in the Nineteenth Century*, 84.

3. For an initial antagonistic philosophical critique of Conrad's Preface, see David Goldknopf, "What's Wrong with Conrad: Conrad on Conrad," *Criticism* 10 (1968): 54–64. For philosophically informed arguments on the side of Conrad, see J. Hillis Miller, *Poets of Reality: Six Twentieth-Century Writers* (Cambridge, MA: Harvard University Press, 1965), 26–39; Watt, *Conrad in the Nineteenth Century*, 76–88; Mark Stockdale, "Art, Language, and Invisible Truth: A Reappraisal of Conrad's Preface," *Colloquy: Text Theory Critique* 8 (2004). For a mimetic account of Conrad's 1914 preface, see William A. Johnsen, "'To My Readers of America': Conrad's 1914 Preface to *The Nigger of the "Narcissus,"* *Conradiana* 35.1–2 (2003): 105–22.

4. See Isaiah Berlin, *The Roots of Romanticism*, ed. Henry Hardy (Princeton, NJ: Princeton University Press, 2001). On the specific shift from a mimetic to an expressive theory of art, see M. H. Abrams, *The Mirror and the Lamp: Romantic Theory and the Critical Tradition* (Oxford: Oxford University Press, 1971).

5. See Philippe Lacoue-Labarthe, "The Horror of the West," J. Hillis Miller, "Prologue: Revisiting '*Heart of Darkness* Revisited' (in the Company of Philippe Lacoue-Labarthe)," Jonathan Dollimore, "Civilization and Its Darkness," and Henry Staten Conrad's Dionysian Elegy" in *Conrad's* Heart of Darkness *and Contemporary Thought Revisiting the Horror with Lacoue-Labarthe*, ed. Nidesh Lawtoo (London: Bloomsbury, 2012).

6. Albert Guerard, *Conrad the Novelist* (Cambridge, MA: Harvard University Press, 1958), 107; Brian W. Shaffer, "The Nigger of the 'Narcissus,'" in *A Joseph Conrad Companion*, ed. Leonard Orr and Ted Billy (London: Greenwood Press, 1999), 49–64, 52.

7. Arthur Schopenhauer, *The World as Will and Idea*, vol. 1, tr. R. B. Haldane and J. Kemp (London: Routledge, Kegan & Paul, 1948), 16.

8. See also Schopenhauer's account of the sublime where he speaks of "Nature convulsed by a storm;

the sky darkened by black threatening thunder clouds" and of a "storm of tempestuous seas, where the mountain waves rise and fall" (*WWI* 264, 265).

9. For an account of the epistemology of impressionism attentive to the way this aesthetics "blurs" the boundaries between self and Others, see John Peters, *Conrad and Impressionism* (Cambridge: Cambridge University Press, 2001) 61–85.

10. André Breton, "Manifesto of Surrealism," in André Breton, *Manifestoes of Surrealism*, tr. Richard Seaver and Helen R. Lane (Ann Arbor: University of Michigan Press, 1974), 1–48, 27, 47.

11. André Breton, "Second Manifesto of Surrealism," in Breton, *Manifestoes of Surrealism*, 117–94, 136–37.

12. Georges Dumézil, quoted in Claudine Frank, introduction to *The Edge of Surrealism: A Roger Caillois Reader*, ed. Claudine Frank, tr. Claudine Frank and Camille Naish (Durham, NC: Duke University Press, 2003), 1–57, 9.

13. Roger Caillois, *Le Mythe et l'homme* (Paris: Gallimard, 1938).

14. Caillois's objection to this evolutionary hypothesis is that some of these mimetic insects are actually inedible, or, alternatively, that disappearing against a given background (such as edible plants) may actually diminish, rather than increase, the chances of survival.

15. Mikkel Borch-Jacobsen and Sonu Shamdasani, in their revisionist, historical account of Freud's "triumph" over his rivals, put it succinctly: "What was good in psychoanalysis was not new, and stemmed from Janet's work. What was new was not good, and could safely be left to Freud." Mikkel Borch-Jacobsen and Sonu Shamdasani, *The Freud Files: An Inquiry into the History of Psychoanalysis* (Cambridge: Cambridge University Press, 2012), 75. For a historical reevaluation of the role of Janet in the discovery of the unconscious, see Henry Ellenberger, *The Discovery of the Unconscious: The History and Evolution of Dynamic Psychiatry* (New York: Basic Books, 1970), chap. 6.

16. Janet defines "psychasthenia" as a "trouble in the apprehension of present reality, both with respect to perception and action." Pierre Janet, *Les Névroses* (Paris: Flammarion, 1927), 358. Characteristic symptoms include fatigue, vulnerability to emotions, loss of will, daydreaming, inability to act in the present, lack of self-confidence, unfounded fears. For Janet's detailed account of psychasthenia, see Pierre Janet, *Les Obsessions et la psychasthénie* (Paris: Félix Alcan, 1903), 260–442. For Janet's summary of his diagnostic of psychasthenia, see Janet, *Les Névroses*, 349–67. For a concise and informed account of this pathology, see Karl Jaspers, *General Psychopathology*, vol. 1, tr. J. Hoenig and M. W. Hamilton (Baltimore: Johns Hopkins University Press, 1997), 422. For an account of the modernist dissolution of the ego from the angle of Janet's psychology, see Nidesh Lawtoo, *The Phantom of the Ego: Modernism and the Mimetic Unconscious* (East Lansing: Michigan State University Press, 2013), 266–77.

17. Jacques Lacan, "Le Stade du miroir comme formateur de la function du Je," in *Écrits* (Paris: Seuil, 1966), 92.

18. Lacan, "Miroir," 92.

19. Janet, *Névroses*, 359.

20. See Martin Bock, *Joseph Conrad and Psychological Medicine* (Lubbock: Texas Tech University Press, 2002), chap. 3.

21. Miller, *Poets of Reality*, 39.

22. Roger Caillois, "Le surréalisme comme univers de signes," in *Œuvres*, ed. Dominique Rabourdin (Paris: Gallimard, 2008), 227–34, 228.

23. Stephen Ross, "*The Nigger of the 'Narcissus'* and Modernist Haunting," *Novel* 44.2 (2011): 268–91, 271.

24. William Deresiewicz, for instance, adopts a mimetic frame as he says that "the drama within the page mirrors the drama within the author." William Deresiewicz, "Conrad's Impasse: *The Nigger of the 'Narcissus'* and the Invention of Marlow," *Conradiana* 38.3 (2006): 205–26, 214. Brian Richardson, on the other hand, argues that "it is precisely the mimetic conventions of realism that Conrad transcends in this work." Brian Richardson, "Conrad and Posthumanist Narration: Fabricating Class and Consciousness on Board the *Narcissus*," in *Conrad in the Twenty-First Century: Contemporary Approaches and Perspectives*, ed. Carola M. Kaplan, Peter Mallios, and Andrea White (New York: Routledge, 2005), 213–22, 219.

25. Diegesis, writes Plato in Republic, is a narrative mode whereby the "poet himself is the speaker and does not even attempt to suggest that anyone else but himself is the speaker," whereas in mimesis as in tragedy, "the poet delivers a speech as if he were someone else ... assimilating thereby his own diction as far as possible to that of the person whom he announces as about to speak." Plato, *Republic*, in *The Collected Dialogues of Plato*, ed. E. Hamilton and H. Cairns (New York: Pantheon Books, 1963), 575–844, 637, 638.

26. Philippe Lacoue-Labarthe, "The Horror of the West," in Lawtoo, *Conrad's* Heart of Darkness, 112.

27. Miller, *Poets of Reality*, 37.

28. Breton, "Manifesto of Surrealism," 26–27.

### Chapter 7. Rebirth of Tragedy: *Almayer's Folly* to *Apocalypse Now*

1. As J. Hillis Miller puts it, the best readers of Conrad are still "unanimous in not taking seriously any 'metaphysical' dimension of Conrad's work." J. Hillis Miller, foreword to *Conrad in the Twenty-First Century: Contemporary Approaches and Perspectives*, ed. Carola M. Kaplan, Peter Mallios, and Andrea White (New York: Routledge, 2005), 1–14, 6.

2. See Royal Roussel, *The Metaphysics of Darkness: A Study in the Unity and Development of Conrad's Fiction* (Baltimore: Johns Hopkins University Press, 1971); J. Hillis Miller, *Poets of Reality: Six Twentieth-Century Writers* (Cambridge, MA: Harvard University Press, 1965), 13–39; Daphna Erdinast-Vulcan, *Joseph Conrad and the Modern Temper* (Oxford: Clarendon Press, 1991), 86–138.

3. Carola Kaplan, Peter Lancelot Mallios, Andrea White, introduction to Kaplan, Mallios, and White, *Conrad in the Twenty-First Century*, xiii–xxii, xv.

4. Miller, foreword to Kaplan, Mallios, and White, *Conrad in the Twenty-First Century* 5.

5. See Nidesh Lawtoo, ed., *Conrad's* Heart of Darkness *and Contemporary Thought: Revisiting the Horror with Lacoue-Labarthe* (London: Bloomsbury, 2012).

6. Adriana Cavarero, *Horrorism: Naming Contemporary Violence*, tr. William McCuaig (New York: Columbia University Press, 2011), 116. I thank Rachel Falconer for suggesting Cavarero's work for the first session of a memorable theory reading group at the University of Lausanne in the fall of 2012.

7. Rita Felski, introduction to *Rethinking Tragedy*, ed. Rita Felski (Baltimore: Johns Hopkins University Press, 2008), 6.

8. Friedrich Nietzsche, *Beyond Good and Evil: Prelude to a Philosophy of the Future*, tr. R. J. Hollingdale (London: Penguin Books, 2003), 37.

9. On the tension between Conrad's Romantic and idealistic father, Apollo Korzeniowski, and the pragmatic and realistic maternal uncle, Tadeusz Bobrowksi, who served as a tutor and substitute father figure, see Zdzisław Najder, *Joseph Conrad: A Chronicle* (Cambridge: Cambridge University Press, 1983), 4–23, 145–65.

10. On the biographical sources of this story, see Ian Watt, *Conrad in the Nineteenth Century* (London: Chatto, 1980), 34–41.

11. See Aristotle, *The Poetics of Aristotle*, tr. Stephen Halliwell (Chapel Hill: University of North Carolina Press), chap. 4.

12. Albert Guerard, *Conrad the Novelist* (Cambridge, MA: Harvard University Press, 1958), 71.

13. Nietzsche, *Beyond Good and Evil*, 193.

14. Michel Onfray, *Cosmos: Une ontologie matérialiste* (Paris: Flammarion, 2015), my translation. For Onfray's full discussion of the *sipo matador*, see 139–53.

15. James G. Frazer, *The Golden Bough* (New York: Gramercy Books, 1981), 321.

16. Frazer, *Golden Bough*, 322.

17. Friedrich Nietzsche, *The Birth of Tragedy*, in *The Birth of Tragedy and The Case of Wagner*, tr. Walter Kaufmann (New York: Vintage Books, 1967), 59.

18. Frazer, *Golden Bough*, 321.

19. In Fried's view, this impressionistic aesthetics reflects Conrad's preoccupations with writing in general and the blank page in particular. As he puts it: it reflects "a particular fantasmatic relation to the blank page [that] lies at the heart not only of *Almayer's Folly* but of Conrad's fictions generally." Michael Fried, "Almayer's Face: On 'Impressionism' in Conrad, Crane, and Norris," *Critical Inquiry* 17.1 (1990): 193–236, 199. I would like to thank Michael for friendly and stimulating exchanges on Conrad and other aesthetic matters during my stay at Hopkins.

20. Aristotle famously writes in chapter four of *Poetics*, "We take pleasure in contemplating the most precise images of things whose sight in itself causes us pain—such as the appearance of basest animals, or of corpses" (*P* 34).

21. In his first book Lacoue-Labarthe defines "Dionysus as the only veritable hero of tragedy." Philippe Lacoue-Labarthe, *The Subject of Philosophy*, ed. Thomas Trezise, tr. Thomas Trezise, Hugh J. Silverman, Gary M. Cole, Timothy D. Bent, Karen McPherson, and Claudette Sartiliot (Minneapolis: University of Minnesota Press, 1993), 67.

22. For critics who have explored the common artistic metaphysics between Nietzsche and Conrad, see Edward Said, "Nietzsche and Contradiction," in *Joseph Conrad: A Commemoration*, ed. Norman Sherry (London: Macmillan, 1976), 65–76; Erdinast-Vulcan, *Conrad and the Modern Temper*, 9–19, 139–43; Nic Panagopoulos, Heart of Darkness *and* The Birth of Tragedy: *A Comparative Study* (Athens: Kardamista, 2002); Nidesh Lawtoo, *The Phantom of the Ego: Modernism and the Mimetic Unconscious* (East Lansing: Michigan State University Press, 2013), chap. 2. My current approach furthers this literary-philosophical connection by foregrounding the

underlying mimetic principles that structure the Apollonian/Dionysian dichotomy along lines informed by the recent philosophical turn in Conrad studies mentioned above.

23. Erwin Rohde, *Psyche: The Cult of Souls and the Belief in Immortality among the Greeks* (New York: Routledge, 2001), 261.

24. Rohde, *Psyche*, 257–58.

25. On Dionysus and Greek tragedy, see E. R. Dodds, *The Greeks and the Irrational* (Berkeley: University of California Press, 1964), 270–78. On Dionysus and mimesis, see René Girard, *Violence and the Sacred*, tr. Patrick Gregory (Baltimore: Johns Hopkins University Press, 1977), chap. 5.

26. It is possible that Conrad had first- or secondhand knowledge of *The Birth of Tragedy*, but my argument takes mimesis beyond questions of influence in order articulate the metaphysics that emerge from the text itself. I mention in passing that Conrad's critique of what he calls "Nietzsche's mad individualism" (just as his critique of Dostoevsky) should be taken with a grain of salt; it suggests a type of mimetic rivalry of the sort we have seen at work in Achebe.

27. See Jonathan Dollimore, "Civilization and Its Darkness," in Lawtoo, *Conrad's* Heart of Darkness *and Contemporary Thought*, 67–86, 76–84; Henry Staten, "Conrad's Dionysian Elegy," in Lawtoo, *Conrad's* Heart of Darkness *and Contemporary Thought*, 201–20.

28. Girard writes: "If the art of tragedy is to be defined in a single phrase, we might do worse than calling attention to one of its most characteristic traits: the opposition of symmetrical elements" (*VS* 44) by which he means Apollonian and Dionysian elements (*VS* 55; trans. modified).

29. Rohde will also speak of "reconciliation between the Apolline and the Dionysian," indicating that "in the end the distinction between them seems to disappear entirely." Rohde, *Psyche*, 287–88.

30. For Miller, this passage deconstructs typical views of form as simple container (or shell) that can be peeled off from content (or nut), suggesting that a "preordained correspondence" between the luminous form (or glow) and meaning that "magically brings the 'unseen' meaning [or haze] out and makes it visible." J. Hillis Miller, "*Heart of Darkness* Revisited," in Lawtoo, *Conrad's* Heart of Darkness *and Contemporary Thought*, 39–54, 42; see also 41–46.

31. See M. H. Abrams, *The Mirror and the Lamp: Romantic Theory and the Critical Tradition* (Oxford: Oxford University Press, 1971), chap. 1–3.

32. Miller, "Prologue," 45.

33. William Hazlitt quoted in Abrams, *The Mirror and the Lamp*, 52.

34. References to the moon to reflect on mimetic, ontological, psychological, and aesthetic principles are a defining feature of Conrad's poetics. Compare this passage in *Lord Jim*: "There's something haunting in the light of the moon; it has all the dispassionateness of a disembodied soul, and something of its inconceivable mystery. It is to our sunshine which—say what you like—is all we have to live by, what the echo is to the sound: misleading and confusing whether the note be mocking or sad. It robs all forms of matter—which, after all, is our domain—of their substance and gives a sinister reality to shadows alone. And the shadows were very real around us, but Jim by my side looked very stalwart, as though nothing—not even the occult power of moonlight— could rob him of his reality in my eyes" (186–87).

35. Henry Staten carefully traces the "structural design" of this sequence to cast light on the Intended's "Dionysian cry," which, in his view, serves as the driving telos of this narrative qua myth. Staten, "Conrad's Dionysian Elegy," 206–10.

36. Euripides, *The Bacchae*, tr. William Arrowsmith, in *The Complete Greek Tragedies*, vol. 4, ed. David Grene and Richard Lattimore (Chicago: University of Chicago Press), 543–608, 592.

37. Terry Eagleton, *Sweet Violence: The Idea of the Tragic* (Oxford: Blackwell, 2003), 56.

38. Dollimore, "Civilization and Its Darkness," 84.

39. Eagleton, *Sweet Violence*, 56.

40. Walter Kaufmann, *Tragedy and Philosophy* (Princeton, NJ: Princeton University Press, 1968), 85.

41. For a penetrating reading of *Heart of Darkness*'s insights into the horror of death in light of X-ray technology, see Martine Hennard Dutheil de la Rochère, "Sounding the Hollow Heart of the West: X-rays and the *Technique de la Mort*," in *Conrad's* Heart of Darkness *and Contemporary Thought: Revisiting the Horror with Lacoue-Labarthe*, ed. Nidesh Lawtoo, London: Bloomsbury, 2012, 222–38.

42. *Apocalypse Now Redux*, directed by Francis Ford Coppola, Zoetrope Studios, USA 2001.

43. Jean Baudrillard, *Simulacres et simulation* (Paris: Galilée, 1981), 90.

44. As Rachel Falconer points out in her wide-ranging account of contemporary narratives of the descent to Hell (or *katabasis*), of which *Heart of Darkness* and *Apocalypse Now* are paradigmatic examples: "Along with *Platoon* and *Full Metal Jacket*, *Apocalypse Now* is watched by American soldiers in their preparation for war because such films, the soldiers say, 'celebrate the terrible and despicable beauty of their fighting skills.'" Rachel Falconer, *Hell in Contemporary Literature: Western Descent Narratives since 1945* (Edinburgh: Edinburgh University Press, 2007), 198.

45. Francis Ford Coppola, quoted in Margot Norris, "Modernist and Vietnam: Francis Ford Coppola's *Apocalypse Now*," *Modern Fiction Studies* 44.3 (1998): 730–66, 730.

46. Neither the tiger nor the caribou is mentioned in *Heart of Darkness*, yet they are in line with its tragic foundations for both animals are Oriental counterparts of Dionysian animal manifestations, such as the leopard and the bull.

47. Holger Bachmann, "Hollow Men in Vietnam: A Reading of the Concluding Sequence of *Apocalypse Now*," *Forum for Modern Language Studies* 34.4 (1998): 314–34, 320.

48. Frazer, *Golden Bough*, 326. The general trajectory of *Apocalypse Now* is faithful to Frazer's idea that "the man-god must be killed as soon as he shows symptoms that his powers are beginning to fail, and his soul must be transferred to a vigorous successor before it has been seriously impaired by the threatened decay" (215).

49. See Girard, *Violence and the Sacred*, chap. 2 and esp. chap. 5 devoted to Dionysus. On Girard and *Apocalypse Now*, see also Garrett Stewart, "Coppola's Conrad: The Repetitions of Complicity," *Critical Inquiry* 7.3 (1981): 455–74, 456–57, 469–70.

50. *Hearts of Darkness: A Filmmaker's Apocalypse*, directed by Fax Bahr, George Hickenlooper, Eleanor Coppola, American Zoetrope, USA, 1991.

51. Speaking of the sacrifice of a bull in the context of Greek fertility rites linked to the cult of Dionysus, Jane Harrison writes: "The holy flesh is not offered to a god, it is eaten—to every man his portion—by each and every citizen that he may get his share of the strength of the Bull." Jane Harrison, *Ancient Art and Ritual* (New York: Greenwood Press, 1969), 89. Harrison is talking about Greek religion here, yet her theory of ritual was an important influence on Jessie Weston's *From Ritual to Romance* (the other book on Kurtz's desk, along with Frazer's *The Golden Bough*) and is thus directly relevant for the anthropology of *Apocalypse Now*.

52. Along with René Girard and Georges Bataille, the mythologist Joseph Campbell is one of the few contemporary thinkers who, on the broad shoulders of figures like Nietzsche, Frazer, and Harrison, dares to propose a general comparative theory of sacrifice. Particularly resonant with our discussion is Campbell's wide-ranging and beautifully illustrated account of "sacrificial festivals" in Southeast Asia, where he also uses Nietzsche's take on the Dionysian and the Apollonian to frame the metaphysical violence of the sacred. Joseph Campbell, *Historical Atlas of World Mythology*, vol. 2, *The Way of the Seeded Earth. Part 1: The Sacrifice* (New York: Harper & Row, 1988), 54–73.

53. Georges Bataille, "Hegel, la mort, le sacrifice," in *Oeuvres Complètes*, vol. 12, 326–45 (my translation).

54. Mircea Eliade, *Shamanism: Archaic Techniques of Ecstas*, tr. Willard R. Trask (Princeton, NJ: Princeton University Press, 1974), 510.

55. Speaking of the aesthetic principle that animates *Apocalypse Now*, Coppola stated that "he tried to make it more an experience than a movie," yet the medium of the movie is the source of this experience. Francis Ford Coppola, quoted in Bachmann, "Hollow Men," 318.

### Chapter 8. Hypermimesis: Horrorism Redux in *The Secret Agent*

1. Adriana Cavarero, *Horrorism: Naming Contemporary Violence*, tr. William McCuaig (New York: Columbia University Press, 2011).

2. For an informed collection of early reviews and criticism until the 1970s, see Ian Watt, ed., *Conrad: The Secret Agent (A Casebook)* (London: Macmillan, 1973).

3. On Kazynski's "misreading" of Conrad's *The Secret Agent*, see James Guimond and Katherine K. Maynard, "Kaczynski, Conrad and Terrorism," *Conradiana* 31.1 (1999): 3–25.

4. Margaret Scanlan, *Plotting Terror: Novelists and Terrorists in Contemporary Fiction* (Charlottesville: University of Virginia Press, 2001), 14.

5. Slavoj Žižek, *Welcome to the Desert of the Real: Five Essays on September 11* (London: Verso, 2002), 16.

6. Jean Baudrillard, *The Spirit of Terrorism and Other Essays*, tr. Chris Turner (London: Verso, 2003), 5, 7.

7. Baudrillard acknowledges that "the terrorist act is generated by models," but eventually dismisses this mimetic hypothesis as "reductive." Baudrillard, *Spirit of Terrorism*, 72–73.

8. Oscar Wilde, "The Decay of Lying," in *The Complete Works of Oscar Wilde*, vol. 4, ed. Josephine M. Guy (Oxford: Oxford University Press, 2007), 94.

9. See Žižek, *Welcome to the Desert*, 17.

10. For an informed account of post-9/11 media responses to *The Secret Agent*, see Peter Lancelot Mallios, "Afterword: The Deserts of Conrad," in Joseph Conrad, *The Secret Agent*, ed. Peter Mallios (New York: Modern Library, 2004), 261–90, esp. 261–63; Terry Eagleton, *Holy Terror* (Oxford: Oxford University Press, 2005), 121.

11. Mallios, "Afterword," 279. See also see Peter Lancelot Mallios, "Reading *The Secret Agent* Now: The Press, the Police, the Premonition of Simulation," in *Conrad in the Twenty-First Century: Contemporary Approaches and Perspectives*, ed. Carola M. Kaplan, Peter Mallios, and Andrea White (New York: Routledge, 2005), 155–72.

12. Mallios, "Afterword," 280. Notice that Mallios's hermeneutical recuperation of the real Conrad from the "desert of Conrad" does not rest on a postmodern ontology. For Baudrillard, in fact, "there is no point of attacking the virtual, if it means falling back into reality." Baudrillard, *Spirit of Terrorism*, 72.

13. Adriana Cavarero, "Appendix: The Horror! The Horror! Rereading Conrad," in Cavarero, *Horrorism*, 117–24.

14. Jacques Berthoud, "The Secret Agent," in *The Cambridge Companion to Joseph Conrad*, ed. J. H. Stape (Cambridge: Cambridge University Press, 1996), 100–121, 103.

15. As Alex Houen points out, types of "contagion" that cross borders between fiction and reality "remain largely unexamined in terrorism studies." Alex Houen, *Terrorism and Modern Literature: From Joseph Conrad to Ciaran Carson* (Oxford: Oxford University Press, 2002), 18. What we must add is that Conrad already examined this disconcerting form of contagion in *The Secret Agent*.

16. John Gray, "The NS Essay—A Target for Destructive Ferocity," *New Statesman*, April 29, 2002.

17. On the historical sources of *The Secret Agent*, see Norman Sherry, "The Greenwich Bomb: Outrage and *The Secret Agent*," in Watt, *Conrad*, 202–28.

18. Cavarero argues that contrary to "terror" (from Latin, *tremo*, root, *ter* indicating the act of trembling), "horror" (from Latin, *orreo*, bristling sensation) is beyond fear and escape: it leaves bodies frozen and paralyzed in front of a scene, and, as she specifies, "more than fear, horror has to do with repugnance" in face of a "form of violence that is more inadmissible than death" (*H* 4, 5).

19. Eagleton, *Holy Terror*, chap. 1.

20. As Hillis Miller puts it, "the theme of *The Secret Agent* is the universal death which underlies life. As the characters get closer to death, they approach a condition in which they are the equivalents of one another." J. Hillis Miller, *Poets of Reality: Six Twentieth-Century Writers* (Cambridge, MA: Harvard University Press, 1965), 66. This "equivalence" entails a return to a mimetic metaphysics that, for Conrad, is the very foundation, seat, or ground of the subject.

21. Cavarero does not directly address the horrorism of mimesis, yet mimetic phantoms surface at times from the interstices of her argument. For instance, she writes: "Phantasmic copies of real torturers known to history, the Abu Gharib tormentors and their victims appear as specters, personified citations of horror, grotesque mimes from a gallery of infamy" (*H* 111).

22. Aristotle, *The Poetics of Aristotle*, tr. Stephen Halliwell (Chapel Hill: University of North Carolina Press, 1987), 34.

23. Fredric Jameson, *The Political Unconscious: Narrative as a Socially Symbolic Act* (Ithaca, NY: Cornell University Press, 1981), 217.

24. Georges Bataille, *Erotism: Death and Sensuality*, tr. Mary Dalwood (San Francisco: City Lights Books, 1962), 11.

25. Recall that Stevie, as a reaction to a feeling of "compassion," which, we are told, could be wrought to "the pitch of that frenzy," nearly explodes himself by "letting off fireworks on the staircase" (13).

26. In his commentary on *The Secret Agent*, Thomas Mann touches on an essential point as he says that "the striking feature of modern art is that it has ceased to recognize the categories of tragic and comic, or the dramatic classifications, tragedy and comedy. It sees life as a tragi-comedy, with the result that the grotesque is its most genuine style." Thomas Mann, "Joseph Conrad's *The Secret Agent* (1926)," in Watt, *Conrad*, 98–112, 106.

27. Mark Wollaeger, *Modernism, Media, and Propaganda: British Narrative from 1900 to 1945* (Princeton, NJ: Princeton University Press, 2006), 60.

28. Baudrillard, *Spirit of Terrorism*, 26, 30.

29. Eagleton, *Holy Terror*, 91.

30. Eagleton, *Holy Terror*, 92. On early-modernist writers such as Conrad and James who anticipate contemporary concerns such as "the tendency of art to convert violence into an enthralling spectacle," see also Scanlan, *Plotting Terror*, 10.

31. Gabriel Tarde, *Les lois de l'imitation* (Paris: Seuil, 2001), vii.

32. Mallios, "Reading *The Secret Agent*," 158, 163.

33. Wollaeger, *Modernism, Media, and Propaganda*, 35; see also chap. 1.

34. Raymond Williams, *Keywords: A Vocabulary of Culture and Society* (New York: Oxford University Press, 1983), 193.

35. See Nidesh Lawtoo, *The Phantom of the Ego: Modernism and the Mimetic Unconscious* (East Lansing: Michigan State University Press, 2013), 105–17.

36. Mallios, "Reading *The Secret Agent*," 170.

37. Mallios, "Reading *The Secret Agent*," 170.

38. See Friedrich Nietzsche, *Twilight of the Idols*, in *The Portable Nietzsche*, tr. Walter Kaufmann (New York: Viking Press, 1954), 463–563, 485–86.

39. Mallios stresses the media's "controlling" power, whereas Wollaeger stresses that they "go unread." Mallios, "Reading *The Secret Agent*," 162; Wollaeger, *Modernism, Media, and Propaganda*, 50.

40. In a letter to Cunninghame Graham, Joseph Conrad famously compared the universe to a "knitting machine," not, of course, a typographic machine. Here is the original version, for the record: "There is a—let us say—a machine. It evolved itself (I am severely scientific) out of a chaos of scraps of iron and behold!—it knits. I am horrified at the horrible work and stand appalled. I feel it ought to embroider—but it goes on knitting. You come and say: 'this is all right; it's only a question of the right kind of oil. Let us use this—for instance—celestial oil and the machine shall embroider the most beautiful design in purple and gold.' Will it? Alas no. You cannot by any special lubrication make embroidery with a knitting machine. And the most withering thought is that the infamous thing has made itself: made itself without thought, without conscience, without foresight, without eyes, without heart. It is a tragic accident—and it has happened. . . . It knits us in and it knits us out. It has knitted time, space, pain, death, corruption, despair and all the illusions—and nothing matters" (*CL*, I, 495).

41. Susan Sontag, *Regarding the Pain of Others* (New York: Ferrar, Strauss and Giroux, 2003).

42. Baudrillard, *Spirit of Terrorism*, 7.

### Coda: Conrad's Neuroplasticity

1. A number of scholars on both sides of the science/humanities divide have recently come to this realization. Thus one of the most visible figures in contemporary brain research, V. S. Ramachandran, affirms that his goal is "ultimately, to bridge the gap that now separates C. P. Snow's 'two cultures'—the sciences and the humanities." V. R. Ramachandran, *A Brief Tour of Human Consciousness: From Impostor Poodles to Purple Numbers* (New York: PI Press, 2004),

ix. Along similar lines, historians of science Nikolas Rose and Joelle Abi-Rached state that we
are now confronted with "a new opportunity for collaboration across 'two cultures.'" Nikolas
Rose and Joelle Abi-Rached, *Neuro: The New Brain Sciences and the Management of the Mind*
(Princeton, NJ: Princeton University Press, 2013), 142. And on the literary front, Paul Armstrong
speaks of an "opportunity for exchange" that should not be missed. Paul B. Armstrong, *How
Literature Plays with the Brain: The Neuroscience of Reading and Art* (Baltimore: Johns Hopkins
University Press, 2013), xi.

2. Armstrong, *How Literature Plays with the Brain*, 10.

3. Norman Doidge, *The Brain that Changes Itself: Stories of Personal Triumph from the Frontiers
of Brain Science* (London: Penguin Books, 2007), xv. Jeffrey Schwartz and Sharon Begley
supplement this definition as follows: "*Neuroplasticity* refers to the ability of neurons to forge
new connections, to blaze new paths through the cortex, even to assume new roles. In short,
neuroplasticty means rewiring of the brain." Jeffrey M. Schwartz and Sharon Begley, *The Mind
and the Brain: Neuroplasticity and the Power of Mental Force* (New York: ReganBooks, 2002),
15. For an informed historical account of neuroplasticity, see also Rose and Abi-Rached, *Neuro*,
48–51, 221–26.

4. Catherine Malabou, *What Should We Do with Our Brain?* tr. Sebastian Rand (New York:
Fordham University Press, 2008), 1.

5. See Omri Moses, *Out of Character: Modernism, Vitalism, Psychic Life* (Stanford, CA: Stanford
University Press, 2014); Nidesh Lawtoo, *The Phantom of the Ego: Modernism and the Mimetic
Unconscious* (East Lansing: Michigan State University Press, 2013).

6. On the biographical continuities between Conrad and Razumov, see Keith Carabine, *The Life
and the Art: A Study of Conrad's* Under Western Eyes (Amsterdam: Rodopi, 1997), chapt. 3.
For a historically informed account of Conrad's conflicted relation to his "Slavic profile" as it is
configured in *A Personal Record* and *Under Western Eyes*, see Christopher GoGwilt, *The Invention
of the West: Joseph Conrad and the Double-Mapping of Europe and Empire* (Stanford: Stanford
University Press, 1995), 131–55.

7. As Geoffrey Harpham also recognizes, Conrad was "intimate to a degree we can scarcely imagine
with the human capacity for adaptation." And he adds: "Conrad's acquired sensitivity to the
human capacity to assume different forms became the basis for both his self understanding and his
understanding of human beings generally." Geoffrey Galt Harpham, "Beyond Mastery," in *Conrad
in the Twenty-First Century: Contemporary Approaches and Perspectives*, ed. Carola M. Kaplan,
Peter Mallios, and Andrea White (New York: Routledge, 2005), 17–38, 18.

8. Zdzisław Najder and J. H. Stape recognize that "if there are few tangible connections between
the two books [*A Personal Record* and *Under Western Eyes*], an underlying emotional link exists
between them" ("Introduction," *PR* xxv). What follows suggests that the so far unexplored
problematic of plasticity gives form to this emotional link, a mimetic link that, at a higher level of
generality, informs Conrad's corpus as a whole.

9. Plato, *Republic*, in *The Collected Dialogues of Plato*, ed. Edith Hamilton and Huntington Cairns
(New York: Pantheon Books, 1963), 575–844, 820.

10. For an informed account of the role mimesis plays in the Plato's take on education, see Eric A.
Havelock, *Preface to Plato* (Cambridge, MA: Harvard University Press, 1963), chapt. 2.

11. Jean-Jacques Rousseau, *Émile ou de l'éducation* (Paris: Flammarion, 1966), 40 (my translation).

12. Rousseau, *Émile*, 139.

13. Philippe Lacoue-Labarthe, *Typography: Mimesis, Philosophy, Politics*, ed. Christopher Fynsk (Cambridge, MA: Harvard University Press, 1989), 126–27.

14. Lacoue-Labarthe, *Typography*, 115.

15. Doidge, *Brain That Changes Itself*, xvi.

16. Rose and Abi-Rached, *Neuro*, 48.

17. Following her thesis on plasticity and Hegel, in her most recent writings Malabou continues to ground the philosophical foundations of plasticity at the dusk of the history of philosophy. As she puts it, "the concept of plasticity" was "discovered for the first time in the preface to Hegel's *Phenomenology of Spirit*." Catherine Malabou, *Plasticity at the Dusk of Writing: Dialectic, Destruction, Deconstruction*, tr. Carolyn Sheared (New York: Columbia University Press, 2010), 8. Malabou's general philosophical ambition is to inaugurate a new paradigm that is supposed to dislocate—in a move not deprived of mimetic rivalry—the ontology of writing she inherited from Jacques Derrida. Hence she posits what she calls "the style of an era" predicated on the realization that "form is plastic." (1). Given the emphasis on both "form" and "plasticity," Malabou is strangely silent on the concept of mimesis. Yet she acknowledges, in a Freudian mood, that "because plasticity never presents itself without form, plastic is always thought as a factor of identification" (74). Since Malabou reads the formative and deformative power of plasticity from a deconstructive perspective heavily in-*formed* by Derrida—and, less explicitly but not less importantly, by Lacoue-Labarthe—she remains, nolens volens, in line with pharmaceutical, mimetic principles that were discovered for the first time in Plato's *Republic*.

18. Armstrong, *How Literature Plays with the Brain*, 19–20; see also chapt. 5.

19. Derrida's diagnostic of writing is also a perfect picture of Razumov: "This signifier of little, this discourse that doesn't amount to much, is like all ghosts: errant. It rolls (*kulindeitai*) this way and that like someone who has lost his way, who doesn't know where he is going, having strayed from the correct path, the right direction, the rule of rectitude, the norm; but also like someone who has lost his rights, an outlaw, a pervert, a bad seed, a vagrant, an adventurer, a bum. Wandering in the streets, he doesn't even know who he is, what his identity—if he has one—might be, what his name is, what his father's name is. . . . Uprooted, anonymous, unattached to any house or country, this almost insignificant signifier is at everyone's disposal." Jacques Derrida, "Plato's Pharmacy," in *Dissemination*, tr. Barbara Johnson (Chicago: University of Chicago Press, 1981), 143–44.

20. For an informed account of critics interested in "the author's psychology, opinions and the facts of his life" see Najder and Stape's introduction (*PR* xliii–xlvii).

21. Harpham perceptively adds that "both adoption and identification involve similar principles" and that by "depicting the identification of one character with another, Conrad was casting into narrative form the very struggle he was experiencing with respect to his medium." Harpham, "Beyond Mastery," 22. What follows supplements this perspective from the angle of mimetic plasticity.

22. Paul Armstrong perceptively notices that, "How to render the subjective experience of a sensation or a perception with paint or words is the distinctive challenge of impressionist art," and sets out to enlist Conrad, Ford Madox Ford, and Henry James as figures who cast light on the "riddle of consciousness" along lines that anticipate what neurosciences now call "the problem of qualia." Paul B. Armstrong "What Is It Like to Be Conscious: Impressionism and the Problem of Qualia," in *A History of the Modernist Novel*, ed. Gregory Castle (Cambridge: Cambridge University Press, 2015), 66–85, 66.

23. Ford Madox Ford, *Joseph Conrad: A Personal Remembrance* (New York: Octagon Books, 1971), 255.

24. René Girard, *To Double Business Bound: Essays on Literature, Mimesis, and Anthropology* (Baltimore: Johns Hopkins University Press, 1978), 201.

25. Schwartz and Begley, *The Mind and the Brain*, 15.

26. Doidge, *Brain That Changes Itself*, 207, 214.

27. Doidge, *Brain That Changes Itself*, xv.

# Bibliography

Abrams, M. H. *The Mirror and the Lamp: Romantic Theory and the Critical Tradition*. Oxford: Oxford University Press, 1971.

Achebe, Chinua. *The African Trilogy: Things Fall Apart, No Longer at Ease, Arrow of God*. New York: Everyman's Library, 2010.

———. "Africa's Tarnished Image." In *Things Fall Apart*, edited by Abiola Irele, 209–20. New York: W. W. Norton, 2009.

———. *Conversations with Chinua Achebe*. Edited by Bernth Lindfors. Jackson: University Press of Mississippi, 1997.

———. *Hopes and Impediments: Selected Essays 1965–1987*. Oxford: Heinemann, 1988.

———. "An Image of Africa: Racism in Conrad's *Heart of Darkness*." In *Heart of Darkness*, 4th ed., edited by Paul B. Armstrong, 336–49. New York: W. W. Norton, 2006.

———. *Things Fall Apart*. Edited by Francis Abiola Irele. New York: W. W. Norton, 2009.

Adekoya, Olusegun. "Criticising the Critic: Achebe on Conrad." In *Things Fall Apart*, by Chinua Achebe, edited by Francis Abiola Irele, 189–99. New York: W. W. Norton, 2009.

Anderson, Benedict. *Imagined Communities: Reflections on the Origins and Spread of Nationalism*. London: Verso, 1991.

Antonello, Pierpaolo, and Paul Gifford, eds. *Can We Survive Our Origins? Readings in René Girard's Theory of Violence and the Sacred*. East Lansing: Michigan State University Press, 2015.

Appiah, Anthony Kwame. Introduction to *Things Fall Apart*, by Chinua Achebe, v–xxvi. New York: Knopf, 1992.

Aristotle. *The Poetics of Aristotle*. Translated by Stephen Halliwell. Chapel Hill: University of North Carolina Press, 1987.

Armstrong, Paul B. *How Literature Plays with the Brain: The Neuroscience of Reading and Art*. Baltimore: Johns Hopkins University Press, 2013.

———. "Reading, Race and Representing Others." In *Heart of Darkness*, edited by Paul B. Armstrong, 429–44. New York: W. W. Norton, 2006.

———. "What Is It like to Be Conscious? Impressionism and the Problem of Qualia." In *A History of the Modernist Novel*, edited by Gregory Castle, 66–85. Cambridge: Cambridge University Press, 2015.

Aron, Raymond. *Penser la guerre, Clausewitz*. Vols. 1–2. Paris: Gallimard, 1976.

———. *Sur Clausewitz*. Paris: Editions Complexe, 1987.

Arvamudan, Srinivas. "The Catachronism of Climate Change." *Diacritics* 41.3 (2013): 6–31.

Bachmann, Holger. "Hollow Men in Vietnam: A Reading of the Concluding Sequence of *Apocalypse Now*." *Forum for Modern Language Studies* 34. 4 (1998): 314–34.

Basden, G. T. *Among the Ibos of Nigeria*. London: Frank Cass, 1966.

Bassford, Christopher. *Clausewitz in English: The Reception of Clausewitz in Britain and America*. Oxford: Oxford University Press, 1994.

Bataille, Georges. *Erotism: Death and Sensuality*. Translated by Mary Dalwood. San Francisco: City Lights Books, 1962.

———. "Hegel, la mort, le sacrifice." In *Oeuvres Complètes*, Vol. 12, 326–45. Paris: Gallimard, 1988.

Bateson, Gregory. *Steps to an Ecology of Mind: A Revolutionary Approach to Man's Understanding of Himself*. New York: Ballantine Books, 1972.

Baudrillard, Jean. *Simulacres et simulation*. Paris: Galilée, 1981.

———. *The Spirit of Terrorism and Other Essays*. Translated by Chris Turner. London: Verso, 2003.

Bell, Catherine. *Ritual Perspectives and Dimensions*. Oxford: Oxford University Press, 1997.

Benjamin, Walter. "The Mimetic Faculty." In *Reflections: Essays Aphorisms, Autobiographical Writings*, translated by Edmund Jephcott, edited by Peter Demetz, 333–36. New York: Schocken Books, 1978.

Bennett, Jane. *Vibrant Matter: A Political Ecology of Things*. Durham, NC: Duke University Press, 2010.

Benson, Carl. "Two Stories of Initiation." *PMLA* 69.1 (1954): 46–56.

Berlin, Isaiah. *The Roots of Romanticism*. Edited by Henry Hardy. Princeton, NJ: Princeton University Press, 2001.

Berthoud, Jacques. "The Secret Agent." In *The Cambridge Companion to Joseph Conrad*, edited by J. H. Stape, 100–121. Cambridge: Cambridge University Press, 1996.

Bhabha, Homi K. *The Location of Culture*. London: Routledge, 1994.

Bianchi, Aristide, and Leonid Kharlamov. "Les Écrits sur l'Occident de Philippe Lacoue-Labarthe." In *La Réponse d'Ulysse*, by Philippe Lacoue-Labarthe, edited by Aristide Bianchi and Leonid Kharlamov, 145–83. Lignes/Imec, 2012.

Bock, Martin. "Joseph Conrad and Germ Theory: Why Captain Allistoun Smiles Thoughtfully." *The Conradian* 31.2 (2006): 1–14.

———. *Joseph Conrad and Psychological Medicine.* Lubbock: Texas Tech University Press, 2002.

Borch-Jacobsen, Mikkel. *The Emotional Tie: Psychoanalysis, Affect, Mimesis.* Translated by Douglass Brick et al. Stanford, CA: Stanford University Press, 1992.

———. *The Freudian Subject.* Translated by Catherine Porter. Stanford, CA: Stanford University Press, 1988.

———. *Lacan: The Absolute Master.* Translated by Douglas Brick. Stanford, CA: Stanford University Press, 1991.

Borch-Jacobsen, Mikkel, and Sonu Shamdasani. *The Freud Files: An Inquiry into the History of Psychoanalysis.* Cambridge: Cambridge University Press, 2012.

Breton, André. *Manifestoes of Surrealism.* Translated by Richard Seaver and Helen R. Lane. Ann Arbor: University of Michigan Press, 1974.

Bull, Malcolm. "What Is the Rational Response?" *London Review of Books* 34.10 (2012): 3–6.

Butler, Judith. *The Psychic Life of Power: Theories in Subjection.* Stanford, CA: Stanford University Press, 1997.

Caillois, Roger. *Le Mythe et l'homme.* Paris: Gallimard, 1938.

———. "Le Surréalisme comme univers de signes." In *Œuvres,* edited by Dominique Rabourdin, 227–34. Paris: Gallimard, 2008.

Caminero-Santangelo, Byron. *African Fiction and Joseph Conrad: Reading Postcolonial Intertextuality.* Albany: State University of New York Press, 2005.

Campbell, Joseph. *Historical Atlas of World Mythology.* Vol. 2, *The Way of the Seeded Earth. Part 1: The Sacrifice.* New York: Harper & Row, 1988.

Carabine, Keith. *The Life and the Art: A Study of Conrad's* Under Western Eyes. Amsterdam: Rodopi, 1997.

Cary, Joyce. *Mister Johnson.* London: Michael Joseph, 1975.

Cavarero, Adriana. *Horrorism: Naming Contemporary Violence.* Translated by William McCuaig. New York: Columbia University Press, 2011.

———. *Orrorismo: Ovvero della violenza sull'inerme.* Milan: Feltrinelli, 2007.

Chakrabarty, Dipesh. "The Climate of History: Four Theses." *Critical Inquiry* 35.2 (2009): 197–222.

Chomsky, Noam, and Laray Polok. *Nuclear War and Environmental Catastrophe.* New York: Seven Stories Press, 2013.

Clausewitz, Carl. *On War.* Translated by Michael Howard and Peter Paret. Oxford: Oxford University Press, 2008.

———. *Vom Kriege.* Bonn: Dummler, 1973.

Clendinnen, Inga. "Preempting Postcolonial Critique: Europeans in *Heart of Darkness.*" *Common Knowledge* 13.1 (2007): 1–17.

Clifford, James. *The Predicament of Culture: Twentieth-Century Ethnography, Literature, and Art.* Cambridge, MA: Harvard University Press, 1988.

Collits, Terry. *Postcolonial Conrad: Paradoxes of Empire*. New York: Routledge, 2005.

Connolly, William E. *The Fragility of Things: Self-Organizing Processes, Neoliberal Fantasies, and Democratic Activism*. Durham, NC: Duke University Press, 2013.

Coppola, Francis Ford. *Apocalypse Now Redux*, Zoetrope Studios, USA, 2001.

Crutzen, Paul J., and Eugene Stoermer F. "The Anthropocene." *IGBP [International Geosphere-Biosphere Programme] Newsletter* 41 (2000): 12–15.

Curley, Daniel. "The Writer and His Use of Material: The Case of 'The Secret Sharer.'" *Modern Fiction Studies* 13.2 (1967): 179–94.

Damasio, Antonio. *Descartes' Error: Emotion, Reason, and the Human Brain*. New York: Penguin Books, 2005.

Darwin, Charles. *The Descent of Man*. In *Darwin: A Norton Critical Edition*, 2nd ed., edited by Philip Appelman. London: W. W. Norton, 1970.

Davis, Eugene. "The Structure of Justice in 'The Secret Sharer.'" *Conradiana* 27.1 (1995): 64–73.

Davis, Mike. *The Monster at Our Door: The Global Threat of Avian Flu*. New York: Owl Books, 2005.

De Heusch, Luc. *La transe et ses entours*. Paris: Éditions complexe, 2006.

Deleuze, Gilles, and Félix Guattari. *A Thousand Plateaus: Capitalism and Schizophrenia*. Translated by Brian Massumi. London: Continuum, 2004.

Deresiewicz, William. "Conrad's Impasse: *The Nigger of the 'Narcissus'* and the Invention of Marlow." *Conradiana* 38.3 (2006): 205–26.

Derrida, Jacques. "Plato's Pharmacy." In *Dissemination*, translated by Barbara Johnson, 61–171. Chicago: University of Chicago Press, 1981.

Dodds, E. R. *The Greeks and the Irrational*. Berkeley: University of California Press, 1964.

Doidge, Norman. *The Brain that Changes Itself: Stories of Personal Triumph from the Frontiers of Brain Science*. London: Penguin Books, 2007.

Dollimore, Jonathan. "Civilization and Its Darkness." In *Conrad's* Heart of Darkness *and Contemporary Thought: Revisiting the Horror with Lacoue-Labarthe*, edited by Nidesh Lawtoo, 67–86. London: Bloomsbury, 2012.

Donato, Eugenio, and Richard Macksey. *The Structuralist Controversy: The Languages of Criticism and the Sciences of Man*. Baltimore: Johns Hopkins University Press, 1970.

Dupré, Marie-Claude, ed. *Familiarité avec les dieux: transe et possession (Afrique Noire, Madagascar, La Réunion)*. Clermont-Ferrand, France: Presses Universitaires Blaise Pascal, 2001.

Dupuy, Jean-Pierre. *The Mark of the Sacred*. Translated by M. B. Debevoise. Stanford, CA: Stanford University Press, 2013.

———. *La Panique*. Paris: Seuil, 1991.

———. *Pour un catastrophisme éclairé: Quand l'impossible est certain*. Paris: Seuil, 2002.

Durkheim, Émile. *The Elementary Forms of Religious Life*. Translated by Carol Cosman. Oxford: Oxford University Press, 2001.

Eagleton, Terry. *Exiles and Émigrés: Studies in Modern Literature*. New York: Schocken Books, 1970.

————. *Holy Terror*. Oxford: Oxford University Press, 2005.

————. *Literary Theory: An Introduction*. Oxford: Blackwell, 2008.

————. *Sweet Violence: The Idea of the Tragic*. Oxford: Blackwell, 2003.

Eliade, Mircea. *Shamanism: Archaic Techniques of Ecstasy*. Translated by Willard R. Trask. Princeton, NJ: Princeton University Press, 1974.

Ellenberger, Henry. *The Discovery of the Unconscious: The History and Evolution of Dynamic Psychiatry*. New York: Basic Books, 1970.

Erdinast-Vulcan, Daphna. *Joseph Conrad and the Modern Temper*. Oxford: Clarendon Press, 1991.

————. *The Strange Short Fiction of Joseph Conrad: Writing, Culture, and Subjectivity*. Oxford: Oxford University Press, 1999.

Euripides. *The Bacchae*. Translated by William Arrowsmith. In *The Complete Greek Tragedies*, Vol. 4, edited by David Grene and Richard Lattimore, 543–608. Chicago: University of Chicago Press, 1958.

Falconer, Rachel. *Hell in Contemporary Literature: Western Descent Narratives since 1945*. Edinburgh: Edinburgh University Press, 2007.

Felski, Rita. Introduction to *Rethinking Tragedy*, edited by Rita Felski, 1–25. Baltimore: Johns Hopkins University Press, 2008.

Ford, Ford Madox. *Joseph Conrad: A Personal Remembrance*. New York: Octagon Books, 1971.

Forster, E. M. *Abinger Harvest*. London: Edward Arnold, 1936.

Foucault, Michel. "Two Lectures." In *Power/Knowledge: Selected Interviews & Other Writings 1972–1977*, edited by Colin Gordon, 78–108. New York: Pantheon Books, 1980.

————. "What Is an Author." In *Critical Theory since 1965*, edited by Hazard Adams and Leroy Searle, 138–47. Tallahassee: Florida State University Press, 1989.

Frank, Claudine. Introduction to *The Edge of Surrealism: A Roger Caillois Reader*, edited by Claudine Frank, translated by Claudine Frank and Camille Naish, 1–57. Durham, NC: Duke University Press, 2003.

Frazer, James G. *The Golden Bough*. New York: Gramercy Books, 1981.

Freud, Sigmund. *Group Psychology and the Analysis of the Ego*. Translated by James Strachey. New York: W. W. Norton, 1959.

Fried, Michael. "Almayer's Face: On 'Impressionism' in Conrad, Crane, and Norris." *Critical Inquiry* 17.1 (1990): 193–236.

Fumaroli, Marc. *Les abeilles et les araignées*. In *La Querrelle des Anciens et des Modernes*, edited by Anne-Marie Lecoq, 7–218. Paris: Gallimard, 2001.

Gallese, Vittorio. "The Two Sides of Mimesis: Mimetic Theory, Embodied Simulation, and Social Identification." In *Mimesis and Science: Empirical Research on Imitation and the Mimetic Theory of Culture and Religion*, edited by Scott R. Garrels, 87–108. East Lansing: Michigan State University Press, 2011.

Garber, Marjorie, and Barbara Johnson. "Secret Sharing: Reading Conrad Psychoanalytically." *College English* 49.6 (1987): 628–40.

Gardiner, Stephen. *A Perfect Moral Storm: The Ethical Tragedy of Climate Change.* Oxford: Oxford University Press, 2011.

Garrels, Scott R., ed. *Mimesis and Science: Empirical Research on Imitation and the Mimetic Theory of Culture and Religion.* East Lansing: Michigan State University Press, 2011.

Garrett, Laurie. *The Coming Plague: Newly Emerging Diseases in a World Out of Balance.* London: Penguin, 1995.

Gebauer, Gunter, and Christopher Wulf. *Mimesis: Culture—Art—Society.* Translated by Don Reneau. Berkeley: University of California Press, 1995.

Gikandi, Simon. "Foreword: Chinua Achebe and the Institution of African Literature." In *The Chinua Achebe Encyclopedia*, edited by M. Keith Booker, vii–xvi. Westport, CT: Greenwood Press, 2003.

———. "Theory after Postcolonial Theory: Rethinking the Work of Mimesis." In *Theory after Theory*, edited by Jane Elliott and Derek Attridge, 163–78. New York: Routledge, 2011.

Girard, René. *Achever Clausewitz: Entretiens avec Benoît Chantre.* Paris: Carnets Nord, 2007.

———. *Battling to the End: Conversations with Benoît Chantre.* Translated by Mary Baker. East Lansing: Michigan State University Press, 2010.

———. *Le Bouc émissaire.* Paris: Éditions Grasset et Fasquelle, 1982.

———. *Deceit, Desire, and the Novel.* Translated by Yvonne Freccero. Baltimore: Johns Hopkins University Press, 1965.

———. *To Double Business Bound: Essays on Literature, Mimesis, and Anthropology.* Baltimore: Johns Hopkins University Press, 1978.

———. *Violence and the Sacred.* Translated by Patrick Gregory. Baltimore: Johns Hopkins University Press, 1977.

———. *La Violence et le sacré.* Paris: Éditions Albin Michel, 1990.

Girard, René, Pierpaolo Antonello, and João Cezar de Castro Rocha. *Evolution and Conversion: Dialogues on the Origins of Culture.* London: Continuum, 2007.

GoGwilt, Christopher. *The Invention of the West: Joseph Conrad and the Double-Mapping of Europe and Empire.* Stanford, CA: Stanford University Press, 1995.

Goldknopf, David. "What's Wrong with Conrad: Conrad on Conrad." *Criticism* 10 (1968): 54–64.

Gore, Al. *An Inconvenient Truth.* Directed by Davis Guggenheim. Paramount Classics, USA, 2006.

Gray, John. "The NS Essay—A Target for Destructive Ferocity." *New Statesman*, April 29, 2002. Http://www.newstatesman.com/node/155451.

Griffith, John W. *Joseph Conrad and the Anthropological Dilemma.* Oxford: Clarendon Press, 1995.

Guerard, Albert. *Conrad the Novelist.* Cambridge, MA: Harvard University Press, 1958.

Guimond, James, and Katherine K. Maynard. "Kaczynski, Conrad and Terrorism." *Conradiana* 31.1 (1999): 3–25.

Hampson, Robert. *Conrad's Secrets.* London: Palgrave Macmillan, 2012.

Handke, Barbara. *First Command: A Psychological Reading of Joseph Conrad's "The Secret Sharer" and The Shadow-Line.* Berlin: Galda Verlag, 2010.

Harpham, Geoffrey Galt. "Beyond Mastery: Future of Conrad's Beginnings." In *Conrad in the Twenty-First Century: Contemporary Approaches and Perspectives*, edited by Carola M. Kaplan, Peter Mallios, and Andrea White, 17–37. New York: Routledge, 2005.

Harrison, Jane. *Ancient Art and Ritual*. New York: Greenwood Press, 1969.

Harrison, Nicholas. *Postcolonial Criticism: History, Theory and the Work of Fiction*. Malden, MA: Polity Press, 2003.

Havelock, Eric A. *Preface to Plato*. Cambridge, MA: Harvard University Press, 1963.

Hawkins, Hunt. "*Heart of Darkness* and Racism." In *Heart of Darkness*, by Joseph Conrad, edited by Paul B. Armstrong, 365–75. New York: W. W. Norton, 2006.

Hawkins, Hunt, and Brian W. Shaffer, eds. *Approaches to Teaching "Heart of Darkness" and "The Secret Sharer."* New York: Modern Language Association of America, 2002.

*Hearts of Darkness: A Filmmaker's Apocalypse*. Directed by Fax Bahr, George Hickenlooper, and Eleanor Coppola. American Zoetrope, USA 1991.

Hell, Bertrand. *Possession et chamanisme: Les maîtres du désordre*. Paris: Flammarion, 1999.

Hennard Dutheil de la Rochère, Martine. "Sounding the Hollow Heart of the West: X-rays and the *Technique de la Mort*." In *Conrad's* Heart of Darkness *and Contemporary Thought: Revisiting the Horror with Lacoue-Labarthe*, edited by Nidesh Lawtoo, 222–38. London: Bloomsbury, 2012.

Herdman, John. *The Double in Nineteenth-Century Fiction*. London: Macmillan, 1990.

Houen, Alex. *Terrorism and Modern Literature: From Joseph Conrad to Ciaran Carson*. Oxford: Oxford University Press, 2002.

Iacoboni, Marco. *Mirroring People: The New Science of How We Connect with Others*. New York: Farrar, Straus and Giroux, 2008.

Irele, Abiola. "The Crisis of Cultural Memory in Chinua Achebe's *Things Fall Apart*." In *Things Fall Apart*, by Chinua Achebe, edited by Abiola Irele, 453–91. New York: W. W. Norton, 2009.

James, William. *Psychology: The Briefer Course*. Edited by Gordon Allport. Notre Dame, IN: University of Notre Dame Press, 1985.

Jameson, Fredric. *The Political Unconscious: Narrative as a Socially Symbolic Act*. Ithaca, NY: Cornell University Press, 1981.

Janet, Pierre. *Les Névroses*. Paris: Flammarion, 1927.

———. *Les Obsessions et la psychasthénie*. Paris: Félix Alcan, 1903.

JanMohamed, Abdul. "Sophisticated Primitivism: The Syncretism of Oral and Literate Modes in Achebe's *Things Fall Apart*." In *Things Fall Apart*, by Chinua Achebe, edited by Abiola Irele, 571–86. New York: W. W. Norton, 2009.

Jaspers, Karl. *General Psychopathology*, Vol. 1. Translated by J. Hoenig and M. W. Hamilton. Baltimore: Johns Hopkins University Press, 1997.

Johnsen, William A. "'To My Readers of America': Conrad's 1914 Preface to *The Nigger of the "Narcissus."* *Conradiana* 35.1–2 (2003): 105–22.

———. *Violence and Modernism: Ibsen, Joyce, and Woolf*. Gainesville: University Press of Florida, 2003.

Jullien, François. *Traité de l'efficacité*. Paris: Grasset, 1996.

Kaufmann, Walter. *Tragedy and Philosophy*. Princeton, NJ: Princeton University Press, 1968.

Lacan, Jacques. "Le Stade du miroir comme formateur de la function du Je." In *Écrits*, 89–97. Paris: Seuil, 1966.

Lacoue-Labarthe, Philippe. "Le Chant des Muses." In *Pour n'en pas finir: Écrits sur la musique*, edited by Aristide Bianchi and Leonid Kharlamov, 27–54. Paris: Christian Bourgeois Éditeur, 2015.

———. "The Horror of the West." Translated by Nidesh Lawtoo and Hannes Opelz. In Lawtoo, *Conrad's* Heart of Darkness *and Contemporary Thought: Revisiting the Horror with Lacoue-Labarthe*, edited by Nidesh Lawtoo, 111–22. London: Bloomsbury, 2012.

———. *L'Imitation des modernes (Typographie 2)*. Paris: Galilée, 1986.

———. *La Réponse d'Ulysse: Et autres textes sur L'Occident*. Edited by Aristide Bianchi and Leonid Kharlamov. Lignes/Imec, 2012.

———. "The Response of Ulysses." In *Who Comes after the Subject*, edited by Eduardo Cadava, Peter Connor, and Jean-Luc Nancy, 198–205. New York: Routledge, 1991.

———. *The Subject of Philosophy*. Edited by Thomas Trezise, translated by Thomas Trezise et al. Minneapolis: University of Minnesota Press, 1993.

———. *Typography: Mimesis, Philosophy, Politics*. Edited by Christopher Fynsk. Cambridge, MA: Harvard University Press, 1989.

Lacoue-Labarthe, Philippe, and Jean-Luc Nancy. "The Unconscious Is Destructed Like an Affect (Part I of The Jewish People Do Not Dream)." *Stanford Literature Review* 6.2 (1989): 191–209.

———. "From Where Is Psychoanalysis Possible (Part II of The Jewish People Do Not Dream)." *Stanford Literature Review* 8.1–2 (1991): 19–55.

———. "The Nazi Myth." Translated by Bian Holmes. *Critical Inquiry* 16.2 (1990): 291–312.

———. "La Panique Politique." In *Retreating the Political*, edited by Simon Sparks, 1–28. New York: Routledge, 1977.

Lapassade, Georges. *Les États modifiés de conscience*. Paris: Presses Universitaires de France, 1987.

———. *Les Rites de possession*. Paris: Anthropos, 1997.

———. *La Transe*. Paris: Presses Universitaires de France, 1990.

Lawtoo, Nidesh. "*Avatar* Simulation in 3Ts: Techne, Trance, Transformation," *Science Fiction Studies* 125.42 (2015): 132–50.

———, ed. *Conrad's* Heart of Darkness *and Contemporary Thought: Revisiting the Horror with Lacoue-Labarthe*. London: Bloomsbury, 2012.

———. "A Frame for 'The Horror of the West.'" In *Conrad's* Heart of Darkness *and Contemporary Thought: Revisiting the Horror with Lacoue-Labarthe*, edited by Nidesh Lawtoo, 89–108. London: Bloomsbury, 2012.

———. "The Horror of Mimesis: Echoing Lacoue-Labarthe." In *Conrad's* Heart of Darkness *and Contemporary Thought: Revisiting the Horror with Lacoue-Labarthe*, edited by Nidesh Lawtoo, 239–59. London: Bloomsbury, 2012.

———. *The Phantom of the Ego: Modernism and the Mimetic Unconscious*. East Lansing: Michigan State University Press, 2013.

Leavis, F. R. *The Great Tradition: George Eliot, Henry James, Joseph Conrad.* New York: New York University Press, 1964.

Leitch, Vincent B. *Literary Criticism in the 21st Century: Theory Renaissance.* London: Bloomsbury, 2014.

Leiter, Louis H. "Echo Structures: Conrad's 'The Secret Sharer.'" *Twentieth Century Literature* 5.4 (1960): 159–75.

Levinas, Emmanuel. *Autrement qu'être ou au delà de l'essence.* Paris: Seuil, 1990.

Lévi-Strauss, Claude, and Didier Eribon. *Conversations with Claude Lévi-Strauss.* Translated by Paula Wissing. Chicago: University of Chicago Press, 1991.

Magnusson, Bruce, and Zahi Zalloua, eds. *Contagion: Health, Fear, Sovereignty.* Seattle: University of Washington Press, 2012.

Mallios, Peter Lancelot. "Afterword: The Deserts of Conrad." In *The Secret Agent*, by Joseph Conrad, edited by Peter Mallios, 261–90. New York: Modern Library, 2004.

———. "Reading *The Secret Agent* Now: The Press, the Police, the Premonition of Simulation." In *Conrad in the Twenty-First Century: Contemporary Approaches and Perspectives*, edited by Carola M. Kaplan, Peter Mallios, and Andrea White, 155–72. New York: Routledge, 2005.

Malabou, Catherine. *Plasticity at the Dusk of Writing: Dialectic, Destruction, Deconstruction.* Translated by Carolyn Sheared. New York: Columbia University Press, 2010.

———. *Que faire de notre cerveau?* Paris: Bayard, 2004.

———. *What Should We Do with Our Brain?* Translated by Sebastian Rand. New York: Fordham University Press, 2008.

Mann, Thomas. "Joseph Conrad's *The Secret Agent* (1926)." In *Conrad: The Secret Agent (A Casebook)*, edited by Ian Watt, 98–112. London: Macmillan, 1973.

Massumi, Brian. *Parables for the Virtual: Movement, Affect, Sensation.* Durham, NC: Duke University Press, 2002.

McKenna, Andrew. *Violence and Difference: Girard, Derrida, and Deconstruction.* Urbana: University of Illinois Press, 1991.

Meltzoff, Andrew, and Keith Moore. "Persons and Representation: Why Infant Imitation Is Important for Theories of Human Development." In *Imitation in Infancy*, edited by Jacqueline Nadel and George Butterworth, 9–35. Cambridge: Cambridge University Press, 1999.

Meyers, Jeffrey. "The Duel in Fiction." *North Dakota Quarterly* 51.4 (1983): 129–50.

Miller, Hillis J. Foreword to *Conrad in the Twenty-First Century*, edited by Carola M. Kaplan, Peter Mallios, and Andrea White, 1–14. New York: Routledge, 2005.

———. "*Heart of Darkness* Revisited." In *Conrad's* Heart of Darkness *and Contemporary Thought: Revisiting the Horror with Lacoue-Labarthe*, edited by Nidesh Lawtoo, 39–54. London: Bloomsbury, 2012.

———. *Poets of Reality: Six Twentieth-Century Writers.* Cambridge, MA: Harvard University Press, 1965.

———. "Prologue: Revisiting '*Heart of Darkness* Revisited' (in the Company of Philippe

Lacoue-Labarthe)." In *Conrad's* Heart of Darkness *and Contemporary Thought: Revisiting the Horror with Lacoue-Labarthe*, edited by Nidesh Lawtoo, 17–35. London: Bloomsbury, 2012.

Mongia, Padmini. "The Rescue: Conrad, Achebe, and the Critics." *Conradiana* 33.2 (2001): 153–63.

Morin, Edgar. *La Méthode 6: Éthique*. Paris: Seuil, 2004.

Moses, Michael Valdez. *The Novel and the Globalization of Culture*. Oxford: Oxford University Press, 1995.

Moses, Omri. *Out of Character: Modernism, Vitalism, Psychic Life*. Stanford, CA: Stanford University Press, 2014.

Mozina, Andrew. *Joseph Conrad and the Art of Sacrifice: The Evolution of the Scapegoat Theme in Joseph Conrad's Fiction*. London: Routledge, 2001.

Murfin, Ross C., ed. *Heart of Darkness: Case Studies in Contemporary Criticism*, 3rd ed. Boston: Bedford/St. Martin's, 2011.

Najder, Zdzisław. *Joseph Conrad: A Chronicle*. Cambridge: Cambridge University Press, 1983.

Nancy, Jean-Luc. *Being Singular Plural*. Translated by Robert D. Richardson. Stanford, CA: Stanford University Press, 2000.

———. *L'Équivalence des catastrophes (Après Fukushima)*. Paris: Galilée, 2012.

———. *The Inoperative Community*. Translated by Peter Connor. Minneapolis: University of Minnesota Press, 1991.

Nietzsche, Friedrich. *Beyond Good and Evil: Prelude to a Philosophy of the Future*. Translated by R. J. Hollingdale. London: Penguin Books, 2003.

———. *The Birth of Tragedy and The Case of Wagner*. Translated by Walter Kaufmann. New York: Vintage Books, 1967.

———. *Ecce Homo*. Translated by R. J. Hollingdale. New York: Penguin Books, 1980.

———. *Sämtliche Werke: Kritische Studienausgabe*. 15 vols. Edited by Giorgio Colli and Mazzino Montinari. Berlin: Walter de Gruyter, 1967–77.

———. *Twilight of the Idols*. In *The Portable Nietzsche*. Translated by Walter Kaufmann, 463–563. New York: Viking Press, 1954.

———. *The Will to Power*. Translated by Walter Kaufmann and R. J. Hollingdale. New York: Vintage Books, 1968.

Norris, Margot. "Modernist and Vietnam: Francis Ford Coppola's *Apocalypse Now*." *Modern Fiction Studies* 44.3 (1998): 730–66.

Nwosu, Maik. "The River, the Earth and the Spirit of the World: Joseph Conrad, Chinua Achebe, Ben Okri and the Novel in Africa." *Matatu Journal for African Culture and Society* 35 (2007): 93–109.

Onfray, Michel. *Cosmos: Une ontologie matérialiste*. Paris: Flammarion, 2015.

Panagopoulos, Nic. Heart of Darkness *and* The Birth of Tragedy*: A Comparative Study*. Athens: Kardamista, 2002.

Pandurang, Mala. "Chinua Achebe and the 'African Experience': A Socio-Literary Perspective." In *Things Fall Apart*, by Chinua Achebe, edited by Abiola Irele, 343–58. New York: W. W. Norton, 2009.

Peters, John. *Conrad and Impressionism*. Cambridge: Cambridge University Press, 2001.

———. *Joseph Conrad's Critical Reception*. Cambridge: Cambridge University Press, 2013.

Phillips, Caryl. "Was Joseph Conrad Really a Racist?" *Philosophia Africana* 10.1 (2007): 59–66.

Plato. *The Collected Dialogues of Plato*. Edited by Edith Hamilton and Huntington Cairns. New York: Pantheon Books, 1963.

———. *Republic*. In *The Collected Dialogues of Plato*, edited by Edith Hamilton and Huntington Cairns. 575–844. New York: Pantheon Books, 1963.

Potolsky, Matthew. *Mimesis*. London: Routledge, 2006.

Ramachandran, V. R. *A Brief Tour of Human Consciousness: From Impostor Poodles to Purple Numbers*. New York: PI Press, 2004.

Ressler, Steve. "Conrad's 'The Secret Sharer': Affirmation of Action." *Conradiana* 16.3 (1984): 195–214.

Richardson, Brian. "Conrad and Posthumanist Narration: Fabricating Class and Consciousness on Board the *Narcissus*." In *Conrad in the Twenty-First Century: Contemporary Approaches and Perspectives*, edited by Carola M. Kaplan, Peter Mallios, and Andrea White, 213–22. New York: Routledge, 2005.

Rizzolatti, Giacomo, and Corrado Sinigaglia. *Mirrors in the Brain: How Our Minds Share Actions and Emotions*. Translated by Frances Anderson. Oxford: Oxford University Press, 2008.

Rohde, Erwin. *Psyche: The Cult of Souls and the Belief in Immortality among the Greeks*. New York: Routledge, 2001.

Romanick Baldwin, Debra. "*Victory* (1916) and *The Shadow-Line* (1916)." In *A Joseph Conrad Companion*, edited by Orr Leonard and Ted Billy, 231–51. London: Greenwood Press, 1999.

Rose, Nikolas, and Joelle M. Abi-Rached. *Neuro: The New Brain Sciences and the Management of the Mind*. Princeton, NJ: Princeton University Press, 2013.

Ross, Stephen. "*The Nigger of the 'Narcissus'* and Modernist Haunting." *NOVEL: A Forum on Fiction* 44.2 (2011): 268–91.

Rouch, Jean. *Les maîtres fous. Jean Rouch*. DVD. Edition Montparnasse, 2004.

Rouget, Gilbert. *Music and Trance: A Theory of the Relations between Music and Possession*. Translated by Brunhilde Biebuyck. Chicago: University of Chicago Press, 1985.

Rousseau, Jean-Jacques. *Émile ou de l'éducation*. Paris: Flammarion, 1966.

Roussel, Royal. *The Metaphysics of Darkness: A Study in the Unity and Development of Conrad's Fiction*. Baltimore: Johns Hopkins University Press, 1971.

Said, Edward. *Culture and Imperialism*. New York: Vintage Books, 1994.

———. *Joseph Conrad and the Fiction of Autobiography*. Cambridge, MA: Harvard University Press, 1966.

———. "Nietzsche and Contradiction." In *Joseph Conrad: A Commemoration*, edited by Norman Sherry, 65–76. London: Macmillan, 1976.

———. "The Problem of Textuality: Two Exemplary Traditions." *Critical Inquiry* 4.4 (1978): 673–714.

Said, Edward, and Peter Mallios. "An Interview with Edward Said." In *Conrad in the Twenty-First*

*Century: Contemporary Approaches and Perspectives*, edited by Carola M. Kaplan, Peter Mallios, and Andrea White, 283–303. New York: Routledge, 2005.

Sarvan, C. P. "Racism and the *Heart of Darkness*." In *Heart of Darkness* by Joseph Conrad, 3rd ed., edited by Robert Kimbrough, 280–84. New York: W. W. Norton, 1988.

Scanlan, Margaret. *Plotting Terror: Novelists and Terrorists in Contemporary Fiction*. London: University of Virginia Press, 2001.

Schopenhauer, Arthur. *The World as Will and Idea*, Vol. 1. Translated by R. B. Haldane and J. Kemp. London: Routledge, Kegan & Paul, 1948.

Schwarz, Daniel R. "A Critical History of 'The Secret Sharer.'" In *The Secret Sharer: Case Studies in Contemporary Criticism*, edited by Daniel R. Schwarz, 63–78. Boston: Bedford Books, 1997.

Schwartz, Jeffrey M., and Sharon Begley. *The Mind and the Brain: Neuroplasticity and the Power of Mental Force*. New York: Regan Books, 2002.

Serres, Michel. *The Natural Contract*. Translated by Elizabeth MacArthur and William Paulson. Ann Arbor: University of Michigan Press, 1995.

Shaffer, Brian W. "The Nigger of the 'Narcissus.'" In *A Joseph Conrad Companion*, edited by Leonard Orr and Ted Billy, 49–64. London: Greenwood Press, 1999.

Sherry, Norman. "The Greenwich Bomb: Outrage and *The Secret Agent*." In *Conrad: The Secret Agent (A Casebook)*, edited by Ian Watt, 202–28. London: Macmillan, 1973.

Sontag, Susan. *Regarding the Pain of Others*. New York: Farrar, Straus and Giroux, 2003.

Spariosu, Mihai, ed. *Mimesis in Contemporary Theory: An Interdisciplinary Approach*. Vol. 1, *The Literary and Philosophical Debate*. Philadelphia: John Benjamin Publishing Company, 1984.

Spivak, Gayatri Chakravorty. *A Critique of Postcolonial Reason: Towards a History of the Vanishing Present*. Cambridge, MA: Harvard University Press, 1999.

Stape, J. H. "Conrad's 'The Duel': A Reconsideration." *The Conradian* 11.1 (1986): 42–46.

Staten, Henry. "Conrad's Dionysian Elegy." In *Conrad's* Heart of Darkness *and Contemporary Thought: Revisiting the Horror with Lacoue-Labarthe*, edited by Nidesh Lawtoo, 201–20. London: Bloomsbury, 2012.

———. "Tracking the 'Native Informant:' Cultural Translation as the Horizon of Literary Translation." In *Nation, Language, and the Ethics of Translation*, edited by Sandra Bermann and Michael Wood, 111–26. Princeton, NJ: Princeton University Press, 2005.

Stewart, Garrett. "Coppola's Conrad: The Repetitions of Complicity." *Critical Inquiry* 7.3 (1981): 455–74.

Stockdale, Mark. "Art, Language, and Invisible Truth: A Reappraisal of Conrad's Preface." *Colloquy: Text Theory Critique* 8 (2004).

Tarde, Gabriel. *Les lois de l'imitation*. Paris: Seuil, 2001.

Thompson, Christina A. "Anthropology's Conrad: Malinowski's in the Tropics and What He Read." *The Journal of Pacific History* 30.1 (1995): 53–75.

Torgovnick, Marianna. *Gone Primitive: Savage Intellects, Modern Lives*. Chicago: University of Chicago Press, 1990.

Tylor, E. B. *Primitive Culture*, Vol. 1. London: Murray, 1871.

Tzu, Sun. *The Art of War*. Translated by Yuan Shibing. Ware, UK: Wordsworth Editions, 1998.

Vardoulakis, Dimitris. *The Doppelgänger: Literature's Philosophy*. New York: Fordham University Press, 2010.

Warin, François. "Philippe's Lessons of Darkness." In *Conrad's* Heart of Darkness *and Contemporary Thought: Revisiting the Horror with Lacoue-Labarthe*, edited by Nidesh Lawtoo, 123–42. London: Bloomsbury, 2012.

Watt, Ian, ed. *Conrad: The Secret Agent (A Casebook)*. London: Macmillan, 1973.

———. *Conrad in the Nineteenth Century*. London: Chatto, 1980.

Watts, Cedric. "'A Bloody Racist': About Achebe's View of Conrad." *The Yearbook of English Studies* 13 (1983): 196–209.

———. *Conrad's* Heart of Darkness*: A Critical and Contextual Discussion*. New York: Rodopi, 2012.

———. *The Deceptive Text: An Introduction to Cover Plots*. Sussex: Harvester Press, 1984.

———. "The Mirror-tale: An Ethico Structural Analysis of Conrad's 'The Secret Sharer.'" *Critical Quarterly* 19.3 (1977): 25–37.

———. *A Preface to Conrad*. London: Longman, 1993.

Weisman, Alan. *The World without Us*. New York: St. Martin's Press, 2007.

Wilde, Oscar. "The Decay of Lying." In *The Complete Works of Oscar Wilde*, Vol. 4, edited by Josephine M. Guy, 73–103. Oxford: Oxford University Press, 2007.

Williams, Raymond. *Keywords: A Vocabulary of Culture and Society*. New York: Oxford University Press, 1983.

Wollaeger, Mark A. *Joseph Conrad and the Fictions of Skepticism*. Stanford, CA: Stanford University Press, 1990.

———. *Modernism, Media, and Propaganda: British Narrative from 1900 to 1945*. Princeton, NJ: Princeton University Press, 2006.

Woolf, Virginia. "Joseph Conrad." In *The Essays of Virginia Woolf*. Vol. 4, *1925–1928*, edited by Andrew McNeillie, 227–33. London: Hogarth Press, 1994.

Young, Robert. *White Mythologies: Writing History and the West*. London: Routledge, 1990.

Žižek, Slavoj. *Welcome to the Desert of the Real: Five Essays on September 11*. London: Verso, 2002.

# Index